The
Random
House
Basic Dictionary

German-English
English-German

The Random House Basic Dictionary

German-English
English-German

by Jenni Karding Moulton

Under the General Editorship of
Professor William G. Moulton
Princeton University

The Ballantine Reference Library

Ballantine Books · New York

Library of Congress Catalog Card Number: 67-20647
ISBN 0-345-29619-2
This edition published by arrangement with Random House, Inc. Previously published as *The German Vest Pocket Dictionary* and *The Random House German Dictionary*.

Manufactured in the United States of America
First Ballantine Books Edition: August 1981

Concise Pronunciation Guide

Consonants

b Usually like English *b:* **Bett, graben.** But when final or before *s* or *t*, like English *p:* **das Grab, des Grabs, er gräbt.**

c In foreign words only. Before *a, o, u,* like English *k:* **Café′.** Before *ä, e, i* in words borrowed from Latin, like English *ts:* **Cicero;** otherwise usually with the foreign pronunciation.

ch After *a, o, u, au,* a scraping sound like Scottish *ch* in *loch,* made between the back of the tongue and the roof of the mouth: **Dach, Loch, Buch, auch.** In other positions, much like English *h* in *hue:* **Dächer, Löcher, Bücher, ich, manch, welch, durch.** In words borrowed from Greek or Latin, initial *ch* before *a, o, u, l, r* is like English *k:* **Charak′ter, Chor, Christ.** In words borrowed from French it is like German *sch:* **Chance.**

chs As a fixed combination, like English *ks:* **der Dachs,** *the badger.* But when the *s* is an ending, like German *ch* plus *s:* **des Dachs,** genitive of **das Dach,** *the roof.*

ck As in English: **backen, Stock.**

d Usually like English *d:* **Ding, Rede.** But when final or before *s,* like English *t:* **das Band, des Bands.**

dt Like English *tt:* **Stadt** just like **statt.**

f As in English: **Feuer, Ofen, Schaf.**

g Usually like English *g* in *get:* **Geld, schlagen, Könige, reinigen.** But when final or before *s* or *t,* like English *k:* **der Schlag, des Schlags, er schlägt.** However, *ig* when final or before *s* or *t* is like German *ich:* **der König, des Königs, er reinigt.** In words borrowed from French, *g* before *e* is like English *z* in *azure:* **Loge.**

h As in English: **hier.** But after vowels it is only a sign of vowel length, and is not pronounced: **gehen, Bahn, Kuh.**

j Like English *y:* **Jahr.** In a few words borrowed from French, like English *z* in *azure:* **Journal′.**

k As in English: **kennen, Haken, buk.**

l Not the "dark *l*" of English *mill, bill,* but the "bright *l*" of English *million, billion:* **lang, fallen, hell.**

m As in English: **mehr, kommen, dumm.**

n As in English: **neu, kennen, kann.**

ng Always like English *ng* in *singer,* never like English *ng + g* in *finger.* German **Finger, Hunger.**

p As in English: **Post, Rippe, Tip.**

pf Like English *pf* in *cupful:* **Kopf, Apfel, Pfund.**

ph As in English: **Philosophie′**.

qu Like English *kv:* **Quelle, Aqua′rium**.

r When followed by a vowel, either a gargled sound made between the back of the tongue and the roof of the mouth, or (less commonly) a quick flip of the tongue tip against the gum ridge: **Ring, Haare, bessere**. When not followed by a vowel, a sound much like the *ah* of English *yeah*, or the *a* of *sofa:* **Haar, besser**.

Consonants

s Usually like English *z* in *zebra*, or *s* in *rose:* **sie, Rose**. But when final or before a consonant, like English *s* in *this:* **das, Wespe, Liste, Maske**.

sch Like English *sh* in *ship*, but with the lips rounded: **Schiff, waschen, Tisch**.

sp } At the beginning of a word,
st } like *sch* + *p*, *sch* + *t:* **Spiel, Stahl**.

ss } Like English *ss* in *miss*. *ss* is
ß } written only after a short vowel when another vowel follows: **müssen**. Otherwise ß is written: finally **muß**, before a consonant **mußte**, or after a long vowel **Muße**.

t As in English: **tun, bitter, Blatt**.

th Always like *t:* **Thea′ter**; never like English *th*.

tion Pronounced *tsyohn:* **Nation′, Aktion′**.

tsch Like *t* + *sch:* **deutsch**.

tz Like English *ts:* **sitzen, Platz**.

v In German words, like English *f:* **Vater, Frevel**. In foreign words, like English *v:* **Novem′ber, Moti′ve**; but finally and before *s*, like *f* again: **das Motiv′, des Motivs′**.

w Like English *v:* **Wagen, Löwe**.

x As in English: **Hexe**.

z Always like English *ts:* **zehn, Kreuz, Salz**.

Short vowels

a	Satz	Between English *o* in *hot* and *u* in *hut*.
ä } **e**	Sätze } setze	Like English *e* in *set*.
i	sitze	Like English *i* in *sit*.
o	Stock	Like English *o* in *gonna*, or the "New England short *o*" in *coat, road;* shorter than English *o* in *cost*.
ö	Stöcke	Tongue position as for short *e*, lips rounded as for short *o*.
u	Busch	Like English *u* in *bush*.
ü } **y**	Büsche } mystisch	Tongue position as for short *i*, lips rounded as for short *u*.

Unaccented short e

e	beginne	Like English *e* in *begin, pocket*.

Long vowels

a } **ah** } **aa**	Tal } Zahl } Saal	Like English *a* in *father*.
ä } **äh**	Täler } zählen	In elevated speech, like English *ai* in *fair;* otherwise just like German long *e*.
e } **eh** } **ee**	wer } mehr } Meer	Like English *ey* in *they*, but with no glide toward a *y* sound.

i	mir	
ih	ihr	Like English *i* in *machine*, but with no glide toward a *y* sound.
ie	Bier	

ü	Hüte	
üh	Kühe	Tongue position as for long *i*, lips rounded as for long *u*.
y	Typ	

long vowels

o	Ton	
oh	Sohn	Like English *ow* in *slow*, but with no glide toward a *w* sound.
oo	Boot	

Diphthongs

ei	Seite	Like English *i* in *side*. Also spelled *ey, ay* in names: *Meyer, Bayern*.
ai	Saite	

ö	Töne	Tongue position as for long *e*, lips rounded as for long *o*.
öh	Sohne	

au	Haut	Like English *ou* in *out*.

eu	heute	Like English *oi* in *oil*.
äu	Häute	

u	Hut	
uh	Kuh	Like English *u* in *rule*, but with no glide toward a *w* sound.

The Spelling of vowel length

An accented vowel is always short when followed by a doubled consonant letter, but nearly always long when followed by a single consonant letter.

Short	Long
schlaff	Schlaf
wenn	wen
still	Stil
offen	Ofen
öffnen	Öfen
Butter	Puter
dünne	Düne

Note that

ck counts as the doubled form of k:
tz counts as the doubled form of z:
ss counts as the doubled form of ß:
Vowels are always long when followed by (unpronounced) h:

hacken	Haken
putzen	duzen
Masse	Maße
wann	Wahn
stelle	stehle
irre	ihre
Wonne	wohne
gönne	Söhne
Rum	Ruhm
dünn	kühn

Vowels are always long when they are written double:

Stadt	Staat
Bett	Beet
Gott	Boot

In this respect, ie counts as the doubled form of i:

bitte	biete

German Accentuation

Most German words are accented on the first syllable: **Mo'nate, ar'beitete, Düsenkampfflugzeuge.** However, the prefixes **be-, emp-, ent-, er-, ge-, ver-, zer-** are never accented: **befeh'len, der Befehl', empfan'gen, der Empfang',** etc. Other prefixes are usually accented in nouns: **der Un'terricht,** but unaccented in verbs: **unterrich'ten.** Foreign words are often accented on a syllable other than the first: **Hotel'. Muse'um, Photographie'.**

Note particularly the accentuation of such forms as **übertre'ten, ich übertre'te** *I overstep,* where **über** is a prefix; but **ü'bertreten, ich trete... über** *I step over* where **über** is a separate word, despite the fact that **ü'bertreten** is spelled without a space. These two types will be distinguished in this dictionary by writing **übertre'ten** but **über•treten.**

German spelling does not indicate the place of the accent. In this dictionary, accent will be marked when it falls on a syllable other than the first: **Befehl', unterrich'ten, Photographie'.** Where it is not marked, the accent is on the first syllable: **Monate, arbeitete, Düsenkampfflugzeuge, Unterricht, über•treten.**

Nouns

This listing	means this
Wagen,-	plural is **Wagen.**
Vater,¨	plural is **Väter.**
Tisch,-e	plural is **Tische.**
Sohn,¨e	plural is **Söhne.**
Bild,-er	plural is **Bilder.**
Haus,¨er	plural is **Häuser.**
Auge,-n	plural is **Augen.**
Ohr,-en	plural is **Ohren.**
Hotel',-s	plural is **Hotels'.**
Muse'um,-e'en	plural is **Muse'en.**
Doktor,-o'ren	plural is **Dokto'ren.**
Kopie',-i'en	plural is **Kopi'en,** with three syllables.
Kuß,¨sse	final ß changes to medial ss because the ü is short.
Fuß,¨e	final ß kept in all forms because the ü is long.
Junge,-n,-n	nominative singular is **Junge,** all other forms are **Jungen.**
Name(n),-	declined like **Wagen** (above), except that nominative singular is **Name.**
Beamt'-	takes adjective endings: **ein Beamter, der Beamte, zwei Beamte, die zwei Beamten.**
Milch	has no plural.
Leute, *n.pl.*	has no singular.

From almost any German noun meaning some kind of man or boy, a noun meaning the corresponding woman or girl can be formed by adding **-in: der Arbeiter** *worker (man or boy),* **die Arbeiterin** *worker (woman or girl);* **der Russe** *Russian (man or boy),* **die Russin** *Russian (woman or girl).* Such feminine nouns will not usually be listed in this dictionary, unless they involve some sort of irregularity: **der Franzo'se,** *Frenchman,* **die Franzö'sin** *Frenchwoman* (irregular because of the umlaut).

Adjectives

Most German adjectives can also be used, without ending, as adverbs: **schlecht** *bad, badly*. The few which never occur without ending as adverbs are listed with a following hyphen: **link-** *left*, **ober-** *upper*, **zweit-** *second*. (The corresponding adverbs are **links** *to the left*, **oben** *above*, **zweitens** *secondly*.)

Adjectives which take umlaut in the comparative and superlative are listed as follows: **lang (¨)**, i.e., the comparative and superlative are **länger**, **längst-**.

Limiting or determining adjectives are listed in the nominative singular masculine, with an indication of the nominative singular neuter and feminine: **der, das, die, dieser,-es,-e; ein,-,-e.**

Descriptive adjectives take the following endings:

	Strong endings				Weak endings			
	masc.	neut.	fem.	pl.	masc.	neut.	fem.	pl.
nom.	-er	-es	-e	-e	-e	-e	-e	-en
acc.	-en	-es	-e	-e	-en	-e	-e	-en
dat.	-em	-em	-er	-en	-en	-en	-en	-en
gen.	-en	-en	-er	-er	-en	-en	-en	-en

Weak endings are used if the adjective is preceded by an inflected form of a limiting (determining) adjective; strong endings are used otherwise.

Verbs

Regular weak verbs are listed simply in the infinitive: **machen**. If a verb is used with a separable prefix (accented adverb), this is indicated by a raised dot: **auf·machen** (i.e., the infinitive is **aufmachen**, the present **ich mache... auf**, the past **ich machte...auf**, the past participle **aufgemacht**). An asterisk after a verb refers to the following lists of irregular weak and strong verbs. The sign † means that a verb takes the auxiliary verb **sein**; the sign ‡ means that a verb can take either **sein** or **haben**.

Irregular weak verbs

Infinitive	3rd sg. present	Past	Subjunctive	Past participle
haben	hat	hatte	hätte	gehabt
bringen	bringt	brachte	brächte	gebrach
denken	denkt	dachte	dächte	gedacht
dünken	dünkt, deucht	dünkte, deuchte	dünkte, deuchte	gedünkt, gedeucht
brennen	brennt	brannte	brennte	gebrannt
kennen	kennt	kannte	kennte	gekannt
nennen	nennt	nannte	nennte	genannt
†rennen	rennt	rannte	rennte	gerannt
senden	sendet	sandte	sendete	gesandt
wenden	wendet	wandte	wendete	gewandt
dürfen	darf	durfte	dürfte	gedurft

Infinitive	3rd sg. present	Past	Subjunctive	Past participle
können	kann	konnte	könnte	gekonnt
mögen	mag	mochte	mohe	gemocht
müssen	muß	mußte	müßte	gemußt
sollen	soll	sollte	sollte	gesollt
wollen	will	wollte	wollte	gewollt
wissen	weiß	wußte	wüßte	gewußt

Strong verbs

If a derived or compound verb is not listed, its forms may be found by consulting the simple verb. The sign + means that a regular weak form is also used.

Infinitive	3rd sg. present	Past	Subjunctive	Past participle
backen	bäckt	+buk	+büke	gebacken
befehlen	befiehlt	befahl	beföhle	befohlen
beginnen	beginnt	begann	begönne, begänne	begonnen
beißen	beißt	biß	bisse	gebissen
bergen	birgt	barg	bärge	geborgen
†bersten	birst	barst	bärste	geborsten
bewegen	bewegt	bewog	bewöge	bewogen
‡beigen	biegt	bog	böge	gebogen
bieten	bietet	bot	böte	geboten
binden	bindet	band	bände	gebunden
bitten	bittet	bat	bäte	gebeten
blasen	bläst	blies	bliese	gablasen
†bleiben	bleibt	blieb	bliebe	geblieben
braten	brät	briet	briete	gebraten
brechen	bricht	brach	bräch	gebrochen
dingen	dingt	+dang	+dänge	+gedungen
dreschen	drischt	drosch, drasch	drösche, dräsche	gedroschen
†dringen	dringt	drang	dränge	gedrungen
†erbleichen	erbleicht	+erblich	+erbliche	+erblichen
erlöschen	erlischt	erlosch	erlösche	erloschen
essen	ißt	aß	äße	gegessen
‡fahren	fährt	fuhr	führe	gefahren
†fallen	fällt	fiel	fiele	gefallen
fangen	fängt	fing	finge	gefangen
fechten	ficht	focht	föchte	gefochten
finden	findet	fand	fände	gefunden
flechten	flicht	flocht	flöchte	geflochten
‡fliegen	fliegt	flog	flöge	geflogen
†fliehen	flieht	floh	flöhe	geflohen
†fließen	fließt	floß	flösse	geflossen
fressen	frißt	fraß	fräße	gefressen
frieren	friert	fror	fröre	gefroren
gären	gärt	+gor	+göre	+gegoren
gebären	gebiert	gebar	gebäre	geboren
geben	gibt	gab	gäbe	gegeben
†gedeihen	gedeiht	gedieh	gediehe	gediehen
†gehen	geht	ging	ginge	gegangen
†gelingen	gelingt	gelang	gelänge	gelungen

Infinitive	3rd sg. present	Past	Subjunctive	Past participle
gelten	gilt	galt	gölte, gälte	gegolten
†genesen	genest	genas	genäse	genesen
genießen	genießt	genoß	genösse	genossen
†geschehen	geschieht	geschah	geschähe	geschehen
gewinnen	gewinnt	gewann	gewönne gewänne	gewonnen
gießen	gießt	goß	gösse	gegossen
gleichen	gleicht	glich	gliche	geglichen
†gleiten	gleitet	glitt	glitte	geglitten
glimmen	glimmt	+glomm	+glömme	+geglommen
graben	gräbt	grub	grübe	gegraben
greifen	greift	griff	griffe	gegriffen
halten	hält	hielt	hielte	gehalten
hängen	hängt	hing	hinge	gehangen
hauen	haut	+hieb	+hiebe	gehauen
heben	hebt	hob, hub	höbe, hübe	gehoben
heißen	heißt	hieß	heiße	geheißen
helfen	hilft	half	hülfe, hälfe	geholfen
klimmen	klimmt	+klomm	+klömme	+geklommen
klingen	klingt	klang	klänge	geklungen
kneifen	kneift	kniff	kniffe	gekniffen
†kommen	kommt	kam	käme	gekommen
†kriechen	kriecht	kroch	kröche	gekrochen
laden	lädst	lud	lüde	geladen
lassen	läßt	ließ	leiße	gelassen
†laufen	läuft	lief	liefe	gelaufen
leiden	leidet	litt	litte	gelitten
leihen	leiht	lieh	liehe	geliehen
lesen	liest	las	läse	gelesen
liegen	liegt	lag	läge	gelegen
lügen	lügt	log	löge	gelogen
meiden	meidet	mied	miede	gemieden
melken	+milkt	+molk	+mölke	+gemolken
messen	mißt	maß	mäße	gemessen
mißlingen	mißlingt	mißlang	mißlänge	mißlungen
nehmen	nimmt	nahm	näme	genommen
pfeifen	pfeift	pfiff	pfiffe	gepfiffen
preisen	preist	pries	priese	gepriesen
quellen	quillt	quoll	quölle	gequollen
raten	rät	riet	riete	geraten
reiben	reibt	rieb	riebe	gerieben
‡reißen	reißt	riß	risse	gerissen
‡reiten	reitet	ritt	ritte	geritten
riechen	riecht	roch	röche	gerochen

Infinitive	3rd sg. present	Past	Subjunctive	Past participle
ringen	ringt	rang	ränge	gerungen
rinnen	rinnt	rann	ränne, rönne	geronnen
rufen	ruft	rief	riefe	gerufen
saufen	säuft	soff	söffe	gesoffen
saugen	saugt	+sog	+söge	+gesogen
schaffen	schafft	schuf	schüfe	geschaffen
schallen	schallt	+scholl	+schölle	geschallt
‡scheiden	scheidet	schied	schiede	geschieden
scheinen	scheint	schien	schiene	geschienen
schelten	schilt	schalt	schölte	gescholten
scheren	schert	+schor	+schöre	+geschoren
schieben	schiebt	schob	schöbe	geschoben
schießen	schießt	schoß	schösse	geschossen
schinden	schindet	schund	schünde	geschunden
schlafen	schläft	schlief	schliefe	geschlafen
schlagen	schlägt	schlug	schlüge	geschlagen
†schleichen	schleicht	schlich	schliche	geschlichen
schleifen	schleift	schliff	schliffe	geschliffen
schließen	schließt	schloß	shlösse	geschlossen
schlingen	schlingt	schlang	schlänge	geschlungen
schmeißen	schmeißt	schmiß	schmisse	geschmissen
schmeizen	schmilzt	schmolz	schmölze	geschmolzen
schnauben	schnaubt	+schnob	+schnöbe	+geschnoben
schneiden	schneidet	schnitt	schnitte	geschnitten
schrecken	schrickt	schrak	schräke	geschrocken
schreiben	schreibt	schrieb	schriebe	geschrieben
schreien	schreit	schrie	schriee	geschrie(e)n
†schreiten	schreitet	schritt	schritte	geschritten
schweigen	schweigt	schwieg	schwiege	geschwiegen
schwellen	schwillt	schwoll	schwölle	geschwollen
‡schwimmen	schwimmt	schwamm	schwömme, schwämme	geschwommen
†schwinden	schwindet	schwand	schwände	geschwunden
schwingen	schwingt	schwang	schwänge	geschwungen
schwören	schwört	+schwur, schwor	+schwüre	+geschworen
sehen	sieht	sah	sähe	gesehen
sein	ist	war	wäre	gewesen
sieden	siedet	+sott	+sötte	+gesotten
singen	singt	sang	sänge	gesungen
†sinken	sinkt	sank	sänke	gesunken
sinnen	sinnt	sann	sänne, sönne	gesonnen
sitzen	sitzt	saß	säße	gesessen
speien	speit	spie	spiee	gespie(e)n

Infinitive	3rd sg. present	Past	Subjunctive	Past participle
spinnen	spinnt	spann	spönne, spänne	gesponnen
spleißen	spleißt	spliß	splisse	gesplissen
sprechen	spricht	sprach	spräche	gesprochen
sprießen	sprießt	sproß	sprösse	gesprossen
†springen	springt	sprang	spränge	gesprungen
stechen	sticht	stach	stäche	gestochen
stecken	steckt	+stak	+stäke	gesteck
stehen	steht	stand	stände, stünde	gestanden
stehlen	stiehlt	stahl	stähle, stöhle	gestohlen
†steigen	steigt	stieg	stiege	gestiegen
†sterben	stirbt	starb	stürbe	gestorben
‡stieben	stiebt	+stob	+stöbe	+gestoben
stinken	stinkt	stank	stänke	gestunken
‡stoßen	stößt	stieß	stieße	gestoßen
streichen	streicht	strich	striche	gestrichen
streiten	streitet	stritt	stritte	gestritten
tragen	trägt	trug	trüge	getragen
treffen	trifft	traf	träfe	getroffen
‡treiben	treibt	trieb	triebe	getrieben
‡treten	tritt	trat	träte	getreten
trinken	trinkt	trank	tränke	getrunken
trügen	trügt	trog	tröge	getrogen
tun	tut	tat	täte	getan
verbleichen	verbleicht	verblich	verbliche	verblichen
verderben	verdirbt	verdarb	verdürbe	verdorben
verdrießen	verdrießt	verdroß	verdrösse	verdrossen
vergessen	vergißt	vergaß	vergäße	vergessen
verlieren	verliert	verlor	verlöre	verloren
†wachsen	wächst	wuchs	wüchse	gewachsen
wägen	wägt	wog	wöge	gewogen
waschen	wäscht	wusch	wüsche	gewaschen
weben	webt	+wob	+wöbe	+gewoben
weichen	weicht	wich	wiche	gewichen
weisen	weist	wies	wiese	gewiesen
werben	wirbt	warb	würbe	geworben
†werden	wird	wurde, (ward)	würde	geworden
werfen	wirft	warf	würfe	geworfen
wiegen	wiegt	wog	wöge	gewogen
winden	windet	wand	wände	gewunden
wringen	wringt	wrang	wränge	gewrungen
zeihen	zeiht	zieh	ziehe	geziehen
‡ziehen	zieht	zog	zöge	gezogen
zwingen	zwingt	zwang	zwänge	gezwungen

Abbreviations

abbr.	abbreviation	*intr.*	intransitive
adj.	adjective	*jur.*	juridical
adv.	adverb	*m.*	masculine
arch.	architecture	*math.*	mathematics
art.	article	*med.*	medicine
bot.	botany	*mil.*	military
chem.	chemistry	*n.*	noun
comm.	commercial	*naut.*	nautical
conj.	conjunction	*nt.*	neuter
cpds.	compounds	*num.*	number
eccles.	ecclesiastical	*pl.*	plural
econ.	economics	*pol.*	politics
elec.	electricity	*pred.*	predicate
f.	feminine	*prep.*	preposition
fam.	familiar	*pron.*	pronoun
fig.	figuratively	*sg.*	singular
geogr.	geography	*tech.*	technical
geom.	geometry	*tr.*	transitive
gov't.	government	*typogr.*	typography
gram.	grammar	*vb.*	verb
interj.	interjection	*zool.*	zoology

Useful Phrases

Hello (or) How do you do?   Guten Tag.
Good morning.   Guten Morgen.
Good evening.   Guten Abend.
How are you?   Wie geht es Ihnen?
Fine, thanks, and you?   Gut, danke, und Ihnen?
I'm fine, too, thanks.   Auch gut, danke.
Please.   Bitte.
Thank you.   Danke schön.
You're welcome.   Bitte schön.
Good luck.   Alles Gute.
Good night.   Gute Nacht.
Good-bye.   Auf Wiedersehen.

Can you please help me?   Können Sie mir bitte helfen?
Do you understand me?   Verste'hen Sie mich?
I don't understand you.   Ich verste'he Sie nicht.
Please speak slowly.   Sprechen Sie bitte langsam.
Please say it again.   Sagen Sie es bitte noch einmal.
I don't speak German very well.   Ich spreche nicht sehr gut Deutsch.
Do you speak English?   Sprechen Sie Englisch?
What do you call that in German?   Wie heißt das auf deutsch?
How do you say…in German?   Wie sagt man…auf deutsch?
What's your name, please?   Wie heiß en Sie bitte?
My name is…   Ich heiße…

What time is it?   Wieviel Uhr ist es?
How much does that cost?   Wieviel kostet das?
I'd like to buy…   Ich möchte gern…kaufen.
I'd like to eat.   Ich möchte gernessen.
Where is there a good restaurant?   Wo ist hier ein gutes Restaurant?
I'm hungry (thirsty).   Ich habe Hunger (Durst).

Waiter, the check, please.   Herr Ober, bitte zahlen.
Where is there a good hotel?   Wo ist hier ein gutes Hotel'?

How do I get to the station?   Wie komme ich zum Bahnhof?
I'm sick.   Ich bin krank.
I need a doctor.   Ich brauche einen Arzt.
I want to send a telegram.   Ich möchte gern ein Telegramm' schicken.

Where can I change money?   Wo kann ich hier Geld wechseln?
Do you accept travelers checks?   Nehmen Sie Reiseschecks?
Right away.   Sofort'.
Help!   Hilfe!
Come in.   Herein'.
Hello (*on telephone*).   Hier...(*say your name*).
Stop.   Halt.
Hurry.   Schnell.
To the right.   Rechts.
To the left.   Links.
Straight ahead.   Gera'de aus.

Signs

Vorsicht   Caution
Achtung   Watch out
Ausgang   Exit
Eingang   Entrance
Halt   Stop
Geschlossen   Closed
Geöffnet   Open
Langsam   Slow
Verboten   Prohibited
Gesperrt   Road closed
Einbahnstraße   One way street
Raucher   For smokers
Nichtraucher   For non-smokers
Rauchen verboten   No smoking
Kein Zutritt   No admittance
Damen (*or*) **Frauen**   Women
Herren (*or*) **Männer**   Men
Abort   Toilet

Weights and Measures

The Germans use the *Metric System* of weights and measures, which is a decimal system in which multiples are shown by the prefixes: Dezi- (one tenth); Zenti- (one hundredth); Milli- (one thousandth); Deka- (ten); Hekto- (hundred); Kilo- (thousand).

1 Zentimeter	=	.3937 inches
1 Meter	=	39.37 inches
1 Kilometer	=	.621 mile
1 Zentigramm	=	.1543 grain
1 Gramm	=	15.432 grains
1 Pfund (½ Kilogramm)	=	1.1023 pounds
1 Kilogramm	=	2.2046 pounds
1 Tonne	=	2,204 pounds
1 Zentiliter	=	.338 ounces
1 Liter	=	1.0567 quart (liquid); .908 quart (dry)
1 Kiloliter	=	264.18 gallons

Numerals

Cardinal

1	eins		32	zweiunddreißig
2	zwei		40	vierzig
3	drei		43	dreiundvierzig
4	vier			
5	fünf		50	fünfzig
6	sechs		54	vierundfünfzig
7	sieben		60	sechzig
8	acht		65	fünfundsechzig
9	neun			
10	zehn		70	siebzig
11	elf		76	sechsundsiebzig
12	zwölf		80	achtzig
13	dreizehn		87	siebenundachtzig
14	vierzehn			
15	fünfzehn		90	neunzig
16	sechzehn		98	achtundneunzig
17	siebzehn			
18	achtzehn		100	hundert
19	neunzehn		101	hunderteins
20	zwanzig		202	zweihundertzwei
21	einundzwanzig			
30	dreißig		1,000	tausend
			1,000,000	eine Million'

Ordinal

1st	erst-		14th	vierzehnt-
2nd	zweit-		15th	fünfzehnt-
3rd	dritt-		16th	sechzehnt-
4th	viert-		17th	siebzehnt-
5th	fünft-		18th	achtzehnt-
6th	sechst-		19th	neunzehnt-
7th	sieb(en)t-		20th	zwanzigst-
8th	acht-		21st	einundzwanzigst-
9th	neunt-		30th	dreißigst-
10th	zehnt-		32nd	zweiunddreißigst-
11th	elft-		40th	vierzigst-
12th	zwölft-		43rd	dreiundvierzigst-
13th	dreizehnt-		50th	fünfzigst-

54th	vierundfünfzigst-	90th	neunzigst-
60th	sechzigst-	98th	achtundneunzigst-
65th	fünfundsechzigst-	100th	hundertst-
70th	siebzigst-	101st	hunderterst-
76th	sechsundsiebzigst-	202nd	zweinhundertzweit-
80th	achtzigst-	1,000th	tausendst-
87th	siebenundachtzigst-	1,000,000	millionst'-

Decimals

Instead of a decimal point, a comma is used:

> *English:* 3.82 "three point eight two"
> *German:* 3,82 „drei Komma acht zwei"

Fractions

the half; half a pound	die Hälfte; ein halbes Pfund
one and a half	anderthalb, eineinhalb
the third; two-thirds	das Drittel; zweidrittel
the fourth; three-fourths	das Viertel; dreiviertel
the fifth; four-fifths	das Fünftel; vierfünftel

Days of the Week

Sunday	der Sonntag
Monday	der Montag
Tuesday	der Dienstag
Wednesday	der Mittwoch
Thursday	der Donnerstag
Friday	der Freitag
Saturday	der Sonnabend
	or der Samstag

Months

January	der Januar	July	der Juli
February	der Februar	August	der August'
March	der März	September	der Septem'ber
April	der April'	October	der Okto'ber
May	der Mai	November	der Novem'ber
June	der Juni	December	der Dezem'ber

German-English

A

Aachen, *n.nt.* Aachen, Aix-la-Chapelle.

Aal, -e, *n.m.* eel.

ab, *adv.* down; off; **(ab Berlin)** leaving Berlin; **(ab heute)** from today on.

ab·ändern, *vb.* revise.

Abänderung, -en, *n.f.* variation, revision.

Abart, -en, *n.f.* variety, species.

Abbau, *n.m.* working; reduction, razing.

ab·bauen, *vb.* raze; mine.

Abbild, -er, *n.nt.* image, effigy.

ab·blenden, *vb.* dim (headlights).

ab·brechen*, *vb.* break off; cease, stop.

Abbruch, -e, *n.m.* breaking off; cessation; damage.

ab·danken, *vb.* abdicate.

Abdankung, -en, *n.f.* abdication.

Abdruck, -e, *n.m.* (printed) impression, copy.

Abdruck, -̈e, *n.m.* impress, mark, cast.

Abend, -e, *n.m.* evening; **(zu A. essen*)** dine, have dinner.

Abendbrot, -e, *n.nt.* supper.

Abenddämmerung, -en, *n.f.* dusk.

Abendessen, -, *n.nt.* dinner, supper.

Abendland, *n.nt.* Occident.

abendländisch, *adj.* occidental.

abendlich, *adj.* evening.

Abendmahl, -e, *n.nt.* Holy Communion, Lord's Supper.

abends, *adv.* in the evening.

Abenteuer, -, *n.nt.* adventure.

abenteuerlich, *adj.* adventurous.

Abenteurer, -, *n.m.* adventurer.

aber, *conj.* but.

Aberglaube(n), -, *n.m.* superstition.

abergläubisch, *adj.* superstitious.

abermals, *adv.* once again.

Abessi'nien, *n.nt.* Abyssinia.

ab·fahren*, *vb.* leave, depart.

Abfahrt, -en, *n.f.* departure.

Abfall, -e, *n.m.* slope; decrease; defection; rubbish.

ab·fallen*, *vb.* fall off; decrease; revolt.

abfällig, *adj.* precipitous; derogatory.

ab·fangen*, *vb.* intercept.

ab·fassen, *vb.* draw up, compose.

ab·fertigen, *vb.* take care of, expedite.

ab·feuern, *vb.* discharge (gun).

ab·finden*, *vb.* **(sich a. mit)** put up with.

Abfluß, -̈sse, *n.m.* drain(age), outlet.

ab·führen, *vb.* lead off.

Abführmittel, -, *n.nt.* laxative.

Abgabe, -n, *n.f.* levy.

Abgasbestimmungen, *n.f.pl.* emission controls.

ab·geben*, *vb.* hand over; check (baggage); cast (vote).

abgebrüht, *adj.* hard-boiled.

abgedroschen, *adj.* trite.

abgelegen, *adj.* remote.

abgemacht, *adj.* settled, agreed.

abgeneigt, *adj.* averse, disinclined.

abgenutzt, *adj.* worn-out.

Abgeordnet-, *n.m.&f.* representative, deputy.

abgeschieden, *adj.* separated, secluded; departed.

abgesehen von, *prep.* aside from.

ab·gewinnen*, *vb.* gain from.

Abgott, -̈er, *n.m.* idol.

Abgötterei', -en, *n.f.* idolatry.

Abgrenzung, -en, *n.f.* demarcation.

Abgrund, -̈e, *n.m.* abyss, precipice.

ab·halten*, *vb.* hold off, restrain, detain.

abhan'den, *adv.* missing; **(a. kommen*)** get lost.

Abhandlung, -en, *n.f.* treatise.

Abhang, -̈e, *n.m.* slope.

ab·hängen*, *vb.* depend.

abhängig, *adj.* dependent.

Abhängigkeit, *n.f.* dependence.

ab·härten, *vb.* harden.

ab·helfen*, *vb.* remedy.

Abhilfe, -n, *n.f.* remedy, relief.

abhold, *adj.* averse, disinclined.

ab·holen, *vb.* go and get, pick up, call for.

ab·hören, *vb.* listen to, monitor.

Abitur', -e, *n.nt.* final examination at end of secondary school; high school degree.

Abkehr, *n.f.* turning away.

Abkomme, -n, *n.m.* descendant, offspring.

Abkommen, -, *n.nt.* convention; agreement.

Abkömmling, -e, *n.m.* offspring, descendant; derivative.

ab·kühlen, *vb.* cool off.

ab·kürzen, *vb.* abbreviate; abridge.

Abkürzung, -en, *n.f.* abbreviation; abridgment.

ab·laden*, *vb.* unload.

Ablage, -n, *n.f.* depot, place of deposit.

ablaß, -̈sse, *n.m.* letting off, drainage; *(eccles.)* indulgence.

ab·lassen*, *vb.* let off, drain; desist.

Ablativ, -e, *n.m.* ablative.

Ablauf, *n.m.* running off, expiration.

ab·laufen*, *vb.* run off, expire.

Ablaut, -e, *n.m.* ablaut (vowel alteration, as in singen, sang, gesungen).

ab·legen, *vb.* discard, take off.

ab·lehnen, *vb.* decline, reject.

Ablehnung, -en, *n.f.* rejection.

ab·leiten, *vb.* derive.

Ableitung, -en, *n.f.* derivation.

ab·lenken, *vb.* divert, distract.

Ablenkung, -en, *n.f.* diversion, distraction.

ab·leugnen, *vb.* deny, disavow.

Ableugnung, -en, *n.f.* denial, disavowal.

Ablichtung, -en, *n.f.* photocopy.

ab·liefern, *vb.* deliver.

Ablieferung, -en, *n.f.* delivery.

ab·lösen, *vb.* relieve.

Ablösung, -en, *n.f.* relief.

Abmarsch, -̈e, *n.m.* marching off, departure.

ab·melden, *vb.* report the departure of.

Abnahme, -n, *n.f.* decrease.

abnehmbar, *adj.* removable.

ab·nehmen*, *vb.* *(tr.)* take off, remove; *(intr.)* decrease, lose weight.

Abnehmer, -, *n.m.* purchaser.

Abneigung, -en, *n.f.* antipathy, dislike, aversion.

abnorm', *adj.* abnormal.

ab·nötigen, *vb.* force from.

ab·nutzen, *vb.* wear (something) out.

Abnutzung, *n.f.* wearing out.

Abonnement', -s, *n.nt.* subscription.

abonnie'ren, *vb.* subscribe.

Abordnung, -en, *n.f.* delegation.

Abort, -e, *n.m.* toilet.

Abort', -e, *n.m.* abortion.

ab·rackern, *vb.* **(sich a.)** drudge.

ab·raten*, *vb.* dissuade.

ab·räumen, *vb.* clear off.

ab·rechnen, *vb.* settle accounts.

Abrechnung, -en, *n.f.* settlement of accounts.

Abrede, -n, *n.f.* **(in A. stellen)** deny.

Abreise, -n, *n.f.* departure.

ab·reisen, *vb.* depart.

ab·reißen*, *vb.* tear off; demolish.

Abriß, -sse. *n.m.* outline, summary.

ab·rüsten, *vb.* disarm.

Abrüstung, -en, *n.f.* disarmament.

Absage, -n, *n.f.* refusal (of an invitation), calling off.

ab·sagen, *vb.* decline, revoke.

Absatz, -̈e, *n.m.* paragraph; heel; landing; sale, market.

ab·schaben, *vb.* scrape off, abrade.

ab·schaffen*, *vb.* abolish.

Abschaffung, -en, *n.f.* abolition.

ab·schätzen, *vb.* appraise, estimate.

Abschätzung, -en, *n.f.* appraisal, estimate.

Abschaum, *n.m.* dregs.

Abscheu, -e, *n.m.* abhorrence, loathing.

abscheu'lich, *adj.* abominable, detestable.

Abschied, -e, *n.m.* departure, leave, farewell.

Abschlag, -e, *n.m.* chips; repulse; refusal.

ab·schlagen*, *vb.* chip off; repel; refuse.

abschlägig, *adj.* negative, refusing.

ab·schleifen*, *vb.* grind off, abrade.

ab·schließen*, *vb.* lock up, close off; conclude.

Abschluß, -sse, *n.m.* conclusion.

ab·schneiden*, *vb.* cut off.

Abschnitt, -e, *n.m.* section.

ab·schrecken, *vb.* frighten off.

abschreckend, *adj.* forbidding.

Abschreckung, *n.f.* deterrence.

Abschreckungsmittel, -, *n.nt.* deterrent.

ab·schreiben*, *vb.* copy.

Abschrift, -en, *n.f.* copy.

abschüssig, *adj.* precipitous.

ab·schweifen, *vb.* digress.

ab·schwören*, *vb.* abjure.

Abschwörung, -en, *n.f.* abjuration.

absehbar, *adj.* foreseeable.

ab·sehen*, *vb.* look away; see from; **(a. von)** give up; **(auf mich abgesehen)** aimed at me; **(ist abzusehen)** can be seen.

abseits, *adv.* aside, apart.

ab·senden*, *vb.* send off, mail.

Absender, -, *n.m.* sender.

Absendung, -en, *n.f.* dispatch.

ab·setzen, *vb.* set off, set down, depose.

Absicht, -en, *n.f.* intent, purpose; **(mit A.)** on purpose.

absichtlich, *adj.* intentional.

absolut', *adj.* absolute.

absolvie'ren, *vb.* absolve; complete; finish (school); pass (an examination).

abson'derlich, *adj.* peculiar.

ab·sondern, *vb.* separate, detach; secrete.

absorbie'ren, *vb.* absorb.

Absorbie'rungsmittel, -, *n.nt.* absorbent.

Absorption', -en, *n.f.* absorption.

ab·spannen, *vb.* loosen (tension), relax.

ab·spielen, *vb.* **(sich a.)** occur, take place.

ab·splittern, *vb.* chip.

Absprache, -n, *n.f.* agreement.

ab·sprechen*, *vb.* deny.

ab·springen*, *vb.* jump down, bail out (of a plane).

Absprung, -e, *n.m.* jump down, parachute jump; digression.

ab·stammen, *vb.* be descended.

Abstammung, -en, *n.f.* descent, ancestry; derivation.

Abstand, -e, *n.m.* distance, interval; **(von etwas A. nehmen*)** renounce.

ab·statten, *vb.* grant; **(einen Besuch a.)** pay a visit.

ab·stauben, *vb.* dust.

Abstecher, -, *n.m.* digression, side trip.

ab·stehen*, *vb.* stand off, stick out.

ab·steigen*, *vb.* descend, dismount; put up at (an inn).

ab·stellen*, *vb.* put away; turn off.

ab·stempeln, *vb.* stamp, cancel.

ab·sterben*, *vb.* die out.

Abstieg, -e, *n.m.* descent.

ab·stimmen, *vb.* vote.

Abstimmung, -en, *n.f.* vote, plebiscite.

abstinent', *adj.* abstinent.

Abstinenz', *n.f.* abstinence.

ab·stoßen*, *vb.* knock off, repel, repulse.

abstoßend, *adj.* repulsive.

abstrahie'ren, *vb.* abstract.

abstrakt', *adj.* abstract.

Abstraktion', -en, *n.f.* abstraction.

ab·streifen, *vb.* strip.

Abstufung, -en, *n.f.* gradation.

ab·stumpfen, *vb.* become dull, blunt; make dull, blunt.

Absturz, -e, *n.m.* fall, crash.

ab·stürzen, *vb.* fall, crash.

absurd', *adj.* absurd.

Abszeß', -sse, *n.m.* abscess.

Abtei', -en, *n.f.* abbey.

Abteil, -e, *n.nt.* compartment.

Abtei'lung, -en, *n.f.* division, section.

ab·tragen*, *vb.* wear out.

ab·treiben*, *vb.* drive off; cause an abortion.

Abtreibung, -en, *n.f.* abortion.

ab·trennen, *vb.* detach.

ab·treten*, *vb.* cede.

Abtretung, -en, *n.f.* withdrawal, cession, surrender.

Abtritt, -e, *n.nt.* departure, exit; latrine.

ab·tun*, *vb.* put aside, settle.

ab·wägen*, *vb.* weigh out, consider.

ab·wandeln, *vb.* change, inflect.

ab·wandern, *vb.* depart, migrate.

ab·warten, *vb.* wait (to see what will happen), bide one's time.

abwärts, *adv.* downwards.

ab·waschen*, *vb.* wash off.

Abwaschung, -en, *n.f.* ablution.

ab·wechseln, *vb.* alternate, take turns.

abwechselnd, *adj.* alternate.

Abwechs(e)lung, -en, *n.f.* change, alternation.

Abweg, -e, *n.m.* wrong way,

devious path; **(auf A.e gera'ten*)** go astray.

abwegig, *adj.* errant.

Abwehr, *n.f.* warding off, defense.

Abwehrdienst, -e, *n.m.* counterintelligence service.

ab·wehren, *vb.* ward off, prevent.

ab·weichen*, *vb.* deviate, depart.

Abweichung, -en, *n.f.* deviation, departure.

ab·weisen*, *vb.* send away, repulse.

ab·wenden*, *vb.* turn away, deflect, avert.

ab·werfen*, *vb.* throw down, shed.

ab·werten, *vb.* devaluate.

Abwertung, -en, *n.f.* devaluation.

abwesend, *adj.* absent.

Abwesend-, *n.m.&f.* absent person, absentee.

Abwesenheit, -en, *n.f.* absence.

ab·wickeln, *vb.* unwind.

ab·winken, *vb.* gesture "no".

Abwurf, -, *n.m.* throwing down; thing thrown down.

ab·zahlen, *vb.* pay off.

ab·zählen, *vb.* count off.

ab·zapfen, *vb.* draw off, tap.

ab·zehren, *vb.* waste away, consume.

Abzeichen, -, *n.nt.* badge, medal, insignia.

ab·ziehen*, *vb.* *(tr.)* draw off, subtract, deduct; *(intr.)* march off.

Abzug, -e, *n.m.* marching off, departure; drawing off, subtraction, drain; print; trigger.

ab·zwingen*, *vb.* force away from, extort.

Acetylen', *n.nt.* acetylene.

ach, *interj.* oh.

Achat', -e, *n.m.* agate.

Achse, -n, *n.f.* axis, axle.

Achsel, -n, *n.f.* shoulder.

acht, *num.* eight.

acht-, *adj.* eighth.

Acht, *n.f.* attention, care; **(sich in A. nehmen*)** watch out, be on one's guard; **(außer A. lassen*)** pay no attention to, neglect.

Achtel, -, *n.nt.* eighth part; **(ein a.)** one-eighth.

achten, *vb.* respect; **(a. auf)** pay attention to.

ächten, *vb.* outlaw, ostracise.

achtern, *adv.* aft.

acht·geben*, *vb.* watch out, pay attention.

acht·haben*, *vb.* watch out, pay attention.

achtlos, *adj.* heedless.

achtsam, *adj.* attentive.

Achtung, *n.f.* attention, regard, esteem; **(A.!)** watch out! attention!

achtzehn, *num.* eighteen.

achtzehnt-, *adj.* eighteenth.

achtzig, *num.* eighty.

achtzigst-, *adj.* eightieth.
Achtzigstel, -, *n.nt.* eightieth part; **(ein a.)** one-eightieth.
ächzen, *vb.* groan, moan.
Acker, ⸗, *n.m.* field.
Ackerbau, *n.m.* farming.
addie'ren, *vb.* add.
ade', *interj.* adieu.
Adel, *n.m.* nobility.
Ader, -n, *n.f.* vein.
adieu, *interj.* adieu.
Adjektiv, -e, *n.nt.* adjective.
adjekti'visch, *adj.* adjectival.
Adjutant', -en, -en, *n.m.* adjutant, aide, aide-de-camp.
Adler, -, *n.m.* eagle.
Adler-, *cpds.* aquiline.
Adlig, *adj.* noble.
Adlig-, *n.m.&f.* nobleman, -woman.
Admiral', -e, *n.m.* admiral.
Admiralität', -en, *n.f.* admiralty.
adoptie'ren, *vb.* adopt.
Adoption', -en, *n.f.* adoption.
Adres'se, -n, *n.f.* address.
adressie'ren, *vb.* address.
adrett', *adj.* trim, smart.
Advent', -e, *n.m.* Advent, each of the four Sundays before Christmas.
Adverb', -ien, *n.nt.* adverb.
adverbial', *adj.* adverbial.
Advokat', -en, -en, *n.m.* lawyer.
Aeronau'tik, *n.f.* aeronautics.
Affä're, -n, *n.f.* affair, love affair.
Affe, -n, -n, *n.m.* ape, monkey.
Affekt', -e, *n.m.* affect.
affektiert', *adj.* affected.
Affektiert'heit, -en, *n.f.* affectation.
äffen, *vb.* ape, mock.
Affix, -e, *n.nt.* affix.
Affront', -s, *n.m.* affront, snub.
Afrika, *n.nt.* Africa.
Afrika'ner, -, *n.m.* African.
afrika'nisch, *adj.* African.
AG, *abbr.* (= Aktiengesellschaft) company.
Agent', -en, -en, *n.m.* agent.
Agentur', -en, *n.f.* agency.
Aggression', -en, *n.f.* aggression.
aggressiv', *adj.* aggressive.
agie'ren, *vb.* act.
Agno'stiker, -, *n.m.* agnostic.
agno'stisch, *adj.* agnostic.
Ägyp'ten, *n.nt.* Egypt.
Ägyp'ter, -, *n.m.* Egyptian.
ägyp'tisch, *adj.* Egyptian.
Ahn, -en, *n.m.* ancestor.
Ahne, -n, *n.f.* ancestress.
ähneln, *vb.* resemble.
ahnen, *vb.* have any idea (that something will happen); forebode.
ähnlich, *adj.* similar.
Ähnlichkeit, -en, *n.f.* similarity.
Ahnung, -en, *n.f.* foreboding; hunch; **(ich habe keine A.)** I have no idea.
ahnungslos, *adj.* unsuspecting.
ahnungsvoll, *adj.* ominous.

Ahorn, -e, *n.m.* maple tree.
Ähre, -n, *n.f.* ear (of grain).
Ajatol'lah, -s, *n.m.* ayatollah.
Akademie', -i'en, *n.f.* academy.
akade'misch, *adj.* academic.
Aka'zie, -n, *n.f.* acacia.
Akkord', -e, *n.m.* chord.
akkrediti'ren, *vb.* accredit.
Akkumula'tor, -to'ren, *n.m.* battery.
Akkusativ', -e, *n.m.* accusative.
Akne, -n, *n.f.* acne.
Akrobat', -en, -en, *n.m.* acrobat.
Akt, -e, *n.m.* act; nude (drawing).
Akte, -n, *n.f.* document, dossier, file.
Aktenmappe, -n, *n.f.* brief case.
Aktie, -n, *n.f.* share (of stock).
Aktiengesellschaft, -en, *n.f.* corporation, stock company.
Aktion', -en, *n.f.* action, undertaking.
Aktionär', -e, *n.m.* stockholder.
aktiv', *adj.* active.
aktivie'ren, *vb.* activate.
Aktivie'rung, -en, *n.f.* activation.
aktuell', *adj.* topical.
Akupunktur', -en, *n.f.* acupuncture.
Aku'stik, *n.f.* acoustics.
aku'stisch, *adj.* acoustic.
akut', *adj.* acute.
Akzent', -e, *n.m.* accent.
akzentuie'ren, *vb.* accentuate.
Alarm', -e, *n.m.* alarm, alert.
alarmie'ren, *vb.* alarm, alert.
Alaun', -e, *n.m.* alum.
albern, *adj.* silly.
Albi'no, -s, *n.m.* albino.
Album, -ben, *n.nt.* album.
Alchimie', *n.f.* alchemy.
Alchimist', -en, -en, *n.m.* alchemist.
Alge, -n, *n.f.* alga.
Algebra, *n.f.* algebra.
algebra'isch, *adj.* algebraic.
alias, *adv.* alias.
Alibi, -s, *n.nt.* alibi.
Aliment', -e, *n.nt.* alimony.
Alka'li, -en, *n.nt.* alkali.
alka'lisch, *adj.* alkaline.
Alkohol, -e, *n.m.* alcohol.
Alkoho'liker, -, *n.m.* alcoholic.
alkoho'lisch, *adj.* alcoholic.
Alko'ven, -, *n.m.* alcove.
All, *n.nt.* universe.
all; **aller**, -es, -e, *pron.&adj.* all.
Allee', -e'en, *n.f.* avenue.
Allegorie', -i'en, *n.f.* allegory.
allein', **1.** *adv.* alone. **2.** *conj.* but.
allei'nig, *adj.* sole, only.
allemal, *adv.* always; **(ein für a.)** once and for all.
allenfalls, *adv.* in any case.
allenthal'ben, *adv.* everywhere.
aller-, *cpds.* of all; **allerbest'**, best of all; etc.
allerart, *adv.* all sorts of.
allerdings', *adv.* certainly, to be sure, indeed.
Allergie', -i'en, *n.f.* allergy.

allerhand, *adv.* all sorts of; **(das ist ja a.)** that's tremendous, that's the limit.
allerlei, *adv.* all sorts of.
alles, *pron.* everything.
allgemein, *adj.* general, common; **(im a. en)** generally, in general.
Allgemein'heit, -en, *n.f.* generality, general public.
Allianz', -en, *n.f.* alliance.
Alliga'tor, -o'ren, *n.m.* alligator.
alliie'ren, *vb.* ally.
Alliiert'-, *n.m.&f.* ally.
alljähr'lich, *adj.* annual.
allmäch'tig, *adj.* almighty, omnipotent.
allmäh'lich, *adj.* gradual.
allmo'natlich, *adj.* monthly.
allnächt'lich, *adj.* nightly.
Alltag, -e, *n.m.* weekday, tedium.
alltäg'lich, *adj.* daily, routine.
allzu, *adv.* all too.
Almanach, -e, *n.m.* almanac.
Almo'sen, -, *n.nt.* alms.
Alpdruck, ⸗e, *n.m.* nightmare.
Alpen, *n.pl.* Alps.
Alphabet', -e, *n.nt.* alphabet.
alphabe'tisch, *adj.* alphabetical.
alphabetisie'ren, *vb.* alphabetize.
als, *conj.* as, when; than.
alsbald', *adv.* immediately.
alsdann', *adv.* thereupon.
also, *adv.* so, thus, and so, hence, therefore.
alt, *adj.* old.
Alt, -e, *n.m.* alto.
Altar', ⸗e, *n.m.* altar.
Altar'diener, -, *n.m.* acolyte.
Alter, -, *n.nt.* age.
altern, *vb.* age.
alternativ', *adj.* alternative.
Alternati've, -n, *n.f.* alternative.
Altertum, -ümer, *n.nt.* antiquity.
altertümlich, *adj.* archaic.
Altertumskunde, *n.f.* archaeology.
Ältest-, *n.m.* elder.
alther'gebracht, *adj.* traditional.
Altjahrsa'bend, -e, *n.m.* New Year's Eve.
altklug, ⸗, *adj.* precocious.
ältlich, *adj.* elderly.
altmodisch, *adj.* old-fashioned.
Altruis'mus, *n.m.* altruism.
Altstimme, -n, *n.f.* alto.
Alumi'nium, *n.nt.* aluminum.
Amalgam', -e, *n.nt.* amalgam.
amalgamie'ren, *vb.* amalgamate.
Amateur', -e, *n.m.* amateur.
Amboß, -sse, *n.m.* anvil.
ambulant', *adj.* ambulatory.
Ameise, -n, *n.f.* ant.
Ame'rika, *n.nt.* America.
Amerika'ner, -, *n.m.* American.
amerika'nisch, *adj.* American.

Amethyst', -e, *n.m.* amethyst.

Ammoni'ak, *n.nt.* ammonia.

Amnestie', -i'en, *n.f.* amnesty.

Amö'be, -n, *n.f.* amoeba.

amoralisch, *adj.* amoral.

amortisie'ren, *vb.* amortize.

Ampere, -, *(pron. Ampär')* *n.nt.* ampere.

amphi'bisch, *adj.* amphibious.

amputie'ren, *vb.* amputate.

Amputiert'-, -, *n.m.&f.* amputee.

Amt, -er, *n.nt.* office.

amtie'ren, *vb.* officiate.

amtlich, *adj.* official.

Amtseinführung, -en, *n.f.* inauguration.

Amtsschimmel, *n.m.* red tape.

Amtstratsch, *n.m.* grapevine, gossip.

amüsie'ren, *vb.* amuse; (**sich a.**) have a good time.

an, *prep.* at, on, to.

Anachronis'mus, -men, *n.m.* anachronism.

analog', *adj.* analogous.

Analogie', -i'en, *n.f.* analogy.

analo'gisch, *adj.* analogical.

Analphabet', -en, -en, *n.m.* illiterate.

Analphabe'tentum, *n.nt.* illiteracy.

Analy'se, -n, *n.f.* analysis.

analysie'ren, *vb.* analyze.

Analy'tiker, -, *n.m.* analyst.

analy'tisch, *adj.* analytic(al).

Anarchie', -i'en, *n.f.* anarchy.

Anästhesie', *n.f.* anesthesia.

Anatomie', -i'en, *n.f.* anatomy.

Anbau, -ten, *n.m.* cultivation; addition (to a house).

Anbeginn, *n.m.* origin.

anbei', *adv.* inclosed, herewith.

an·beten, *vb.* worship, adore.

Anbetracht, *n.m.* (**in A.**) in view of.

Anbetung, -en, *n.f.* adoration.

an·bieten*, *vb.* ofier.

Anblick, -e, *n.m.* sight, view, appearance.

an·brechen*, *vb.* begin; break; (**der Tag bricht an**) day breaks, dawns.

Anbruch, -e, *n.m.* beginning, (day)break, (night)fall.

Andacht, -en, *n.f.* devotion.

andächtig, *adj.* devout.

andauernd, *adj.* continual.

Andenken, -, *n.nt.* memory, memorial, souvenir.

ander-, *adj.* other, different.

and(e)rerseits, *adv.* on the other hand.

ändern, *vb.* change, alter.

anders, *adv.* otherwise, else.

anderswie, *adv.* otherwise.

anderswo, *adv.* elsewhere.

anderthalb, *num.* one and a half.

Änderung, -en, *n.f.* change, alteration.

an·deuten, *vb.* indicate, imply.

Andeutung, -en, *n.f.* indication, implication.

Andrang, *n.m.* rush, crowd.

an·drehen, *vb.* turn on.

an·eignen, *vb.* seize, appropriate.

Aneignung, -en, *n.f.* seizure, appropriation.

aneinan'der, *adv.* to one another, together.

Anekdo'te, -n, *n.f.* anecdote.

an·ekeln, *vb.* disgust.

an·erkennen* (*or* **anerkennen***), *vb.* acknowledge.

anerkennenswert, *adj.* creditable.

Anerkennung, -en, *n.f.* acknowledgment, recognition.

anfahren*, *vb.* drive up against, collide with, hit; speak sharply to.

Anfall, -e, *n.m.* attack.

an·fallen*, *vb.* fall upon, attack.

Anfang, -e, *n.m.* beginning.

an·fangen*, *vb.* begin.

Anfänger, -, *n.m.* beginner.

anfänglich, *adj.* initial.

anfangs, *adv.* in the beginning.

an·fassen*, *vb.* take hold of, grasp.

an·fechten*, *vb.* assail.

an·fertigen, *vb.* prepare, manufacture.

an·feuchten, *vb.* moisten.

an·feuern, *vb.* fire, incite, inspire.

an·flehen, *vb.* beseech.

an·fliegen*, *vb.* fly at.

Anflug, -e, *n.m.* approach flight, slight attack, touch.

an·fordern, *vb.* claim, demand.

Anfrage, -n, *n.f.* inquiry, application.

an·freunden, *vb.* (**sich a. mit**) befriend.

an·führen, *vb.* lead on; allege; cite; dupe.

Anführung, -en, *n.f.* leadership; quotation, allegation.

Anführungsstrich, -e, *n.m.* quotation mark.

Anführungszeichen, *n.nt.* quotation mark.

Angabe, -n, *n.f.* fact cited, statement, assertion; (*pl.*) data.

an·geben*, *vb.* cite as a fact, state, assert; brag, boast.

Angeber, -, *n.m.* boaster.

Angeberei', -en, *n.f.* boast, boastfulness.

angeberisch, *adj.* boastful.

angeblich, *adj.* as stated, alleged.

angeboren, *adj.* innate, congenital.

Angebot, -e, *n.nt.* bid, offer.

angebracht, *adj.* proper.

angeheiratet, *adj.* related by marriage.

an·gehen*, *vb.* concern.

angehend, *adj.* beginning, incipient.

an·gehören, *vb.* belong to.

angehörig, *adj.* belonging to.

Angehörig-, *n.m.&f.* dependent.

Angeklagt-, *n.m.&f.* accused, defendant.

Angel, -n, *n.f.* hinge, axis; fishing tackle.

angelegen, *adj.* important, of concern.

Angelegenheit, -en, *n.f.* matter, concern, affair.

angelehnt, *adj.* leaned against, ajar.

angeln, *vb.* fish, angle.

angemessen, *adj.* adequate, appropriate, suitable.

angenehm, *adj.* pleasant, agreeable.

angesehen, *adj.* respected, respectable.

Angesicht, -er, *n.nt.* face.

Angestellt-, *n.m.&f.* employee.

angewandt, *adj.* applied.

an·gewöhnen, *vb.* accustom to.

Angewohnheit, -en, *n.f.* habit, custom.

an·gleichen*, *vb.* assimilate, adjust.

Angleichung, -en, *n.f.* assimilation.

Angler, -, *n.m.* fisherman.

an·gliedern, *vb.* affiliate.

Angliederung, -en, *n.f.* affiliation.

angreifbar, *adj.* assailable.

an·greifen*, *vb.* attack, assault.

Angreifer, -, *n.m.* attacker, aggressor.

an·grenzen, *vb.* abut, border on.

angrenzend, *adj.* contiguous.

Angriff, -e, *n.m.* attack, aggression.

Angriffslust, *n.f.* aggressiveness.

Angst, -e, *n.f.* fear; (**A. haben***, **A. sein***) be afraid.

ängstigen, *vb.* frighten.

ängstlich, *adj.* timid, anxious.

an·haben*, *vb.* have on, wear

Anhalt, -e, *n.m.* hold; basis.

an·halten*, *vb.* (*tr.*) stop, arrest; (*intr.*) last, continue.

anhaltend, *adj.* lasting.

Anhaltspunkt, -e, *n.m.* point of reference, basis, clue.

Anhang, -e, *n.m.* appendix; adherents.

Anhänger, -, *n.m.* follower; pendant; trailer.

an·häufen, *vb.* amass, accumulate.

Anhäufung, -en, *n.f.* accumulation.

an·heften, *vb.* affix, attach.

anheim'stellen, *vb.* submit.

Anhieb, -e, *n.m.* first stroke; (**auf A.**) right away, right off the bat.

an·hören, *vb.* listen to.

Anilin', *n.nt.* aniline.

Ankauf, -e, *n.m.* purchase.

an·kaufen, *vb.* buy.

Anker, -, *n.m.* anchor.

Ankerplatz, -e, *n.m.* anchorage.

an·ketten, *vb.* chain.

Anklage, -n, n.f. accusation, indictment, impeachment.

an·klagen, vb. accuse, indict, impeach.

Ankläger, -, n.m. accuser, plaintiff.

an·klammern, vb. fasten (with a clamp); (sich a.) cling.

an·kommen*, vb. arrive; (a. auf) depend upon.

an·kündigen, vb. announce.

Ankunft, -̈e, n.f. arrival.

an·kurbeln, vb. crank up, get started.

Anlage, -n, n.f. arrangement, disposition, investment; enclosure; (pl.) grounds.

an·langen, vb. (tr.) concern; (intr.) arrive.

Anlaß, -̈sse, n.m. cause, motivating factor.

an·lassen*, vb. leave on; start.

Anlasser, -, n.m. starter.

anläßlich, prep. on the occasion of.

Anlauf, -̈e, n.m. start, warmup; attack.

an·laufen*, vb. run at, make for; swell, rise.

an·legen*, vb. put on; invest; land.

an·lehnen, vb. lean against, leave ajar.

Anleihe, -n, n.f. loan.

an·leiten, vb. lead to, instruct.

Anleitung, -en, n.f. instruction.

an·lernen, vb. train.

an·machen, vb. fix, attach, turn on.

an·maßen, vb. assume, presume.

anmaßend, adj. arrogant, presumptuous.

Anmaßung, -en, n.f. arrogance, presumption.

an·melden, vb. announce.

Anmeldung, -en, n.f. announcement, report, registration.

an·merken, vb. note.

Anmerkung, -en, n.f. (foot)note.

an·messen*, vb. measure for, fit.

Anmut, n.f. grace, charm.

anmutig, adj. graceful.

an·nähern, vb. approach.

annähernd, adj. approximate.

Annäherung, -en, n.f. approach, approximation.

Annahme, -n, n.f. acceptance, adoption; assumption, supposition.

annehmbar, adj. acceptable.

an·nehmen*, vb. accept, assume, suppose, infer.

Annehmlichkeit, -en, n.f. pleasure, agreeableness.

Annon'ce, -n, n.f. advertisement.

annoncie'ren, vb. advertise.

annulie'ren, vb. annul.

Anomalie, -i'en, n.f. anomaly.

anonym', adj. anonymous.

an·ordnen, vb. order, arrange.

Anordnung, -en, n.f. order, arrangement.

an·packen, vb. grab hold of, get started with.

an·passen, vb. adapt, fit, try on; (sich a.) conform.

Anpassung, -en, n.f. adaptation.

anpassungsfähig, adj. adaptable, adaptive.

Anprall, n.m. collision, impact.

an·preisen*, vb. praise, recommend.

Anprobe, -n, n.f. fitting.

Anrecht, -e, n.nt. right, claim.

Anrede, -n, n.f. address, speech.

an·reden, vb. speak to, accost.

an·regen, vb. stimulate, incite.

Anregung, -en, n.f. stimulation; suggestion.

Anreiz, -e, n.m. stimulus, incentive.

an·reizen, vb. incite.

Anruf, -e, n.m. appeal, (telephone) call.

an·rufen*, vb. appeal to, invoke; call up.

Anrufung, n.f. invocation.

an·rühren, vb. touch; (cooking) mix.

an·sagen, vb. announce.

Ansager, -, n.m. announcer.

an·sammeln, vb. amass; (sich a.) congregate, gather.

Ansammlung, -en, n.f. collection, backlog.

ansässig, adj. resident.

Ansatz, -̈e, n.m. start; estimate; charge; added piece.

an·schaffen*, vb. get, obtain.

Anschaffung, -en, n.f. acquisition.

an·schauen, vb. look at.

anschaulich, adj. graphic, clear.

Anschauung, -en, n.f. view, opinion.

Anschein, -e, n.m. appearance.

anscheinend, adj. apparent.

Anschlag, -̈e, n.m. stroke; poster; estimate; plot.

an·schlagen*, vb. (tr.) strike, affix, fasten, post; estimate; (intr.) work, start to function.

an·schließen*, vb. fasten with a lock, adjoin; (sich a.) join; fit tight.

Anschluß, -sse, n.m. connection, annexation.

an·schnallen, vb. buckle on.

an·schneiden*, vb. start cutting.

an·schreiben*, vb. write down, score, charge.

Anschrift, -en, n.f. address.

an·sehen*, vb. look at.

Ansehen, n.nt. reputation, repute.

ansehnlich, adj. handsome; considerable, notable.

an·setzen, vb. fix, affix; set, schedule; estimate.

Ansicht, -en, n.f. view, opinion.

an·siedeln, vb. settle, colonize.

an·spannen, vb. stretch, strain; harness.

Anspannung, -en, n.f. strain, tension.

an·spielen, vb. start to play; allude.

Anspielung, -en, n.f. allusion.

an·spornen, vb. spur on.

Ansprache, -n, n.f. pronunciation; talk.

an·sprechen*, vb. address, accost.

ansprechend, adj. attractive.

Anspruch, -̈e, n.m. claim; (A. machen auf) lay claim to; (in A. nehmen*) require, take up.

anspruchslos, adj. unassuming.

anspruchsvoll, adj. pretentious.

an·stacheln, vb. goad, incite.

Anstalt, -en, n.f. arrangement, institution.

Anstand, n.m. propriety; objection.

anständig, adj. decent.

Anständigkeit, -en, n.f. decency.

anstatt', adv. instead of.

an·stecken, vb. pin on, put on; light, set fire to; infect.

ansteckend, adj. contagious.

Ansteckung, -en, n.f. contagion.

an·stehen*, vb. line up, stand in line.

an·steigen*, vb. rise.

an·stellen*, vb. place; hire, employ.

Anstellung, -en, n.f. employment.

Anstieg, -e, n.m. rise.

an·stiften, vb. incite, instigate.

an·stimmen, vb. intone, tune up.

Anstoß, -̈e, n.m. shock; impetus; offense.

an·stoßen*, vb. knock, bump against, nudge; offend; clink glasses.

anstoßend, adj. adjoining.

anstößig, adj. offensive.

an·streben, vb. strive for.

an·streichen*, vb. paint; underline; mark.

an·strengen, vb. strain; (sich a.) exert oneself, try hard.

anstrengend, adj. strenuous.

Anstrengung, -en, n.f. effort, exertion.

Anstrich, -e, n.m. coat of paint; appearance; touch.

Ansturm, -̈e, n.m. assault, run (on a bank).

Antark'tis, n.f. Antarctic.

antark'tisch, adj. antarctic.

Anteil, -e, n.m. share.

Anten'ne, -n, n.f. antenna.

antik', adj. antique.

Anti'ke, n.f. antiquity, classical times.

Antilo'pe, -n, n.f. antelope.

Antimon', n.nt. antimony.

antinuklear', adj. antinuclear.

Antipathie', -i'en, n.f. antipathy.

Antiquar', -e, *n.m.* second-hand bookdealer, antique dealer.

Antiquariat', -e, *n.nt.* second-hand bookstore.

antiqua'risch, *adj.* second-hand.

antisep'tisch, *adj.* antiseptic.

antisozial', *adj.* antisocial.

Antlitz, -e, *n.nt.* countenance.

Antrag, ⸗e, *n.m.* offer, proposal, motion.

an-treffen*, *vb.* meet up with.

an-treiben*, *vb.* drive on, propel, incite.

an-treten*, *vb.* enter into (office), start out on, step forward.

Antrieb, -e, *n.m.* impulse, impetus, force.

Antritt, -e, *n.m.* entrance into, start.

an-tun*, *vb.* put on, inflict, cause.

Antwort, -en, *n.f.* answer.

antworten, *vb.* answer.

an-vertrauen, *vb.* entrust; (sich a.) confide.

an-wachsen*, *vb.* grow, increase.

Anwalt, ⸗e, *n.m.* attorney, advocate.

Anwärter, -, *n.m.* applicant, aspirant.

an-weisen*, *vb.* instruct, direct; assign.

Anweisung, -en, *n.f.* instruction, assignment; money order.

anwendbar, *adj.* applicable.

an-wenden*, *vb.* apply, use.

Anwendung, -en, *n.f.* application, use.

anwesend, *adj.* present.

Anwesenheit, -en, *n.f.* presence.

Anwurf, ⸗e, *n.m.* slur.

Anzahl, *n.f.* quantity, number.

an-zahlen, *vb.* make a down payment.

Anzahlung, -en, *n.f.* down payment.

an-zapfen, *vb.* tap.

Anzeichen, -, *n.nt.* sign, symptom.

an-zeichnen, *vb.* mark, note.

Anzeige, -n, *n.f.* notice, advertisement; denunciation.

an-zeigen, *vb.* announce, advertise; denounce.

Anzeiger, -, *n.m.* advertiser; informer.

an-ziehen*, *vb.* draw along, attract; put on, dress; rise.

anziehend, *adj.* attractive.

Anziehungskraft, ⸗e, *n.f.* attraction; (A. der Erde) gravity.

Anzug, ⸗e, *n.m.* suit; approach.

an-zünden, *vb.* ignite, light.

an-zweifeln, *vb.* doubt, question.

apart, *adj.* out of the ordinary.

Apart'heid, *n.f.* apartheid.

Apathie', -i'en, *n.f.* apathy.

apa'thisch, *adj.* apathetic.

Apfel, ⸗, *n.m.* apple.

Apfelmus, *n.nt.* applesauce.

Apfelsi'ne, -n, *n.f.* orange.

apoplek'tisch, *adj.* apoplectic.

Apos'tel, -, *n.m.* apostle.

aposto'lisch, *adj.* apostolic.

Apothe'ke, -n, *n.f.* pharmacy.

Apothe'ker, -, *n.m.* pharmacist.

Apparat', -e, *n.m.* apparatus.

appellie'ren, *vb.* appeal.

Appetit', -e, *n.m.* appetite.

appetit'lich, *adj.* appetizing, inviting.

applaudie'ren, *vb.* applaud.

Applaus', -e, *n.m.* applause.

Apriko'se, -n, *n.f.* apricot.

April', *n.m.* April.

Aquarell', -e, *n.nt.* watercolor.

Aqua'rium, -ien, *n.nt.* aquarium.

Äqua'tor, *n.m.* equator.

äquatorial', *adj.* equatorial.

Araber, -, *n.m.* Arab.

ara'bisch, *adj.* Arabic, Arabian.

Arbeit, -en, *n.f.* work.

arbeiten, *vb.* work.

Arbeiter, -, *n.m.* worker, workman, laborer.

Arbeiterschaft, *n.f.* labor.

Arbeitge'ber, -, *n.m.* employer.

arbeitslos, *adj.* unemployed.

Arbeitslosigkeit, *n.f.* unemployment.

Arbeitszimmer, -, *n.nt.* study.

Archäologie', *n.f.* archaeology.

Archipel', -e, *n.m.* archipelago.

Architekt', -en, -en, *n.m.* architect.

architekto'nisch, *adj.* architectural.

Architektur', -en, *n.f.* architecture.

Archiv', -e, *n.nt.* archives.

Are'na, -nen, *n.f.* arena.

arg, *adj.* bad.

Argenti'nien, *n.nt.* Argentina.

Ärger, *n.m.* anger, annoyance, bother.

ärgerlich, *adj.* angry, annoying.

ärgern, *vb.* annoy, make angry, bother; (sich ä.) be angry.

Ärgernis, -se, *n.nt.* nuisance.

Arglist, *n.f.* guile.

arglos, *adj.* harmless, unsuspecting.

Argument', -e, *n.nt.* argument.

argumentie'ren, *vb.* argue.

Argwohn, *n.m.* suspicion.

argwöhnisch, *adj.* suspicious.

Arie, -n, *n.f.* aria.

Aristokrat', -en, -en, *n.m.* aristocrat.

Aristokratie', -i'en, *n.f.* aristocracy.

aristokra'tisch, *adj.* aristocratic.

Arithmetik', *n.f.* arithmetic.

Arka'de, -n, *n.f.* arcade.

arktisch, *adj.* arctic.

arm (⸗), *adj.* poor.

Arm, -e, *n.m.* arm.

Arm-, *n.m.&f.* pauper.

Armband, ⸗er, *n.nt.* bracelet.

Armbanduhr, -en, *n.f.* wristwatch.

Armee', -me'en, *n.f.* army.

Ärmel, -, *n.m.* sleeve.

Armleuchter, -, *n.m.* candelabrum.

armselig, *adj.* beggarly, miserable.

Armut, *n.f.* poverty, destitution.

Aro'ma, -s, *n.nt.* aroma.

arrangie'ren, *vb.* arrange.

arrogant', *adj.* arrogant.

Arroganz', -en, *n.f.* arrogance.

Arsen', *n.nt.* arsenic.

Art, -en, *n.f.* kind, sort, species; way, manner; (A. und Weise) way.

Arte'rie, -i'en, *n.f.* artery.

Arthri'tis, *n.f.* arthritis.

artig, *adj.* good, well-behaved.

Arti'kel, -, *n.m.* item, article.

artikulie'ren, *vb.* articulate.

Artillerie', -i'en, *n.f.* artillery.

Artischo'cke, -n, *n.f.* artichoke.

Arzt, ⸗e, *n.m.* physician, doctor; (praktischer A.) general practitioner.

ärztlich, *adj.* medical.

As, -se, *n.nt.* ace.

Asbest', -e, *n.m.* asbestos.

Asche, -n, *n.f.* ash; (glühende A.) embers.

Asch(en)becher, -, *n.m.* ashtray.

aschgrau, *adj.* ashen.

Asiat', -en, -en, *n.m.* Asian.

asia'tisch, *adj.* Asian.

Asien, *n.nt.* Asia.

Asket', -en, -en, *n.m.* ascetic.

aske'tisch, *adj.* ascetic.

Asphalt', -e, *n.m.* asphalt.

Aspirin', *n.nt.* aspirin.

assimilie'ren, *vb.* assimilate.

Assistent', -en, -en, *n.m.* assistant.

assoziie'ren, *vb.* associate.

Ast, ⸗e, *n.m.* branch.

ästhe'tisch, *adj.* aesthetic.

Asthma, *n.nt.* asthma.

Astigmatis'mus, -men, *n.m.* astigmatism.

Astrologie', -i'en, *n.f.* astrology.

Astronaut', -en, -en, *n.m.* astronaut.

Astronomie', -i'en, *n.f.* astronomy.

Asyl', -e, *n.nt.* asylum.

Atelier', -s, *n.nt.* studio.

Atem, -, *n.m.* breath.

atemlos, *adj.* breathless.

Atempause, -n, *n.f.* respite.

Atheist', -en, -en, *n.m.* atheist.

Äther, *n.m.* ether.

äthe'risch, *adj.* ethereal.

Athlet', -en, -en, *n.m.* athlete.

athle'tisch, *adj.* athletic.

Atlan'tik, *n.m.* Atlantic Ocean.

atlan'tisch, *adj.* Atlantic.

Atlas, -lan'ten, *n.m.* atlas.

atmen, *vb.* breathe.

Atmen, *n.nt.* breathing.

Atmosphä're, -n, *n.f.* atmosphere.

atmosphä'risch, *adj.* atmospheric.

Atmung, *n.f.* respiration.

Atom', *-e, n.nt.* atom.

atomar', *adj.* atomic.

atomisie'ren, *vb.* atomize.

Atom'müll, *n.m.* nuclear waste.

Atomsperr'vertrag, *-̈e, n.m.* non-proliferation treaty.

Attaché', *-s, n.m.* attaché.

Attentat', *-e, n.nt.* attempt on someone's life.

Attentä'ter, *-, n.m.* assassin.

Attest', *-e, n.nt.* certificate.

ätzen, *vb.* etch; *(med.)* cauterize.

au, *interj.* ouch.

auch, *adv.* also, too; **(a. nicht)** not . . . either; **(a. jetzt)** even now.

Audienz', *-en, n.f.* audience.

audiovisuell', *adj.* audiovisual.

Audito'rium, -rien, *n.nt.* auditorium.

auf, *prep.* on, onto.

auf·atmen, *vb.* breathe a sigh of relief.

Aufbau, *n.m.* erection, construction; structure.

auf·bauen, *vb.* erect.

auf·blasen*, *vb.* inflate.

auf·brechen*, *vb.* break open; start out.

auf·decken, *vb.* uncover, unearth.

auf·drängen, *vb.* obtrude; **(sich a.)** obtrude.

aufdringlich, *adj.* obtrusive, importunate.

aufeinan'derfolgend, *adj.* successive, consecutive.

Aufenthalt, *n.m.* stay.

auf·erlegen, *vb.* impose.

Auferstehung, *n.f.* resurrection.

auf·fallen*, *vb.* be conspicuous.

auffällig, *adj.* noticeable, conspicuous, flashy.

Auffälligkeit, -en, *n.f.* conspicuousness, flashiness.

auf·fangen*, *vb.* catch; intercept.

auf·fassen, *vb.* conceive, interpret.

Auffassung, -en, *n.f.* conception, interpretation.

auf·flammen, *vb.* flash, flare up.

auf·fordern, *vb.* ask, invite, summon.

Aufforderung, -en, *n.f.* invitation, summons.

auf·frischen, *vb.* refresh.

auf·führen, *vb.* list; (theater) perform.

Aufführung, -en, *n.f.* performance.

Aufgabe, -n, *n.f.* task, assignment; (school) lesson.

Aufgang, -̈e, n.m. rise.

auf·geben*, *vb.* give up, abandon; (luggage) check

through; (food) serve; *(jur.)* waive.

Aufgebot, -e, n.nt. banns.

aufgebracht, *adj.* angry, provoked.

auf·gehen*, *vb.* (sun etc.) rise; *(math.)* leave no remainder; *(fig.)* be absorbed in.

auf·halten*, *vb.* hold open; stop, detain; **(sich a.)** stay.

auf·hängen*, *vb.* suspend; hang.

auf·heben*, *vb.* revoke, nullify; **(zeitweilig a.)** suspend.

Aufheben, *n.nt.* ado, fuss.

Aufhebung, -en, *n.f.* revocation, abolition.

auf·heitern, *vb.* cheer up.

auf·hören, *vb.* stop, quit.

Aufhören, *n.nt.* cessation.

auf·klären, *vb.* enlighten; **(sich a.)** clear.

Aufklärung, *n.f.* enlightenment.

auf·kommen*, *vb.* come into use; **(a. für)** be responsible for.

Auflage, -n, *n.f.* printing, circulation.

Auflauf, -̈e, n.m. crowd, mob; soufflé.

auf·lösen, *vb.* dissolve.

Auflösung, -en, *n.f.* dissolution.

auf·machen, *vb.* open; **(sich a.)** set out for.

Aufmachung, -en, *n.f.* make-up.

aufmerksam, *adj.* attentive, polite; alert.

Aufmerksamkeit, -en, *n.f.* attention, attentiveness.

auf·muntern, *vb.* cheer up.

Aufnahme, -n, *n.f.* reception; (photo) shot; (phonograph, tape) recording.

auf·nehmen*, *vb.* take in; (phonograph, tape) record; film, photograph.

auf·opfern, *vb.* **(sich a.)** sacrifice oneself.

auf·passen, *vb.* pay attention, look out for.

auf·raffen, *vb.* **(sich a.)** bestir oneself.

auf·räumen, *vb.* put in order; **(mit etwas a.)** debunk.

aufrecht, *adj.* upright.

aufrecht·erhalten*, *vb.* maintain, uphold.

Aufrechterhaltung, *n.f.* maintenance.

auf·regen, *vb.* excite, agitate; **(sich a.)** get excited.

Aufregung, -en, *n.f.* excitement.

aufreibend, *adj.* exhausting.

auf·reihen, *vb.* string.

auf·reißen*, *vb.* tear open.

auf·richten, *vb.* erect.

aufrichtig, *adj.* sincere, heartfelt.

Aufruf, -e, n.m. proclamation.

Aufruhr, *n.m.* riot; **(in A. geraten*)** riot.

aufrührerisch, *adj.* insurgent; inflammatory.

auf·sagen, *vb.* recite.

aufsässig, *adj.* rebellious.

Aufsatz, -̈e, n.m. essay.

auf·saugen, *vb.* suck up, absorb.

auf·schieben*, *vb.* postpone, delay, procrastinate.

Aufschlag, -̈e, n.m. surtax; (trousers, sleeve) cuff.

auf·schlagen*, *vb.* open; hit the ground.

auf·schließen*, *vb.* unlock.

Aufschluß, -̈sse, n.m. information.

aufschlußreich, *adj.* informative.

Aufschnitt, *n.m.* cut; **(kalter A.)** cold cuts.

Aufschrift, -en, *n.f.* inscription; address.

Aufschub, *n.m.* postponement, stay.

Aufschwung, *n.m.* upward swing, boost.

auf·sehen*, *vb.* look up.

Aufsehen, *n.nt.* sensation.

aufsehenerregend, *adj.* spectacular.

auf·setzen, *vb.* put on.

Aufsicht, *n.f.* supervision.

auf·speichern, *vb.* store up.

auf·springen*, *vb.* leap up; fly open; (skin) chap.

Aufstand, -̈e, n.m. uprising, insurrection.

aufständisch, *adj.* insurgent.

Aufständisch-, *n.m.* insurgent.

auf·stapeln, *vb.* stack.

auf·stehen*, *vb.* get up, rise, arise.

auf·steigen*, *vb.* mount, ascend, rise.

auf·stellen, *vb.* put up; nominate.

Aufstieg, -e, n.m. ascent, advancement.

auf·suchen, *vb.* look up; seek.

auf·tauchen, *vb.* emerge.

Auftrag, -̈e, n.m. instruction, order.

auf·tragen*, *vb.* instruct, assign; lay on; wear out; (food) serve up.

auf·treiben*, *vb.* raise.

auf·trennen, *vb.* rip.

auf·treten*, *vb.* appear; act.

Auftreten, *n.nt.* appearance; **(sicheres A.)** poise.

auf·wachen, *vb.* awake.

Aufwand, *n.m.* expenditure, display.

auf·warten, *vb.* wait upon; wait up.

aufwärts, *adv.* upward(s).

auf·wecken, *vb.* wake up.

auf·wenden*, *vb.* expend.

auf·wiegen*, *vb.* balance.

auf·zählen, *vb.* enumerate; itemize.

auf·zeichnen, *vb.* record.

auf·ziehen*, *vb.* draw open; (watch) wind; (knitting) unravel; (child) rear.

Aufzug, ¨-e, *n.m.* lift, hoist, elevator; procession; (theater) act.

auf·zwingen*, *vb.* force upon.

Auge, -n, *n.nt.* eye; **(blaues A.)** black eye.

Augenarzt, ¨-e, *n.m.* oculist.

Augenblick, -e, *n.m.* moment, instant.

augenblicklich, *adj.* momentary, instant.

Augenbraue, -n, *n.f.* eyebrow.

Augenglas, -er, *n.nt.* eyeglass.

Augenhöhle, -n, *n.f.* eye socket.

Augenlid, -er, *n.nt.* eyelid.

Augenschein, *n.m.* evidence.

augenscheinlich, *adj.* ostensible.

Augensicht, *n.f.* eyesight.

Augenwimper, -n, *n.f.* eyelash.

August´, *n.m.* August.

aus, *prep.* out of, from.

aus·arbeiten, *vb.* elaborate.

aus·arten, *vb.* degenerate.

aus·atmen, *vb.* exhale.

aus·bessern, *vb.* repair, mend.

aus·beuten, *vb.* exploit.

aus·bilden, *vb.* educate, train.

aus·bleiben*, *vb.* stay out; fail to materialize.

Ausblick, -e, *n.m.* outlook; view.

aus·brechen*, *vb.* erupt.

aus·breiten, *vb.* spread, expand.

aus·brennen*, *vb.* burn out; *(med.)* cauterize.

Ausbruch, ¨-e, *n.m.* outbreak, outburst, eruption.

aus·brüten, *vb.* hatch.

aus·buchten, *vb.* (sich a.) bulge.

Ausdauer, *n.f.* endurance, stamina.

ausdauernd, *adj.* enduring.

aus·dehnen, *vb.* expand, extend; prolong; **(sich a.)** distend, dilate.

Ausdehnung, -en, *n.f.* expanse, expansion.

aus·denken*, *vb.* think up, invent.

aus·drehen, *vb.* turn out.

Ausdruck, ¨-e, *n.m.* expression, term.

aus·drücken, *vb.* express, phrase.

ausdrücklich, *adj.* explicit.

ausdrucksvoll, *adj.* expressive.

auseinan´der, *adv.* apart, asunder.

auseinan´der·gehen*, *vb.* part; diverge.

auseinan´der·nehmen*, *vb.* take apart.

auseinan´der·reißen*, *vb.* tear apart, disrupt.

auserlesen, *adj.* choice.

aus·fallen*, *vb.* fall out, not take place.

Ausflug, ¨-, *n.m.* excursion, outing.

aus·fragen, *vb.* interrogate, quiz.

Ausfuhr, *n.f.* export.

aus·führen, *vb.* carry out, execute; export.

ausführend, *adj.* executive.

ausführlich, *adj.* detailed, explicit.

Ausführung, -en, *n.f.* execution; statement.

aus·füllen, *vb.* fill out.

Ausgabe, -n, *n.f.* expense, expenditure; issuance; edition; (computer) output.

Ausgang, ¨-e, *n.m.* exit; end.

aus·geben*, *vb.* give out; spend, expend; issue; **(sich a. für)** pose as.

ausgefallen, *adj.* rare; odd.

aus·gehen*, *vb.* go out; date.

ausgelassen, *adj.* hilarious.

ausgenommen, *adj.* except for.

ausgestorben, *adj.* extinct.

ausgesucht, *adj.* select.

ausgezeichnet, *adj.* excellent.

aus·gleichen*, *vb.* balance, adjust.

aus·gleiten*, *vb.* slip.

Ausguß, -sse, *n.m.* sink.

aus·halten*, *vb.* hold out; bear.

aus·händigen, *vb.* hand out, over.

Aushilfe, -n, *n.f.* assistance; stopgap.

aus·hungern, *vb.* starve out.

aus·kleiden, *vb.* undress.

aus·kommen*, *vb.* get along (with).

Auskommen, *n.nt.* livelihood.

Auskunft, ¨-e, *n.f.* information.

aus·lachen, *vb.* laugh at.

aus·laden*, *vb.* unload.

Auslage, -n, *n.f.* outlay; display.

Ausland, *n.nt.* foreign country; **(im A.)** abroad.

Ausländer, -, *n.m.* foreigner, alien.

ausländisch, *adj.* foreign, alien.

aus·lassen*, *vb.* leave out; let out.

aus·legen, *vb.* lay out; interpret; (money) advance.

Auslegung, -en, *n.f.* interpretation.

Auslese, -n, *n.f.* selection.

aus·liefern, *vb.* extradite.

aus·löschen, *vb.* extinguish, efface.

aus·lösen, *vb.* release, unleash.

Ausmaß, -e, *n.nt.* dimension.

Ausnahme, -n, *n.f.* exception.

aus·nutzen, *vb.* utilize; exploit.

aus·packen, *vb.* unpack.

aus·pressen, *vb.* squeeze.

Auspuff, -e, *n.m.* exhaust.

aus·radieren, *vb.* erase, obliterate.

aus·rangieren, *vb.* scrap.

aus·rechnen, *vb.* figure out.

aus·reichen, *vb.* suffice.

aus·reißen*, *vb.* run away, bolt.

aus·renken, *vb.* dislocate.

aus·richten, *vb.* align; execute; deliver (a message).

aus·rotten, *vb.* exterminate, eradicate.

Ausruf, -e, *n.m.* exclamation.

aus·rufen*, *vb.* proclaim, exclaim.

Ausrufungszeichen, -, *n.nt.* exclamation point.

aus·ruhen, *vb.* rest.

ausruhsam, *adj.* restful.

aus·rüsten, *vb.* equip.

Aussage, -n, *n.f.* statement; testimony.

aus·sagen, *vb.* testify.

Aussatz, *n.m.* leprosy.

aus·schalten, *vb.* eliminate; *(elec.)* disconnect.

Ausschalter, -, *n.m.* *(elec.)* cutout.

aus·scheiden*, *vb.* eliminate; *(med.)* secrete; retire, withdraw.

Ausscheidung, -en, *n.f.* elimination.

aus·schelten*, *vb.* berate.

aus·schimpfen, *vb.* scold, bawl out.

aus·schlafen*, *vb.* sleep as long as one wants to.

Ausschlag, ¨-e, *n.m.* *(med.)* rash; **(den A. geben*)** clinch the matter.

aus·schließen*, *vb.* shut out, exclude.

ausschließlich, *adj.* exclusive.

Ausschluß, *n.m.* exclusion.

aus·schmücken, *vb.* embellish.

Ausschnitt, -e, *n.m.* section; clipping; neck (of dress).

aus·schöpfen, *vb.* bail out (water), exhaust.

Ausschuß, ¨-sse, *n.m.* committee, board.

aus·schweifen, *vb.* go far afield; dissipate.

aus·sehen*, *vb.* look, appear.

außen, *adv.* outside; **(nach a.)** outward.

Außenbezirk, -e, *n.m.* outskirts.

Außenseite, -n, *n.f.* outside.

Außenwelt, *n.f.* outside.

außer, *prep.* beside(s); except; out of; **(a. sich)** beside oneself.

äußer-, *adj.* exterior, external.

außerdem, *adv.* besides.

außergewöhnlich, *adj.* extraordinary.

äußerlich, *adj.* outward.

äußern, *vb.* utter.

außerordentlich, *adv.* exceedingly.

äußerst-, *adj.* extreme.

äußerst, *adv.* extremely.

Äußerst-, *n.nt.* extremity.

außerstan´de, *adv.* unable.

Äußerung, -en, *n.f.* utterance.

aus·setzen, *vb.* set out; expose; subject.

Aussetzung, -en, *n.f.* exposure.

Aussicht, -en, *n.f.* view; prospect.

aus·speien*, *vb.* disgorge.

Aussprache, -n, *n.f.* pronunciation.

aus·sprechen*, *vb.* enunciate,

pronounce; (falsch a.) mispronounce.

aus·spucken, vb. spit (out).

aus·spülen, vb. rinse.

Ausstand, -e, n.m. strike.

aus·statten, vb. equip, endow.

Ausstattung, -en, n.f. equipment, décor.

aus·stehen*, vb. bear, stand.

aus·steigen*, vb. get out.

aus·stellen, vb. show, exhibit; issue.

Ausstellung, -en, n.f. exhibit, exhibition.

aus·sterben*, vb. die out.

Aussterben, n.nt. extinction.

aus·stoßen*, vb. expel.

aus·strahlen, vb. radiate.

Ausstrahlung, -en, n.f. radiation.

aus·streichen*, vb. delete.

aus·strömen, vb. emanate.

aus·suchen, vb. choose, select.

Austausch, n.m. exchange.

austauschbar, adj. exchangeable.

aus·tauschen, vb. exchange.

aus·teilen, vb. distribute.

Auster, -n, n.f. oyster.

aus·tilgen, vb. expunge.

aus·tragen*, vb. deliver.

aus·treiben*, vb. drive out, exorcise.

aus·treten*, vb. step out; resign; secede.

aus·üben, vb. exercise, practice.

Ausübung, -en, n.f. exercise, practice.

Ausverkauf, n.m. sale.

Auswahl, -en, n.f. choice, selection, assortment.

aus·wählen, vb. select, pick.

aus·walzen, vb. roll out, laminate.

Auswanderer, -, n.m. emigrant.

aus·wandern, vb. emigrate.

auswärtig, adj. external.

Ausweg, -e, n.m. way out, escape.

aus·weichen*, vb. evade, dodge.

ausweichend, adj. evasive.

Ausweis, -e, n.m. pass, identification.

aus·weisen*, vb. evict; (sich a.) identify oneself.

Ausweisung, -en, n.f. eviction.

auswendig, adj. by heart; (a. lernen) memorize.

aus·werten, vb. evaluate; reclaim.

Auswertung, -en, n.f. evaluation; reclamation.

aus·wickeln, vb. unwrap.

aus·wirken, vb. work out; (sich a.) have an effect.

Auswirkung, -en, n.f. effect, impact.

aus·wischen, vb. wipe out.

Auswuchs, -e, n.m. protuberance, excrescence.

aus·zahlen, vb. pay out.

aus·zeichnen, vb. distinguish; (sich a.) excel.

aus·ziehen*, vb. move out; (clothes) take off; (sich a.) undress.

Auszug, -e, n.m. exodus; excerpt, extract.

authen'tisch, adj. authentic.

Auto, -s, n.nt. auto.

Autobahn, -en, n.f. superhighway.

Autobus, -se, n.m. bus.

Autogramm', -e, n.nt. autograph.

Automat', -en, -en, n.m. automat; automaton.

Automation', n.f. automation.

automa'tisch, adj. automatic.

autonom', adj. autonomous.

autoritär', adj. authoritarian.

Autorität', -en, n.f. authority.

Axt, -e, n.f. axe.

azur'blau, adj. azure.

B

Baby, -s, n.nt. baby.

Bach, -e, n.m. brook.

Backe, -n, n.f. cheek, jowl.

backen*, vb. bake.

Bäcker, -, n.m. baker.

Bäckerei', -en, n.f. bakery, pastry shop.

Backpflaume, -n, n.f. prune.

Backstein, -e, n.m. brick.

Bad, -er, n.nt. bath.

Badeanstalt, -en, n.f. public bath.

Badeanzug, -e, n.m. bathing suit.

Bademantel, -, n.m. bathrobe.

baden, vb. bathe.

Badeort, -e, n.m. bathing resort.

Badewanne, -n, n.f. bathtub.

Badezimmer, -, n.nt. bathroom.

Bahn, -en, n.f. path, course.

Bahnhof, -e, n.m. station.

Bahnsteig, -e, n.m. platform.

Bahre, -n, n.f. bier.

Bajonett', -e, n.nt. bayonet.

Bakte'rie, -n, n.f. germ.

Bakte'rium, -rien, n.nt. bacterium.

balancie'ren, vb. balance.

bald, adv. soon, shortly.

Balken, -, n.m. beam.

Balkon', -s or -e, n.m. balcony.

Ball, -e, n.m. ball.

ballen, vb. (fist) clench.

Balleri'na, -nen, n.f. ballerina.

Ballon', -s, n.m. balloon.

Balsam, -e, n.m. balsam, balm.

balsamie'ren, vb. embalm.

Bambus, -se, n.m. bamboo.

banal', adj. banal.

Bana'ne, -n, n.f. banana.

Band, -e, n.nt. bond, tie.

Band, -e, n.m. (book) volume.

Band, -er, n.nt. band, ribbon, tape.

Bande, -n, n.f. band, gang.

bändigen, vb. tame.

Bandit', -en, -en, n.m. bandit, desperado.

bang(e), adj. afraid.

Bank, -e, n.f. bench.

Bank, -en, n.f. bank.

Bankgeschäft, -e, n.nt. banking; banking firm.

Bankier', -s, n.m. banker.

bankrott', adj. bankrupt.

Bankrott', n.m. bankruptcy.

Bann, -e, n.m. ban; (eccles.) excommunication.

bannen, vb. banish, outlaw.

Banner, -, n.nt. banner.

bar, adj. cash.

Bar, -s, n.f. bar.

Bär, -en, -en, n.m. bear; (Große B.) Big Dipper.

Barbar', -en, -en, n.m. barbarian.

Barbarei', -en, n.f. barbarism.

barba'risch, adj. barbarian, barbarous.

barfuß, adj. barefoot.

Bargeld, -er, n.nt. cash.

Bariton, -e, n.m. baritone.

Barium, n.nt. barium.

Barke, -n, n.f. bark.

barmher'zig, adj. merciful.

Barmixer, -, n.m. bartender.

barock', adj. baroque.

Barome'ter, -, n.nt. barometer.

barome'trisch, adj. barometric.

Baron', -e, n.m. baron.

Barones'se, -n, n.f. baroness.

Barrika'de, -n, n.f. barricade.

Bart, -e, n.m. beard.

Barthaar, -e, n.nt. whisker.

bärtig, adj. bearded.

bartlos, adj. beardless.

Barzahlung, -en, n.f. cash payment.

Baseball-Spiel, -e, n.nt. baseball.

basie'ren, vb. base.

Basis, -sen, n.f. basis.

Baß, -sse, n.m. bass.

Bastard, -e, n.m. bastard.

Bataillon', -e, n.nt. battalion.

Batist', -e, n.m. cambric; batiste.

Batterie', -i'en, n.f. battery.

Bau, -ten, n.m. construction; building; structure.

Bauch, -e, n.m. belly.

bauen, vb. build, construct.

Bauer, -n, n.m. farmer, peasant; (chess) pawn.

Bauernhaus, -er, n.nt. farmhouse.

Bauernhof, -e, n.m. farmyard.

baufällig, adj. dilapidated.

Baukunst, n.f. architecture.

Baum, -, n.m. tree.

Baumeister, -, n.m. builder.

baumeln, vb. dangle; (b. lassen*) dangle.

bäumen, vb. (sich b.) rear.

Baumstamm, -e, n.m. log.

Baumwolle, n.f. cotton.

bauschig, adj. baggy.

Bauunternehmer, -, n.m. contractor.

Bazar', -e, n.m. bazaar.

Bazil'lus, -len, n.m. bacillus.

beab'sichtigen, vb. intend.

beach'ten, vb. notice, pay attention to.

beach'tenswert, adj. noteworthy.

beacht'lich, adj. remarkable.

Beach'tung, -en, n.f. notice, consideration.

Beamt'-, n.m. official.

bean'spruchen, vb. lay claim to.

bean'standen, vb. object to.

bean'tragen, vb. propose, move.

beant'worten, vb. answer.

bear'beiten, vb. work; adapt; handle, process.

beauf'sichtigen, vb. supervise.

beauf'tragen, vb. commission.

Beauf'tragt-, n.m. commissioner.

bebau'en, vb. till; build on.

beben, vb. quake, tremble.

Becher, -, n.m. beaker, goblet.

Becken, -, n.nt. basin; pelvis.

Bedacht', n.m. deliberation, care.

bedäch'tig, adj. cautious, deliberate.

bedan'ken, vb. (sich bei jemandem für etwas b.) thank someone for something.

Bedarf', n.m. need, demand.

bedau'erlich, adj. regrettable.

bedau'ern, vb. regret.

Bedau'ern, n.nt. regret.

bede'cken, vb. cover over.

beden'ken*, vb. bear in mind.

Beden'ken, -, n.nt. compunction, misgiving.

bedeu'ten, vb. mean, signify.

bedeu'tend, adj. significant, important.

Bedeu'tung, -en, n.f. significance, meaning.

bedeu'tungslos, adj. insignificant.

bedie'nen, vb. serve, wait on; operate (machine); follow suit (cards); (sich b.) help oneself.

Bedie'ner, -, n.m. operator (of a machine).

Bedient'-, n.m.&f. servant, attendant.

Bedie'nung, n.f. service.

bedingt', adj. conditional, qualified.

Bedin'gung, -en, n.f. condition.

bedin'gungslos, adj. unconditional.

bedrän'gen, vb. beset.

bedro'hen, vb. menace, threaten.

bedrü'cken, vb. oppress.

bedrü'ckend, adj. oppressive.

bedür'fen*, vb. have need of.

Bedürf'nis, -se, n.nt. need, requirement.

Bedürf'nisanstalt, -en, n.f. comfort station.

bedürf'tig, adj. indigent, needy; in need of.

Beefsteak, -s, n.nt. beefsteak.

beeh'ren, vb. honor.

beei'len vb. (sich b.) hurry.

beein'drucken, vb. impress.

beein'flussen, vb. influence.

beein'trächtigen, vb. impair.

been'den, vb. end, finish.

been'digen, vb. end, finish.

beer'digen, vb. inter, bury.

Beer'digung, -en, n.f. funeral.

Beere, -n, n.f. berry.

befä'higen, vb. enable, qualify.

befahr'bar, adj. passable.

befal'len*, vb. fall upon, attack.

befan'gen, adj. embarrassed.

befas'sen, vb. touch; (sich b. mit) take up, attend to, deal with.

Befehl', -e, n.m. command, order.

befeh'len*, vb. command, order.

Befehls'haber, -, n.m. commander.

befes'tigen, vb. fasten, fortify, confirm.

befeuch'ten, vb. moisten.

befin'den*, vb. find; deem; (sich b.) be located, feel.

befle'cken, vb. stain.

beflei'ßigen, vb. (sich b.) endeavor, take pains.

befol'gen, vb. follow, observe, obey.

beför'dern, vb. advance, promote, transport.

Beför'derungsmittel, n.nt. conveyance.

befra'gen, vb. question, interrogate.

befrei'en, vb. liberate, exempt.

Befrei'ung, -en, n.f. liberation, release.

befrem'den, vb. appear strange to, alienate.

befreun'den, vb. befriend; (sich b. mit) make friends with.

befrie'digen, vb. satisfy.

befrie'digend, adj. satisfactory.

Befrie'digung, -en, n.f. satisfaction.

befruch'ten, vb. fertilize, fructify.

Befug'nis, -se, n.f. authority.

befugt', adj. authorized.

befüh'len, vb. feel, finger.

Befund', -e, n.m. finding(s).

befürch'ten, vb. fear.

befür'worten, vb. advocate, recommend.

begabt', adj. gifted.

Bega'bung, -en, n.f. talent.

bege'ben*, vb. (sich b.) betake oneself; occur.

begeg'nen, vb. meet, encounter.

Begeg'nung, -en, n.f. meeting, encounter.

bege'hen*, vb. commit.

begeh'ren, vb. desire, covet.

begeis'tern, vb. inspire.

begeis'tert, adj. enthusiastic.

Begeis'terung, n.f. enthusiasm.

Begier'de, -n, n.f. desire, lust.

begie'rig, adj. eager, desirous.

begie'ßen*, vb. water.

Beginn', n.m. beginning.

begin'nen*, vb. begin.

Begin'nen, n.nt. inception.

beglau'bigen, vb. certify, accredit.

Beglau'bigungsschreiben, n.nt. credentials.

beglei'chen*, vb. settle.

beglei'ten, vb. accompany.

beglei'tend, adj. concomitant.

Beglei'ter, -, n.m. companion, escort; accompanist.

Beglei'tung, -en, n.f. accompaniment.

beglück'wünschen, vb. congratulate.

begna'digen, vb. pardon.

begnü'gen, vb. (sich b. mit) content oneself with.

begra'ben*, vb. bury.

Begräb'nis, -se, n.nt. burial, funeral.

begrei'fen*, vb. comprehend.

begreif'lich, adj. understandable.

begren'zen, vb. limit.

Begren'zung, -en, n.f. limitation.

Begriff', -e, n.m. concept; (im B. sein*) be about to.

begrün'den, vb. establish; justify.

begrü'ßen, vb. greet.

Begrü'ßung, -en, n.f. greeting, salutation.

begüns'tigen, vb. favor, support.

Begüns'tigung, -en, n.f. favoritism, encouragement.

behä'big, adj. portly.

beha'gen, vb. please.

Beha'gen, n.nt. comfort, pleasure.

behag'lich, adj. comfortable, pleasant.

behal'ten*, vb. keep.

Behäl'ter, -, n.m. container.

behan'deln, vb. treat.

Behand'lung, -en, n.f. treatment.

Behang', -e, n.m. drapery.

behar'ren, vb. persevere, insist.

beharr'lich, adj. constant, persistent.

Beharr'lichkeit, n.f. perseverance.

behaup'ten, vb. assert, maintain; allege.

Behaup'tung, -en, n.f. assertion.

behe'ben*, vb. remove.

Behelf', -e, n.m. expedient, makeshift.

behel'fen*, vb. (sich b. mit) make do with.

behel'ligen, vb. bother.

behen'd(e), adj. nimble, agile.

beher'bergen, vb. shelter, lodge.

beherr'schen, vb. rule, govern; control, master; dominate.

Beherr'schung, n.f. rule, mastery.

beher'zigen, vb. take to heart.

beherzt, *adj.* courageous, game.

behilf'lich, *adj.* helpful.

behin'dern, *vb.* impede.

Behin'derung, -en, *n.f.* impediment.

Behör'de, -n, *n.f.* governing office, authority.

Behuf', **-e,** *n.m.* purpose; benefit.

behufs', *prep.* for the purpose of.

behü'ten, *vb.* guard, protect, keep from; **(Gott behüte)** God forbid.

behut'sam, *adj.* cautious.

bei, *prep.* at, near, by; in connection with; **(b. mir)** at my house, on my person.

bei·behalten*, *vb.* retain.

Beibehaltung, -en, *n.f.* retention.

Beiblatt, ̈er, *n.nt.* supplement.

bei·bringen*, *vb.* bring forward; **(jemandem etwas b.)** make something clear to someone, teach someone something.

Beichte, -n, *n.f.* confession.

beichten, *vb.* confess.

Beichtstuhl, ̈e, *n.m.* confessional.

Beichtvater, ̈, *n.m.* confessor.

beide, *adj.&pron.* both.

Beifall, -e, *n.m.* applause.

Beifallsruf, -e, *n.m.* cheer.

bei·fügen, *vb.* add, enclose, attach, include.

Beifügung, -en, *n.f.* attachment.

Beihilfe, -n, *n.f.* assistance.

bei·kommen*, *vb.* get at.

Beil, -e, *n.nt.* hatchet.

Beilage, -n, *n.f.* enclosure; supplement.

beiläufig, *adj.* incidental.

bei·legen, *vb.* add, attach to, enclose.

Beileid, *n.nt.* condolence.

bei·messen*, *vb.* attribute.

Beimessung, -en, *n.f.* attribution.

Beimischung, -en, *n.f.* admixture.

Bein, -e, *n.nt.* leg.

beinahe, *adv.* almost.

bei·ordnen, *vb.* adjoin, coordinate.

bei·pflichten, *vb.* agree with.

beir'ren, *vb.* confuse.

beisam'men, *adv.* together.

Beisein, *n.nt.* presence.

beisei'te, *adv.* aside, apart.

Beispiel, -e, *n.nt.* example.

beispiellos, *adj.* unheard of.

beißen*, *vb.* bite.

beißend, *adj.* biting, acrid.

Beistand, ̈e, *n.m.* assistance.

bei·stimmen, *vb.* agree.

Beitrag, ̈e, *n.m.* contribution.

bei·tragen*, *vb.* contribute.

Beiträger, -, *n.m.* contributor.

bei·treten*, *vb.* join.

Beitritt, -e, *n.m.* joining.

bei·wohnen, *vb.* attend, witness.

Beiwort, -e, *n.nt.* epithet.

Beize, -n, *n.f.* corrosion, stain.

beizei'ten, *adv.* in good time.

beizen, *vb.* corrode, stain.

bejah'en, *vb.* affirm, say yes to.

bejah'end, *adj.* affirmative.

bejahrt', *adj.* aged.

bejam'mern, *vb.* deplore.

bejam'mernswert, *adj.* deplorable.

bekämp'fen, *vb.* combat.

bekannt', *adj.* well-known; acquainted.

Bekannt'-, n.m.&f. acquaintance.

bekannt'-geben*, *vb.* make known, announce.

bekannt'lich, *adv.* as is well known.

bekannt'-machen, *vb.* acquaint, make known.

Bekannt'machung, -en, *n.f.* proclamation.

Bekannt'schaft, -en, *n.f.* acquaintance.

bekeh'ren, *vb.* convert.

beken'nen*, *vb.* confess.

Bekennt'nis, -se, *n.nt.* confession.

bekla'gen, *vb.* deplore, lament; **(sich b. über)** complain about.

bekla'genswert, *adj.* deplorable, lamentable.

Beklagt'-, n.m.&f. accused, defendant.

beklei'den, *vb.* clothe, cover; fill (a position).

Beklei'dung, -en, *n.f.* clothing, covering.

beklem'men*, *vb.* oppress.

Beklom'menheit, *n.f.* anxiety.

bekom'men*, *vb.* get, obtain, receive; agree with, suit.

bekös'tigen, *vb.* feed, board.

bekräf'tigen, *vb.* confirm, corroborate.

beküm'mern, *vb.* grieve, distress.

Beküm'mernis, -se, *n.f.* grief, distress.

bekun'den, *vb.* manifest.

bela'den*, *vb.* load, burden.

Belag', ̈e, *n.m.* covering, surface; (food) spread.

bela'gern, *vb.* besiege.

Bela'gerung, -en, *n.f.* siege.

Belang', -e, *n.m.* importance.

belan'gen, *vb.* concern; sue.

belang'los, *adj.* unimportant, irrelevant.

belang'reich, *adj.* important, relevant.

belas'ten, *vb.* load, burden, strain; incriminate.

beläs'tigen, *vb.* annoy, bother, molest.

Belas'tung, -en, *n.f.* strain; inconvenience; incrimination.

belau'fen*, *vb.* **(sich b. auf)** amount to.

bele'ben, *vb.* animate, enliven.

Beleg', -e, *n.m.* proof, evidence, documentation.

bele'gen, *vb.* attest; reserve (seat); sign up for (academic subject).

belegt', *adj.* **(b. es Brot)** sandwich.

beleh'ren, *vb.* teach.

belei'digen, *vb.* insult.

Belei'digung, -en, *n.f.* insult.

beleuch'ten, *vb.* illuminate.

Beleuch'tung, -en, *n.f.* illumination.

Belgien, *n.nt.* Belgium.

Belgier, -, *n.m.* Belgian.

belgisch, *adj.* Belgian.

belich'ten, *vb.* expose.

Belich'tung, -en, *n.f.* exposure.

belie'ben, *vb.* please; **(wie beliebt?)** I beg your pardon?

Belie'ben, *n.nt.* pleasure, discretion; **(nach B.)** as you please.

belie'big, *adj.* any (you wish); **(eine b.e Zahl)** any number you want.

beliebt', *adj.* popular.

Beliebt'heit, *n.f.* popularity.

bellen, *vb.* bark.

beloh'nen, *vb.* reward.

Beloh'nung, -en, *n.f.* reward.

belü'gen*, *vb.* lie to.

belus'tigen, *vb.* amuse, entertain.

bema'len, *vb.* paint up.

beman'nen, *vb.* man.

bemerk'bar, *adj.* noticeable, perceptible.

bemer'ken, *vb.* notice; remark.

bemer'kenswert, *adj.* notable.

Bemer'kung, -en, *n.f.* remark.

bemü'hen, *vb.* trouble; **(sich b.)** take pains, try hard.

benach'bart, *adj.* neighboring.

benach'richtigen, *vb.* notify.

Benach'richtigung, -en, *n.f.* notification.

benach'teiligen, *vb.* put at a disadvantage, handicap.

beneh'men*, *vb.* take away; **(sich b.)** behave.

Beneh'men, *n.nt.* behavior.

benei'den, *vb.* envy.

benei'denswert, *adj.* enviable.

benom'men, *adj.* groggy, confused.

benö'tigen, *vb.* need.

benut'zen, *vb.* use.

Benut'zung, -en, *n.f.* use.

Benzin', n.nt. gas, gasoline.

beob'achten, *vb.* observe.

Beob'achtung, -en, *n.f.* observation.

bequem', *adj.* comfortable, convenient.

Bequem'lichkeit, -en, *n.f.* comfort.

bera'ten*, *vb.* advise; **(sich b.)** deliberate.

Bera'ter, -, *n.m.* adviser, consultant.

berau'ben, *vb.* rob, deprive of.

Berau'bung, -en, *n.f.* deprivation.

berau'schen, *vb.* intoxicate.

bere'chenbar, *adj.* calculable.
berech'nen, *vb.* calculate, compute.
berech'nend, *vb.* calculating.
Berech'nung, -en, *n.f.* calculation, computation.
berech'tigen, *vb.* justify, entitle.
Berech'tigung, -en, *n.f.* justification.
bere'den, *vb.* persuade.
Bered'samkeit, *n.f.* eloquence.
beredt', *adj.* eloquent.
Bereich', -e, *n.m.* domain, scope.
berei'chern, *vb.* enrich.
berei'sen, *vb.* tour.
bereit', *adj.* ready, prepared.
berei'ten, *vb.* make ready, prepare.
bereits', *adv.* already.
bereit'willig, *adj.* willing (to oblige).
bereu'en, *vb.* repent, regret.
Berg, -e, *n.m.* mountain.
bergab', *adv.* downhill.
bergan', *adv.* uphill.
Bergarbeiter, -, *n.m.* miner.
bergauf', *adv.* uphill.
Bergbau, *n.m.* mining.
Bergkette, -n, *n.f.* mountain range.
Bergsteiger, -, *n.m.* mountain climber.
Bergung, *n.f.* salvage.
Bergwerk, -e, *n.nt.* mine.
Bericht', -e, *n.m.* report.
berich'ten, *vb.* report.
Bericht'erstatter, -, *n.m.* reporter.
berich'tigen, *vb.* report.
Berich'tigung, -en, *n.f.* correction.
bersten*, *vb.* burst.
berüch'tigt, *adj.* notorious.
berück'sichtigen, *vb.* consider, take into consideration; allow for.
Beruf', -e, *n.m.* profession.
beru'fen*, *vb.* call, appoint; **(sich b. auf)** refer to, appeal to.
berufs'mäßig, *adj.* professional.
Beru'fung, -en, *n.f.* summons; appointment; appeal.
beru'hen, *vb.* rest, be based.
beru'higen, *vb.* quiet, calm.
Beru'higungsmittel, -, *n.nt.* sedative.
berühmt', *adj.* famous.
Berühmt'heit, -en, *n.f.* celebrity.
berüh'ren, *vb.* touch.
Berüh'rung, -en, *n.f.* touch.
besa'gen, *vb.* say, indicate, mean.
besagt', *adj.* (afore)said.
besänf'tigen, *vb.* soften, soothe.
Besatz', ¨-e, *n.m.* border, trimming, facing.
Besat'zung, -en, *n.f.* occupying forces; crew.
beschä'digen, *vb.* damage.

Beschä'digung, -en, *n.f.* damage.
beschaf'fen, *vb.* get, obtain, procure; provide.
beschaf'fen, *adj.* constituted; **(so b.)** of such a nature.
Beschaf'fenheit, -en, *n.f.* nature, quality.
beschäf'tigen, *vb.* employ, occupy, keep busy.
beschäf'tigt, *adj.* busy, engaged.
Beschäf'tigung, -en, *n.f.* occupation, employment.
beschä'men, *vb.* shame.
beschämt', *adj.* ashamed.
beschat'ten, *vb.* shade.
beschau'en, *vb.* look at, contemplate.
beschau'lich, *adj.* contemplative.
Bescheid', -e, *n.m.* answer, decision; information; **(B. geben*)** let know; **(B. wissen* über)** know all about.
beschei'den*, *vb.* allot, apportion; inform.
beschei'den, *adj.* modest.
Beschei'denheit, *n.f.* modesty.
beschei'nigen, *vb.* certify.
Beschei'nigung, -en, *n.f.* certificate, certification.
beschen'ken, *vb.* **(b. mit)** make a present of.
beschie'ßen*, *vb.* shoot at, shell, bombard.
Beschie'ßung, -en, *n.f.* bombardment.
beschimp'fen, *vb.* abuse, insult.
Beschim'pfung, -en, *n.f.* abuse, insult.
beschir'men, *vb.* protect.
Beschlag', ¨-e, *n.m.* metal fitting, coating, condensation; **(in B. nehmen*)** confiscate.
beschla'gen*, *vb.* cover with, coat, mount; **(sich b.)** become coated, tarnish.
beschla'gen, *adj.* experienced, proficient.
Beschlag'nahme, -n, *n.f.* seizure, confiscation.
beschlag'nahmen, *vb.* seize, confiscate.
beschleu'nigen, *vb.* quicken, accelerate.
beschlie'ßen*, *vb.* finish, conclude, decide, make up one's mind.
Beschluß', ¨-sse, *n.m.* decision, conclusion.
beschmie'ren, *vb.* smear, spread on.
beschmut'zen, *vb.* make dirty, soil.
beschnei'den*, *vb.* cut off, clip, circumcise.
beschö'nigen, *vb.* make pretty; gloss over, excuse.
beschrän'ken, *vb.* limit.
beschränkt', *adj.* limited, of limited abilities.
Beschrän'kung, -en, *n.f.* limitation.
beschrei'ben*, *vb.* describe.

Beschrei'bung, -en, *n.f.* description.
beschul'digen, *vb.* blame, accuse, incriminate.
Beschul'digung, -en, *n.f.* incrimination.
beschüt'zen, *vb.* protect.
Beschwer'de, -n, *n.f.* complaint, burden, trouble.
beschwe'ren, *vb.* burden; **(sich bei jemandem über etwas b.)** complain to someone about something.
beschwer'lich, *adj.* burdensome.
beschwich'tigen, *vb.* appease, soothe.
Beschwich'tigung, -en, *n.f.* appeasement.
beschwipst', *adj.* tight.
beschwö'ren*, *vb.* swear to; implore.
Beschwö'rung, -en, *n.f.* swearing by oath; entreaty; exorcism.
besei'tigen, *vb.* remove.
Besei'tigung, *n.f.* removal.
Besen, -, *n.m.* broom.
beses'sen, *adj.* mad, possessed.
beset'zen, *vb.* occupy, fill; trim.
Beset'zung, *n.f.* occupation.
besich'tigen, *vb.* view, inspect, look around in.
Besich'tigung, -en, *n.f.* view, inspection, sight-seeing.
besie'deln, *vb.* settle, colonize.
Besie'd(e)lung, -en, *n.f.* settlement, colonization.
besie'geln, *vb.* steal.
besie'gen, *vb.* defeat.
besin'nen*, *vb.* **(sich b.)** remember, think over; **(sich anders b.)** change one's mind.
Besin'nung, -en, *n.f.* consideration, recollection; senses, consciousness.
besin'nungslos, *adj.* senseless, unconscious.
Besitz', *n.m.* possession, property.
besit'zen*, *vb.* possess, own.
Besit'zer, -, *n.m.* proprietor.
besit'zgierig, *adj.* possessive.
Besit'zung, -en, *n.f.* possession.
besof'fen, *adj.* drunk.
besoh'len, *vb.* sole.
beson'der-, *adj.* special.
Beson'derheit, -en, *n.f.* peculiarity.
beson'ders, *adv.* especially.
beson'nen, *adj.* thoughtful, cautious.
besor'gen, *vb.* take care of, get.
Besorg'nis, -se, *n.f.* apprehension, anxiety.
besorgt', *adj.* anxious, worried.
Besor'gung, -en, *n.f.* management, care; errand.
bespöt'teln, *vb.* ridicule.
bespre'chen*, *vb.* discuss, talk over.
Bespre'chung, -en, *n.f.* discussion, review, conference.
besprit'zen, *vb.* spatter.

besser, *adj.* better.

bessern, *vb.* make better, improve.

Besserung, -en, *n.f.* amelioration, improvement; (gute B.!) I hope you get well soon.

best-, *adj.* best.

Bestand´, ¨e, *n.m.* duration, stability; supply, stock.

bestän´dig, *adj.* steady, stable, constant.

Bestand´teil, -e, *n.m.* constituent, ingredient.

bestär´ken, *vb.* strengthen.

bestä´tigen, *vb.* confirm, acknowledge, verify.

Bestä´tigung, -en, *n.f.* confirmation, verification.

bestat´ten, *vb.* bury.

Bestat´tung, -en, *n.f.* burial.

beste´chen*, *vb.* bribe.

beste´chend, *adj.* attractive, tempting.

Beste´chung, -en, *n.f.* bribery, graft, corruption.

Besteck´, -e, *n.nt.* set of implements; knife, fork, and spoon.

beste´hen*, *vb.* exist; (test) undergo, pass; (b. auf) insist on; (b. aus) consist of.

Beste´hen, *n.nt.* existence; insistence.

besteh´len*, *vb.* steal from, rob.

bestei´gen*, *vb.* climb up, ascend; mount; go on board.

bestel´len, *vb.* order; send for; give a message; appoint; till.

Bestel´lung, -en, *n.f.* order; message; appointment; cultivation.

bestens, *adv.* very well.

besteu´ern, *vb.* tax.

Besteu´erung, -en, *n.f.* taxation.

Bestie, *n.f.* beast.

bestimm´bar, *adj.* definable, ascertainable, assignable.

bestim´men, *vb.* determine, decide, specify, designate, destine, dispose.

bestimmt´, *adj.* definite.

Bestim´mungsort, -e, *n.m.* destination.

bestra´fen, *vb.* punish.

bestrah´len, *vb.* irradiate, treat with rays.

bestre´ben, *vb.* (sich b.) strive.

Bestre´bung, -en, *n.f.* effort.

bestreit´bar, *adj.* disputable.

bestrei´ten*, *vb.* contest, dispute, deny.

bestri´cken, *vb.* entangle, ensnare, captivate, charm.

bestür´men, *vb.* storm, attack, implore.

bestürzt´, *adj.* dismayed.

Bestür´zung, -en, *n.f.* dismay.

Besuch´, -e, *n.m.* visit, call; visitor, company; attendance.

besu´chen, *vb.* visit, attend.

Besu´cher, -, *n.m.* visitor.

betagt´, *adj.* aged.

betä´tigen, *vb.* operate; show; (sich b.) be active.

betäu´ben, *vb.* stun, deafen, stupefy.

betäu´bend, *adj.* stupefying; narcotic, anesthetic.

Bete, -n, *n.f.* beet.

betei´ligen, *vb.* cause to share in; (sich b.) take part.

Betei´ligung, -en, *n.f.* participation.

beten, *vb.* pray.

beteu´ern, *vb.* assert, swear.

Beteu´erung, -en, *n.f.* assertion.

beti´teln, *vb.* entitle.

Beton´, -s, *n.m.* concrete.

beto´nen, *vb.* stress.

Beto´nung, -en, *n.f.* stress.

betö´ren, *vb.* infatuate.

Betracht´, *n.m.* consideration.

betrach´ten, *vb.* look at, consider, observe, contemplate.

beträcht´lich, *adj.* considerable.

Betrach´tung, -en, *n.f.* consideration, contemplation.

Betrag´, ¨e, *n.m.* amount, sum.

betra´gen*, *vb.* amount to; (sich b.) behave.

Betra´gen, *n.nt.* behavior.

betrau´ern, *vb.* mourn for, deplore.

Betreff´, *n.m.* (in B.) in regard to.

betref´fen*, *vb.* affect, concern.

betreffs´, *prep.* in regard to.

betrei´ben*, *vb.* carry on.

betre´ten*, *vb.* step upon, enter.

betreu´en, *vb.* take care of.

Betrieb´, -e, *n.m.* works, management, activity; (in B.) running.

betrin´ken*, *vb.* (sich b.) get drunk.

betrof´fen, *adj.* taken aback; affected.

betrü´ben, *vb.* grieve.

Betrüb´nis, -se, *n.f.* grief.

Betrug´, *n.m.* deceit, deception, fraud.

betrü´gen*, *vb.* deceive, cheat.

betrü´gerisch, *adj.* deceitful, crooked.

betrun´ken, *adj.* drunk, drunken.

Bett, -en, *n.nt.* bed.

Bettdecke, -n, *n.f.* bedspread.

betteln, *vb.* beg.

Bettler, -, *n.m.* beggar.

Bettplatz, ¨e, *n.m.* berth.

Bettzeug, *n.nt.* bedding, bedclothes.

beugen, *vb.* bend.

Beugung, -en, *n.f.* bend; inflection.

Beule, -n, *n.f.* swelling, bump, lump.

beun´ruhigen, *vb.* disturb, agitate.

Beun´ruhigung, -en, *n.f.* alarm, agitation.

beur´kunden, *vb.* authenticate.

beur´lauben, *vb.* give leave (of absence) to.

beur´teilen, *vb.* judge.

Beute, -n, *n.f.* booty, loot.

Beutel, -, *n.m.* bag, purse, pouch.

Bevöl´kerung, -en, *n.f.* population.

bevoll´mächtigen, *vb.* authorize, give full power to.

Bevoll´mächtigung, -en, *n.f.* authorization.

bevor´, *conj.* before.

bevor´-stehen*, *vb.* be about to happen, be in store for.

bevor´stehend, *adj.* imminent.

bevor´zugen, *vb.* favor.

bewa´chen, *vb.* guard, watch.

bewaff´nen, *vb.* arm.

Bewaff´nung, -en, *n.f.* armament.

bewah´ren, *vb.* keep, preserve.

bewäh´ren, *vb.* (sich b.) prove itself.

Bewah´rung, -en, *n.f.* conservation.

bewäl´tigen, *vb.* overcome, master.

bewan´dert, *adj.* (b. in) experienced in, conversant with.

bewe´gen*, *vb.* induce.

bewe´gen, *vb.* move.

Beweg´grund, ¨e, *n.m.* motive.

beweg´lich, *adj.* movable, active.

Bewe´gung, -en, *n.f.* movement, motion, exercise.

bewe´gungslos, *adj.* motionless.

bewei´nen, *vb.* bewail, deplore.

Beweis´, -e, *n.m.* proof, evidence.

bewei´sen*, *vb.* prove, demonstrate.

bewer´ben*, *vb.* (sich b. um) apply for.

Bewer´ber, -, *n.m.* applicant, contestant, suitor.

Bewer´bung, -en, *n.f.* application.

bewer´ten, *vb.* evaluate, grade.

bewil´ligen, *vb.* approve, appropriate.

Bewil´ligung, -en, *n.f.* approval, appropriation.

bewir´ken, *vb.* cause, effect.

bewir´ten, *vb.* be host to, entertain.

bewohn´bar, *adj.* habitable.

bewoh´nen, *vb.* inhabit.

Bewoh´ner, -, *n.m.* inhabitant, occupant.

bewölkt´, *adj.* cloudy.

bewun´dern, *vb.* admire.

bewun´dernswert, *adj.* admirable.

Bewun´derung, *n.f.* admiration.

bewußt´, *adj.* conscious, aware.

bewußt´los, *adj.* unconscious.

Bewußt´sein, *n.nt.* consciousness; (bei B.) conscious.

bezah´len, *vb.* pay.

Bezah´lung, -en, *n.f.* pay, payment.

bezau'bern, *vb.* bewitch, enchant.

bezeich'nen, *vb.* mark, designate, signify.

bezeich'nend, *adj.* characteristic.

Bezeich'nung, -en, *n.f.* designation.

bezeu'gen, *vb.* testify, attest.

bezie'hen*, *vb.* cover with, upholster, put on clean sheets; move into; draw (pay); **(sich b.)** cloud over; **(sich b. auf)** refer to.

Bezie'hung, -en, *n.f.* reference, relation; pull, drag.

Bezirk', -e, *n.m.* district.

Bezug', ⁻e, *n.m.* cover(ing), case; supply; reference.

Bezug'nahme, -n, *n.f.* reference.

bezwe'cken, *vb.* have as one's purpose, aim at.

bezwei'feln, *vb.* doubt.

Bibel, -n, *n.f.* Bible.

Biber, -, *n.m.* beaver.

Bibliothek', -en, *n.f.* library.

Bibliothekar', -e, *n.m.* librarian.

Bibliotheka'rin, -nen, *n.f.* librarian.

biblisch, *adj.* Biblical.

bieder, *adj.* upright, bourgeois.

biegen*, *vb.* bend; **(sich b.)** buckle.

biegsam, *adj.* flexible, pliable.

Biegung, -en, *n.f.* bend.

Biene, -n, *n.f.* bee.

Bier, -e, *n.nt.* beer.

Bierlokal, -e, *n.nt.* tavern, pub.

Biest, -er, *n.nt.* beast; brute.

bieten*, *vb.* bid, offer.

Bieter, -, *n.m.* bidder.

bifokal', *adj.* bifocal.

Bigamie', *n.f.* bigamy.

bigott', *adj.* bigoted.

Bild, -er, *n.nt.* picture, painting.

bilden, *vb.* form.

bildend, *adj.* educational, formative.

Bildhauer, -, *n.m.* sculptor.

bildhauern, *vb.* sculpture.

bildlich, *adj.* figurative.

Bildung, *n.f.* learning, education, refinement.

Billard, *n.nt.* billiards.

Billett', -e, *n.nt.* ticket.

billig, *adj.* cheap; equitable.

billigen, *vb.* approve.

Billigkeit, -en, *n.f.* cheapness; justness.

Billion', -en, *n.f.* billion.

Binde, -n, *n.f.* bandage; **(Damenbinde)** sanitary napkin.

binden*, *vb.* tie; bind.

bindend, *adj.* binding.

Bindestrich, -e, *n.m.* hyphen.

Bindfaden, ⁻, *n.m.* string.

Bindung, -en, *n.f.* tie, bond; (ski) binding; *(fig.)* obligation.

binnen, *prep.* within.

Binnenland, ⁻er, *n.nt.* inland.

Biographie', -i'en, *n.f.* biography.

biogra'phisch, *adj.* biographical.

Biologie', -i'en, *n.f.* biology.

biolo'gisch, *adj.* biological.

Biosignalrück'gabe, -n, *n.f.* biofeedback.

Birke, -n, *n.f.* birch.

Birne, -n, *n.f.* pear.

bis, *adv.&prep.* till, until.

Bischof, ⁻e, *n.m.* bishop.

bisher', *adv.* hitherto.

Biskuit', -e, *n.nt.* biscuit.

Bißchen, -, *n.nt.* bit; **(ein b.)** a bit, a little.

Bissen, -, *n.m.* bite, mouthful.

Bit, -, *n.nt.* (computer) bit.

bitte, *interj.* please; you are welcome.

Bitte, -n, *n.f.* request, plea.

bitten*, *vb.* ask, request; beg.

bitter, *adj.* bitter.

bizarr', *adj.* bizarre, freak.

Bizeps, -n, *n.m.* biceps.

blähen, *vb.* bloat, puff up.

Blama'ge, -n, *n.f.* disgrace.

blamie'ren, *vb.* disgrace.

blank, *adj.* bright, shining; (without money) broke.

Blase, -n, *n.f.* bubble; bladder; blister.

Blasebalg, ⁻e, *n.m.* bellows.

blasen*, *vb.* blow.

blaß, *adj.* pale.

Blässe, *n.f.* paleness.

Blatt, ⁻er, *n.nt.* leaf.

Blattern, *n.pl.* smallpox.

blau, *adj.* blue.

Blaubeere, -n, *n.f.* blueberry.

Blech, *n.nt.* tin.

Blei, *n.nt.* lead.

bleiben*, *vb.* stay, remain.

bleich, *adj.* pale; **(b. werden)** blanch.

bleichen, *vb.* bleach.

bleiern, *adj.* leaden.

bleifrei, *adj.* unleaded.

Bleistift, -e, *n.m.* pencil.

blenden, *vb.* blind, dazzle.

Blick, -e, *n.m.* look, glance.

blicken, *vb.* look, glance.

blind, *adj.* blind.

Blinddarm, ⁻e, *n.m.* appendix.

Blinddarmentzündung, -en, *n.f.* appendicitis.

Blindheit, -en, *n.f.* blindness.

blinken, *vb.* blink.

Blinklicht, -er, *n.nt.* blinker.

blinzeln, *vb.* blink; wink.

Blitz, -e, *n.m.* lightning.

blitzen, *vb.* flash, emit lightening.

blitzsauber, *adj.* immaculate.

Block, -s, *n.m.* bloc; block; (paper) pad.

Blocka'de, -n, *n.f.* blockade.

blockfrei, *adj.* non-aligned.

blockie'ren, *vb.* block; (account) freeze.

blöde, *adj.* stupid, dumb.

Blödsinn, *n.m.* idiocy, nonsense.

blödsinnig, *adj.* idiotic.

blond, *adj.* blond.

bloß, 1. *adj.* bare. 2. *adv.* only, merely.

Blöße, -n, *n.f.* nakedness; *(fig.)* weak spot.

Bloßstellung, -en, *n.f.* exposure.

Bluejeans, *n.pl.* blue jeans.

Bluff, -s, *n.m.* bluff.

bluffen, *vb.* bluff.

blühen, *vb.* bloom; flourish.

blühend, *adj.* prosperous.

Blume, -n, *n.f.* flower.

Blumengeschäft, -e, *n.nt.* flower shop.

Blumenhändler, -, *n.m.* florist.

Blumenkohl, -e, *n.m.* cauliflower.

Blumenstrauß, ⁻e, *n.m.* bouquet.

blumig, *adj.* flowery.

Bluse, -n, *n.f.* blouse.

Blut, *n.nt.* blood.

blutarm, *adj.* anemic; *(fig.)* penniless.

Blutarmut, *n.f.* anemia.

Blutdruck, -e, *n.m.* blood pressure.

Blüte, -n, *n.f.* bloom, blossom; *(fig.)* prime.

bluten, *vb.* bleed.

blütenreich, *adj.* florid.

Bluterguß, ⁻sse, *n.m.* hemorrhage.

Bluterkrankheit, *n.f.* hemophilia.

blutig, *adj.* bloody.

blutlos, *adj.* bloodless.

blutunterlaufen, *adj.* bloodshot.

Blutvergießen, *n.nt.* bloodshed.

Blutvergiftung, -en, *n.f.* blood poisoning.

Bö, -en, *n.f.* squall.

Bock, ⁻e, *n.m.* buck.

bockig, *adj.* obstinate.

Bockwurst, ⁻e, *n.f.* sausage.

Boden, ⁻, *n.m.* ground, soil, bottom, floor; attic; **(Grund und B.)** real estate.

bodenlos, *adj.* bottomless.

Bodensatz, *n.m.* dregs.

Bogen, ⁻, *n.m.* arch; bow; (paper) sheet.

Bogenschießen, *n.nt.* archery.

Bogenschütze, -n, -n, *n.m.* archer.

Böhme, -n, -n, *n.m.* Bohemian.

Böhmen, *n.nt.* Bohemia.

böhmisch, *adj.* Bohemian.

Bohne, -n, *n.f.* bean; **(grüne B.)** string bean.

bohren, *vb.* bore, drill.

Bohrer, -, *n.m.* drill.

Boli'vien, *n.nt.* Bolivia.

Bollwerk, -e, *n.nt.* bulwark.

bombardie'ren, *vb.* bombard.

Bombe, -n, *n.f.* bomb, bombshell.

bomben, *vb.* bomb.

Bombenflugzeug, -e, *n.nt.* bomber.

bombensicher, adj. bombproof.

Boot, -e, n.nt. boat.

Bord, -e, n.nt. shelf; board; **(an B.)** aboard; **(an B. gehen)** board.

Bordell', -e, n.nt. brothel.

Bordstein, -e, n.m. curb, curbstone.

borgen, vb. borrow.

borniert', adj. stupid.

Börse, -n, n.f. purse; stock exchange.

Borste, -n, n.f. bristle.

Borte, -n, n.f. trimming, braid.

Bös-, n.nt. evil.

bösartig, adj. malicious; (med.) malignant.

Böschung, -en, n.f. bank, embankment.

böse, adj. bad, evil; angry, mad.

Bösewicht, -e, n.m. scoundrel.

boshaft, adj. malicious.

Bosheit, -en, n.f. malice.

böswillig, adj. malevolent.

Bota'nik, n.f. botany.

bota'nisch, adj. botanical.

Bote, -n, -n, n.m. messenger.

Botschaft, -en, n.f. message; embassy.

Botschafter, -, n.m. ambassador.

Bouillon', -s, n.f. consommé.

boxen, vb. box, spar.

Boxen, n.nt. boxing.

Boxkampf, -e, n.m. boxing match.

Boykott', -e, n.m. boycott.

boykotti'ren, vb. boycott.

Brand, -e, n.m. conflagration; blight.

branden, vb. surge.

brandmarken, vb. brand.

Brandstifter, -, n.m. arsonist.

Brandstiftung, -en, n.f. arson.

Brandung, -en, n.f. surf, breakers.

Branntwein, -e, n.m. brandy.

Brasi'lien, n.nt. Brazil.

braten*, vb. roast, fry.

Braten, -, n.m. roast.

Bratpfanne, -n, n.f. frying pan, griddle.

Bratrost, -e, n.m. oven rack; broiler.

Bratsche, -n, n.f. viola.

Bräu, n.nt. brew.

Brauch, -e, n.m. custom, usage.

brauchbar, adj. useful.

brauchen, vb. need, require; use.

brauen, vb. brew.

Brauer, -, n.m. brewer.

Brauerei', -en, n.f. brewery.

braun, adj. brown.

bräunen, vb. brown; tan.

brausen, vb. roar.

Braut, -e, n.f. bride.

Brautführer, -, n.m. usher (at a wedding).

Bräutigam, -e, n.m. bridegroom.

Brautjungfer, -n, n.f. bridesmaid.

brav, adj. upright; (of children) good.

Bravour', n.f. bravado.

brechen*, vb. break; (med.) fracture.

Brechmittel, -, n.nt. emetic.

Brei, -e, n.m. pap; (fig.) pulp.

breit, adj. broad, wide.

Breite, -n, n.f. breadth, width; latitude.

Bremse, -n, n.f. brake; gadfly.

bremsen, vb. brake, put on the brake.

brennbar, adj. combustible.

brennen*, vb. burn, scorch.

brennend, adj. burning; fervid.

Brenner, -, n.m. burner.

Brennholz, n.nt. firewood.

Brennpunkt, -e, n.m. focus.

Brennstoff, -e, n.m. fuel.

brenzlich, adj. risky, precarious.

Brett, -er, n.nt. board, plank.

Bretterbude, -n, n.f. shack.

Brezel, -n, n.f. pretzel.

Brief, -e, n.m. letter.

Briefkasten, -, n.m. mailbox.

Briefmarke, -n, n.f. stamp.

Briefpapier, n.nt. stationery.

Brieftasche, -n, n.f. wallet, billfold.

Briefträger, -, n.m. postman.

Briefumschlag, -e, n.m. envelope.

Briefwechsel, n.m. correspondence.

Briga'de, -n, n.f. brigade.

Brille, -n, n.f. spectacles, glasses.

bringen*, vb. bring; take.

Brise, -n, n.f. breeze.

Britan'nien, n.nt. Britain.

Brite, -n, -n, n.m. Briton.

britisch, adj. British.

Brocken, -, n.m. crumb.

Brombeere, -n, n.f. blackberry.

bronchial', adj. bronchial.

Bronchi'tis, n.f. bronchitis.

Bronze, -n, n.f. brooch.

Broschü're, -n, n.f. pamphlet, booklet.

Brot, -e, n.nt. bread; **(beleg'tes B.)** sandwich.

Brötchen, -, n.nt. roll, bun.

Bruch, -e, n.m. break, breach, fracture; hernia; (fig.) violation.

brüchig, adj. brittle.

Bruchrechnung, n.f. fractions.

Bruchstück, -e, n.nt. fragment.

Bruchteil, -e, n.m. fraction.

Brücke, -n, n.f. bridge.

Bruder, -, n.m. brother.

brüderlich, adj. brotherly, fraternal.

Brüderschaft, -en, n.f. fraternity.

Brühe, -n, n.f. broth.

brühen, vb. scald.

brüllen, vb. yell, bellow, howl.

brummen, vb. hum, buzz; grumble.

Brünet'te, -n, n.f. brunette.

Brunnen, -, n.m. well, fountain.

brünstig, adj. fervent.

brüsk, adj. brusque.

Brust, -e, n.f. breast, chest.

brüsten, vb. (sich b.) boast.

Brut, -en, n.f. brood.

brutal', adj. brutal.

Brutalität', -en, n.f. brutality.

brüten, vb. brood.

brutto, adj. gross.

Bube, -n, -n, n.m. boy; (cards) jack.

Buch, -er, n.nt. book.

Buchbinder, -, n.m. bookbinder.

Buchbinderei', -ei'en, n.f. bookbindery.

Buche, -n, n.f. beech.

buchen, vb. book, reserve (plane seat, hotel).

Bücherei', -en, n.f. library.

Bücherschrank, -e, n.m. bookcase.

Buchführung, -en, n.f. accounting, bookkeeping.

Buchhalter, -, n.m. accountant, bookkeeper.

Buchhändler, -, n.m. bookseller.

Buchhandlung, -en, n.f. bookstore.

Büchse, -n, n.f. can.

Büchsenöffner, -, n.m. can opener.

Buchstabe(n), -, (or -n, -n), n.m. letter (of the alphabet).

buchstabie'ren, vb. spell; **(falsch b.)** misspell.

buchstäblich, adj. literal.

Bucht, -en, n.f. bay.

Buchweizen, n.m. buckwheat.

Buckel, -, n.m. hump, protuberance; hunchback.

buckelig, adj. hunchbacked.

bücken, vb. (sich b.) bend down, stoop.

Bude, -n, n.f. booth, stall, stand.

Büfett', -s, n.nt. buffet.

Büffel, -, n.m. buffalo.

Bug, -e, n.m. bow.

Bügeleisen, -, n.nt. flatiron.

bügeln, vb. iron, press.

Bühne, -n, n.f. stage.

Bühnenausstattung, -en, n.f. scenery.

Bulldogge, -n, n.f. bulldog.

Bulle, -n, -n, n.m. bull.

Bummel, -n, n.m. spree.

bummeln, vb. gallivant.

Bund, -e, n.m. league, federation.

Bund, -e, n.nt. bunch, bundle.

Bündel, -, n.nt. bundle.

Bundes, cpds. federal.

Bundesbahn, n.f. West German Federal Railway.

Bundeskanzler, n.m. chancellor of West Germany.

Bundesrat, n.m. upper house of West German parliament.

bundesstaatlich, adj. federal.

Bundestag, n.m. lower house of West German parliament.

Bündnis, -se, n.nt. alliance.

bunt, *adj.* colorful; varicolored, motley.

Bürde, -n, *n.f.* burden.

Bürge, -n, -n, *n.m.* sponsor, guarantor.

Bürger, -, *n.m.* citizen.

bürgerlich, *adj.* civil; bourgeois.

Bürgermeister, -, *n.m.* mayor.

Bürgerschaft, *n.f.* citizenry.

Bürgersteig, -e, *n.m.* sidewalk.

Burgfriede(n), -n, *n.m.* truce.

Bürgschaft, -en, *n.f.* guaranty, bond, bail.

Burgun′der, -, *n.m.* burgundy (wine).

Büro′, -s, *n.nt.* office, bureau.

Bursche, -n, -n, *n.m.* chap, fellow.

Bürste, -n, *n.f.* brush.

bürsten, *vb.* brush.

Bus, -se, *n.m.* bus.

Busch, -e, *n.m.* bush, shrub.

Büschel, -, *n.nt.* bunch.

buschig, *adj.* bushy.

Busen, -, *n.m.* bosom.

Buße, -n, *n.f.* atonement, penitence; fine, penalty.

büßen, *vb.* do penance, atone for.

Büste, -n, *n.f.* bust.

Büstenhalter, -, *n.m.* brassiere.

Butter, *n.f.* butter.

Butterblume, -n, *n.f.* buttercup.

Butterbrot, -e, *n.nt.* slice of bread and butter.

Buttermilch, *n.f.* buttermilk.

buttern, *vb.* churn.

C

Café′, -s, *n.nt.* café.

Cellist′, -en, -en, *n.m.* cellist.

Cello, -s, *n.nt.* cello.

Chance, -n, *n.f.* opportunity, odds.

chao′tisch, *adj.* chaotic.

Charak′ter, -e′re, *n.m.* character.

charakterisie′ren, *vb.* characterize.

charakteris′tisch, *adj.* characteristic.

Charis′ma, *n.nt.* charisma.

Charme, *n.m.* charm.

Charterflug, -e, *n.m.* charter flight.

Chauffeur′, -e, *n.m.* chauffeur.

Chaussee′, -e′en, *n.f.* highway.

Chef, -s, *n.m.* chef; boss.

Chemie′, *n.f.* chemistry.

Chemika′lien, *n.pl.* chemicals.

Chemiker, -, *n.m.* chemist.

chemisch, *adj.* chemical.

Chemotherapie′, *n.f.* chemotherapy.

Chiffre, -n, *n.f.* cipher.

China, *n.nt.* China.

Chine′se, -n, -n, *n.m.* Chinese.

chine′sisch, *adj.* Chinese.

Chinin′, *n.nt.* quinine.

Chiroprak′tiker, -, *n.m.* chiropractor.

Chirurg′, -en, -en, *n.f.* surgeon.

Chirurgie′, *n.f.* surgery.

Chlor, -s, *n.nt.* chlorine.

Chloroform′, *n.nt.* chloroform.

Cholera, *n.f.* cholera.

chole′risch, *adj.* choleric.

Chor, -e, *n.m.* choir; chorus.

Chorgang, -e, *n.m.* aisle.

Chorsänger, -, *n.m.* chorister.

Christ, -en, -en, *n.m.* Christian.

Christenheit, *n.f.* Christendom.

Christentum, *n.nt.* Christianity.

christlich, *adj.* Christian.

Christus, *n.m.* Christ.

Chrom, *n.nt.* chrome, chromium.

Chronik, -en, *n.f.* chronicle.

chronisch, *adj.* chronic.

Chronologie′, -i′en, *n.f.* chronology.

chronolo′gisch, *adj.* chronological.

Chrysanthe′me, -en, *n.f.* chrysanthemum.

Clown, -s, *n.m.* clown.

Cocktail, -s, *n.m.* cocktail.

College, -s, *n.nt.* college.

Couch, -es, *n.f.* couch.

Coupon′, -s, *n.m.* coupon.

Cousin, -s, *n.m.* (male) cousin.

Cousi′ne, -en, *n.f.* (female) cousin.

Cowboy, -s, *n.m.* cowboy.

Crème, -s, *n.f.* cream.

D

da, 1. *conj.* because, since, as. **2.** *adv.* there; here; then.

dabei′, *adv.* near it; present; in so doing, at the same time.

Dach, -er, *n.nt.* roof.

Dachrinne, -n, *n.f.* eaves.

Dachstube, -n, *n.f.* garret.

Dachtraufe, -n, *n.f.* gutter.

dadurch, *adv.* thereby.

dafür, *adv.* for that; instead.

dage′gen, *adv.* against it; on the other hand.

daher, *adv.* therefore, hence.

dahin, *adv.* (to) there.

dahin′ter, *adv.* behind it.

damals, *adv.* then, at that time.

Dame, -n, *n.f.* lady.

Damebrett, -er, *n.nt.* checkerboard.

Damenhut, -e, *n.m.* lady's hat.

Damenunterwäsche, *n.f.* lingerie.

Damespiel, *n.nt.* checkers.

damit′, 1. *conj.* in order that. **2.** *adv.* with it, with them, at that.

Damm, -e, *n.m.* dam, causeway, levee.

dämmern, *vb.* dawn.

Dämmerung, -en, *n.f.* twilight.

Dämon, -o′nen, *n.m.* demon.

Dampf, -e, *n.m.* steam, vapor fume.

Dampfboot, -e, *n.nt.* steamboat.

dampfen, *vb.* steam.

dämpfen, *vb.* muffle; (cooking) steam.

Dampfer, -, *n.m.* steamship.

Däne, -n, -n, *n.m.* Dane.

Dänemark, *n.nt.* Denmark.

dänisch, *adj.* Danish.

dank, *prep.* owing to.

Dank, *n.m.* thanks.

dankbar, *adj.* thankful, grateful.

Dankbarkeit, -en, *n.f.* gratitude.

danken, *vb.* thank.

dann, *adv.* then, after that.

darauf, *adv.* on it, on them; after that, thereupon.

dar′bieten*, *vb.* present.

Darbietung, -en, *n.f.* presentation; entertainment.

dar′legen, *vb.* state.

Darlegung, -en, *n.f.* exposé, exposition.

Darlehen, -, *n.nt.* loan.

Darm, -e, *n.m.* intestine.

dar′stellen, *vb.* represent, constitute; present; portray.

Darstellung, -en, *n.f.* presentation; representation, depiction; **(graphische D.)** diagram.

Dasein, *n.nt.* existence.

daß, *conj.* that.

Datenverarbeitung, -en, *n.f.* data processing.

datie′ren, *vb.* date.

Dattel, -n, *n.f.* date.

Datum, -ten, *n.nt.* date.

Dauer, *n.f.* duration, length.

dauerhaft, *adj.* durable, lasting.

Dauerhaftigkeit, *n.f.* durability.

dauern, *vb.* last, continue; take (a while).

dauernd, *adj.* lasting, continual.

Dauerwelle, -n, *n.f.* permanent wave.

Daumen, -, *n.m.* thumb.

Daune, -n, *n.f.* down.

dazu′, *adv.* in addition.

dazwi′schen-kommen*, *vb.* intervene.

dazwi′schen-treten*, *vb.* intercede.

Dazwischentreten, *n.nt.* intervention.

DDR (Deutsche Demokratische Republik) East Germany (German Democratic Republic).

Deba′kel, -, *n.nt.* debacle.

Debat′te, -n, *n.f.* debate.

Debet, -s, *n.nt.* debit.

Debüt′, -s, *n.nt.* debut.

Debütan′tin, -nen, *n.f.* debutante.

Deck, -s, *n.nt.* deck.

Decke, -n, *n.f.* cover; blanket; ceiling.

Deckel, -n, *n.m.* lid.

decken, *vb.* cover; **(sich d.)** coincide, jibe.

Deckung, -en, *n.f.* cover(ing); collateral.

defekt', *adj.* defective.

Defekt', -e, *n.m.* defect.

Defensi've, -n, *n.f.* defensive.

Definition', -en, *n.f.* definition.

definitiv', *adj.* definite; definitive.

Defizit, -e, *n.nt.* deficit.

Deflation', -en, *n.f.* deflation.

Degen, -, *n.m.* sword; epée.

Degeneration', *n.f.* degeneration.

degeneriert', *adj.* degenerate.

degradie'ren, *vb.* demote.

dehnen, *vb.* stretch; expand; drawl.

Dehnung, -en, *n.f.* stretch(ing), expansion.

Deich, -e, *n.m.* dike.

Dekan', -e, *n.m.* dean.

Deklamation', -en, *n.f.* declamation.

deklamie'ren, *vb.* declaim.

deklarie'ren, *vb.* declare.

Deklination', -en, *n.f.* declension.

deklinie'ren, *vb.* decline.

Dekorateur', -e, *n.m.* decorator.

dekorativ', *adj.* decorative, ornamental.

dekorie'ren, *vb.* decorate.

Dekret', -e, *n.nt.* decree.

Delegation', -en, *n.f.* delegation.

delegie'ren, *vb.* delegate.

Delegiert', -, *n.m.&f.* delegate.

delikat', *adj.* delicate, dainty.

Delikates'se, -n, *n.f.* delicacy.

Deli'rium, -rien, *n.nt.* delirium.

Demago'ge, -n, -n, *n.m.* demagogue.

demgemäß, *adv.* accordingly.

demnächst', *adv.* shortly, soon.

demobilisie'ren, *vb.* demobilize.

Demobilisie'rung, -en, *n.f.* demobilization.

Demokrat', -en, -en, *n.m.* democrat.

Demokratie', -n, *n.f.* democracy.

demokra'tisch, *adj.* democratic.

demolie'ren, *vb.* wreck.

demonstrativ', *adj.* demonstrative.

demonstrie'ren, *vb.* demonstrate.

demoralisie'ren, *vb.* demoralize.

Demut, *n.f.* humility.

demütig, *adj.* humble.

demütigen, *vb.* humiliate.

Demütigung, -en, *n.f.* humiliation.

demzufolge, *adv.* accordingly; consequently.

denkbar, *adj.* imaginable.

denken*, *vb.* think, reason.

Denker, -, *n.m.* thinker.

Denkmal, ⁻er, *n.nt.* monument, memorial.

Denkungsart, *n.f.* mode of thinking, mentality.

denkwürdig, *adj.* memorable.

denn, 1. *conj.* for. **2.** *adv.* do tell me; I wonder.

dennoch, *adv.* still, yet, nevertheless.

denunzie'ren, *vb.* denounce, inform.

Deportation', -en *n.f.* deportation.

deportie'ren, *vb.* deport.

Depot', -s, *n.nt.* depot.

Depression', -en, *n.f.* depression.

deprimie'ren, *vb.* depress.

der, das, die, 1. *art.&adj.* the, that. **2.** *pron.* he, she, it, they; that one. **3.** *rel. pron.* who, which, that.

derart, 1. *adj.* such, of such a kind. **2.** *adv.* in such a way.

derb, *adj.* coarse; stout; earthy.

dermaßen, *adv.* to such a degree, in such a manner.

Deserteur', -e, *n.m.* deserter.

Desertion', -en, *n.f.* desertion.

deshalb, *adv.* therefore, hence.

desinfizie'ren, *vb.* disinfect.

desodorisie'ren, *vb.* deodorize.

Despot', -en, -en, *n.m.* despot.

despo'tisch, *adj.* despotic.

Destillation', -en, *n.f.* distillation.

destille'ren, *vb.* distill.

desto, *adv.* **(d. besser)** so much the better; **(je mehr, d. besser)** the more the better.

deswegen, *adv.* therefore, that's why.

Detail', -s, *n.nt.* detail.

Detektiv', -e, *n.m.* detective.

deuten, *vb.* interpret; point.

deutlich, *adj.* clear, distinct.

deutsch, *adj.* German.

Deutsch-, *n.m.&f.* German.

Deutschland, *n.nt.* Germany.

Deutung, -en, *n.f.* interpretation.

Dezem'ber, -, *n.m.* December.

dezentralisie'ren, *vb.* decentralize.

Dezi'bel, -n, *n.f.* decibel.

Dezimal'-, *cpds.* decimal.

dezimie'ren, *vb.* decimate.

Diagno'se, -n, *n.f.* diagnosis.

diagnostizie'ren, *vb.* diagnose.

diagonal', *adj.* diagonal.

Diagramm', -e, *n.nt.* graph.

Dialekt', -e, *n.m.* dialect.

Dialog', -e, *n.m.* dialogue.

Diamant', -en, *n.m.* diamond.

diametral', *adj.* diametrical.

Diät', -en, *n.f.* diet.

diätgemäß, *adj.* dietary.

dicht, *adj.* dense, thick; tight.

Dichte, *n.f.* density.

Dichter, -, *n.m.* poet.

dichterisch, *adj.* poetic.

Dichtheit, *n.f.* thickness.

Dichtung, -en, *n.f.* poetry; *(tech.)* packing, gasket.

dick, *adj.* thick, fat, stout.

Dicke, *n.f.* thickness.

dicken, *vb.* thicken.

Dickicht, *n.nt.* thicket, brush.

dicklich, *adj.* chubby.

Dieb, -e, *n.m.* thief, robber.

Diebstahl, ⁻e, *n.m.* theft, larceny.

Diele, -n, *n.f.* hall, hallway.

dienen, *vb.* serve.

Diener, -, *n.m.* valet, butler.

Dienerschaft, -en, *n.f.* servant.

Dienst, -e, *n.m.* service.

Dienstag, -e, *n.m.* Tuesday.

dienstbeflissen, *adj.* assiduous; officious.

Dienstmädchen, -, *n.nt.* maid.

Dienstpflicht, *n.f.* compulsory military service, draft.

Dienstvorschrift, -en, *n.f.* regulation.

Dieselmotor, -en, *n.m.* diesel engine.

dieser, -es, -e, *pron.&adj.* this.

differential', *adj.* differential.

differenzie'ren, *vb.* differentiate.

Diktat', -e, *n.nt.* dictation.

Dikta'tor, -o'ren, *n.m.* dictator.

diktato'risch, *adj.* dictatorial.

Diktatur', -en, *n.f.* dictatorship.

diktie'ren, *vb.* dictate.

Dilem'ma, -s, *n.nt.* dilemma, predicament.

Dilettant', -en, -en, *n.m.* dilettante.

Dill, *n.m.* dill.

Ding, -e, *n.nt.* thing.

dingen*, *vb.* hire.

Diphtherie', *n.f.* diphtheria.

Diplom', -e, *n.nt.* diploma.

Diplomat', -en, -en, *n.m.* diplomat.

Diplomatie', *n.f.* diplomacy.

diploma'tisch, *adj.* diplomatic.

direkt', *adj.* direct; downright.

Direkti've, -n, *n.f.* directive.

Direk'tor, -o'ren, *n.m.* director.

Direkto'rium, -rien, *n.nt.* directorate, directory.

Dirigent', -en, -en, *n.m.* conductor.

dirigie'ren, *vb.* conduct.

Diskont', -e, *n.m.* discount.

Diskont'satz, ⁻e, *n.m.* interest rate.

Diskothek', -en, *n.f.* discotheque.

diskret', *adj.* discreet.

Diskretion', *n.f.* discretion.

diskriminie'ren, *vb.* discriminate.

Diskriminie'rung, -en, *n.f.* discrimination.

Diskussion', -en, *n.f.* discussion.

diskutie'ren, *vb.* discuss.

disqualifizie'ren, *vb.* disqualify.

Dissertation', -en, *n.f.* dissertation.

Disziplin', *n.f.* discipline.

disziplinie'ren, *vb.* discipline.

Diva, -s, *n.f.* diva.

divers', *adj.* miscellaneous.

Division', -en, *n.f.* division.

D-Mark, -, *n.f.* (= deutsche Mark) mark, West German unit of currency.

doch, 1. *conj.* yet. 2. *adv.* yet; indeed; oh yes.

Docht, -e, *n.m.* wick.

Dock, -s, *n.nt.* dock.

docken, *vb.* dock.

Dogma -men, *n.nt.* dogma.

dogma'tisch, *adj.* dogmatic.

Doktor, -o'ren, *n.m.* doctor.

Doktorat', -e, *n.nt.* doctorate.

doktrinär', *adj.* doctrinaire.

Dokument', -e, *n.nt.* document.

dokumenta'risch, *adj.* documentary.

dokumentie'ren, *vb.* document, authenticate.

Dolch, -e, *n.m.* dagger.

Dollar, -s, *n.m.* dollar.

dolmetschen, *vb.* interpret.

Dolmetscher, -, *n.m.* interpreter.

Dom, -e, *n.m.* cathedral, dome.

Domi'nion, -s, *n.nt.* dominion.

Donau, *n.f.* Danube.

Donner, -, *n.m.* thunder.

donnern, *vb.* thunder.

Donnerstag, -e, *n.m.* Thursday.

Donnerwetter, *n.nt.* (**zum D.**) confound it!; (what) in thunder.

Doppel-, *cpds.* double, dual.

Doppelgänger, -, *n.m.* double.

doppelkohlensaur, *adj.* (**d. es Natron**) bicarbonate of soda.

Doppelpunkt, -e, *n.m.* colon.

doppelt, *adj.* double.

Dorf, ¨er, *n.nt.* village.

Dorn, -en, *n.m.* thorn.

dörren, *vb.* dry, parch.

dort, *adv.* there.

Dose, -n, *n.f.* (small) box, can.

dösen, *vb.* doze.

Dosie'rung, -en, *n.f.* dosage.

Dosis, -sen, *n.f.* dose.

Drache, -n, -n, *n.m.* dragon.

Draht, ¨e, *n.m.* wire.

Drahtaufnahmegerät, -e, *n.nt.* wire recorder.

drahtlos, *adj.* wireless.

drall, *adj.* buxom.

Drama, -men, *n.nt.* drama.

Drama'tiker, -, *n.m.* dramatist.

drama'tisch, *adj.* dramatic.

dramatisie'ren, *vb.* dramatize.

Drang, ¨e, *n.m.* urge.

drängeln, *vb.* crowd.

drängen, *vb.* urge, press.

Drangsal, -e, *n.f.* distress.

drapie'ren, *vb.* drape.

drastisch, *adj.* drastic.

draußen, *adv.* outside.

Dreck, *n.m.* dirt, mud.

dreckig, *adj.* filthy.

Drehbuch, ¨er, *n.nt.* scenario (film).

drehen, *vb.* turn; make (a movie).

Drehpunkt, -e, *n.m.* pivot, fulcrum.

Drehung, -en, *n.f.* turning.

drei, *num.* three.

Dreieck, -e, *n.nt.* triangle.

dreifach, *adj.* triple.

dreifältig, *adj.* threefold.

dreimal, *adv.* thrice, three times.

dreißig, *num.* thirty.

dreißigst-, *adj.* thirtieth.

Dreißigstel, -, *n.nt.* thirtieth part; (**ein d.**) one-thirtieth.

dreist, *adj.* bold; fresh, nervy.

dreizehn, *num.* thirteen.

dreschen*, *vb.* thresh, thrash.

Drill, -, *n.m.* drill.

Drillbohrer, -, *n.m.* drill.

dringen*, *vb.* force one's way, penetrate; insist.

dringend, *adj.* urgent.

dringlich, *adj.* pressing.

Dringlichkeit, *n.f.* urgency.

drinnen, *adv.* inside.

dritt-, *adj.* third.

Drittel, -, *n.nt.* third part; (**ein d.**) one-third.

drittens, *adv.* in the third place, thirdly.

Dritte Welt, *n.f.* Third World.

drittletzt, *adj.* third from last.

Droge, -n, *n.f.* drug.

Drogerie', -i'en, *n.f.* drug store.

Drogist, -en, *n.m.* druggist.

drohen, *vb.* threaten.

dröhnen, *vb.* sound, boom, roar.

Drohung, -en, *n.f.* threat.

drollig, *adj.* droll, funny.

Droschke, -n, *n.f.* hack, cab.

Drossel, -n, *n.f.* thrush.

drosseln, *vb.* throttle, cut down.

drüben, *adv.* over there.

Druck, -e, *n.m.* print(ing), impression.

Druck, ¨e, *n.m.* pressure.

drucken, *vb.* print.

Drucken, *n.nt.* printing.

drücken, *vb.* press, squeeze; oppress; (**sich d.**) get out of work, shirk.

drückend, *adj.* pressing, oppressive.

Druckerpresse, -n, *n.f.* printing-press.

drunter, *adv.* underneath.

Drüse, -n, *n.f.* gland.

Dschungel, -, *n.m. or nt.* (*-n f.*), jungle.

du, *pron.* you (familiar); thou.

ducken, *vb.* (**sich d.**) duck.

Duell', -e, *n.nt.* duel.

Duett', -e, *n.nt.* duet.

Duft, ¨e, *n.m.* fragrance.

duftig, *adj.* fragrant.

dulden, *vb.* tolerate.

duldsam, *adj.* tolerant.

Duldsamkeit, *n.f.* tolerance.

dumm(-), *adj.* stupid, dumb.

Dummheit, -en, *n.f.* stupidity.

Dummkopf, ¨e, *n.m.* dullard, idiot.

dumpf, *adj.* dull, musty.

Düne, -n, *n.f.* dune.

Dung, *n.m.* dung.

düngen, *vb.* fertilize.

Dünger, *n.m.* fertilizer, manure.

dunkel, *adj.* dark; obscure.

Dunkel, *n.nt.* dark(ness).

Dünkel, *n.m.* pretension.

dünken*, *vb.* seem; (**mich dünkt**) methinks.

dünn, *adj.* thin.

Dunst, ¨e, *n.m.* haze, vapor.

dunsten, *vb.* steam, fume.

dünsten, *vb.* steam, stew.

dunstig, *adj.* hazy.

Duplikat', -e, *n.nt.* duplicate.

Dur, *n.nt.* major; (**A-Dur**) A-major.

durch, *prep.* through; by means of.

durchaus', *adv.* entirely, by all means.

durchblät'tern, *vb.* leaf through.

Durchblick, -e, *n.m.* view (through something).

durch-blicken, *vb.* look through; be visible.

durchbli'cken, *vb.* see through, discern.

durchboh'ren, *vb.* pierce.

Durchbruch, ¨e, *n.m.* breakthrough.

durchdacht', *adj.* thought out.

durch-drehen, *vb.* panic.

durch-dringen*, *vb.* force one's way through, penetrate.

durchdrin'gen*, *vb.* permeate, impregnate.

durcheinan'der, *adv.* through one another; all mixed up.

Durcheinan'der, *n.nt.* confusion, turmoil, mess.

Durchfahrt, -en, *n.f.* passage, transit.

Durchfall, *n.m.* diarrhea.

durch-fallen*, *vb.* fail (a test).

durchführbar, *adj.* practicable.

durch-führen, *vb.* carry out.

Durchgang, ¨e, *n.m.* passage through; passageway; (**D. gesperrt!**) closed to traffic.

durch-gehen*, *vb.* go through; bolt, run away.

durchgehend, *adj.* nonstop.

durch-helfen*, *vb.* help through; (**sich d.**) get along somehow.

durch-kreuzen, *vb.* cross out.

durchkreu'zen, *vb.* cross, intersect; thwart.

durch-leuchten, *vb.* shine through.

durchleuch'ten, *vb.* illuminate, irradiate, X-ray.

durchlö'chern, *vb.* perforate, puncture.

Durchlö'cherung, -en, *n.f.* perforation.

Durchmesser, -, *n.m.* diameter.

durchnäs'sen, *vb.* drench, soak.

Durchreise, -n, *n.f.* journey through; (**auf der D.**) passing through.

durch-schauen, *vb.* look through.

durchschau'en, *vb.* see through, understand.

durch·schnei·den*, vb. cut in two.

durchschnei'den*, vb. cut, bisect, intersect.

Durchschnitt, -e, n.m. average.

durchschnittlich, adj. average.

durch·sehen*, vb. see through.

durchse'hen*, vb. look over, scrutinize; revise.

durch·setzen, vb. put through, get accepted.

durchset'zen, vb. intersperse, permeate.

Durchsicht, n.f. view; perusal.

durchsichtig, adj. transparent.

durch·sickern, vb. leak through, seep through.

durch·stechen*, vb. stick through.

durchste'chen*, vb. puncture, pierce.

durchsu'chen, vb. search.

Durchsu'chung, -en, n.f. search.

durchwüh'len, vb. ransack.

dürfen*, vb. be permitted, may.

dürftig, adj. meager.

dürr, adj. dry, barren.

Dürre, -n, n.f. drought, barrenness.

Durst, n.m. thirst.

dürsten, vb. thirst.

durstig, adj. thirsty.

Dusche, -n, n.f. shower.

Düse, -n, n.f. nozzle, jet.

Dusel, n.m. good luck.

duselig, adj. fizzy; stupid.

Düsenflugzeug, -e, n.nt. jet plane.

Düsenkampfflugzeug, n.nt. jet fighter plane.

düster, adj. gloomy.

Düsterheit, n.f. gloom.

Dutzend, -e, n.nt. dozen.

duzen, vb. call a person du.

Dyna'mik, n.f. dynamics.

dyna'misch, adj. dynamic.

Dynamit', n.nt. dynamite.

Dyna'mo, -s, n.m. dynamo.

Dynastie', -i'en, n.f. dynasty.

Dyslexie', n.f. dyslexia.

D-Zug, ∹e, n.m. (= Durchgangszug) train with corridors in the cars; express train.

E

Ebbe, n.f. low tide.

ebben, vb. ebb.

eben, adj. even, level.

eben, adv. just; exactly.

Ebene, -n, n.f. plain, level ground; plane.

ebenfalls, adv. likewise.

ebenso, adv. likewise; (e. groß) just as big.

ebnen, vb. level, make smooth.

Echo, -s, n.nt. echo.

echt, adj. genuine.

Echtheit, -en, n.f. authenticity, genuineness.

Ecke, -n, n.f. corner.

eckig, adj. angular.

edel, adj. noble.

Edelstein, -e, n.m. jewel.

Efeu, n.m. ivy.

EG (Europäische Gemeinschaft), n.f. Common Market.

egal', adj. equal; (es ist mir e.) I don't care, it makes no difference to me.

Egois'mus, n.m. egoism.

Egoist', -en, -en, n.m. egotist.

Egotis'mus, n.m. egotism.

ehe, conj. before.

Ehe, -n, n.f. marriage, matrimony.

Ehebrecher, -, n.m. adulterer.

Ehebrecherin, -nen, n.f. adulteress.

Ehebruch, ∹e, n.m. adultery.

ehedem, adv. formerly.

Ehefrau, -en, n.f. wife.

Ehegatte, -n, -n, n.m. spouse; husband.

Ehegattin, -nen, n.f. wife.

Eheleute, n.pl. married people.

ehelich, adj. marital; legitimate.

ehelos, adj. celibate.

Ehelosigkeit, n.f. celibacy.

ehemalig, adj. former.

ehemals, adv. formerly.

Ehemann, ∹er, n.m. husband.

Ehepaar, -e, n.nt. married couple.

eher, adv. sooner, earlier; rather.

ehern, adj. brazen, brass.

Ehescheidung, -en, n.f. divorce.

Ehestand, n.m. matrimony.

ehrbar, adj. honorable.

Ehre, -n, n.f. honor.

ehren, vb. honor.

ehrenamtlich, adj. honorary, unpaid.

Ehrengast, ∹e, n.m. guest of honor.

Ehrenplatz, ∹e, n.m. place of honor.

ehrenvoll, adj. honorable.

ehrenwert, adj. worthy.

ehrerbietig, adj. respectful.

Ehrerbietung, -en, n.f. reverence, obeisance.

Ehrfurcht, n.f. awe, respect, reverence.

Ehrgeiz, n.m. ambition.

ehrgeizig, adj. ambitious.

ehrlich, adj. honest, sincere.

Ehrlichkeit, -en, n.f. honesty.

ehrlos, adj. dishonorable.

Ehrlosigkeit, n.f. dishonor.

ehrsam, adj. honest, respectable.

Ehrsamkeit, n.f. respectability.

Ehrung, -en, n.f. tribute.

ehrwürdig, adj. reverend, venerable.

Ei, -er, n.nt. egg.

Eiche, -n, n.f. oak.

Eichhörnchen, -, n.nt. squirrel.

Eid, -e, n.m. oath.

Eidam, -e, n.m. son-in-law.

eidesstattlich, adj. under oath; (e.e Erklä'rung) affidavit.

Eidgenosse, -n, -n, n.m. confederate.

Eidgenossenschaft, -en, n.f. confederation; (Schweizerische E.) Swiss Confederation.

eidgenössisch, adj. federal; Swiss.

Eifer, n.m. zeal, eagerness.

Eifersucht, n.f. jealousy.

eifersüchtig, adj. jealous.

eifrig, adj. zealous, eager, ardent.

Eigelb, n.nt. yolk.

eigen, adj. own; typical of.

Eigenart, -en, n.f. peculiarity, inherent nature.

eigenartig, adj. peculiar.

Eigenheit, -en, n.f. peculiarity.

eigenmächtig, adj. arbitrary.

Eigenname(n), -, n.m. proper name.

Eigennutz, n.m. selfishness.

eigennützig, adj. selfish.

Eigenschaft, -en, n.f. quality.

Eigenschaftswort, ∹er, n.nt. adjective.

Eigensinn, n.m. obstinacy, willfulness.

eigensinnig, adj. obstinate, willful.

eigentlich, 1. adj. actual. 2. adv. as a matter of fact.

Eigentum, n.nt. property.

Eigentümer, -, n.m. owner.

Eigentumswohnung, -en, n.f. condominium.

eignen, vb. (sich e.) be suited.

Eilbote, -n, -n, n.m. special delivery messenger; (per E.n) by special delivery.

Eilbrief, -e, n.m. special delivery letter.

Eile, n.f. haste, hurry.

eilen, vb. hurry.

eilig, adj. hasty, urgent.

Eilpost, n.f. special delivery.

Eimer, -, n.m. pail.

ein, -, -e, art. & adj. a, an; (stressed) one.

einan'der, pron. one another, each other.

ein·äschern, vb. cremate.

Einäscherung, -en, n.f. cremation.

ein·atmen, vb. inhale.

Einbahn-, cpds. one-way.

Einband, ∹e, n.m. binding.

ein·bauen, vb. install.

ein·behalten*, vb. withhold.

ein·berufen*, vb. summon, convoke.

ein·bilden, vb. (sich e.) imagine.

Einbildung, -en, n.f. imagination; conceit.

ein·binden*, vb. bind.

Einblick, -e, n.m. insight.

Einbrecher, -, n.m. burglar.

ein·bringen*, vb. yield.

Einbruch, ∹e, n.m. burglary.

Einbuchtung, -en, n.f. dent; bay.

ein·bürgern, *vb.* naturalize.

Einbuße, *n.f.* forfeiture.

ein·büßen, *vb.* forfeit.

ein·dämmen, *vb.* dam.

eindeutig, *adj.* clear, unequivocal.

ein·drängen, *vb.* (sich e.) encroach upon.

ein·dringen*, *vb.* penetrate, intrude, invade.

Eindringling, -e, *n.m.* intruder.

Eindruck, ⁀e, *n.m.* impression.

eindrucksvoll, *adj.* impressive.

ein·engen, *vb.* hem in.

einer, -es, -e, *pron.* one, a person; one thing.

einerlei', *adj.* of one kind; (es ist mir e.) it's all the same to me.

einerseits, *adv.* on the one hand.

einfach, *adj.* simple, plain.

Einfachheit, *n.f.* simplicity.

Einfahrt, -en, *n.f.* gateway, entrance.

Einfall, ⁀e, *n.m.* collapse; bright idea.

ein·fallen*, *vb.* fall in; invade; occur to.

einfältig, *adj.* simple.

ein·fassen, *vb.* edge, trim.

ein·finden*, *vb.* (sich e.) present oneself, show up.

ein·flößen, *vb.* instill with.

Einfluß, ⁀sse, *n.m.* influence.

einflußreich, *adj.* influential.

ein·fordern, *vb.* demand, reclaim.

einförmig, *adj.* uniform.

ein·fügen, *vb.* insert; (sich e.) adapt oneself.

Einfuhr, *n.f.* import, importation.

ein·führen, *vb.* import, induct.

Einführung, -en, *n.f.* induction; introduction.

Eingabe, -n, *n.f.* petition; (computer) input.

Eingang, ⁀e, *n.m.* entrance.

ein·geben*, *vb.* give; inspire.

eingebildet, *adj.* conceited.

eingeboren, *adj.* native, indigenous.

Eingeboren-, *n.m.&f.* native.

Eingebung, -en, *n.f.* inspiration.

eingedenk, *adj.* mindful.

eingefleischt, *adj.* inveterate.

ein·gehen*, *vb.* enter; shrink; cease, perish.

eingehend, *adj.* detailed, thorough.

Eingemacht-, *n.nt.* preserves.

eingenommen, *adj.* partial, prejudiced.

Eingesessen-, *n.m.&f.* inhabitant.

Eingeständnis, -se, *n.nt.* confession, admission.

ein·gestehen*, *vb.* confess, admit.

Eingeweide, *n.npl.* intestines.

ein·gewöhnen, *vb.* acclimate.

ein·graben*, *vb.* bury.

ein·greifen*, *vb.* interfere.

Eingriff, -e, *n.m.* intervention.

ein·halten*, *vb.* check, stop; observe, keep.

ein·händigen, *vb.* hand in.

einheimisch, *adj.* native.

Einheimisch-, *n.m.&f.* native.

Einheit, -en, *n.f.* unit.

einheitlich, *adj.* uniform.

einher', *adv.* along.

ein·holen, *vb.* gather; overtake.

ein·hüllen, *vb.* wrap up, enfold.

einig, *adj.* united, agreed.

einige, *pron.&adj.* some, several.

einigen, *vb.* unite; (sich e.) agree.

einigermaßen, *adv.* to some extent.

Einigkeit, *n.f.* unity.

ein·impfen, *vb.* inoculate.

ein·kassieren, *vb.* collect.

Einkauf, ⁀e, *n.m.* purchase.

ein·kaufen, *vb.* purchase.

ein·kehren, *vb.* put up (at an inn).

ein·kerkern, *vb.* incarcerate.

ein·klammern, *vb.* bracket; put in parentheses.

Einklang, ⁀e, *n.m.* harmony.

ein·kleiden, *vb.* clothe.

ein·klemmen, *vb.* wedge in.

Einkommen, -, *n.nt.* income.

Einkommensteuer, -n, *n.f.* income tax.

ein·kreisen, *vb.* encircle.

Einkünfte, *n.pl.* revenue.

ein·laden*, *vb.* invite.

Einladung, -en, *n.f.* invitation.

Einlage, -n, *n.f.* enclosure, filling; deposit.

Einlaß, ⁀sse, *n.m.* admission, entrance.

ein·laufen*, *vb.* enter; shrink.

ein·legen, *vb.* insert; deposit; pickle.

ein·leiten, *vb.* introduce.

einleitend, *adj.* introductory.

Einleitung, -en, *n.f.* introduction.

ein·leuchten, *vb.* make sense.

einleuchtend, *adj.* plausible.

ein·lösen, *vb.* redeem.

Einlösung, -en, *n.f.* redemption.

ein·machen, *vb.* preserve, can.

einmal, *adv.* once; (auf e.) all of a sudden; (noch e.) once again; (nicht e.) not even.

einmalig, *adj.* occurring only once, single, unique.

Einmarsch, ⁀e, *n.m.* marching into, entry.

ein·mauern, *vb.* wall in.

ein·mengen, *vb.* mix in; (sich e.) interfere.

ein·mischen, *vb.* mix in; (sich e.) intervene, meddle.

Einmischung, -en, *n.f.* intervention.

Einnahme, -n, *n.f.* receipt; capture.

ein·nehmen*, *vb.* take; captivate.

Einöde, *n.f.* desolate place, solitude.

ein·ordnen, *vb.* arrange, file.

ein·packen, *vb.* pack up, wrap up.

ein·pflanzen, *vb.* plant.

ein·prägen, *vb.* impress.

ein·rahmen, *vb.* frame.

ein·räumen, *vb.* concede.

ein·rechnen, *vb.* include, allow for.

Einrede, -n, *n.f.* objection.

ein·reden, *vb.* talk into, persuade.

ein·reihen, *vb.* arrange.

ein·reißen*, *vb.* tear down.

ein·richten, *vb.* furnish, arrange, establish.

Einrichtung, -en, *n.f.* arrangement, institution.

ein·rücken, *vb.* move in; indent.

eins, *num.* one.

einsam, *adj.* lone(ly), lonesome.

Einsamkeit, *n.f.* loneliness, solitude.

ein·sammeln, *vb.* gather in.

Einsatz, ⁀e, *n.m.* inset; stake (in betting); (mil.) sortie.

ein·schalten, *vb.* switch on, shift into, tune in.

ein·schärfen, *vb.* inculcate.

ein·schätzen, *vb.* assess, estimate.

ein·schiffen, *vb.* embark.

ein·schlafen*, *vb.* go to sleep.

Einschlag, ⁀e, *n.m.* impact, envelope.

ein·schlagen*, *vb.* drive in; strike, break; take.

einschlägig, *adj.* pertinent, relevant.

ein·schließen*, *vb.* lock up in, enclose, include, involve.

einschliesslich, *adj.* inclusive.

ein·schmeicheln, *vb.* (sich e.) insinuate oneself.

ein·schnappen*, *vb.* snap shut; get annoyed.

Einschnitt, -e, *n.m.* cut, notch, segment.

ein·schränken, *vb.* limit, restrict.

Einschränkung, -en, *n.f.* restriction.

Einschreibebrief, -e, *n.m.* registered letter.

ein·schreiben*, *vb.* inscribe; register.

ein·schüchtern, *vb.* intimidate.

Einschüchterung, -en, *n.f.* intimidation.

ein·segnen, *vb.* consecrate, confirm.

ein·sehen*, *vb.* look into, realize.

ein·seifen, *vb.* soap, lather.

einseitig, *adj.* one-sided.

ein·setzen, *vb.* set in; appoint; install.

Einsicht, -en, *n.f.* insight; inspection.

Einsiedler, -, *n.m.* hermit.

ein·spannen, *vb.* stretch; harness, enlist.

ein·sperren, *vb.* lock up, imprison.

ein·spritzen, *vb.* inject.

Einspritzung, -en, *n.f.* injection.

Einspruch, ⸚e, *n.m.* protest; **(E. erhe′ben*)** to protest.

einst, *adv.* once, one day.

ein·stecken, *vb.* put in one's pocket.

ein·stehen*, *vb.* **(e. für)** stand up for, take the place of.

ein·steigen*, *vb.* get in; **(e.!)** allaboard!

ein·stellen, *vb.* put in, tune in, engage; stop, suspend.

Einstellung, -en, *n.f.* attitude; adjustment; suspension.

ein·stimmen, *vb.* chime in, join in, agree.

einstimmig, *adj.* unanimous.

Einstimmigkeit, *n.f.* unanimity.

ein·studieren, *vb.* practice, rehearse.

Einsturz, ⸚e, *n.m.* collapse.

einstweilen, *adv.* in the meantime.

ein·tauchen, *vb.* dip.

ein·tauschen, *vb.* exchange, swap.

ein·teilen, *vb.* divide, arrange, classify.

Einteilung, -en, *n.f.* classification.

eintönig, *adj.* monotonous.

Eintracht, *n.f.* harmony, concord.

ein·tragen*, *vb.* register, enter, record; bring in.

einträglich, *adj.* profitable.

Eintragung, -en, *n.f.* entry.

ein·treffen*, *vb.* arrive, happen.

ein·treten*, *vb.* enter.

Eintritt, -e, *n.m.* entry; beginning.

Eintrittskarte, -n, *n.f.* ticket of admission.

ein·üben, *vb.* practice.

ein·verleiben, *vb.* incorporate, annex.

Einvernehmen, -, *n.nt.* accord.

Einverständnis, -se, *n.nt.* agreement.

Einwand, ⸚e, *n.m.* objection.

Einwanderer, -, *n.m.* immigrant.

ein·wandern, *vb.* immigrate.

Einwanderung, -en, *n.f.* immigration.

einwandfrei, *adj.* sound, unobjectionable.

ein·wechseln, *vb.* change, cash.

ein·weichen, *vb.* soak.

ein·weihen, *vb.* consecrate, initiate.

Einweihung, -en, *n.f.* consecration, inauguration.

ein·wenden*, *vb.* wrap up.

ein·werfen*, *vb.* throw in; object, interject.

ein·wickeln, *vb.* wrap up.

ein·willigen, *vb.* consent.

Einwilligung, -en, *n.f.* consent, approval.

Einwirkung, -en, *n.f.* influence.

Einwohner, -, *n.m.* inhabitant, resident.

Einwurf, ⸚e, *n.m.* slot; objection.

ein·zahlen, *vb.* pay in, deposit.

Einzahlung, -en, *n.f.* deposit.

Einzäunung, -en, *n.f.* enclosure.

ein·zeichnen, *vb.* inscribe.

Einzelheit, -en, *n.f.* detail.

einzeln, *adj.* single, individual.

ein·ziehen*, *vb. (tr.)* pull in, furl, seize, draft; *(intr.)* move in, march in.

einzig, *adj.* only, sole, single.

einzigartig, *adj.* unique.

Einzug, ⸚e, *n.m.* entry.

ein·zwängen, *vb.* force in, squeeze in.

Eis, *n.nt.* ice.

Eisberg, -e, *n.m.* iceberg.

Eisen, -, *n.nt.* iron.

Eisenbahn, -en, *n.f.* railroad.

Eisenbahnwagen, -, *n.m.* railroad coach.

Eisenwaren, *n.pl.* hardware.

eisern, *adj.* iron.

eisig, *adj.* icy.

Eisregen, -, *n.m.* sleet.

Eisschrank, ⸚e, *n.m.* ice-box, refrigerator.

eitel, *adj.* vain.

Eitelkeit, *n.f.* vanity.

Eiter, -, *n.m.* pus.

Eiterbeule, -n, *n.f.* abscess.

Eitergeschwulst, ⸚e, *n.f.* abscess.

Eiweiß, *n.nt.* white of egg.

Ekel, *n.m.* disgust.

ekelerregend, *adj.* nauseating.

ekelhaft, *adj.* disgusting.

ekeln, *vb.* arouse disgust; **(sich e. vor)** be disgusted by.

EKG (Elektrokardiogramm′, -e), *n.nt.* electrocardiogram.

Eksta′se, -n, *n.f.* ecstasy.

eksta′tisch, *adj.* ecstatic.

Ekzem′, -e, *n.nt.* eczema.

elas′tisch, *adj.* elastic.

Elefant′, -en, -en, *n.m.* elephant.

elegant′, *adj.* elegant, chic, smart.

Eleganz′, *n.f.* elegance.

elektrifizie′ren, *vb.* electrify.

Elek′triker, -, *n.m.* electrician.

elek′trisch, *adj.* electric.

Elektrizität′, *n.f.* electricity.

Elek′tron, -o′nen, *n.nt.* electron.

Elektro′nenrechner, -, *n.m.* computer.

Elektro′nenwissenschaft, *n.f.* electronics.

Element′, -e, *n.nt.* element.

elementar′, *adj.* elemental, elementary.

Elend, *n.nt.* misery.

elend, *adj.* miserable, wretched; sick.

elf, *num.* eleven.

Elfenbein, *n.nt.* ivory.

elft-, *adj.* eleventh.

Elftel, -, *n.nt.* eleventh part; **(ein e.)** one-eleventh.

Eli′te, *n.f.* elite.

Elixier′, -e, *n.nt.* elixir.

Ellbogen, -, *n.m.* elbow.

Elle, -, *n.f.* ell, yard.

Elsaß, *n.nt.* Alsace.

elterlich, *adj.* parental.

Eltern, *n.pl.* parents.

Emai′lle, *n.f.* enamel.

emanzipie′ren, *vb.* emancipate.

Embar′go, -s, *n.nt.* embargo.

Emblem′, -e, *n.nt.* emblem.

Embryo, -s, *n.m.* embryo.

Empfang′, ⸚e, *n.m.* reception.

empfan′gen*, *vb.* receive; conceive (child).

Empfän′ger, -, *n.m.* receiver, recipient, addressee.

empfäng′lich, *adj.* susceptible.

empfeh′len*, *vb.* recommend, commend.

empfeh′lenswert, *adj.* (re)commendable.

Empfeh′lung, -en, *n.f.* recommendation.

empfin′den*, *vb.* feel, sense.

empfind′lich, *adj.* sensitive.

empfind′sam, *adj.* sentimental.

Empfin′dung, -en, *n.f.* feeling, sensation.

empfin′dungslos, *adj.* insensitive.

empor′, *adv.* upward, aloft.

empö′ren, *vb.* make indignant; **(sich e.)** be furious; rebel.

empor′·ragen, *vb.* rise up, tower.

empor′·schwingen*, *vb.* **(sich e.)** soar upward.

Empö′rung, -en, *n.f.* indignation; rebellion.

emsig, *adj.* busy, industrious.

Emulsion′, -en, *n.f.* emulsion.

Ende, -n, *n.nt.* end.

enden, *vb.* end.

endgültig, *adj.* definitive, conclusive, final.

endigen, *vb.* end.

endlich, 1. *adj.* final; finite. **2.** *adv.* at last.

endlos, *adj.* endless.

Endstation, -en, *n.f.* terminus.

Energie′, -n, *n.f.* energy.

energie′los, *adj.* languid.

ener′gisch, *adj.* energetic.

eng, *adj.* narrow, tight.

engagie′ren, *vb.* engage, hire.

Enge, -n, *n.f.* narrowness; narrow place; **(in die E. trei′ben*)** drive into a corner.

Engel, -, *n.m.* angel.

England, *n.nt.* England.

Engländer, -, *n.m.* Englishman.

englisch, *adj.* English.

Enkel, -, *n.m.* grandson.

Enkelin, -nen, *n.f.* granddaughter.

Enkelkind, -er, *n.nt.* grandchild.

enorm′, *adj.* enormous.

Ensem′ble, -s, *n.nt.* ensemble.

entar′ten, *vb.* degenerate.

entbeh′ren, *vb.* go without.

entbehr'lich, *adj.* dispensable.

Entbeh'rung, -en, *n.f.* privation.

entbin'den*, *vb.* set free; deliver.

Entbin'dung, -en, *n.f.* delivery.

entblö'ßen, *vb.* denude, uncover, bare.

entde'cken, *vb.* discover.

Entde'ckung, -en, *n.f.* discovery.

Ente, -n, *n.f.* duck.

enteh'ren, *vb.* dishonor.

enteig'nen, *vb.* dispossess.

entfa'chen, *vb.* kindle.

entfal'len*, *vb.* fall to; slip from (memory).

entfal'ten, *vb.* unfold.

entfer'nen, *vb.* remove.

entfernt', *adj.* removed; distant.

Entfer'nung, -en, *n.f.* removal; distance.

entfes'seln, *vb.* unchain, release.

entflam'men, *vb.* inflame.

entflie'hen*, *vb.* flee, escape.

entfrem'den, *vb.* estrange, alienate.

entfüh'ren*, *vb.* carry off, abduct, kidnap.

Entfüh'rung, -en, *n.f.* abduction.

entge'gen, *adv.&prep.* opposite, contrary to; towards.

entge'gengesetzt, *adj.* opposite.

entge'gen-kommen*, *vb.* come towards; be obliging.

entge'gen-setzen, *vb.* oppose.

entgeg'nen, *vb.* reply, retort.

entge'hen*, *vb.* elude.

Entgelt', *n.nt.* remuneration.

entglei'sen*, *vb.* jump the track; make a slip.

Entglei'sung, -en, *n.f.* derailment; blunder.

enthal'ten*, *vb.* hold, contain; (sich e.) refrain.

enthalt'sam, *adj.* abstemious.

Enthalt'samkeit, -en, *n.f.* abstinence.

Enthal'tung, *n.f.* forbearance.

enthe'ben*, *vb.* oust.

Enthe'bung, -en, *n.f.* ouster.

enthül'len, *vb.* unveil, disclose.

Enthül'lung, -en, *n.f.* disclosure, exposé.

Enthusiast', -en, -en, *n.m.* enthusiast.

entklei'den, *vb.* undress, divest.

entkom'men*, *vb.* escape.

entkräf'ten*, *vb.* debilitate.

entla'den*, *vb.* unload.

entlang', *adv.&prep.* along.

entlas'sen*, *vb.* dismiss, release.

Entlas'sung, -en, *n.f.* dismissal, release.

entlau'fen*, *vb.* run away.

entle'digen, *vb.* free from, exempt.

entle'gen, *adj.* remote.

entmilitarisie'ren, *vb.* demilitarize.

entmu'tigen, *vb.* discourage.

Entmu'tigung, -en, *n.f.* discouragement.

entneh'men*, *vb.* take from, infer from.

entrah'men, *vb.* skim.

entrit'seln, *vb.* decipher.

entrei'ßen*, *vb.* snatch from.

entrich'ten, *vb.* pay, settle.

entrin'nen*, *vb.* run away from.

entrüs'ten, *vb.* make indignant; (sich e.) become indignant.

entrüs'tet, *adj.* indignant.

Entrüs'tung, -en, *n.f.* indignation.

entsa'gen, *vb.* renounce, abjure.

entschä'digen, *vb.* compensate, indemnify.

Entschä'digung, -en, *n.f.* compensation, indemnification.

entschei'den*, *vb.* decide.

entschei'dend, *adj.* decisive.

Entschei'dung, -en, *n.f.* decision.

entschie'den, *adj.* decided, definite.

entschlie'ßen*, *vb.* (sich e.) decide.

entschlos'sen, *adj.* determined.

Entschlos'senheit, *n.f.* determination.

entschlüp'fen, *vb.* slip away from.

Enschluß', -sse, *n.m.* decision.

entschul'digen, *vb.* excuse; (sich e.) apologize.

Entschul'digung, -en, *n.f.* excuse, apology.

entset'zen, *vb.* dismiss; horrify; (sich e.) be horrified.

Entset'zen, *n.nt.* horror.

entsetz'lich, *adj.* horrible.

entsin'nen*, *vb.* (sich e.) recollect.

entspan'nen, *vb.* relax.

Entspan'nung, *n.f.* détente.

entspre'chen*, *vb.* correspond.

entspre'chend, *adj.* corresponding (to), respective.

entste'hen*, *vb.* arise, originate.

entstel'len, *vb.* disfigure, deform, distort, mutilate, garble.

enttäu'schen, *vb.* disappoint.

Enttäu'schung, -en, *n.f.* disappointment.

entthro'nen, *vb.* dethrone.

entwaff'nen, *vb.* disarm.

entwä's'sern, *vb.* drain.

entwe'der, *conj.* (e. . . . oder) either . . . or.

entwei'chen*, *vb.* escape.

entwen'den*, *vb.* steal.

entwer'fen*, *vb.* sketch, draft, plan.

entwer'ten, *vb.* depreciate; cancel.

entwi'ckeln, *vb.* develop.

Entwick'ler, -, *n.m.* developer.

Entwicklung, -en, *n.f.* development.

Entwick'lungshilfe, *n.f.* foreign aid.

Entwick'lungsland, ⁼er, *n.nt.* developing nation.

entwir'ren, *vb.* disentangle.

entwi'schen, *vb.* slip away from.

entwür'digen, *vb.* dishonor.

Entwurf', ⁼e, *n.m.* sketch, design, draft, plan.

entzie'hen*, *vb.* remove, extract.

entzü'cken, *vb.* delight.

Entzü'cken, -, *n.nt.* delight.

entzü'ckend, *adj.* delightful, charming.

Entzü'ckung, -en, *n.f.* rapture.

entzünd'bar, *adj.* inflammable.

entzün'den, *vb.* inflame.

entzün'det, *adj.* infected.

Entzün'dung, -en, *n.f.* inflammation, infection.

entzwei', *adv.* in two, apart.

Enzy'klika, -ken, *n.f.* encyclical.

Enzyklopädie', -i'en, *n.f.* encyclopaedia.

Epidemie', -i'en, *n.f.* epidemic.

epide'misch, *adj.* epidemic.

Epilepsie', *n.f.* epilepsy.

Epilog', -e, *n.m.* epilogue.

Episo'de, -n, *n.f.* episode.

Epo'che, -n, *n.f.* epoch.

Epos (*pl.* Epopen) *n.f.* epic poem.

er, *pron.* he, it.

erach'ten, *vb.* consider.

erbar'men, *vb.* have pity; (sich e.) pity.

Erbar'men, *n.nt.* pity.

erbärm'lich, *adj.* pitiful.

erbar'mungslos, *adj.* pitiless.

erbau'en, *vb.* construct; edify.

erbau'lich, *adj.* edifying.

Erbau'ung, *n.f.* edification.

Erbe, -n, -n, *n.m.* heir.

Erbe, *n.nt.* inheritance, heritage.

erben, *vb.* inherit.

Erbfolge, *n.f.* succession.

erbie'ten*, *vb.* (sich e.) offer, volunteer.

erbit'ten, *vb.* ask for.

erbit'tern, *vb.* embitter.

erblas'sen, *vb.* turn pale.

erblei'chen*, *vb.* turn pale.

erblich, *adj.* hereditary.

Erblichkeit, *n.f.* heredity.

erblicken, *vb.* catch sight of.

erbo'sen, *vb.* make angry; (sich e.) get angry.

erbre'chen*, *vb.* break open; (sich e.) vomit.

Erbschaft, -en, *n.f.* inheritance.

Erbse, -n, *n.f.* pea.

Erbstück, -e, *n.nt.* heirloom.

Erdbeben, -, *n.nt.* earthquake.

Erdbeere, -n, *n.f.* strawberry.

Erdboden, *n.m.* ground, soil.

Erde, *n.f.* earth.

erden, *vb.* ground.

erden'ken*, *vb.* think up.

erdenk'lich, *adj.* imaginable.

Erdgeschoß, *n.nt.* ground floor.

Erdhügel, -, *n.m.* mound.

erdich'ten, *vb.* invent, imagine.

erdich'tet, *adj.* fictional.

Erdich'tung, *n.f.* fiction.

erdig, *adj.* earthy.

Erdkreis, -e, *n.m.* sphere.

Erdkugel, -n, *n.f.* globe.

Erdkunde, *n.f.* geography.

Erdnuß, ¨sse, *n.f.* peanut.

Erdöl, -e, *n.nt.* petroleum.

erdrei'sten, *vb.* (sich e.) be so bold.

erdros'seln, *vb.* strangle.

erdrü'cken, *vb.* crush (to death), stifle.

Erdteil, -e, *n.m.* continent.

erdul'den, *vb.* endure.

ereig'nen, *vb.* (sich e.) happen.

Ereig'nis, -se, *n.nt.* event.

erig'nisreich, *adj.* eventful.

erfah'ren*, *vb.* come to know, learn, experience.

erfah'ren, *adj.* experienced, adept.

Erfah'rung, -en, *n.f.* experience.

erfas'sen, *vb.* grasp, realize; apprehend.

erfin'den*, *vb.* invent; contrive.

Erfin'der, -, *n.m.* inventor.

erfin'derisch, *adj.* inventive; ingenious.

Erfin'dung, -en, *n.f.* invention.

Erfolg', -e, *n.m.* success.

erfolg'los, *adj.* unsuccessful.

erfolg'reich, *adj.* successful; (e. sein*) to succeed.

erfor'derlich, *adj.* required.

erfor'dern, *vb.* require.

Erfor'dernis, -se, *n.nt.* requirement, requisite.

erfor'schen, *vb.* explore.

Erfor'schung, -en, *n.f.* exploration.

erfreu'en, *vb.* delight, gratify; (sich e.) enjoy.

erfreu'lich, *adj.* enjoyable.

erfrie'ren*, *vb.* freeze.

erfri'schen, *vb.* refresh, invigorate.

Erfri'schung, -en, *n.f.* refreshment.

erfül'len, *vb.* fill; fulfill.

Erfül'lung, -en, *n.f.* fulfillment.

ergän'zen, *vb.* supplement; amend.

Ergän'zung, -en, *n.f.* supplement, complement.

erge'ben*, *vb.* yield; result in; (sich e.) result, follow; surrender.

erge'ben, *adj.* devoted.

Ergeb'nis, -se, *n.nt.* result, outcome.

ergie'big, *adj.* productive.

ergöt'zen, *vb.* delight.

ergötz'lich, *adj.* delectable.

ergrei'fen*, *vb.* grasp, seize.

Ergrif'fenheit, *n.f.* emotion.

Erguß', ¨sse, *n.m.* effusion.

erha'ben, *adj.* elevated; lofty, sublime.

Erha'benheit, *n.f.* grandeur.

erhal'ten*, *vb.* maintain, preserve; get, obtain.

Erhal'tung, *n.f.* maintenance, preservation; acquisition.

erhär'ten, *vb.* harden.

erha'schen, *vb.* snatch.

erhe'ben*, *vb.* raise, heighten; ennoble.

erheb'lich, *adj.* considerable.

erhei'tern, *vb.* brighten, cheer.

erhel'len, *vb.* illuminate.

erhit'zen, *vb.* heat.

erhö'hen, *vb.* raise, heighten; ennoble.

Erhö'hung, -en, *n.f.* elevation, rise; enhancement.

erho'len, *vb.* (sich e.) get better, recuperate.

Erho'lung, *n.f.* recuperation, recreation.

erhö'ren, *vb.* hear.

erin'nern, *vb.* remind; (sich e.) remember, recollect.

Erin'nerung, -en, *n.f.* remembrance, memory.

erkäl'ten, *vb.* (sich e.) catch cold.

Erkäl'tung, -en, *n.f.* cold.

erken'nen*, *vb.* recognize.

erkennt'lich, *adj.* recognizable; thankful.

Erkennt'nis, -se, *n.f.* realization, knowledge.

erklä'ren, *vb.* explain, declare.

erklä'rend, *adj.* explanatory.

Erklä'rung, -en, *n.f.* explanation; declaration.

erklet'tern, *vb.* climb up, scale.

erklin'gen*, *vb.* (re)sound.

erkran'ken, *vb.* be taken ill.

erkun'digen, *vb.* (sich e.) inquire.

Erkun'digung, -en, *n.f.* inquiry.

erlan'gen, *vb.* obtain, attain.

Erlaß', ¨sse, *n.m.* decree.

erlas'sen*, *vb.* decree; forgive.

erlau'ben, *vb.* allow, permit.

Erlaub'nis, *n.f.* permission, permit.

erläu'tern, *vb.* illustrate; elucidate.

Erläu'terung, -en, *n.f.* illustration; elucidation.

Erleb'nis, -se, *n.nt.* event, experience.

erle'digen, *vb.* take care of, settle.

erle'digt, *adj.* settled; exhausted.

erleich'tern, *vb.* lighten, facilitate; relieve.

Erleich'terung, -en, *n.f.* ease, relief.

erlei'den*, *vb.* suffer.

erle'sen, *adj.* chosen.

erleuch'ten, *vb.* illuminate.

erlie'gen*, *vb.* succumb.

Erlös', -e, *n.m.* proceeds.

erlö'schen*, *vb.* go out, be extinguished; become extinct.

erlö'sen, *vb.* deliver, redeem.

Erlö'ser, *n.m.* redeemer.

Erlö'sung, -en, *n.f.* deliverance, redemption.

ermäch'tigen, *vb.* empower, enable.

Ermäch'tigung, -en, *n.f.* authorization.

ermah'nen, *vb.* admonish.

erman'geln, *vb.* lack.

ermä'ßigen, *vb.* reduce.

Ermä'ßigung, -en, *n.f.* reduction.

ermat'ten, *vb.* tire.

ermes'sen*, *vb.* calculate; comprehend.

ermit'teln, *vb.* ascertain.

Ermitt'lung, -en, *n.f.* detection.

ermög'lichen, *vb.* make possible, enable.

ermor'den, *vb.* murder.

Ermor'dung, -en, *n.f.* murder, assassination.

ermü'den, *vb.* tire.

ermun'tern, *vb.* rouse; cheer up.

ermu'tigen, *vb.* encourage.

Ermu'tigung, -en, *n.f.* encouragement.

ernäh'ren, *vb.* nourish, nurture.

Ernäh'rung, *n.f.* nourishment, nutrition.

ernen'nen*, *vb.* appoint, nominate.

Ernen'nung, -en, *n.f.* appointment, nomination.

erneu'ern, *vb.* renew.

Erneu'erung, -en, *n.f.* renewal.

ernie'drigen, *vb.* debase, degrade.

Ernie'drigung, -en, *n.f.* degradation.

ernst, *adj.* earnest; severe, serious.

Ernst, *n.m.* earnestness; gravity, seriousness.

Ernte, -n, *n.f.* harvest, crop.

ernten, *vb.* harvest, reap.

Ero'berer, -, *n.m.* conqueror.

ero'bern, *vb.* conquer.

Ero'berung, -en, *n.f.* conquest.

eröff'nen, *vb.* open.

Eröff'nung, -en, *n.f.* opening.

erör'tern, *vb.* discuss, debate.

Erör'terung, -en, *n.f.* discussion, debate.

Ero'tik, *n.f.* eroticism.

ero'tisch, *adj.* erotic.

erpicht', *adj.* intent.

erpres'sen, *vb.* blackmail.

Erpres'sung, -en, *n.f.* blackmail, extortion.

erqui'cken, *vb.* refresh.

erra'ten*, *vb.* guess.

erre'gen, *vb.* arouse, excite.

Erre'gung, -en, *n.f.* excitement; emotion.

errei'chen, *vb.* reach; achieve.

errich'ten, *vb.* erect, establish.

Errich'tung, -en, *n.f.* erection.

errin'gen*, *vb.* achieve; gain.

Errun'genschaft, -en, *n.f.* achievement, attainment.

Ersatz', *n.m.* compensation; substitute; *cpds.* spare.

erschaf'fen*, *vb.* create.

Erschaf'fung, -en, *n.f.* creation.

erschei'nen*, *vb.* appear.

Erschei'nung, -en, *n.f.* appearance; apparition; phenomenon.

erschie'ßen*, *vb.* shoot (dead).

erschla'gen*, *vb.* slay.

erschlie'ßen*, *vb.* open, unfold.

erschöp'fen, *vb.* exhaust.

erschöpft', *adj.* weary, exhausted.

Erschöp'fung, *n.f.* exhaustion.

erschre'cken, *vb.* scare, frighten, startle.

erschre'cken*, *vb.* become scared, become frightened, be startled.

erschüt'ttern, *vb.* shake, shock.

Erschüt'terung, -en, *n.f.* shock; vibration.

erschwe'ren, *vb.* make more difficult, aggravate.

erschwing'lich, *adj.* within one's means.

erse'hen*, *vb.* see, learn.

erset'zen, *vb.* make good, replace; supersede.

ersicht'lich, *adj.* evident.

ersin'nen*, *vb.* devise.

erspa'ren, *vb.* save.

erst, 1. *adj.* first. 2. *adv.* not until, only.

erstar'ren, *vb.* get numb, stiffen; congeal.

erstat'ten, *vb.* refund, recompense.

erstau'nen, *vb.* astonish, amaze.

Erstau'nen, *n.nt.* amazement, astonishment.

erstaun'lich, *adj.* amazing.

erste'hen*, *vb.* arise; get, obtain.

erstei'gen*, *vb.* climb.

erstens, *adv.* in the first place, firstly.

erster-, *adj.* former.

ersti'cken, *vb.* stifle, suffocate, smother.

Ersti'ckung, -en, *n.f.* suffocation, asphyxiation, choking.

erstklassig, *adj.* first-class, first-rate.

erstre'ben, *vb.* aspire to.

erstreck'en, *vb.* (sich e.) extend, range.

ersu'chen, *vb.* request.

ertap'pen, *vb.* catch, surprise.

ertei'len, *vb.* give, administer.

Ertrag', ¨e, *n.m.* yield, return.

ertrag'bar, *adj.* bearable.

ertra'gen*, *vb.* bear, endure.

erträg'lich, *adj.* passable.

erträn'ken, *vb.* (tr.) drown.

ertrin'ken*, *vb.* (intr.) drown.

erü'brigen, *vb.* (sich e.) not be necessary.

erwa'chen, *vb.* wake.

erwach'sen*, *vb.* arise, grow.

erwach'sen, *adj.* grown, grown-up, adult.

Erwach'sen-, *n.m.&f.* adult.

erwä'gen*, *vb.* deliberate, ponder.

Erwä'gung, -en, *n.f.* consideration.

erwäh'nen, *vb.* mention.

Erwäh'nung, -en, *n.f.* mention.

erwar'ten, *vb.* expect, await.

Erwar'tung, -en, *n.f.* expectation, anticipation.

erwe'cken, *vb.* awaken.

erwei'chen, *vb.* soften, mollify; (sich e. lassen*) relent.

erwei'sen*, *vb.* prove; render.

erwei'tern, *vb.* widen, extend.

erwer'ben*, *vb.* acquire.

Erwer'bung, -en, *n.f.* acquisition.

erwi'dern, *vb.* reply; return, reciprocate.

Erwi'derung, -en, *n.f.* reply; return.

erwir'ken, *vb.* bring about.

erwi'schen, *vb.* catch, get hold of.

erwünscht', *adj.* desired.

erwür'gen, *vb.* strangle.

erzäh'len, *vb.* tell, narrate, relate.

Erzäh'lung, -en, *n.f.* story, narrative, tale.

Erzbischof, ¨e, *n.m.* archbishop.

Erzdiözese, -n, *n.f.* archdiocese.

erzeu'gen, *vb.* create, produce; (elec.) generate.

Erzeug'nis, -se, *n.nt.* product.

Erzherzog, ¨e, *n.m.* archduke.

erzie'hen*, *vb.* educate.

Erzie'her, -, *n.m.* educator.

Erzie'herin, -nen, *n.f.* governess.

erzie'herisch, *adj.* education; breeding.

erzür'nen, *vb.* (sich e.) become angry.

erzwin'gen*, *vb.* force.

es, *pron.* it.

Esche, -n, *n.f.* ash (tree).

Esel, -, *n.m.* donkey, ass, jackass.

Eskalation', *n.f.* escalation.

eskalie'ren, *vb.* escalate.

eßbar, *adj.* edible.

essen*, *vb.* eat.

Essen, *n.nt.* food.

Essenz', -en, *n.f.* essence; flavoring.

Essig, *n.m.* vinegar.

Esslöffel, -, *n.m.* tablespoon.

Eta'ge, -n, *n.f.* floor, story.

Etat', -s, *n.m.* budget.

ethnisch, *adj.* ethnic.

Etikett', -e, *n.nt.* tag, label, sticker.

Etiket'te, *n.f.* etiquette.

etliche, *pron.* several.

etwa, *adv.* about, approximately, more or less, maybe.

etwaig, *adj.* eventual.

etwas, 1. *pron.* something. 2. *adv.* somewhat.

Eule, -n, *n.f.* owl.

Euro'pa, *n.nt.* Europe.

Europä'er, -, *n.m.* European.

europä'isch, *adj.* European.

evakuie'ren, *vb.* evacuate.

evange'lisch, *adj.* evangelical, Protestant.

Evangelist', -en, -en, *n.m.* evangelist.

Evange'lium, *n.nt.* gospel.

Eventualität', -en, *n.f.* contingency.

eventuell', *adj.* possible, potential.

ewig, *adj.* eternal, everlasting. 2. *adv.* forever.

Ewigkeit, -en, *n.f.* eternity.

Exa'men, -, *n.nt.* examination.

Exemplar', -e, *n.nt.* specimen, copy.

exerzie'ren, *vb.* drill.

Existenz', -en, *n.f.* existence.

existie'ren, *vb.* exist.

exo'tisch, *adj.* exotic.

Experiment', -e, *n.nt.* experiment.

experimentie'ren, *vb.* experiment.

explodie'ren, *vb.* explode, detonate.

Explosion', -en, *n.f.* explosion.

explosiv', *adj.* explosive.

Export', -e, *n.m.* export.

exportie'ren, *vb.* export.

Expreß', -sse, *n.m.* express train.

extra, *adj.* extra.

Extravaganz, -en, *n.f.* extravagance.

extrem', *adj.* extreme.

Exzellenz', -en, *n.f.* Excellency.

exzen'trisch, *adj.* eccentric.

Exzentrizität', -en, *n.f.* eccentricity.

F

Fabel, -n, *n.f.* fable.

fabelhaft, *adj.* fabulous, wonderful.

Fabrik', -en, *n.f.* factory, plant.

Fabrikant', -en, -en, *n.m.* manufacturer.

Fabrikat', -e, *n.nt.* manufactured article; (deutsches F.) made in Germany.

Fach, ¨er, *n.nt.* compartment; profession; (academic) subject.

Fächer, -, *n.m.* fan.

fächern, *vb.* fan.

fachmännisch, *adj.* professional.

Fackel, -, *n.f.* torch.

fade, *adj.* flavorless, insipid.

Faden, -, *n.m.* thread, filament.

fadenscheinig, *adj.* threadbare.

fähig, *adj.* able, capable, competent.

Fähigkeit, -en, *n.f.* ability, capability, competence.

fahnden, *vb.* search.

Fahne, -n, *n.f.* flag.

Fahnenflucht, *n.f.* desertion.

Fahnenflüchtig-, *n.m.* deserter.

Fähnrich, -e, *n.m.* ensign.

Fahrbahn, -en, *n.f.* lane.

Fähre, -n, *n.f.* ferry.

fahren*, *vb.* drive, ride, go.

Fahrer, -, *n.m.* driver.
Fahrgeld, -er, *n.nt.* fare.
Fahrkarte, -n, *n.f.* ticket.
fahrlässig, *adj.* negligent.
Fahrplan, ⁼e, *n.m.* timetable, schedule.
fahrplanmäßig, *adj.* scheduled.
Fahrpreis, -e, *n.m.* fare.
Fahrrad, ⁼er, *n.nt.* bicycle.
Fahrrinne, -n, *n.f.* lane.
Fahrstuhl, ⁼e, *n.m.* elevator.
Fahrt, -en, *n.f.* ride; trip.
Fährte, -n, *n.f.* track, trail.
Fahrzeug, -e, *n.nt.* vehicle, conveyance.
Faktor, -o'ren, *n.m.* factor.
Fakultät', -en, *n.f.* faculty.
fakultativ', *adj.* optional.
Fall, ⁼e, *n.m.* fall; case.
Falle, -n, *n.f.* trap; pitfall.
fallen*, *vb.* fall, drop; **(f. lassen*)** drop.
fällen, *vb.* fell.
fällig, *adj.* due; **(f. werden*)** become due, mature.
Fälligkeit, *n.f.* maturity.
falls, *conj.* in case, if.
falsch, *adj.* false, wrong; fake; deceitful.
fälschen, *vb.* forge, counterfeit.
Fälscher, -, *n.m.* forger.
Falschheit, -en, *n.f.* falseness, deceit.
Fälschung, -en, *n.f.* forgery.
Falte, -n, *n.f.* fold, crease, pleat; wrinkle.
falten, *vb.* fold, pleat, crease.
familiär', *adj.* familiar; intimate.
Fami'lie, -n, *n.f.* family.
Fami'lienname(n), -, *n.m.* surname.
famos', *adj.* splendid.
Fana'tiker, -n, *n.m.* fanatic.
fana'tisch, *adj.* fanatic, rabid.
Fanatis'mus, *n.m.* fanaticism.
Fanfa're, -n, *n.f.* fanfare.
Fang, ⁼e, *n.m.* catch.
fangen*, *vb.* catch, capture.
Fänger, -, *n.m.* catcher.
Farbe, -n, *n.f.* color; paint; dye; (cards) suit.
färben, *vb.* color, dye.
farbenreich, *adj.* colorful.
Färber, -, *n.m.* dyer.
farbig, *adj.* colored.
farblos, *adj.* colorless, drab.
Farbstoff, -e, *n.m.* dye (stuff).
Farbton, ⁼e, *n.m.* shade.
Farbtönung, -en, *n.f.* tint.
Färbung, -en, *n.f.* coloring, hue.
Farce, -n, *n.f.* farce.
Farmer, -, *n.m.* farmer.
Fasching, *n.m.* carnival, Mardi Gras.
Faschis'mus, *n.m.* fascism.
Faschist', -en, -en, *n.m.* fascist.
faschis'tisch, *adj.* fascist.
faseln, *vb.* talk nonsense.
Faser, -n, *n.f.* fiber.
Faß, ⁼sser, *n.nt.* barrel, keg, vat, cask.
Fassa'de, -n, *n.f.* façade.
fassen, *vb.* grasp, seize; **(sich**

f.) compose oneself; **(fasse dich kurz!)** make it short.
Fasson', -s, *n.f.* shape.
Fassung, -en, *n.f.* version; gem setting; *(fig.)* composure; **(aus der F. bringen*)** rattle.
fassungslos, *adj.* bewildered, staggered.
Fassungsvermögen, -, *n.nt.* capacity; comprehension.
fast, *adv.* almost, nearly.
fasten, *vb.* fast.
Fastenzeit, -f Lent.
faszinie'ren, *vb.* fascinate.
fauchen, *vb.* puff; (of cats) spit.
faul, *adj.* lazy; rotten.
faulenzen, *vb.* loaf.
Faulenzer, -n, *n.m.* loafer.
Fäulnis, *n.f.* decay, putrefaction.
Faultier, -e, *n.nt.* sloth.
Faust, ⁼e, *n.f.* fist.
Februar, -e, *n.m.* February.
fechten*, *vb.* fence.
Feder, -n, *n.f.* feather, plume; pen.
federleicht, *adj.* feathery.
federn, *vb.* feather; have good springs.
Fee, Fe'en, *n.f.* fairy.
Fegefeuer, *n.nt.* purgatory.
Fehde, -n, *n.f.* feud.
fehlbar, *adj.* fallible.
fehlen, *vb.* lack; be absent or missing.
Fehler, -, *n.m.* mistake, error; flaw, imperfection, defect; blunder.
fehlerfrei, *adj.* flawless.
fehlerhaft, *adj.* faulty, imperfect, defective.
fehlerlos, *adj.* faultless.
fehl-gebären*, *vb.* abort, have a miscarriage.
Fehlgeburt, -en, *n.f.* miscarriage, abortion.
fehl-gehen*, *vb.* err, go astray.
Fehlschlag, ⁼e, *n.m.* failure; setback.
Fehltritt, -e, *n.m.* slip.
Feier, -n, *n.f.* celebration.
feierlich, *adj.* ceremonious; solemn.
Feierlichkeit, -en, *n.f.* ceremony, solemnity.
feiern, *vb.* celebrate.
Feiertag, -e, *n.m.* holiday.
feige, *adj.* cowardly.
Feige, -n, *n.f.* fig.
Feigheit, -en, *n.f.* cowardice.
Feigling, -e, *n.m.* coward.
Feile, -n, *n.f.* file.
feilen, *vb.* file.
feilschen, *vb.* bargain, haggle.
fein, *adj.* fine, delicate; elegant; subtle.
Feind, -e, *n.m.* foe, enemy.
feindlich, *adj.* hostile.
Feindschaft, -en, *n.f.* enmity; feud.
Feindseligkeit, -en, *n.f.* purity; delicacy; elegance; subtlety.
Feingefühl, *n.nt.* sensitivity.

Feinheit, -en, *n.f.* purity; delicacy; elegance; subtlety.
feinsinnig, *adj.* ingenious.
feist, *adj.* fat, plump.
Feld, -er, *n.nt.* field.
Feldbett, -en, *n.nt.* cot.
Feldherr, -n, -en, *n.m.* commander.
Feldstecher, -, *n.m.* binoculars.
Feldzug, ⁼e, *n.m.* campaign.
Fell, -e, *n.nt.* skin, pelt, hide.
Fels(en), -, *n.m.* rock, boulder.
Felsblock, ⁼e, *n.m.* boulder.
felsig, *adj.* rocky, craggy.
Fenster, -, *n.nt.* window.
Fensterladen, ⁼, *n.m.* shutter.
Fensterscheibe, -n, *n.f.* windowpane.
Ferien, *n.pl.* vacation.
Ferienort, -e, *n.m.* resort.
fern, *adj.* far, distant, remote.
Fernanruf, -e, *n.m.* long-distance call.
ferner, *adv.* moreover, furthermore.
Ferngespräch, -e, *n.nt.* long-distance call.
Fernglas, ⁼er, *n.nt.* binocular(s).
Fernrohr, -e, *n.nt.* telescope.
Fernsehapparat, -e, *n.m.* television set.
Fernsehen, *n.nt.* television.
Fernsprecher, -, *n.m.* telephone.
Ferse, -n, *n.f.* heel.
fertig, *adj.* finished, complete, ready, done; **(f. sein*)** be through; **(f. bringen*)** complete, accomplish.
Fertigkeit, -en, *n.f.* dexterity, knack.
fesch, *adj.* chic.
Fessel, -n, *n.f.* fetter, irons, handcuffs; ankle.
Fesselgelenk, -e, *n.nt.* ankle.
fesseln, *vb.* chain; (fig.) captivate, fascinate.
fest, *adj.* firm, solid; fixed, steady; tight.
Fest, -e, *n.nt.* feast, celebration.
Feste, -n, *n.f.* fort, stronghold.
Festessen, -, *n.nt.* banquet, feast.
fest-fahren*, *vb.* run aground; *(fig.)* come to an impasse.
fest-halten*, *vb.* hold fast to, adhere to; detain.
festigen, *vb.* solidify, consolidate.
Festigkeit, *n.f.* firmness, solidity.
fest-klammern, *vb.* clamp; **(sich f.)** hold fast.
Festland, *n.nt.* mainland.
fest-legen, *vb.* fix, lay down.
festlich, *adj.* festive.
Festlichkeit, -en, *n.f.* festivity.
fest-machen, *vb.* fasten, make fast.
Festmahl, -e, *n.nt.* feast.
fest-nehmen*, *vb.* arrest.
fest-setzen, *vb.* fix, establish; determine.

Festspiel, -e, *n.nt.* festival.

fest·stehen*, *vb.* be stable; be certain.

feststehend, *adj.* stationary.

fest·stellen, *vb.* determine, ascertain; state.

Festtag, -e, *n.m.* holiday.

Festung, -en, *n.f.* fortress.

fett, *adj.* fat, greasy.

Fett, -e, *n.nt.* fat, grease.

fetten, *vb.* grease.

fettig, *adj.* fatty, greasy, oily.

fettleibig, *adj.* obese.

Fetzen, -, *n.m.* rag; scrap.

feucht, *adj.* moist, damp, humid.

Feuchtigkeit, *n.f.* moisture, dampness, humidity.

feuchtkalt, *adj.* clammy.

Feuer, -, *n.nt.* fire, *(fig.)* verve.

Feueralarm, -e, *n.m.* fire alarm.

feuergefährlich, *adj.* inflammable.

Feuerleiter, -n, *n.f.* fire escape.

Feuermelder, -, *n.m.* fire alarm (box).

feuern, *vb.* fire.

Feuersbrunst, *n.f.* conflagration.

Feuerspritze, -n, *n.f.* fire engine.

Feuerstein, -e, *n.m.* flint.

Feuerwaffe, -n, *n.f.* firearm.

Feuerwechsel, -, *n.m.* skirmish.

Feuerwehrmann, -̈er, *n.m.* fireman.

Feuerwerk, -e, *n.nt.* foreworks.

Feuerzeug, -e, *n.nt.* cigarette lighter.

feurig, *adj.* fiery.

Fichte, -n, *n.f.* pine, fir.

fidel', *adj.* jolly.

Fieber, *n.nt.* fever.

fieberhaft, *adj.* feverish.

fiebern, *vb.* be feverish.

Fieberwahnsinn, -e, *n.m.* delirium.

Fiedel, -n, *n.f.* fiddle.

Figur', -en, *n.f.* figure.

figür'lich, *adj.* figurative.

Fiktion', -en, *n.f.* figment.

Filet', -s, *n.nt.* fillet.

Film, -e, *n.m.* film, movie, motion-picture.

filmen, *vb.* film.

Filmschauspieler, -, *n.m.* movie actor.

Filter, -, *n.m.* filter.

filtrie'ren, *vb.* filter.

Filz, -e, *n.m.* felt.

Fina'le, -s, *n.nt.* finale.

Finan'zen, *n.pl.* finances.

finanziell', *adj.* financial.

finanzie'ren, *vb.* finance.

Finanz'mann, -̈er, *n.m.* financier.

Finanz'wirtschaft, -en, *n.f.* finance.

finden*, *vb.* find, locate.

Finderlohn, *n.m.* reward (for returning lost articles).

findig, *adj.* ingenious, resourceful.

Findigkeit, *n.f.* ingenuity.

Findling, -e, *n.m.* foundling.

Finger, -, *n.m.* finger.

Fingerabdruck, -̈e, *n.m.* fingerprint.

Fingernagel, -̈, *n.m.* fingernail.

fingie'ren, *vb.* feign, simulate.

fingiert', *adj.* fictitious.

finster, *adj.* dark; saturnine.

Finsternis, -se, *n.f.* darkness; eclipse.

Firma (*pl.* **Firmen**), *n.f.* firm, company.

Firnis, -se, *n.m.* varnish.

firnissen, *vb.* varnish.

Fisch, -e, *n.m.* fish.

fischen, *vb.* fish.

Fischer, -, *n.m.* fisherman.

Fischgeschäft, -e, *n.nt.* fish-store.

Fixie'rung, -en, *n.f.* fixation.

flach, *adj.* flat, shallow.

Fläche, -n, *n.f.* plane, area.

Flachheit, -en, *n.f.* flatness.

Flachs, *n.m.* flax.

flackern, *vb.* flare, flicker.

Flagge, -n, *n.f.* flag.

Flak, -(s), *n.f.* (= Fliegerabwehrkanone) antiaircraft (fire, troops).

Flak-, *cpds.* antiaircraft.

Flame, -n, *n.m.* Fleming.

Flamme, -n, *n.f.* flame, blaze.

flammend, *adj.* flaming; *(fig.)* enthusiastic.

Flanell', -e, *n.m.* flannel.

Flanke, -n, *n.f.* flank.

flankie'ren, *vb.* flank.

Flasche, -n, *n.f.* bottle, flask.

flattern, *vb.* flutter, flap.

flau, *adj.* slack, dull.

Flaum, *n.m.* down, fuzz.

flaumig, *adj.* downy, fuzzy, fluffy.

Flechte, -n, *n.f.* braid.

Fleck, -e, *n.m.* spot, stain, blotch.

Fledermaus, -̈e, *n.f.* bat.

Flegel, -, *n.m.* rowdy, boor.

flehen, *vb.* implore, beseech.

flehentlich, *adj.* beseeching.

Fleisch, *n.nt.* flesh, meat.

fleischig, *adj.* fleshy.

fleischlich, *adj.* carnal.

Fleiß, *n.m.* diligence, hard work.

fleißig, *adj.* industrious, hard working.

flicken, *vb.* patch.

Flicken, -, *n.m.* patch.

Flickwerk, *n.nt.* patchwork.

Flieder, -, *n.m.* lilac.

Fliege, -n, *n.f.* fly.

fliegen*, *vb.* fly.

Flieger, -, *n.m.* flier, aviator.

fliehen*, *vb.* flee.

Fliese, -n, *n.f.* tile, flagstone.

Fluß, *n.m.* flow.

fließend, *adj.* fluent.

flimmern, *vb.* flicker.

flink, *adj.* nimble, spry.

Flirt, -s, *n.m.* flirt, flirtation.

flirten, *vb.* flirt.

Flitterwochen, *n.pl.* honeymoon.

Flocke, -n, *n.f.* flake.

Floh, -̈e, *n.m.* flea.

Floß, -̈e, *n.m.* float, raft.

Flosse, -n, *n.f.* fin.

Flöte, -n, *n.f.* whistle; flute.

flott, *adj.* afloat; smart, dashing.

Flotte, -n, *n.f.* fleet, navy.

Fluch, -̈e, *n.m.* curse.

fluchen, *vb.* swear, curse.

Fluchen, *n.nt.* profanity.

Flucht, *n.f.* escape, flight, getaway; (in die F. schlagen*) rout.

flüchten, *vb.* flee.

flüchtig, *adj.* fleeting, cursory; superficial.

Flüchtling, -en, *n.m.* refugee, fugitive.

Flug, -̈e, *n.m.* flight.

Flugblatt, -̈er, *n.nt.* leaflet.

Flügel, -, *n.m.* wing.

Flughafen, -̈, *n.m.* airport.

Flugpersonal, *n.nt.* flight attendants.

Flugzeug, -e, *n.nt.* airplane.

Flunder, -n, *n.nf.* flounder.

flunkern, *vb.* fib.

fluoreszie'rend, *adj.* fluorescent.

Fluß, -̈sse, *n.m.* river; flux.

flüssig, *adj.* liquid; fluid; (f. machen) liquefy.

Flüssigkeit, -en, *n.f.* fluid, liquid.

flüstern, *vb.* whisper.

Flut, -en, *n.f.* flood, high tide.

fluten, *vb.* flood.

Folge, -n, *n.f.* consequence, outgrowth; succession; (zur F. haben*) result in.

folgen, *vb.* follow; succeed.

folgend, *adj.* subsequent.

folgenreich, *adj.* consequential.

folgenschwer, *adj.* momentous.

folgerichtig, *adj.* consistent.

folgern, *vb.* infer, deduce.

Folgerung, -en, *n.f.* inference, deduction.

folglich, *adv.* consequently.

Folter, -n, *n.f.* torture.

Fond, -s, *n.m.* fund.

Fondant', -s, *n.m.* bonbon.

Förderer, -, *n.m.* sponsor.

förderlich, *adj.* helpful, conducive.

fordern, *vb.* demand.

fördern, *vb.* promote, further; (mining) mine, haul.

Forderung, -en, *n.f.* demand, claim.

Förderung, -en, *n.f.* furtherance, advancement.

Forel'le, -n, *n.f.* trout.

Form, -en, *n.f.* form, shape; mold; (in F. sein*) be fit, be in fine shape.

Formalität', -en, *n.f.* formality.

Format', -e, *n.nt.* format; *(fig.)* stature.

Formation', -en, *n.f.* formation.

Formel, -n, *n.f.* formula.

formell', *adj.* formal.

formen, *vb.* form, shape, mold.

Förmlichkeit, -en, *n.f.* formality.

formlos, *adj.* formless.

Formular', -e, *n.nt.* form, blank.

formulie'ren, *vb.* formulate.

forschen, *vb.* explore, search.

Forscher, -, *n.m.* explorer.

Forschung, -en, *n.f.* research.

fort, *adv.* away, gone; forward.

Fortdauer, *n.f.* continuity.

fortdauernd, *adj.* continuous.

fort·fahren*, *vb.* drive away; proceed, continue.

fort·gehen*, *vb.* leave; continue.

fortgeschritten, *adj.* advanced.

fort·pflanzen, *vb.* propagate.

fort·schreiten*, *vb.* progress.

Fortschritt, -e, *n.m.* progress, advance.

fortschrittlich, *adj.* progressive.

fort·setzen, *vb.* continue.

Fortsetzung, -en, *n.f.* continuation.

fortwährend, *adj.* continuous.

Foyer', -s, *n.nt.* foyer.

Fracht, -en, *n.f.* freight, cargo.

Frachtbrief, -e, *n.m.* bill of lading.

Frachter, -, *n.m.* freighter.

Frachtschiff, -e, *n.nt.* freighter.

Frachtspesen, *n.pl.* freight charges.

Frage, -n, *n.f.* question.

Fragebogen, -, *n.m.* questionnaire.

fragen, *vb.* ask, inquire.

fragend, *adj.* interrogative.

Fragezeichen, -, *n.nt.* question mark.

fraglich, *adj.* questionable.

fragmenta'risch, *adj.* fragmentary.

fragwürdig, *adj.* questionable.

Fraktur', n.f. (*med.*) fracture; German type (print).

Frankreich, -, *n.f.* France.

Franse, -n, *n.f.* fringe.

Franzo'se, -n, -n, *n.m.* Frenchman.

Franzö'sin, -nen, *n.f.* Frenchwoman.

franzö'sisch, *adj.* French.

frappant', *adj.* striking.

fraternisie'ren, *vb.* fraternize.

Fratze, -n, *n.f.* grimace; face, mug.

Frau, -en, *n.f.* woman, wife; Mrs.

Frauenarzt, -e, *n.m.* gynecologist.

Fräulein, -, *n.nt.* Miss.

fraulich, *adj.* womanly.

frech, *adj.* impudent; saucy.

Frechheit, -en, *n.f.* impertinence, effrontery.

frei, *adj.* free; frank; vacant.

Frei-, *n.nt.* outdoors.

Freier, -, *n.m.* suitor.

freigebig, *adj.* generous.

Freigebigkeit, *n.f.* liberality, generosity.

freigestellt, *adj.* optional.

frei·halten*, *vb.* keep free; treat.

Freiheit, -en, *n.f.* liberty, freedom.

Freiherr, -n, -en, *n.m.* baron.

frei·lassen*, *vb.* free; leave blank.

freilich, *adv.* to be sure.

Freimarke, -n, *n.f.* stamp.

Freimaurer, -, *n.m.* Mason.

freimütig, *adj.* candid, heart-to-heart.

freisinnig, *adj.* liberal.

frei·sprechen*, *vb.* acquit, absolve.

Freispruch, -e, *n.m.* acquittal.

Freitag, -e, *n.m.* Friday.

freiwillig, *adj.* voluntary; (**sich f. melden**) volunteer; enlist.

Freiwillig-, *n.m.&f.* volunteer.

Freizeit, *n.f.* leisure time.

fremd, *adj.* strange; foreign; alien.

Fremd-, *n.m.&f.* stranger.

Fremdenführer, -, *n.m.* guide.

Fremdenzimmer, -, *n.nt.* guest room, room to let.

frequentie'ren, *vb.* habituate.

Frequenz', -en, *n.f.* frequency.

Fresko, -ken, *n.nt.* fresco.

fressen*, *vb.* (of animals) eat; stuff oneself.

Freude, -n, *n.f.* joy, pleasure.

Freudenfeuer, -, *n.nt.* bonfire.

freudig, *adj.* joyful, joyous.

freudlos, *adj.* cheerless.

freuen, *vb.* make glad; (**sich f.**) be glad, rejoice.

Freund, -e, *n.m.* friend.

Freundin, -nen, *n.f.* friend (female).

freundlich, *adj.* friendly, kind.

freundlicherweise, *adv.* kindly.

Freundlichkeit, *n.f.* kindness, friendliness.

freundlos, *adj.* friendless.

Freundschaft, -en, *n.f.* friendship.

freundschaftlich, *adj.* amicable.

Frevel, -, *n.m.* outrage.

frevelhaft, *adj.* sacrilegious; flagrant.

Friede(n), *n.m.* peace.

Friedensvertrag, -e, *n.m.* peace treaty.

friedfertig, *adj.* peaceable.

Friedhof, -e, *n.m.* cemetery, graveyard.

friedlich, *adj.* peaceable, peaceful.

frieren*, *vb.* freeze.

Frikassee', -s, *n.nt.* fricassee.

frisch, *adj.* fresh, crisp.

Frische, *n.f.* freshness.

Friseur', -e, *n.m.* barber, hairdresser.

Friseu'se, -n, *n.f.* hairdresser (female).

frisie'ren, *vb.* dress the hair; (*fig.*) tamper with.

Frist, -en, *n.f.* limited period; respite.

Frisur', -en, *n.f.* coiffure, hairdo.

frivol', *adj.* frivolous.

froh, *adj.* glad.

fröhlich, *adj.* gay, cheerful.

Fröhlichkeit, *n.f.* cheerfulness, merriment.

frohlocken, *vb.* rejoice.

frohlo'ckend, *adj.* jubilant.

fromm (-, -) *adj.* pious, religious, devout.

Frömmelei', -en, *n.f.* bigotry.

Frömmigkeit, *n.f.* piety.

Frömmler, -, *n.m.* bigot.

frönen, *vb.* indulge.

Front, -en, *n.f.* front.

Frosch, -e, *n.m.* frog.

Frost, -e, *n.m.* frost, chill.

frösteln, *vb.* feel chilly.

frostig, *adj.* frosty.

Frucht, -e, *n.f.* fruit.

fruchtbar, *adj.* fruitful, fertile; prolific.

Fruchtbarkeit, *n.f.* fertility.

fruchtlos, *adj.* fruitless.

früh, *adj.* early.

früher, *adj.* earlier; former.

Frühjahr, -e, *n.nt.* spring.

Frühling, -e, *n.m.* spring.

frühreif, *adj.* precocious.

Frühstück, -e, *n.nt.* breakfast.

frühzeitig, *adj.* early.

Fuchs, -e, *n.m.* fox.

fügen, *vb.* join; (**sich f.**) comply, submit.

fügsam, *adj.* docile.

fühlbar, *adj.* tangible.

fühlen, *vb.* feel, sense.

führen, *vb.* lead, guide, direct.

Führer, -, *n.m.* leader, guide.

Führerschein, -e, *n.m.* driver's license.

Fülle, *n.f.* fullness, wealth; (**in Hülle und F.**) galore.

füllen, *vb.* fill.

Füllfederhalter, -, *n.m.* fountain pen.

Füllung, -en, *n.f.* filling.

Fund, -e, *n.m.* find, discovery.

Fundament', -e, *n.nt.* foundation.

fundie'ren, *vb.* base.

fünf, *num.* five.

fünft-, *adj.* fifth.

Fünftel, -, *n.nt.* fifth part; (**ein f.**) one-fifth.

fünfzig, *num.* fifty.

fünfzigst-, *adj.* fiftieth.

Fünfzigstel, -, *n.nt.* fiftieth part; (**ein f.**) one-fiftieth.

Funke(n), -, *n.m.* spark.

funkeln, *vb.* sparkle.

funkelnagelneu, *adj.* brand-new.

funken, *vb.* radio.

Funktion', -en, *n.f.* function.

Funktionär', -e, *n.m.* functionary.

funktionie'ren, *vb.* function.

für, *prep.* for.

Furche, -n, *n.f.* furrow.

Furcht, *n.f.* fright, fear, dread.

furchtbar, *adj.* terrible.

fürchten, *vb.* fear; (**sich f. vor**) be afraid of.

furchtlos, *adj.* fearless.

Furchtlosigkeit, *n.f.* fearlessness.

furchtsam, *adj.* fearful.

Fürst, -en, -en, *n.m.* prince, ruler.

fürstlich, *adj.* princely.

Furt, -en, *n.f.* ford.

Furun'kel, -n, *n.f.* boil.

Fürwort, -er, *n.nt.* pronoun.

Fusion', -en, *n.f.* fusion, merger.

Fuß, -̈e, *n.m.* foot.

Fußball, -̈e, *n.m.* football.

Fußboden, -̈, *n.m.* floor; flooring.

Fußgänger, -, *n.m.* pedestrian.

Fußnote, -n, *n.f.* footnote.

Fußpfleger, -, *n.m.* chiropodist.

Futter, -, *n.nt.* feed, fodder; lining.

füttern, *vb.* feed; (clothing) line.

Futurologie', *n.f.* futurology.

G

Gabardine, *n.m.* gabardine.

Gabe, -n, *n.f.* gift, donation; faculty.

Gabel, -n, *n.f.* fork.

gaffen, *vb.* gape.

gähnen, *vb.* yawn.

galant', *adj.* gallant.

Galanterie', -en, *n.f.* gallantry.

Gala-Uniform, *n.f.* full dress.

Galerie', -i'en, *n.f.* gallery.

Galgen, -, *n.m.* gallows.

Galle, -n, *n.f.* gall, bile.

Gallenblase, -n, *n.f.* gall bladder.

gallertartig, *adj.* gelatinous.

gallig, *adj.* bilious.

Galopp', -s, *n.m.* gallop; (leichter G.) canter.

galoppie'ren, *vb.* gallop.

galvanisie'ren, *vb.* galvanize.

Gama'sche, -n, *n.f.* gaiters, leggings.

Gang, -̈e, *n.m.* walk; corridor, aisle; course; (auto) gear.

Gangrän', -e, *n.f.* gangrene.

Gangster, -, *n.m.* gangster.

Gans, -̈e, *n.f.* goose.

Gänsemarsch, *n.m.* single file.

ganz, 1. *adj.* whole, entire. **2.** *adv.* quite, rather; (**g. gut**) pretty good; (**g. und gar**) completely.

Ganz-, *n.nt.* whole (thing).

Ganzheit, *n.f.* entirety.

gänzlich, *adj.* complete.

gar, 1. *adj.* cooked, done. **2.** *adv.* (**g. nicht**) not at all; (**g. nichts**) nothing at all.

Gara'ge, -n, *n.f.* garage.

Garantie', -i'en, *n.f.* guarantee.

garantie'ren, *vb.* guarantee, warrant.

Garbe, -n, *n.f.* sheaf.

Gardero'be, -n, *n.f.* clothes; cloakroom.

gären*, *vb.* ferment.

Garn, -e, *n.nt.* yarn; thread.

Garne'le, -n, *n.f.* shrimp.

garnie'ren, *vb.* garnish.

Garnison', -en, *n.f.* garrison.

Garnitur', -en, *n.f.* set.

garstig, *adj.* nasty.

Garten, -̈, *n.m.* garden, yard.

Gartenbau, *n.m.* horticulture.

Gärtner, -, *n.m.* gardener.

Gas, -e, *n.nt.* gas.

Gashebel, -, *n.m.* accelerator.

gasig, *adj.* gassy.

Gasse, -n, *n.f.* narrow street, alley.

Gast, -̈e, *n.m.* guest.

Gastarbeiter, -, *n.m.* foreign worker.

gastfrei, *adj.* hospitable.

Gastfreiheit, *n.f.* hospitality.

gastfreundlich, *adj.* hospitable.

Gastfreundschaft, *n.f.* hospitality.

Gastgeber, -, *n.m.* host.

Gastgeberin, -nen, *n.f.* hostess.

Gasthaus, -̈er, *n.nt.* inn.

gastrono'misch, *adj.* gastronomical.

Gaststube, -n, *n.f.* taproom.

Gatte, -n, -n, *n.m.* husband.

Gattin, -nen, *n.f.* wife.

Gattung, -en, *n.f.* species, genus.

Gau, -e, *n.m.* district, province.

Gaul, -̈e, *n.m.* nag.

Gaumen, -, *n.m.* palate.

Gaze, -n, *n.f.* gauze.

Geäch'tet, *n.m.* outlaw.

Gebäck', -, *n.nt.* pastry.

Gebär'de, -n, *n.f.* gesticulation; gesture.

geba'ren, *vb.* (**sich g.**) behave.

gebä'ren*, *vb.* bear.

Gebäu'de, -, *n.nt.* building.

geben*, *vb.* give; deal (cards); (**es gibt**) there is, there are.

Geber, -, *n.m.* giver.

Gebet', -e, *n.nt.* prayer.

Gebiet', -e, *n.nt.* territory, region, field.

gebie'ten*, *vb.* command.

Gebie'ter, -, *n.m.* master.

Gebil'de, -, *n.nt.* form, structure.

gebil'det, *adj.* educated, civilized, cultured.

Gebir'ge, -, *n.nt.* mountainous area, mountains; mountain range.

gebir'gig, *adj.* mountainous.

Gebiß', -sse, *n.nt.* teeth; denture; (horse) bit.

Geblüt', *n.nt.* descent, family.

gebo'ren, *adj.* born.

Gebor'genheit, *n.f.* safety.

Gebot', -e, *n.nt.* command(ment).

Gebräu', -e, *n.nt.* brew, concoction.

Gebrauch', -̈e, *n.m.* use; usage, custom.

gebrau'chen, *vb.* use.

gebräuch'lich, *adj.* customary.

Gebrauchs'anweisung, -en, *n.f.* directions (for use).

Gebre'chen, -, *n.nt.* infirmity.

gebrech'lich, *adj.* decrepit.

Gebrü'der, *n.pl.* brothers.

Gebrüll', *n.nt.* roar, howl.

gebückt', *adj.* stooped.

Gebühr', -en, *n.f.* charge, fee; (**nach G.**) duly; (**über alle G.**) excessively.

gebüh'ren, *vb.* be due; (**sich g.**) be proper.

gebüh'rend, *adj.* duly.

gebühr'lich, *adj.* proper.

Geburt', -en, *n.f.* birth; childbirth; (**von G. an**) congenital.

Gebur'tenkontrolle, *n.f.* birth control.

gebür'tig, *adj.* native.

Geburts'datum, -ten, *n.nt.* date of birth.

Geburts'helfer, -, *n.m.* obstetrician.

Geburts'ort, -e, *n.m.* birthplace.

Geburts'schein, -e, *n.m.* birth certificate.

Geburts'tag, -e, *n.m.* birthday.

Gebüsch', -e, *n.nt.* bushes, shrubbery.

Geck, -en, -en, *n.m.* dandy.

Gedächt'nis, -se, *n.nt.* memory.

Gedächt'nisfeier, -n, *n.f.* commemoration.

Gedan'ke(n), -, *n.m.* thought, idea.

gedan'kenlos, *adj.* thoughtless, unthinking.

gedan'kenvoll, *adj.* thoughtful.

Gedeck', -e, *n.nt.* cover, table setting.

gedei'hen*, *vb.* thrive.

geden'ken*, *vb.* remember; commemorate.

Gedicht', -e, *n.nt.* poem.

gedie'gen, *adj.* solid.

Gedrän'ge, -, *n.nt.* crush.

gedrängt', *adj.* concise.

Geduld', *n.f.* patience.

gedul'den, *vb.* (**sich g.**) have patience, forbear.

gedul'dig, *adj.* patient.

geeig'net, *adj.* qualified; suitable.

Gefahr', -en, *n.f.* danger, jeopardy.

gefähr'den, *vb.* endanger, jeopardize.

gefähr'lich, *adj.* dangerous.

gefahr'los, *adj.* without danger.

Gefähr'te, -n, -n, *n.m.* companion.

gefal'len*, *vb.* please; (**es gefällt mir**) I like it.

Gefal'len, -, *n.m.* favor.

gefäl'lig, *adj.* obliging, pleasing.

Gefan'gen-, *n.m.&f.* prisoner, captive.

Gefan'gennahme, -n, *n.f.* capture.

Gefan'genschaft, -en, *n.f.* captivity.

Gefäng'nis, -se, *n.nt.* prison, jail.

Gefäng'niswärter, -, *n.m.* jailer.

Gefäß', -e, *n.nt.* container.

gefaßt', *adj.* composed.

Gefecht', -e, *n.nt.* battle, engagement.

gefeit', adj. fortified against.

Gefie'der, n.nt. plumage.

gefleckt', adj. dappled.

geflis'sentlich, adj. intentional; studied.

Geflü'gel, n.nt. poultry.

Geflüs'ter, n.nt. whispering.

Gefol'ge, n.nt. retinue.

gefrä'ßig, adj. gluttonous.

Gefreit'-, n.m. corporal.

gefrie'ren*, vb. freeze.

Gefrier'fach, ⁻er, n.nt. freezer (in refrigerator).

Gefro'ren -, n.nt. ice (cream).

gefü'gig, adj. compliant.

Gefühl', -e, n.nt. feeling, sensation; emotion, sentiment.

gefühl'los, adj. insensible, callous.

gefühls'mäßig, adj. emotional.

gefühl'voll, adj. sentimental.

gegen, prep. against; toward; about.

Gegenangriff', -e, n.m. counterattack.

Gegend, -en, n.f. region.

Gegengewicht', -e, n.nt. counterbalance.

Gegengift', -e, n.nt. antidote, antitoxin.

Gegenmaßnahme, -n, n.f. countermeasure.

Gegensatz', ⁻e, n.m. contrast, opposite.

gegenseitig, adj. mutual.

Gegenstand', ⁻e, n.m. object.

Gegenteil', n.nt. reverse, opposite.

gegenü'ber, prep.&adv. opposite.

gegenü'ber-stellen, vb. confront.

Gegenwart', n.f. present, presence.

gegenwärtig, adj. present.

Gegenwirkung, -en, n.f. counteraction.

Gegner, -, n.m. adversary, opponent.

Gehalt', -e, n.m. content, substance.

Gehalt', ⁻er, n.nt. salary, pay.

gehar'nischt, adj. armed; (fig.) vehement.

gehäs'sig, adj. malicious.

Gehäu'se, -, n.nt. casing.

geheim', adj. secret, cryptic.

Geheim'dienst, -e, n.m. secret service.

geheim'-halten*, vb. keep secret.

Geheim'nis, -se, n.nt. secret, mystery.

geheim'nisvoll, adj. secretive, mysterious.

Geheiß', n.nt. command, behest.

gehen*, vb. go, walk; (wie geht es Ihnen?) how are you?

gehen-lassen*, vb. (sich g.) let oneself go.

Gehil'fe, -n, -n, n.m. helper, assistant.

Gehirn', -e, n.nt. brain.

Gehöft', -e, n.nt. farmstead.

Gehölz', -e, n.nt. woods.

Gehör', n.nt. hearing.

gehor'chen, vb. obey.

gehö'ren, vb. belong to.

gehö'rig, adj. belonging to; thorough, sound; appropriate.

gehor'sam, adj. obedient.

Gehor'sam, n.m. obedience, allegiance.

Geige, -n, n.f. violin.

Geisel, -n, n.m. hostage.

Geiser, -, n.m. geyser.

Geißel, -n, n.f. whip, scourge.

geißeln, vb. flagellate, scourge.

Geist, -er, n.m. mind, spirit; ghost; (Heiliger G.) Holy Spirit, Ghost.

geistesabwesend, adj. absentminded.

Geistesgegenwart, n.f. presence of mind.

geistesgestört, adj. deranged.

Geisteswissenschaften, n.pl. arts.

geistig, adj. mental, spiritual.

geistlich, adj. ecclesiastic(al).

Geistlich -, n.m. minister, clergyman.

Geistlichkeit, n.f. clergy.

geistlos, adj. inane, vacuous.

geistreich, adj. bright, witty.

geisttötend, adj. dull.

Geiz, n.m. avarice.

Geizhals, ⁻e, n.m. miser.

geizig, adj. avaricious, miserly.

Geklap'per, n.nt. clatter.

Gekrit'zel, n.nt. scribbling.

gekün'stelt, adj. contrived.

Geläch'ter, n.nt. laughter.

Gela'ge, -, n.nt. banquet.

gelähmt', adj. crippled.

Gelän'de, -, n.nt. terrain.

Gelän'der, -, n.nt. railing, banister.

gelan'gen, vb. reach, get to.

gelas'sen, adj. placid, composed.

Gelati'ne, -n, n.f. gelatine.

geläu'fig, adj. familiar, fluent.

Geläu'figkeit, n.f. fluency.

gelaunt', adj. (gut g.) in good humor.

gelb, adj. yellow.

gelbbraun, adj. tan.

Geld, -er, n.nt. money.

Geldbeutel, -, n.m. purse.

geldlich, adj. monetary.

Geldschein, -, n.m. bill.

Geldschrank, ⁻e, n.m. safe.

Geldstrafe, -n, n.f. fine; (zu einer G. verurteilen) fine.

Geldwechsler, -, n.m. moneychanger.

Gelee', -s, n.nt. jelly.

gele'gen, adj. situated; opportune.

Gele'genheit, -en, n.f. occasion, chance.

gele'gentlich, adj. occasional.

Gelehr'samkeit, n.f. erudition, scholarship.

gelehrt', adj. learned, erudite.

Gelehr't-, n.m.&f. scholar.

Gelei'se, -, n.nt. track.

Geleit', n.nt. accompaniment; (freies G.) safe conduct.

gelei'ten, vb. escort.

Geleit'zug, ⁻e, n.m. convoy.

Gelenk', -e, n.nt. joint.

gelen'kig, adj. supple.

geliebt', adj. beloved.

Gelieb'te, -n, n.f. beloved; mistress.

gelind', adj. mild, light.

gellen, vb. shriek.

gellend, adj. shrill.

gelo'ben, vb. vow, pledge.

gelten*, vb. be valid, apply, hold; be intended for; be considered; (das gilt nicht) that's not fair.

Geltung, n.f. standing, value.

Gelüb'de, -, n.nt. vow.

Gelüst', -e, n.nt. lust.

gemach', adv. slowly, gently.

Gemach', ⁻er, n.nt. chamber.

gemäch'lich, adj. leisurely, slow and easy.

Gemahl', -e, n.m. husband, consort.

gemäß', prep. according to.

gemä'ßigt, adj. moderate.

gemein', 1. adj. mean, vile, vicious. 2. adv. in common.

Gemein'de, -n, n.f. community; municipality; congregation.

gemein'gültig, adj. generally accepted.

Gemein'platz, ⁻e, n.m. platitude.

gemein'sam, adj. common, joint.

Gemein'schaft, n.f. community, fellowship.

Gemur'mel, -, n.nt. murmur.

Gemü'se, -, n.nt. vegetable.

Gemüt', -er, n.nt. mind, spirit, temper, heart.

gemüt'lich, adj. comfortable, homey, genial.

Gemüts'art, -en, n.f. temperament.

Gemüts'ruhe, n.f. placidity.

genau', adj. accurate, exact; fussy.

Genau'igkeit, -en, n.f. accuracy.

geneh'migen, vb. grant, approve.

Geneh'migung, -en, n.f. permission, license.

geneigt', adj. inclined.

General', ⁻e, n.m. general.

Genera'tor, -o'ren, n.m. generator.

gene'sen*, vb. recover.

Gene'sung, n.f. convalescence, recovery.

genial', adj. ingenious, having genius.

Genialität', n.f. ingenuity, genius.

Genie', -s, n.nt. genius.

genie'ßen*, vb. enjoy, relish.

Genitiv, -e, n.m. genitive.

Genos'se, -n, n.m. companion; (derogatory) character.

Genos'senschaft, -en, n.f. association, co-operative society.

genug', *adj.* enough.

genü'gen, *vb.* be enough, suffice.

genü'gend, *adj.* satisfactory, sufficient.

genüg'sam, *adj.* modest.

Genüg'samkeit, *n.f.* frugality.

Genug'tuung, **-en**, *n.f.* satisfaction.

Genuß', **-sse**, *n.m.* enjoyment; relish.

Geograph', **-en**, **-en**, *n.m.* geographer.

Geographie', *n.f.* geography.

geogra'phisch, *adj.* geographical.

Geometrie', *n.f.* geometry.

geome'trisch, *adj.* geometric.

geord'net, *adj.* orderly.

Gepäck', *n.nt.* luggage, baggage.

Gepäck'träger, **-**, *n.m.* porter.

Gepäck'schein, **-e**, *n.m.* baggage check.

Geplau'der, *n.nt.* chat, small talk.

Geprä'ge, *n.nt.* stamp; character.

gera'de, **1.** *adj.* straight, even. **2.** *adv.* just; **(g. aus)** straight ahead.

gera'destehen*, *vb.* stand straight; answer for.

geradezu', *adv.* downright.

Gerad'heit, *n.f.* erectness; directness.

Gerät', **-e**, *n.nt.* tool, appliance, utensil.

Geratewohl', *n.* **(aufs G.)** at random, haphazardly.

geraum', *adj.* considerable.

geräu'mig, *adj.* spacious.

Geräusch', **-e**, *n.nt.* noise.

geräusch'los, *adj.* noiseless.

gerben, *vb.* tan.

gerecht', *adj.* just, fair.

Gerech'tigkeit, *n.f.* justice.

Gere'de, *n.nt.* chatter; **(ins G. bringen)** make someone the talk of the town.

gereift', *adj.* mellow.

gereizt', *adj.* irritated, edgy.

Gereizt'heit, *n.f.* irritability.

gereu'en, *vb.* repent, regret.

Gericht', **-e**, *n.nt.* court, bar, tribunal; (food) course; **(Jüngstes G.)** doomsday, judgment day.

gericht'lich, *adj.* legal, judicial, forensic.

Gerichts'barkeit, *n.f.* jurisdiction.

Gerichts'gebäude, **-**, *n.nt.* courthouse.

Gerichts'saal, **-säle**, *n.m.* courtroom.

Gerichts'verhandlung, **-en**, *n.f.* court proceedings, trial.

gerie'ben, *adj.* cunning, sly.

gering', *adj.* slight, slim.

gering'achten, *vb.* look down upon.

gering'fügig, *adj.* negligible, petty.

gering'schätzen, *vb.* hold in low esteem.

gering'schätzig, *adj.* disparaging, derogatory.

gerin'nen*, *vb.* curdle, clot, coagulate.

Gerip'pe, **-**, *n.nt.* skeleton.

geris'sen, *adj.* shrewd.

Germa'ne, **-n**, **-n**, *n.m.* Teuton.

germa'nisch, *adj.* Germanic.

gern, *adv.* gladly, readily; **(g. haben*)** like, be fond of; **(g. tun*)** like to do.

Gerste, **-n**, *n.f.* barley.

Gerstenkorn, **-er**, *n.nt.* barleycorn; sty.

Geruch', **-e**, *n.m.* smell, odor, scent.

Gerücht', **-e**, *n.nt.* rumor.

geru'hen, *vb.* deign.

Gerüst', **-e**, *n.nt.* scaffold, scaffolding.

gesamt', *adj.* total.

Gesamt'heit, *n.f.* entirety.

Gesandt'-, *n.m.* ambassador, envoy.

Gesandt'schaft, **-en**, *n.f.* legation.

Gesang', **-e**, *n.m.* song, chant.

Gesang'buch, **-er**, *n.nt.* hymnal.

Geschäft', **-e**, *n.nt.* business, deal; shop, store.

geschäf'tig, *adj.* busy.

Geschäf'tigkeit, **-en**, *n.f.* bustle.

Geschäfts'mann, **-er**, *or* **-leute**, *n.m.* businessman.

geschäfts'mäßig, *adj.* businesslike.

Geschäfts'viertel, **-**, *n.nt.* downtown, business section.

gesche'hen*, *vb.* occur, happen.

Gesche'hnis, **-se**, *n.nt.* happening, occurrence.

gescheit', *adj.* bright, clever.

Geschenk', **-e**, *n.nt.* present.

Geschich'te, **-n**, *n.f.* story; history.

Geschick', *n.nt.* skill.

Geschick'lichkeit, **-en**, *n.f.* dexterity, facility.

geschickt', *adj.* skillful, clever, deft.

Geschirr', **-e**, *n.nt.* dishes; harness.

Geschlecht', **-er**, *n.nt.* genus, sex; gender; lineage, family.

geschlecht'lich, *adj.* sexual.

Geschmack', **-e**, *n.m.* taste, flavor.

geschmack'los, *adj.* tasteless; in bad taste.

geschmei'dig, *adj.* lithe.

Geschöpf', **-e**, *n.nt.* creature.

Geschoß', **-sse**, *n.nt.* missile, projectile.

Geschrei', *n.nt.* clamor.

Geschütz', **-e**, *n.nt.* gun.

Geschwa'der, **-**, *n.nt.* squadron.

Geschwätz', *n.nt.* idle talk, babble.

geschwät'zig, *adj.* talkative, gossipy.

geschwind', *adj.* swift.

Geschwin'digkeit, **-en**, *n.f.* speed, velocity.

Geschwin'digkeitsgrenze, **-n**, *n.f.* speed limit.

Geschwo'ren-, *n.m.&f.* juror; *(pl.)* jury.

Geschwulst', **-e**, *n.nt.* swelling, growth.

Geschwür', **-e**, *n.nt.* abscess, ulcer.

geseg'net, *adj.* blessed.

Gesel'le, **-n**, **-n**, *n.m.* journeyman; fellow.

gesel'len, *vb.* **(sich g.)** join.

gesel'lig, *adj.* sociable, gregarious.

Gesell'schaft, **-en**, *n.f.* society; company; party.

Gesell'schafterin, **-nen**, *n.f.* companion.

gesell'schaftlich, *adj.* social.

Gesell'schaftskleidung, **-en**, *n.f.* evening dress, dress clothes.

Gesell'schaftsreise, **-n**, *n.f.* group tour.

Gesetz', **-e**, *n.nt.* law, act.

Gesetz'antrag, **-e**, *n.m.* bill.

gesetz'gebend, *adj.* legislative.

Gesetz'geber, **-**, *n.m.* legislator.

Gesetz'gebung, *n.f.* legislation.

gesetz'lich, *adj.* lawful, legal.

gesetz'los, *adj.* lawless.

gesetz'mäßig, *adj.* legal.

Gesetz'mäßigkeit, *n.f.* legality.

gesetz'widrig, *adj.* illegal, unlawful.

Gesicht', **-er**, *n.nt.* face.

Gesichts'ausdruck, **-e**, *n.m.* facial expression, mien.

Gesichts'farbe, *n.f.* complexion.

Gesichts'kreis, *n.m.* horizon.

Gesichts'massage, **-n**, *n.f.* facial.

Gesichts'punkt, **-e**, *n.m.* point of view, aspect.

Gesichts'zug, **-e**, *n.m.* feature.

Gesin'del, *n.nt.* rabble.

gesinnt', *adj.* **(g. sein*)** be of a mind, be disposed.

Gesin'nung, **-en**, *n.f.* attitude, way of thinking, views.

gesit'tet, *adj.* well-mannered, civilized.

gespannt', *adj.* tense; eager to know, curious.

Gespenst', **-er**, *n.nt.* ghost.

Gespie'le, **-n**, **-n**, *n.m.* playmate.

Gespräch', **-e**, *n.nt.* talk, conversation.

gesprä'chig, *adj.* talkative.

Gestalt', **-en**, *n.f.* figure, form, shape.

gestal'ten, *vb.* form, shape, fashion.

Gestal'tung, **-en**, *n.f.* formation, fashioning.

Gestam'mel, *n.nt.* stammering.

gestän'dig, *adj.* **(g. sein*)** make a confession.

Geständ'nis, **-se**, *n.nt.* confession, avowal.

Gestank', *n.m.* stench.

gestat'ten, *vb.* permit.

Geste, -n, *n.f.* gesture.

geste'hen*, *vb.* confess, avow.

Gestein', *n.nt.* rock.

Gestell', -e, *n.nt.* stand, rack, frame.

gestern, *adv.* yesterday.

gestikulie'ren, *vb.* gesticulate.

Gestirn', -e, *n.nt.* star; constellation.

Gestirns'bahn, -en, *n.f.* orbit.

Gestrüpp', *n.nt.* scrub, brush.

Gesuch', -e, *n.nt.* application, petition, request.

gesucht', *adj.* far-fetched, contrived.

gesund', *adj.* healthy, sound, wholesome.

gesun'den, *vb.* recover.

Gesund'heit, *n.f.* health, fitness; (geistige G.) sanity.

Gesund'heitsattest, -e, *n.nt.* certificate of health.

gesund'heitsschädlich, *adj.* unhealthy.

Gesund'heitswesen, *n.nt.* sanitation.

Gesun'dung, *n.f.* recovery.

Getö'se, *n.nt.* uproar.

Getränk', -e, *n.nt.* drink, beverage; (alkoholfreies G.) soft drink.

getrau'en, *vb.* (sich g.) dare.

Getrei'de, *n.nt.* grain, cereal.

getrennt', *adj.* separate.

getreu', *adj.* faithful.

Getrie'be, -n, *n.nt.* gear.

getrost', *adv.* confidently.

Getu'e, *n.nt.* affectation, goings-on.

geübt', *adj.* experienced.

Gewächs', -e, *n.nt.* growth.

gewagt', *adj.* daring, hazardous.

Gewähr', *n.f.* guarantee.

gewäh'ren, *vb.* grant.

gewähr'leisten, *vb.* warrant, guarantee.

Gewahr'sam, *n.m.* custody.

Gewalt', -en, *n.f.* force, power.

Gewalt'herrschaft, *n.f.* despotism.

gewal'tig, *adj.* powerful, tremendous.

gewalt'sam, *adj.* forcible, violent.

gewalt'tätig, *adj.* violent.

Gewalt'tätigkeit, -en, *n.f.* violence.

Gewand', -̈er, *n.nt.* garb, garment.

gewandt', *adj.* facile, versatile.

Gewandt'heit, -en, *n.f.* deftness.

gewär'tig, *adv.* (g. sein*) prepared.

Gewäs'ser, *n.nt.* waters.

Gewe'be, -, *n.nt.* tissue, texture.

Gewehr', -e, *n.nt.* rifle, gun.

Gewer'be, -, *n.nt.* trade, business.

Gewerk'schaft, -en, *n.f.* labor union.

Gewicht' -e, *n.nt.* weight.

gewiegt', *adj.* crafty.

gewillt', *adj.* willing.

Gewinn', -e, *n.m.* gain, profit.

gewinn'bringend, *adj.* lucrative.

gewin'nen*, *vb.* win, gain.

Gewin'ner, -, *n.m.* winner.

gewinn'süchtig, *adj.* mercenary, greedy.

Gewirr', *n.nt.* tangle, confusion.

gewiß', *adj.* certain.

Gewis'sen, -, *n.nt.* conscience.

gewis'senhaft, *adj.* conscientious.

gewis'senlos, *adj.* unprincipled.

Gewis'sensbiß, -sse, *n.m.* remorse, qualms.

gewisserma'ßen, *adv.* so to speak, as it were.

Gewiß'heit, -en, *n.f.* certainty.

Gewit'ter, -, *n.nt.* thunderstorm.

gewit'zigt, *adj.* clever.

gewo'gen, *adj.* (g. sein*) disposed towards.

gewöh'nen, *vb.* accustom; (sich g. an) become accustomed to.

Gewohn'heit, -en, *n.f.* habit, custom, practice.

gewohn'heitsmäßig, *adj.* customary, habitual.

gewöhn'lich, *adj.* ordinary, usual, regular; common, vulgar.

gewohnt', *adj.* accustomed.

Gewöl'be, -, *n.nt.* vaulting, vault.

Gewühl', *n.nt.* shuffle, melee.

gewun'den, *adj.* coiled; sinuous.

Gewürz', -e, *n.nt.* spice, condiment, seasoning.

Gewürz'kraut -̈er, *n.nt.* herb.

Gezei'ten, *n.pl.* tide.

gezie'men, *vb.* be proper, befit.

Gicht, -en, *n.f.* gout, arthritis.

Giebel, -, *n.m.* gable.

Gier, *n.f.* greed(iness).

gierig, *adj.* greedy.

gießen*, *vb.* pour; cast (metal).

Gift, -e, *n.nt.* poison.

giftig, *adj.* poisonous.

Gilde, -n, *n.f.* guild.

Gin, -s, *n.m.* gin.

Gipfel, -, *n.m.* peak.

gipfeln, *vb.* culminate.

Gips, -e, *n.m.* gypsum, plaster.

Giraf'fe, -n, *n.f.* giraffe.

Girant', -en, -en, *n.m.* endorser.

Girat', -en, -en, *n.m.* endorsee.

girie'ren, *vb.* endorse (a check, note, etc.), put into circulation.

Giro, -s, *n.nt.* endorsement, circulation (of endorsed notes, etc.).

Gischt, -e, *n.m.* spray, foam.

Gitar're, -n, *n.f.* guitar.

Gitter, -, *n.nt.* grating; gate.

Gitterwerk, -e, *n.nt.* grating.

glaciert', *adj.* glacé.

Glanz, *n.m.* shine, sheen, gloss; brilliance, splendor.

glänzen, *vb.* shine.

glänzend, *adj.* shiny, brilliant.

Glas, -̈er, *n.nt.* glass.

Glaser, -, *n.m.* glazier.

gläsern, *adj.* made of glass.

glasie'ren, *vb.* glaze.

glasig, *adj.* glassy.

Glasscheibe, -n, *n.f.* pane.

Glasur, -en, *n.f.* glaze.

Glasware, -n, *n.f.* glassware.

glatt, *adj.* smooth, slippery; outright.

glätten, *vb.* smooth.

Glatzkopf, -̈e, *n.m.* bald head.

Glaube(n), -, *n.m.* belief, faith.

glauben, *vb.* believe.

Glaubensbekenntnis, -se, *n.nt.* confession of faith; creed.

glaubhaft, *adj.* believable.

gläubig, *adj.* believing, devout.

Gläubig-, -, *n.m.&f.* believer; creditor.

glaublich, *adj.* credible.

glaubwürdig, *adj.* credible.

Glaubwürdigkeit, *n.f.* credibility.

gleich, 1. *adj.* equal, same, even. **2.** *adv.* right away.

gleichaltig, *adj.* of the same age.

gleichartig, *adj.* similar, homogeneous.

gleichberechtigt, *adj.* having equal rights.

Gleichberechtigung, -en, *n.f.* equality of rights.

gleichen*, *vb.* be like, equal, resemble.

gleichfalls, *adv.* likewise.

gleichförmig, *adj.* uniform.

gleichgesinnt, *adj.* likeminded.

gleichgestellt, *adj.* coordinate.

Gleichgewicht, *n.nt.* equilibrium.

gleichgültig, *adj.* indifferent.

Gleichgültigkeit, *n.f.* indifference.

Gleichheit, *n.f.* equality.

gleich-machen, *vb.* equalize.

Gleichmaß, *n.nt.* proportion, symmetry.

gleichmäßig, *adj.* even, regular.

Gleichmut, *n.m.* equanimity.

gleichmütig, *adj.* even-tempered.

Gleichnis, -se, *n.nt.* simile, parable.

gleichsam, *adv.* as it were.

gleichseitig, *adj.* equilateral.

gleich-setzen, *vb.* equate.

Gleichstrom, -̈e, *n.m.* direct current.

gleich-tun*, *vb.* do like, match up to.

Gleichung, -en, *n.f.* equation.

gleichwertig, *adj.* equivalent.

gleichwie, *adv.&conj.* just as.

gleichwohl, *adv.* nevertheless.

gleichzeitig, *adj.* simultaneous.

Gleis, -e, *n.nt.* track.

gleiten*, *vb.* glide, slide, slip.

Gletscher, -, *n.m.* glacier.

Gletscherspalte, -n, *n.f.* crevasse.

Glied, -er, *n.nt.* limb; link.

gliedern, *vb.* segment, classify.

Gliederung, -en, *n.f.* arrangement, structure.

Gliedmaßen, *n.pl.* limbs, extremities.

glitzern, *vb.* glitter.

Globus, -ben (-busse), *n.m.* globe.

Glocke, -n, *n.f.* bell.

Glockenschlag, ∹e, *n.m.* stroke of the clock.

Glockenspiel, -e, *n.nt.* chimes, carillon.

Glockenturm, ∹, *n.m.* belfry, bell-tower.

Glorie, -n, *n.f.* glory.

Glorienschein, -e, *n.m.* halo.

glorreich, *adj.* glorious.

glotzen, *vb.* stare.

Glück, *n.nt.* happiness, luck.

gluckern, *vb.* gurgle.

glücklich, *adj.* happy.

glücklicherweise, *adj.* fortunately.

glückselig, *adj.* blissful.

Glückseligkeit, -en, *n.f.* bliss.

glucksen, *vb.* gurgle.

Glücksfall, ∹e, *n.m.* stroke of luck.

Glücksspiel, -e, *n.nt.* gamble; gambling.

Glücksspieler, -, *n.m.* gambler.

Glückwunsch, ∹e, *n.m.* congratulation.

Glühbirne, -n, *n.f.* electric light bulb.

glühen, *vb.* glow.

glühend, *adj.* glowing, incandescent; ardent.

Glut, -en, *n.f.* heat, live coals; ardor, passion.

Glyzerin', *n.nt.* glycerine.

G.m.b.H., *abbr.* (= Gesell'-schaft mit beschränk'ter Haftung) incorporated, inc.

Gnade, *n.f.* grace, mercy.

gnadenreich, *adj.* merciful.

gnädig, *adj.* gracious, merciful; (g.e Frau) madam.

Gold, *n.nt.* gold.

Goldbarren, -, *n.m.* bullion.

golden, *adj.* golden.

Goldfisch, -e, *n.m.* goldfish.

goldig, *adj.* darling, cute.

Goldschmied, -e, *n.m.* goldsmith.

Golf, -e, *n.m.* gulf, bay.

Golf, *n.nt.* golf.

Golfplatz, ∹e, *n.m.* golf course.

Gondel, -n, *n.f.* gondola.

gönnen, *vb.* grant, not begrudge; (sich g.) allow oneself; (das gönne ich ihm!) that serves him right!

Gör, -en, *n.nt.* brat, girl.

Goril'la, -s, *n.m.* gorilla.

Gosse, -n, *n.f.* gutter, drain.

gotisch, *adj.* Gothic.

Gotik, *n.f.* Gothic architecture.

Gott, ∹er, *n.m.* god, deity.

gottähnlich, *adj.* godlike.

Götterdämmerung, *n.f.* twilight of the gods.

Gottesacker, ∹, *n.m.* cemetery.

Gottesdienst, -e, *n.m.* (church) service.

Gottesgabe, -n *f.* godsend.

Gotteshaus, ∹er, *n.nt.* church.

Gotteslästerung, -en, *n.f.* blasphemy.

Gottheit, -en, *n.f.* deity, divinity.

Göttin, -nen, *n.f.* goddess.

göttlich, *adj.* godly, divine.

gottlob', *interj.* praise God.

gottlos, *adj.* godless.

Götze, -n, -n, *n.m.* idol, false god.

Götzenbild, -er, *n.nt.* idol.

Götzendienst, -e, *n.m.* idolatry.

Gouvernan'te, -n, *n.f.* governess.

Gouverneur', -e, *n.m.* governor.

Gouverneurs'amt, ∹er, *n.nt.* governorship.

Grab, ∹er, *n.nt.* grave.

graben*, *vb.* dig.

Graben, ∹, *n.m.* trench, ditch.

Grablegung, -en, *n.f.* burial.

Grabmal, ∹er, *n.nt.* tomb(-stone).

Grabschrift, -en, *n.f.* epitaph.

Grabstein, -e, *n.m.* gravestone.

Grad, -e, *n.m.* degree.

Graf, -en, -en, *n.m.* count.

Gräfin, -nen, *n.f.* countess.

Grafschaft, -en, *n.f.* county.

Gram, *n.m.* grief, care.

grämen, *vb.* (sich g.) grieve, fret.

Gramm, -, *n.nt.* gram.

Gramma'tik, -en, *n.f.* grammar.

Gramma'tiker, -, *n.m.* grammarian.

gramma'tisch, *adj.* grammatical.

Grammophon', -e, *n.nt.* phonograph.

Grammophon'platte, -n, *n.f.* phonograph record.

Granat', -e, *n.m.* garnet.

Grana'te, -n, *n.f.* grenade.

Granit', *n.m.* granite.

granulie'ren, *vb.* granulate.

Graphiker, -, *n.m.* illustrator, commercial artist.

graphisch, *adj.* graphic.

Gras, ∹er, *n.nt.* grass.

grasartig, *adj.* grasslike, grassy.

grasen, *vb.* graze.

grasig, *adj.* grassy.

gräßlich, *adj.* hideous.

Grat, -e, *n.m.* ridge.

Gräte, -n, *n.f.* bone (of a fish).

gratis, *adj.* gratis.

gratulie'ren, *vb.* congratulate.

grau, *adj.* gray.

Grauen, *n.nt.* horror.

grauenhaft, *adj.* ghastly.

grausam, *adj.* cruel.

grausig, *adj.* lurid.

Graveur', -e, *n.m.* engraver.

gravie'ren, *vb.* engrave.

gravitie'ren, *vb.* gravitate.

Grazie, -n, *n.f.* grace, charm.

graziös', *adj.* graceful.

greifbar, *adj.* tangible.

greifen*, *vb.* seize, grasp.

Greis, -e, *n.m.* old man.

Greisenalter, -, *n.nt.* old age.

Greisin, -nen, *n.f.* old woman.

grell, *adj.* garish, gaudy, shrill.

Grenze, -n, *n.f.* limit, border, boundary.

grenzen, *vb.* (g. an) border on.

grenzenlos, *adj.* boundless.

Greuel, -, *n.m.* horror, outrage.

greulich, *adj.* horrible.

Grieche, -n, -n, *n.m.* Greek.

Griechenland, *n.nt.* Greece.

griechisch, *adj.* Greek.

Griesgram, -e, *n.m.* grouch.

griesgrämig, *adj.* sullen.

Grieß, -e, *n.m.* semolina, coarse meal; gravel.

Griff, -e, *n.m.* grasp, grip, handle.

Grill, -s, *n.m.* grill; grillroom.

Grille, -n, *n.f.* cricket; whim.

grillen, *vb.* broil.

grillenhaft, *adj.* whimsical.

Grimas'se, -n, *n.f.* grimace.

Grimm, *n.m.* anger.

grimmig, *adj.* angry.

grinsen, *vb.* grin.

Grinsen, *n.nt.* grin.

Grippe, -n, *n.f.* grippe, influenza.

grob(-), *adj.* coarse, rough, crude.

Grobian, *n.m.* boor, ruffian.

Grog, -s, *n.m.* grog.

Groll, *n.m.* anger, grudge.

grollen, *vb.* be angry, bear a grudge.

Gros, -se, *n.nt.* gross.

Groschen, -, *n.m.* ten pfennig piece; 1/100 of an Austrian schilling.

groß(-), *adj.* big, tall, great.

großartig, *adj.* grand, magnificent.

Großbritan'ien, *n.nt.* Great Britain.

Größe, -n, *n.f.* size, height, greatness.

Großeltern, *n.pl.* grandparents.

großenteils, *adv.* in large part, largely.

Großhandel, -, *n.m.* wholesale trade.

großherzig, *adj.* magnanimous.

großjährig, *adj.* of age.

Großmacht, ∹e, *n.f.* major power.

Großmut, *n.m.* magnanimity, generosity.

großmütig, *adj.* magnanimous, generous.

Großmutter, ∹, *n.f.* grandmother.

Grossrechenanlage, -n, *n.f.* (computer) mainframe.

großsprecherisch, *adj.* boastful.

Großstaat, -en, *n.m.* major power.

Großstadt, ∹e, *n.f.* large city, metropolis.

Großstädter, -e, *n.m.* big city person.

größtenteils, *adv.* for the most part, mostly.

groß-tun*, *vb.* act big, boast.

Großvater, :, *n.m.* grandfather.

groß-ziehen*, *vb.* bring up, raise.

großzügig, *adj.* on a grand scale, generous, broad-minded.

grotesk', *adj.* grotesque.

Grotte, -n, *n.f.* grotto.

Grube, -n, *n.f.* pit; mine.

grübeln, *vb.* brood.

Grubenarbeiter, -, *n.m.* miner.

Gruft, :e, *n.f.* crypt, vault.

grün, *adj.* green.

Grund, :e, *n.m.* ground, bottom, basis, reason; **(G. und Boden)** land, real estate.

Grundbegriff, -e, *n.m.* basic concept.

Grundbesitz, -e, *n.m.* landed property.

Grundbesitzer, -, *n.m.* landholder.

gründen, *vb.* found.

Grundgesetz, -e, *n.nt.* basic law; constitution.

Grundlage, -n, *n.f.* basis.

grundlegend, *adj.* fundamental.

gründlich, *adj.* thorough.

Grundlinie, -n, *n.f.* base.

grundlos, *adj.* bottomless; unfounded.

Grundriß, -sse, *n.m.* outline, sketch.

Grundsatz, :e, *n.m.* principle.

grundsätzlich, *adj.* fundamental, on principle.

Grundschule, -n, *n.f.* elementary school.

Grundstoff, -e, *n.m.* basic material.

Grundstück, -e, *n.nt.* lot.

Gründung, -en, *n.f.* founding, establishment.

grunzen, *vb.* grunt.

Gruppe, -n, *n.f.* group.

gruppie'ren, *vb.* group.

gruselig, *adj.* uncanny, creepy.

Gruß, :e, *n.m.* greeting; salute.

grüßen, *vb.* greet; salute.

gucken, *vb.* look.

gültig, *adj.* valid.

Gültigkeit, *n.f.* validity.

Gummi, -s, *n.m.* rubber; eraser.

Gummi, -s, *n.nt.* gum.

gummiartig, *adj.* gummy.

Gummiband, :er, *n.nt.* elastic (band).

Gummischuhe, *n.pl.* overshoes, galoshes, rubbers.

Gunst, :e, *n.f.* favor.

günstig, *adj.* favorable.

Günstling, -e, *n.m.* favorite.

Gurgel, -n, *n.f.* throat, gullet.

gurgeln, *vb.* gargle.

Gurke, -n, *n.f.* cucumber; **(saure G.)** pickle.

Gurt, -e, *n.m.* girth, harness.

Gürtel, -, *n.m.* belt, girdle.

gürten, *vb.* gird.

Guru, -s, *n.m.* guru.

Guß, :sse, *n.m.* downpour; frosting; casting.

Gußstein, -e, *n.m.* sink, drain.

gut, 1. *adj.* good. **2.** *adv.* well.

Gut, :er, *n.nt.* property; landed estate; *(pl.)* goods.

Gutachten, -, *n.nt.* (expert) opinion, (legal) advice.

gutaussehend, *adj.* good-looking.

Gutdünken, *n.nt.* opinion, discretion.

Güte, *n.f.* kindness; quality, purity.

gutgläubig, *adj.* credulous.

Guthaben, -, *n.nt.* credit; assets.

gut-heißen*, *vb.* approve.

gutherzig, *adj.* good-hearted.

gütig, *adj.* kind, friendly, gracious.

gütlich, *adj.* kind, friendly.

gut-machen, *vb.* make good; **(wieder g.)** make amends for.

gutmütig, *adj.* good-natured.

gut-schreiben*, *vb.* credit.

Gutschrift, -en, *n.f.* credit.

Gymna'sium, -ien, *n.nt.* secondary school preparing for university.

Gymnas'tik, *n.f.* gymnastics.

gymnas'tisch, *adj.* gymnastic.

H

ha, *abbr.* (= Hektar') hectare.

Haar, -e, *n.nt.* hair.

haarig, *adj.* hairy.

Haarklammer, -n, *n.f.* bobby pin.

Haarnadel, -n, *n.f.* hairpin.

haarscharf, *adj.* very sharp.

Haarschneiden, *n.nt.* haircut.

Haarschnitt, -e, *n.m.* (style of) haircut.

Haarspray, *n.m.* hairspray.

Habe, -n, *n.f.* property; **(Hab und Gut)** goods and chattels, all one's property.

haben*, *vb.* have.

Haben, *n.nt.* credit; **(Soll und H.)** debit and credit.

Habgier, *n.f.* greed.

habgierig, *adj.* greedy.

Habseligkeiten, *n.pl.* belongings.

Habsucht, *n.f.* greed.

habsüchtig, *adj.* greedy.

Hacke, -n, *n.f.* hoe, pick; heel.

hacken, *vb.* chip.

Hader, -n, *n.m.* quarrel, strife.

hadern, *vb.* quarrel.

Hafen, -, *n.m.* harbor, port.

Hafenstadt, :e, *n.f.* seaport.

Hafer, n.m. oats.

Hafergrütze, *n.f.* oatmeal.

Haft, *n.f.* arrest, detention.

haftbar, *adj.* liable.

Haftbefehl, -e, *n.m.* warrant.

haften, *vb.* stick, adhere; be responsible.

Haftpflicht, -en, *n.f.* liability.

Hagel, *n.m.* hail.

Hagelwetter, -, *n.nt.* hailstorm.

hager, *adj.* gaunt.

Hahn, :e, *n.m.* rooster; faucet.

Haifisch, -e, *n.m.* shark.

Hain, -e, *n.m.* grove.

Haken, -, *n.m.* hook.

halb, *adj.* half.

halber, *prep.* because of, for the sake of.

halbie'ren, *vb.* halve.

Halbinsel, -n, *n.f.* peninsula.

halbjährlich, *adj.* semiannual.

Halbkreis, -e, *n.m.* semicircle.

Halbkugel, -n, *n.f.* hemisphere.

Halbmesser, -, *n.m.* radius.

Halbschuhe, *n.pl.* low shoes, oxfords.

halbwegs, *adv.* halfway.

Hälfte, -n, *n.f.* half.

Halfter, -, *n.nt.* halter.

Halle, -n, *n.f.* hall.

hallen, *vb.* sound, echo.

Halm, -e, *n.m.* blade, stalk.

hallo, *interj.* hello.

Hals, :e, *n.m.* neck.

Halsband, :er, *n.nt.* necklace.

halsbrecherisch, *adj.* breakneck.

Halskette, -n, *n.f.* necklace.

Halsschmerzen, *n.pl.* sore throat.

halsstarrig, *adj.* obstinate.

Halstuch, :er, *n.nt.* kerchief.

Halsweh, *n.nt.* sore throat.

halt, *interj.* halt.

halt, *adv.* after all, I think.

Halt, -e, *n.m.* halt; hold, support.

haltbar, *adj.* tenable.

halten*, *vb.* hold, keep, stop; **(h. für)** consider as.

Halter, -, *n.m.* holder.

Haltestelle, -n, *n.f.* stop.

halt-machen, *vb.* halt, stop.

Haltung, -en, *n.f.* attitude, posture.

Hammelbraten, -, *n.m.* roast mutton.

Hammelfleisch, *n.nt.* mutton.

Hammelkeule, -n, *n.f.* leg of mutton.

Hammer, :, *n.m.* hammer.

hämmern, *vb.* hammer.

Hämorrhoi'de, -n, *n.f.* hemorrhoid.

hamstern, *vb.* hoard.

Hand, :e, *n.f.* hand.

Handarbeit, -en, *n.f.* manual labor; needlework.

Handbremse, -n, *n.f.* hand brake, emergency brake.

Handbuch, :er, *n.nt.* handbook, manual.

Händedruck, *n.m.* clasp (of hands).

Handel, *n.m.* trade, commerce.

handeln, *vb.* act, trade, deal; **(es handelt sich um . . .)** it is a question of . . .

Handelsgeist, *n.m.* commercialism.

Handelsmarine, *n.f.* merchant marine.

Handelsreisend-, n.m. traveling salesman.
handfest, adj. sturdy.
Handfläche, -n, n.f. palm.
Handgelenk, -e, n.nt. wrist.
handhaben, vb. handle, manage.
Handikap, -s, n.nt. handicap.
Handlanger, -, n.m. handy man, general worker.
Händler, -, n.m. dealer, trader.
handlich, adj. handy.
Handlung, -en, n.f. action; plot.
Handschelle, -n, n.f. handcuff.
Handschrift, -en, n.f. handwriting.
Handschuh, -e, n.m. glove.
Handtasche, -n, n.f. pocketbook.
Handtuch, ̈er, n.nt. towel.
Handvoll, n.f. handful.
Handwerk, -e, n.nt. handicraft, handiwork.
Handwerker, -, n.m. craftsman, artisan.
Hang, ̈e, n.m. slope; inclination.
Hängebrücke, -n, n.f. suspension bridge.
Hängematte, -n, n.f. hammock.
hängen*, vb. (intr.) hang, be suspended; (an jemandem h.) be attached to someone.
hängen(*), vb. (tr.) hang, suspend.
Hans, n.m. Hans; (H. Dampf in allen Gassen) jack-of-all-trades.
hänseln, vb. tease.
hantie'ren, vb. handle, manipulate.
hapern, vb. get stuck, be wrong.
Happen, -, n.m. morsel.
Harfe, -n, n.f. harp.
Harke, -n, n.f. rake.
harken, vb. rake.
Harm, n.m. grief.
harmlos, adj. harmless.
Harmonie', -i'en, n.f. harmony.
Harmo'nika, -s, n.f. harmonica.
harmo'nisch, adj. harmonious.
harmonisie'ren, vb. harmonize.
Harn, n.m. urine.
Harnblase, -n, n.f. (urinary) bladder.
harnen, vb. urinate.
Harnisch, -e, n.m. harness; armor.
Harpu'ne, -n, n.f. harpoon.
hart (̈-), adj. hard, severe.
Härte, -n, n.f. hardness, severity.
härten, vb. harden, temper.
hartgekocht, adj. hard-boiled.
hartherzig, adj. hard-hearted.
hartnäckig, adj. stubborn.
Harz, -e, n.nt. resin, rosin.
Hasch, n.m. & nt. marijuana.
haschen, vb. catch, snatch.
Hase, -n, -n, n.m. hare.
Haselnuß, ̈-sse, n.f. hazelnut.

Hasenbraten, -, n.m. roast hare.
Haspe, -n, n.f. hasp, hinge.
Haß, n.m. hatred.
hassen, vb. hate.
häßlich, adj. ugly.
Häßlichkeit, n.f. ugliness.
Hast, n.f. haste, hurry.
hasten, vb. hasten, hurry.
hastig, adj. hasty.
Haube, -n, n.f. hood.
Hauch, -e, n.m. breath.
hauchdünn, adj. extremely thin.
hauen*, vb. hew, chop, strike, spank; (sich h.) fight.
Haufen, -, n.m. pile, heap; crowd; large amount.
häufen, vb. heap.
häufig, adj. frequent.
Häufigkeit, -en, n.f. frequency.
Häufung, -en, n.f. accumulation.
Haupt, ̈er, n.nt. head.
Hauptamt, ̈er, n.nt. main office.
Hauptbahnhof, ̈e, n.m. main railroad station.
Häuptling, -e, n.m. chieftain.
Hauptmann, -leute, n.m. captain.
Hauptquartier, -e, n.nt. headquarters.
Hauptsache, -n, n.f. main, essential thing; principal matter.
hauptsächlich, adj. main, principal.
Hauptstadt, ̈e, n.f. capital.
Hauptwort, ̈er, n.nt. noun, substantive.
Haus, ̈er, n.nt. house.
Hausangestellt -, n.m.&f. servant.
Hausarbeit, -en, n.f. housework.
Hausaufgabe, -n, n.f. homework.
hausbacken, adj. homemade; plain.
hausen, vb. dwell, reside.
Häuserblock, -s, n.m. block.
Hausfrau, -en, n.f. housewife.
Haushalt, -e, n.m. household.
haus·halten*, vb. economize.
Haushälterin, -nen, n.f. housekeeper.
Haushaltung, n.f. housekeeping.
hausie'ren, vb. peddle.
hausie'ren, vb. peddle.
Hausie'rer, -, n.m. peddler.
häuslich, adj. domestic.
Hausmeister, -, n.m. janitor.
Hausrat, n.m. household goods.
Hausschuh, -e, n.m. slipper.
Haut, ̈e, n.f. skin, hide.
hautstraffend, adj. astringent.
Hebamme, -n, n.f. midwife.
Hebel, -, n.m. lever.
heben*, vb. raise, lift.
Hebrä'er, -, n.m. Hebrew.
hebrä'isch, adj. Hebrew.
hecheln, vb. heckle.

Hecht, -e, n.m. pike (fish).
Heck, -e, n.nt. stern, rear, tail.
Hecke, -n, n.f. hedge.
Heer, -e, n.nt. army.
Heft, -e, n.nt. notebook; handle, hilt.
heften, vb. fasten, pin, stitch, tack.
Hefter, -, n.m. folder.
heftig, adj. vehement.
Heftigkeit, n.f. vehemence.
hegen, vb. nurture.
Heide, -n, -n, n.m. heathen.
Heide, -n, n.f. heath.
Heidelbeere, -n, n.f. huckleberry.
heidnisch, adj. heathen.
heikel, adj. ticklish, tricky, delicate.
Heil, n.nt. welfare, safety, salvation.
heil, adj. whole; well, healed, unhurt.
Heiland, n.m. Savior.
Heilbad, ̈er, n.nt. spa.
heilbar, adj. curable.
Heilbutt, -e, n.m. halibut.
heilen, vb. heal, cure.
heilig, adj. holy, sacred.
Heilig, -, n.m.&f. saint.
heiligen, vb. hallow, sanctify.
Heiligenschein, -e, n.m. halo.
Heiligkeit, n.f. holiness, sanctity.
Heiligtum, ̈er, n.nt. sanctuary.
Heiligung, -en, n.f. sanctification, consecration.
Heilmittel, -, n.nt. remedy, cure.
Heilung, -en, n.f. healing, cure.
Heim, -e, n.nt. home.
heim, adv. home.
Heimat, n.f. home (town, country).
Heimatland, ̈er, n.nt. homeland.
heimatlich, adj. native.
heimatlos, adj. homeless.
Heimchen, -, n.nt. cricket.
heimisch, adj. domestic, homelike.
heimlich, adj. secret.
heim·suchen, vb. scourge.
Heimsuchung, -en, n.f. scourge.
heimtückisch, adj. malicious, treacherous.
heimwärts, adv. homeward.
Heimweh, n.nt. homesickness.
Heirat, -en, n.f. marriage.
heiraten, vb. marry.
Heiratsantrag, ̈e, n.m. proposal.
heiser, adj. hoarse.
heiß, adj. hot.
heissen*, vb. be called, be named; mean; call, order.
heiter, adj. cheerful; clear.
heizen, vb. heat, have the heat on.
Heizkörper, -, n.m. radiator.
Heizvorrichtung, -en, n.f. heater.
Hektar', -e, n.m. hectare.
hektisch, adj. hectic.

Hektogramm', -e, *n.nt.* hectogram.

Held, -en, -en, *n.m.* hero.

heldenhaft, *adj.* heroic.

Heldenmut, - *n.m.* heroism.

Heldin, -nen, *n.f.* heroine.

helfen*, *vb.* help, aid, assist.

Helfer, -, *n.m.* helper.

Helfershelfer, -, *n.m.* confederate, accomplice.

hell, *adj.* bright, light.

Helligkeit, *n.f.* brightness.

Helm, -e, *n.m.* helmet.

Hemd, -en, *n.nt.* shirt.

hemmen, *vb.* stop, hinder.

Hemmnis, -se, *n.nt.* hindrance, obstacle.

Hemmschuh, -e, *n.m.* brake, drag, skid.

Hemmung, -en, *n.f.* restraint, inhibition.

Henkel, -, *n.m.* handle.

Henna, *n.f.* henna.

Henne, -n, *n.f.* hen.

her, *adv.* towards here; ago.

herab', *adv.* downwards.

herab'hängen, *vb.* droop.

herab'lassen*, *vb.* let down; (**sich h.**) condescend.

herab'lassend, *adj.* condescending.

Herab'lassung, -en, *n.f.* condescension.

herab'setzen, *vb.* set down, lower, reduce, disparage.

Herab'setzung, -en, *n.f.* reduction, disparagement.

heran', *adv.* up to, toward.

heran'gehen*, *vb.* walk up to, approach.

heran'nahen, *vb.* approach, draw near.

heran'wachsen*, *vb.* grow up.

herauf', *adv.* upwards.

heraus', *adv.* out.

heraus'bringen*, *vb.* bring out, publish.

Heraus'forderer, -, *n.m.* challenger.

heraus'fordern, *vb.* challenge.

heraus'fordernd, *adj.* defiant.

Heraus'forderung, -en, *n.f.* challenge, defiance.

heraus'geben*, *vb.* edit, publish.

Heraus'geber, -, *n.m.* editor, publisher.

heraus'kommen*, *vb.* come out, be published.

heraus'lassen*, *vb.* let out.

heraus'putzen, *vb.* dress up.

heraus'stellen, *vb.* put out; (**sich h.**) turn out to be.

heraus'ziehen*, *vb.* extract.

herb, *adj.* tart, bitter.

herbei', *adv.* toward here.

herbei'schaffen, *vb.* procure.

Herberge, -n, *n.f.* hostel.

herbergen, *vb.* shelter, lodge.

Herbheit, -en, *n.f.* tartness.

Herbst, -e, *n.m.* fall, autumn.

herbstlich, *adj.* autumnal.

Herd, -e, *n.m.* kitchen stove; hearth.

Herde, -n, *n.f.* herd.

herein', *adv.* in; (**h.!**) come in!

Hergang, -e, *n.m.* course of events.

hergebracht, *adj.* customary.

hergelaufen, *adj.* of uncertain origin.

Hering, -e, *n.m.* herring.

Herkommen, -, *n.nt.* tradition; origin.

Herkömmlich, *adj.* traditional.

Herkunft, -e, *n.f.* origin, extraction.

her·leiten, *vb.* derive.

herme'tisch, *adj.* hermetic.

hernach', *adv.* afterwards.

hernie'der, *adv.* downwards, from above.

Herr, -n, -en, *n.m.* Mr., gentleman, lord, master.

Herrenbekleidung, *n.f.* menswear.

Herrenfriseur, -e, *n.m.* men's barber.

Herrenvolk, -er, *nt.* master race.

her·richten, *vb.* set up, arrange.

Herrin, -nen, *n.f.* mistress.

herrisch, *adj.* imperious.

herrlich, *adj.* wonderful, splendid.

Herrlichkeit, *n.f.* glory, magnificence.

Herrschaft, *n.f.* rule, reign; estate.

Herrschaften, *n.pl.* master and mistress of the house; people of high rank; (**meine H.**) ladies and gentlemen.

herrschen, *vb.* rule, reign.

herrschend, *adj.* ruling, prevailing.

Herrscher, -, *n.m.* ruler.

herrschsüchtig, *adj.* imperious, tyrannical.

her·sagen, *vb.* recite.

her·stellen, *vb.* make, manufacture.

Herstellung, -n, *n.f.* manufacture.

Hertz, *n.nt.* hertz.

herü'ber, *adv.* over (towards here).

herum', *adv.* around, about.

herum'kriegen, *vb.* talk over, win over.

herum'lungern, *vb.* loaf around.

herum'nörgeln, *vb.* nag.

herum'pfuschen, *vb.* tamper.

herum'schnüffeln, *vb.* pry, snoop.

herum'stehen*, *vb.* stand around, loiter.

herun'ter, *adv.* down.

herun'tergekommen, *adj.* rundown, down at the heels.

herun'ter·lassen*, *vb.* lower.

herun'ter·machen, *vb.* dress down, tear apart, pan.

hervor', *adv.* forth, forward.

hervor'brechen*, *vb.* erupt.

hervor'bringen*, *vb.* bring forth, produce.

hervor'heben*, *vb.* emphasize.

hervor'quellen*, *vb.* gush; ooze.

hervor'ragend, *adj.* prominent, outstanding, superb.

hervor'rufen*, *vb.* evoke; provoke.

hervor'schießen*, *vb.* spurt.

hervor'stehen*, *vb.* protrude.

Herz(en), -, *n.nt.* heart.

her·zeigen, *vb.* show.

herzen, *vb.* hug, cuddle.

herzhaft, *adj.* hearty.

herzig, *adj.* lovable, darling.

Herzinfarkt, -e, *n.m.* heart attack.

herzlich, *adj.* cordial, affectionate.

Herzlichkeit, *n.f.* cordiality.

herzlos, *adj.* heartless.

Herzog, -e, *n.m.* duke.

Herzogin, -nen, *n.f.* duchess.

Herzogtum, -er, *n.nt.* dukedom, duchy.

heterosexuell', *adj.* heterosexual.

Hetze, -n, *n.f.* rush; agitation, inflammatory talk; hassle.

hetzen, *vb.* rush; hound, agitate, rabble-rouse.

Hetzerei', -en, *n.f.* rush; demagoguery.

hetzerisch, *adj.* inflammatory, demagogic.

Hetzredner, -, *n.m.* rabble rouser, demagogue.

Heu, *n.nt.* hay.

Heuchelei', -en, *n.f.* hypocrisy.

heucheln, *vb.* fake, feign; play the hypocrite.

Heuchler, -, *n.m.* hypocrite.

heuchlerisch, *adj.* hypocritical.

heuer, *adv.* this year.

Heugabel, -n, *n.f.* pitchfork.

Heuhaufen, -, *n.m.* haystack.

heulen, *vb.* howl; cry.

heurig, *adj.* of this year.

Heuschnupfen, -, *n.m.* hay fever.

heute, *adv.* today; (**h. abend**) tonight.

heutig, *adj.* today's.

Heuwiese, -n, *n.f.* hayfield.

Hexe, -n, *n.f.* witch.

hexen, *vb.* perform witchcraft; be a magician.

Hexenschuß, *n.m.* lumbago.

Hieb, -e, *n.m.* blow, stroke.

hienie'den, *adv.* here below.

hier, *adv.* here.

hierar'chisch, *adj.* hierarchical.

hierbei, *adv.* hereby.

hierher, *adv.* hither.

hiermit, *adv.* hereby, herewith.

Hifi, *n.nt.* high fidelity.

Hilfe, -n, *n.f.* help, aid.

hilfeflehend, *adj.* imploring.

Hilfeleistung, -en, *n.f.* assistance, aid.

hilflos, *adj.* helpless, defenseless.

Hilflosigkeit, *n.f.* helplessness.

hilfreich, *adj.* helpful.

hilfsbedürftig, *adj.* needy.

hilfsbereit, *adj.* cooperative.

Hilfsquelle, -n, *n.f.* resource.

Himbeere, -n, *n.f.* raspberry.

Himmel, -, *n.m.* heaven, sky.

Himmelfahrt, -en, *n.f.* ascension to heaven; **(H. Christi)** Ascension (Day) (40 days after Easter); **(Mari'ä H.)** Assumption (of the Blessed Virgin) (August 15).

himmelhochjauchzend, *adj.* jubilant.

himmelschreiend, *adj.* scandalous.

Himmelsrichtung, -en, *n.f.* point of the compass, direction.

himmlisch, *adj.* heavenly.

hin, *adv.* to there; gone; **(h. und her)** back and forth; **(h. und wieder)** now and then.

hinab', *prep.* down.

hinaus', *adv.* out.

hinaus'zögern, *vb.* procrastinate.

Hinblick, *n.m.* aspect. **(in H. auf . . .)** with regard to . . .

hinderlich, *adj.* hindering, inconvenient.

hindern, *vb.* hinder, deter.

Hindernis, -se, *n.nt.* hindrance, obstacle.

hin·deuten, *vb.* point to.

hinein', *adv.* in.

Hingabe, *n.f.* fervency.

hin·geben*, *vb.* give away; up; **(sich h.)** devote oneself; surrender.

Hingebung, *n.f.* devotion.

hingestreckt, *adj.* prostrate.

hin·halten*, *vb. (fig.)* delay.

hinken, *vb.* limp.

hin·legen, *vb.* lay down; **(sich h.)** lie down.

hin·purzeln, *vb.* tumble.

hin·reißen*, *vb.* **(sich h. lassen)** let oneself be carried away.

hinreißend, *adj.* captivating, ravishing.

hin·richten, *vb.* execute.

Hinrichtung, -en, *n.f.* execution.

Hinsicht, -en, *n.f.* respect, regard.

hinsichtlich, *prep.* in regard to, regarding, concerning.

hinten, *adv.* behind.

hintenherum', *adv.* from behind; *(fig.)* roundabout, through the back door.

hinter, *prep.* behind, beyond.

hinter-, *adj.* hind, back.

Hintergedanke(n), -, *n.m.* ulterior motive.

hinterge'hen*, *vb.* doublecross.

Hintergrund, ¨e, *n.m.* background.

Hinterhalt, -e, *n.m.* ambush.

hinterher', *adv.* afterward(s).

Hinterland, -, *n.nt.* hinterland.

hinterle'gen, *vb.* deposit.

Hinterlist, *n.f.* insidiousness, underhanded act.

hinterlistig, *adj.* insidious, designing, underhanded.

Hintertreffen, *n.nt.* **(ins H. geraten)** fall behind.

Hintertür, -en, *n.f.* back door; *(fig.)* loophole.

hinterzie'hen*, *vb. (fig.)* defraud.

hinü'ber, *adv.* over, across.

hinun'ter, *adv.* down.

Hinweis, -e, *n.m.* reference; indication.

hin·weisen*, *vb.* point, refer, allude.

hinzu'fügen, *vb.* add.

Hirn, -e, *n.nt.* brain.

Hirsch, -e, *n.nt.* stag.

Hirschleder, -, *n.nt.* deerskin.

Hirt, -en, -en *(Biblical* **Hirte,** -n, -n), *n.m.* shepherd.

hissen, *vb.* hoist.

Histo'riker, -, *n.m.* historian.

histo'risch, *adj.* historic(al).

Hitze, *n.f.* heat.

hitzig, *adj.* heated, fiery, heady.

hitzköpfig, *adj.* hot-headed.

Hitzschlag, ¨e, *n.m.* heatstroke.

Hobel, -, *n.m.* plane.

hobeln, *vb.* plane.

hoch (hoh-, höher, höchst), **1.** *adj.* high, tall. **2.** *adv.* up.

Hochebene, -n, *n.f.* plateau.

hocherfreut, *adj.* elated.

hochgradig, *adj.* intense, extreme.

Hochmut, *n.m.* haughtiness, pride.

hochmütig, *adj.* haughty, arrogant.

hoch·schätzen, *vb.* treasure.

Hochschule, -n, *n.f.* university.

Hochsommer, -, *n.m.* midsummer.

höchst, *adv.* highly, extremely.

Hochstapler, -, *n.m.* swindler, impersonator.

höchstenfalls, *adv.* at best, the outside.

höchstens, *adv.* at best, at the outside.

Höchstgrenze, -n, *n.f.* top limit.

hochtrabend, *adj.* pompous, grandiloquent.

Hochverrat, *n.m.* high treason.

Hochzeit, -en, *n.f.* wedding.

Hochzeitsreise, -n, *n.f.* honeymoon.

hoch·ziehen*, *vb.* hoist.

hocken, *vb.* squat.

Hocker, -, *n.m.* stool.

Höcker, -, *n.m.* bump, hump.

Hockey, *n.nt.* hockey.

Hof, ¨e, *n.m.* court, courtyard; **(den H. machen)** court.

hoffen, *vb.* hope.

hoffentlich, *adv.* I hope.

Hoffnung, -en, *n.f.* hope.

hoffnungslos, *adj.* hopeless.

hoffnungsvoll, *adj.* hopeful.

höfisch, *adj.* courtly.

höflich, *adj.* polite, courteous, respectful, civil.

Höflichkeit, -en, *n.f.* courtesy.

Höhe, -n, *n.f.* height, altitude, elevation.

Hoheit, -en, *n.f.* Highness.

Höhepunkt, -e, *n.m.* high point, highlight, climax, culmination.

höher, *adj.* higher.

hohl, *adj.* hollow.

Höhle, -n, *n.f.* cave, den.

Hohlraum, ¨e, *n.m.* hollow space, vacuum.

Hohn, *n.m.* mockery, derision.

höhnisch, *adj.* derisive, mocking.

hohn·lächeln, *vb.* sneer, deride.

hold, *adj.* gracious, lovely.

holdselig, *adj.* gracious.

holen, *vb.* (go and) get, fetch.

Holland, *n.nt.* Holland.

Holländer, -, *n.m.* Dutchman.

holländisch, *adj.* Dutch.

Hölle, *n.f.* inferno, hell.

höllisch, *adj.* infernal, hellish.

Hologramm', -e, *n.nt.* hologram.

Holographie', *n.f.* holography.

holprig, *adj.* bumpy.

Holz, ¨er, *n.nt.* wood, lumber, timber.

hölzern, *adj.* wooden.

Holzklotz, ¨e, *n.m.* block (of wood); log.

Holzkohle, -n, *n.f.* charcoal.

Holzschnitt, -e, *n.m.* woodcut.

Honig, *n.m.* honey.

Honorar', -e, *n.nt.* honorarium.

honorie'ren, *vb.* honor; remunerate.

Hopfen, -, *n.m.* hop(s).

hopsen, *vb.* hop, skip.

hops·gehen*, *vb.* go down the drain, go west.

hörbar, *adj.* audible.

horchen, *vb.* listen to; eavesdrop.

Horde, -n, *n.f.* horde.

hören, *vb.* hear.

Hörensagen, *n.nt.* hearsay.

Hörer, -, *n.m.* (telephone) receiver; (student) auditor.

hörig, *adj.* submissive; subservient.

Horizont', -e, *n.m.* horizon.

horizontal', *adj.* horizontal.

Hormon', -e, *n.nt.* hormone.

Horn, ¨er, *n.nt.* horn.

hörnern, *adj.* horny.

Hornhaut, ¨e, *n.f.* callous skin; cornea.

hornig, *adj.* horny.

Hornis'se, -en, *n.f.* horoscope.

Horoskop', -e, *n.nt.* horoscope.

Hort, -e, *n.m.* hoard; refuge, retreat.

Hörweite, *n.f.* earshot.

Hose, -n, *n.f.* trousers, pants.

Hosenband, ¨er, *n.nt.* garter.

Hostie, *n.f.* host.

Hotel', -s, *n.nt.* hotel.

Hotel'boy, -s, *n.m.* bellboy.

Hovercraft, *n.nt.* hovercraft.

hübsch, *adj.* pretty, handsome.

Hubschrauber, -, *n.m.* helicopter.

Huf, -e, *n.nt.* hoof.

Hüfte, -n, *n.f.* hip.

Hügel, -, *n.m.* hill.

Huhn, ¨er, *n.nt.* chicken, fowl.

Hühnerauge, -n, *n.nt.* corn (on the foot).

huldigen, *vb.* do homage to.

Hülle, -n, *n.f.* covering, casing; **(in H. und Fülle)** abundantly, in profusion.

hüllen, *vb.* clothe, wrap, envelop.

Hülse, -n, *n.f.* hull, husk; case.

human', *adj.* humane.

Humanis'mus, *n.m.* humanism.

Humanist', -en, -en, *n.m.* humanist.

humanitär', *adj.* humanitarian.

Humanität', *n.f.* humanity.

Hummel, -n, *n.f.* bumblebee.

Hummer, -, *n.m.* lobster.

Humor', *n.m.* humor, wit.

Humorist', -en, -en, *n.m.* humorist.

humor'voll, *adj.* humorous.

humpeln, *vb.* starve.

Hund, -e, *n.m.* dog, hound.

hundert, *num.* a hundred.

Hundert, -e, *n.nt.* hundred.

Hundertjahr'feier, -n, *n.f.* centenary, centennial.

hundertjährig, *adj.* centennial.

hundertst -, *adj.* hundredth.

Hundertstel, -, *n.nt.* hundredth part; **(ein h.)** one one-hundredth.

Hundezwinger, -, *n.m.* kennel.

Hündin, -nen, *n.f.* bitch.

hünenhaft, *adj.* gigantic.

Hunger, *n.m.* hunger.

hungern, *vb.* starve.

Hungersnot, -̈e, *n.f.* famine.

Hungertod, *n.m.* starvation.

hungrig, *adj.* hungry.

Hupe, -n, *n.f.* auto horn.

hupen, *vb.* blow the horn.

hüpfen, *vb.* hop.

Hürde, -n, *n.f.* hurdle.

Hure, -n, *n.f.* whore.

husten, *vb.* cough.

Husten, -n, *n.m.* cough.

Hut, -̈e, *n.m.* hat.

Hut, *n.f.* care, protection; **(auf der H. sein*)** be on the alert.

hüten, *vb.* tend; **(sich h.)** beware, be careful not to do.

Hütte, -n, *n.f.* hut; shed, hovel; *(tech.)* foundry.

Hyazin'the, -n, *n.f.* hyacinth.

Hydrant', -en, -en, *n.m.* hydrant.

Hygie'ne, *n.f.* hygiene.

hygie'nisch, *adj.* hygienic, sanitary.

Hymne, -n, *n.f.* hymn, anthem.

Hypno'se, -n, *n.f.* hypnosis.

hypno'tisch, *adj.* hypnotic.

hypnotisie'ren, *vb.* hypnotize.

Hypothek', -en, *n.f.* mortgage.

Hypothe'se, -n, *n.f.* hypothesis.

hypothe'tisch, *adj.* hypothetical.

Hysterie', *n.f.* hysteria, hysterics.

hyste'risch, *adj.* hysterical.

I

ich, *pron.* I.

Ich, *n.nt.* ego.

ideal', *adj.* ideal.

Ideal', -e, *n.nt.* ideal.

idealisie'ren, *vb.* idealize.

Idealis'mus, *n.m.* idealism.

Idee', -e'en, *n.f.* idea, notion; **(fixe I.)** obsession.

identifizier'bar, *adj.* identifiable.

identifizie'ren, *vb.* identify.

iden'tisch, *adj.* identical.

Identität', -en, *n.f.* identity.

Idiot', -en, -en, *n.m.* idiot.

idio'tisch, *adj.* idiotic.

Idyll', -e, *n.nt.* idyl.

idyl'lisch, *adj.* idyllic.

ignorie'ren, *vb.* ignore.

illuminie'ren, *vb.* illuminate.

illuso'risch, *adj.* illusive, illusory.

Illustration', -en, *n.f.* illustration.

illustrie'ren, *vb.* illustrate.

imaginär', *adj.* imaginary.

Imam, -e, *n.m.* imam.

Imbiß, -sse, *n.m.* snack.

Imita'tor, -o'ren, *n.m.* impersonator.

imitie'ren, *vb.* imitate.

immatrikulie'ren, *vb.* **(sich i.)** register in a university.

immer, *adv.* always.

immergrün, *adj.* evergreen.

immerhin', *adv.* after all, anyway.

Immobi'lien, *n.pl. real* estate.

immun', *adj.* immune.

Immunität', -en, *n.f.* immunity.

Imperfekt, -e, *n.nt.* imperfect tense.

Imperialis'mus, *n.m.* imperialism.

imperialis'tisch, *adj.* imperialist.

impfen, *vb.* vaccinate.

Impfstoff, -e, *n.m.* vaccine.

Impfung, -en, *n.f.* vaccination.

impli'cite, *adv.* by implication.

implizie'ren, *vb.* imply, implicate.

Import', -e, *n.m.* import.

importie'ren, *vb.* import.

imposant', *adj.* imposing.

impotent', *adj.* impotent.

Impotenz', *n.f.* impotence.

imprägnie'ren, *vb.* waterproof.

Impresa'rio, -s, *n.m.* impresario.

improvisie'ren, *vb.* improvise.

Impuls', -e, *n.m.* impulse.

impulsiv', *adj.* impulsive.

Impulsivität', *n.f.* spontaneity.

imstan'de, *adj.* able, capable.

in, *prep.* in, into.

Inbegriff, -e, *n.m.* essence, embodiment.

inbegriffen, *adj.* included; implicit.

Inbrunst, *n.f.* ardor, fervor.

inbrünstig, *adj.* zealous, ardent.

Inder, -, *n.m.* Indian.

Index, -e *or* **-dizes,** *n.m.* index.

India'ner, -, *n.m.* (American) Indian.

india'nisch, *adj.* (American) Indian.

Indien, *n.nt.* India.

Indikativ, -e, *n.m.* indicative.

Indika'tor, -o'ren, *n.m.* indicator.

indirekt, *adj.* indirect.

indisch, *adj.* Indian.

indiskret, *adj.* indiscreet.

Individualität', -en, *n.f.* individuality.

individuell', *adj.* individual.

Indivi'duum, -duen, *n.nt.* individual.

Indone'sien, *n.nt.* Indonesia.

Induktion', -en, *n.f.* induction.

induktiv', *adj.* inductive.

Industrie', -i'en, *n.f.* industry.

industriell', *adj.* industrial.

Industriell'e, -n, -n, *n.m.* industrialist.

induzie'ren, *vb.* induce.

infam', *adj.* infamous; beastly.

Infanterie, -n, *n.f.* infantry.

Infanterist, -en, -en, *n.m.* infantryman.

infiltrie'ren, *vb.* infiltrate.

Infinitiv, -e, *n.m.* infinitive.

infizie'ren, *vb.* infect.

Inflation', -en, *n.f.* inflation.

infolgedes'sen, *adv.* consequently.

informie'ren, *vb.* inform.

Ingenieur', -e, *n.m.* engineer.

Ingwer, *n.m.* ginger.

Inhaber, -, *n.m.* proprietor; (of an apartment) occupant.

Inhalt, *n.m.* content, volume, capacity.

Inhaltsangabe, -n, *n.f.* table of contents.

inhaltschwer, *adj.* momentous, weighty.

Inhaltsverzeichnis, -se, *n.nt.* table of contents, index.

Initiati've, -n, *n.f.* initiative.

inkog'nito, *adv.* incognito.

Inland, -e, *n.nt.* homeland; **(im In- und Ausland)** at home and abroad.

inländisch, *adj.* domestic.

inmit'ten, *prep.* amid, in the midst of.

innen, *adv.* inside.

Innen-, *cpds.* interior, inner; domestic.

Innenpolitik, *n.f.* domestic policy.

Innenseite, -n, *n.f.* inside.

inner-, *adj.* inner, interior, internal.

Inner-, *n.nt.* interior, inside; soul.

innerhalb, *prep.* within.

innerlich, *adj.* inward, intrinsic.

innerst-, *adj.* innermost.

innig, *adj.* intimate; fervent.

Innigkeit, *n.f.* fervor.

Innung, -en, *n.f.* guild.

Input, -s, *n.m.* input.

Insasse, -n, -n, *n.m.* occupant; inmate.

insbeson'dere, *adv.* especially.

Inschrift, -en, *n.f.* inscription.

Insekt', -en, *n.nt.* insect.

Insek'tenpulver, -, *n.nt.* insecticide.

Insel, -n, *n.f.* island.

Inserat', -e, *n.nt.* advertisement.

Inserent', -en, -en, *n.m.* advertiser.

insgeheim', *adv.* secretly.

insgesamt', *adv.* altogether.

Insig'nien, *n.pl.* insignia.

insofern', insoweit, *adv.* to that extent, to this extent.

insofern', insoweit, *conj.* insofar as, to the extent that.

Inspek'tor, -o'ren, *n.m.* inspector.

inspizie'ren, *vb.* inspect.

Installation', -en, *n.f.* installation.

instand-'halten*, *vb.* keep up, keep in good repair.

Instand'haltung, *n.f.* maintenance.

instän'dig, *adj.* earnest.

instand' setzen, *vb.* repair, recondition; enable.

Instanz', -en, *n.f.* instance.

Instan'zenweg, -e, *n.m.* stages of appeal, channels.

Instinkt', -e, *n.m.* instinct.

instinktiv', *adj.* instinctive.

Institut', -e, *n.nt.* institute, institution.

Instrument', -e, *n.nt.* instrument.

Insulin', *n.nt.* insulin.

inszenie'ren, *vb.* stage.

Inszenie'rung, -en, *n.f.* scenario.

intakt', *adj.* intact.

integrie'ren, *vb.* integrate.

Intellekt', *n.m.* intellect.

intellektuell', *adj.* intellectual.

Intellektuell'-, *n.m. & f.* intellectual, highbrow, egghead.

intelligent', *adj.* intelligent.

Intelligenz', *n.f.* intelligence.

intensiv', *adj.* intense, intensive.

interessant', *adj.* interesting.

Interes'se, -n, *n.nt.* interest, concern.

interessie'ren, *vb.* interest.

Interjektion', -en, *n.f.* interjection.

international', *adj.* international.

internie'ren, *vb.* intern.

Internist', -en, -en, *n.m.* specialist for internal medicine.

interpretie'ren, *vb.* interpret.

interpunktie'ren, *vb.* punctuate.

Interpunktion', *n.f.* punctuation.

Interview', -s, *n.nt.* interview.

interview'en, *vb.* interview.

intim', *adj.* intimate.

Intoleranz', *n.f.* intolerance.

intransitiv', *adj.* intransitive.

intravenös', *adj.* intravenous.

Intri'ge, -n, *n.f.* intrigue.

intrigie'ren, *vb.* plot, scheme.

Intuition', -en, *n.f.* intuition.

intuitiv', *adj.* intuitive.

Invali'de, -n, -n, *n.m.* invalid.

Invasion', -en, *n.f.* invasion.

Inventar', -e, *n.nt.* inventory.

Inventur', -en, *n.f.* inventory.

investie'ren, *vb.* invest.

inwendig, *adj.* inward, inner.

inzwi'schen, *adv.* in the meantime.

Irak', *n.nt.* Iraq.

Iran', *n.nt.* Iran.

irdisch, *adj.* earthly.

Ire, -n, -n, *n.m.* Irishman.

irgendein, -, -e *adj.* any (at all), any old.

irgendeiner, -e, *pron.* anyone, anybody.

irgendetwas, *pron.* something or other, anything at all.

irgendjemand, *pron.* somebody or other.

irgendwann', *adv.* sometime.

irgendwelcher, -es, -e, *adj.* any.

irgendwie', *adv.* somehow.

irgendwo', *adv.* somewhere, anywhere.

irgendwohin', *adv.* (to) somewhere, anywhere.

irisch, *adj.* Irish.

Irland, *n.nt.* Ireland.

Irländer, -, *n.m.* Irishman.

Ironie', *n.f.* irony.

iro'nisch, *adj.* ironical.

irre, *adj.* astray, wrong; wandering, lost; insane.

irre-führen, *vb.* mislead.

irreführend, *adj.* misleading.

irren, *vb.* err, go astray; (sich i.) err, be mistaken.

irrig, *adj.* mistaken.

irritie'ren, *vb.* irritate, annoy.

Irrsinn, *n.m.* nonsense, lunacy.

irrsinnig, *adj.* lunatic.

Irrtum, -er, *n.m.* error.

irrtümlich, *adj.* erroneous.

Isolationist', -en, -en, *n.m.* isolationist.

Isola'tor, -o'ren, *n.m.* insulator.

isolie'ren, *vb.* isolate; insulate.

Isolie'rung, -en, *n.f.* isolation; insulation.

Israel, *n.nt.* Israel.

Israe'li, -s, *n.m.* Israeli.

israe'lisch, *adj.* Israeli.

Israelit', -en, -en, *n.m.* Israelite.

Ita'lien, *n.nt.* Italy.

Italie'ner, -, *n.m.* Italian.

italie'nisch, *adj.* Italian.

J

ja, 1. *interj.* yes. **2.** *adv.* as is well known, to be sure.

Jacht, -en, *n.f.* yacht.

Jacke, -n, *n.f.* jacket.

Jade, *n.m.* jade.

Jagd, -en, *n.f.* hunt; chase, pursuit.

jagen, *vb.* hunt; chase.

Jäger, -, *n.m.* hunter.

jäh, *adj.* sudden.

Jahr, -e, *n.nt.* year.

jahraus', jahrein', *adv.* year in, year out.

Jahrbuch, -er, *n.nt.* yearbook, almanac, annual; *(pl.)* annals.

Jahrestag, -e, *n.m.* anniversary.

Jahreszeit, -en, *n.f.* season.

Jahrgang, -e, *n.m.* (school) class; (wine) vintage.

Jahrhun'dert, -e, *n.nt.* century.

jährlich, *adj.* yearly, annual.

Jahrmarkt, -e, *n.m.* fair.

Jahrzehnt', -e, *n.nt.* decade.

Jähzorn, *n.m.* quick temper.

jähzornig, *adj.* quick-tempered.

Jammer, *n.m.* misery.

jämmerlich, *adj.* miserable; dismal.

Januar, -e, *n.m.* January.

Japan, *n.nt.* Japan.

Japa'ner, -, *n.m.* Japanese.

japa'nisch, *adj.* Japanese.

Jargon', -s, *n.m.* jargon, slang.

jäten, *vb.* weed.

jauchzen, *vb.* jubilate, cheer.

jawohl', *interj.* yes, sir.

Jazz, *n.m.* jazz.

je, *adv.* ever; apiece, each; (j. nach) in each case according to; (j. nachdem') according to whether, as the case may be; (je mehr, je [desto, umso] besser) the more the better.

Jeans, *n.pl.* jeans.

Jeansstoff, -e, *n.m.* denim.

jeder, -es, -e, *pron. & adj.* each, every.

jedoch', *conj.* yet; nevertheless.

jemals, *adv.* ever.

jemand, *pron.* someone, somebody; anyone, anybody.

jener, -es, -e, *pron & adj.* that, yonder; the former.

jenseits, *adv. & prep.* beyond, on the other side.

Jenseits, *n.nt.* beyond, life after death.

Jeru'salem, *n.nt.* Jerusalem.

Jesuit', -en, -en, *n.m.* Jesuit.

jetzig, *adj.* present.

jetzt, *adv.* now.

jeweilig, *adj.* in question, under consideration.

Joch, -e, *n.nt.* yoke.

Jockei, -s, *n.m.* jockey.

Jod, *n.nt.* iodine.

jodeln, *vb.* yodel.

Joghurt', *n.m. or nt.* yogurt.

johlen, *vb.* howl.

Joker, -, *n.m.* joker.

jonglie'ren, *vb.* juggle.

Jota, -s, *n.nt.* iota.

Journalist', -en, -en, *n.m.* journalist.

Jubel, *n.m.* jubilation, rejoicing.

jubeln, *vb.* shout with joy, rejoice.

Jubiläum, -en, *n.nt.* jubilee.

jucken, *vb.* itch.

Jude, -n, -n, *n.m.* Jew.

Judentum, *n.nt.* Judaism, Jewry.

Judenverfolgung, -en, *n.f.* pogrom.

jüdisch, *adj.* Jewish.

Jugend, *n.f.* youth.

jugendlich, *adj.* youthful; adolescent, juvenile.

Jugendverbrecher, -, *n.m.* juvenile delinquent.

Jugendzeit, -en, *n.f.* youth, adolescence.

Jugoslawe, -n, -n, *n.m.* Yugoslav.

Jugoslawien, *n.nt.* Yugoslavia.

jugoslawisch, *adj.* Yugoslavian.

Juli, *n.m.* July.

jung (-), *adj.* young.

Jung-, *n.nt.* young (of an animal).

Junge, -n, -n, *n.m.* boy.

jungenhaft, *adj.* boyish.

Jünger, -, *n.m.* disciple.

Jungfer, -n, *n.f.* (**alte J.**) old maid, spinster.

Jungfrau, -en, *n.f.* virgin.

Junggeselle, -n, -n, *n.m.* bachelor.

Jüngling, -e, *n.m.* young man.

Juni, *n.m.* June.

Junker, -, *n.m.* aristocratic landowner (especially in Prussia).

Jurist, -en, -en, *n.m.* jurist; law student.

juristisch, *adj.* juridical, legal.

Justiz, *n.f.* justice.

Juwel, -en, *n.nt.* jewel.

Juwelier, -e, *n.m.* jeweler.

Jux, *n.m.* fun.

K

Kabarett, -e, *n.nt.* cabaret.

Kabel, -, *n.nt.* cable; cablegram.

Kabeljau, -e, *n.m.* cod.

kabeln, *vb.* cable.

Kabine, -n, *n.f.* cabin, stateroom.

Kabinett, -e, *n.nt.* cabinet.

Kabriolett, -s, *n.nt.* convertible.

Kachel, -n, *n.f.* tile.

Kadaver, -, *n.m.* carcass.

Kadett, -en, -en, *n.m.* cadet.

Käfer, -, *n.m.* beetle, bug.

Kaffee, *n.m.* coffee.

Kaffein, *n.nt.* caffeine.

Käfig, -e, *n.m.* cage.

kahl, *adj.* bald; bare.

Kahn, ⁓e, *n.m.* boat, barge.

Kaiser, -, *n.m.* emperor.

Kajüte, -n, *n.f.* cabin (on a boat).

Kakao, -s, *n.m.* cocoa.

Kalb, ⁓er, *n.nt.* calf.

Kalbfleisch, *n.nt.* veal.

Kalbleder, -, *n.nt.* calfskin.

Kalender, -, *n.m.* calendar.

Kali, *n.nt.* potash, potassium.

Kaliber, -, *n.nt.* caliber.

Kalium, *n.nt.* potassium.

Kalk, *n.m.* lime, chalk, calcium.

Kalkstein, *n.m.* limestone.

Kalorie, -ien, *n.f.* calorie.

kalt (⁓), *adj.* cold.

kaltblütig, *adj.* cold-blooded.

Kälte, -n, *n.f.* cold(ness).

Kalvarienberg, *n.m.* Calvary.

Kalzium, *n.nt.* calcium.

Kamee, -n, *n.f.* cameo.

Kamel, -e, *n.nt.* camel.

Kamera, -s, *n.f.* camera.

Kamerad, -en, -en, *n.m.* comrade.

Kameradschaft, -en, *n.f.* comradeship, camaraderie.

Kamille, -n, *n.f.* camomile.

Kamin, -e, *n.m.* fireplace, hearth; fireside.

Kamm, ⁓e, *n.m.* comb; (mountain) crest.

kämmen, *vb.* comb.

Kammer, -n, *n.f.* room; chamber.

Kammermusik, *n.f.* chamber music.

Kampagne, -n, *n.f.* campaign.

Kampf, ⁓e, *n.m.* fight, fighting, combat.

kämpfen, *vb.* fight.

Kampfer, *n.m.* camphor.

Kämpfer, -, *n.m.* fighter, combatant; champion.

kampfunfähig, *adj.* disabled.

Kanada, *n.nt.* Canada.

Kanadier, -, *n.m.* Canadian.

kanadisch, *adj.* Canadian.

Kanal, ⁓e, *n.m.* canal, channel; duct.

Kanalisation, *n.f.* canalization; sewer.

kanalisieren, *vb.* canalize; drain by sewer.

Kanarienvogel, ⁓, *n.m.* canary.

Kandare, -n, *n.f.* curb (of a horse); (**an die K. nehmen**) take a person in hand.

Kandidat, -en, -en, *n.m.* candidate, nominee.

Kandidatur, -en, *n.f.* candidacy, nomination.

kandiert, *adj.* candied.

Känguruh, -s, *n.nt.* kangaroo.

Kaninchen, -, *n.nt.* rabbit, bunny.

Kanne, -n, *n.f.* can, jug, pitcher.

Kannibale, -n, -n, *n.m.* cannibal.

Kanon, -s, *n.m.* canon.

Kanonade, -n, *n.f.* cannonade.

Kanone, -n, *n.f.* cannon.

Kanonenboot, -e, *n.nt.* gunboat.

Kanonier, -e, *n.m.* cannoneer.

kanonisch, *adj.* canonical.

kanonisieren, *vb.* cannonize.

Kantate, -n, *n.f.* cantata.

Kante, -n, *n.f.* edge, border.

Kantine, -n, *n.f.* canteen.

Kanu, -s, *n.nt.* canoe.

Kanzel, -n, *n.f.* pulpit.

Kanzlei, -en, *n.f.* chancellery.

Kanzler, -, *n.m.* chancellor.

Kap, -s, *n.nt.* cape.

Kapaun, -e, *n.m.* capon.

Kapelle, -n, *n.f.* chapel; orchestra, band.

Kapellmeister, -, *n.m.* conductor, bandmaster.

kapern, *vb.* capture.

kapieren, *vb.* understand.

kapital, *adj.* capital.

Kapital, -ien, *n.nt.* capital.

kapitalisieren, *vb.* capitalize.

Kapitalismus, *n.m.* capitalism.

kapitalistisch, *adj.* capitalistic.

Kapitän, -e, *n.m.* captain.

Kapitel, -, *n.nt.* chapter.

kapitulieren, *vb.* capitulate.

Kappe, -n, *n.f.* cap, hood.

Kapsel, -n, *n.f.* capsule.

kaputt, *adj.* broken, busted; (**k. machen**) bust, wreck.

Kapuze, -n, *n.f.* hood.

Karabiner, -, *n.m.* carbine.

Karaffe, -n, *n.f.* decanter, carafe.

Karamel, *n.nt.* caramel.

Karate, *n.nt.* karate.

Karawane, -n, *n.f.* caravan.

Karbid, *n.nt.* carbide.

Karbunkel, -, *n.m.* carbuncle.

Kardinal, ⁓e, *n.m.* cardinal.

Karfreitag, *n.m.* Good Friday.

Karies, *n.f.* caries.

Karikatur, -en, *n.f.* caricature; cartoon.

karikieren, *vb.* caricature.

karminrot (⁓), *adj.* crimson.

Karneval, -s, *n.m.* carnival.

Karo, -n, *n.nt.* (cards) diamond(s).

Karpfen, -, *n.m.* carp.

Karre, -n, *n.f.* cart.

Karree, -s, *n.nt.* square.

Karren, -, *n.m.* cart.

Karriere, -n, *n.f.* career; (**K. machen**) be successful, get far in one's profession.

Karte, -n, *n.f.* card; chart, map.

Kartei, -en, *n.f.* card index, file.

Kartell, -e, *n.nt.* cartel.

Kartenspiel, -e, *n.nt.* card game; deck of cards.

Kartoffel, -n, *n.f.* potato.

Karton, -s, *n.m.* carton.

Karussell, -s, *n.nt.* merry-go-round.

Karwoche, *n.f.* Holy Week.

Kaschmir, -e, *n.m.* cashmere.

Käse, *n.m.* cheese.

Kaserne, -n, *n.f.* barracks.

Kasino, -s, *n.nt.* casino.

Kasse, -n, *n.f.* cash box; cash register; box-office; (**bei K. sein***) be flush; (**an der K. bezahlen**) pay the cashier.

Kassenzettel, -, *n.m.* sales slip.

Kassette, -n, *n.f.* cassette.

kassieren, *vb.* collect (money due); dismiss.

Kassierer, -, *n.m.* teller, cashier.

Kaste, -n, *n.f.* caste.

kastei'en, vb. chastise, mortify.
Kasten, ", n.m. box, case.
Katalog', -e, n.m. catalogue.
Katapult', -e, n.m. catapult.
Katarrh', -e, n.m. catarrh.
Katas'ter, -, n.nt. register.
katastrophal', adj. disastrous, ruinous.
Katechis'mus, -men, n.m. catechism.
Kategorie', -i'en, n.f. category.
katego'risch, adj. categorical.
Kater, -, n.m. tomcat; hangover.
Kathedra'le, -n, n.f. cathedral.
Katho'de, -n, n.f. cathode.
Katholik', -en, -en, n.m. Catholic.
katho'lisch, adj. Catholic.
Katholizis'mus, -men, n.m. Catholicism.
Kattun', -e, n.m. gingham, calico.
Kätzchen, -, n.nt. kitten.
Katze, -n, n.f. cat.
katzenartig, adj. feline.
Katzenjammer, n.m. hangover.
kauen, vb. chew.
kauern, vb. crouch, cower.
Kauf, "e, n.m. purchase.
kaufen, vb. purchase, buy.
Käufer, -, n.m. buyer.
Kaufkontrakt, -e, n.m. bill of sale.
Kaufmann, -leute, n.m. businessman, merchant.
kaufmännisch, adj. commercial.
Kaugummi, -s, n.nt. chewing gum.
kaum, adv. scarcely, hardly, barely.
Kausalität', -en, n.f. causation.
Kaution', -en, n.f. surety; security; bail.
Kavalier', -e, n.m. cavalier.
Kavallerie, -n, n.f. cavalry.
Kaviar, n.m. caviar.
keck, adj. saucy.
Kegel, -, n.m. cone.
kegelförmig, adj. conic.
kegeln, vb. bowl.
Kehle, -n, n.f. throat.
Kehlkopfentzündung, -en, n.f. laryngitis.
kehren, vb. turn; brush, sweep.
Kehricht, n.m. sweepings; garbage.
Kehrseite, -n, n.f. reverse side; other side of the picture.
kehrt-machen, vb. turn around, about-face.
Kehrtwendung, n.f. about face.
keifen, vb. nag, scold.
Keil, -e, n.m. wedge.
Keilerie', -en, n.f. fracas, brawl.
Keim, -e, n.m. germ, bud.
keimen, vb. germinate.
keimfrei, adj. germ free, sterile.
keimtötend, adj. germicidal.
kein, -, -e, adj. not a, not any, no.

keiner, -es, -e, pron. no one, not any, none.
keinerlei, adj. not of any sort.
keineswegs, adv. by no means.
Keks, -e, n.m. biscuit, cookie.
Kelch, -e, n.m. cup, goblet, chalice; calyx.
Kelchglas, "er, n.nt. goblet.
Kelle, -n, n.f. ladle, scoop.
Keller, -, n.m. cellar.
Kellner, -, n.m. waiter.
Kellnerin, -nen, n.f. waitress.
kennen*, vb. know, be acquainted with.
kennen-lernen, vb. meet, become acquainted with.
Kenner, -, n.m. connoisseur.
Kennkarte, -n, n.f. identity card.
kenntlich, adj. recognizable.
Kenntnis, -se, n.f. knowledge, notice.
Kennzeichen, -, n.nt. sign, distinguishing mark, feature.
kennzeichnen, vb. mark, stamp, distinguish, characterize.
kentern, vb. capsize.
Kera'mik, -en, n.f. ceramics.
kera'misch, adj. ceramic.
Kerbe, -n, n.f. notch.
kerben, vb. notch.
Kerker, -, n.m. jail, prison.
Kerl, -e, n.m. fellow, guy.
Kern, -e, n.m. kernel, pit, core; nucleus; gist.
Kernenergie, n.f. nuclear energy.
Kerngehäuse, -, n.nt. core.
Kernhaus, "er, n.nt. core.
Kernphysik, n.f. nuclear physics.
Kernspaltung, -en, n.f. nuclear fission.
Kerosin', n.nt. kerosene.
Kerze, -n, n.f. candle.
Kessel, -, n.m. kettle, boiler.
Kette, -n, n.f. chain.
ketten, vb. chain, link.
Kettenreaktion, -en, n.f. chain reaction.
Ketzer, -, n.m. heretic.
Ketzerei', n.f. heresy.
keuchen, vb. gasp.
Keuchhusten, n.m. whooping-cough.
Keule, -n, n.f. club, cudgel; (meat) leg, joint.
keusch, adj. chaste.
Keuschheit, n.f. chastity.
kichern, vb. giggle.
Kiefer, -, n.m. jaw.
Kiefer, -n, n.f. pine.
Kiel, -e, n.m. keel.
Kielwasser, n.nt. wake.
Kieme, -n, n.f. gill.
Kiepe, -n, n.f. basket (carried on the back).
Kies, -e, n.m. gravel.
Kilo, -, n.nt. kilogram.
Kilohertz, n.nt. kilohertz.
Kilome'ter, n.m. or nt. kilometer.
Kilowatt', -, n.nt. kilowatt.
Kind, -er, n.nt. child.

Kinderarzt, "e, n.m. pediatrician.
Kinderbett, -en, n.nt. crib.
Kindergarten, ", n.m. kindergarten.
Kinderlähmung, -en, n.f. infantile paralysis, polio.
kinderlos, adj. childless.
Kinderraub, n.m. kidnapping.
Kinderräuber, -, n.m. kidnapper.
Kindersportwagen, -, n.m. stroller.
Kinderwagen, -, n.m. baby carriage.
Kinderzimmer, -, n.nt. nursery.
Kindheit, -en, n.f. childhood.
kindisch, adj. childish.
kindlich, adj. childlike.
Kinn, -e, n.nt. chin.
Kino, -s, n.nt. movie theater.
Kiosk', -e, n.m. kiosk, newsstand.
kippen, vb. tip, tilt.
Kirche, -n, n.f. church.
Kirchenlied, -er, n.nt. hymn.
Kirchenschiff, -e, n.nt. nave.
Kirchenstuhl, "e, n.m. pew.
Kirchhof, "e, n.m. churchyard.
kirchlich, adj. ecclesiastical.
Kirchspiel, -e, n.nt. parish.
Kirchturm, "e, n.m. steeple.
Kirsche, -n, n.f. cherry.
Kissen, -e, n.nt. cushion, pillow.
Kissenbezug, "e, n.m. pillowcase.
Kiste, -n, n.f. crate, chest.
Kitsch, n.m. trash.
Kittel, -, n.m. smock.
kitzeln, vb. tickle.
kitzlig, adj. ticklish.
klaffen, vb. gape, yawn.
Klage, -n, n.f. complaint; suit.
Kläger, -, n.m. plaintiff.
kläglich, adj. miserable.
Klammer, -n, n.f. clamp, clasp; parenthesis.
Klamot'ten, n.pl. duds, rags, stuff.
Klampe, -n, n.f. cleat.
Klang, "e, n.m. sound, ring(-ing).
Klappbett, -en, n.nt. folding bed.
Klappe, -n, n.f. flap, lid, valve.
klappen, vb. flap, fold; come out right.
klappern, vb. clatter, chatter, rattle.
Klaps, -e, n.m. slap.
klar, adj. clear.
klären, vb. clear.
Klarheit, -en, n.f. clarity.
Klarinet'te, -n, n.f. clarinet.
klar-legen, vb. clarify.
klar-stellen, vb. clarify.
Klasse, -n, n.f. class.
Klassenkamerad, -en, -en, n.m. classmate.
Klassenzimmer, -, n.nt. classroom.
klassifizie'ren, vb. classify.
Klassifizie'rung, -en, n.f. classification.

klassisch, *adj.* classic(al).
Klatsch, *n.m.* gossip.
klatschen, *vb.* clap; gossip.
Klaue, -n, *n.f.* claw.
klauen, *vb.* snitch.
Klausel, -n, *n.f.* clause, proviso.
Klavier', -e, *n.nt.* piano.
Klebemittel, -, *n.nt.* glue, adhesive.
kleben, *vb.* paste; stick.
Klebgummi, *n.m.* mucilage.
klebrig, *adj.* sticky.
Klebstoff, -e, *n.m.* paste.
kleckern, *vb.* spill, make a spot.
Klecks, -e, *n.m.* spot, stain.
Klee, *n.m.* clover.
Kleid, -er, *n.nt.* dress; *(pl.)* clothes.
kleiden, *vb.* clothe, dress.
Kleiderbügel, -, *n.m.* hanger.
Kleiderhändler, -, *n.m.* clothier.
Kleiderschrank, *:e*, *n.m.* clothes closet, wardrobe.
kleidsam, *adj.* becoming.
Kleidung, -en, *n.f.* clothing.
Kleidungsstück, -e, *n.nt.* garment.
klein, *adj.* little, small.
Kleingeld, -er, *n.nt.* change.
Kleinheit, -en, *n.f.* smallness.
Kleinigkeit, -en, *n.f.* trifle.
kleinlaut, *adj.* meek, subdued.
kleinlich, *adj.* petty.
Kleinod, -ien, *n.nt.* jewel, gem.
Kleister, -, *n.m.* paste.
Klemme, -n, *n.f.* clamp; dilemma, jam, tight spot.
klemmen, *vb.* pinch, jam.
Klempner, -, *n.m.* plumber.
Klepper, -, *n.m.* hack.
klerikal', *adj.* clerical.
Kleriker, -, *n.m.* clergyman.
Klerus, *n.m.* clergy.
klettern, *vb.* climb.
Klient', -en, -en, *n.m.* client.
Klima, -a'te, *n.nt.* climate.
Klimaanlage, -n, *n.f.* air conditioning (system).
klima'tisch, *adj.* climatic.
klimatisie'ren, *vb.* air-condition.
klimmen*, *vb.* climb.
Klinge, -n, *n.f.* blade.
Klingel, -n, *n.f.* (small) bell; buzzer.
klingeln, *vb.* ring.
klingen*, *vb.* ring, sound.
Klinik, -en, *n.f.* clinic, hospital.
klinisch, *adj.* clinical.
Klippe, -n, *n.f.* cliff, crag.
Klistier', -e, *n.nt.* enema.
Klo, -s, *n.nt.* (short for Klosett') bathroom, toilet.
Kloa'ke, -n, *n.f.* sewer, drain.
klobig, *adj.* clumsy.
klopfen, *vb.* knock, beat.
Klops, -e, *n.m.* meatball.
Klosett', -e, *n.nt.* water closet.
Kloß, *:e*, *n.m.* clump; dumpling.
Kloster, *::*, *n.nt.* monastery, nunnery.

Klosterbruder, *::*, *n.m.* friar.
Klostergang, *:e*, *n.m.* cloister(s).
Klotz, *:e*, *n.m.* block.
Klub, -s, *n.m.* club (social).
Kluft, *:e*, *n.f.* gap, cleft, fissure.
klug(-), *adj.* clever.
Klugheit, -en, *n.f.* cleverness.
Klumpen, -, *n.m.* lump.
klumpig, *adj.* lumpy.
knabbern, *vb.* nibble.
Knabe, -n, -n, *n.m.* lad, youth.
knacken, *vb.* click.
Knall, -e, *n.m.* bang, crack, pop.
knallen, *vb.* bang, pop.
knapp, *adj.* scarce, scant, tight, terse.
Knappheit, -en, *n.f.* scarcity, shortage, terseness.
knarren, *vb.* creak, rattle.
Knäuel, -, *n.m.* or *nt.* clew, ball; throng, crowd.
knauserig, *adj.* niggardly.
Knebel, -, *n.m.* cudgel; gag.
knebeln, *vb.* bind, gag.
Knecht, -e, *n.m.* servant, farm hand.
Knechtschaft, -en, *n.f.* bondage, servitude.
kneifen*, *vb.* pinch.
Kneifzange, -n, *n.f.* pliers.
Kneipe, -n, *n.f.* tavern, pub, joint.
kneten, *vb.* knead.
Knick, -e, *n.m.* bend, crack.
knicken, *vb.* bend, fold, crack.
Knicks, -e, *n.m.* curtsy.
Knie, -i'e, *n.nt.* knee.
kni'en, *vb.* kneel.
Kniff, -e, *n.m.* pinch; trick.
knifflig, *adj.* tricky.
knipsen, *vb.* snap, punch (ticket), take a snapshot, snap one's fingers.
knirschen, *vb.* grate, crunch; gnash (teeth).
knistern, *vb.* crackle.
knittern, *vb.* wrinkle.
Knöchel, -, *n.m.* knuckle.
Knochen, -, *n.m.* bone.
knochenlos, *adj.* boneless.
knochig, *adj.* bony.
Knödel, -, *n.m.* dumpling.
Knopf, *:e*, *n.m.* button.
Knopfloch, *:er*, *n.nt.* buttonhole.
Knorpel, -, *n.m.* cartilage.
Knorren, -, *n.m.* knot, gnarl.
knorrig, *adj.* knotty, gnarled.
Knospe, -n, *n.f.* bud.
knospen, *vb.* bud.
Knoten, -, *n.m.* knot.
knoten, *vb.* knot.
Knotenpunkt, -e, *n.m.* junction.
knüpfen, *vb.* tie, knot.
Knüppel, -, *n.m.* cudgel, club.
knurren, *vb.* growl.
knusp(e)rig, *adj.* crisp, crusty.
Kobalt, *n.m.* cobalt.
Koch, *:e*, *n.m.* cook.
Kochbuch, *:er*, *n.nt.* cookbook.
kochen, *vb.* cook, boil.
Köchin, -nen, *n.f.* cook.

Kode, -s, *n.m.* code.
Kodein', *n.nt.* codein.
ködern, *vb.* decoy.
Kodex, -dizes, *n.m.* code.
kodifizie'ren, *vb.* codify.
Koffein', -e, *n.nt.* caffeine.
koffein'frei, *adj.* decaffeinated.
Koffer, -, *n.m.* suitcase, trunk.
Kofferkuli, -s, *n.m.* baggage cart (airport).
Kognak, -s, *n.m.* brandy, cognac.
Kohl, -e, *n.m.* cabbage.
Kohle, -n, *n.f.* coal.
kohlen, *vb.* char.
Kohlenoxyd', *n.nt.* carbon monoxide.
Kohlenstoff, -e, *n.m.* carbon.
Koje, -n, *n.f.* bunk.
Kokain', *n.nt.* cocaine.
kokett', *adj.* coquettish.
Koket'te, -n, *n.f.* coquette.
kokettie'ren, *vb.* flirt.
Kokon', -s, *n.m.* cocoon.
Koks, -e, *n.m.* coke.
Kolben, -, *n.m.* butt; piston.
Kolle'ge, -n, -n, *n.m.* colleague.
kollektiv', *adj.* collective.
Koller, *n.m.* rage, frenzy.
kölnisch Wasser, *n.nt.* eau-de-cologne.
kolonial', *adj.* colonial.
Kolonial'waren, *n.pl.* groceries.
Kolonial'warenhändler, -, *n.m.* grocer.
Kolonie', -i'en, *n.f.* colony.
Kolonisation', *n.f.* colonization.
kolonisie'ren, *vb.* colonize.
Kolon'ne, -n, *n.f.* column.
kolorit', -e, *n.nt.* color(ing).
kolossal', *adj.* colossal.
Koma, *n.nt.* coma.
kombinie'ren, *vb.* combine.
Komet', -en, -en, *n.m.* comet.
Komiker, -, *n.m.* comedian.
Komikerin, -nen, *n.f.* comedienne.
komisch, *adj.* funny.
Komitee', -s, *n.nt.* committee.
Komma, -s, *(or* -ta), *n.nt.* comma.
Kommandant', -en, -en, *n.m.* commandant, commanding officer.
Kommandantur', -en, *n.f.* commander's office.
kommen*, *vb.* come.
Kommentar', -e, *n.m.* commentary.
Kommenta'tor, -o'ren, *n.m.* commentator.
kommentie'ren, *vb.* comment on.
Kommissar', -e, *n.m.* commissary, commissioner.
Kommission', -en, *n.f.* commission.
Kommo'de, -n, *n.f.* bureau.
kommunal', *adj.* communal, municipal.
Kommunikant', -en, -en, *n.m.* communicant.
Kommunion', -en, *n.f.* communion.

Kommuniqué, -s, *n.nt.* communiqué.
Kommunis'mus, *n.m.* communism.
Kommunist', -en, -en, *n.m.* communist.
kommunis'tisch, *adj.* communistic.
kommunizie'ren, *vb.* commune; communicate.
Komödiant', -en, -en, *n.m.* comedian.
Komö'die, -n, *n.f.* comedy.
Kompagnon, -s, *n.m.* (business) partner.
kompakt', *adj.* compact.
Komparative, -e, *n.m.* comparative (degree).
Kompaß, -sse, *n.m.* compass.
kompensie'rend, *adj.* compensatory.
kompetent', *adj.* competent, authoritative.
Kompetenz', -en, *n.f.* competence, authority, jurisdiction.
komplex', *adj.* complex.
Komplex', -e, *n.m.* complex.
Komplikation', -en, *n.f.* complication.
Kompliment', -e, *n.nt.* compliment.
Kompli'ze, -n, -n, *n.m.* accomplice.
komplizie'ren, *vb.* complicate.
kompliziert', *adj.* complicated.
Komplott', -e, *n.nt.* plot.
komponie'ren, *vb.* compose.
Komponist', -en, -en, *n.m.* composer.
Komposition', -en, *n.f.* composition.
Kompott', -e, *n.nt.* compote.
Kompres'se, -n, *n.f.* compress.
Kompression', -en, *n.f.* compression.
Kompres'sor, -o'ren, *n.m.* compressor.
Kompromiß', -sse, *n.m.* compromise.
kompromittie'ren, *vb.* compromise.
Kompu'ter, -, *n.m.* computer.
Kondensation', -en, *n.f.* condensation.
Kondensa'tor, -o'ren, *n.m.* condenser.
kondensie'ren, *vb.* condense.
Kondi'tor, -o'ren, *n.m.* confectioner, pastry baker.
Konditorei', -ei'en, *n.f.* café and pastry shop.
Konfekt', -e, *n.nt.* candy.
Konfektion', *n.f.* ready-made clothing.
Konferenz', -en, *n.f.* conference.
Konfirmation', -en, *n.f.* confirmation.
konfiszie'ren, *vb.* confiscate.
Konfiti're, -n, *n.f.* jam.
Konflikt', -e, *n.m.* conflict.
konform', *adj.* in conformity.
konfrontie'ren, *vb.* confront.
konfus', *adj.* confused.

Kongreß', -sse, *n.m.* congress.
König, -e, *n.m.* king.
Königin, -nen, *n.f.* queen.
königlich, *adj.* royal.
Königreich, -e, *n.nt.* kingdom.
Königtum, *n.nt.* kingship, royalty.
Konjugation', -en, *n.f.* conjugation.
konjugie'ren, *vb.* conjugate.
Konjunktion', -en, *n.f.* conjunction.
Konjunktiv, -e, *n.m.* subjunctive.
konkav', *adj.* concave.
konkret', *adj.* concrete.
Konkurrent', -en, -en, *n.m.* competitor.
Konkurrenz', -en, *n.f.* competition.
konkurrie'ren, *vb.* compete.
Konkurs', -e, *n.m.* bankruptcy.
können*, *vb.* can, be able.
konsequent', *adj.* consistent.
Konservatis'mus, *n.m.* conservatism.
konservativ', *adj.* conservative.
Konservato'rium, -en, *n.nt.* conservatory.
Konser'venfabrik, -en, *n.f.* cannery.
konservie'ren, *vb.* preserve.
Konservie'rung, -en, *n.f.* conservation.
Konsistenz', -n *n.f.* consistency.
konsolidie'ren, *vb.* consolidate.
Konsonant', -en, -en, *n.m.* consonant.
konstant', *adj.* constant.
Konstellation', -en, *n.f.* constellation.
konstitue'ren, *vb.* constitute.
Konstitution', -en, *n.f.* constitution.
konstitutionell', *adj.* constitutional.
konstruie'ren, *vb.* construct.
Konstrukteur', -e, *n.m.* constructor, designer.
Konstruktion', -en, *n.f.* construction.
Konsul, -n, *n.m.* consul.
konsula'risch, *adj.* consular.
Konsulat', -e, *n.nt.* consulate.
Konsum', -s, *n.m.* consumption; (short for **Konsum'laden, ¨,** *n.m.*) cooperative store, co-op.
Konsument', -en, -en, *n.m.* consumer.
Konsum'verein, -e, *n.m.* cooperative (society).
Kontakt', -e, *n.m.* contact.
Kontinent, -e, *n.m.* continent.
kontinental', *adj.* continental.
Konto, -s *or* **-ten** *or* **-ti,** *n.nt.* account.
Kontobuch, ¨er, *n.nt.* bankbook, account book.
Kontor', -e, *n.nt.* office.
Kontorist', -en, -en, *n.m.* clerk.
Kontroll'abschnitt, -e, *n.m.* stub.
Kontrol'le, -n, *n.f.* control, check.

kontrollier'bar, *adj.* controllable.
kontrollie'ren, *vb.* control, check.
Kontroll'marke, -n, *n.f.* check.
Kontur', -en, *n.f.* contour, outline.
Konvaleszenz', *n.f.* convalescence.
Konvention', -en, *n.f.* convention.
konventionell', *adj.* conventional.
konvergie'ren, *vb.* converge.
konvertie'ren, *vb.* convert.
konvex', *adj.* convex.
Konvulsion', -en, *n.f.* convulsion.
konvulsiv', *adj.* convulsive.
Konzentration', -en, *n.f.* concentration.
Konzentrations'lager, -, *n.nt.* concentration camp.
konzentrie'ren, *vb.* concentrate.
konzen'trisch, *adj.* concentric.
Konzept', -e, *n.nt.* plan, draft; **(aus dem K. bringen*)** confuse.
Konzern', -e, *n.m.* (business) trust, pool.
Konzert', -e, *n.nt.* concert.
Konzession', -en, *n.f.* concession.
koordinie'ren, *vb.* coordinate.
Kopf, ¨e, *n.m.* head.
Kopfhaut, ¨e, *n.f.* scalp.
Kopfhörer, -, *n.m.* earphone.
Kopfkissen, -, *n.nt.* pillow.
Kopfsalat, -e, *n.m.* lettuce.
Kopfschmerzen, *n.pl.* headache.
Kopfsprung, ¨e, *n.m.* dive.
Kopftuch, ¨er, *n.nt.* kerchief.
Kopie, -i'en, *n.f.* copy.
kopie'ren, *vb.* copy, duplicate.
Kopier'maschine, -n, *n.f.* photocopier; copying machine.
koppeln, *vb.* couple.
Koral'le, -n, *n.f.* coral.
Korb, ¨e, *n.m.* basket.
Korbball, ¨e, *n.m.* basketball.
Korbwiege, -n, *n.f.* bassinet.
Korduanleder, -, *n.nt.* cordovan.
Kore'a, *n.nt.* Korea.
Korin'the, -n, *n.f.* currant.
Kork, -e, *n.m.* cork (material).
Korken, -, *n.m.* cork (stopper).
Korkenzieher, -, *n.m.* corkscrew.
Korn, -, *n.m.* grain whiskey.
Korn, -e, *n.nt.* (type of) grain.
Korn, ¨er, *n.nt.* (individual) grain.
Körnchen, -, *n.nt.* granule.
Kornett, -e, *n.nt.* cornet.
körnig, *adj.* granular.
Kornkammer, -n, *n.f.* granary.
Kornspeicher, -, *n.m.* granary.
Körper, -, *n.m.* body.
Körperbau, -ten *n.m.* physique.
Körperbehinderung, -en, *n.f.* physical disability.

Körperchen, -, n.nt. corpuscle.

Körperkraft, n.f. physical strength.

körperlich, adj. physical, corporeal.

Körperschaft, -en, n.f. corporation.

Korps, -, n.nt. corps.

korpulent', adj. corpulent.

korrekt', adj. correct.

Korrekt'heit, -en, n.f. correctness.

korrektiv', adj. corrective. dent.

Korrespondent', -en, -en, n.m. correspondent.

Korrespondenz', -en, n.f. correspondence.

korrespondie'ren, vb. correspond.

Korridor, -e, n.m. corridor.

korrigie'ren, vb. correct.

korrumpie'ren, vb. corrupt.

korrupt', adj. corrupt.

Korruption', -en, n.f. corruption.

Korsett', -s, n.nt. corset.

kosen, vb. fondle, caress.

Kosename(n), -, n.m. pet name.

kosme'tisch, adj. cosmetic.

kosmisch, adj. cosmic.

kosmopoli'tisch, adj. cosmopolitan.

Kosmos, n.m. cosmos.

Kost, n.f. food, fare, board.

kostbar, adj. costly, precious.

kosten, vb. cost; taste.

Kosten, n.pl. cost, charges, expenses.

Kostenanschlag, -̈e, n.m. estimate.

kostenfrei, adj. free of charge.

kostenlos, adj. free, without cost.

Kostgänger, -, n.m. boarder.

köstlich, adj. delicious.

kostspielig, adj. expensive.

Kostspieligkeit, -en, n.f. costliness.

Kostüm', -e, n.nt. costume; matching coat and skirt.

Kot, n.m. dirt, mud, filth.

Kotelett', -s, n.nt. cutlet, chop.

Köter, -, n.m. cur.

kotzen, vb. vomit.

Krabbe, -n, n.f. shrimp, crab.

Krach, -e, or -s, n.m. bang, crash, racket; row, fight.

krachen, vb. crash.

Kraft, -̈e, n.f. strength, force, power.

kraft, prep. by virtue of.

Kraftbrühe, -, n.f. bouillon.

Kraftfahrer, -, n.m. motorist.

Kraftfahrzeug, -e, n.nt. motor vehicle.

kräftig, adj. strong.

kraftlos, adj. powerless.

kraftstrotzend, adj. vigorous.

kraftvoll, adj. powerful.

Kraftwagen, -, n.m. automobile.

Kragen, -, n.m. collar.

Krähe, -n, n.f. crow.

Kralle, -n, n.f. claw.

Kram, -̈e, n.m. stuff, junk; business, affairs; retail trade, goods.

kramen, vb. rummage.

Krämer, -, n.m. small tradesman.

Krampf, -̈e, n.m. cramp, spasm.

krampfhaft, adj. spasmodic.

Kran, -̈e, n.m. crane, derrick.

Kranich, -e, n.m. crane.

krank(-), adj. sick.

kranken, vb. suffer from, ail.

kränken, vb. offend.

Krankenauto, -s, n.nt. ambulance.

Krankenhaus, -̈er, n.nt. hospital.

Krankenschwester, -n, n.f. nurse.

Krankenwagen -, n.m. ambulance.

krankhaft, adj. morbid.

Krankheit, -en, n.f. sickness, disease.

kränklich, adj. sickly.

Kränkung, -en, n.f. offense.

Kranz, -̈e, n.m. wreath.

kraß, adj. crass, gross.

Kraßheit, -en, n.f. grossness.

kratzen, vb. scrape, scratch.

kraulen, vb. crawl.

kraus, adj. curly, crisp.

Krause, -n, n.f. frill.

kräuseln, vb. curl, ruffle.

Kraut, -̈er, n.nt. herb, plant.

Krawat'te, -n, n.f. necktie.

Krebs, -e, n.m. crayfish; (med.) cancer.

krebserregend, adj. carcinogenic.

kreden'zen, vb. serve, offer.

Kredit', -e, n.m. credit.

Kredit'karte, -n, n.f. credit card.

Kreide, -n, n.f. chalk.

kreidig, adj. chalky.

Kreis, -e, n.m. circle; district.

Kreisbahn, -en, n.f. orbit.

kreischen, vb. shriek.

Kreisel, -, n.m. top.

kreiseln, vb. spin like a top, gyrate.

kreisen, vb. circle, revolve.

kreisförmig, adj. circular.

Kreislauf, -̈e, n.m. circulation, circuit.

Kremato'rium, -ien, n.nt. crematorium.

Krempe, -n, n.f. brim.

Krepp, n.m. crepe.

Kretonn'e, -s, n.m. cretonne.

Kreuz, -e, n.nt. cross; back; (music) sharp.

kreuzen, vb. cross; cruise, tack.

Kreuzer, -, n.m. cruiser.

Kreuzgang, -̈e, n.m. cloister.

kreuzigen, vb. crucify.

Kreuzigung, -en, n.f. crucifixion.

kreuz und quer, adv. crisscross.

Kreuzung, -en, n.f. cross(-breed); crossing, intersection.

Kreuzverhör, -e, n.nt. cross-examination.

Kreuzzug, -̈e, n.m. crusade.

Kreuzzügler, -, n.m. crusader.

kribbelig, adj. jittery.

kriechen*, vb. crawl, creep; grovel.

Krieg, -e, n.m. war.

kriegen, vb. get.

Krieger, -, n.m. warrior.

kriegerisch, adj. warlike.

Kriegsdienst, -e, n.m. military service.

Kriegsdienstverweigerer, -, n.m. conscientious objector.

Kriegsgefangen-, n.m. prisoner of war.

Kriegsgericht, -e, n.nt. court-martial.

Kriegslist, -en, n.f. stratagem.

Kriegslust, -̈e, n.f. belligerence.

kriegslustig, adj. bellicose.

Kriegsmacht, -̈e, n.f. military forces.

Kriegsschiff, -e, n.nt. warship.

kriegsversehrt, adj. disabled (by war).

Kriegszug, -̈e, n.m. military expedition.

Kriegszustand, -̈e, n.m. state of war.

kriminal', adj. criminal.

Krippe, -n, n.f. crib.

Krise, -n, n.f. crisis.

Kristall', -e, n.m. crystal.

kristal'len, adj. crystal, crystalline.

kristallisie'ren, vb. crystallize.

Kritik', -en, n.f. criticism, critique, review.

Kritiker, -, n.m. critic.

kritisch, adj. critical.

kritisie'ren, vb. criticize.

kritzeln, vb. scribble.

Krocket'spiel, -e, n.nt. croquet.

Krokodil', -e, n.nt. crocodile.

Krone, -n, n.f. crown.

krönen, vb. crown.

Kronleuchter, -, n.m. chandelier.

Kronprinz, -en, -en, n.m. crown prince.

Krönung, -en, n.f. coronation.

Kropf, -̈e, n.m. crop; goiter.

Krücke, -n, n.f. crutch.

Krug, -̈e, n.m. pitcher.

Krümel, -, n.m. crumb.

krümeln, vb. crumble.

krumm (-, -), adj. crooked.

krümmen, vb. bend; (sich k.) warp, buckle, double up (with pain or laughter).

Krümmung, -en, n.f. bend; curve; curvature.

Krüppel, -, n.m. cripple.

Kruste, -n, n.f. crust.

Kruzifix, -e, n.nt. crucifix.

Kübel, -, n.m. bucket.

Kubik'-, cpds. cubic.

kubisch, adj. cubic.

Küche, -n, n.f. kitchen.

Kuchen, -, n.m. cake.

Küchenchef, -s, n.m. chef.

Küchenzettel, -, n.m. menu, bill of fare.

44

Kugel, -n, *n.f.* sphere, ball, bullet.

kugelförmig, *adj.* spherical; globular.

Kuh, -̈e, *n.f.* cow.

kühl, *adj.* cool.

Kühle, *n.f.* coolness.

kühlen, *vb.* cool.

Kühler, -, *n.m.* auto radiator.

Kühlschrank, -̈e, *n.m.* refrigerator.

kühn, *adj.* bold.

Kühnheit, -en, *n.f.* boldness.

Küken, -, *n.nt.* chick.

kulina'risch, *adj.* culinary.

Kult, -e, *n.m.* cult.

kultivie'ren, *vb.* cultivate.

kultiviert', *adj.* cultured.

Kultivie'rung, *n.f.* cultivation.

Kultur', -en, *n.f.* culture.

kulturell', *adj.* cultural.

Kümmel, *n.m.* caraway.

Kummer, -, *n.m.* sorrow, grief.

kümmerlich, *adj.* miserable.

kümmern, *vb.* grieve, trouble, concern; **(sich k. um)** care about, look out for.

kummervoll, *adj.* sorrowful.

kund, *adj.* known.

Kunde, -n, -n, *n.m.* customer, client.

Kunde, -n, *n.f.* knowledge, information.

kund-geben*, *vb.* make known.

Kundgebung, -en, *n.f.* demonstration.

kundig, *adj.* well informed, knowing.

kündigen, *vb.* give notice; cancel.

Kündigung, -en, *n.f.* cancellation.

Kundschaft, -en, *n.f.* clientele.

künftig, *adj.* future.

Kunst, -̈e, *n.f.* art.

künsteln, *vb.* contrive.

kunstfertig, *adj.* skillful.

Künstler, -, *n.m.* artist.

künstlerisch, *adj.* artistic.

Künstlertum, *n.nt.* artistry.

künstlich, *adj.* artificial.

kunstlos, *adj.* artless.

Kunstseide, -n, *n.f.* rayon.

Kunststoff, -e, *n.m.* plastic.

Kunststück, -e, *n.nt.* feat, stunt.

kunstvoll, *adj.* artistic.

Kunstwerk, -e, *n.nt.* work of art.

Kunstwissenschaft, *n.f.* fine arts.

Kupfer, *n.nt.* copper.

kuppeln, *vb.* couple, join; pander.

Kupplung, -en, *n.f.* clutch.

Kur, -en, *n.f.* cure.

Kurbel, -n, *n.f.* crank.

Kürbis, -se, -e, *n.m.* pumpkin, gourd.

Kurier', -e, *n.m.* courier.

kurie'ren, *vb.* cure.

kurios', *adj.* odd, strange.

Kuriosität', -en, *n.f.* curio.

Kurio'sum, -sa, *n.nt.* freak.

Kurort, -e, *n.m.* resort.

Kurs, -e, *n.m.* course; rate of exchange.

Kursbuch, -̈er, *n.nt.* timetable.

kursie'ren, *vb.* circulate.

kursiv', *adj.* italic.

Kursus, Kurse, *n.m.* course.

Kurve, -n, *n.f.* curve.

kurz(-), *adj.* short; **(k. und bündig)** short and to the point.

Kürze, -n, *n.f.* shortness, brevity.

kürzen, *vb.* shorten.

kürzlich, *adj.* recently.

kurzsichtig, *adj.* near-sighted.

kurzum', *adv.* in short.

Kürzung, -en, *n.f.* shortening, cut.

Kurzwaren, *n.pl.* notions.

Kuß, -̈sse, *n.m.* kiss.

küssen, *vb.* kiss.

Küste, -n, *n.f.* coast, shore.

Küster, -, *n.m.* sexton.

Kutsche, -n, *n.f.* coach.

Kuvert', -s, *n.nt.* envelope.

L

Labe, -n, *n.f.* refreshment, comfort.

laben, *vb.* refresh, comfort.

Laborato'rium, -rien, *n.nt.* laboratory.

Labsal, -e, *n.nt.* refreshment, comfort.

Labyrinth', -e, *n.nt.* labyrinth.

Lache, -n, *n.f.* puddle.

lächeln, *vb.* smile.

Lächeln, *n.nt.* smile.

lachen, *vb.* laugh.

Lachen, *n.nt.* laugh(ing).

lächerlich, *adj.* ridiculous.

Lachs, *n.m.* salmon.

Lack, -e, *n.m.* lacquer.

Lackleder, *n.nt.* patent leather.

Lade, -n, *n.f.* box, chest, drawer.

laden*, *vb.* load, charge; summon.

Laden, -̈, *n.m.* shop; shutter.

Ladenkasse, -n, *n.f.* till.

Ladentisch, -e, *n.m.* counter.

Ladung, -en, *n.f.* load, cargo, shipment; charge.

Lage, -n, *n.f.* location, situation, condition.

Lager, -, *n.nt.* camp, lair, bed; deposit, depot, supply; bearing.

Lagerhaus, -̈er, *n.nt.* storehouse.

lagern, *vb.* lay down, store, deposit; **(sich l.)** camp; be deposited.

Lagerung, -en, *n.f.* storage, bearing; stratification, grain.

Lagu'ne, -n, *n.f.* lagoon.

lahm, *adj.* lame.

lähmen, *vb.* lame, cripple, paralyze.

Lähmung, -en, *n.f.* paralysis.

Laib, -e, *n.m.* loaf.

Laie, -n, -n, *n.m.* layman.

Laienstand, *n.m.* laity.

Laken, -, *n.nt.* sheet.

Lamm, -̈er, *n.nt.* lamb.

Lampe, -n, *n.f.* lamp.

lancie'ren, *vb.* launch.

Land, -̈er, *n.nt.* land, country.

Landbau, *n.m.* agriculture.

Landebahn, -en, *n.f.* flight strip, runway.

landen, *vb.* land.

Landesverrat, *n.m.* high treason.

Landkarte, -n, *n.f.* map.

landläufig, *adj.* usual, ordinary.

ländlich, *adj.* rural.

Landschaft, -en, *n.f.* landscape, countryside.

Landser, -, *n.m.* common soldier, GI.

Landsmann, -leute, *n.m.* compatriot.

Landstraße, -e, *n.f.* highway.

Landstrich, -e, *n.m.* region.

Landung, -en, *n.f.* landing.

Landwirt, -e, *n.m.* farmer.

Landwirtschaft, *n.f.* agriculture.

landwirtschaftlich, *adj.* agricultural.

lang (-), *adj.* long, tall.

lange, *adv.* for a long time.

Länge, -n, *n.f.* length; longitude.

langen, *vb.* hand; suffice.

Langeweile, *n.f.* boredom.

langlebig, *adj.* long-lived.

länglich, *adj.* oblong.

Langmut, *n.f.* patience.

langmütig, *adj.* long-suffering.

längs, *adv. & prep.* along.

langsam, *adj.* slow.

Langsamkeit, *n.f.* slowness.

längst, *adv.* long since.

langweilen, *vb.* bore.

langweilig, *adj.* boring.

langwierig, *adj.* lengthy.

Lanze, -n, *n.f.* lance.

Lappa'lie, -n, *n.f.* trifle.

Lappen, -, *n.m.* rag; lobe.

Lärm, *n.m.* noise.

Larve, -n, *n.f.* mask; larva.

Laserstrahl, -en, *n.m.* laser beam.

lassen*, *vb.* let, permit; cause to, have (someone do something, something done); leave; leave off, stop.

lässig, *adj.* indolent, careless.

Last, -en, *n.f.* burden, encumbrance; load, weight, cargo.

Lastauto, -s, *n.nt.* truck.

lasten, *vb.* weigh heavily, be a burden.

Laster, -, *n.nt.* vice.

lasterhaft, *adj.* vicious, wicked.

lästern, *vb.* slander, blaspheme.

lästig, *adj.* troublesome, disagreeable.

Lastkraftwagen, -, *n.m.* (motor) truck.

Lastwagen, -n, *n.m.* (motor) truck.

Latein', *n.nt.* Latin.

latei'nisch, *adj.* Latin.

Later'ne, -n, n.f. lantern.
Latri'ne, -n, n.f. latrine.
latschen, vb. shuffle, slouch.
Latz, ¨-e, n.m. bib, flap.
lau, adj. tepid, lukewarm.
Laub, n.nt. foliage.
Lauer, n.f. ambush.
lauern, vb. lurk, lie in wait for.
Lauf, ¨-e, n.m. course, race, run; (gun) barrel.
Laufbahn, -en, n.f. career; runway, race track.
laufen*, vb. run, walk.
laufend, adj. running, current.
Läufer, -, n.m. runner; stair carpet; (chess) bishop.
Lauge, -n, n.f. lye.
Laune, -n, n.f. whim, caprice, fancy; mood, humor.
launenhaft, adj. capricious.
launig, adj. humorous.
launisch, adj. moody.
Laus, ¨-e, n.f. louse.
lauschen, vb. listen.
lausig, adj. lousy.
laut, adj. loud, aloud.
laut, prep. according to.
Laut, -e, n.m. sound.
Laute, -n, n.f. lute.
lauten, vb. read, say.
läuten, vb. ring, peal, sound.
lauter, adj. pure, sheer, nothing but.
Lauterkeit, -en, n.f. purity.
läutern, vb. purify.
lautlos, adj. soundless, silent.
Lautsprecher, -, n.m. loudspeaker.
lauwarm, adj. lukewarm; halfhearted.
Lava, n.f. lava.
Laven'del, n.m. lavender.
lax, adj. lax.
Laxheit, n.f. laxity.
leben, vb. live, be alive.
Leben, -, n.nt. life.
lebend, adj. living.
leben'dig, adj. living, alive; lively.
Leben'digkeit, n.f. liveliness, vivacity.
lebenserfahren, adj. experienced, sophisticated.
Lebensgefahr, -en, n.f. danger (to life).
lebensgefährlich, adj. highly dangerous.
Lebenskraft, n.f. vitality.
lebenslänglich, adj. lifelong, for life.
Lebensmittel, n.pl. provisions, groceries.
Lebensmittelgeschäft, -e, n.nt. grocery store.
Lebensstil, n.m. life style.
Lebensunterhalt, n.m. livelihood.
Leber, -n, n.f. liver.
Lebewesen, -, n.nt. living being, organism.
lebewohl', interj. farewell, adieu.
lebhaft, adj. lively.
leblos, adj. lifeless.
Lebzeiten, n.pl. lifetime.

lechzen, vb. thirst, languish.
leck, adj. leaky, having a leak.
Leck, -e, n.nt. leak.
lecken, vb. leak; lick.
lecker, adj. tasty, appetizing.
Leder, -, n.nt. leather.
ledern, adj. leather(y).
ledig, adj. unmarried, single; vacant; exempt.
lediglich, adv. merely.
leer, adj. empty, vacant, blank.
Leere, -, n.f. emptiness.
leeren, vb. empty.
Leerlauf, n.m. neutral (gear).
legal', adj. legal.
legalisie'ren, vb. legalize.
Legat', -e, n.nt. bequest.
legen, vb. lay, place, put; (sich l.) lie down, subside.
legendär', adj. legendary.
Legen'de, -n, n.f. legend.
Legie'rung, -en, n.f. alloy.
Legion', -en, n.f. legion.
legitim', adj. legitimate.
legitimie'ren, vb. legitimize; (sich l.) prove one's identity.
Lehm, n.m. loam, clay.
Lehne, -n, n.f. back, arm (of a chair), support.
lehnen, vb. lean.
Lehnstuhl, ¨-e, n.m. armchair.
Lehrbuch, ¨-er, n.nt. textbook.
Lehre, -n, n.f. doctrine, teaching, lesson; apprenticeship.
lehren, vb. teach.
Lehrer, -, n.m. teacher.
Lehrgang, ¨-e, n.m. course of instruction.
Lehrplan, ¨-e, n.m. curriculum.
lehrreich, adj. instructive.
Lehrsatz, ¨-e, n.m. proposition.
Lehrstunde, -n, n.f. lesson.
Leib, -er, n.m. body; abdomen; womb.
leibhaft(ig), adj. incarnate, personified.
leiblich, adj. bodily.
Leiche, -n, n.f. corpse.
leicht, adj. light; easy.
Leichter, -, n.m. barge.
leichtfertig, adj. frivolous.
Leichtfertigkeit, n.f. frivolity.
leichtgläubig, adj. gullible, credulous.
Leichtigkeit, -en, n.f. ease.
Leichtsinn, n.m. frivolity.
leichtsinnig, adj. frivolous, reckless.
leid, adj. (es tut* mir l.) I'm sorry.
Leid, n.nt. suffering, sorrow, harm.
leiden*, vb. suffer; stand, endure; (gern l. mögen*) like.
Leiden, -, n.nt. suffering; illness.
Leidenschaft, -en, n.f. passion.
leidenschaftlich, adj. passionate.
leidenschaftslos, adj. dispassionate.
leider, adv. unfortunately.
leidig, adj. unpleasant.
leidlich, adj. tolerable.
Leier, -n, n.f. lyre.

leihen*, vb. lend; borrow.
leihweise, adv. on loan.
Leim, n.m. glue.
leimen, vb. glue.
Leine, -n, n.f. line, leash.
leinen, adj. linen.
Leinen, -, n.nt. linen.
Leinsamen, n.m. linseed.
Leinwand, n.f. canvas; (movie) screen.
leise, adj. soft, quiet, gentle.
leisten, vb. perform, accomplish; (sich l.) afford.
Leisten, -, n.m. last.
Leistung, -en, n.f. performance, accomplishment, achievement, output.
leistungsfähig, adj. efficient.
Leitartikel, -, n.nt. editorial.
leiten, vb. lead, direct, conduct, manage.
Leiter, -, n.m. leader, director, manager.
Leiter, -n, n.f. ladder.
Leitfaden, ¨-, n.m. key, guide.
Leitsatz, ¨-e, n.m. guiding principle.
Leitung, -en, n.f. guidance, direction, management; wire, line, duct, tube; conduit.
Leitungsrohr, -e, n.nt. conduit.
Lektion', -en, n.f. lesson.
Lektor, -o'ren, n.m. university instructor.
Lektü're, -n, n.f. reading.
Lende, -n, n.f. loin.
Lendenstück, -e, n.nt. sirloin.
lenkbar, adj. steerable, dirigible, manageable.
lenken, vb. direct, steer, guide.
Lenkung, -en, n.f. guidance, steering, control.
Lenz, -e, n.m. spring.
Leopard', -en, -en, n.m. leopard.
Lerche, -n, n.f. lark.
lernen, vb. learn.
Lesart, -en, n.f. reading, version.
lesbar, adj. legible; worth reading.
lesbisch, adj. lesbian.
Lese, -n, n.f. vintage.
Lesebuch, ¨-er, n.nt. reader.
lesen*, vb. read; lecture; gather.
Leser, -, n.m. reader.
leserlich, adj. legible.
Lethargie', n.f. lethargy.
lethar'gisch, adj. lethargic.
Lettland, n.nt. Latvia.
letzt-, adj. last.
letzter-, adj. latter.
leuchten, vb. give forth light, shine.
Leuchter, -, n.m. candlestick.
Leuchtschirm, -e, n.m. fluorescent screen, television screen.
Leuchtsignal, -e, n.nt. flare.
Leuchtturm, ¨-e, n.m. lighthouse.
leugnen, vb. deny.
Leukoplast', n.nt. adhesive tape, band-aid.

Leumund, -e, *n.m.* reputation.

Leute, *n.pl.* people.

Leutnant, -s *or* -e, *n.m.* lieutenant.

leutselig, *adj.* affable.

Lexikon, -ka, *n.nt.* dictionary.

Liaison', -s, *n.f.* liaison.

liberal', *adj.* liberal.

Liberalis'mus, *n.m.* liberalism.

Libret'to, -s, *n.nt.* libretto.

Licht, -er, *n.nt.* light.

Lichtbild, -er, *n.nt.* photograph.

Lichtschimmer, -, *n.m.* glint.

Lichtspiel, -e, *n.nt.* moving picture.

Lid, -er, *n.nt.* eyelid.

lieb, *adj.* dear.

liebäugeln, *vb.* make eyes at.

Liebchen, -, *n.nt.* dearest, darling.

Liebe, -n, *n.f.* love.

Liebelei', -en, *n.f.* flirtation.

liebeln, *vb.* flirt, make love.

lieben, *vb.* love.

liebenswert, *adj.* lovable.

liebenswürdig, *adj.* amiable, kind.

lieber, *adv.* rather.

Liebesaffäre, -n, *n.f.* love affair.

liebevoll, *adj.* loving, affectionate.

lieb·haben*, *vb.* love.

Liebhaber, -, *n.m.* lover.

Liebhaberei', -en, *n.f.* hobby.

liebkosen, *vb.* fondle, caress.

Liebkosung, -en, *n.f.* caress.

lieblich, *adj.* lovely.

Liebling, -e, *n.m.* darling.

Lieblings-, *cpds.* favorite.

lieblos, *adj.* loveless.

Liebreiz, -e, *n.m.* charm.

Liebschaft, -en, *n.f.* love affair.

Liebst-, *n.m. & f.* dearest, sweetheart.

Lied, -er, *n.nt.* song.

liederlich, *adj.* slovenly; dissolute.

Lieferant', -en, -en, *n.m.* supplier.

liefern, *vb.* supply, deliver.

Lieferung, -en, *n.f.* delivery.

Lieferwagen, -, *n.m.* delivery van.

liegen*, *vb.* lie, be located.

Lift, -e, *n.m.* elevator.

Likör', -e, *n.m.* liqueur.

lila, *adj.* lilac, purple.

Lilie, -n, *n.f.* lily.

Limona'de, -n, *n.f.* lemonade.

Limo'ne, -n, *n.f.* lime.

Limousi'ne, -n, *n.f.* limousine, sedan.

lind, *adj.* mild, gentle.

lindern, *vb.* alleviate, ease, soothe.

Lineal', -e, *n.nt.* ruler.

linear', *adj.* linear.

Linguist', -en, -en, *n.m.* linguist.

linguis'tisch, *adj.* linguistic.

Linie, -n, *n.f.* line.

link-, *adj.* left.

Link-, *n.f.* left.

linkisch, *adj.* awkward, clumsy.

links, *adv.* to the left.

Linse, -n, *n.f.* lens; lentil.

Lippe, -n, *n.f.* lip.

Lippenstift, -e, *n.m.* lipstick.

liquidie'ren, *vb.* liquidate.

lispeln, *vb.* lisp, whisper.

List, -en, *n.f.* cunning, trick, ruse.

Liste, -n, *n.f.* list.

listig, *adj.* cunning, crafty.

Litanei', *n.f.* litany.

Litauen, *n.nt.* Lithuania.

Liter, -, *n.m. or nt.* liter.

litera'risch, *adj.* literary.

Literatur', -en, *n.f.* literature.

Lithographie', -i'en, *n.f.* lithograph(y).

Liturgie', -i'en, *n.f.* liturgy.

litur'gisch, *adj.* liturgical.

Livree', -e'en, *n.f.* livery.

Lizenz', -en, *n.f.* license.

Lob, -e, *n.nt.* praise.

loben, *vb.* praise.

lobenswert, *adj.* praiseworthy.

löblich, *adj.* praiseworthy.

lobpreisen, *vb.* praise, extol.

Lobrede, -n, *n.f.* eulogy.

Loch, -er, *n.nt.* hole.

lochen, *vb.* put a hole in, punch.

Locke, -n, *n.f.* lock, curl.

locken, *vb.* curl; lure.

locker, *adj.* loose.

lockern, *vb.* loosen.

lockig, *adj.* curly.

lodern, *vb.* blaze.

Löffel, -, *n.m.* spoon.

Logbuch, -er, *n.nt.* log.

Loge, -n, *n.f.* loge, box; (fraternal) lodge.

Logik, *n.f.* logic.

logisch, *adj.* logical.

Lohn, -e, *n.m.* reward; wages.

lohnen, *vb.* reward, pay, be of value; (**sich l.**) be worth the trouble.

lokal', *adj.* local.

Lokal', -e, *n.nt.* night club, bar, place of amusement; premises.

Lokomoti've, -n, *n.f.* locomotive.

Lokus, -se, *n.m.* toilet.

los, *adj.* loose; wrong; (**was ist l.?**) what's the matter?

Los, -e, *n.nt.* lot.

lösbar, *adj.* soluble.

los·binden*, *vb.* untie.

Löschblatt, -er, *n.nt.* blotter.

löschen, *vb.* extinguish, quench; unload.

lose, *adj.* loose, slack, lax, dissolute.

Lösegeld, -er, *n.nt.* ransom.

lösen, *vb.* undo, solve, dissolve; buy (a ticket).

los·fahren*, *vb.* start out.

los·gehen*, *vb.* start out, go off, begin.

los·kommen*, *vb.* get loose.

los·lassen*, *vb.* get loose, let go.

los·lösen, *vb.* disconnect.

los·machen, *vb.* unfasten, free.

Lösung, -en, *n.f.* solution.

Lösungsmittel, -, *n.nt.* solvent.

los·werden*, *vb.* get rid of.

Lot, -e, *n.nt.* lead, plumbline.

löten, *vb.* solder.

lotrecht, *adj.* perpendicular.

Lotse, -n, -n, *n.m.* pilot.

lotsen, *vb.* pilot.

Lotterie', -i'en, *n.f.* lottery.

Löwe, -n, -n, *n.m.* lion.

Lücke, -n, *n.f.* gap.

lückenhaft, *adj.* with gaps, incomplete.

lückenlos, *adj.* without gaps, complete.

Luder, -, *n.nt.* scoundrel, slut; carrion.

Luft, -e, *n.f.* air.

Luftabwehr, *n.f.* anti-aircraft, air defense.

Lutfangriff, -e, *n.m.* air raid.

Luftballon, -s, *n.m.* balloon.

Luftblase, -n, *n.f.* bubble.

Luftbrücke, -n, *n.f.* air lift.

luftdicht, *adj.* airtight.

Luftdruck, -e, *n.m.* air pressure.

lüften, *vb.* air, ventilate.

Luftfahrt, *n.nt.* aviation.

Luftflotte, -n, *n.f.* air fleet.

luftig, *adj.* airy.

luftkrank, -, *adj.* air-sick.

Luftlinie, -n, *n.f.* air line.

Luftpirat, -en, -en, *n.m.* hijacker.

Luftpost, *n.f.* airmail.

Luftsack, -e, *n.m.* airbag (automobile).

Luftschiff, -e, *n.nt.* airship, dirigible.

Luftsprung, -e, *n.m.* caper.

Luftstützpunkt, -e, *n.m.* air base.

Lüftung, *n.f.* ventilation.

Luftverpestung, *n.f.* air pollution.

Luftwaffe, -n, *n.f.* air force.

Luftzug, -e, *n.m.* draft.

Lüge, -n, *n.f.* lie.

lugen, *vb.* peep.

lügen*, *vb.* lie.

Lügner, -, *n.m.* liar.

Lümmel, -, *n.m.* lout.

Lump, -en, -en, *n.m.* bum.

Lumpen, -, *n.m.* rag.

Lunge, -n, *n.f.* lung.

Lungenentzündung, -en, *n.f.* pneumonia.

Lust, -e, *n.f.* pleasure, desire; (**L. haben***) feel like (doing something).

lüstern, *adj.* lecherous.

lustig, *adj.* merry, gay.

Lüstling, -e, *n.m.* libertine.

lustlos, *adj.* listless.

Lustspiel, -e, *n.nt.* comedy.

Luthera'ner, -, *n.m.* Lutheran.

lutherisch, *adj.* Lutheran.

lutschen, *vb.* suck.

Luxus, *n.m.* luxury.

Luxus-, *cpds.* de luxe.

Lymphe, -n, *n.f.* lymph.

lynchen, *vb.* lynch.

Lyrik, *n.f.* lyric poetry.

lyrisch, *adj.* lyric.

Lyze'um, -e'en, *n.nt.* girls' high school.

M

Maat, -e, *n.m.* mate.

machen, *vb.* make, do.

Macht, ⸚e, *n.f.* power.

Machterweiterung, -en, *n.f.* aggrandizement.

mächtig, *adj.* powerful.

machtlos, *adj.* powerless.

Mädchen, -, *n.nt.* girl.

mädchenhaft, *adj.* girlish.

Mädel, -, *n.nt.* girl.

Mafia, *n.f.* mafia.

Magazin', -e, *n.nt.* magazine, storeroom, store.

Magd, ⸚e, *n.f.* hired girl.

Magen, - or ⸚, *n.m.* stomach.

Magenbeschwerden, *n.pl.* indigestion.

Magengeschwür, -e, *n.nt.* stomach ulcer.

Magenschmerzen, *n.pl.* stomach ache.

Magenverstimmung, -en, *n.f.* stomach upset.

mager, *adj.* lean.

Magermilch, *n.f.* skim milk.

Magie', *n.f.* magic.

magisch, *adj.* magic.

Magnat', -en, -en, *n.m.* magnate, tycoon.

Magne'sium, *n.nt.* magnesium.

Magnet', -e, or -en, -en, *n.m.* magnet.

magne'tisch, *adj.* magnetic.

Magnetophon', -e, *n.nt.* tape recorder.

Mahago'ni, *n.nt.* mahogany.

mähen, *vb.* mow.

Mahl, -e, or ⸚er, *n.nt.* meal, repast.

mahlen, *vb.* grind.

Mahlzeit, -en, *n.f.* meal.

mahnen, *vb.* remind, urge, warn, dun.

Mahnung, -en, *n.f.* admonition, warning.

Mähre, -n, *n.f.* mare.

Mai, *n.m.* May.

Mais, *n.m.* corn, maize.

Maiskolben, -, *n.m.* corncob.

Majestät', -en, *n.f.* majesty.

majestä'tisch, *adj.* majestic.

Major', -e, *n.m.* major.

Majorität', -en, *n.f.* majority.

Majus'kel, -n, *n.f.* capital letter.

Makel, -, *n.m.* stain, blemish, flaw.

makellos, *adj.* spotless, flawless, immaculate.

Makkaro'ni, *n.pl.* macaroni.

Makre'le, -n, *n.f.* mackerel.

Makro'ne, -n, *n.f.* macaroon.

¹Mal, -e, *n.nt.* mark, sign, spot, mole.

²Mal, -e, *n.nt.* time; (das erste

M.) the first time; (2 mal 2) 2 times 2.

mal, *adv.* (= einmal) once, just; (nicht m.) not even.

Mala'ria, *n.f.* malaria.

malen, *vb.* paint.

Maler, -, *n.m.* painter.

Malerei', -en, *n.f.* painting.

malerisch, *adj.* picturesque.

Malz, *n.nt.* malt.

man, *pron.* one, a person.

Manager, -, *n.m.* manager.

mancher, -es, -e, *pron. & adj.* many, many a.

mancherlei, *adj.* various.

manchmal, *adv.* sometimes.

Mandat', -e, *n.nt.* mandate.

Mandel, -n, *n.f.* almond; tonsil.

Mandoli'ne, -n, *n.f.* mandolin.

Mangel, ⸚, *n.m.* lack, dearth, defect.

Mangel, -n, *n.f.* mangle.

mangelhaft, *adj.* faulty.

mangeln, *vb.* be lacking, deficient; (es mangelt mir an ....) I lack ....

mangels, *prep.* for lack of.

Manie', -i'en, *n.f.* mania.

Manier', -en, *n.f.* manner.

manier'lich, *adj.* mannerly, polite.

manikü'ren, *vb.* manicure.

manipulie'ren, *vb.* manipulate.

Manko, -s, *n.nt.* defect, deficiency.

Mann, ⸚er, *n.m.* man, husband.

Männchen, -, *n.nt.* male (animal).

Mannesalter, *n.nt.* manhood.

mannhaft, *adj.* manly.

mannigfach, *adj.* manifold.

mannigfaltig, *adj.* manifold.

Mannigfaltigkeit, -en, *n.f.* diversity.

männlich, *adj.* male, masculine.

Männlichkeit, *n.f.* manliness.

Mannschaft, -en, *n.f.* crew, team, squad; (pl.) enlisted men.

Manö'ver, -, *n.nt.* maneuver.

manövrie'ren, *vb.* maneuver.

Manschet'te, -n, *n.f.* cuff.

Mantel, ⸚, *n.m.* overcoat.

Manufaktur', -en, *n.f.* manufacture, factory.

Manuskript', -e, *n.nt.* manuscript.

Mappe, -n, *n.f.* portfolio, briefcase, folder.

Märchen, -, *n.nt.* fairy tale.

märchenhaft, *adj.* fabulous.

Märchenland, ⸚er, *n.nt.* fairyland.

Margari'ne, *n.f.* margarine.

Marihua'na, *n.nt.* marijuana.

Mari'ne, *n.f.* navy.

marinie'ren, *vb.* marinate.

Marionet'te, -n, *n.f.* marionette, puppet.

Mark, -, *n.f.* mark (unit of money); (deutsche M.) West German mark.

Mark, -en, *n.f.* border(land).

Marke, -n, *n.f.* mark; brand, sort; postage stamp, check, ticket.

markie'ren, *vb.* mark.

Marki'se, -n, *n.f.* awning.

Markstein, -e, *n.m.* boundary stone, landmark.

Markt, ⸚e, *n.m.* market.

Marktplatz, ⸚e, *n.m.* market place.

Marmela'de, -n, *n.f.* jam.

Marmor, -, *n.m.* marble.

Maro'ne, -n, *n.f.* chestnut.

Marot'te, -n, *n.f.* whim, fad.

Marsch, ⸚e, *n.m.* march.

Marsch, -en, *n.f.* marsh.

Marschall, ⸚e, *n.m.* marshal.

marschie'ren, *vb.* march.

Marter, -n, *n.f.* torture.

martern, *vb.* torture.

Märtyrer, -, *n.m.* martyr.

Märtyrertum, *n.nt.* martyrdom.

März, *n.m.* March.

Marzipan', -e, *n.m.* or nt. marzipan, almond paste.

Masche, -n, *n.f.* stitch, mesh.

Maschi'ne, -n, *n.f.* machine.

Maschi'nenbau, *n.m.* engineering.

Maschi'nengewehr, -e, *n.nt.* machine gun.

Maschinist', -en, -en, *n.m.* machinist.

Masern, *n.pl.* measles.

Maske, -n, *n.f.* mask.

Maskera'de, -n, *n.f.* masquerade.

maskie'ren, *vb.* mask.

Maskot'te, -n, *n.f.* mascot.

maskulin', *adj.* masculine.

Maß, -e, *n.nt.* measure(ment), dimension, extent, rate, proportion.

Massa'ge, -n, *n.f.* massage.

Masse, -n, *n.f.* mass.

massenhaft, *adj.* in large quantity.

Massenversammlung, -en, *n.f.* mass meeting.

massenweise, *adv.* in large numbers.

Masseur', -e, *n.m.* masseur.

maßgebend, *adj.* authoritative, standard.

maßgeblich, *adj.* authoritative, standard.

massie'ren, *vb.* massage.

massig, *adj.* bulky, solid.

mäßig, *adj.* moderate.

mäßigen, *vb.* moderate.

Mäßigkeit, *n.f.* temperance.

Mäßigung, *n.f.* moderation.

massiv', *adj.* massive.

maßlos, *adj.* immoderate, excessive.

Maßnahme, -n, *n.f.* measure, step.

Maßregel, -n, *n.f.* measure, step.

maßregelnd, *adj.* disciplinary.

Maßstab, ⸚e, *n.m.* scale, rate, gauge, standard.

maßvoll, *adj.* moderate.

Mast, -e or -en, *n.m.* mast.

mästen, *vb.* fatten.
Material', **-ien**, *n.nt.* material.
Materialis'mus, *n.m.* materialism.
Mate'rie, **-n**, *n.f.* matter, stuff.
materiell', *adj.* material.
Mathematik', *n.f.* mathematics.
Mathema'tiker, **-**, *n.m.* mathematician.
mathema'tisch, *adj.* mathematical.
Matrat'ze, **-n**, *n.f.* mattress.
Mätres'se, **-n**, *n.f.* mistress.
Matro'se, **-n**, **-n**, *n.m.* sailor.
matschig, *adj.* muddy, slushy; pulpy.
matt, *adj.* dull, tired.
Matte, **-n**, *n.f.* mat.
Mattigkeit, *n.f.* lassitude.
Mätzchen, **-**, *n.nt.* antic, foolish trick.
Mauer, **-n**, *n.f.* (outside) wall.
Maul, **-er**, *n.nt.* mouth, snout.
Maulkorb, **-e**, *n.m.* muzzle.
Maultier, **-e**, *n.nt.* mule.
Maulwurf, **-e**, *n.m.* mole.
Maure, **-n**, **-n**, *n.m.* Moor.
Maurer, **-**, *n.m.* mason, bricklayer.
Maus, **-e**, *n.f.* mouse.
Mausole'um, **-le'en**, *n.nt.* mausoleum.
maximal', *adj.* maximum.
Maximum, **-ma**, *n.nt.* maximum.
Mayonnai'se, **-n**, *n.f.* mayonnaise.
m. E., *abbr.* (= meines Erach'tens) in my opinion.
Mecha'nik, *n.f.* mechanics, mechanism.
Mecha'niker, **-**, *n.m.* mechanic.
mecha'nisch, *adj.* mechanical.
mechanisie'ren, *vb.* mechanize.
Mechanis'mus, **-men**, *n.m.* mechanism.
Medai'lle, **-n**, *n.f.* medal.
Medikament', **-e**, *n.nt.* drug, medicine.
Medium, **-ien**, *n.nt.* medium.
Medizin', **-en**, *n.f.* medicine.
Medizi'ner, **-**, *n.m.* medical man, medical student.
medizi'nisch, *adj.* medical.
Meer, **-e**, *n.nt.* sea.
Meerbusen, **-**, *n.m.* bay.
Meerenge, **-n**, *n.f.* strait.
Meeresboden, *n.m.* seabed.
Meeresbucht, **-en**, *n.f.* bay.
Meerrettich, **-e**, *n.m.* horseradish.
Megahertz, *n.nt.* megahertz.
Mehl, *n.nt.* flour, meal.
mehr, *adj.* more.
mehren, *vb.* increase.
mehrere, *adj.* several.
mehrfach, *adj.* multiple.
Mehrheit, **-en**, *n.f.* majority.
mehrmalig, *adj.* repeated.
mehrmals, *adv.* repeatedly.
Mehrwertsteuer, **-n**, *n.f.* value-added tax.
Mehrzahl, **-en**, *n.f.* majority; plural.

meiden*, *vb.* avoid.
Meile, **-n**, *n.f.* mile.
Meilenstein, **-e**, *n.m.* milestone.
mein, **-**, **-e**, *adj.* my.
meinen, *vb.* mean, think.
meiner, **-es**, **-e**, *pron.* mine.
meinetwegen, *adv.* for my sake; for all I care.
Meinung, **-en**, *n.f.* opinion.
Meinungsumfrage, **-n**, *n.f.* poll.
Meißel, **-**, *n.m.* chisel.
meist, **1.** *adj.* most (of). **2.** *adv.* mostly, usually.
meistens, *adv.* mostly, usually.
Meister, **-**, *n.m.* master; champion.
meisterhaft, *adj.* masterly.
Meisterschaft, **-en**, *n.f.* championship.
Meisterstück, **-e**, *n.nt.* masterpiece.
Melancholie', *n.f.* melancholy.
melancho'lisch, *adj.* melancholy.
Melas'se, *n.f.* molasses.
melden, *vb.* announce, notify, report.
Meldung, **-en**, *n.f.* announcement, notification, report.
melken*, *vb.* milk.
Melodie', **-i'en**, *n.f.* melody, tune.
melo'disch, *adj.* melodious.
Melo'ne, **-n**, *n.f.* melon; derby.
Membra'ne, **-n**, *n.f.* membrane.
Memoi'ren, *n.pl.* memoirs.
Memoran'dum, **-den**, *n.nt.* memorandum.
Menagerie', **-i'en**, *n.f.* menagerie.
Menge, **-n**, *n.f.* quantity; crowd, multitude; **(eine M.)** a lot.
Mensch, **-en**, **-en**, *n.m.* human being, person; man.
Menschenfeind, **-e**, *n.m.* misanthrope.
Menschenfreund, **-e**, *n.m.* humanitarian.
Menschenliebe, *n.f.* philanthropy.
Menschenmenge, **-n**, *n.f.* mob.
Menschenrechte, *n.pl.* human rights.
Menschenverstand, *n.m.* **(gesunder M.)** common sense.
Menschheit, *n.f.* mankind, humanity.
menschlich, *adj.* human; humane.
Menschlichkeit, *n.f.* humanity.
Menstruation', *n.f.* menstruation.
Mentalität', *n.f.* mentality.
Menthol', *n.nt.* menthol.
Menü, **-s**, *n.nt.* menu.
merken, *vb.* realize, notice; **(sich m.)** keep in mind; **(sich nichts m. lassen*)** not give oneself away.
Merkmal, **-e**, *n.nt.* mark, characteristic.

merkwürdig, *adj.* peculiar, odd, queer.
Messe, **-n**, *n.f.* fair; *(eccles.)* mass.
messen*, *vb.* measure; gauge; **(sich m.)** match.
Messer, **-**, *n.nt.* knife.
Messi'as, *n.m.* Messiah.
Messing, *n.nt.* brass.
Metall', **-e**, *n.nt.* metal.
metal'len, *adj.* metallic.
Metall'waren, *n.pl.* hardware.
Meteor', **-e**, *n.m. or nt.* meteor.
Meteorologie', *n.f.* meteorology.
Meter, **-**, *n.m. or nt.* meter.
Metho'de, **-n**, *n.f.* method.
metrisch, *adj.* metric.
Metzger, **-**, *n.m.* butcher.
Metzgerei', **-en**, *n.f.* butcher shop.
Meuterei', **-en**, *n.f.* mutiny.
meutern, *vb.* mutiny.
Mexika'ner, **-**, *n.m.* Mexican.
mexika'nisch, *adj.* Mexican.
Mexiko, *n.nt.* Mexico.
Mieder, **-**, *n.nt.* bodice.
Miene, **-n**, *n.f.* mien.
Mienenspiel, **-e**, *n.nt.* pantomime.
Miete, **-n**, *n.f.* rent, rental.
mieten, *vb.* rent, lease, hire.
Mieter, **-**, *n.m.* tenant.
Mietvertrag, **-e**, *n.m.* lease.
Mietwohnung, **-en**, *n.f.* flat, apartment.
Migrä'ne, *n.f.* migraine.
Mikro'be, **-n**, *n.f.* microbe.
Mikrofilm, **-e**, *n.m.* microfilm.
Mikrophon', **-e**, *n.nt.* microphone.
Mikroskop', **-e**, *n.nt.* microscope.
Milbe, **-n**, *n.f.* mite.
Milch, *n.f.* milk.
Milchhändler, **-**, *n.m.* dairyman.
milchig, *adj.* milky.
Milchmann, **-er**, *n.m.* milkman.
Milchwirtschaft, **-en**, *n.f.* dairy.
mild, *adj.* mild, gentle, lenient.
Milde, *n.f.* mildness, leniency, clemency.
mildern, *vb.* mitigate, alleviate, soften; **(mildernde Umstände)** extenuating circumstances.
Milderung, **-en**, *n.f.* alleviation.
Militär', **-s**, *n.nt.* military.
Militär'dienstpflicht, **-en**, *n.f.* conscription.
militä'risch, *adj.* military.
Militaris'mus, *n.m.* militarism.
militaris'tisch, *adj.* militaristic.
Miliz', **-en**, *n.f.* militia.
Millime'ter, **-**, *n.nt.* millimeter.
Million', **-en**, *n.f.* million.
Millionär', **-e**, *n.m.* millionaire.
Milz, **-en**, *n.f.* spleen.
Minderheit, **-en**, *n.f.* minority.
minderjährig, *adj.* minor, not of age.
Minderjährigkeit, *n.f.* minority.

mindern, vb. reduce.

minderwertig, adj. inferior.

mindestens, adv. at least.

Mine, -n, n.f. mine.

Mineral', -e or **ien,** n.nt. mineral.

minera'lisch, adj. mineral.

Miniatur', -en, n.f. miniature.

minimal', adj. minimum, minute.

Minimum, -ma, n.nt. minimum.

Mini'ster, -, n.m. (cabinet) minister.

Ministe'rium, -rien, n.nt. ministry, department.

Mini'sterpräsident, -en, -en, n.m. prime minister.

minus, adv. minus.

Minu'te, -n, n.f. minute.

Minz'e, -n, n.f. mint.

mischen, vb. mix, mingle, blend.

Mischmasch, -e, n.m. hodgepodge.

Mischung, -en, n.f. mixture, blend.

mißachten, vb. disregard; slight.

Mißachtung, -en, n.f. disdain.

Mißbildung, -en, n.f. abnormality, deformity.

mißbilligen, vb. disapprove.

Mißbrauch, -̈e, n.m. abuse, misuse.

mißbrau'chen, vb. abuse.

mißdeu'ten, vb. misconstrue.

missen, vb. do without.

Mißerfolg, -e, n.m. failure.

Missetat, -en, n.f. misdeed, crime.

Missetäter, -, n.m. offender.

mißfal'len*, vb. displease.

Mißfallen, n.nt. displeasure.

Mißgeburt, -en, n.f. freak.

Mißgeschick, -e, n.nt. adversity, misfortune.

mißglü'cken, vb. fail.

mißglückt', adj. unsuccessful, abortive.

mißgön'nen, vb. begrudge.

mißhan'deln, vb. mistreat, maltreat.

Mission', -en, n.f. mission.

Missionar', -e, n.m. missionary.

Mißklang, -̈e, n.m. discord.

mißlin'gen*, vb. miscarry, fail.

mißra'ten, adj. ill-bred, low.

mißtrau'en, vb. distrust.

Mißtrauen, n.nt. distrust.

mißtrauisch, adj. suspicious, distrustful.

mißvergnügt, adj. cranky.

Mißverhältnis, -se, n.nt. disproportion.

Mißverständnis, -se, n.nt. misunderstanding.

mißverstehen*, vb. misunderstand.

Mist, n.m. manure, muck.

mistig, adj. misty.

mit, prep. with.

Mitarbeit, n.f. cooperation, collaboration.

mitarbeiten, vb. collaborate.

Mitarbeiter, -, n.m. collaborator; **(anonymer M.)** ghost writer.

Mitbewerber, -, n.m. competitor.

mitbringen*, vb. bring along; bring a present.

Mitbürger, -, n.m. fellow citizen.

miteinan'der, adv. together, jointly.

mitein'begriffen, adj. included; implied.

mitempfunden, adj. sympathizing; vicarious.

mitfühlen, vb. sympathize.

mitfühlend, adj. sympathetic.

Mitgefühl, n.nt. sympathy.

mitgenommen, adj. the worse for wear.

Mitgift, -en, n.f. dowry.

Mitglied, -er, n.nt. member, fellow.

Mitgliedschaft, n.f. membership.

Mithelfer, -, n.m. accessory.

Mitleid, n.nt. pity, compassion; mercy.

mitleidig, adj. compassionate.

mitmachen, vb. string along, join, conform.

Mitmacher, -, n.m. conformer.

Mitmensch, -en, -en, n.m. fellow-man.

Mitschuld, n.f. complicity.

mitschuldig, adj. being an accessory.

Mitschüler, -, n.m. classmate.

Mitspieler, -, n.m. player.

Mittag, -e, n.m. midday, noon.

Mittagessen, -, n.nt. noon meal, lunch, dinner.

Mittäter, -, n.m. accomplice.

Mitte, -n, n.f. middle, midst, center.

mitteilbar, adj. communicable.

mitteilen, vb. inform, communicate.

Mitteilung, -en, n.f. information, communication.

Mittel, -, n.nt. means, measure, expedient; medium.

mittel, adj. mean.

Mittelalter, n.nt. Middle Ages.

mittelalterlich, adj. medieval.

mittellos, adj. penniless, destitute.

mittelmäßig, adj. mediocre.

Mittelmeer, n.nt. Mediterranean Sea.

Mittelpunkt, -e, n.m. center, focus.

mittels, prep. by means of.

Mittelstand, n.m. middle class.

Mitternacht, n.f. midnight.

mittler-, adj. medium, middle.

Mittler-Osten, n.m. Middle East.

mittschiffs, adv. amidships.

Mittwoch, -e, n.m. Wednesday.

mitwirken, vb. cooperate, assist, contribute.

mitwirkend, adj. contributory.

Möbel, -, n.nt. piece of furniture; (pl.) furniture.

Möbelwagen, -, n.m. moving van.

mobil', adj. mobile; (fig.) hale and hearty.

mobilisie'ren, vb. mobilize.

mobilisiert', adj. mobile.

möblie'ren, vb. furnish.

Mode, -n, n.f. mode, fashion.

Modell', -e, n.nt. model.

modellie'ren, vb. model.

Modenschau, n.f. fashion show.

modern, vb. rot.

modern', adj. modern, fashionable.

modernisie'ren, vb. modernize.

Modeschöpfer, -, n.m. designer.

modifizie'ren, vb. modify.

modisch, adj. modish, fashionable.

Mofa, -s, n.nt. moped.

mögen*, vb. like; may.

möglich, adj. possible; potential.

möglicherweise, adv. possibly.

Möglichkeit, -en, n.f. possibility; potential; facility.

Mohr, -en, -en, n.m. Moor.

Mohrrübe, -n, n.f. carrot.

Mole, -n, n.f. mole, jetty, breakwater.

Molkerei', -en, n.f. dairy.

Moll, n.nt. minor.

mollig, adj. plump; snug.

Moment', -e, n.m. moment, instant.

Moment', -e, n.nt. factor, impulse, motive.

momentan', adj. momentary.

Monarch', -en, -en, n.m. monarch.

Monarchie', -i'en, n.f. monarchy.

Monat, -e, n.m. month.

monatlich, adj. monthly.

Monatschrift, -en, n.f. monthly.

Mönch, -e, n.m. monk.

Mond, -e, n.m. moon.

Mondschein, n.m. moonlight.

Mondsichel, -n, n.f. crescent moon.

Monolog', -e,, n.m. monologue.

Monopol', -e, n.nt. monopoly.

monopolisie'ren, vb. monopolize.

monoton', adj. monotonous.

Monotonie', n.f. monotony.

monströs', adj. monstrous, freak.

Montag, -e, n.m. Monday.

Montan'union, n.f. European Coal and Steel Community.

montie'ren, vb. assemble, mount.

monumental', adj. monumental.

Moor, -e, n.nt. moor.

Moos, -e, n.nt. moss.

Mop, -s, n.m. mop.

Moral', *n.f.* morals; morality; morale.

mora'lisch, *adj.* moral, ethical.

Moralist', **-en, -en,** *n.m.* moralist.

Morast', **-e,** *n.m.* morass, bog.

Mord, **-e,** *n.m.* murder, assassination.

morden, *vb.* murder.

Mörder, **-,** *n.m.* murderer.

Mords-, *cpds.* mortal; heck of a . . . .

morgen, *adv.* tomorrow.

Morgen, **-,** *n.m.* morning; acre.

Morgendämmerung, **-en,** *n.f.* dawn.

Morgenrock, **-e,** *n.m.* dressing gown.

morgens, *adv.* in the morning.

Morphium, *n.nt.* morphine.

morsch, *adj.* rotten.

Mörser, **-,** *n.m.* mortar.

Mörtel, **-,** *n.m.* mortar.

Mosaik', **-e,** *n.nt.* mosaic.

Most, **-e,** *n.m.* grape juice, new wine; (Apfelmost) cider.

Mostrich, *n.m.* mustard.

Motiv', **-e,** *n.nt.* motif.

motivie'ren, *vb.* motivate.

Motivie'rung, **-en,** *n.f.* motivation.

Motor('), **-o'ren,** *n.m.* motor, engine.

motorisie'ren, *vb.* motorize, mechanize.

Motor'rad, **-er,** *n.nt.* motorcycle.

Motte, **-n,** *n.f.* moth.

Motto, **-s,** *n.nt.* motto.

Mücke, **-n,** *n.f.* mosquito.

mucksen, *vb.* stir.

müde, *adj.* tired, sleepy; weary.

Müdigkeit, *n.f.* fatigue.

Muff, **-e,** *n.m.* muff.

muffig, *adj.* musty.

Mühe, **-n,** *n.f.* trouble, inconvenience; effort; (machen Sie sich keine M.) don't bother.

mühelos, *adj.* effortless.

mühen, *vb.* (sich m.) try, take the trouble.

Mühle, **-n,** *n.f.* mill.

Muhme, **-n,** *n.f.* aunt.

Mühsal, **-e,** *n.f.* trouble, hardship.

mühsam, *adj.* difficult, tedious, inconvenient.

mühselig, *adj.* laborious.

Mull, *n.m.* gauze.

Müll, *n.m.* garbage.

Mullah, **-s,** *n.m.* mullah.

Müller, **-,** *n.m.* miller.

multinational', *adj.* multinational.

Multiplikation', **-en,** *n.f.* multiplication.

multiplizie'ren, *vb.* multiply.

Mumie, **-n,** *n.f.* mummy.

Mund, **-er,** *n.m.* mouth.

Mundart, **-en,** *n.f.* dialect.

Mündel, **-,** *n.nt.* ward.

münden, *vb.* run, flow into, end.

mündlich, *adj.* oral, verbal.

Mündung, **-en,** *n.f.* (river) mouth; (gun) muzzle.

Munition', **-en,** *n.f.* ammunition, munition.

munkeln, *vb.* rumor.

munter, *adj.* awake; sprightly, lusty.

Münze, **-n,** *n.f.* coin; mint.

mürbe, *adj.* mellow; (meat) tender; (cake) crisp; (fig.) weary.

murmeln, *vb.* murmur, mutter.

murren, *vb.* grumble.

mürrisch, *adj.* disgruntled, petulant, glum.

Mürrischkeit, *n.f.* glumness.

Muschel, **-n,** *n.f.* shell; mussel, clam.

Muse, **-n,** *n.f.* muse.

Muse'um, **-e'en,** *n.nt.* museum.

Musik', *n.f.* music.

musika'lisch, *adj.* musical.

Musikant', **-en, -en,** *n.m.* musician.

Musiker, **-,** *n.m.* musician.

Musik'kapelle, **-n,** *n.f.* band, orchestra.

Musik'pavillon, **-s,** *n.m.* bandstand.

Muskat', **-n,** *n.m.* nutmeg.

Muskel, **-n,** *n.m.* muscle.

Muskelkraft, **-e,** *n.f.* muscular strength, brawn.

muskulös', *adj.* muscular.

Muße, *n.f.* leisure.

Musselin', **-e,** *n.m.* muslin.

müssen*, *vb.* must, have to.

müßig, *adj.* idle.

Müßigkeit, *n.f.* idleness.

Muster, **-,** *n.nt.* model; sample; pattern, design.

Musterbeispiel, **-e,** *n.nt.* paragon, perfect example.

mustergültig, *adj.* exemplary, model.

musterhaft, *adj.* exemplary.

mustern, *vb.* examine; (mil.) muster.

Musterung, **-en,** *n.f.* examination; (mil.) muster; (pattern) figuring.

Mut, *n.m.* courage, fortitude.

Mutation', **-en,** *n.f.* mutation.

mutig, *adj.* courageous.

Mutigkeit, *n.f.* pluck.

mutmaßen, *vb.* conjecture.

mutmaßlich, *adj.* presumable.

Mutmaßung, **-en,** *n.f.* conjecture.

Mutter, **-,** *n.f.* mother.

Mutterleib, *n.m.* womb.

mütterlich, *adj.* maternal.

Mutterschaft, *n.f.* maternity.

mutterseelenallein', *adj.* all alone.

Muttersprache, **-n,** *n.f.* native language.

mutwillig, *adj.* deliberate, wilful.

Mütze, **-n,** *n.f.* cap, bonnet.

Myrte, **-n,** *n.f.* myrtle.

mysteriös', *adj.* mysterious.

Mystik, *n.f.* mysticism.

mystisch, *adj.* mystic.

Mythe, **-n,** *n.f.* myth.

N

na, *interj.* well; (n. also) there you are; (n. und ob) I should say so.

Nabe, **-n,** *n.f.* hub.

nach, *prep.* towards, to; after; according to; (n. und n.) by and by, gradually.

nach-affen, *vb.* ape, imitate.

nach-ahmen, *vb.* imitate, simulate.

Nachahmung, **-en,** *n.f.* imitation.

Nachbar, **(-n,) -n,** *n.m.* neighbor.

Nachbarschaft, **-en,** *n.f.* neighborhood.

nachdem', *conj.* after.

nach-denken*, *vb.* think, meditate, reflect.

nachdenklich, *adj.* contemplative, pensive.

Nachdruck, *n.m.* emphasis.

nachdrücklich, *adj.* emphatic.

nach-eifern, *vb.* emulate.

Nachfolger, **-,** *n.m.* successor.

Nachforschung, **-en,** *n.f.* investigation; research.

Nachfrage, **-n,** *n.f.* inquiry; (Angebot und N.) supply and demand.

nach-fühlen, *vb.* understand, appreciate.

nach-füllen, *vb.* refill.

nach-geben*, *vb.* give in, yield.

nach-gehen*, *vb.* follow; seek; (clock) be slow.

nachgiebig, *adj.* compliant.

nachhaltig, *adj.* lasting.

nach-helfen*, *vb.* assist, boost.

nachher, *adv.* afterward(s).

Nachhilfe, *n.f.* assistance.

Nachhilfelehrer, **-,** *n.m.* tutor.

nach-holen, *vb.* make up for.

Nachkomme, **-n, -n,** *n.m.* descendant.

Nachlaß, **-sse,** *n.m.* estate.

nach-lassen*, *vb.* abate, subside.

nachlässig, *adj.* negligent, careless, derelict.

Nachlässigkeit, **-en,** *n.f.* negligence, carelessness.

nach-machen, *vb.* imitate.

Nachmittag, **-e,** *n.m.* afternoon.

Nachmittagsvorstellung, **-en,** *n.f.* matinée.

Nachnahme, **-n,** *n.f.* (per N.) C.O.D.

nach-prüfen, *vb.* check up, verify.

Nachricht, **-en,** *n.f.* information, message; notice; (pl.) news.

Nachrichtensendung, *n.f.* newscast.

nach-schlagen*, *vb.* look up, refer to.

Nachschrift, **-en,** *n.f.* postscript.

nach-sehen*, *vb.* look after;

look up; examine, check; (fig.) excuse, indulge.

Nachsehen, n.nt. (**das N. haben***) be the loser.

Nachsicht, -en, n.f. indulgence, forbearance.

nachsichtig, adj. lenient, indulgent.

Nachspiel, -e, n.nt. postlude.

nach·spüren, vb. track down.

nächst-, adj. next nearest.

nach·stehen*, vb. be inferior.

nach·stellen, vb. pursue; (clock) put back.

Nächstenliebe, n.f. charity.

nächstens, adv. soon.

Nacht, ¨-e, n.f. night.

Nachteil, -e, n.m. disadvantage, drawback.

nachteilig, adj. disadvantageous, adverse.

Nachthemd, -en, n.nt. nightgown.

Nachtigall, -en, n.f. nightingale.

Nachtisch, -e, n.m. dessert.

nächtlich, adj. nocturnal.

Nachtlokal, -e, n.nt. night club.

Nachtrag, ¨-e, n.m. supplement.

nach·tragen*, vb. carry behind; (fig.) resent, bear a grudge.

Nachtwache, -n, n.f. vigil.

Nachweis, -e, n.m. proof, certificate.

nachweisbar, adj. demonstrable.

nach·weisen*, vb. demonstrate, prove.

Nachwelt, n.f. posterity.

Nachwirkung, -en, n.f. aftereffect.

nach·zählen, vb. count over again, count up.

nach·zeichnen, vb. trace.

nackt, adj. naked, nude; bare.

Nacktheit, n.f. nakedness, bareness.

Nadel, -n, n.f. needle, pin.

Nagel, ¨-, n.m. nail.

nagen, vb. gnaw.

Nagetier, -e, n.nt. rodent.

nah(e) (**näher, nächst-**), adj. near.

Nähe, n.f. vicinity, proximity.

nähen, vb. sew.

Näherin, -nen, n.f. seamstress.

nähern, vb. (**sich n.**) approach.

nähren, vb. nourish; nurture.

nahrhaft, adj. nutritious, nourishing.

Nahrung, -en, n.f. nourishment, food.

Nahrungsmittel, n.pl. foodstuffs.

Naht, ¨-e, n.f. seam.

naiv', adj. naïve.

Name(n), -, n.m. name.

namentlich, adv. by name, namely; considerable.

namhaft, adj. renowned.

nämlich, adv. that is to say, namely.

nanu', interj. well, what do you know?

Naphtha, n.nt. naphtha.

Narbe, -n, n.f. scar.

Narko'se, -n, n.f. anesthetic.

narko'tisch, adj. narcotic, anesthetic.

Narr, -en, -en, n.m. fool; (**zum N. halten***) fool, make a fool of.

narrensicher, adj. foolproof.

närrisch, adj. foolish, daffy.

Narzis'se, -n, n.f. narcissus; (**gelbe N.**) daffodil.

nasal', adj. nasal.

naschen, vb. nibble (secretly) on sweets.

Nase, -n, n.f. nose.

Nasenbluten, n.nt. nosebleed.

Nasenloch, ¨-er, n.nt. nostril.

Nasenschleim, n.m. mucus.

naseweis, adj. fresh, know-it-all.

naß(-), adj. wet.

Nässe, n.f. wetness, moisture.

nässen, vb. wet.

Nation', -en, n.f. nation.

national', adj. national.

Nationalis'mus, n.m. nationalism.

Nationalität', -en, n.f. nationality.

National'ökonomie, n.f. political economics.

Natrium, n.nt. sodium.

Natron, n.nt. sodium.

Natur', -en, n.f. nature.

Natura'lien, n.pl. food produce.

naturalisie'ren, vb. naturalize.

Naturalist', -en, -en, n.m. naturalist.

Natur'forscher, -, n.m. naturalist.

Natur'kunde, n.f. nature study.

natür'lich, 1. adj. natural. 2. adv. of course.

Natür'lichkeit, n.f. naturalness.

Natur'wissenschaftler, n.m. scientist.

nautisch, adj. nautical.

Navigation', n.f. navigation.

Nebel, -, n.m. fog, mist.

Nebelfleck, -e, n.m. nebula.

nebelhaft, adj. nebulous.

neb(e)lig, adj. foggy.

neben, prep. beside.

Nebenanschluß, ¨-sse, n.m. (telephone) extension.

nebenbei', adv. besides; by the way, incidentally.

Nebenbuhler, -, n.m. rival.

nebeneinan'der, adv. beside one another, abreast.

Nebengebäude, -, n.nt. annex.

Nebenprodukt, -e, n.nt. by-product.

Nebensache, -n, n.f. incidental matter.

nebensächlich, adj. incidental, irrelevant.

Nebenweg, -e, n.m. byway.

nebst, prep. with, including.

necken, vb. tease, kid.

neckisch, adj. playful, cute.

Neffe, -n, -n, n.m. nephew.

negativ, adj. negative.

Negativ, -e, n.nt. negative.

Neger, -, n.m. Negro.

Negligé, -s, n.nt. negligée.

nehmen*, vb. take.

Neid, n.m. envy.

neidisch, adj. envious.

neigen, vb. (tr.) incline, bow, bend; (intr.) lean, slant; (fig.) tend.

Neigung, -en, n.f. inclination; slant; tendency, trend; affection.

nein, interj. no.

Nelke, -n, n.f. carnation.

nennen*, vb. name, call.

nennenswert, adj. considerable, worth mentioning.

Nenner, -, n.m. denominator.

Nennwert, -e, n.m. denomination; face value.

Neon, n.nt. neon.

Nerv, -en, n.m. nerve.

Nervenkitzel, -, n.m. thrill.

nervös', adj. nervous, jittery; high-strung.

Nervosität', n.f. nervousness.

Nerz, -e, n.m. mink.

Nessel, -n, n.f. nettle.

Nest, -er, n.nt. nest.

nett, adj. nice, enjoyable.

netto, adj. net.

Netz, -e, n.nt. net, web; network.

Netzhaut, ¨-e, n.f. retina.

neu, adj. new; (**aufs neue, von neuem**) anew.

Neubelebung, -en, n.f. revival.

Neuerung, -en, n.f. innovation.

Neugierde, n.f. curiosity.

neugierig, adj. curious, inquisitive.

Neuheit, -en, n.f. novelty.

Neuigkeit, -en, n.f. news; novelty.

Neujahr, n.nt. New Year; (**Fröhliches N.**) Happy New Year.

neulich, adv. the other day, recently.

Neuling, -e, n.m. novice.

neun, num. nine.

neunt-, adj. ninth.

Neuntel, -, n.nt. ninth part; (**ein n.**) one-ninth.

neunzig, num. ninety.

neunzigst-, adj. ninetieth.

Neunzigstel, -, n.nt. ninetieth part; (**ein n.**) one-ninetieth.

Neuralgie', n.f. neuralgia.

neuro'tisch, adj. neurotic.

neutral', adj. neutral.

Neutralität', n.f. neutrality.

Neutron, -o'nen, n.nt. neutron.

Neutro'nenbombe, -n, n.f. neutron bomb.

nicht, adv. not; (**n. wahr**) isn't that so, don't you, aren't we, won't they, etc.

Nichtachtung, n.f. disregard, disrespect.

Nichtanerkennung, -en, n.f. nonrecognition; repudiation.

Nichtbeachtung, n.f. disregard.

Nichte, -n, n.f. niece.

nichtig, adj. null, void.

nichts, pron. nothing.

Nichts, *n.nt.* nothingness, non-entity.

nichtsdestoweniger, *adv.* notwithstanding, nevertheless.

Nichtswisser, -, *n.m.* ignoramus.

nichtswürdig, *adj.* worthless, condemnable.

Nickel, *n.nt.* nickel.

nicken, *vb.* nod.

nie, *adv.* never.

nieder, *adv.* down.

Niedergang, *n.m.* decline.

niedergedrückt, *adj.* depressed.

niedergeschlagen, *adj.* dejected.

Niederkunft, *n.f.* childbirth.

Niederlage, -n, *n.f.* defeat; branch office.

Niederlande, *n.pl.* Netherlands.

Niederländer, -, *n.m.* Netherlander, Dutchman.

niederländisch, *adj.* Netherlandic, Dutch.

nieder·lassen*, *vb.* (**sich n.**) settle.

Niederlassung, -en, *n.f.* settlement.

nieder·metzeln, *vb.* massacre.

Niederschlag, ⸚e, *n.m.* precipitation; sediment.

Niedertracht, *n.f.* meanness, infamy.

niederträchtig, *adj.* mean, vile, infamous.

niedlich, *adj.* pretty, cute.

niedrig, *adj.* low; base, menial.

niemals, *adv.* never.

niemand, *pron.* no one, nobody.

Niere, -n, *n.f.* kidney.

nieseln, *vb.* drizzle.

niesen, *vb.* sneeze.

Niete, -n, *n.f.* rivet; (lottery) blank; failure, washout.

Nihilis'mus, *n.m.* nihilism.

Nikotin', *n.nt.* nicotine.

nimmer, *adv.* never.

nimmermehr, *adv.* never again.

nirgends, nirgendwo, *adv.* nowhere.

Nische, -n, *n.f.* recess, niche.

nisten, *vb.* nestle.

Niveau', -s, *n.nt.* level.

nobel, *adj.* noble; liberal.

noch, *adv.* still, yet; (**n. einmal**) once more; (**n. ein**) another, an additional; (**weder . . . n.**) neither . . . nor.

nochmalig, *adj.* additional, repeated.

nochmal(s), *adv.* once more.

Noma'de, -n, -n, *n.m.* nomad.

nominal', *adj.* nominal.

Nonne, -n, *n.f.* nun.

Nonnenkloster, ⸚e, *n.nt.* convent.

Nord, Norden, *n.m.* north.

nördlich, *adj.* northern; to the north.

Nordos'ten, *n.m.* northeast.

nordöst'lich, *adj.* northeastern; to the northeast.

Nordpol, *n.m.* North Pole.

Nordwes'ten, *n.m.* northwest.

nordwest'lich, *adj.* northwestern; to the northwest.

nörgeln, *vb.* gripe.

Norm, -en, *n.f.* norm, standard.

normal', *adj.* normal.

Norwegen, *n.nt.* Norway.

Norweger, -, *n.m.* Norwegian.

norwegisch, *adj.* Norwegian.

Not, ⸚e, *n.f.* need, necessity; hardship; distress.

Notar', -e, *n.m.* notary.

Notbehelf, *n.m.* makeshift, stop-gap.

Notdurft, *n.f.* want; need.

notdürftig, *adj.* scanty, bare.

Note, -n, *n.f.* note.

Notfall, ⸚e, *n.m.* emergency.

notgedrungen, *adv.* perforce.

notie'ren, *vb.* note, make a note.

Notie'rung, -en, *n.f.* quotation.

nötig, *adj.* necessary.

nötigen, *vb.* urge.

Notiz', -en, *n.f.* note.

Notiz'block, ⸚e, *n.m.* notepaper pad.

Notiz'buch, ⸚er, *n.nt.* notebook.

notleidend, *adj.* needy.

notwendig, *adj.* necessary.

Notwendigkeit, -en, *n.f.* necessity.

Novel'le, -n, *n.f.* short story.

Novem'ber, *n.m.* November.

Nu, *n.m.* jiffy.

nüchtern, *adj.* sober; (**auf nüchternen Magen**) on an empty stomach.

Nüchternheit, *n.f.* sobriety; unimaginativeness.

Nudeln, *n.pl.* noodles.

nuklear', *adj.* nuclear.

Null, -en, *n.f.* cipher; zero.

numerie'ren, *vb.* number.

nun, *adv.* now; (**von n. an**) henceforth.

nur, *adv.* only.

Nuß, ⸚sse, *n.f.* nut.

Nußschale, -n, *n.f.* nutshell.

Nüster, -n, *n.f.* nostril.

Nutzbarkeit, *n.f.* utility.

Nutzen, -, *n.m.* benefit.

nützen, *vb.* use, utilize; *(intr.)* be of use, help, benefit.

nützlich, *adj.* useful, beneficial.

nutzlos, *adj.* useless, futile.

Nutzlosigkeit, *n.f.* futility.

Nylon, *n.nt.* nylon.

Nymphe, -n, *n.f.* nymph.

O

Oa'se, -n, *n.f.* oasis.

ob, *conj.* whether; (**als o.**) as if.

Obdach, *n.nt.* shelter.

obdachlos, *adj.* homeless.

oben, *adv.* above; upstairs.

ober-, *adj.* upper.

Ober, -, *n.m.* (= Oberkellner) headwaiter, waiter; (**Herr O.!**) waiter!

Oberbefehlshaber, -, *n.m.* commander-in-chief.

Oberfläche, -n, *n.f.* surface.

oberflächlich, *adj.* superficial.

Oberhaupt, ⸚er, *n.nt.* chief.

Oberherrschaft, *n.f.* sovereignty.

Oberschicht, *n.f.* upper stratum; upper classes; (**geistige O.**) intelligentsia.

oberst-, *adj.* supreme, paramount.

Oberst, -en, -en, *n.m.* colonel.

Oberstleut'nant, -s, *n.m.* lieutenant colonel.

obgleich', *conj.* although.

Obhut, *n.f.* keeping, charge.

obig, *adj.* above, aforesaid.

Objekt' -e, *n.nt.* object.

objektiv', *adj.* objective.

Objektiv', -e, *n.nt.* objective; lens.

Objektivität', *n.f.* objectivity, detachment.

Obliegenheit, -en, *n.f.* duty, obligation.

Obligation', -en, *n.f.* bond; obligation.

obligato'risch, *adj.* obligatory.

Obrigkeit, -en, *n.f.* authorities, government.

obschon', *conj.* although.

ob·siegen, *vb.* be victorious over.

Obst, *n.nt.* fruit.

Obstgarten, ⸚, *n.m.* orchard.

obszön', *adj.* obscene.

Obus, -se, *n.m.* (= Oberleitungsomnibus) trolley bus.

ob·walten, *vb.* prevail, exist.

obwohl', *conj.* although.

Ochse, -n, -n or **Ochs, -en, -en,** *n.m.* ox.

öde, *adj.* bleak, desolate.

Öde, -n, *n.f.* bleakness, waste place.

oder, *conj.* or.

Ofen, ⸚, *n.m.* stove, oven, furnace.

offen, *adj.* open, frank.

offenbar, *adj.* evident.

offenba'ren, *vb.* reveal.

Offenba'rung, -en, *n.f.* revelation.

Offenba'rungsschrift, -en, *n.f.* scripture.

Offenheit, *n.f.* frankness.

offenkundig, *adj.* manifest.

offensichtlich, *adj.* obvious.

Offensi've, -n, *n.f.* offense, offensive.

öffentlich, *adj.* public.

Öffentlichkeit, *n.f.* public.

offiziell', *adj.* official.

Offizier', -e, *n.m.* officer.

öffnen, *vb.* open.

Öffnung, -en, *n.f.* opening, aperture.

oft (⸚), *adv.* often.

öfters, *adv.* quite often.

oftmals, *adv.* often (times).

Oheim, -e, *n.m.* uncle.

ohne, *prep.* without.

ohnglei'chen, *adv.* unequalled.

ohnehin, *adv.* in any case.

Ohnmacht, *n.f.* faint, unconsciousness; **(in O. fallen*)** faint.

ohnmächtig, *adj.* in a faint, powerless.

Ohr, -en, *n.nt.* ear.

Öhr, -e, *n.nt.* eye (of a needle, etc.).

Ohrenschmerzen, *n.pl.* earache.

Ohrring, -e, *n.m.* earring.

okay, *pred. adv.* okay.

okkult', *adj.* occult.

Ökologie', *n.f.* ecology.

ökologisch, *adj.* ecological.

Ökonom', -en, -en, *n.m.* farmer, manager.

Ökonomie', -i'en, *n.f.* economy; agriculture.

ökono'misch, *adj.* economical.

Okta've, -n, *n.f.* octave.

Okto'ber, *n.m.* October.

ökume'nisch, *adj.* ecumenical.

Okzident, *n.m.* occident.

Öl, -e, *n.nt.* oil.

ölen, *vb.* oil.

ölig, *adj.* oily.

Oli've, -n, *n.f.* olive.

Ölung, -en, *n.f.* oiling; anointment; **(letzt Ö.)** extreme unction.

Oma, -s, *n.f.* granny, grandma.

Ombudsmann, ¨er, *n.m.* ombudsman.

Omelett', -e, *n.nt.* omelet.

Omnibus, -se, *n.m.* (omni)bus.

ondulie'ren, *vb.* wave (hair).

Onkel, -, *n.m.* uncle.

Opa, -s, *n.m.* grandpa.

Opal', -e, *n.m.* opal.

Oper, -n, *n.f.* opera.

Operation', -en, *n.f.* operation.

operativ', *adj.* operative.

Operet'te, -n, *n.f.* operetta.

operie'ren, *vb.* operate.

Opernglas, ¨er, *n.nt.* opera glasses.

Opfer, -, *n.nt.* offering, sacrifice; victim, casualty.

opfern, *adv.* sacrifice.

Opium, *n.nt.* opium.

opponie'ren, *vb.* oppose.

Opposition', -en, *n.f.* opposition.

Optik, *n.f.* optics.

Optiker, -, *n.m.* optician.

Optimis'mus, *n.m.* optimism.

optimis'tisch, *adj.* optimistic.

optisch, *adj.* optic.

Oran'ge, -n, *n.f.* orange.

Orches'ter, -, *n.nt.* orchestra.

Orchide'e, -n, *n.f.* orchid.

Orden, -, *n.m.* order, medal, decoration.

ordentlich, *adj.* orderly, decent, regular.

ordinär', *adj.* vulgar.

ordnen, *vb.* put in order, sort, arrange.

Ordnung, -en, *n.f.* order.

Organ', -e, *n.nt.* organ.

Organisation', -en, *n.f.* organization.

orga'nisch, *adj.* organic.

organisie'ren, *vb.* organize; scrounge.

Organis'mus, -men, *n.m.* organism.

Organist', -en, -en, *n.m.* organist.

Orgel, -n, *n.f.* organ.

Orgie, -n, *n.f.* orgy.

Orient, *n.m.* Orient.

orienta'lisch, *adj.* oriental.

orientie'ren, *vb.* orient(ate).

Orientie'rung, -en, *n.f.* orientation.

Original', -e, *n.nt.* original.

Originalität', -en, *n.f.* originality.

originell', *adj.* original.

Ort, -e, *n.m.* place, locality, town.

Orter, -, *n.m.* navigator.

orthodox', *adj.* orthodox.

örtlich, *adj.* local.

ortsansässig, *adj.* resident, indigenous.

Ortschaft, -en, *n.f.* town, village.

Ost, Osten, *n.m.* east.

Ostblockstaaten, *n.m.pl.* Eastern European Nations.

Ostern, *n.nt.* Easter.

Österreich, *n.nt.* Austria.

Österreicher, -, *n.m.* Austrian.

österreichisch, *adj.* Austrian.

östlich, *adj.* eastern, easterly.

Ostsee, *n.f.* Baltic Sea.

ostwärts, *adv.* eastward.

Otter, -, *n.m.* otter.

Otter, -n, *n.f.* adder.

Ouvertü're, -n, *n.f.* overture.

oval', *adj.* oval.

Ozean, -e, *n.m.* ocean.

Ozeandampfer, -, *n.m.* ocean liner.

Ozon', -e, *n.nt.* ozone.

P

Paar, -e, *n.nt.* pair, couple; **(ein paar)** a few.

paaren, *vb.* mate.

Pacht, -en, *n.f.* lease, tenure.

Pachtbrief, -e, *n.m.* lease (document).

pachten, *vb.* lease (from).

Pächter, -, *n.m.* tenant.

Pachtzins, *n.m.* rent (money).

Pack, ¨e, *n.m.* pack; rabble.

Päckchen, -, *n.nt.* parcel.

packen, *vb.* pack, seize, thrill.

Packen, -, *n.m.* pack.

Packung, -en, *n.f.* packing, wrapper, pack(age).

Pädago'ge, -n, -n, *n.m.* pedagogue.

Pädago'gik, *n.f.* pedagogy.

Paddel, -, *n.nt.* paddle.

paff, *interj.* bang.

Page, -n, *n.m.* page.

Paket', -e, *n.nt.* package.

Pakt, -e, *n.m.* pact.

Palast', ¨e, *n.m.* palace.

Palet'te, -n, *n.f.* palette.

Palme, -n, *n.f.* palm.

Pampelmu'se, -n, *n.f.* grapefruit.

Panik, *n.f.* panic.

Panne, -n, *n.f.* breakdown; flat tire.

Panora'ma, -men, *n.nt.* panorama.

Panther, -, *n.m.* panther.

Pantof'fel, -n, *n.f.* slipper.

Pantomi'me, -n, *n.f.* pantomime.

Panzer, -, *n.m.* armor; tank.

Panzer-, *cpds.* armored.

Papagei', -en, -en, *n.m.* parrot.

Papier', -e, *n.nt.* paper.

Papier'bogen, ¨, *n.m.* sheet of paper.

Papier'korb, ¨e, *n.m.* wastebasket.

Papier'krieg, -e, *n.m.* red tape, paperwork.

Papier'waren, *n.pl.* stationery.

Papp, -e, *n.m.* pap, paste.

Pappe, -n, *n.f.* cardboard.

Papst, ¨e, *n.m.* pope.

päpstlich, *adj.* papal.

Papsttum, *n.nt.* papacy.

Para'de, -n, *n.f.* parade.

Paradies', *n.nt.* paradise.

paradox', *adj.* paradoxical.

Paradox', -e, *n.nt.* paradox.

Paraffin', -e, *n.nt.* paraffin.

Paragraph', -en, -en, *n.m.* paragraph.

parallel', *adj.* parallel.

Paralle'le, -n, *n.f.* parallel.

Paraly'se, -n, *n.f.* paralysis.

Parenthe'se, -n, *n.f.* parenthesis.

Parfüm', -e, *n.nt.* perfume.

pari, *adv.* at par.

Pari, *n.nt.* par.

Paris', *n.nt.* Paris.

Pari'ser, -, *n.m.* Parisian.

Park, -e *or* -s, *n.m.* park.

parken, *vb.* park.

Parkuhr, -en, *n.f.* parking meter.

Parkverbot, -e, *n.nt.* no parking.

Parlament', -e, *n.nt.* parliament.

parlamenta'risch, *adj.* parliamentary.

Parodie', -i'en, *n.f.* parody.

Paro'le, -n, *n.f.* password.

Partei', -en, *n.f.* party.

Partei'genosse, -n, -n, *n.m.* party comrade.

partei'isch, *adj.* partisan, biased.

partei'lich, *adj.* partisan, biased.

partei'los, *adj.* impartial.

Parter're, -s, *n.nt.* ground floor; orchestra (seats in the ater).

Partie', -i'en, *n.f.* match.

Partisan', (-en,) -en, *n.m.* partisan; guerilla.

Partitur', -en, *n.f.* score.

Partizip', -ien, *n.nt.* participle.

Partner, -, *n.m.* partner, associate.

Parzel'le, -n, *n.f.* lot, plot.

Paß, =sse, *n.m.* pass; passport.

passa'bel, *adj.* passable.

Passagier', -e, *n.m.* passenger.

Passant', -en, -en, *n.m.* passer-by.

passen, *vb.* suit, fit; (p. zu) match.

passend, *adj.* fitting, suitable, proper.

passie'ren, *vb.* happen; pass.

Passion', *n.f.* passion.

passiv, *adj.* passive.

Passiv, -e, *n.nt.* passive.

Pasta, -sten, *n.f.* paste.

Paste, -n, *n.f.* paste.

Paste'te, -n, *n.f.* meat pie.

pasteurisie'ren, *vb.* pasteurize.

Pastil'le, -n, *n.f.* lozenge.

Pastor, -o'ren, *n.m.* minister.

Pate, -n, -n, *n.m.* godfather.

Pate, -n, *n.f.* godmother.

Patenkind, -er, *n.nt.* godchild.

Patenonkel, -, *n.m.* godfather.

Patent', -e, *n.nt.* patent.

Patentante, -n, *n.f.* godmother.

Pathos, *n.nt.* pathos.

Patient', -en, -en, *n.m.* patient.

Patin, -nen, *n.f.* godmother.

Patriot', -en, -en, *n.m.* patriot.

patrio'tisch, *adj.* patriotic.

Patriotis'mus, *n.m.* patriotism.

Patro'ne, -n, *n.f.* cartridge; pattern.

Patrouil'le, -n, *n.f.* patrol.

Pauschal'preis, -e, *n.m.* total price.

Pause, -n, *n.f.* pause, intermission, recess.

Pavillon, -s, *n.m.* pavillion.

Pazifis'mus, *n.m.* pacifism.

Pazifist', -en, -en, *n.m.* pacifist.

Pech, *n.nt.* pitch, bad luck.

Pedal', -e, *n.nt.* pedal.

Pedant', -en, -en, *n.m.* pedant.

Pein, *n.f.* pain, agony.

peinigen, *vb.* torment.

peinlich, *adj.* embarrassing; meticulous.

Peitsche, -n, *n.f.* whip.

peitschen, *vb.* whip.

Pelz, -e, *n.m.* fur.

Pelzhändler, -, *n.m.* furrier.

Pendel, -, *n.m.* or *nt.* pendulum.

pendeln, *vb.* swing, oscillate.

Pendler, -, *n.m.* commuter.

Penicillin', *n.nt.* penicillin.

Pension', -en, *n.f.* pension; board, boarding house.

pensionie'ren, *vb.* pension; (sich p. lassen*) retire.

per, *prep.* per, by, with.

perfekt', *adj.* perfect.

Perfekt', -e, *n.nt.* perfect (tense).

Pergament', -e, *n.nt.* parchment.

Perio'de, -n, *n.f.* period, term.

perio'disch, *adj.* periodic.

Peripherie', -i'en, *n.f.* periphery.

Perle, -n, *n.f.* pearl.

Perlmutter, *n.f.* mother-of-pearl.

Persia'ner, *n.m.* Persian lamb.

Persien, *n.nt.* Persia.

Person', -en, *n.f.* person.

Personal', *n.pl.* personnel, staff.

Persona'lien, *n.pl.* personal data.

persön'lich, *adj.* personal.

Persön'lichkeit, -en, *n.f.* personage; personality.

Perspekti've, -n, *n.f.* perspective.

pervers', *adj.* perverse.

Pessimis'mus, *n.m.* pessimism.

pessimis'tisch, *adj.* pessimistic.

Pest, *n.f.* plague, pestilence.

Petersi'lie, *n.f.* parsley.

Petro'leum, *n.nt.* petroleum.

Petschaft, -en, *n.f.* seal.

Pfad, -e, *n.m.* path.

Pfadfinder, -, *n.m.* boy scout.

Pfahl, =e, *n.m.* pole, pile, stake.

Pfand, =er, *n.m.* pawn, pledge, security.

Pfandbrief, -e, *n.m.* bond, mortgage bond.

pfänden, *vb.* seize, attach, impound.

Pfandhaus, =er, *n.nt.* pawnshop.

Pfanne, -n, *n.f.* pan.

Pfannkuchen, -, *n.m.* pancake.

Pfarrer, -, *n.m.* minister, priest.

Pfau, -e, *n.m.* peacock.

Pfeffer, -, *n.m.* pepper.

Pfefferkuchen, -, *n.m.* gingerbread.

Pfeffermin'ze, *n.f.* peppermint.

Pfeife, -n, *n.f.* pipe, whistle.

pfeifen*, *vb.* whistle.

Pfeil, -e, *n.m.* arrow.

Pfeiler, -, *n.m.* pillar, pier.

Pfennig, -e, *n.m.* penny.

Pferd, -e, *n.nt.* horse.

Pferdestärke, -n, *n.f.* horse-power.

Pfiff, -e, *n.m.* whistle; trick.

pfiffig, *adj.* tricky, sly.

Pfingsten, *n.m.* Pentecost, Whitsuntide.

Pfirsich, -e, *n.m.* peach.

Pflanze, -n, *n.f.* plant.

pflanzen, *vb.* plant.

Pflaster, -, *n.nt.* plaster; pavement.

pflastern, *vb.* plaster, pave.

Pflaume, -n, *n.f.* plum.

Pflege, -n, *n.f.* care, nursing, cultivation.

Pflegeeltern, *n.pl.* foster parents.

pflegen, *vb.* take care of, nurse, cultivate; be accustomed.

Pflicht, -en, *n.f.* duty.

pflichtgemäß, *adj.* dutiful.

Pflock, =e, *n.m.* peg.

pflücken, *vb.* pick, gather.

Pflug, =e, *n.m.* plow.

pflügen, *vb.* plow.

Pforte, -n, *n.f.* gate, door, entrance.

Pförtner, -, *n.m.* janitor, doorman.

Pfosten, -, *n.m.* post, jamb.

Pfote, -n, *n.f.* paw.

Pfropfen, -, *n.m.* stopper, plug.

pfropfen, *vb.* graft.

pfrofen, *vb.* botch, bungle.

Pfütze, -n, *n.f.* puddle.

Phänomen', -e, *n.nt.* phenomenon.

Phantasie', -i'en, *n.f.* fantasy.

phantas'tisch, *adj.* fantastic.

Phase, -n, *n.f.* phase.

Philosoph', -en, -en, *n.m.* philosopher.

Philosophie', -i'en, *n.f.* philosophy.

philoso'phisch, *adj.* philosophical.

phlegma'tisch, *adj.* phlegmatic.

phone'tisch, *adj.* phonetic.

Phosphor, *n.m.* phosphorus.

Photoapparat, -e, *n.m.* camera.

photoelek'trisch, *adj.* photoelectric.

Photograph', -en, -en, *n.m.* photographer.

Photographie', -i'en, *n.f.* photograph(y).

Photokopie', -n, *n.f.* photocopy.

photokopie'ren, *vb.* photocopy.

Photokopier'maschine, -n, *n.f.* photocopier.

Physik', *n.f.* physics.

Physiker, -, *n.m.* physicist.

Physiologie', *n.f.* physiology.

physisch, *adj.* physical.

Pianist', -en, -en, *n.m.* pianist.

Pickel, -, *n.m.* pimple; ice axe.

picken, *vb.* peck.

Picknick, -s, *n.nt.* picnic.

piepsen, *vb.* peep.

Pier, -s, *n.m.* pier.

Pietät', *n.f.* piety.

Pigment', -e, *n.nt.* pigment.

pikant', *adj.* piquant.

Pilger, -, *n.m.* pilgrim.

Pille, -n, *n.f.* pill.

Pilot', -en, -en, *n.m.* pilot.

Pilz, -e, *n.m.* mushroom.

Pinsel, -, *n.m.* brush.

Pionier', -e, *n.m.* pioneer; (*mil.*) engineer.

Pisto'le, -n, *n.f.* pistol.

Pisto'lenhalter, -, *n.m.* holster.

Pizza, -s, *n.f.* pizza.

Plackerei', -en, *n.f.* drudgery.

plädie'ren, *vb.* plead.

Plädoyer', -s, *n.nt.* plea.

Plage, -n, *n.f.* trouble, affliction.

plagen, *vb.* plague, annoy, afflict.

Plagiat', *n.nt.* plagiarism.

Plakat', -e, *n.nt.* placard, poster.

Plan, =e, *n.m.* plan.

planen, *vb.* plan.

Planet', -en, -en, *n.m.* planet.

Planke, -n, *n.f.* plank.

planlos, *adj.* aimless.

planmäßig, *adj.* according to plan.

planschen, *vb.* splash.

Planta'ge, -n, *n.f.* plantation.

Plappermaul, ¨-er, *n.nt.* chatterbox.

plappern, *vb.* babble.

Plasma, -men, *n.nt.* plasma.

Plastik, -en, *n.f.* sculpture.

plastisch, *adj.* plastic.

Plateau', -s, *n.nt.* plateau.

Platin, *n.nt.* platinum.

platt, *adj.* flat.

Plättbrett, -er, *n.nt.* ironing board.

Platte, -n, *n.f.* plate, slab, sheet, tray; (photographic) slide; (phonograph) record.

Plätteisen, -, *n.nt.* (flat) iron.

plätten, *vb.* iron.

Plattenspieler, -, *n.m.* record player.

Plattform, -en, *n.f.* platform.

Plattfuß, ¨-e, *n.m.* flat foot.

plattie'ren, *vb.* plate.

Platz, ¨-e, *n.m.* place, seat, square.

platzen, *vb.* burst.

Plauderei', -en, *n.f.* chat.

plaudern, *vb.* chat.

pleite, *adj.* broke.

Plombe, -n, *n.f.* (tooth) filling.

plötzlich, *adj.* sudden.

plump, *adj.* clumsy, tactless.

Plunder, *n.m.* old clothes, rubbish.

plündern, *vb.* plunder, pillage.

Plünderung, -en, *n.f.* pillage.

Plural, -e, *n.m.* plural.

plus, *adv.* plus.

Plüsch, -e, *n.m.* plush.

Plutokrat', -en, -en, *n.m.* plutocrat.

pneuma'tisch, *adj.* pneumatic.

Pöbel, *n.m.* mob, rabble.

pöbelhaft, *adj.* vulgar.

pochen, *vb.* knock, throb.

Pocke, -n, *n.f.* pock; (pl.) smallpox.

Podium, -ien, *n.nt.* rostrum.

Poesie', I'en, *n.f.* poetry.

Poet', -en, -en, *n.m.* poet.

poe'tisch, *adj.* poetic.

Poin'te, -n, *n.f.* point (of a joke), punch line.

Pokal', -e, *n.m.* goblet, cup.

Pol, -e, *n.m.* pole.

polar', *adj.* polar.

Polar'stern, *n.m.* North Star.

Pole, -n, -n, *n.m.* Pole.

Polen, *n.nt.* Poland.

Poli'ce, -n, *n.f.* (insurance) policy.

polie'ren, *vb.* polish.

Politik', *n.f.* politics, policy.

Poli'tiker, -, *n.m.* politician.

poli'tisch, *adj.* politic(al).

Politur', -en, *n.f.* polish.

Polizei', -en, *n.f.* police.

polizei'lich, *adj.* by the police.

Polizei'präsident, -en, -en, *n.m.* chief of police.

Polizei'präsidium, -ien, *n.nt.* police headquarters.

Polizei'revier, -e, *n.nt.* police station.

Polizei'richter, -, *n.m.* police state.

Polizei'staat, -en, *n.m.* police state.

Polizei'stunde, -n, *n.f.* curfew.

Polizei'wache, -n, *n.f.* police station.

Polizist', -en, -en, *n.m.* policeman.

polnisch, *adj.* Polish.

Poloni'se, -n, *n.f.* polonaise.

Polster, -, *n.nt.* pad, cushion.

polstern, *vb.* pad, upholster.

Polsterung, -en, *n.f.* padding, upholstery.

poltern, *vb.* rattle, bluster.

Polygamie', *n.f.* polygamy.

Poly'pen, *n.pl.* adenoids.

Polytech'nikum, -ken, *n.nt.* technical college.

Pomeran'ze, -n, *n.f.* orange.

Pony, -s, *n.nt.* pony; (pl.) bangs.

populär', *adj.* popular.

popularisie'ren, *vb.* popularize.

Popularität', *n.f.* popularity.

Pore, -n, *n.f.* pore.

porös', *adj.* porous.

Portal', -e, *n.nt.* portal.

Portefeuille', -s, *n.nt.* portfolio.

Portemonnaie', -s, *n.nt.* purse.

Portier', -s, *n.m.* doorman, concierge.

Portion', -en, *n.f.* portion, helping.

Porto, *n.nt.* postage.

Porträt', -s, *n.nt.* portrait.

Portugal, *n.nt.* Portugal.

Portugie'se, -n, -n, *n.m.* Portuguese.

portugie'sisch, *adj.* Portuguese.

Porzellan', -en, *n.nt.* porcelain, china.

Posau'ne, -n, *n.f.* trumpet.

Pose, -n, *n.f.* pose.

posie'ren, *vb.* strike a pose.

Position', -en, *n.f.* position.

positiv, *adj.* positive.

Posse, -n, *n.f.* prank, antic; farce.

Post, *n.f.* mail; post office.

Postamt, ¨-er, *n.nt.* post office.

Postanweisung, -en, *n.f.* money order.

Postbote, -n, -n, *n.m.* postman.

Posten, -, *n.m.* post; station; item.

Postfach, ¨-er, *n.nt.* post office box.

Postkarte, -n, *n.f.* post card.

postlagernd, *adv.* general delivery.

Postleitzahl, -en, *n.f.* zip code.

Poststempel, -, *n.m.* post mark.

Pracht, *n.f.* splendor.

prächtig, *adj.* splendid.

prachtvoll, *adv.* gorgeous.

Prädikat', -e, *n.nt.* predicate.

Präfix, -e, *n.nt.* prefix.

prägen, *vb.* stamp, coin, impress.

Prägung, -en, *n.f.* coinage.

prähistorisch, *adj.* prehistoric.

prahlen, *vb.* boast.

praktisch, *adj.* practical.

Prali'ne, -n, *n.f.* chocolate candy.

prallen, *vb.* bounce, be reflected.

Prämie, -n, *n.f.* premium, prize.

präparie'ren, *vb.* prepare.

Präposition', -en, *n.f.* preposition.

Präsens, *n.nt.* present.

präsentie'ren, *vb.* present.

Präsident', -en, -en, *n.m.* president.

prasseln, *vb.* patter, crackle.

Praxis, *n.f.* practice; doctor's office.

Präzedenz'fall, ¨-e, *n.m.* precedent.

Präzision', *n.f.* precision.

predigen, *vb.* preach.

Prediger, -, *n.m.* preacher.

Predigt, -en, *n.f.* sermon.

Preis, -e, *n.m.* price, cost; prize, praise.

Preiselbeere, -n, *n.f.* cranberry.

preisen*, *vb.* praise.

Preisgabe, -n, *n.f.* surrender, abandonment.

preis-geben*, *vb.* surrender, abandon.

prellen, *vb.* toss; cheat.

Premie're, -n, *n.f.* première.

Premier'minister, -, *n.m.* prime minister.

Presse, *n.f.* press.

pressen, *vb.* press.

Prestige', *n.nt.* prestige.

Preuße, -n, -n, *n.m.* Prussian.

Preußen, *n.nt.* Prussia.

preußisch, *adj.* Prussian.

Priester, -, *n.m.* priest.

prima, *adj.* first class, swell.

primär, *adj.* primary.

Primel, -n, *n.f.* primrose.

primitiv', *adj.* primitive.

Prinz, -en, -en, *n.m.* prince.

Prinzes'sin, -nen, *n.f.* princess.

Prinzip', -ien, *n.nt.* principle.

Priorität', -en, *n.f.* priority.

Prise, -n, *n.f.* pinch.

Prisma, -men, *n.nt.* prism.

privat', *adj.* private.

Privileg', -ien, *n.nt.* privilege.

pro, *prep.* per.

Probe, -n, *n.f.* experiment, test; rehearsal; sample.

proben, *vb.* rehearse.

probeweise, *adj.* tentative.

Probezeit, -en, *n.f.* probation.

probie'ren, *vb.* try (out).

Problem', -e, *n.nt.* problem.

Produkt', -e, *n.nt.* product.

Produktion', *n.f.* production.

produktiv', *adj.* productive.

Produzent', -en, -en, *n.m.* producer.

produzie'ren, *vb.* produce.

profan', *adj.* profane.

Profes'sor, -o'ren, *n.m.* professor.

Profil', -e, *n.nt.* profile.

Profit', -e, *n.m.* profit.

profitie'ren, *vb.* profit.

Progno'se, -n, *n.f.* prognosis.

Programm', -e, *n.nt.* program.

Projekt', -e, *n.nt.* project.

Projektion', -en, n.f. projection.

Projek'tor, -o'ren, n.m. projector.

projizie'ren, vb. project.

Proklamation', -en, n.f. proclamation.

Prokurist', -en, -en, n.m. manager.

Proletariat', n.nt. proletariat.

Proleta'rier, -, n.m. proletarian.

proleta'risch, adj. proletarian.

Prolog', -e, n.m. prologue.

prominent', adj. prominent.

Prono'men, -mina, n.nt. pronoun.

Propagan'da, n.f. propaganda, publicity.

Propel'ler, -, n.m. propeller.

Prophet', -en, -en, n.m. prophet.

prophe'tisch, adj. prophetic.

prophezei'en, vb. prophesy.

Prophezei'ung, -en, n.f. prophecy.

Proportion', -en, n.f. proportion.

proppenvoll, adj. chock full.

Prosa, n.f. prose.

prosa'isch, adj. prosaic.

Prospekt', -e, n.m. prospectus.

Prostituiert'-, n.m. prostitute.

Protein', n.nt. protein.

Protest', -e, n.m. protest.

Protestant', -en, -en, n.m. Protestant.

protestie'ren, vb. protest.

Protokoll', -e, n.nt. minutes, record.

protzen, vb. show off.

protzig, adj. gaudy.

Proviant', n.m. food, supplies.

Provinz', -en, n.f. province.

provinziell', adj. provincial.

Provision', -en, n.f. commission.

proviso'risch, adj. temporary.

Provokation', -en, n.f. provocation.

provozie'ren, vb. provoke.

Prozent', -e, n.nt. per cent.

Prozent'satz, -̈e, n.m. percentage.

Prozeß', -sse, n.m. process; trial, lawsuit.

Prozession', -en, n.f. procession.

prüde, adj. prudish.

prüfen, vb. test, examine, verify.

Prüfung, -en, n.f. test, examination, scrutiny.

Prügel, -, n.m. cudgel; (pl.) beating.

Prügelei', -en, n.f. brawl.

prügeln, vb. beat, thrash.

Prunk, n.m. pomp, show.

prunkvoll, adj. pompous, showy.

PS, abbr. (= Pferdestärke) horsepower.

Psalm, -en, n.m. psalm.

Pseudonym', -e, n.nt. pseudonym.

psychede'lisch, adj. psychedelic.

Psychia'ter, -, n.m. psychiatrist.

Psychiatrie', n.f. psychiatry.

Psychoanaly'se, -n, n.f. psychoanalysis.

Psycholo'ge, -n, -n, n.m. psychologist.

Psychologie', n.f. psychology.

psycho'gisch, adj. psychological.

Psycho'se, -n, n.f. psychosis.

Publikation', -en, n.f. publication.

Publikum, n.nt. public, audience.

publizie'ren, vb. publish.

Pudding, -e, n.m. pudding.

Pudel, -, n.m. poodle.

Puder, -, n.m. powder.

Puderdose, -n, n.f. compact.

pudern, vb. powder.

Puderquaste, -n, n.f. powder puff.

Puffer, -, n.m. buffer; potato pancake.

Pullo'ver, -, n.m. sweater.

Puls, -e, n.m. pulse.

Pulsader, -n, n.f. artery.

Pulsar, -s, n.m. pulsar.

pulsie'ren, vb. pulsate, throb.

Pult, -e, n.nt. desk, lectern.

Pulver, -, n.nt. powder.

Pumpe, -n, n.f. pump.

pumpen, vb. pump; borrow, lend.

Pumps, n.pl. pumps.

Punkt, -e, n.m. point, dot, period.

Punktgleichheit, n.f. tie.

Punktion', -en, n.f. puncture.

pünktlich, adj. punctual.

Punktzahl, -en, n.f. score.

Punsch, -e, n.m. punch.

Pupil'le, -n, n.f. pupil.

Puppe, -n, n.f. doll; chrysalis.

pur, adj. pure; (alcohol) straight.

Püree', -s, n.nt. purée.

Purpur, n.m. purple.

purpurn, adj. purple.

Puter, -, n.m. turkey.

Putsch, -e, n.m. attempt to overthrow the government.

Putz, n.m. finery.

putzen, vb. clean, polish.

Putzfrau, -en, n.f. cleaning woman.

putzig, adj. funny, droll, quaint.

Putzwaren, n.pl. millinery.

Puzzle, -s, n.nt. puzzle.

Pyja'ma, -s, n.m. pajamas.

Pyrami'de, -n, n.f. pyramid.

Q

quadraphon', adj. quadraphonic.

Quadrat', -e, n.nt. square.

Quadrat'-, cpds. square.

quadra'tisch, adj. square.

quaken, vb. quack, croak.

Qual, -en, n.f. torment, agony, ordeal.

quälen, vb. torment, torture.

Qualifikation', -en, n.f. qualification.

qualifizie'ren, vb. qualify.

Qualität', -en, n.f. quality.

qualmen, vb. smoke.

qualvoll, adj. agonizing.

Quantität', -en, n.f. quantity.

Quaranti'ne, -n, n.f. quarantine.

Quark, n.m. curds.

Quarkkäse, n.m. cottage cheese.

Quartal', -e, n.nt. quarter of a year.

Quartett', -e, n.nt. quartet.

Quartier', -e, n.nt. lodging, billet.

Quarz, -e, n.m. quartz.

Quasar, n.m. quasar.

Quaste, -n, n.f. tuft.

Quatsch, n.m. nonsense, bunk, baloney.

Quecksilber, n.nt. mercury.

Quelle, -n, n.f. spring, source, well, fountain.

quellen*, vb. well, gush, flow.

quer, adj. cross(wise), diagonal.

Querschnitt, -, n.m. cross section.

Querstraße, -n, n.f. cross street.

Querverweis, -e, n.m. cross reference.

quetschen, vb. squeeze, bruise.

Quetschung, -en, n.f. contusion.

quietschen, vb. squeak.

Quintett', -e, n.nt. quintet.

quitt, adj. quits, even, square.

quittie'ren, vb. receipt.

Quittung, -en, n.f. receipt.

Quote, -n, n.f. quota.

R

Rabatt', -e, n.m. discount.

Rabau'ke, -n, -n, n.m. tough.

Rabbi'ner, -, n.m. rabbi.

Rabe, -n, -n, n.m. raven.

Rache, n.f. revenge.

rächen, vb. revenge, avenge.

Rachen, -, n.m. throat, jaws.

Rad, -̈er, n.nt. wheel.

Radar, n.nt. radar.

Radau', n.m. noise, racket.

radeln, vb. (bi)cycle.

rad-fahren*, vb. (bi)cycle.

Radfahrer, -, n.m. (bi)cyclist.

radie'ren, vb. erase; etch.

Radier'gummi, -s, n.m. (rubber) eraser.

Radie'rung, -en, n.f. etching.

Radies'chen, -, n.nt. radish.

radikal', adj. radical.

Radio, -s, n.nt. radio.

radioaktiv', adj. radioactive.

radioaktiv'-Niederschlag, n.m. fallout.

Radioapparat, -e, *n.m.* radio set.

Radioempfänger, -, *n.m.* radio receiver.

Radiosender, -, *n.m.* radio transmitter, broadcasting station.

Radiosendung, -en, *n.f.* radio broadcast.

Radium, *n.nt.* radium.

Radius, -ien, *n.m.* radius.

Radspur, -en, *n.f.* rut.

raffinie'ren, *vb.* refine.

raffiniert', *adj.* tricky, shrewd; sophisticated.

ragen, *vb.* extend, loom.

Rahm, *n.m.* cream.

rahmen, *vb.* frame.

Rahmen, -, *n.m.* frame.

Rake'te, -n, *n.f.* rocket.

Rake'tenwaffe, -n, *n.f.* missile.

rammen, *vb.* ram.

Rampe, -n. *n.f.* ramp.

Rand, ⁻er, *n.m.* edge, brim, margin.

Rang, ⁻e, *n.m.* rank.

rangie'ren, *vb.* switch, shunt.

Rangordnung, -en, *n.f.* hierarchy.

ranzig, *adj.* rancid.

Rapier', -e, *n.nt.* foil.

rasch, *adj.* quick.

rascheln, *vb.* rustle.

rasen, *vb.* rage.

Rasen, *n.m.* lawn, turf.

rasend, *adj.* frenzied.

Raserei', -en, *n.f.* frenzy.

Rasierapparat, -e, *n.m.* safety razor.

rasie'ren, *vb.* shave.

Rasier'klinge, -n, *n.f.* razor blade.

Rasier'messer, -, *n.nt.* (straight) razor.

Rasse, -n, *n.f.* race; breed.

rasseln, *vb.* rattle.

Rast, -en, *n.f.* rest.

rasten, *vb.* rest.

rastlos, *adj.* restless.

Rasur', -en, *n.f.* erasure; shave.

Rat, ⁻e, *n.m.* advice; councilor.

Rate, -n, *n.f.* payment, installment.

raten*, *vb.* guess, advise.

Ratenzahlung, *n.f.* payment by installments.

ratifizie'ren, *vb.* ratify.

Ration', -en, *n.f.* ration.

rationell', *adj.* rational, reasonable.

rationie'ren, *vb.* ration.

ratlos, *adj.* helpless, perplexed, at one's wit's end.

Ratlosigkeit, *n.f.* perplexity.

ratsam, *adj.* advisable.

Ratsamkeit, *n.f.* advisability.

Rätsel, -, *n.nt.* riddle, puzzle; enigma, mystery.

rätselhaft, *adj.* puzzling, mysterious.

Ratte, -n, *n.f.* rat.

rattern, *vb.* rattle.

Raub, *n.m.* robbery, plunder.

rauben, *vb.* rob.

Räuber, -, *n.m.* robber.

Rauch, *n.m.* smoke.

rauchen, *vb.* smoke.

Raucher, -, *n.m.* smoker.

räuchern, *vb.* smoke (fish, meat).

raufen, *vb.* pull, tear; (sich r.) fight, brawl.

Rauferei', -en, *n.f.* brawl.

rauh, *adj.* rough; harsh; rugged.

Rauheit, -en, *n.f.* roughness.

Raum, ⁻e, *n.m.* room, space.

räumen, *vb.* vacate.

Raumfahrt, *n.f.* space travel.

Rauminhalt, *n.m.* volume, capacity, contents.

räumlich, *adj.* spatial.

Raumtransporter, *n.m.* space shuttle.

Räumung, -en, *n.f. (comm.)* clearance; *(mil.)* evacuation.

raunen, *vb.* whisper.

Rausch, ⁻e, *n.m.* intoxication.

rauschen, *vb.* roar, rustle.

Rauschgift, -e, *n.nt.* narcotic, dope.

Razzia, -ien, *n.f.* raid.

reagie'ren, *vb.* react, respond.

Reaktion', -en, *n.f.* reaction, response.

Reaktionär', -e, *n.m.* reactionary.

reaktionär', *adj.* reactionary.

reaktivie'ren, *vb.* recommission.

Reak'tor, -o'ren, *n.m.* reactor.

realisie'ren, *vb.* realize, put into effect.

Realisie'rung, -en, *n.f.* realization.

Realis'mus, *n.m.* realism.

Realist', -en, -en, *n.f.* realist.

Realität', -en, *n.f.* reality.

Rebe, -n, *n.f.* vine; grape.

Rebstock, ⁻e, *n.m.* vine.

Rechen, -, *n.m.* rake.

Rechenaufgabe, -n, *n.f.* arithmetic problem.

Rechnen, *n.nt.* arithmetic.

Rechenmaschine, -n, *n.f.* calculating machine.

Rechenschaft, *n.f.* account, responsibility; (R. ablegen) account for.

Rechenschieber, -, *n.m.* slide rule.

rechnen, *vb.* count, do sums, figure.

Rechnen, *n.nt.* arithmetic.

Rechnung, -en, *n.f.* figuring, computation; bill; (R. tragen*) take into account.

Rechnungsbuch, ⁻er, *n.nt.* account book.

recht, *adj.* right; (r. haben*) be right.

Recht, -e, *n.nt.* right; (system of) law.

Rechteck, -e, *n.nt.* rectangle.

rechteckig, *adj.* rectangular, oblong.

rechtfertigen, *vb.* justify; vindicate.

Rechtfertigung, -en, *n.f.* justification.

rechtlich, *adj.* legal, judicial.

rechtmäßig, *adj.* lawful.

rechts, *adv.* (to the) right.

Rechtsanwalt, ⁻e, *n.m.* lawyer.

rechtschaffen, *adj.* honest, righteous.

Rechtschaffenheit, *n.f.* honesty, righteousness.

Rechtschreibung, *n.f.* orthography, spelling.

Rechtsgelehrt-, *n.m.* jurist.

Rechtsprechung, *n.f.* jurisdiction.

Rechtsspruch, ⁻e, *n.m.* judgment, sentence.

Rechtsstreit, -e, *n.m.* litigation.

Rechtswissenschaft, *n.f.* jurisprudence.

recken, *vb.* stretch.

Redakteur', -e, *n.m.* editor.

Redaktion', -en, *n.f.* editorial office; editor.

Rede, -n, *n.f.* speech, talk; (eine R. halten*) give a speech; (keine R. sein* von) be no question of; (jemanden zur R. stellen) confront a person with, take to task.

redegewandt, *adj.* eloquent.

Redekunst, *n.f.* rhetoric, oratory.

reden, *vb.* talk, speak; (vernünftig r. mit) reason with.

Redensart, -en, *n.f.* way of speaking; saying, idiom.

Redeteil, -e, *n.nt.* part of speech.

Redewendung, -en, *n.f.* phrase, figure of speech.

redlich, *adj.* honest, upright.

Redner, -, *n.m.* speaker, orator.

redselig, *adj.* loquacious.

Reduktion', -en, *n.f.* reduction.

reduzie'ren, *vb.* reduce.

reell', *adj.* honest, sound.

reflektie'ren, *vb.* reflect.

Reflex', -e, *n.m.* reflex.

Reflexion', -en, *n.f.* reflection.

Reform', -en, *n.f.* reform.

reformie'ren, *vb.* reform.

Refrain', -s, *n.m.* refrain.

Regal', -e, *n.nt.* shelf.

rege, *adj.* alert; active.

Regel, -n, *n.f.* rule.

regelmäßig, *adj.* regular.

Regelmäßigkeit, *n.f.* regularity.

regeln, *vb.* regulate.

regelrecht, *adj.* regular, downright.

Regelung, -en, *n.f.* regulation.

regen, *vb.* stir, move.

Regen, *n.m.* rain.

Regenbogen, ⁻, *n.m.* rainbow.

Regenguß, ⁻sse, *n.m.* downpour.

Regenmantel, ⁻, *n.m.* raincoat.

Regenschirm, -e, *n.m.* umbrella.

Regie', *n.f.* direction.

regie'ren, *vb.* govern.

Regie'rung, -en, *n.f.* government.

Regi'me, -s, *n.nt.* regime.

Regiment', -er, *n.nt.* regiment.

Region', -en, *n.f.* region.

Regisseur', -e, *n.m.* director.
Regis'ter, -, *n.nt.* register, index.
Registrie'rung, -en, *n.f.* registration.
regnen, *vb.* rain.
regnerisch, *adj.* rainy.
regsam, *adj.* alert, quick.
regulie'ren, *vb.* regulate.
Reh, -e, *n.nt.* deer, roe.
rehabilitie'ren, *vb.* rehabilitate.
Rehleder, -, *n.nt.* deerskin.
Reibe, -n, *n.f.* grater.
reiben*, *vb.* rub; grate; chafe.
Reibung, -en, *n.f.* friction.
reich, *adj.* rich.
Reich, -e, *n.nt.* kingdom, empire, realm.
reichen, *vb.* (tr.) pass, hand, reach; (intr.) extend.
reichlich, *adj.* plentiful, ample, abundant.
Reichtum, ̈er, *n.m.* wealth, affluence.
Reichweite, -n, *n.m.* reach, range.
reif, *adj.* ripe, mature.
Reife, *n.f.* maturity.
reifen, *vb.* ripen, mature.
Reifen, -, *n.m.* hoop; (auto, etc.) tire.
Reifenpanne, -n, *n.f.* puncture, blowout.
reiflich, *adj.* carefully considerate.
Reigen, -, *n.m.* (dance) round; (music) song.
Reihe, -n, *n.f.* row; series, succession.
reihen, *vb.* (sich r.) rank.
Reihenfolge, -n, *n.f.* sequence, succession.
Reim, -, *n.m.* rhyme.
rein, *adj.* clean, pure.
Reinfall, ̈e, *n.m.* flop.
rein'fallen*, *vb.* be taken in.
Reinheit, *n.f.* purity.
reinigen, *vb.* clean, cleanse.
Reinigung, -en, *n.f.* cleaning, cleansing; (chemische R.) dry-cleaner, dry-cleaning.
rein'legen, *vb.* trick, take in.
Reis, *n.m.* rice.
Reise, -n, *n.f.* trip, journey.
Reiseandenken, -, *n.nt.* souvenir.
Reisebüro, -s, *n.nt.* travel agency.
Reiseführer, -, *n.m.* guidebook.
reisen, *vb.* travel.
Reisend-, *n.m.&f.* traveler.
Reiseroute, -n, *n.f.* itinerary.
Reisescheck, -s, *n.m.* traveler's check.
reißen*, *vb.* rip, tear; (sich r. um) scramble for.
reißend, *adj.* rapid, racing.
Reißer, -, *n.m.* thriller, bestseller.
reiten*, *vb.* ride, horseback.
Reiter, -, *n.m.* rider.
Reiz, -e, *n.m.* charm, appeal; irritation.
reizbar, *adj.* sensitive, irritable.
reizen, *vb.* excite, tempt; irritate.

reizend, *adj.* adorable, lovely.
Reizfaktor, -en, *n.m.* irritant.
Reizmittel, -, *n.nt.* stimulant.
Reizung, -en, *n.f.* irritation.
rekeln, *vb.* (sich r.) stretch, sprawl.
Rekla'me, *n.f.* advertisement, advertising, publicity.
reklamie'ren, *vb.* reclaim; complain.
Rekord', -e, *n.m.* record.
Rekrut', -en, -en, *n.m.* draftee, recruit.
Rektor, -o'ren, *n.m.* headmaster; (university) president, chancellor.
relativ', *adj.* relative.
Religion', -en, *n.f.* religion.
religiös', *adj.* religious.
Rendezvous, -, *n.nt.* rendezvous, tryst.
Rennen, -, *n.nt.* race.
rennen*, *vb.* run, dash; race.
Renntier, -e, *n.nt.* reindeer.
renta'bel, *adj.* profitable.
Rente, -n, *n.f.* pension, income.
rentie'ren, *vb.* (sich r.) be profitable.
Reparation', -en, *n.f.* reparation.
Reparatur', -en, *n.f.* repair.
reparie'ren, *vb.* repair.
repatriie'ren, *vb.* repatriate.
Repertoire', -s, *n.nt.* repertoire.
Repor'ter, -, *n.m.* reporter.
Repräsentant', -en, -en, *n.m.* representative.
Repräsentation', -en, *n.f.* representation.
reproduzie'ren, *vb.* reproduce.
Reptil', -e *or* -ien, *n.nt.* reptile.
Republik', -en, *n.f.* republic.
republika'nisch, *adj.* republican.
requirie'ren, *vb.* requisition.
Requisition', -en, *n.f.* requisition.
Reservation', -en, *n.f.* reservation.
Reser've, -n, *n.f.* reserve.
reservie'ren, *vb.* reserve.
Reservoir', -s, *n.nt.* reservoir.
Residenz', -en, *n.f.* residence.
Resignation', -en, *n.f.* resignation.
resignie'ren, *vb.* resign.
resolut', *adj.* determined.
resonant', *adj.* resonant.
Resonanz', -en, *n.f.* resonance.
Respekt', *n.m.* respect, regard.
Rest, -e, *n.m.* rest, remnant.
Restaurant', -s, *n.nt.* restaurant.
restaurie'ren, *vb.* restore.
Restbestand, ̈e, *n.m.* residue.
restlos, *adj.* without remainder, entire.
Resultat', -e, *n.nt.* result.
Resümee', -s, *n.nt.* résumé.
retten, *vb.* rescue, save, salvage.
Retter, -, *n.m.* savior.
Rettung, -en, *n.f.* rescue; salvation.

Rettungsboot, -e, *n.nt.* lifeboat.
rettungslos, *adj.* irretrievable, hopeless.
Rettungsring, -e, *n.m.* life preserver.
Reue, *n.f.* repentance.
reuevoll, *adj.* repentant.
reuig, *adj.* penitent.
Revan'che, -n, *n.f.* revenge; return match.
Revers', -, *n.m.* lapel.
revidie'ren, *vb.* revise.
Revier', -e, *n.nt.* district.
Revision', -en, *n.f.* revision.
Revol'te, -n, *n.f.* revolt.
revoltie'ren, *vb.* revolt.
Revolution', -en, *n.f.* revolution.
revolutionär', *adj.* revolutionary.
Revol'ver, -, *n.m.* revolver, gun.
Rezept', -e, *n.nt.* receipt, recipe; prescription.
Rhabar'ber, *n.m.* rhubarb.
Rhapsodie', -i'en, *n.f.* rhapsody.
Rhein, *n.m.* Rhine.
rheto'risch, *adj.* rhetorical.
Rheuma, *n.nt.* rheumatism.
Rheumatis'mus, *n.m.* rheumatism.
rhythmisch, *adj.* rhythmical.
Rhythmus, -men, *n.m.* rhythm.
richten, *vb.* set right; (r. auf) turn to; (sich r. an) turn to; (sich r. nach) go by, be guided by, depend on; (jur.) judge.
Richter, -, *n.m.* judge.
richterlich, *adj.* judicial, judiciary.
Richterstand, *n.m.* judiciary.
richtig, *adj.* true, correct.
Richtigkeit, *n.f.* correctness.
Richtung, -en, *n.f.* direction; tendency.
riechen*, *vb.* smell.
Riecher, -, *n.m.* (fig.) hunch.
Riegel, -, *n.m.* bolt.
Riemen, -, *n.m.* strap; oar.
Riese, -n, -n, *n.m.* giant.
riesenhaft, *adj.* gigantic.
riesig, *adj.* tremendous, vast.
rigoros', *adj.* rigorous.
Rind, -er, *n.nt.* ox, cow, cattle.
Rinde, -n, *n.f.* bark.
Rindfleisch, *n.nt.* beef.
Rindsleder, -, *n.nt.* cowhide.
Ring, -e, *n.m.* ring.
ringeln, *vb.* curl.
ringen*, *vb.* struggle, wrestle.
Ringkampf, ̈e, *n.m.* wrestling match.
Rinne, -n, *n.f.* rut, groove.
Rinnstein, -e, *n.m.* curb, gutter.
Rippe, -n, *n.f.* rib.
Rippenfellentzündung, -en, *n.f.* pleurisy.
Risiko, -s, *n.nt.* risk, hazard, gamble.
riskie'ren, *vb.* risk, gamble.
Riß, -sse, *n.m.* tear, crack.
Ritt, -e, *n.m.* ride.

Ritter, -, *n.m.* knight.
ritterlich, *adj.* chivalrous.
rittlings, *adv.* astride.
Rituele´, -, *n.nt.* ritual.
rituell´, *adj.* ritual.
Ritus, -en, *n.m.* rite.
Ritze, -n, *n.f.* crack.
Riva´le, -n, -n, *n.m.* rival.
rivalisie´ren, *vb.* rival.
Rivalität´, -en, *n.f.* rivalry.
Rizinusöl, *n.nt.* castor oil.
Robbe, -n, *n.f.* seal.
Roboter, -, *n.m.* robot.
robust´, *adj.* robust.
röcheln, *vb.* breathe heavily.
Rock, ¨e, *n.m.* (men) jacket; (women) skirt; (music) rock.
Rockmusik, *n.f.* rock music.
rodeln, *vb.* go sledding.
Rodelschlitten, -, *n.m.* sled.
Rogen, -, *n.m.* roe.
Roggen, *n.m.* rye.
roh, *adj.* raw, crude; *(fig.)* brutal.
Roheit, -en, *n.f.* crudeness, brutality.
Rohling, -e, *n.m.* rowdy.
Rohr, -e, *n.nt.* pipe; (gun) barrel; (bamboo, sugar) cane.
Röhre, -n, *n.f.* pipe, tube.
Rohrflöte, -n, *n.f.* reed pipe.
Rolle, -n, *n.f.* roll, coil; spool; role, part.
rollen, *vb.* roll.
Roller, -, *n.m.* scooter.
Rolltreppe, -n, *n.f.* escalator.
Rom, *n.nt.* Rome.
Roman´, -e, *n.m.* novel.
roma´nisch, *adj.* Romance.
Roman´schriftsteller, -, *n.m.* novelist.
Roman´tisch, *adj.* romantic.
Roman´ze, -n, *n.f.* romance.
Römer, -, *n.m.* Roman.
römisch, *adj.* Roman.
röntgen, *vb.* x-ray.
Röntgenaufnahme, -n, *n.f.* x-ray.
Röntgenstrahlen, *n.pl.* x-rays.
rosa, *adj.* pink.
Rose, -n, *n.f.* rose.
Rosenkranz, ¨e, *n.m.* rosary.
rosig, *adj.* rosy.
Rosi´ne, -n, *n.f.* raisin.
Roß, -sse, *n.nt.* horse, steed.
Rost, -e, *n.m.* rust; (oven) grate.
rosten, *vb.* rust.
rösten, *vb.* roast; toast.
rostig, *adj.* rusty.
rot (¨), *adj.* red.
rotbraun, -e, *adj.* red-brown, maroon.
Röteln, *n.pl.* German measles.
rotie´ren, *vb.* rotate.
Rotwein, -e, *n.m.* red wine, claret.
Roué´, -s, *n.m.* roué, rake.
Rouge, *n.nt.* rouge.
Roula´de, -n, *n.f.* meat roll.
Route, -n, *n.f.* route.
Routi´ne, -n, *n.f.* routine.
routiniert´, *adj.* experienced.
Rowdy, -s, *n.m.* hoodlum.

Rübe, -n, *n.f.* **(gelbe R.)** carrot; **(rote R.)** beet; **(weisse R.)** turnip.
Rubin´, -e, *n.m.* ruby.
Rubrik´, -en, *n.f.* category, heading.
ruchbar, *adj.* notorious.
ruchlos, *adj.* infamous, profligate.
Ruck, -e, *n.m.* jerk, wrench.
Rückantwort, -en, *n.f.* reply.
ruckartig, *adj.* jerky.
rückbezüglich, *adj.* reflexive.
Rückblick, -e, *n.m.* retrospect.
rücken, *vb.* move, move over.
Rücken, -, *n.m.* back.
rückerstatten, *vb.* refund.
Rückfahrkarte, -n, *n.f.* return ticket.
Rückfahrt, -en, *n.f.* return trip.
Rückfall, ¨e, *n.m.* relapse.
Rückgabe, *n.f.* return, restitution.
Rückgang, ¨e, *n.m.* retrogression, decline.
rückgängig, *adj.* declining; (r. machen) cancel, revoke.
Rückgrat, -e, *n.nt.* spine, backbone.
Rückhalt, -e, *n.m.* support, reserve.
rückhaltlos, *adj.* unreserved, frank.
Rückhand, ¨, *n.f.* backhand.
Rückkaufswert, -e, *n.m.* equity (mortgage, etc.).
Rückkehr, *n.f.* return; reversion.
Rückkopplung, -en, *n.f.* feedback.
Rückmarsch, ¨e, *n.m.* retreat.
Rucksack, ¨e, *n.m.* knapsack.
Rückschlag, ¨e, *n.m.* reverse, upset.
Rückschluß, ¨sse, *n.m.* conclusion.
Rückseite, -n, *n.f.* reverse, rear.
Rücksicht, -en, *n.f.* consideration.
Rücksichtnahme, *n.f.* consideration.
rücksichtslos, *adj.* inconsiderate; reckless, ruthless.
Rücksichtslosigkeit, -en, *n.f.* lack of consideration, ill-mannered behavior; ruthlessness.
rücksichtsvoll, *adj.* thoughtful, considerate.
Rückstand, ¨e, *n.m.* arrears; (in R. geraten*) fall behind, lag.
rückständig, *adj.* in arrears; backward, antiquated.
Rücktritt, -e, *n.m.* resignation.
rückwärts, *adv.* backward(s).
Rückwärtsgang, ¨e, *n.m.* reverse (gear).
ruckweise, *adv.* by fits and starts.
Rückzug, ¨e, *n.m.* retreat.
Rudel, -, *n.m.* pack.
Ruder, -, *n.nt.* oar.
Ruderboot, -e, *n.nt.* rowboat.
rudern, *vb.* row.

Ruf, -e, *n.m.* call; reputation, standing.
rufen*, *vb.* call, shout.
Rufnummer, -n, *n.f.* (telephone) number.
Rüge, -n, *n.f.* reprimand.
rügen, *vb.* reprimand.
Ruhe, *n.f.* rest; calmness, tranquility; silence.
ruhelos, *adj.* restless.
ruhen, *vb.* rest, repose.
Ruhestand, *n.m.* retirement.
Ruhestätte, -n, *n.f.* resting place.
ruhig, *adj.* calm, composed; quiet; (das kannst du r. machen) go ahead and do it.
Ruhm, *n.m.* fame, glory.
rühmen, *vb.* praise, extol.
rühmenswert, *adj.* praiseworthy.
rühmlich, *adj.* laudable.
ruhmlos, *adj.* inglorious.
ruhmreich, *adj.* glorious.
Ruhr, *n.f.* dysentery.
Rührei, -er, *n.nt.* scrambled eggs.
rühren, *vb.* move, stir; (sich r.) stir.
rührend, *adj.* touching, pathetic.
rührig, *adj.* lively, bustling.
Rührung, *n.f.* emotion, compassion.
Rui´ne, -n, *n.f.* ruin.
ruinie´ren, *vb.* ruin.
Rum, *n.m.* rum.
Rummel, *n.m.* hubbub, racket.
rumpeln, *vb.* rumble.
Rumpf, -e, *n.m.* torso, fuselage, hull.
rund, *adj.* round, circular.
Runde, -n, *n.f.* round; (sports) lap.
Rundfunk, *n.m.* radio.
Rundfunksendung, -en, *n.f.* broadcast.
Rundfunksprecher, -, *n.m.* broadcaster.
Rundfunkübertragung, -en, *n.f.* broadcast.
rundlich, *adj.* plump.
Rundschreiben, -, *n.nt.* circular.
Runzel, -n, *n.f.* wrinkle.
runzeln, *vb.* wrinkle; (die Stirn r.) frown.
rupfen, *vb.* pluck.
Rüsche, -n, *n.f.* ruffle.
Ruß, *n.m.* soot, grime.
Russe, -n, *n.m.* Russian.
Rüssel, -n, *n.m.* trunk.
russisch, *adj.* Russian.
Rußland, *n.nt.* Russia.
rüsten, *vb.* prepare; *(mil.)* arm.
rüstig, *adj.* vigorous, spry.
Rüstung, -en, *n.f.* armament; armor.
rutschen, *vb.* slide, skid.
rütteln, *vb.* shake, jolt.

S

Saal, Säle, *n.m.* large room, hall.

Saat, -en, *n.f.* seed, sowing.

Sabbat, -en, *n.m.* Sabbath.

Säbel, -, *n.m.* saber.

Sabota'ge, *n.f.* sabotage.

Saboteur', -e, *n.m.* saboteur.

sabotie'ren, *vb.* sabotage.

Sacharin', *n.nt.* saccharine.

Sache, -n, *n.f.* thing, matter; cause.

Sachkundig-, *n.m.* expert.

sachlich, *adj.* objective, relevant, matter-of-fact; (art) functional.

Sachlichkeit, *n.f.* objectivity, detachment.

sacht, *adj.* soft.

sachte, *adv.* cautiously, gingerly.

Sachverständig-, *n.m.* expert.

Sack, ¨e, *n.m.* sack, bag.

Sadis'mus, *n.m.* sadism.

Sadist', -en, -en, *n.m.* sadist.

sadis'tisch, *adj.* sadistic.

säen, *vb.* sow.

Saft, ¨e, *n.m.* juice, sap.

saftig, *adj.* juicy, succulent.

Sage, -n, *n.f.* myth.

Säge, -n, *n.f.* saw.

sagen, *vb.* say, tell.

sägen, *vb.* saw.

sagenhaft, *adj.* mythical, fabulous.

Sago, *n.nt.* tapioca.

Sahne, *n.f.* cream.

Sahneeis, *n.nt.* ice cream.

Saison', -s, *n.f.* season.

Saite, -n, *n.f.* string, chord.

Sakrament', -e, *n.nt.* sacrament.

Sakrileg', -e, *n.nt.* sacrilege.

Sakristei, -en, *n.f.* sacristy, vestry.

Salat', -e, *n.m.* salad.

Salat'soße, -n, *n.f.* salad dressing.

Salbe, -n, *n.f.* salve, ointment.

salben, *vb.* anoint.

Saldo, -den, *n.m.* balance, remainder.

Salm, -e, *n.m.* salmon.

Salon', -s, *n.m.* salon.

salopp', *adj.* nonchalant.

salutie'ren, *vb.* salute.

Salve, -n, *n.f.* salvo.

Salz, -e, *n.nt.* salt.

salzen, *vb.* salt.

salzig, *adj.* salty.

Salzwasser, -, *n.nt.* brine.

Samen, -, *n.m.* seed.

sammeln, *vb.* collect, gather; (sich s.) (*mil.*) rally.

Sammler, -, *n.m.* collector.

Sammlung, -en, *n.f.* collection.

Samstag, -e, *n.m.* Saturday.

Samt, *n.m.* velvet.

samt, *adv.&prep.* together with.

sämtlich, *adj.* entire.

Sanato'rium, -rien, *n.nt.* sanatorium.

Sand, -e, *n.m.* sand.

Sanda'le, -n, *n.f.* sandal.

sandig, *adj.* sandy.

Sandtorte, -n, *n.f.* pound cake.

sanft, *adj.* gentle, meek.

Sanftmut, *n.m.* gentleness.

sanftmütig, *adj.* gentle, meek.

Sänger, -, *n.m.* singer.

sang- und klanglos, *adv.* quietly.

Sankt, *adj.* Saint.

Saphir', -e, *n.m.* sapphire.

Sardel'le, -n, *n.f.* anchovy.

Sardi'ne, -n, *n.f.* sardine.

Sarg, ¨e, *n.m.* coffin.

Sarkas'mus, *n.m.* sarcasm.

sarkas'tisch, *adj.* sarcastic.

Satan, *n.m.* Satan.

sata'nisch, *adj.* diabolical.

Satellit', -en, -en, *n.m.* satellite.

Satin', -s, *n.m.* satin.

Sati're, -n, *n.f.* satire.

sati'risch, *adj.* satirical.

satt, *adj.* satiated; (ich bin s.) I have had enough to eat; (ich habe es s.) I am sick of it; (sich s. essen*, sehen*) have one's fill.

Sattel, -, *n.m.* saddle.

satteln, *vb.* saddle.

sättigen, *vb.* satiate, saturate.

Sättigung, *n.f.* satiation, saturation.

sattsam, *adv.* sufficiently.

Satz, ¨e, *n.m.* (*gram.*) sentence, clause; (music) movement; (dishes, tennis) set.

Satzlehre, *n.f.* syntax.

Satzung, -en, *n.f.* statute, bylaw.

Satzzeichen, -, *n.nt.* punctuation mark.

Sau, ¨e, *n.f.* sow.

sauber, *adj.* clean, neat.

Sauberkeit, *n.f.* cleanliness, neatness.

säuberlich, *adj.* clean, careful.

säubern, *vb.* cleanse, purge.

Säuberungsaktion, -en, *n.f.* purge.

sauer, *adj.* sour, acid.

Säuerlichkeit, -en, *n.f.* acidity.

Sauerstoff, *n.m.* oxygen.

saufen*, *vb.* drink heavily, guzzle.

Säufer, -, *n.m.* drunkard.

saugen*, *vb.* suck.

Saugen, *n.nt.* suction.

Sauger, -, *n.m.* nipple (baby's bottle).

Säugling, -e, *n.m.* infant, baby.

Säule, -n, *n.f.* pillar, column.

Saum, ¨e, *n.m.* seam, hem.

säumen, *vb.* hem; delay.

säumig, *adj.* tardy, delinquent.

Säure, -n, *n.f.* acid.

säuseln, *vb.* rustle.

sausen, *vb.* (wind) whistle; run, dash.

schaben, *vb.* scrape.

Schabernack, -e, *n.m.* hoax.

schäbig, *adj.* shabby.

Schach, *n.nt.* chess; (in S. halten*) keep at bay.

Schachbrett, -er, *n.nt.* chessboard.

Schachfigur, -en, *n.f.* chessman.

schachmatt', *adj.* checkmate; (*fig.*) exhausted.

Schachspiel, -e, *n.nt.* chess.

Schacht, ¨e, *n.m.* shaft.

Schachtel, -n, *n.f.* box.

schade, *adv.* too bad.

Schädel, -, *n.m.* skull.

schaden, *vb.* harm; be harmful.

Schaden, ¨, *n.m.* harm, damage.

Schadenersatz, *n.m.* indemnity, compensation, damages.

schadenfroh, *adj.* gloating; (s. sein*) gloat.

schadhaft, *adj.* defective.

schädigen, *vb.* wrong, damage.

schädlich, *adj.* harmful, injurious.

Schädling, -e, *n.m.* pest, destructive insect.

Schaf, -e, *n.nt.* sheep.

Schäfer, -, *n.m.* shepherd.

schaffen*, *vb.* make, create.

schaffen, *vb.* get done, achieve; (sich zu s. machen mit) to busy oneself with, tangle.

Schaffner, -, *n.m.* conductor.

Schafott', -e, *n.nt.* scaffold.

Schafskopf, ¨e, *n.m.* idiot.

Schaft, ¨e, *n.m.* shaft.

Schakal', -e, *n.m.* jackal.

Schal, -s, *n.m.* shawl, scarf.

schal, *adj.* stale.

Schale, -n, *n.f.* skin, rind; shell; dish, bowl.

schälen, *vb.* pare, peel.

Schalk, ¨e, *n.m.* rogue.

schalkhaft, *adj.* roguish.

Schall, ¨e, *n.m.* sound, ring.

Schalldämpfer, -, *n.m.* (auto) muffler; (gun) silencer.

Schallgrenze, -n, *n.f.* sound barrier.

Schallplatte, -n, *n.f.* phonograph record.

Schalot'te, -n, *n.f.* scallion.

Schaltanlage, -n, *n.f.* switchboard.

Schaltbrett, -er, *n.nt.* switchboard; control panel.

schalten, *vb.* shift; command; (s. und walten) do as one pleases.

Schalter, -, *n.m.* (elec.) switch; (ticket, etc.) window.

Schaltjahr, -e, *n.nt.* leap year.

Schaltung, -en, *n.f.* (elec.) connection; (auto) shift.

Scham, *n.f.* shame; chastity.

schämen, *vb.* shame; (sich s.) be ashamed.

Schamgefühl, -e, *n.nt.* sense of modesty.

schamhaft, *adj.* modest, chaste.

schamlos, *adj.* shameless, infamous.

Schamlosigkeit, *n.f.* shamelessness.

Schampun', -s, *n.nt.* shampoo.

schandbar, *adj.* shameful, disgraceful.

Schande, *n.f.* shame, dishonor.

schänden, *vb.* dishonor, ravish.

Schandfleck, -e, *n.m.* blemish, stigma.

schändlich, *adj.* infamous.

Schandtat, -en, *n.f.* crime.

Schändung, -en, n.f. desecration; rape.

Schankstube, -n, n.f. barroom.

Schanze, -n, n.f. entrenchment; **(sein Leben in die S. schlagen*)** risk one's life.

Schar, -en, n.f. flock, group, host.

scharf (-), adj. sharp, acute, keen.

Scharfblick, n.m. quick eye; acuteness.

Schärfe, -n, n.f. sharpness, acuteness.

schärfen, vb. sharpen.

Scharfrichter, -, n.m. executioner.

Scharfsinn, n.m. acumen, discernment.

scharfsinnig, adj. acute, shrewd.

Scharlach, n.m. scarlet fever.

scharlachrot, adj. scarlet.

Scharnier', -e, n.nt. hinge.

Schärpe, -n, n.f. sash.

Scharte, -n, n.f. crack.

Schatten, -, n.m. shade; shadow.

Schattenbild, -er, n.nt. silhouette.

Schattengestalt, -en, n.f. phantom, phantasm.

Schattenseite, -n, n.f. shady side; (fig.) disadvantage, drawback.

schattie'ren, vb. shade.

schattig, adj. shady.

Schatz, -̈e, n.m. treasure.

schätzen, vb. treasure, prize; estimate, gauge; esteem.

schätzenswert, adj. estimable.

Schatzmeister, -, n.m. treasurer.

Schätzung, -en, n.f. estimate.

schätzungsweise, adv. approximately.

Schau, n.f. show, exhibition; **(zur S. tragen*)** display.

Schauder, -, n.m. shudder, shiver.

schauderhaft, adj. horrible, ghastly.

schaudern, vb. shudder.

schauen, vb. see, look.

Schauer, -, n.m. shower; (fever) chill.

schauerlich, adj. gruesome.

Schaufel, -n, n.f. shovel; dustpan.

Schaufenster, -, n.nt. store window, display window.

Schaukel, -n, n.f. swing.

schaukeln, vb. swing, rock.

Schaukelstuhl, -̈e, n.m. rocking chair.

Schaum, n.m. froth, foam; lather.

schäumen, vb. froth, foam; lather.

Schaumgummi, n.m. foam rubber.

Schaumwein, -e, n.m. champagne.

Schauplatz, -̈e, n.m. scene, theater, locale.

schaurig, adj. horrible.

Schauspiel, -e, n.nt. drama; spectacle.

Schauspieler, -, n.m. actor.

Schauspielerin, -nen, n.f. actress.

Schaustellung, n.f. exhibition; ostentation.

Scheck, -s, n.m. check.

scheel, adj. **(s. an•sehen*)** look askance at.

Scheffel, -, n.m. bushel.

Scheibe, -n, n.f. disk; slice.

Scheide, -n, n.f. sheath; (water) divide; vagina.

scheiden*, vb. leave, part; **(sich s. lassen*)** get divorced.

Scheidewand, -̈e, n.f. partition.

Scheideweg, -e, n.m. crossroads.

Scheidung, -en, n.f. divorce.

Schein, n.m. shine, light, shimmer; brilliance.

scheinbar, adj. apparent, imaginary.

scheinen*, vb. shine; seem.

scheinheilig, adj. hypocritical.

Scheinwerfer, -, n.m. spotlight; headlight.

Scheinwerferlicht, n.nt. floodlight.

Scheitel, -, n.m. part (in the hair).

scheitern, vb. fail.

Schelle, -n, n.f. bell.

schellen, vb. ring.

Schelm, -e, n.m. rogue.

schelmisch, adj. roguish, mischievous.

Schelte, n.f. scolding.

schelten*, vb. scold.

Schema, -s, n.nt. scheme.

Schenke, -n, n.f. tavern, bar.

Schenkel, -, n.m. thigh.

schenken, vb. give (as a present).

Schenkstube, -n, n.f. taproom, bar.

Schenkung, -en, nf. donation.

Schere, -n, n.f. scissors, shears.

scheren*, vb. shear.

Scherere'i, -en, n.f. bother.

Scherz, -e, n.m. joke, jest.

scherzen, vb. joke, jest, kid.

scherzhaft, adj. jocular.

scheu, adj. shy.

Scheu, n.f. timidity.

scheuchen, vb. scare, shoo.

scheuen, vb. shy, shun.

Scheuer, -n, n.f. barn, shed.

scheuern, vb. scour.

Scheuklappe, -n, n.f. blinder.

Scheune, -n, n.f. barn, shed.

Scheusal, -e, n.nt. monster, fright.

scheußlich, adj. horrible.

Schi, -er, n.m. ski.

Schicht, -en, n.f. layer, stratum, class.

schick, adj. chic, stylish.

Schick, n.m. skill; stylishness.

schicken, vb. send; **(sich s.)** be proper.

Schickeri'a, n.f. (slang) jet-set.

schicklich, adj. proper.

Schicksal, -e, n.nt. fate.

schicksalsschwer, adj. fateful.

Schickung, n.f. providence.

schieben*, vb. push, shove; engage in illegal transactions.

Schieber, -, n.m. profiteer.

Schiebung, -en, n.f. racketeering.

Schiedsrichter, -, n.m. umpire, referee.

schief, adj. crooked, askew.

Schiefer, n.m. slate.

schielen, vb. be cross-eyed, look cross-eyed.

Schienbein, -e, n.nt. shin.

Schiene, -n, n.f. rail; (med.) splint.

schier, 1. adj. sheer, pure. **2.** adv. almost.

Schierling, n.m. hemlock.

schießen*, vb. shoot.

Schießgewehr, -e, n.nt. gun.

Schiff, -e, n.nt. ship; nave (of a church).

Schiffahrt, n.f. navigation.

schiffbar, adj. navigable.

Schiffbau, n.m. ship building.

Schiffbruch, -̈e, n.m. shipwreck.

schiffen, vb. ship, navigate.

Schiffer, -, n.m. mariner.

Schiffsrumpf, -̈e, n.m. hull.

schikanie'ren, vb. annoy.

schi•laufen*, vb. ski.

Schild, -e, n.m. shield.

Schild, -er, n.nt. sign.

Schilddrüse, -n, n.f. thyroid gland.

schildern, vb. portray.

Schilderung, -en, n.f. portrayal.

Schildkröte, -n, n.f. turtle, tortoise.

Schilf, n.nt. reed.

Schilift, -s, n.m. ski lift.

schillern, vb. be iridescent.

Schilling, -e, n.m. shilling.

Schimmel, -, n.m. mold, mildew; white horse.

schimmelig, adj. moldy.

Schimmer, -, n.m. glimmer, gleam.

Schimpan'se, -n, -n, n.m. chimpanzee.

Schimpf, -e, n.m. insult, abuse, disgrace.

schimpfen, vb. insult, abuse; complain, gripe.

Schimpfwort, -e, n.nt. term of abuse.

schinden*, vb. flay; (fig.) torment; **(sich s.)** work hard, slave.

Schinken, -, n.m. ham.

Schirm, -e, n.m. screen; umbrella, parasol; shelter.

schirmen, vb. protect.

Schirmherr, -n, -en, n.m. patron.

Schlacht, -en, n.f. battle.

schlachten, vb. slaughter.

Schlächter, -, n.m. butcher.

Schlachtfeld, -er, n.nt. battlefield.

Schlachtschiff, -e, *n.nt.* battleship.

Schlacke, -n, *n.f.* slag, clinker, cinder.

Schlaf, *n.m.* sleep.

Schlafanzug, "e, *n.m.* pajamas.

Schläfe, -n, *n.f.* temple.

schlafen*, *vb.* sleep, be asleep.

Schlafenszeit, -en, *n.f.* bedtime.

schlaff, *adj.* limp.

Schlaffheit, *n.f.* limpness, laxity.

Schlaflosigkeit, *n.f.* insomnia.

Schlafmittel, -, *n.nt.* sleeping pill.

schläfrig, *adj.* sleepy.

Schlafrock, "e, *n.m.* dressing gown.

Schlafwagen, -, *n.m.* sleeping car.

Schlafzimmer, -, *n.nt.* bedroom.

Schlag, "e, *n.m.* blow, stroke, shock.

Schlagader, -n, *n.f.* artery.

Schlaganfall, "e, *n.m.* stroke; apoplexy.

Schlagbaum, "e, *n.m.* wooden bar, (railroad customs) barrier.

schlagen*, *vb.* hit, strike, beat; fell (trees); coin (money).

Schlager, -, *n.m.* hit (song, play, book).

Schläger, -, *n.m.* hitter; bat, club.

Schlägerei', -en, *n.f.* brawl.

Schlagholz, "er, *n.nt.* bat, club.

Schlagobers, *n.nt.* whipped cream.

Schlagsahne, *n.f.* whipped cream.

Schlagseite, *n.f.* list.

Schlagwort, -e, *n.nt.* slogan.

Schlagzeile, -n, *n.f.* headline.

Schlamm, *n.m.* muck, mud.

schlampig, *adj.* frowsy.

Schlange, -n, *n.f.* snake, serpent.

schlängeln, *vb.* (**sich s.**) wind, wriggle.

schlank, *adj.* slender, slim.

schlapp, *adj.* slack, flabby.

Schlappe, -n, *n.f.* rebuff, setback, defeat.

schlau, *adj.* sly, clever, astute.

Schlauch, "e, *n.m.* hose, tube.

Schlaufe, -n, *n.f.* loop.

schlecht, *adj.* bad.

schlechterdings, *adv.* absolutely.

schlechthin, *adv.* quite, simply.

Schlegel, -, *n.m.* mallet, sledge hammer, drumstick.

schleichen*, *vb.* sneak, slink, crawl.

Schleier, -, *n.m.* veil.

schleierhaft, *adj.* veil-like; inexplicable, mysterious.

Schleife, -n, *n.f.* bow.

schleifen, *vb.* drag.

schleifen*, *vb.* grind, polish, sharpen.

Schleifmittel, -, *n.nt.* abrasive.

Schleifstein, -e, *n.m.* grindstone.

Schleim, *n.m.* slime; mucus.

Schleimhaut, "e, *n.f.* mucous membrane.

schleimig, *adj.* slimy; mucous.

schlendern, *vb.* saunter, stroll.

schlenkern, *vb.* shamble, dangle, swing.

Schleppe, -n, *n.f.* train.

schleppen, *vb.* drag, lug, haul, tow.

Schlepper, -, *n.m.* tugboat, tractor.

Schleuder, -n, *n.f.* slingshot, catapult, centrifuge.

schleudern, *vb.* hurl, fling; skid.

schleunig, *adj.* speedy.

Schleuse, -n, *n.f.* sluice, lock.

Schlich, -e, *n.m.* trick.

schlicht, *adj.* plain, simple.

schlichten, *vb.* smooth; arbitrate.

Schlichter, -, *n.m.* arbitrator.

Schlichtung, -en, *n.f.* arbitration.

schließen*, *vb.* shut; close; conclude.

Schliessfach, "er, *n.nt.* baggage locker.

schließlich, 1. *adj.* final. **2.** *adv.* at last.

Schliff, -e, *n.m.* cut, polish(ing), grind(ing); good manners, style; (**letzter S.**) final touch.

schlimm, *adj.* bad, serious.

Schlinge, -n, *n.f.* sling, noose.

schlingen*, *vb.* twist, wind; gulp.

schlingern, *vb.* roll.

Schlips, -e, *n.m.* necktie.

Schlitten, -, *n.m.* sled, sleigh.

Schlittschuh, -e, *n.m.* skate.

schlittschuh-laufen*, *vb.* skate.

Schlitz, -e, *n.m.* slit, slot, slash.

schlitzen, *vb.* slit, slash.

Schloß, "sser, *n.nt.* lock; castle.

Schlot, -e, *n.m.* chimney, flue.

schlottern, *vb.* hang loosely, flop, shake.

Schlucht, -en, *n.f.* gorge, gulch.

schluchzen, *vb.* sob.

Schluck, -e, *n.m.* swallow.

Schluckauf, *n.m.* hiccup(s).

Schlückchen, -, *n.nt.* nip.

schlucken, *vb.* swallow.

Schlummer, *n.m.* slumber.

schlummern, *vb.* slumber.

Schlund, "e, *n.m.* throat, gullet; chasm.

schlüpfen, *vb.* slip.

Schlüpfer, -, *n.m.* panties.

schlüpfrig, *adj.* slippery.

schlürfen, *vb.* sip.

Schluß, "sse, *n.m.* end, close, conclusion.

Schlüssel, -, *n.m.* key.

Schlußfolgerung, -e, *n.f.* deduction, conclusion.

Schmach, *n.f.* disgrace, insult.

schmachten, *vb.* languish.

schmächtig, *adj.* slim, slight.

schmachvoll, *adj.* ignominious.

schmackhaft, *adj.* tasty.

schmähen, *vb.* abuse, revile.

schmal (-, "), *adj.* narrow.

schmälern, *vb.* curtail, detract from.

Schmalz, *n.nt.* lard.

schmarotzen, *vb.* sponge (on).

Schmarot'zer, -, *n.m.* hanger-on; parasite.

schmatzen, *vb.* smack one's lips.

Schmaus, "e, *n.m.* feast.

schmausen, *vb.* feast.

schmecken, *vb.* taste.

Schmeichelei', -en, *n.f.* flattery.

schmeichelhaft, *adj.* flattering.

schmeicheln, *vb.* flatter.

schmeißen*, *vb.* throw, hurl, chuck, hit.

schmelzen*, *vb.* melt.

Schmerz, -en, *n.m.* ache, pain.

schmerzen, *vb.* ache, pain, hurt.

schmerzhaft, *adj.* painful.

Schmetterling, -e, *n.m.* butterfly.

schmettern, *vb.* dash, smash; bray, blare.

Schmied, -e, *n.m.* blacksmith.

Schmiede, -n, *n.f.* forge.

schmieden, *vb.* forge.

schmiegen, *vb.* bend, press close, nestle, cling.

schmiegsam, *adj.* pliant, flexible.

Schmiere, -n, *n.f.* grease.

schmieren, *vb.* grease, smear, scribble; (**wie geschmiert'**) like clockwork.

schmierig, *adj.* greasy, dirty, sordid.

Schmiermittel, -, *n.nt.* lubricant.

Schminke, -n, *n.f.* rouge, make-up, grease paint.

schminken, *vb.* put on make-up.

Schmiß, "sse, *n.m.* stroke, cut; dueling scar; verve.

schmökern, *vb.* browse.

schmollen, *vb.* pout, sulk.

schmoren, *vb.* stew.

schmuck, *adj.* smart, trim.

Schmuck, *n.m.* ornament, jewelry.

schmücken, *vb.* decorate.

Schmucknadel, -n, *n.f.* clip.

Schmuggel, *n.m.* smuggling.

schmuggeln, *vb.* smuggle.

Schmuggelware, -n, *n.f.* contraband.

Schmuggler, -, *n.m.* smuggler.

schmunzeln, *vb.* smirk, grin.

schmusen, *vb.* spoon, neck.

Schmutz, *n.m.* dirt, filth.

schmutzig, *adj.* dirty.

Schnabel, ", *n.m.* beak.

Schnake, -n, *n.f.* gnat.

Schnalle, -n, *n.f.* buckle, clasp.

schnallen, *vb.* buckle.

schnalzen, *vb.* click (one's tongue), snap (one's fingers), crack (a whip).

schnappen, *vb.* snap, snatch, grab, catch, gasp (for breath).

Schnappschuß, ¨sse, *n.m.* snapshot.

Schnaps, ¨, *n.m.* hard liquor, whisky, brandy.

schnarchen, *vb.* snore.

schnarren, *vb.* buzz, whir, rattle, burr.

schnattern, *vb.* cackle.

schnauben, *vb.* pant, snort.

schnaufen, *vb.* breathe hard.

Schnauze, -, *n.f.* snout.

Schnecke, -n, *n.f.* snail.

Schnee, *n.m.* snow.

Schneesturm, ¨e, *n.m.* blizzard.

Schneid, *n.m.* bravado.

Schneide, -n, *n.f.* edge.

schneiden*, *vb.* cut.

schneidend, *adj.* cutting, scathing.

Schneider, -, *n.m.* tailor.

Schneiderin, -nen, *n.f.* dressmaker.

schneidig, *adj.* dashing.

schneien, *vb.* snow.

schnell, *adj.* quick.

schnellen, *vb.* flip, jerk.

Schnelligkeit, -en, *n.f.* swiftness.

Schnellzug, ¨e, *n.m.* express train.

schneuzen, *vb.* (sich s.) blow one's nose.

schnippisch, *adj.* saucy.

Schnitt, -e, *n.m.* cut, slice, incision.

Schnittbohne, -n, *n.f.* string bean.

Schnitte, -n, *n.f.* slice, sandwich.

Schnittlauch, *n.m.* chive(s).

Schnittmuster, -, *n.nt.* pattern.

Schnittpunkt, -e, *n.m.* intersection.

Schnittstelle, -n, *f.* (computer) interface.

Schnittwaren, *n.pl.* dry goods.

Schnittwunde, -n, *n.f.* cut.

Schnitzel, -, *n.nt.* chip; cutlet.

schnitzen, *vb.* carve, whittle.

Schnitzwerk, -e, *n.nt.* carving.

schnodd(e)rig, *adj.* insolent.

schnöde, *adj.* scornful, base.

Schnorchel, -, *n.m.* snorkel.

schnüffeln, *vb.* sniffle, snoop.

Schnuller, -, *n.m.* pacifier.

Schnupfen, -, *n.m.* cold (in the head).

Schnupftuch, ¨er, *n.nt.* handkerchief.

Schnuppe, -n, *n.f.* shooting star; (das ist mir S.) I don't care a hoot.

Schnur, -e, *n.f.* cord, string.

schnüren, *vb.* lace.

Schnurrbart, ¨e, *n.m.* mustache.

Schnürsenkel, -, *n.m.* shoelace.

Schock, -s, *n.m.* shock.

schockie'ren, *vb.* shock.

schofel(ig), *adj.* shabby, mean.

Schokola'de, -n, *n.f.* chocolate.

Scholle, -n, *n.f.* clod, sod.

schon, *adv.* already; even.

schön, *adj.* beautiful, nice.

schonen, *vb.* treat carefully, spare.

Schönheit, -en, *n.f.* beauty.

Schönheitssalon, -s, *n.m.* beauty parlor.

Schonung, -en, *n.f.* careful treatment, consideration.

schonungslos, *adj.* merciless.

Schopf, ¨e, *n.m.* forelock, crown.

schöpfen, *vb.* draw (water, breath); take from.

Schöpfer, *n.m.* creator.

schöpferisch, *adj.* creative.

Schöpfkelle, -n, *n.f.* scoop.

Schöpflöffel, -, *n.m.* ladle, dipper.

Schöpfung, *n.f.* creation.

Schoppen, -, *n.m.* glass of beer or wine; pint.

Schorf, *n.m.* scab.

Schornstein, -e, *n.m.* chimney, smokestack.

Schoß, ¨e, *n.m.* lap.

Schößling, -e, *n.m.* shoot.

Schote, -n, *n.f.* pod.

Schotte, -n, -n, *n.m.* Scotsman.

schottisch, *adj.* Scotch.

Schottland, *n.nt.* Scotland.

schräg, *adj.* oblique.

Schrägschrift, *n.f.* italics.

Schramme, -n, *n.f.* scratch.

Schrank, ¨e, *n.m.* wardrobe, locker, cupboard, cabinet.

Schranke, -n, *n.f.* barrier.

Schrapnell', -s, *n.nt.* shrapnel.

Schraube, -n, *n.f.* screw.

schrauben, *vb.* screw.

Schraubenschlüssel, -, *n.m.* wrench.

Schraubenzieher, -, *n.m.* screwdriver.

Schreck, -e, *n.m.* fright, scare.

Schrecken, -, *n.m.* terror, fear.

schreckhaft, *adj.* easily frightened.

schrecklich, *adj.* awful, terrible.

Schrei, -e, *n.m.* cry, scream, shout.

Schreibdame, -n, *n.f.* typist.

schreiben*, *vb.* write.

Schreiben, -, *n.nt.* letter.

Schreiber, -, *n.m.* clerk, scribe.

Schreibheft, -e, *n.nt.* notebook.

Schreibmaschine, -n, *n.f.* typewriter.

Schreibtisch, -e, *n.m.* desk.

Schreibung, -en, *n.f.* spelling.

Schreibwaren, *n.pl.* stationery.

schreien*, *vb.* cry, scream, shout.

schreiend, *adj.* flagrant.

Schrein, -e, *n.m.* shrine, casket, cabinet.

schreiten*, *vb.* stride, step.

Schrift, -en, *n.f.* writing, script; (Heilige S.) scripture(s).

Schriftführer, -, *n.m.* secretary (of an organization).

schriftlich, *adj.* written, in writing.

Schriftsatz, ¨e, *n.m.* type.

Schriftsteller, -, *n.m.* writer, author.

schrill, *adj.* shrill.

Schritt, -e, *n.m.* step, pace; crotch (of trousers).

schroff, *adj.* steep, abrupt, curt.

Schrotmehl, *n.m.* coarse meal, grits.

schrubbe(r)n, *vb.* scrub.

Schrulle, -n, *n.f.* whim.

schrumpfen, *vb.* shrink.

Schub, ¨e, *n.m.* shove, thrust; batch.

Schublade, -n, *n.f.* drawer.

schüchtern, *adj.* shy, bashful.

Schüchternheit, -en, *n.f.* bashfulness, shyness.

Schuft, -e, *n.m.* cad, scoundrel.

schuften, *vb.* work hard, drudge.

Schuh, -e, *n.m.* shoe.

Schuhmacher, -, *n.m.* shoemaker.

Schuhputzer, -, *n.m.* bootblack.

Schuhwerk, -e, *n.nt.* footwear.

Schularbeiten, *n.pl.* homework.

Schulbeispiel, -e, *n.nt.* typical example.

Schuld, -en, *n.f.* fault, guilt, blame, debt.

schulden, *vb.* owe.

schuldhaft, *adj.* culpable.

schuldig, *adj.* guilty; due, owing.

Schuldigsprechung, -en, *n.f.* conviction.

Schuldirektor, -en, *n.m.* headmaster, principal.

schuldlos, *adj.* guiltless.

Schuldner, -, *n.m.* debtor.

Schule, -n, *n.f.* school.

schulen, *vb.* train, indoctrinate.

Schüler, -, *n.m.* (boy) pupil.

Schülerin, -nen, *n.f.* (girl) pupil.

Schulgeld, -er, *n.nt.* tuition.

Schulter, -n, *n.f.* shoulder.

schultern, *vb.* shoulder.

Schund, *n.m.* trash.

Schupo, -s, *n.m.* (= Schutzpolizist) cop.

Schuppe, -n, *n.f.* scale; (pl.) dandruff.

Schuppen, -, *n.m.* shed, hangar.

schüren, *vb.* poke, stir up, foment.

Schurke, -n, -n, *n.m.* villain, scoundrel.

Schürze, -n, *n.f.* apron.

Schuß, ¨sse, *n.m.* shot.

Schüssel, -n, *n.f.* dish, bowl.

Schuster, -, *n.m.* shoemaker.

Schutt, *n.m.* rubbish.

schütteln, *vb.* shake.

schütten, *vb.* shed, pour.

Schutz, *n.m.* protection.

Schütze, -n, -n, *n.m.* rifleman, marksman, shot.

schützen, *vb.* protect.

Schützengraben, ¨, *n.m.* trench, dugout.

Schutzhaft, *n.f.* protective custody.

Schutzheilig-, *n.m.&f.* patron saint.

Schutzherr, -n, -en, *n.m.* patron.

schutzlos, *adj.* unprotected, defenseless.

Schutzmann, ⸚er, *n.m.* patrolman.

Schutzmarke, -n, *n.f.* trade mark.

schwach (⸚), *adj.* weak.

Schwäche, -n, *n.f.* weakness.

schwächen, *vb.* weaken.

Schwachheit, -en, *n.f.* frailty.

schwächlich, *adj.* feeble.

Schwächling, -e, *n.m.* weakling.

Schwachsinn, *n.m.* feeblemindedness.

schwachsinnig, *adj.* feebleminded.

Schwachsinnig-, *n.m.&f.* moron.

Schwager, ⸚r, *n.m.* brother-in-law.

Schwägerin, -nen, *n.f.* sister-in-law.

Schwalbe, -n, *n.f.* swallow.

Schwall, -e, *n.m.* flood.

Schwamm, ⸚e, *n.m.* sponge.

Schwan, ⸚e, *n.m.* swan.

schwanger, *adj.* pregnant.

Schwangerschaft, -en, *n.f.* pregnancy.

Schwangerschaftsverhütung, *n.f.* contraception.

schwankern, *vb.* totter, sway, vacillate, waver.

Schwankung, -en, *n.f.* fluctuation.

Schwanz, ⸚e, *n.m.* tail.

schwänzen, *vb.* cut (a class).

Schwarm, ⸚e, *n.m.* swarm.

schwärmen, - *n.m.* swarm; (s. für) be crazy about.

Schwärmer, -, *n.m.* enthusiast.

schwarz(⸚), *adj.* black; illegal.

Schwarz-, *n. m. & f.* Black (person).

Schwarzbrot, -e, *n.nt.* black bread.

schwärzen, *vb.* blacken.

Schwarzmarkt, ⸚e, *n.m.* black market.

Schwarzseher, -, *n.m.* alarmist, pessimist.

schwatzen, schwätzen, *vb.* chatter, gab.

Schwebe, *n.f.* suspense, suspension; (in der S.) undecided.

schweben, *vb.* hover, be suspended, be pending.

Schwebezustand, ⸚e, *n.m.* abeyance.

Schwede, -n, -n, *n.m.* Swede.

Schweden, *n.nt.* Sweden.

schwedisch, *adj.* Swedish.

Schwefel, *n.m.* sulphur.

Schweif, -e, *n.m.* tail, train.

schweifen, *vb.* roam, range.

schweigen*, *vb.* keep quiet, be silent.

Schweigen, *n.nt.* silence.

schweigsam, *adj.* silent.

Schwein, -e, *n.nt.* swine, hog, pig; good luck.

Schweinebraten, -, *n.m.* roast of pork.

Schweinefleisch, *n.nt.* pork.

Schweinerei', -en, *n.f.* awful mess, dirty business.

Schweinestall, ⸚e, *n.m.* pigsty.

Schweinsleder, *n.nt.* pigskin.

Schweiß, *n.m.* sweat.

Schweiz, *n.f.* Switzerland.

Schweizer, -, *n.m.* Swiss.

schweizerisch, *adj.* Swiss.

schwelen, *vb.* smolder.

schwelgen, *vb.* revel.

Schwelgerei', -en, *n.f.* revelry.

Schwelle, -n, *n.f.* sill, threshold; (railroad) tie.

schwellen*, *vb.* swell.

schwenken, *vb.* wave, flourish, brandish.

schwer, *adj.* heavy; difficult.

Schwere, *n.f.* heaviness.

schwerfällig, *adj.* clumsy, ponderous, stolid.

Schwergewicht, *n.nt.* heavyweight.

schwerhörig, *adj.* hard of hearing.

Schwerkraft, *n.f.* gravity.

schwerlich, *adj.* with difficulty, hardly.

Schwermut, *n.f.* melancholy.

schwermütig, *adj.* moody, melancholy.

Schwert, -er, *n.nt.* sword; centerboard.

schwerwiegend, *adj.* grave.

Schwester, -n, *n.f.* sister; nurse.

Schwiegereltern, *n.pl.* parents-in-law.

Schwiegermutter, ⸚, *n.f.* mother-in-law.

Schwiegersohn, ⸚e, *n.m.* son-in-law.

Schwiegertochter, ⸚, *n.f.* daughter-in-law.

Schwiegervater, ⸚, *n.m.* father-in-law.

Schwiele, -n, *n.f.* callus.

schwielig, *adj.* callous.

schwierig, *adj.* difficult.

Schwierigkeit, -en, *n.f.* difficulty, trouble.

Schwimmbad, ⸚er, *n.nt.* swimming pool.

schwimmen*, *vb.* swim.

Schwimmweste, -n, *n.f.* lifejacket.

Schwindel, -, *n.m.* dizziness; swindle, hoax; bunk.

Schwindelgefühl, *n.nt.* vertigo.

schwindeln, *vb.* swindle, cheat, fraud.

schwinden*, *vb.* disappear.

Schwindler, -, *n.m.* swindler, cheat, fraud.

schwindlig, *adj.* dizzy.

Schwindsucht, *n.f.* consumption.

schwindsüchtig, *adj.* consumptive.

schwingen*, *vb.* swing, brandish, oscillate.

Schwingung, -en, *n.f.* oscillation.

Schwips, *n.m.* (einen S. haben*) be tipsy.

schwirren, *vb.* whir.

schwitzen, *vb.* sweat.

schwören, *vb.* swear.

schwul, *adj.* homosexual.

schwül, *adj.* sultry, muggy.

Schwulst, ⸚e, *n.m.* bombast.

Schwund, *n.m.* disappearance, loss.

Schwung, ⸚e, *n.m.* swing, verve, animation, motion.

Schwungkraft, *n.f.* drive.

schwunglos, *adj.* lackadaisical.

schwungvoll, *adj.* spirited.

Schwur, ⸚e, *n.m.* oath.

sechs, *num.* six.

sechst-, *adj.* sixth.

Sechstel, -, *n.nt.* sixth part; (ein s.) one-sixth.

sechzig, *num.* sixty.

sechzigst-, *adj.* sixtieth.

Sechzigstel, -, *n.nt.* sixtieth part; (ein s.) one-sixtieth.

See, Se'en, *n.m.* lake.

See, Se'en, *n.f.* sea.

See-, *cpds.* naval, marine.

Seegang, *n.m.* (rough, calm) sea.

Seehund, -e, *n.m.* seal.

seekrank, *adj.* seasick.

Seekrankheit, *n.f.* seasickness.

Seele, -n, *n.f.* soul, spirit, mind.

Seeleute, *n.pl.* seamen.

seelisch, *adj.* spiritual.

Seelsorge, *n.f.* ministry.

Seemann, -leute, *n.m.* mariner.

Seemeile, -n, *n.f.* nautical mile.

Seeräuber, -, *n.m.* pirate.

Seereise, -n, *n.f.* cruise.

Seetang, *n.m.* seaweed.

seetüchtig, *adj.* seaworthy.

Seezunge, -n, *n.f.* sole.

Segel, -, *n.nt.* sail.

Segelboot, -e, *n.nt.* sailboat.

Segelflug, *n.m.* gliding.

Segelflugzeug, -e, *n.nt.* glider, sailplane.

segeln, *vb.* sail.

Segeltuch, *n.nt.* canvas, duck.

Segen, -, *n.m.* blessing.

Segment', -e, *n.nt.* segment.

segnen, *vb.* bless.

Segnung, -en, *n.f.* blessing, benediction.

sehen*, *vb.* see.

sehenswert, *adj.* worth seeing.

Sehenswürdigkeit, -en, *n.f.* sight(s).

Seher, -, *n.m.* seer, prophet.

Sehkraft, ⸚e, *n.f.* (power of) sight, vision.

Sehne, -n, *n.f.* tendon, ligament, sinew.

sehnen, *vb.* (sich s.) long, yearn.

Sehnsucht, *n.f.* longing.

sehnsüchtig, *adj.* longing.

sehnsuchtsvoll, *adj.* longing.

sehr, *adv.* very, much, a lot.
Sehweite, -n, *n.f.* range of sight.
seicht, *adj.* shallow, insipid.
Seide, -n, *n.f.* silk.
Seidel, -, *n.nt.* beer mug.
seiden, *adj.* silk.
Seidenpapier, *n.nt.* tissue paper.
seidig, *adj.* silky.
Seife, -n, *n.f.* soap.
Seifenschaum, *n.m.* suds.
seihen, *vb.* strain.
Seil, -e, *n.nt.* rope, cable.
Seilbahn, -en, *n.f.* cableway.
sein*, *vb.* be.
sein, -, -e, *adj.* his, its.
Sein, *n.nt.* being.
seiner, -es, -e, *pron.* his, its.
seinerseits, *adv.* for his part.
seinerzeit, *adv.* at the time.
seinesgleichen, *pron.* equal to him, such as he.
seinetwegen, *adv.* for his sake; for all he cares.
seinetwillen, (um s.) for his sake, because of him.
seit, 1. *prep.* since, for. **2.** *conj.* since.
seitab', *adv.* aside.
seitdem, 1. *conj.* since. **2.** *adv.* since then.
Seite, -n, *n.f.* side; page.
seitenlang, *adj.* going on for pages.
seitens, *prep.* on behalf of.
Seitensprung, ⸚e, *n.m.* escapade.
Seitenstraße, -n, *n.f.* side street.
Seitenzahl, -en, *n.f.* number of pages.
seither, *adv.* since then.
seitlich, *adj.* lateral.
seitwärts, *adv.* sideways.
Sekretär', -e, *n.m.* secretary.
Sekretä'rin, -nen, *n.f.* secretary.
Sekt, -e, *n.m.* champagne.
Sekte, -n, *n.f.* sect, denomination.
Sekundant', -en, -en, *n.m.* second (at a duel).
sekundär', *adj.* secondary.
Sekun'de, -n, *n.f.* second.
selb-, *adj.* same.
selber, *adj.* the (my-, your-, him-, etc.)self; (our-, your-, them-)selves.
selbst, *adv.* even; (my-, your-, him-, etc.)self; (our-, your-, them-)selves.
Selbstachtung, *n.f.* self-respect.
selbständig, *adj.* independent.
Selbständigkeit, *n.f.* independence.
Selbstbestimmung, *n.f.* self-determination.
selbstbewußt, *adj.* self-conscious.
Selbstbiographie, -n, autobiography.
selbstgefällig, *adj.* self-satisfied, smug.

selbstgefertigt, *adj.* home-made.
selbstgerecht, *adj.* self-righteous.
Selbstgespräch, -e, *n.nt.* monologue.
selbstlos, *adj.* unselfish.
Selbstmord, -e, *n.m.* suicide.
selbstredend, *adj.* self-evident.
selbstsicher, *adj.* self-confident.
Selbstsucht, *n.f.* selfishness.
selbstsüchtig, *adj.* selfish.
selbsttätig, *adj.* automatic.
selbstverständlich, *adj.* obvious.
Selbstverwaltung, *n.f.* home rule.
selbstzufrieden, *adj.* complacent.
Selbstzufriedenheit, *n.f.* complacency.
selig, *adj.* blessed; blissfully happy; deceased, late.
Seligkeit, -en, *n.f.* salvation, bliss.
selig-sprechen*, *vb.* beatify.
Sellerie, -n, *n.f.* celery.
selten, 1. *adj.* rare, scarce. **2.** *adv.* seldom.
Seltenheit, -en, *n.f.* rarity.
Selters, Selter(s)wasser, *n.nt.* soda water.
seltsam, *adj.* strange, queer, curious.
Seman'tik, *n.f.* semantics.
seman'tisch, *adj.* semantic.
Semes'ter, -, *n.nt.* semester, term.
Semiko'lon, -s, *n.nt.* semicolon.
Seminar', -e, *n.nt.* seminar(y).
Semit', -en, -en, *n.m.* Semite.
semi'tisch, *adj.* Semitic.
Semmel, -n, *n.f.* roll.
Senat', -e, *n.m.* senate.
Sena'tor, -o'ren, *n.m.* senator.
senden*, *vb.* send, ship.
senden, *vb.* broadcast.
Sender, -, *n.m.* sender, transmitter, broadcasting station.
Sendung, -en, *n.f.* shipment; broadcast, transmission.
Senf, *n.m.* mustard.
sengen, *vb.* scorch, singe.
Senior, -o'ren, *n.m.* senior citizen.
senken, *vb.* sink, lower, reduce.
senkrecht, *adj.* perpendicular.
Senkung, -en, *n.f.* depression, reduction.
Sensation', -en, *n.f.* sensation, thrill.
sensationell', *adj.* sensational.
Sense, -n, *n.f.* scythe.
sentimental', *adj.* sentimental.
Septem'ber, -, *n.m.* September.
Serbe, -n, -n, *n.m.* Serbian.
Serbien, *n.nt.* Serbia.
serbisch, *adj.* Serbian.
Serie, -n, *n.f.* series.
Serum, -ra, *n.nt.* serum.
Servi'ce, *n.nt.* service, set.
servie'ren, *vb.* serve.
Servier'platte, -n, *n.f.* platter.

Serviet'te, -n, *n.f.* napkin.
Sessel, -, *n.m.* easy-chair.
seßhaft, *adj.* settled, established.
setzen, *vb.* set, put, place; **(sich s.)** sit down.
Seuche, -n, *n.f.* plague, epidemic.
seufzen, *vb.* sigh.
Seufzer, -, *n.m.* sigh.
sexuell', *adj.* sexual.
Siam, *n.nt.* Siam.
Siame'se, -n, -n, *n.m.* Siamese.
siame'sisch, *adj.* Siamese.
Sibi'rien, *n.nt.* Siberia.
sich, *pron.* (him-, her-, it-, your-)self; (them-, your-)-selves; each other, one another.
Sichel, -n, *n.f.* sickle; crescent.
sicher, *adj.* sure, certain, safe, secure.
Sicherheit, -en, *n.f.* safety, security, certainty.
Sicherheitsnadel, -n, *n.f.* safety-pin.
sicherlich, *adv.* surely.
sichern, *vb.* secure, safeguard.
Sicherung, -en, *n.f.* fuse.
Sicht, *n.f.* sight.
sichtbar, *adj.* visible.
sichten, *vb.* sift; sight.
sickern, *vb.* seep.
sie, *pron.* she; they.
Sie, *pron.* you (normal polite).
Sieb, -e, *n.nt.* sieve, strainer.
sieben, *vb.* sift, strain.
sieben, *num.* seven.
sieb(en)t-, *adj.* seventh.
Sieb(en)tel,-, *n.nt.* seventh part; **(ein s.)** one-seventh.
siebzig, *num.* seventy.
siebzigst-, *adj.* seventieth.
Siebzigstel, -, *n.nt.* seventieth part; **(ein s.)** one-seventieth.
siedeln, *vb.* settle.
sieden*, *vb.* boil.
Siedler, -, *n.m.* settler.
Siedlung, -en, *n.f.* settlement.
Sieg, -e, *n.m.* victory.
Siegel, -, *n.nt.* seal.
siegeln, *vb.* seal.
siegen, *vb.* win, be victorious.
Sieger, -, *n.m.* winner, victor.
sieghaft, *adj.* triumphant.
siegreich, *adj.* victorious.
Signal', -e, *n.nt.* signal.
Signal'horn, ⸚er, *n.nt.* bugle.
Silbe, -n, *n.f.* syllable.
Silber, *n.nt.* silver.
silbern, *adj.* silver.
Silberwaren, *n.f.* silverware.
silbisch, *adj.* syllabic.
silbrig, *adj.* silvery.
Silves'ter, *n.nt.* New Year's Eve.
Sims, -e, *n.m.* cornice; ledge, sill, mantelpiece.
singen*, *vb.* sing.
Singular, -e, *n.m.* singular.
sinken*, *vb.* sink, decline, fall.
Sinn, -e, *n.m.* sense, mind, meaning, taste.
Sinnbild, -er, *n.nt.* symbol.

sinnen*, *vb.* think, meditate, plot.

sinnig, *adj.* thoughtful, appropriate.

sinnlich, *adj.* sensual.

sinnlos, *adj.* senseless.

Sintflut, *n.f.* flood, deluge.

Sippe, -n, *n.f.* kin; cian, tribe.

Sire'ne, -n, *n.f.* siren.

Sirup, *n.m.* molasses; syrup.

Sitte, -n, *n.f.* custom; (*pl.*) mores, manners, morals.

Sittenlehre, -n, *n.f.* ethics.

sittenlos, *adj.* immoral.

sittig, *adj.* chaste, well-bred.

sittlich, *adj.* moral.

Situation', -en, *n.f.* situation.

Sitz, -e, *n.m.* seat, residence.

sitzen*, *vb.* sit, be seated; fit; be in jail.

sitzen·bleiben*, *vb.* remain seated; get stuck (with); not be promoted.

sitzen·lassen*, *vb.* jilt.

Sitzplatz, -̈e, *n.m.* seat.

Sitzung, -en, *n.f.* session.

Sizilia'ner, -, *n.m.* Sicilian.

sizilia'nisch, *adj.* Sicilian.

Sizi'lien, *n.nt.* Sicily.

Skala, -len, *n.f.* scale.

Skandal', -e, *n.m.* scandal.

Skandina'vien, *n.nt.* Scandinavia.

Skandina'vier, -, *n.m.* Scandinavian.

skandina'visch, *adj.* Scandinavian.

Skelett', -e, *n.nt.* skeleton.

Skepsis, *n.f.* skepticism.

Skeptiker, -, *n.m.* skeptic.

skeptisch, *adj.* skeptic(al).

ski, -er, *n.m.* ski.

ski·laufen*, *vb.* ski.

skilehrer, -, *n.m.* ski instructor.

skilift, -s, *n.m.* ski lift.

Skizze, -n, *n.f.* sketch.

skizzie'ren, *vb.* sketch.

Sklave, -n, -n, *n.m.* slave.

Sklaverei', *n.f.* slavery.

Skrupel, -, *n.m.* scruple.

Slang, -s, *n.m.* slang.

Slawe, -n, -n, *n.m.* Slav.

slawisch, *adj.* Slavic.

Slowa'ke, -n, -n, *n.m.* Slovak.

Slowakei', *n.f.* Slovakia.

slowa'kisch, *adj.* Slovakian.

Smaragd', -e, *n.m.* emerald.

Smoking, -s, *n.m.* dinner jacket, tuxedo.

Snob, -s, *n.m.* snob.

so, *adv.* so, thus; (**s. groß wie**) as big as.

Socke, -n, *n.f.* sock.

Sockenhalter, -, *n.m.* garter.

Soda, *n.f.* soda.

Sodbrennen, *n.nt.* heartburn.

soe'ben, *adv.* just now.

Sofa, -s, *n.nt.* sofa.

sofort', *adv.* immediately.

sofor'tig, *adj.* instantaneous.

Sog, *n.m.* suction; undertow.

sogar', *adv.* yet, even.

sogenannt, *adj.* so-called.

Sohle, -n, *n.f.* sole.

Sohn, -̈e, *n.m.* son.

solch(er, -es, -e), *adj.* such.

solcherlei, *adj.* of such a kind.

solchermaßen, *adv.* in such a way.

Sold, -e, *n.m.* pay.

Soldat', -en, -en, *n.m.* soldier.

solid', *adj.* solid.

Solidarität', *n.f.* solidarity.

Solist', -en, -en, *n.m.* soloist.

Soll, *n.nt.* debit; quota.

sollen*, *vb.* be supposed to, be said to; shall; (**er sollte gehen***) he should, ought to go; (**er hätte gehen·sollen**) he should, ought to have gone.

Solo, -s, *n.nt.* solo.

Sommer, -, *n.m.* summer.

Sommersprosse, -n, *n.f.* freckle.

Sommerzeit, -en, *n.f.* summer time; daylight-saving time.

Sona'te, -n, *n.f.* sonata.

Sonde, -n, *n.f.* probe.

sonder, *prep.* without.

Sonder, *cpds.* special.

Sonderangebot, -e, *n.nt.* bargain, special sale.

sonderbar, *adj.* strange, queer.

sonderbarerwei'se, *adv.* strange to say.

sondergleĭ'chen, *adv.* without equal, unparalleled.

sonderlich, *adj.* peculiar.

sondern, *vb.* separate.

sondern, *conj.* but (on the contrary).

sondie'ren, *vb.* sound, probe.

Sonett', -e, *n.nt.* sonnet.

Sonnabend, -e, *n.m.* Saturday.

Sonne, -n, *n.f.* sun.

sonnen, *vb.* (**sich s.**) sun oneself, bask.

Sonnenbrand, -̈e, *n.m.* sunburn.

Sonnenbräune, *n.f.* sun tan.

sonnenklar, *adj.* clear as daylight.

Sonnenschein, *n.m.* sunshine.

Sonnenstich, -e, *n.m.* sun stroke.

sonnenverbrannt, *adj.* sunburned.

sonnig, *adj.* sunny.

Sonntag, -e, *n.m.* Sunday.

sonst, *adv.* otherwise, else; formerly.

sonstig, *adj.* other; former.

sonstwie, *adv.* in some other way.

sonstwo, *adv.* somewhere else.

sonstwoher, *adv.* from some other place.

sonstwohin, *adv.* to some other place.

Sopran', -e, *n.m.* soprano.

Sorbett', -e, *n.nt.* sherbet.

Sorge, -n, *n.f.* sorrow; worry, anxiety, apprehension; care.

sorgen, *vb.* (**s. für**) care for, provide; (**sich s.**) worry, concern oneself.

sorgenfrei, *adj.* carefree.

sorgenvoll, *adj.* worried, careworn.

Sorgfalt, *n.f.* care.

sorgfältig, *adj.* careful, meticulous.

sorglos, *adj.* carefree.

sorgsam, *adj.* careful, painstaking.

Sorte, -n, *n.f.* sort, kind.

sortie'ren, *vb.* sort, assort, classify.

Soße, -n, *n.f.* sauce, gravy.

souverän', *adj.* sovereign.

Souveränität', *n.f.* sovereignty.

soviel, *adv.* so much, as much.

sowie', *conj.* as well as; as soon as.

sowieso', *adv.* in any case.

Sowjet, -s, *n.m.* Soviet.

sowje'tisch, *adj.* Soviet.

Sowjetunion', *n.f.* Soviet Union.

sowohl', *adv.* as well; (**s. A als B, s. A wie B**) both A and B.

sozial', *adj.* social.

sozialisie'ren, *vb.* socialize, nationalize.

Sozialis'mus, *n.m.* socialism.

Sozialist', -en, -en, *n.m.* socialist.

sozialis'tisch, *adj.* socialistic.

Soziologie', *n.f.* sociology.

sozusagen, *adv.* as it were, so to speak.

Spaghet'ti, *n.pl.* spaghetti.

Spalt, -e, *n.m.* crack, chink.

spaltbar, *adj.* fissionable.

Spalte, -n, *n.f.* crevice, gap; (newspaper) column.

spalten, *vb.* split.

Spaltung, -en, *n.f.* cleavage; fission.

Spange, -n, *n.m.* clasp, buckle.

Spanien, *n.nt.* Spain.

Spanier, -, *n.m.* Spaniard.

spanisch, *adj.* Spanish.

Spann, -e, *n.m.* arch, instep.

Spanne, -n, *n.f.* span.

spannen, *vb.* stretch; tighten.

spannend, *adj.* exciting, gripping.

Spannkraft, *n.f.* elasticity; (*fig.*) energy.

Spannung, -en, *n.f.* tension; (*fig.*) close attention, suspense.

sparen, *vb.* save.

Spargel, -, *n.m.* asparagus.

Sparkasse, -n, *n.f.* savings bank.

spärlich, *adj.* sparse, meager.

Sparren, -, *n.m.* spar, rafter.

sparsam, *adj.* thrifty, economical.

Sparsamkeit, *n.f.* thrift.

Spaß, -̈e, *n.m.* joke, fun.

spaßeshalber, *adv.* for the fun of it.

spaßig, *adj.* funny.

Spaßmacher, -, *n.m.* jester.

spät, *adj.* late.

Spaten, -, *n.m.* spade.

spätestens, *adv.* at the latest.

Spatz, -en, -en, *n.m.* sparrow.

spazie'ren·gehen*, *vb.* go for a walk, stroll.

Spazier'fahrt, -en, *n.f.* drive.

Spazier'gang, -̈, *n.m.* walk.

Specht, -e, *n.m.* woodpecker.

Speck, *n.m.* fat; bacon.

spedie'ren, *vb.* dispatch.

Spediteur', -e, *n.m.* shipping agent.

Speer, -e, *n.m.* spear; javelin.

Speiche, -n, *n.f.* spoke.

Speichel, *n.m.* saliva.

Speicher, -, *n.m.* loft, storage place.

speien*, *vb.* spit.

Speise, -n, *n.f.* food, nourishment.

Speisekammer, -n, *n.f.* pantry.

Speisekarte, -n, *n.f.* bill of fare, menu.

speisen, *vb. (tr.)* feed; *(intr.)* eat.

Speiseröhre, -n, *n.f.* esophagus.

Speisewagen, -, *n.m.* diner, dining-car.

Speisezettel, -, *n.m.* menu.

Speisung, -en, *n.f.* feeding.

Spekta'kel, *n.m.* noise, racket.

spekulie'ren, *vb.* speculate.

spenda'bel, *adj.* free and easy with money; **(s. sein*)** splurge.

Spende, -n, *n.f.* donation.

spenden, *vb.* give; donate.

Sperling, -e, *n.m.* sparrow.

Sperre, -n, *n.f.* barrier, blockade; gate.

sperren, *vb.* block, obstruct, blockade; (money) freeze.

Sperrfeuer, -, *n.nt.* barrage.

Sperrstunde, -n, *n.f.* curfew.

Spesen, *n.pl.* charges, expenses, **(auf S.)** on an expense account.

spezialisie'ren, *vb.* specialize.

Spezialist', -en, -en, *n.m.* specialist.

Spezialität', -en, *n.f.* specialty.

speziell', *adj.* special, specific.

spezi'fisch, *adj.* specific.

spezifizie'ren, *vb.* specify.

Sphäre, -n, *n.f.* sphere.

Sphinx, -en, *n.f.* sphinx.

spicken, *vb.* lard, interlard.

Spiegel, -, *n.m.* mirror.

spiegeln, *vb.* mirror, reflect.

Spiegelung, -en, *n.f.* reflection.

Spiel, -e, *n.nt.* play, game; gambling; pack (of cards).

Spielbank, -en, *n.f.* gambling casino.

spielen, *vb.* play, act; **(um Geld s.)** gamble.

spielerisch, *adj.* playful.

Spielgefährte, -n, -n, *n.m.* playmate.

Spielplatz, -̈e, *n.m.* playground.

Spielraum, -̈, *n.m.* room for action, range; elbow room; margin.

Spielwaren, *n.pl.* toys.

Spielzeug, -e, *n.nt.* toy.

Spieß, -e, *n.m.* spear; top sergeant.

Spinat', *n.m.* spinach.

Spindel, -n, *n.f.* spindle.

Spinett', -e, *n.nt.* spinet, harpsichord.

Spinne, -n, *n.f.* spider.

spinnen*, *vb.* spin; be crazy.

Spinngewebe, -, *n.nt.* cobweb.

Spion', -e, *n.m.* spy.

Spionag'e, *n.f.* espionage.

spionie'ren, *vb.* spy.

Spira'le, -n, *n.f.* spiral.

spiral'förmig, *adj.* spiral.

Spiritis'mus, *n.m.* spiritism.

Spiritualis'mus, *n.m.* spiritualism.

Spirituo'sen, *n.pl.* liquor, spirits.

spitz, *adj.* pointed, acute.

Spitzbart, -̈e, *n.m.* goatee.

Spitze, -n, *n.f.* point, tip, top; lace.

spitzenartig, *adj.* lacy.

spitzfindig, *adj.* shrewd; subtle.

Spitzhacke, -n, *n.f.* pick.

Spitzname(n), -, *n.m.* nickname.

Splitter, -, *n.m.* splinter, chip.

splittern, *vb.* splinter, shatter.

spontan', *adj.* spontaneous.

spora'disch, *adj.* sporadic.

Sporn, Sporen, *n.m.* spur.

Sport, -e, *n.m.* sport.

Sportler, -, *n.m.* sportsman; athlete.

sportlich, *adj.* athletic; sportsmanlike.

Sportplatz, -̈e, *n.m.* athletic field, stadium.

Spott, *n.m.* mockery, ridicule.

spottbillig, *adj.* dirt cheap.

spotten, *vb.* mock, scoff.

Spötter, -, *n.m.* scoffer.

spöttisch, *adj.* derisive.

Sprache, -n, *n.f.* speech; language.

spracheigen, *adj.* idiomatic.

Sprachfehler, -, *n.m.* speech impediment.

Sprachführer, -, *n.m.* phrase book.

sprachgewandt, *adj.* fluent.

sprachlos, *adj.* speechless.

Sprachschatz, *n.m.* vocabulary.

Sprachwissenschaft, -en, *n.f.* linguistics, philology.

sprechen*, *vb.* speak, talk.

Sprecher, -, *n.m.* speaker, spokesman.

Sprechstunde, -n, *n.f.* office hour.

spreizen, *vb.* spread apart.

sprengen, *vb.* explode, break; sprinkle.

Sprengstoff, -e, *n.m.* explosive.

Sprichwort, -̈er, *n.nt.* proverb, adage.

sprichwörtlich, *adj.* proverbial.

sprießen*, *vb.* sprout.

springen*, *vb.* jump; crack.

Springer, -, *n.m.* (chess) knight.

Springquell, -e, *n.m.* fountain.

sprinten, *vb.* sprint.

Spritze, -n, *n.f.* spray; injection; hypodermic.

spritzen, *vb.* spray, squirt, splash, inject.

spröde, *adj.* brittle; chapped; reserved, prim.

Sproß, -sse, *n.m.* sprout.

Sprößling, -e, *n.m.* shoot; offspring.

Sprotte, -n, *n.f.* sprat.

Spruch, -̈e, *n.m.* saying.

Sprudel, -, *n.m.* bubbling water; soda water.

sprudeln, *vb.* bubble.

Sprudeln, *n.nt.* effervescence.

sprühen, *vb.* spark, sparkle.

Sprühregen, *n.m.* drizzle.

Sprung, -̈e, *n.m.* jump; fissure, crack.

Sprungbrett, -er, *n.nt.* diving board; *(fig.)* stepping stone.

sprunghaft, *adj.* jumpy; erratic.

Sprungschanze, -n, *n.f.* skijump.

Spucke, *n.f.* spit, saliva.

spucken, *vb.* spit.

Spuk, -e, *n.m.* spook, ghost.

Spule, -n, *n.f.* spool, reel; *(elec.)* coil; bobbin.

spulen, *vb.* reel, wind.

spülen, *vb.* rinse, wash; (W.C.) flush.

Spülstein, -e, *n.m.* sink.

Spund, -e, *n.m.* spigot, tap.

Spur, -en, *n.f.* trace, track.

spuren, *vb.* follow the prescribed pattern.

spüren, *vb.* feel; trace.

spurlos, *adj.* without a trace.

Spurweite, -n, *n.f.* width of track, gauge.

sputen, *vb.* **(sich s.)** hurry up.

Staat, -en, *n.m.* state, government.

Staatenbund, -̈e, *n.m.* federation.

staatlich, *adj.* national, governmental.

Staatsangehörig-, *n.m.&f.* national citizen.

Staatsangehörigkeit, -en, *n.f.* citizenship, nationality.

staatsfeindlich, *adj.* subversive.

Staatskunst, *f.* statesmanship.

Staatsmann, -̈er, *n.m.* statesman.

Staatssekretär, -e, *n.m.* undersecretary of a ministry.

Staatsstreich, -e, *n.m.* coup d'état.

Stab, -̈e, *n.m.* staff, rod.

stabil', *adj.* stable.

stabilisie'ren, *vb.* stabilize.

Stabilität', *n.f.* stability.

Stachel, -n, *n.m.* sting, thorn, spike.

Stachelbeere, -n, *n.f.* gooseberry.

Stachelschwein, -e, *n.nt.* porcupine.

Stadion, -dien, *n.nt.* stadium.

Stadium, -dien, *n.nt.* stage.

Stadt, -̈e, *n.f.* town, city.

stadtbekannt, *adj.* known all over town, notorious.

städtisch, *adj.* municipal; urban.

Stadtteil, -e, *n.m.* borough.

Staffel, -n, *n.f.* rung, step; *(mil.)* echelon, squadron.

staffeln, *vb.* graduate, stagger.

Stagflation', *n.f.* stagflation.

stagnie'ren, *vb.* stagnate.

stagnie'rend, *adj.* stagnant.

Stahl, -e, *n.m.* steel.

Stahlhelm, -e, *n.m.* steel helmet.

Stahlwaren, *n.pl.* cutlery; hardware.

Stall, -̈e, *n.m.* stall, stable, barn.

Stamm, -̈e, *n.m.* (tree) trunk; (word) stem; tribe, clan.

Stammbaum, -̈e, *n.m.* family tree; pedigree.

stammeln, *vb.* stammer.

stammen, *vb.* stem, originate, be descended.

Stammgast, -̈e, *n.m.* habitué.

stämmig, *adj.* sturdy, burly.

stampfen, *vb.* stamp, trample.

Stand, -̈e, *n.m.* stand(ing), position; level; status; class, estate.

Standard, -s, *n.m.* standard.

standardisie'ren, *vb.* standardize.

Ständchen, -, *n.nt.* serenade.

Ständer, -, *n.m.* rack, stand.

Standesamt, -̈er, *n.nt.* marriage bureau; registrar.

standesbewußt, *adj.* class-conscious.

standesgemäß, *adj.* according to one's rank.

standhaft, *adj.* steadfast.

Standhaftigkeit, *n.f.* constancy.

stand-halten*, *vb.* hold one's ground, withstand.

Standpunkt, -e, *n.m.* standpoint, point of view.

Stange, -n, *n.f.* rod, bar, pole; carton (of cigarettes).

Stapel, -, *n.m.* pile; stock; (ship) slip; **(vom S. lassen*)** launch.

stapeln, *vb.* pile up.

stapfen, *vb.* stamp, plod.

Star, -e, *n.m.* (eye) cataract; (bird) starling; (film) star.

stark (-), *adj.* strong.

Stärke, -n, *n.f.* strength; starch.

stärken, *vb.* strengthen; starch.

Stärkungsmittel, -, *n.nt.* tonic.

starr, *adj.* rigid.

starren, *vb.* stare.

Starrheit, *n.f.* rigidity.

starrköpfig, *adj.* stubborn, headstrong.

Starrsinn, *n.m.* obstinacy.

Start, -s, *n.m.* start.

Startbahn, -en, *n.f.* runway.

starten, *vb.* start.

Startklappe, -n, *n.f.* choke (auto).

Station', -en, *n.f.* station.

stationär', *adj.* stationary.

Stations'vorsteher, -, *n.m.* station master.

statisch, *adj.* static.

Statist', -en, -en, *n.m.* (theater) extra; *(fig.)* dummy.

Statis'tik, *n.f.* statistics.

Stativ', -e, *n.nt.* (photo) tripod.

statt, *prep.* instead of.

Stätte, -n, *n.f.* place.

statt-finden*, *vb.* take place.

stattlich, *adj.* imposing.

Statue, -n, *n.f.* statue.

Staub, *n.m.* dust.

staubig, *adj.* dusty.

Staudamm, -̈e, *n.m.* dam.

stauen, *vb.* dam up; **(sich s.)** be dammed up, get jammed up.

staunen, *vb.* be astonished, wonder.

Stauung, -en, *n.f.* congestion.

stechen*, *vb.* prick, sting; pierce, stab.

Stechschritt, *n.m.* goose step.

Steckdose, -n, *n.f.* (elec.) outlet, socket.

stecken(*), *vb. intr.* be located, be hidden; **(wo steckt er denn?)** where *is* he, anyhow?; **(s. bleiben*)** get stuck.

stecken, *vb. tr.* put, stick, pin, hide.

Steckenpferd, -e, *n.nt.* hobbyhorse; hobby.

Stecknadel, -n, *n.f.* pin.

Steckrübe, -n, *n.f.* turnip.

Steg, -e, *n.m.* path; footbridge.

stehen*, *vb.* stand, be located; be becoming; **(sich gut s.)** be on good terms; **(es steht dahin')** it has yet to be shown.

stehen-bleiben*, *vb.* stop.

stehen-lassen*, *vb.* leave standing; leave behind, forget.

stehlen*, *vb.* steal.

Stehplatz, -̈e, *n.m.* standing room.

steif, *adj.* stiff, rigid.

Steifheit, -en, *n.f.* stiffness, rigidity.

Steig, -e, *n.m.* path.

steigen*, *vb.* climb, rise.

steigern, *vb.* increase, boost; **(sich s.)** increase, *(fig.)* work oneself up.

Steigung, -en, *n.f.* rise, slope, ascent.

steil, *adj.* steep.

Stein, -e, *n.m.* stone, rock.

Steingut, *n.nt.* earthenware, crockery.

steinigen, *vb.* stone.

Stelldichein, *n.nt.* rendezvous.

Stelle, -n, *n.f.* place, spot, point.

stellen, *vb.* place, put, set.

Stellenangebot, -e, *n.nt.* position offered.

Stellenvermittlung, -en, *n.f.* employment agency.

stellenweise, *adv.* in parts; in places.

Stellung, -en, *n.f.* position, place, stand; job; **(S. nehmen)** comment.

Stellungnahme, -n, *n.f.* comment, attitude.

stellvertretend, *adj.* assistant, deputy.

Stellvertreter, -, *n.m.* representative, deputy, alternate.

stemmen, *vb.* stem; **(sich s. gegen)** oppose, resist.

Stempel, -, *n.m.* stamp.

stempeln, *vb.* stamp; **(s. gehen)** be on the dole.

Stenographie', -i'en, *n.f.* shorthand.

stenographie'ren, *vb.* take shorthand, write shorthand.

Stenotypis'tin, -nen, *n.f.* stenographer.

Steppdecke, -n, *n.f.* quilt comforter.

Steppe, -n, *n.f.* steppe.

steppen, *vb.* stitch.

sterben*, *vb.* die.

sterblich, *adj.* mortal.

stereophon', *adj.* stereophonic, stereo.

steril', *adj.* sterile.

sterilisie'ren, *vb.* sterilize.

Sterilität', *n.f.* sterility.

Sterling, *n.nt.* pound sterling.

Stern, -e, *n.m.* star.

Sternbild, -er, *n.nt.* constellation.

Sternchen, -, *n.nt.* asterisk.

Sternkunde, *n.f.* astronomy.

Sternwarte, -n, *n.f.* observatory.

stet(ig), *adj.* steady.

stets, *adv.* always.

Steuer, -, *n.nt.* rudder, helm.

Steuer, -n, *n.f.* tax.

steuern, *vb.* steer, pilot, navigate.

Steuerruder, -, *n.nt.* rudder.

Steuerzahler, -, *n.m.* taxpayer.

Steward, -s, *n.m.* steward.

Stewardeß, -ssen, *n.f.* stewardess.

Stich, -e, *n.m.* stab; bite, sting; stitch.

stichhaltig, *adj.* valid, sound.

Stichwort, -̈er, *n.nt.* cue.

sticken, *vb.* embroider.

Stickerei', -en, *n.f.* embroidery.

Stickstoff, *n.m.* nitrogen.

Stief-, *cpds.* step-; **(Stiefvater)** stepfather; etc.

Stiefel, -, *n.m.* boot.

Stiel, -e, *n.m.* handle; stalk, stem.

stier, *adj.* glassy (look).

Stier, -e, *n.m.* steer.

stieren, *vb.* stare.

Stift, -e, *n.m.* peg, pin, tack; crayon, pencil.

Stift, -(e)r, *n.nt.* charitable institution.

stiften, *vb.* donate; found; endow.

Stiftung, -en, *n.f.* foundation; donation.

Stil, -e, *n.m.* style.

stilgerecht, *adj.* in good style, in good taste.

still, *adj.* still, quiet.

Stille, -n, *n.f.* stillness, silence.

Stilleben, -, *n.nt.* still-life.

stillen, vb. still, quench; nurse (a baby).

stillos, adj. in bad taste.

stillschweigend, adj. silent; tacit, implicit.

Stillstand, n.m. halt.

Stimmabgabe, -n, n.f. vote; voting.

Stimmband, ̈er, n.nt. vocal cord.

Stimme, -n, n.f. voice; vote.

stimmen, vb. tune; vote; be correct.

Stimmengleichheit, n.f. tie vote.

Stimmenprüfung, -en, n.f. canvass.

Stimmrecht, -e, n.nt. suffrage, franchise.

Stimmung, -en, n.f. mood; morale.

stimmungsvoll, adj. festive, moving; intimate.

Stimmzettel, -, n.m. ballot.

stinken*, vb. stink.

Stinktier, -e, n.nt. skunk.

Stint, -e, n.m. smelt.

Stipen'dium, -dien, n.nt. scholarship, grant.

Stirn, -en, n.f. forehead, brow.

Stirnhöhle, -n, n.f. sinus.

Stock, ̈e, n.m. stick, cane.

stockdunkel, adj. pitch-dark.

stocken, vb. stop, come to a halt; falter.

Stockung, -en, n.f. stop, standstill; deadlock.

Stockwerk, -e, n.nt. floor, story.

Stoff, -e, n.m. matter, substance; material; cloth.

stofflich, adj. material.

stöhnen, vb. groan.

Stoiker, -, n.m. stoic.

stoisch, adj. stoical.

Stola, -len, n.f. stole.

stolpern, vb. stumble, trip.

stolz, adj. proud.

Stolz, n.m. pride.

stolzie'ren, vb. strut.

stopfen, vb. stuff; (socks, etc.) darn.

stoppen, vb. stop.

Stöpsel, -, n.m. stopper; (elec.) plug.

Stör, -e, n.m. sturgeon.

Storch, ̈e, n.m. stork.

stören, vb. disturb, bother.

Störenfried, -e, n.m. intruder, troublemaker.

Störung, -en, n.f. disturbance; (radio) interference, static.

Stoß, ̈e, n.m. blow, hit, thrust.

stoßen*, vb. push, kick, hit, thrust.

Stoßstange, -n, n.f. bumper.

stottern, vb. stutter.

Strafanstalt, -en, n.f. penal institution.

strafbar, adj. liable to punishment.

Strafe, -n, n.f. punishment; fine; sentence.

strafen, vb. punish.

straff, adj. taut, tight.

straffen, vb. tighten.

Strafgebühr, -en, n.f. fine.

Strafgericht, -e, n.nt. criminal court.

Strafkammer, -n, n.f. criminal court.

Sträfling, -e, n.m. convict.

Strafmandat, -e, n.nt. traffic ticket.

Strafporto, n.nt. postage due.

Strahl, -en, n.m. ray, beam; (water) spout.

strahlen, vb. beam, gleam, radiate.

Strahlen, n.nt. radiance.

strahlend, adj. radiant.

Strahlflugzeug, -e, n.nt. jet plane.

Strahlung, -en, n.f. radiation.

Strähne, -n, n.f. strand; streak.

stramm, adj. tight; (fig.) strapping.

strampeln, vb. kick.

Strand, -e, n.m. beach, shore.

stranden, vb. strand.

Strandgut, n.nt. jetsam.

Strang, -e, n.m. rope; (über die Stränge schlagen*) run riot.

Strapa'ze, -n, n.f. exertion, drudgery.

Straße, -n, n.f. street, road.

Straßenbahn, -en, n.f. streetcar, trolley.

Strategie', n.f. strategy.

strate'gisch, adj. strategic.

Stratosphä're, n.f. stratosphere.

sträuben, vb. (sich s.) bristle; (fig.) struggle against, resist.

Strauch, ̈er, n.m. shrub.

straucheln, vb. falter, stumble.

Strauß, ̈e, n.m. bouquet; ostrich.

streben, vb. strive, endeavor, aspire.

Streben, n.nt. pursuit.

Strebepfeiler, -, n.m. flying buttress.

Streber, -, n.m. (school) grind; (society) social climber.

strebsam, adj. zealous.

Strecke, -n, n.f. stretch, distance.

strecken, vb. stretch; (die Waffen s.) lay down one's arms.

Streich, -e, n.m. stroke, blow; prank.

streicheln, vb. stroke, caress.

streichen*, vb. scratch; paint.

Streichholz, ̈er, n.nt. match.

Streife, -n, n.f. patrol.

streifen, vb. touch lightly.

Streifen, -, n.m. strip.

Streik, -s, n.m. strike.

Streikposten, -, n.m. picket.

Streit, n.m. quarrel, dispute.

streiten*, vb. fight; (sich s.) quarrel.

Streitfrage, -n, n.f. controversy.

Streitpunkt, -e, n.m. point at issue.

streitsüchtig, adj. pugnacious.

streng, adj. strict, stern, severe.

strenggläubig, adj. orthodox.

streuen, vb. strew, scatter, sprinkle.

Strich, -e, n.m. stroke, line; (nach S. und Faden) thoroughly; (gegen den S.) against the grain.

Strick, -e, n.m. rope.

stricken, vb. knit.

strittig, adj. controversial.

Stroh, n.nt. straw.

Strolch, -e, n.m. vagabond.

Strom, ̈e, n.m. stream; (elec.) current.

strömen, vb. stream, flow.

Stromkreis, -e, n.m. circuit.

stromlinienförmig, adj. streamlined.

Stromspannung, -en, n.f. voltage.

Strömung, -en, n.f. current; trend, drift.

Strudel, -, n.m. whirlpool.

Struktur', -en, n.f. structure.

Strumpf, ̈e, n.m. stocking.

Strumpfband, ̈er, n.nt. garter.

Strumpfbandgürtel, n.m. girdle.

Strumpfhose, -n, n.f. panty hose.

Strumpfwaren, n.pl. hosiery.

struppig, adj. shaggy.

Stube, -n, n.f. room.

Stuck, n.m. stucco.

Stück, -e, n.nt. piece; (theater) play.

stückeln, vb. patch, piece together.

stücken, vb. piece.

Student', -en, -en, n.m. student.

Studie, -n, n.f. study.

Studiengeld, -er, n.nt. tuition.

studie'ren, vb. study (at a university), be a student.

Studium, -dien, n.nt. study.

Stufe, -n, n.f. step.

stufenweise, adj. gradual, step by step.

Stuhl, ̈e, n.m. chair.

stumm, adj. mute, silent.

Stummel, -, n.m. stub, butt.

Stümper, -, n.m. beginner, amateur.

stumpf, adj. blunt; stupid; (angle) obtuse.

Stumpf, ̈e, n.m. stump.

Stunde, -n, n.f. hour; (school) class.

stündlich, adj. hourly.

stupsen, vb. joggle.

stur, adj. stubborn; obtuse.

Sturm, ̈e, n.m. storm.

stürmen, vb. storm.

stürmisch, adj. stormy.

Sturz, ̈e, n.m. fall; overthrow.

stürzen, vb. plunge, hurl, overthrow; rush, crash.

Stute, -n, n.f. mare.

Stütze, -n, n.f. support, prop, help.

stutzen, vb. trim.

stützen, vb. support.

Stützpunkt, -e, n.m. base.

Subjekt', -e, n.nt. subject.

sublimie'ren, vb. sublimate.

Substantiv, -e, *n.nt.* noun.
Substanz', -en, *n.f.* substance.
subtil', *adj.* subtle.
subtrahie'ren, *vb.* subtract.
Subvention', -en, *n.f.* subvention, subsidy.
Suche, *n.f.* search.
suchen, *vb.* search, seek, look for.
Sucht, *n.f.* addiction.
Süd, Süden, *n.m.* south.
südlich, *adj.* southern; to the south.
Südos'ten, *n.m.* southeast.
südöst'lich, *adj.* southeast.
Südpol, *n.m.* South Pole.
Südwe'sten, *n.m.* southwest.
südwest'lich, *adj.* southwest.
suggerie'ren, *vb.* suggest.
Sühne, -n, *n.f.* atonement, expiation.
sühnen, *vb.* atone for, expiate.
Sülze, *n.f.* jellied meat.
summa'risch, *adj.* summary.
Summe, -n, *n.f.* sum.
summen, *vb.* hum, buzz.
Sumpf, -̈e, *n.m.* swamp, mire.
Sünde, -n, *n.f.* sin.
Sündenvergebung, *n.f.* absolution.
Sünder, -, *n.m.* sinner.
Sündflut, *n.f.* the Flood; cataclysm.
sündhaft, *adj.* sinful.
sündigen, *vb.* sin.
super, *adj.* super.
Superstar, -s, *n.m.* superstar.
Suppe, -n, *n.f.* soup.
surren, *vb.* buzz.
suspendie'ren, *vb.* suspend.
süß, *adj.* sweet.
Süße, *n.f.* sweetness.
Sylve'ster, *n.nt.* New Year's Eve.
symbo'lisch, *adj.* symbolic.
Sympathie', -i'en, *n.f.* sympathy.
sympa'tisch, *adj.* likable, congenial; *(med.)* sympathetic.
Symphonie', -i'en, *n.f.* symphony.
sympho'nisch, *adj.* symphonic.
Symptom', -e, *n.nt.* symptom.
symptoma'tisch, *adj.* symptomatic.
Synago'ge, -n, *n.f.* synagogue.
synchronisie'ren, *vb.* synchronize.
Syndrom', -e, *n.nt.* syndrome.
Synonym', -e, *n.nt.* synonym.
Synthe'se, -n, *n.f.* synthesis.
synthe'tisch, *adj.* synthetic.
Syphilis, *n.f.* syphilis.
System', -e, *n.nt.* system.
systema'tisch, *adj.* systematic.
Szene, -n, *n.f.* scene.

T

Tabak, *n.m.* tobacco.
Tabel'le, -n, *n.f.* chart.
Tablett', -e, *n.nt.* tray.
Tablet'te, -n, *n.f.* tablet.

Tadel, -, *n.m.* reproof, reprimand; (school) demerit.
tadeln, *vb.* reprove, find fault with.
tadelnswert, *adj.* reprehensible.
Tafel, -n, *n.f.* tablet; table; chart; blackboard; bar (of chocolate).
täfeln, *vb.* panel.
Tag, -e, *n.m.* day; **(guten T.)** how do you do.
Tagebuch, -̈er, *n.nt.* diary.
Tagesanbruch, *n.m.* daybreak.
Tageslicht, *n.nt.* daylight.
Tageszeitung, -en, *n.f.* daily newspaper.
täglich, *adj.* daily.
Tagung, -en, *n.f.* convention, meeting.
Taille, -n, *n.f.* waist.
Takt, -e, *n.m.* tact; rhythm.
taktisch, *adj.* tactical.
Tal, -̈er, *n.nt.* valley.
Talent', -e, *n.nt.* talent.
talentiert', *adj.* talented.
tändeln, *vb.* dally.
Tango, -s, *n.m.* tango.
Tank, -s, *n.m.* tank.
Tankstelle, -n, *n.f.* filling station.
Tanne, -n, *n.f.* fir, spruce.
Tante, -n, *n.f.* aunt.
Tantie'me, -n, *n.f.* bonus.
Tanz, -̈e, *n.m.* dance.
tänzeln, *vb.* flounce, caper.
tanzen, *vb.* dance.
Tänzer, -, *n.m.* dancer.
Tanzsaal, -säle, *n.m.* dance hall, ballroom.
Tape'te, -n, *n.f.* wallpaper.
Tapezie'rer, -, *n.m.* upholsterer.
tapfer, *adj.* brave, valiant.
Tapisserie, -i'en, *n.f.* tapestry.
tappen, *vb.* grope.
tapsig, *adj.* gawky.
tarnen, *vb.* screen, camouflage.
Tarnung, -en, *n.f.* screen, camouflage.
Tasche, -n, *n.f.* pocket; handbag.
Taschenausgabe, -n, *n.f.* paperback.
Taschendieb, -e, *n.m.* pickpocket.
Taschenformat, *n.nt.* pocket-size.
Taschengeld, -er, *n.nt.* allowance, pocket money.
Taschenlampe, -n, *n.f.* flashlight.
Taschentuch, -̈er, *n.nt.* handkerchief.
Tasse, -n, *n.f.* cup.
Tastatur', -en, *n.f.* keyboard.
Taste, -n, *n.f.* key.
tasten, *vb.* feel; grope.
Tastsinn, *n.m.* sense of touch.
Tat, -en, *n.f.* act, deed; **(in der T.)** indeed.
Tatbestand, *n.m.* facts, findings.
Täter, -, *n.m.* culprit.
tätig, *adj.* active.
Tätigkeit, -en, *n.f.* activity.

Tatkraft, -̈e, *n.f.* energy.
tatkräftig, *adj.* energetic.
tätlich, *adj.* violent.
Tätlichkeit, -en, *n.f.* violence.
Tatsache, -n, *n.f.* fact.
tatsächlich, *adj.* actual, real.
Tatze, -n, *n.f.* paw, claw.
Tau, -e, *n.nt.* rope.
Tau, -e, *n.m.* dew.
taub, *adj.* deaf.
Taube, -n, *n.f.* pigeon, dove.
tauchen, *vb.* dive, plunge, dip.
Taucher, -, *n.m.* diver.
Taufe, -n, *n.f.* baptism, christening.
taufen, *vb.* baptize, christen.
Taufkapelle, -n, *n.f.* baptistry.
taugen, *vb.* be worth; be of use.
Taugenichts, *n.m.* good-for-nothing.
tauglich, *adj.* useful, qualified.
taumeln, *vb.* stagger.
taumelnd, *adj.* groggy.
Tausch, *n.m.* exchange, trade.
tauschen, *vb.* exchange.
täuschen, *vb.* deceive, delude, fool.
täuschend, *adj.* deceptive.
Tauschhandel, *n.m.* barter.
Täuschung, -en, *n.f.* deception, delusion, fallacy.
tausend, *num.* a thousand.
Tausend, -e, *n.nt.* thousand.
tausendst-, *adj.* thousandth.
Tausendstel, -, *n.nt.* thousandth part; **(ein t.)** one one-thousandth.
Taxe, -n, *n.f.* tax; taxi.
taxie'ren, *vb.* appraise, estimate.
Technik, *n.f.* technique; technology.
technisch, *adj.* technical.
Tee, -s, *n.m.* tea.
Teekanne, -n, *n.f.* tea-pot.
Teelöffel, -, *n.m.* teaspoon.
Teer, *n.m.* tar.
Teich, -e, *n.m.* pond, pool.
Teig, -e, *n.m.* dough, batter.
Teil, -e, *n.m.* part, portion, section.
teilbar, *adj.* divisible.
teilen, *vb.* divide, share.
teil-haben*, *vb.* share.
Teilhaber, -, *n.m.* partner.
Teilnahme, *n.f.* participation; sympathy.
teilnahmslos, *adj.* lethargic.
teil-nehmen*, *vb.* participate, partake.
Teilnehmer, -, *n.m.* participant, partner.
teils, *adv.* partly.
Teilung, -en, *n.f.* partition, division.
teilweise, *adv.* partly.
Teint, -s, *n.m.* complexion.
Telegramm', -e, *n.nt.* telegram.
Telegraph', -en, -en, *n.m.* telegraph.
telegraphie'ren, *vb.* telegraph.
Telephon', -e, *n.nt.* telephone.
Telephon'buch, -̈er, *n.nt.* telephone directory.

Telephon'fräulein, -, *n.nt.* telephone operator.

telephonie'ren, *vb.* telephone.

Teller, -, *n.m.* plate.

Temperament', *n.nt.* temperament, disposition; vivacity.

temperament'voll, *adj.* temperamental; vivacious.

Temperatur', -en, *n.f.* temperature.

Tempo, -s, *n.nt.* speed; tempo.

Tendenz', -en, *n.f.* tendency, trend.

Tender, -, *n.m.* tender.

Tennis, *n.nt.* tennis.

Tennisschläger, -, *n.m.* tennis racket.

Tennisschuh, -e, *n.m.* sneaker.

Tenor', -e, *n.m.* tenor.

Teppich, -e, *n.m.* rug, carpet.

Termin', -e, *n.m.* fixed day, deadline.

Terpentin', *n.nt.* turpentine.

Terras'se, -n, *n.f.* terrace.

Testament', -e, *n.nt.* testament, will.

testamenta'risch, *adj.* testamentary, noted in the will.

teuer, *adj.* expensive, dear.

Teuerung, *n.f.* rising cost of living.

Teufel, -, *n.m.* devil.

teuflisch, *adj.* diabolic.

Text, -e, *n.m.* text.

Texti'lien, *n.pl.* textiles.

Textil'ware, -n, *n.f.* textile.

Thea'ter, -, *n.nt.* theater; spectacle.

Thea'terkasse, -n, *n.f.* box office.

Thea'terstück, -e, *n.nt.* play.

Thea'terwissenschaft, -en, *n.f.* dramatics.

theatra'lisch, *adj.* theatrical.

Thema, -men, *n.nt.* theme, subject, topic.

Theolo'ge, -n, -n, *n.m.* theologian.

theore'tisch, *adj.* theoretical.

Theorie', -l'en, *n.f.* theory.

Therapie', *n.f.* therapy.

Thermome'ter, -, *n.nt.* thermometer.

These, -n, *n.f.* thesis.

Thron, -e, *n.m.* throne.

Thunfisch, -e, *n.m.* tuna.

tief, *adj.* deep, low; profound.

Tiefe, -n, *n.f.* depth.

Tiefebene, -n, *n.f.* plain, lowland.

tiefgründig, *adj.* profound.

Tiefkühler, -, *n.m.* freezer.

Tiefkühltruhe, -n, *n.f.* deep freeze.

tiefsinnig, *adj.* profound; pensive.

tieftraurig, *adj.* heartbroken.

Tier, -e, *n.nt.* animal.

Tierarzt, -e, *n.m.* veterinary.

tierisch, *adj.* animal, bestial.

Tiger, -, *n.m.* tiger.

tilgen, *vb.* obliterate; delete; pay off, amortize.

Tilgung, -en, *n.f.* liquidation, amortization.

Tinte, -n, *n.f.* ink.

Tintenfisch, -e, *n.m.* octopus.

Tip, -s, *n.m.* hint, suggestion.

tippen, *vb.* type.

Tisch, -e, *n.m.* table.

Tischdecke, -n, *n.f.* tablecloth.

Tischler, -, *n.m.* carpenter.

Tischtuch, -er, *n.nt.* tablecloth.

Titel, -, *n.m.* title.

Toast, n.m. toast.

toben, *vb.* rave, rage.

Tochter, -, *n.f.* daughter.

Tod, *n.m.* death.

Todesfall, -e, *n.m.* (case of) death.

Todesstrafe, -n, *n.f.* capital punishment.

tödlich, *adj.* deadly, mortal; lethal.

Toilet'te, -n, *n.f.* toilet.

Toilet'tenartikel, *n.pl.* toilet articles.

tolerant', *adj.* tolerant.

Toleranz', *n.f.* tolerance.

toll, *adj.* mad, crazy.

tollkühn, *adj.* foolhardy.

Tollwut, *n.f.* rabies.

tölpelhaft, *adj.* clumsy.

Toma'te, -n, *n.f.* tomato.

Ton, -e, *n.m.* tone, sound; clay.

tonangebend, *adj.* setting the style.

Tonart, -en, *n.f.* key.

Tonband, -er, *n.nt.* magnetic tape.

Tonbandaufnahme, -n, *n.f.* tape recording.

Tonbandgerät, -e, *n.nt.* tape recorder.

tönen, *vb.* sound, resound, ring.

Tonfall, -e, *n.m.* intonation, inflection.

Tonfilm, -e, *n.m.* sound movie.

Tonhöhe, -n, *n.f.* pitch.

Tonleiter, -n, *n.f.* scale.

Tonne, -n, *n.f.* ton; barrel.

Tonstufe, -n, *n.f.* (music) pitch.

Tonwaren, *n.pl.* earthenware.

Topf, -e, *n.m.* pot.

Töpferware, -n, *n.f.* pottery.

Tor, -en, -en, *n.m.* fool.

Tor, -e, *n.nt.* gate, gateway; (sport) goal.

Torbogen, -, *n.m.* archway.

Torheit, -en, *n.f.* folly.

töricht, *adj.* foolish.

torkeln, *vb.* lurch, stagger.

Torni'ster, -, *n.m.* knapsack, pack.

torpedie'ren, *vb.* torpedo.

Torpe'do, -s, *n.m.* torpedo.

Törtchen, -, *n.nt.* tart.

Torte, -n, *n.f.* tart, layer cake.

Tortur', -en, *n.f.* torture.

tosen, *vb.* rage, roar.

tot, *adj.* dead.

total', *adj.* total.

totalitär', *adj.* totalitarian.

töten, *vb.* kill.

Totenwache, -n, *n.f.* wake.

Toto, *n.m.* lottery.

Totschlag, -e, *n.m.* (case of) manslaughter.

Tour, -en, *n.f.* tour, excursion, trip.

Tourist', -en, -en, *n.m.* tourist.

Trab, *n.m.* trot.

Trabant', -en, -en, *n.m.* henchman.

traben, *vb.* trot.

Tracht, -en, *n.f.* costume.

trachten, *vb.* seek, endeavor.

Tradition', -en, *n.f.* tradition.

traditionell', *adj.* traditional.

Tragbahre, -n, *n.f.* stretcher.

tragbar, *adj.* portable; bearable.

träge, *adj.* indolent, sluggish.

tragen*, *vb.* carry, bear; wear.

Träger, -, *n.m.* carrier; girder; (lingerie) straps.

Tragik, *n.f.* tragic art; calamity.

tragisch, *adj.* tragic.

Tragö'die, -n, *n.f.* tragedy.

Tragweite, -n, *n.f.* range; significance, consequence.

Trainer, -, *n.m.* coach.

trainie'ren, *vb.* train, work out; coach.

Trambahn, -en, *n.f.* trolley.

trampeln, *vb.* trample.

Tranchier'messer, -, *n.nt.* carving-knife.

Träne, -n, *n.f.* tear.

tränen, *vb.* water (eye).

Trank, -e, *n.m.* potion.

tränken, *vb.* water (animals).

Transaktion', -en, *n.f.* transaction.

Transforma'tor, -o'ren, *n.m.* transformer, converter.

Transfusion', -en, *n.f.* transfusion.

transpirie'ren, *vb.* perspire.

transponie'ren, *vb.* transpose.

Transport', -e, *n.m.* transport.

transportie'ren, *vb.* transport.

transsexual', *adj.* transsexual.

Transvestit', -en, *n.m.* transvestite.

Trapez', -e, *n.nt.* trapeze.

Traube, -n, *n.f.* grape.

trauen, *vb.* (*intr.*) trust; (*tr.*) marry, join in marriage.

Trauer, *n.f.* grief; mourning.

trauern, *vb.* grieve, mourn.

trauervoll, *adj.* mournful.

Traufe, -n, *n.f.* gutter; (**vom Regen in die T.**) out of the frying pan into the fire.

Traum, -e, *n.m.* dream; (**böser T.**) nightmare.

träumen, *vb.* dream; (**vor sich hin-t.**) daydream.

Träumer, -, *n.m.* dreamer.

Träumerei', -en, *n.f.* daydream, reverie.

träumerisch, *adj.* fanciful, faraway.

traumhaft, *adj.* dreamlike; dreamy.

traurig, *adj.* sad.

Trauring, -e, *n.m.* wedding ring.

Travelerscheck, -s, *n.m.* traveler's check.

Trecker, -, *n.m.* tractor.

Treff, *n.nt.* clubs (cards).
treffen*, *vb.* hit; meet; (**sich t.**) meet.
treffend, *adj.* pertinent.
Treffer, -, *n.m.* hit.
trefflich, *adj.* excellent.
treiben*, *vb. (tr.)* drive; be engaged in; *(intr.)* drift, float.
Trend, -s, *n.m.* trend.
trenne, *vb.* separate, divide; hyphenate; (**sich t.**) part.
Trennung, -en, *n.f.* separation, division.
treppab', *adv.* down the stairs.
treppauf', *adv.* up the stairs.
Treppe, -n, *n.f.* staircase, stairs.
Tresor', -e, *n.m.* vault.
treten*, *vb.* step, tread.
treu, *adj.* true, faithful, loyal.
Treue, *n.f.* faith, loyalty; allegiance.
Treueid, -e, *n.m.* oath of allegiance.
Treuhänder, -, *n.m.* trustee.
treuherzig, *adj.* trusting, guileless.
treulich, *adv.* faithfully.
treulos, *adj.* disloyal.
Treulosigkeit, -e, *n.f.* disloyalty.
Tribü'ne, -n, *n.f.* grandstand.
Trichter, -, *n.m.* funnel.
Trick, -s, *n.m.* trick.
Trickfilm, -e, *n.m.* animated cartoon.
Tricktrack, *n.nt.* backgammon.
Trieb, -e, *n.m.* sprout; shoot; urge.
Triebfeder, -n, *n.f.* mainspring.
triebhaft, *adj.* instinctive, unrestrained.
Triebwagen, -, *n.m.* railcar.
triefen*, *vb.* drip.
triftig, *adj.* weighty.
Trikot', *n.nt.* knitted cloth.
trimmen, *vb.* trim.
trinkbar, *adj.* drinkable.
trinken*, *vb.* drink.
Trinker, -, *n.m.* drunkard.
Trinkgeld, -er, *n.nt.* tip.
Trinkspruch, ⸚e, *n.m.* toast.
Tripper, *n.m.* gonorrhea.
Tritt, -e, *n.m.* step; kick.
Trittleiter, -n, *n.f.* stepladder.
Triumph', -e, *n.m.* triumph.
triumphie'ren, *vb.* triumph.
trivial', *adj.* trivial.
trocken, *adj.* dry.
Trockenhaube, -n, *n.f.* hair drier.
trocken-legen, *vb.* (land) drain; (baby) change the diapers.
trocknen, *vb.* dry.
trödeln, *vb.* dawdle.
Trog, ⸚e, *n.m.* trough.
trollen, *vb.* (**sich t.**) toddle off.
Trommel, -n, *n.f.* drum.
Trommelfell, -e, *n.nt.* eardrum.
Trompe'te, -n, *n.f.* trumpet.
Tropen, *n.pl.* tropics.
Tropfen, -, *n.m.* drop.
tropfen, *vb.* drip.
Tropfer, -, *n.m.* dropper.
Trophä'e, -n, *n.f.* trophy.

tropisch, *adj.* tropical.
Trost, *n.m.* consolation, solace, comfort.
trösten, *vb.* console, comfort.
trostlos, *adj.* desolate, dreary.
trostreich, *adj.* comforting.
Trott, *n.m.* trot.
Trottel, -, *n.m.* idiot, dope.
Trotz, *n.m.* defiance, spite.
trotz, *prep.* in spite of, despite, notwithstanding.
trotzdem, **1.** *conj.* although, despite the fact that. **2.** *adv.* nevertheless.
trotzen, *vb.* defy.
trotzig, *adj.* defiant.
trübe, *adj.* dim; muddy; cloudy.
Trubel, *n.m.* bustle, confusion.
trüben, *vb.* dim.
Trübsal, *n.f.* misery, sorrow.
trübselig, *adj.* sad, gloomy.
Trübsinn, *n.p.* dejection, gloom.
trübsinnig, *adj.* gloomy.
Trüffel, -n, *n.f.* truffle.
Trug, *n.m.* deceit; delusion.
trügen*, *vb. (tr.)* deceive; *(intr.)* be deceptive.
trügerisch, *adj.* deceptive; illusory; treacherous.
Trugschluß, ⸚sse, *n.m.* fallacy.
Truhe, -n, *n.f.* chest.
Trümmer, *n.p.* ruins, debris.
Trunk, ⸚e, *n.m.* drink; draught.
Trunkenbold, -e, *n.m.* drunkard.
Trunkenheit, *n.f.* drunkenness.
Trupp, -s, *n.m.* troop, squad.
Truppe, -n, *n.f.* troops.
Truppeneinheit, -en, *n.f.* unit, outfit.
Trust, -s, *n.m.* trust.
Truthahn, ⸚e, *n.m.* turkey.
Tscheche, -n, -n, *n.m.* Czech.
Tschechei', *n.f.* Czechoslovakia.
tschechisch, *adj.* Czech.
Tschechoslowa'ke, -n, -n, *n.m.* Czechoslovakian.
Tschechoslowakei', *n.f.* Czechoslovakia.
tschechoslowa'kisch, *adj.* Czechoslovakian.
T-shirt, -s, *n.nt.* T-shirt.
Tube, -n, *n.f.* tube.
Tuberkulo'se, *n.f.* tuberculosis.
Tuch, ⸚er, *n.nt.* cloth.
tüchtig, *adj.* able, efficient.
Tüchtigkeit, *n.f.* ability, efficiency.
Tücke, -n, *n.f.* malice, perfidy.
tückisch, *adj.* malicious, treacherous.
Tugend, -en, *n.f.* virtue.
tugendhaft, *adj.* virtuous.
tugendsam, *adj.* virtuous.
Tüll, *n.m.* tulle.
Tülle, -n, *n.f.* spout.
Tulpe, -n, *n.f.* tulip.
tummeln, *vb.* move about, romp.
Tummelplatz, ⸚e, *n.m.* playground.
Tumor, -o'ren, *n.m.* tumor.

Tümpel, -, *n.m.* pool.
Tumult', -e, *n.m.* tumult, uproar; hubbub.
tun*, *vb.* do.
Tünche, -n, *n.f.* whitewash; *(fig.)* veneer.
Tunichtgut, -e, *n.m.* ne'er-do-well.
Tunke, -n, *n.f.* sauce, gravy.
tunken, *vb.* dunk.
Tunnel, -, *n.m.* tunnel.
tupfen, *vb.* dab.
Tür, -en, *n.f.* door; (**mit der T. ins Haus fallen***) blurt out.
Turbi'nenjäger, -, *n.m.* turbojet plane.
Turbi'nenpropellertriebwerk, -e, *n.nt.* turbo-prop.
Türeingang, ⸚e, *n.m.* doorway.
Türke, -n, -n, *n.m.* Turk.
Türkei', *n.f.* Turkey.
Türkis', -e, *n.m.* turquoise.
türkisch, *adj.* Turkish.
Turm, ⸚e, *n.m.* tower, spire, steeple; (chess) castle, rook; (**spitzer T.**) spire.
türmen, *vb. (tr.)* pile up; *(intr.)* beat it; (**sich t.**) rise high.
turnen, *vb.* do gymnastics.
Turner, -, *n.m.* gymnast.
Turnhalle, -n, *n.f.* gym(nasium).
Turnier', -e, *n.nt.* tournament.
tuscheln, *vb.* whisper.
Tuschkasten, ⸚, *n.m.* paint box.
Tüte, -n, *n.f.* (paper) bag, sack.
Tüttelchen, -, *n.nt.* dot.
Typ, -en, *n.m.* type.
Type, -n, *n.f.* (printing) type.
Typhus, *n.m.* typhus, typhoid fever.
typisch, *adj.* typical.
Typographie', *n.f.* typography.
Tyrann', -en, -en, *n.m.* tyrant.
Tyrannei', *n.f.* tyranny.
tyrannisie'ren, *vb.* tyrannize, oppress.

U

U-Bahn, -en, *n.f.* (= Untergrundbahn) subway.
übel, *adj.* bad; nasty; nauseate.
Übel, *n.nt.* evil; nuisance.
Übelkeit, *n.f.* nausea.
übel-nehmen*, *vb.* hold against, resent.
Übeltat, -en, *n.f.* offence.
Übeltäter, -, *n.m.* offender.
üben, *vb.* practice.
über, *prep.* over, about, above, across, beyond.
überall, *adv.* everywhere.
überar'beiten, *vb.* work over; (**sich ü.**) overwork.
überaus, *adv.* exceedingly.
überbelichten, *vb.* overexpose.
überbie'ten*, *vb.* outbid; surpass.
Überbleibsel, -, *n.nt.* rest, leftover.

Überblick, -e, *n.m.* survey; general view.

überbli'cken, *vb.* survey.

überbrin'gen*, *vb.* deliver.

Überbrin'ger, -, *n.m.* bearer.

überbrü'cken, *vb.* bridge.

überdau'ern, *vb.* outlive, outlast.

überdies', *adv.* furthermore.

Überdruß, *n.m.* boredom; **(bis zum Ü.)** ad nauseam.

überdrüssig, *adj.* tired of, sick of.

übereilt', *adj.* rash, hasty.

übereinan'der, *adv.* one on top of the other.

überein'-kommen*, *vb.* agree.

Überein'kommen, -, *n.nt.* agreement.

Überein'kunft, ⸚e, *n.f.* agreement.

überein'-stimmen, *vb.* agree.

Überein'stimmung, -en, *n.f.* agreement, accord.

überfah'ren*, *vb.* drive over, run over.

Überfahrt, -en, *n.f.* passage, crossing.

Überfall, -⸚, *n.m.* raid; hold-up.

überfallen*, *vb.* attack suddenly, hold up.

überfällig, *adj.* overdue.

überflie'gen*, *vb.* fly over; *(fig.)* scan.

über-fließen*, *vb.* overflow.

überflü'geln, *vb.* surpass.

Überfluß, -⸚sse, *n.m.* abundance.

überflüssig, *adj.* superfluous.

überflu'ten, *vb.* overflow.

überfüh'ren, *vb.* transfer, transport; convict.

Überfüh'rung, -en, *n.f.* transport, transfer; (railroad) overpass.

überfüllt', *adj.* overcrowded, jammed.

Übergabe, *n.f.* delivery; surrender.

Übergang, ⸚e, *n.m.* passage; transition.

überge'ben*, *vb.* hand over, deliver; **(sich ü.)** vomit.

über-gehen*, *vb.* go over to.

überge'hen*, *vb.* pass over, skip.

Übergewicht, *n.nt.* overweight, preponderance; **(das Ü. bekommen*)** get the upper hand.

über-greifen*, *vb.* spread; encroach.

Übergriff, -e, *n.m.* encroachment.

über-haben*, *vb.* be sick of, be fed up with.

überhand'nehmen*, *vb.* spread, become dominant.

überhäu'fen, *vb.* overwhelm.

überhaupt', *adv.* in general; altogether, at all.

überheb'lich, *adj.* overbearing.

überho'len, *vb.* overhaul; drive past, pass.

überholt', *adj.* out-of-date.

überhö'ren, *vb.* purposely not hear, ignore.

überla'den, *adj.* ornate.

überlas'sen*, *vb.* give to, yield, leave to.

über-laufen*, *vb.* overrun; defect, desert.

überlau'fen, *adj.* overrun.

Überläufer, -, *n.m.* deserter.

überle'ben, *vb.* outlive, survive.

Überle'ben, *n.nt.* survival.

überle'gen, *vb.* reflect on, think over.

überle'gen, *adj.* superior.

überlegt', *adj.* deliberate.

Überle'gung, -en, *n.f.* deliberation, consideration.

überlie'fern, *vb.* hand over.

Überlie'ferung, -en, *n.f.* tradition.

Übermacht, *n.f.* superiority.

überman'nen, *vb.* overpower.

Übermaß, *n.nt.* excess.

übermäßig, *adj.* excessive.

Übermensch, -en, -en, *n.m.* superman.

übermit'teln, *vb.* transmit, convey.

übermorgen, *adv.* the day after tomorrow.

Übermü'dung, *n.f.* overfatigue, exhaustion.

Übermut, *n.m.* high spirits; arrogance.

übernächst, *adj.* next but one.

übernach'ten, *vb.* spend the night, stay overnight.

übernatürlich, *adj.* supernatural.

überneh'men*, *vb.* take over.

überparteilich, *adj.* nonpartisan.

überprü'fen, *vb.* examine, check.

Überprü'fung, -en, *n.f.* checking, check-up.

überque'ren, *vb.* cross.

überra'gen, *vb.* surpass.

überra'gend, *adj.* superior.

überra'schen, *vb.* surprise.

Überra'schung, -en, *n.f.* surprise.

überre'den, *vb.* persuade.

Überre'dung, -en, *n.f.* persuasion.

überreich, *adj.* abundant, profuse.

überrei'chen, *vb.* hand over, present.

Überrest, -e, *n.m.* remains, relics.

überrum'peln, *vb.* take by surprise.

Überschallgeschwindigkeit, -en, *n.f.* supersonic speed.

überschat'ten, *vb.* overshadow.

überschät'zen, *vb.* overestimate.

überschau'en, *vb.* survey, get the whole view of.

überschla'fen*, *vb.* oversleep.

Überschlag, ⸚e, *n.m.* estimate.

überschla'gen*, *vb.* pass over, skip; **(sich ü.)** turn over.

Überschrift, -en, *n.f.* title, heading, headline.

Überschuhe, *n.pl.* galoshes.

Überschuß, -⸚sse, *n.m.* surplus.

überschüt'ten, *vb.* overwhelm.

überschwem'men, *vb.* inundate.

Überschwem'mung, -en, *n.f.* flood.

Übersee, *n.f.* oversea(s).

Überseedampfer, -, *n.m.* transoceanic liner.

überseh'bar, *adj.* capable of being taken in at a glance; foreseeable.

überse'hen*, *vb.* view; overlook, not notice, ignore.

Überse'hen, -, *n.nt.* oversight.

übersen'den*, *vb.* send, transmit; consign, remit.

überset'zen, *vb.* translate.

Überset'zung, -en, *n.f.* translation.

Übersicht, -en, *n.f.* overview; summary, outline.

übersichtlich, *adj.* clear; easily understandable.

überspannt', *adj.* eccentric.

übersprin'gen*, *vb.* skip.

übersprudelnd, *adj.* exuberant.

überste'hen*, *vb.* endure, survive.

überstei'gen*, *vb.* surpass.

überstim'men, *vb.* outvote, overrule.

Überstunde, -n, *n.f.* hour of overtime work; *(pl.)* overtime.

überstür'zen, *vb.* precipitate.

überstürzt', *adj.* headlong, precipitate.

übertrag'bar, *adj.* transferable.

übertra'gen*, *vb.* transfer, transmit; translate; **(im Radio ü.)** broadcast; **(im Fernseh ü.)** televise.

Übertra'gung, -en, *n.f.* transfer; translation; broadcast.

übertref'fen*, *vb.* surpass, excel.

übertrei'ben*, *vb.* exaggerate.

Übertrei'bung, -en, *n.f.* exaggeration.

über-treten*, *vb.* go over.

übertre'ten*, *vb.* trespass, violate, infringe.

Übertre'tung, -en, *n.f.* violation, infringement.

übertrie'ben, *adj.* exaggerated, extravagant.

übervor'teilen, *vb.* get the better of (someone).

überwa'chen, *vb.* watch over, keep under surveillance, control.

Überwa'chung, -en, *n.f.* surveillance, control.

überwäl'tigen, *vb.* overpower, overwhelm.

überwei'sen*, *vb.* transfer; remit.

Überwei'sung, -en, *n.f.* remittance.

überwer'fen*, *vb.* **(sich ü.)** have a falling-out with.

überwie'gen*, *vb.* outweigh; predominate.

überwie'gend, *adj.* preponderant.

überwin'den*, *vb.* conquer, overcome.

Überwin'dung, -en, *n.f.* conquest; effort, reluctance.

überwin'tern, *vb.* hibernate.

Überzahl, *n.f.* numerical superiority.

überzählig, *adj.* surplus.

überzeu'gen, *vb.* convince.

überzeu'gend, *adj.* convincing.

Überzeu'gung, -en, *n.f.* conviction.

Überzeu'gungskraft, *n.f.* forcefulness.

Überzieher, -, *n.m.* overcoat.

üblich, *adj.* customary, usual.

U-Boot, -e, *n.nt.* (= Unterseeboot) submarine.

übrig, *adj.* remaining, left over.

übrig·bleiben*, *vb.* be left over; **(es bleibt mir nichts anderes übrig)** I have no other choice.

übrigens, *adv.* incidentally, by the way.

übrig·haben*, *vb.* have left over; **(nichts ü. für)** have no use for.

Übung, -en, *n.f.* practice; exercise.

Übungsbeispiel, -e, *n.nt.* paradigm.

UdSSR, *abbr.* (= Union' der Soziali'stischen Sowjetrepubliken) Union of Soviet Socialist Republics.

Ufer, -, *n.nt.* shore, bank.

Ufereinfassung, -en, *n.f.* embankment.

uferlos, *adj.* limitless.

Uhr, -en, *n.f.* watch, clock; **(wieviel U. ist es?)** what time is it?; **(sieben U.)** seven o'clock.

Uhrmacher, -, *n.m.* watchmaker.

Uhu, -s, *n.m.* owl.

Ulk, -e, *n.m.* fun.

ulkig, *adj.* funny.

Ultra-, *cpds.* ultra.

um, *prep.* around; at (clock time); **(um . . . zu)** in order to; **(u. so mehr)** the more, all the more so.

um·adressieren, *vb.* readdress.

um·arbeiten, *vb.* rework, revise.

umar'men, *vb.* embrace.

Umar'mung, -en, *n.f.* embrace.

um·bauen, *vb.* remodel.

um·biegen*, *vb.* turn, turn around.

um·bringen*, *vb.* kill.

um·drehen, *vb.* turn around, rotate, revolve.

Umdre'hung, -en, *n.f.* turn, revolution, rotation.

um·erziehen*, *vb.* reeducate.

umfah'ren*, *vb.* circumnavigate, circle.

um·fallen*, *vb.* fall over.

Umfang, ∻e, *n.m.* circumference; extent; volume.

umfangreich, *adj.* extensive; comprehensive; voluminous.

umfas'sen, *vb.* enclose, surround; comprise.

umfas'send, *adj.* comprehensive.

um·formen, *vb.* remodel, transform, convert.

Umfrage, -n, *n.f.* inquiry, poll.

Umgang, *n.m.* intercourse, association.

Umgangssprache, *n.f.* colloquial speech, vernacular.

umge'ben*, *vb.* surround.

Umge'bung, -en, *n.f.* surroundings, environment; vicinity.

um·gehen*, *vb.* go around, circulate; **(u. mit)** deal with, handle; **(mit dem Gedanken u.)** contemplate, plan.

umge'hen*, *vb.* evade, circumvent.

Umge'hen, -, *n.nt.* evasion.

Umge'hung, -en, *n.f.* circumvention; *(mil.)* flanking movement.

Umge'hungsstraße, -n, *n.f.* bypass.

umgekehrt, **1.** *adj.* reverse, inverse. **2.** *adv.* the other way round.

um·gestalten, *vb.* transform, alter, modify.

umgren'zen, *vb.* enclose; circumscribe.

um·gucken, *vb.* **(sich u.)** look around.

um·haben*, *vb.* have on.

Umhang, ∻e, *n.m.* wrap.

umher', *adv.* around, about.

umher'·gehen*, *vb.* walk around.

umher'·wandern, *vb.* wander.

Umkehr, *n.f.* return; reversal.

um·kehren, *vb.* turn (back, round, inside out, upside down).

Umkehrung, -en, *n.f.* reversal, reversing.

um·kippen, *vb.* turn over, tip over.

um·kleiden, *vb.* **(sich u.)** change one's clothes.

Umkleideraum, ∻e, *n.m.* dressing-room.

um·kommen*, *vb.* perish.

Umkreis, -e, *n.m.* circumference; range, radius.

umkrei'sen, *vb.* circle around, rotate around.

Umlauf, *n.m.* circulation.

um·laufen*, *vb.* circulate.

um·legen, *vb.* put on; change the position, shift; change the date.

um·leiten, *vb.* divert.

Umleitung, -en, *n.f.* detour.

um·lernen, *vb.* learn anew, readjust one's views.

umliegend, *adj.* surrounding.

umrah'men, *vb.* frame.

umran'den, *vb.* edge.

um·rechnen, *vb.* convert.

umrei'ßen*, *vb.* outline.

umrin'gen, *vb.* surround.

Umriß, -sse, *n.m.* contour, outline.

um·rühren, *vb.* stir.

Umsatz, ∻e, *n.m.* turnover, sales.

Umsatzsteuer, -n, *n.f.* sales tax.

um·schalten, *vb.* switch.

Umschau, *n.f.* **(U. halten*)** look around.

umschichtig, *adv.* in turns.

Umschlag, ∻e, *n.m.* envelope; (book) cover; turnover; compress.

umschlie'ßen*, *vb.* encircle, encompass.

umschlin'gen*, *vb.* embrace.

um·schreiben*, *vb.* rewrite.

umschrei'ben*, *vb.* circumscribe, paraphrase.

Umschrei'bung, -en, *n.f.* paraphrase.

Umschrift, -en, *n.f.* transcription.

Umschwung, ∻e, *n.m.* change, about-face.

um·sehen*, *vb.* **(sich u.)** look around.

um·setzen, *vb.* transpose; (goods) sell.

Umsicht, *n.f.* circumspection.

umsichtig, *adj.* circumspect, prudent.

umso, *adv.* **(u. besser)** so much the better; **(je mehr, u. besser)** the more the better.

umsonst', *adv.* in vain; gratis, free of charge.

Umstand, ∻e, *n.m.* circumstance, condition; *(pl.)* formalities, fuss; **(in anderen Umständen)** pregnant.

umständlich, *adj.* complicated, fussy.

Umstandskleid, -er, *n.nt.* maternity dress.

Umstandswort, ∻er, *n.nt.* adverb.

Umstehend-, *n.m.&f.* bystander.

um·steigen*, *vb.* transfer, change.

Umsteiger, -, *n.m.* transfer (ticket).

um·stellen, *vb.* change the position of; **(sich u. auf)** readjust, convert to; computerize.

umstel'len, *vb.* surround.

um·steuern, *vb.* reverse.

um·stimmen, *vb.* make someone change his mind.

um·stoßen*, *vb.* overturn, overthrow, upset.

umstri'cken, *vb.* ensnare.

Umsturz, ∻e, *n.m.* overthrow, revolution.

um·stürzen, *vb.* overturn.

Umtausch, -e, *n.m.* exchange; **(vom U. ausgeschlossen)** no exchange.

umtauschbar, *adj.* exchangeable.

um·tauschen, *vb.* exchange.

Umtrieb, -e, *n.m.* intrigue, machinations.

um·tun*, *vb.* **(sich nach etwas u.)** look for, apply for.

Umwälzung, -en, *n.f.* upheaval, revolution.

um·wandeln, *vb.* transform; change; convert.

um·wechseln, *vb.* change, convert.

Umweg, -e, *n.m.* detour.

Umwelt, *n.f.* environment.

Umweltschutz, *n.m.* environmental protection.

Umweltschutzler, -, *n.m.* environmentalist.

umwer'ben*, *vb.* woo, court.

Umwer'bung, *n.f.* courtship.

um·werfen*, *vb.* overthrow; upset.

um·ziehen*, *vb.* move; **(sich u.)** change one's clothes.

umzin'geln, *vb.* surround.

Umzug, -̈e, *n.m.* move; procession.

unabhängig, *adj.* independent.

Unabhängigkeit, *n.f.* independence.

unabkömmlich, *adj.* indispensable.

unablässig, *adj.* incessant.

unabseh'bar, *adj.* unforeseeable.

unabwendbar, *adj.* inevitable.

unachtsam, *adj.* inattentive; careless.

unähnlich, *adj.* dissimilar, unlike.

unangebracht, *adj.* out of place.

unangemessen, *adj.* unsuitable, improper.

unangenehm, *adj.* unpleasant, distasteful.

Unannehmlichkeit, -en, *n.f.* trouble.

unansehnlich, *adj.* plain, inconspicuous.

unanständig, *adj.* indecent, obscene.

unanwendbar, *adj.* inapplicable.

unappetitlich, *adj.* unappetizing; nasty.

Unart, -en, *n.f.* rudeness, bad manners.

unartig, *adj.* naughty.

unauffällig, *adj.* inconspicuous.

unaufhörlich, *adj.* incessant.

unaufmerksam, *adj.* inattentive.

Unaufmerksamkeit, -en, *n.f.* inattentiveness; inadvertence.

unaufrichtig, *adj.* insincere.

Unaufrichtigkeit, -en, *n.f.* insincerity; lie.

unausbleiblich, *adj.* inevitable.

unausgeglichen, *adj.* unbalanced, unstable.

unausgesetzt, *adj.* continual.

unausstehlich, *adj.* insufferable.

unbändig, *adj.* unruly; excessive.

unbarmherzig, *adj.* merciless.

unbeabsichtigt, *adj.* unintentional.

unbeachtet, *adj.* unnoticed; **(u. lassen*)** ignore.

unbedacht, *adj.* thoughtless.

unbedenklich, *adj.* harmless.

unbedeutend, *adj.* insignificant.

unbedingt', *adj.* absolute, unconditional.

unbefangen, *adj.* natural, naïve.

unbefleckt, *adj.* immaculate; **(u.e Empfängnis)** Immaculate Conception.

unbefriedigend, *adj.* unsatisfactory.

unbefriedigt, *adj.* dissatisfied.

unbefugt, *adj.* unauthorized.

unbegabt, *adj.* untalented, dumb.

unbegreiflich, *adj.* incomprehensible.

unbegrenzt, *adj.* limitless.

Unbehagen, *n.nt.* discomfort.

unbehaglich, *adj.* uneasy.

unbeholfen, *adj.* awkward, clumsy.

unbekannt, *adj.* unknown, unfamiliar.

unbekümmert, *adj.* unconcerned.

unbeliebt, *adj.* unpopular.

unbemerkbar, *adj.* imperceptible.

unbemerkt, *adj.* unnoticed.

unbenommen, *adj.* **(es bleibt* Ihnen u.)** you are at liberty to.

unbequem, *adj.* inconvenient; uncomfortable.

unbere'chenbar, *adj.* incalculable; unreliable, erratic.

unberechtigt, *adj.* unauthorized; unjustified.

unberufen! *interj.* touch wood!

unbeschädigt, *adj.* undamaged.

unbescheiden, *adj.* immodest; selfish.

Unbescholtenheit, *n.f.* integrity.

unbeschreiblich, *adj.* indescribable.

unbeschrieben, *adj.* blank.

unbesehen, *adj.* unseen.

unbesieg'bar, *adj.* invincible.

unbesonnen, *adj.* thoughtless.

unbesorgt, *adj.* carefree, unconcerned.

unbeständig, *adj.* changeable.

unbestellbar, *adj.* undeliverable.

unbestimmt, *adj.* indefinite, vague.

unbestritten, *adj.* undisputed.

unbeträchtlich, *adj.* inconsiderable.

unbeugsam, *adj.* inflexible; obstinate.

unbewandert, *adj.* inexperienced.

unbewiesen, *adj.* not proved.

unbewohnbar, *adj.* uninhabitable.

unbewohnt, *adj.* uninhabited.

unbewußt, *adj.* unconscious; unknown.

unbezahl'bar, *adj.* priceless.

unbrauchbar, *adj.* useless.

und, *conj.* and.

Undank, *n.m.* ingratitude.

undankbar, *adj.* ungrateful.

undefinierbar, *adj.* indefinable.

undenklich, *adj.* inconceivable; **(seit u. en Zeiten)** since time out of mind.

undeutlich, *adj.* unclear, indistinct.

undicht, *adj.* leaky.

Unding, *n.nt.* absurdity, nonsense.

unduldsam, *adj.* intolerant.

undurchführbar, *adj.* not feasible.

undurchsichtig, *adj.* opaque.

uneben, *adj.* uneven.

unecht, *adj.* not genuine, false, counterfeit; artificial.

unehelich, *adj.* illegitimate.

unehrenhaft, *adj.* dishonorable.

unehrerbietig, *adj.* disrespectful.

unehrlich, *adj.* dishonest; insincere.

uneingeschränkt, *adj.* unlimited.

uneinig, *adj.* **(u. sein*)** disagree.

Uneinigkeit, -en, *n.f.* disagreement, dissension.

unempfindlich, *adj.* insensitive.

unendlich, *adj.* infinite; **(u. klein)** infinitesimal.

Unend'lichkeit, -en, *n.f.* infinity.

unentbehrlich, *adj.* indispensable.

unentgeltlich, *adj.* gratuitous.

unentschieden, *adj.* undecided; **(das Spiel ist u.)** the game is a draw.

unentschlossen, *adj.* undecided.

unentwegt, *adj.* constant.

unerfahren, *adj.* inexperienced.

Unerfahrenheit, -en, *n.f.* inexperience.

unerfreulich, *adj.* unpleasant.

unerheblich, *adj.* insignificant, irrelevant.

unerhört', *adj.* unheard of, outrageous.

unerkannt, *adj.* unrecognized.

unerkennbar, *adj.* unrecognizable.

unerklärlich, *adj.* inexplicable.

unerläßlich, *adj.* indispensable.

unerlaubt, *adj.* unlawful, illegal, illicit.

unermeß'lich, *adj.* immeasurable.

unermüdlich, *adj.* unpleasant.

unerquicklich, *adj.* unpleasant.

unerschrocken, *adj.* intrepid.

unersetzlich, *adj.* irreplaceable.

unersprießlich, *adj.* unpleasant.

unerträglich, *adj.* unbearable, insufferable.

unerwartet, *adj.* unexpected.

unerwünscht, *adj.* unwelcome.

unerzogen, *adj.* ill-bred, ill-mannered.

unfähig, *adj.* unable, incapable, incompetent.

unfair, *adj.* unfair.

Unfall, ¨e, *n.m.* accident.

unfaß'bar, *adj.* incomprehensible.

unfaß'lich, *adj.* incomprehensible.

unfehl'bar, *adj.* infallible.

Unfeinheit, -en, *n.f.* crudeness, crudity.

unförmig, *adj.* shapeless.

unfreiwillig, *adj.* involuntary.

unfreundlich, *adj.* unkind, unfriendly; rude.

unfruchtbar, *adj.* barren, sterile.

Unfug, *n.m.* mischief.

unfügsam, *adj.* unmanageable.

Ungar, -n, -n, *n.m.* Hungarian.

ungarisch, *adj.* Hungarian.

Ungarn, *n.nt.* Hungary.

ungastlich, *adj.* inhospitable.

ungeachtet, *prep.* notwithstanding.

ungebildet, *adj.* uneducated.

ungebührlich, *adj.* improper.

ungebunden, *adj.* free.

Ungeduld, *n.f.* impatience.

ungeduldig, *adj.* impatient.

ungeeignet, *adj.* unqualified, unsuitable.

ungefähr, 1. *adj.* approximate. **2.** *adv.* approximately, about.

ungefährlich, *adj.* harmless.

ungefällig, *adj.* unobliging, impolite.

ungeheuchelt, *adj.* sincere.

ungeheuer, *adj.* tremendous, huge.

Ungeheuer, -, *n.nt.* monster.

ungeheuerlich, *adj.* monstrous.

ungehobelt, *adj.* uncouth.

ungehörig, *adj.* improper, rude.

ungehorsam, *adj.* disobedient.

Ungehorsam, *n.m.* disobedience.

ungekünstelt, *adj.* unaffected, natural.

ungeläufig, *adj.* unfamiliar.

ungelegen, *adj.* inconvenient.

ungelenk, *adj.* clumsy.

ungelernt, *adj.* unskilled.

ungemein, *adv.* uncommonly.

ungemütlich, *adj.* uncomfortable.

ungeneigt, *adj.* disinclined.

ungeniert, *adj.* free and easy.

ungenießbar, *adj.* inedible; unbearable.

ungenügend, *adj.* insufficient; unsatisfactory.

ungerade, *adj.* uneven; (numbers) odd.

ungerecht, *adj.* unjust, unfair.

ungerechtfertigt, *adj.* unwarranted.

Ungerechtigkeit, -en, *n.f.* injustice.

ungeschehen, *adj.* **(u. machen)** to undo.

Ungeschicklichkeit, -en, *n.f.* clumsiness.

ungeschickt, *adj.* clumsy, awkward.

ungeschlacht, *adj.* uncouth.

ungesetzlich, *adj.* illegal.

ungesittet, *adj.* unmannerly.

ungestört, *adj.* undisturbed.

ungestraft, 1. *adj.* unpunished. **2.** *adv.* with impunity.

ungestüm, *adj.* impetuous.

ungesund, *adj.* unhealthy; unsound.

Ungetüm, -e, *n.nt.* monster.

ungewandt, *adj.* awkward.

ungewiß, *adj.* uncertain.

Ungewißheit, -en, *n.f.* uncertainty.

Ungewitter, -, *n.nt.* thunderstorm.

ungewöhnlich, *adj.* unusual, abnormal.

ungewohnt, *adj.* unaccustomed, unfamiliar.

ungewollt, *adj.* unintentional.

ungezählt, *adj.* innumerable.

ungezügelt, *adj.* unrestrained.

ungezwungen, *adj.* easygoing.

Ungläubig-, *n.m.&f.* infidel.

unglaublich, *adj.* incredible.

unglaubwürdig, *adj.* unreliable.

ungleich, *adj.* unequal, uneven, unlike.

ungleichartig, *adj.* dissimilar.

Ungleichheit, -en, *n.f.* unequality, dissimilarity.

Unglück, -e, *n.nt.* misfortune, calamity, disaster, accident.

unglücklich, *adj.* unhappy; unfortunate.

unglücklicherweise, *adv.* unfortunately.

unglückselig, *adj.* disastrous; utterly miserable.

Ungnade, *n.f.* disfavor.

ungnädig, *n.f.* ungracious.

ungültig, *adj.* invalid, void; **(für u. erklären)** annul, declare null and void.

ungünstig, *adj.* unfavorable.

unhalt'bar, *adj.* untenable.

unhandlich, *adj.* unwieldy.

Unheil, *n.nt.* harm, disaster.

unheil'bar, *adj.* incurable.

unheilbringend, *adj.* fatal, ominous.

unheilvoll, *adj.* ominous.

unheimlich, *adj.* scary, sinister.

unhöflich, *adj.* impolite, rude.

unhygienisch, *adj.* unsanitary.

Uniform', -en, *n.f.* uniform.

uninteressant, *adj.* uninteresting.

unisex, *adj.* unisex.

universal', *adj.* universal.

Universität', -en, *n.f.* university.

unkenntlich, *adj.* unrecognizable.

unklar, *adj.* unclear, obscure.

unkleidsam, *adj.* unbecoming.

Unkosten, *n.pl.* expenses, overhead.

unlängst, *adv.* recently.

unlauter, *adj.* impure; unfair.

unleserlich, *adj.* illegible.

unlieb, *adj.* disagreeable.

unliebenswürdig, *adj.* unfriendly, impolite.

unlogisch, *adj.* illogical.

unlustig, *adj.* listless.

unmanierlich, *adj.* unmannered.

unmaßgeblich, *adj.* irrelevant; unauthoritative.

unmäßig, *adj.* immoderate.

Unmenge, -n, *n.f.* enormous quantity.

Unmensch, -en, -en, *n.m.* brute.

unmenschlich, *adj.* inhuman.

unmerklich, *adj.* imperceptible.

unmittelbar, *adj.* immediate.

unmodern, *adj.* old-fashioned, out of style.

unmöglich, *adj.* impossible.

unmoralisch, *adj.* immoral.

unnachahmlich, *adj.* inimitable.

unnah'bar, *adj.* inaccessible.

unnötig, *adj.* needless, unnecessary.

unnütz, *adj.* useless.

unordentlich, *adj.* disorderly, messy.

Unordnung, *n.f.* disorder.

unparteiisch, *adj.* impartial, neutral.

unpassend, *adj.* unsuitable; improper, off-color.

unpassier'bar, *adj.* impassable.

unpäßlich, *adj.* unwell, indisposed.

unpersönlich, *adj.* impersonal.

unpolitisch, *adj.* nonpolitical.

unpraktisch, *adj.* impractical.

unpünktlich, *adj.* not on time.

unrecht, *adj.* wrong; **(u. haben*)** be wrong.

Unrecht, *n.nt.* wrong, harm, injustice.

unreell, *adj.* dishonest.

unregelmäßig, *adj.* irregular.

unreif, *adj.* immature.

unrein, *adj.* unclean; impure.

unrichtig, *adj.* incorrect.

Unruhe, -n, *n.f.* unrest, trouble, disturbance.

unruhig, *adj.* restless, troubled, uneasy.

unschädlich, *adj.* harmless.

unscheinbar, *adj.* insignificant.

unschicklich, *adj.* improper.

unschlüssig, *adj.* undecided.

Unschuld, *n.f.* innocence.

unschuldig, *adj.* innocent.

unselig, *adj.* unhappy, fatal.

unser, -, -e, *adj.* our.

uns(e)rer, -es, -e, *pron.* ours.

unsicher, *adj.* uncertain; unsafe.

Unsicherheit, -en, *n.f.* uncertainty, insecurity.

unsichtbar, *adj.* invisible.

Unsinn, *n.m.* nonsense.

unsinnig, *adj.* absurd, nonsensical.

Unsitte, -n, *n.f.* bad habit.

unsittlich, *adj.* immoral.

unsterblich, *adj.* immortal.

unstet, *adj.* unsteady.

Unstimmigkeit, -en, *n.f.* discrepancy, disagreement.

untauglich, *adj.* unfit.

unteilbar, *adj.* indivisible.

unten, *adv.* below, down, downstairs.

unter, *prep.* under, beneath, below; among; **(u. uns)** just between you and me.

unter-, *adj.* under, lower.

Unterarm, -e, *n.m.* forearm.

unterbewußt, *adj.* subconscious.

Unterbewußtsein, *n.nt.* subconsciousness.

unterbie'ten*, *vb.* undercut; lower.

unterblei'ben*, *vb.* not get done.

unterbre'chen*, *vb.* interrupt.

Unterbre'chung, -en, *n.f.* interruption.

unterbrei'ten, *vb.* submit.

unter-bringen*, *vb.* lodge, accommodate.

unterdes'(sen), *adv.* meanwhile.

unterdrü'cken, *vb.* suppress, oppress, repress, stifle, subdue.

unterdrückt', *adj.* downtrodden.

Unterdrü'ckung, -en, *n.f.* suppression.

untereinan'der, *adv.* among them- (our-, your-)selves.

unterernährt, *adj.* undernourished.

Unterernährung, *n.f.* malnutrition.

Unterfüh'rung, -en, *n.f.* underpass.

Untergang, -̈e, *n.m.* downfall, decline.

unterge'ben, *adj.* subordinate.

Unterge'ben-, *n.m.&f.* subordinate.

unter-gehen*, *vb.* perish; set (sun).

untergeordnet, *adj.* subordinate.

untergra'ben*, *vb.* undermine, subvert.

Untergrundbahn, -en, *n.f.* subway.

unterhalb, *prep.* below.

Unterhalt, *n.m.* maintenance, keep.

unterhal'ten*, *vb.* maintain, support; entertain; **(sich u.)** converse.

Unterhal'tung, -en, *n.f.* maintenance; entertainment, conversation.

Unterhand'lung, -en, *n.f.* negotiation.

Unterhaus, *n.nt.* lower house (of parliament, congress).

Unterhemd, -en, *n.nt.* undershirt.

Unterhose, -n, *n.f.* underpants.

unterjo'chen, *vb.* subjugate.

Unterkunft, -̈e, *n.f.* lodging.

Unterlage, -n, *n.f.* base, bed; evidence; bottom sheet.

unterlas'sen*, *vb.* omit, fail to do.

Unterlas'sung, -en, *n.f.* omission, default.

unterle'gen, *adj.* inferior.

Unterleib, -er, *n.m.* abdomen.

unterlie'gen*, *vb.* succumb to, be overcome by.

Untermieter, -, *n.m.* subtenant.

unterneh'men*, *vb.* undertake.

Unterneh'men, -, *n.nt.* enterprise.

unterneh'mend, *adj.* enterprising.

Unterneh'mer, -, *n.m.* entrepreneur, contractor.

Unterneh'mung, -en, *n.f.* undertaking.

Unteroffizier, -e, *n.m.* noncommissioned officer, sergeant.

Unterpfand, *n.nt.* pledge, security.

Unterre'dung, -en, *n.f.* discussion, parley.

Unterricht, *n.m.* instruction.

unterrich'ten, *vb.* instruct.

Unterrich'tung, *n.f.* guidance.

Unterrock, -̈e, *n.m.* slip, petticoat.

untersa'gen, *vb.* prohibit.

Untersatz, -̈e, *n.m.* base; saucer.

unterschät'zen, *vb.* underestimate.

unterschei'den, *vb.* distinguish, differentiate; **(sich u.)** differ.

Unterschied, -e, *n.m.* difference.

unterschiedslos, *adj.* indiscriminate.

unterschla'gen*, *vb.* embezzle, suppress.

unterschrei'ben*, *vb.* sign (one's name to).

Unterschrift, -en, *n.f.* signature.

Unterseeboot, -e, *n.nt.* submarine.

untersetzt', *adj.* chunky, thickset.

Unterstand, -̈e, *n.m.* dugout.

unterste'hen*, *vb.* **(sich u.)** dare.

Unterstel'lung, -en, *n.f.* innuendo, insinuation.

unterstrei'chen*, *vb.* underline, underscore.

unterstüt'zen, *vb.* support, back.

Unterstüt'zung, -en, *n.f.* support, backing.

untersu'chen, *vb.* investigate, examine.

Untersu'chung, -en, *n.f.* investigation, examination.

Untertan, (-en,) -en, *n.m.* subject.

Untertasse, -n, *n.f.* saucer.

unter-tauchen, *vb.* submerge.

Unterwäsche, *n.f.* underwear.

unterwegs', *adv.* on the way; bound for.

unterwei'sen*, *vb.* instruct.

Unterwei'sung, -en, *n.f.* instruction.

Unterwelt, *n.f.* underworld.

unterwer'fen*, *vb.* subjugate; subject to; **(sich u.)** submit (to).

Unterwer'fung, -en, *n.f.* submission.

unterwor'fen, *adj.* subject (to).

unterwür'fig, *adj.* subservient.

unterzeich'nen, *vb.* sign.

unterzie'hen*, *vb.* **(sich u.)** undergo.

untief, *adj.* shallow.

untreu, *adj.* unfaithful, disloyal.

Untreue, *n.f.* unfaithfulness, disloyalty.

untröstlich, *adj.* disconsolate.

unüberlegt, *adj.* inconsiderate, thoughtless.

unüberwindlich, *adj.* insuperable.

unumgänglich, *adj.* unavoidable.

unveränderlich, *adj.* invariable.

unverantwortlich, *adj.* irresponsible.

unverbesserlich, *adj.* incorrigible.

unverbindlich, *adj.* without obligation.

unverblümt, *adj.* blunt.

unvereinbar, *adj.* incompatible.

unvergeßlich, *adj.* unforgettable.

unvergleichlich, *adj.* incomparable.

unverheiratet, *adj.* unmarried.

unverhohlen, *adj.* frank, aboveboard.

unverkennbar, *adj.* unmistakable.

unvermeidlich, *adj.* inevitable.

unvermittelt, *adj.* abrupt.

unvermutet, *adj.* unexpected.

unverschämt, *adj.* shameless, impudent, nervy.

Unverschämtheit, -en, *n.f.* impertinence, gall.

unversehens, *adv.* unexpectedly.

unverständlich, *adj.* incomprehensible.

unverzüglich, *adj.* speedy, without delay.

unvollendet, *adj.* incomplete, unfinished.

unvollkommen, *adj.* incomplete, imperfect.

unvoreingenommen, *adj.* unbiased.

unvorher'gesehen, *adj.* unforeseen.

unvorsichtig, *adj.* careless.

unwägbar, *adj.* imponderable.

unwahr(haftig), *adj.* untrue.

Unwahrheit, -en, *n.f.* untruth.

unwahrnehmbar, *adj.* imperceptible.

unwahrscheinlich, *adj.* improbable.

unweigerlich, *adj.* unhesitating; without fail.

unwesentlich, *adj.* immaterial, nonessential.

unwiderlegbar, *adj.* irrefutable.

unwiderstehlich, *adj.* irresistible.

unwillkürlich, *adj.* involuntary.

unwirksam, *adj.* ineffectual.

unwissend, *adj.* ignorant.

unwürdig, *adj.* unworthy.

Unzahl, *n.f.* tremendous number.

unzählig, *adj.* countless.

Unze, -n, *n.f.* ounce.

Unzucht, *n.f.* lewdness.

unzüchtig, *adj.* lewd.

unzufrieden, *adj.* dissatisfied.

Unzufriedenheit, -en, *n.f.* dissatisfaction.

unzulänglich, *adj.* insufficient, inadequate.

unzureichend, *adj.* insufficient.

unzuverlässig, *adj.* unreliable.

Ur-, *cpds.* original; very old; tremendously.

uralt, *adj.* very old, ancient.

Uraufführung, -en, *n.f.* première.

Urenkel, -, *n.m.* great-grandson.

Urenkelin, -nen, *n.f.* great-granddaughter.

Urgroßeltern, *n.pl.* great-grandparents.

Urgroßmutter, ¨, *n.f.* great-grandmother.

Urgroßvater, ¨, *n.m.* great-grandfather.

Urheber, -, *n.m.* author, originator.

Urheberrecht, -e, *n.nt.* copyright.

Urin', -e, *n.nt.* urine.

urinie'ren, *vb.* urinate.

Urkunde, -n, *n.f.* document.

Urlaub, -e, *n.m.* leave, furlough.

Urne, -n, *n.f.* urn; ballot box.

Urquell, -e, *n.m.* fountainhead.

Ursache, -n, *n.f.* cause; (keine U.) don't mention it.

Ursprung, ¨e, *n.m.* origin.

ursprünglich, *adj.* original.

Urteil, -e, *n.nt.* judgment, sentence.

urteilen, *vb.* judge.

usurpie'ren, *vb.* usurp.

usw., *abbr.* (= und so weiter) etc., and so forth.

V

Vagabund', -en, -en, *n.m.* tramp.

vage, *adj.* vague.

Valu'ta, -ten, *n.f.* value; (foreign) currency.

Vanil'le, *n.f.* vanilla.

Variation', -en, *n.f.* variation.

Varieté', *n.nt.* variety show, vaudeville.

variie'ren, *vb.* vary.

Vase, -n, *n.f.* vase.

Vater, ¨, *n.m.* father.

Vaterland, *n.nt.* fatherland.

väterlich, *adj.* fatherly, paternal.

vaterlos, *adj.* fatherless.

Vaterschaft, -en, *n.f.* fatherhood, paternity.

Vaterun'ser, *n.nt.* Lord's Prayer.

Veilchen, -, *n.nt.* violet.

Vene, -n, *n.f.* vein.

vene'risch, *adj.* venereal.

Ventil', -e, *n.nt.* valve.

Ventilation', *n.f.* ventilation.

Ventila'tor, -o'ren, *n.m.* ventilator, fan.

ventilie'ren, *vb.* ventilate.

verab'reden, *vb.* agree upon; (sich v.) make an appointment, date.

Verab'redung, -en, *n.f.* appointment, engagement, date.

verab'scheuen, *vb.* abhor, detest.

verab'schieden, *vb.* dismiss; pass (a bill); (sich v.) take one's leave.

verach'ten, *vb.* scorn, despise.

verach'tenswert, *adj.* despicable.

verächt'lich, *adj.* contemptuous.

Verach'tung, -en, *n.f.* contempt.

verallgemei'nern, *vb.* generalize.

Verallgemei'nerung, -en, *n.f.* generalization.

veral'tet, *adj.* obsolete.

Veran'da, -den, *n.f.* porch.

verän'derlich, *adj.* changeable.

verän'dern, *vb.* change.

Verän'derung, -en, *n.f.* change.

veran'kern, *vb.* anchor, moor.

veran'lassen*, *vb.* cause, motivate.

Veran'lassung, -en, *n.f.* cause, motivation.

veran'schaulichen, *vb.* illustrate.

veran'stalten, *vb.* arrange, put on.

Veran'staltung, -en, *n.f.* arrangement, performance.

verant'wortlich, *adj.* responsible.

Verant'wortlichkeit, -en, *n.f.* responsibility.

Verant'wortung, -en, *n.f.* responsibility; accounting, justification.

verant'wortungslos, *adj.* irresponsible.

verant'wortungsvoll, *adj.* carrying responsibility.

verar'beiten, *vb.* process.

verär'gern, *vb.* exasperate.

verar'men, *vb.* become poor.

Verb, -en, *n.nt.* verb.

verbal', *adj.* verbal.

Verband', ¨e, *n.m.* association; bandage, dressing.

verban'nen, *vb.* banish, exile.

Verban'nung, -en, *n.f.* banishment, exile.

verbau'en, *vb.* build badly; obstruct.

verber'gen*, *vb.* hide.

verbes'sern, *vb.* improve, correct.

Verbes'serung, -en, *n.f.* improvement, correction.

verbeu'gen, *vb.* (sich v.) bow.

Verbeu'gung, -en, *n.f.* bow.

verbeu'len, *vb.* dent, batter.

verbie'gen*, *vb.* bend (out of shape).

verbie'ten*, *vb.* forbid, prohibit, ban.

verbie'terisch, *adj.* prohibitive.

verbin'den*, *vb.* connect, join, combine; bandage.

verbind'lich, *adj.* binding, obligatory.

Verbin'dung, -en, *n.f.* connection, combination; (chemical) compound; (student) fraternity; (in V. stehen* mit) be in touch with; (sich in V. setzen mit) get in touch with.

verbis'sen, *adj.* suppressed; dogged.

verbit'ten*, *vb.* decline; not stand for.

verbit'tern, *vb.* embitter.

verblas'sen, *vb.* turn pale, fade.

Verbleib', *n.m.* whereabouts.

verblei'chen*, *vb.* grow pale, fade.

verblüf'fen, *vb.* dumbfound, flabbergast.

verbo'gen, *adj.* bent.

verbor'gen, *adj.* hidden.

Verbot', -e, *n.nt.* prohibition.

Verbrauch', *n.m.* consumption.

verbrau'chen, *vb.* consume, use up, wear out.

Verbrau'cher, -, *n.m.* consumer.

Verbrauchs'steuer, -n, *n.f.* excise tax.

Verbre'chen, -, *n.nt.* crime.

Verbre'cher, -, *n.m.* criminal.

verbre'cherisch, *adj.* criminal.

verbrei'ten, *vb.* disseminate, propagate, diffuse.

verbrenn'bar, *adj.* combustible.

verbren'nen*, *vb.* burn; cremate.

Verbren'nung, *n.f.* burning; cremation; combustion.

verbrin'gen*, *vb.* spend (time).

verbrü'hen, *vb.* scald.

verbun'den, *adj.* indebted, obliged.

verbün'den, *vb.* ally.

Verbün'det-, *n.m.* ally, confederate.

verbür'gen, *vb.* guarantee.

Verdacht', *n.m.* suspicion.

verdäch'tig, *adj.* suspicious, suspected.

verdam'men, *vb.* damn, condemn.

verdam'menswert, *adj.* damnable.

Verdamm'nis, *n.f.* (eternal) damnation.

verdammt', *adj.* damned; damn it!

Verdam'mung, -en, *n.f.* damnation.

verdam'pfen, *vb.* evaporate.

verdan'den, *vb.* owe (something to someone), be indebted to.

verdau'en, *vb.* digest.

verdau'lich, *adj.* digestible.

Verdau'ung, *n.f.* digestion.

Verdau'ungsstörung, -en, *n.f.* indigestion.

Verdeck', -e, *n.nt.* deck covering; top (of an auto).

verden'ken*, *vb.* take amiss.

verder'ben*, *vb.* perish, spoil, ruin.

Verder'ben, *n.nt.* perdition, ruin, doom.

verderb'lich, *adj.* ruinous; perishable.

verderbt', *adj.* corrupt.

verdeut'lichen, *vb.* make clear.

verdich'ten, *vb.* thicken, solidify.

verdie'nen, *vb.* earn, deserve.

Verdienst', -e, *n.m.* earnings.

Verdienst', -e, *n.nt.* merit.

verdienst'lich, *adj.* meritorious.

verdient', *adj.* deserving, deserved.

verdol'metschen, *vb.* interpret, translate.

verdop'peln, *vb.* double.

Verdop'pelung, -en, *n.f.* doubling.

verdor'ren, *vb.* wither.

verdrängen, *vb.* push out, displace; suppress, inhibit.

Verdrän'gung, -en, *n.f.* displacement; repression, inhibition.

verdre'hen, *vb.* twist, distort, pervert.

verdrie'ßen*, *vb.* grieve, vex, annoy.

verdrieß'lich, *adj.* morose, sulky.

Verdruß, *n.m.* vexation, irritation.

verdun'keln, *vb.* darken.

Verdun'kelung, -en, *n.f.* blackout.

verdün'nen, *vb.* thin, dilute, rarefy.

verdut'zen, *vb.* bewilder.

vereh'ren, *vb.* adore, respect, revere.

Vereh'rer, -, *n.m.* admirer.

Vereh'rung, *n.f.* adoration, reverence.

verei'digen, *vb.* administer an oath to.

Verei'digung, -en, *n.f.* swearing-in.

Verein', -e, *n.m.* association.

verein'bar, *adj.* compatible.

verein'baren, *vb.* come to an agreement, reconcile.

Verein'barkeit, *n.f.* compatibility.

Verein'barung, -en, *n.f.* agreement.

verei'nen, *vb.* unify.

verein'fachen, *vb.* simplify.

verein'heitlichen, *vb.* standardize, make uniform.

verei'nigen, *vb.* unite.

Verei'nigten Staaten von Ame'rika, die, *n.pl.* United States of America.

Verei'nigung, -en, *n.f.* union, alliance, association, merger.

Verein'te Natio'nen, die, *n.pl.* United Nations.

verein'zelt, *adj.* isolated, individual; scattered, stray.

verei'teln, *vb.* thwart, foil.

verer'ben, *vb.* bequeath.

vererb'lich, *adj.* hereditary.

Verer'bung, -en, *n.f.* heredity.

verfah'ren*, *vb.* act, proceed, deal; (sich v.) lose one's way.

Verfah'ren, -, *n.nt.* procedure, process.

Verfall', *n.m.* decay, decline, disrepair.

verfal'len*, *vb.* decay, decline, deteriorate; fall due, lapse.

verfäl'schen, *vb.* falsify, adulterate.

Verfäl'schung, -en, *n.f.* falsification, adulteration.

verfäng'lich, *adj.* captious, insidious.

verfas'sen, *vb.* compose, write.

Verfas'ser, -, *n.m.* author.

Verfas'sung, -en, *n.f.* composition; state, condition; constitution.

verfas'sungsmäßig, *adj.* constitutional.

verfas'sungswidrig, *adj.* unconstitutional.

verfau'len, *vb.* rot.

verfault', *adj.* putrid.

verfecht'bar, *adj.* defensible.

verfeh'len, *vb.* miss.

verfei'nern, *vb.* refine.

Verfei'nerung, -en, *n.f.* refinement.

verfer'tigen, *vb.* manufacture.

verfil'men, *vb.* film, make a movie of.

verflie'ßen*, *vb.* flow away, lapse.

verflu'chen, *vb.* curse, damn.

verflucht', *adj.* cursed, damned; damn it!

verfol'gen, *vb.* pursue, haunt, persecute.

Verfol'gung, -en, *n.f.* pursuit, persecution.

Verfrach'ter, -, *n.m.* shipper.

verfrüht', *adj.* premature.

verfüg'bar, *adj.* available.

verfü'gen, *vb.* enact, order; (v. über) have at one's disposal.

Verfü'gung, -en, *n.f.* disposition, instruction, enactment; (mir zur V. stehen*) be at my

disposal; (mir zur V. stellen) place at my disposal.

verfüh'ren, *vb.* lead astray, entice, pervert, seduce.

verfüh'rerisch, *adj.* seductive.

vergan'gen, *adj.* past, last.

Vergan'genheit, *n.f.* past.

vergäng'lich, *adj.* ephemeral, transitory.

Verga'ser, -, *n.m.* carburetor.

verge'ben*, *vb.* forgive; (sich v.) misdeal (at cards); (sich etwas v.) compromise oneself.

verge'bens, *adv.* in vain.

vergeb'lich, *adj.* vain, futile.

Verge'bung, *n.f.* forgiveness.

vergegenwär'tigen, *vb.* envisage, picture to oneself.

verge'hen*, *vb.* pass, elapse; (sich v.) err, sin, commit a crime.

Verge'hen, -, *n.nt.* misdemeanor.

vergel'ten*, *vb.* repay; retaliate.

Vergel'tung, -en, *n.f.* recompense; retaliation.

Vergel'tungsmaßnahme, -n, *n.f.* reprisal.

verges'sen*, *vb.* forget.

Verges'senheit, *n.f.* oblivion.

vergeß'lich, *adj.* forgetful.

vergeu'den, *vb.* squander.

vergewal'tigen, *vb.* use force on, rape.

Vergewal'tigung, -en, *n.f.* rape.

vergewis'sern, *vb.* confirm; reassure.

vergie'ßen*, *vb.* shed.

vergif'ten, *vb.* poison.

Vergiß'meinnicht, -e, *n.nt.* forget-me-not.

Vergleich', -e, *n.m.* comparison.

vergleich'bar, *adj.* comparable.

verglei'chen*, *vb.* compare.

vergnü'gen, *vb.* amuse.

Vergnü'gen, *n.nt.* fun; (viel V.) have a good time.

vergnügt', *adj.* in good spirits, gay.

Vergnü'gung, -en, *n.f.* pleasure, amusement, diversion.

vergöt'tern, *vb.* idolize.

vergrei'fen*, *vb.* (sich v.) do the wrong thing; (sich an etwas v.) attack, misappropriate.

vergrö'ßern, *vb.* enlarge, magnify.

Vergrö'ßerung, -en, *n.f.* enlargement.

vergrö'ßerungsapparat, -e, *n.m.* enlarger.

Vergün'stigung, -en, *n.f.* favor; reduction.

vergü'ten, *vb.* pay back.

verhaf'ten, *vb.* arrest.

Verhaftung, -en, *n.f.* arrest.

verhal'ten*, *vb.* hold back; (sich v.) be, behave.

verhal'ten, *adj.* suppressed.

Verhal'ten, *n.nt.* behavior.

Verhält'nis, -se, *n.nt.* relation(ship), proportion, ratio; love affair; (pl.) circumstances, conditions.

verhält'nismäßig, adj. relative, comparative.

verhan'deln, vb. negotiate.

Verhand'lung, -en, n.f. negotiation.

Verhand'lungsweise, n.f. procedure.

Verhäng'nis, -se, n.nt. fate, destiny.

verhäng'nisvoll, adj. fatal, fateful.

verhar'ren, vb. remain, persist.

verhär'ten, vb. harden, stiffen.

verhaßt', adj. hateful, odious.

verhau'en*, vb. beat up; make a mess of.

verhed'dern, vb. (sich v.) get snarled, caught.

verhee'ren, vb. desolate.

verhee'rend, adj. disastrous.

verheim'lichen, vb. conceal.

verhei'raten, vb. marry off; (sich v.) get married.

verherr'lichen, vb. glorify.

verhin'dern, vb. prevent, hinder.

Verhin'derung, n.f. prevention, hindrance.

verhoh'len, adj. hidden, clandestine.

Verhör', -e, n.nt. interrogation, hearing.

verhö'ren, vb. interrogate.

verhun'gern, vb. starve to death.

verhü'ten, vb. prevent.

Verhü'tung, -en, n.f. prevention.

Verhü'tungsmittel, -, n.nt. contraceptive device.

verir'ren, vb. (sich v.) lose one's way, go astray.

Verkauf', "-e, n.m. sale.

verkau'fen, vb. sell.

Verkäu'fer, -, n.m. clerk, salesman.

verkäuf'lich, adj. saleable.

Verkehr', n.m. trade, traffic; relations, intercourse.

verkeh'ren, vb. (tr.) change; (intr.) run, go; associate, consort, frequent.

Verkehrs'ampel, -n, n.f. traffic light.

Verkehrs'flugzeug, -e, n.nt. air liner.

Verkehrs'licht, -er, n.nt. traffic light.

verkehrt', adj. reversed, wrong, backwards.

verken'nen*, vb. mistake, misunderstand.

verket'ten, vb. link.

verkla'gen, vb. sue, accuse.

Verklagt'-, n.m.&f. defendant.

verklärt', adj. transfigured, radiant.

verklei'den, vb. disguise; panel.

verklei'nern, vb. make smaller; belittle.

Verklei'nerung, -en, n.f. diminution; disparagement.

verknüp'fen, vb. connect, relate.

verkom'men*, vb. decay, come down in the world, die.

verkom'men, adj. squalid, dissolute.

verkör'pern, vb. embody.

verkör'pert, adj. incarnate.

Verkör'perung, -en, n.f. embodiment, epitome.

verkrüp'pelt, adj. crippled.

verküm'mern, vb. wither.

verkün'd(ig)en, vb. announce, proclaim.

Verkün'd(ig)ung, -en, n.f. announcement, Annunciation.

verkür'zen, vb. shorten.

verla'den*, vb. load, ship.

Verla'der, -, n.m. shipper.

Verlag', -e, n.m. publishing house.

verla'gern, vb. shift, displace.

verlan'gen, vb. demand, require, ask; (v. nach) desire, long for.

Verlan'gen, n.nt. demand, request, craving.

verlän'gern, vb. lengthen, prolong, extend, renew.

Verlän'gerung, -en, n.f. prolongation, extension, renewal.

verlas'sen*, vb. leave, abandon, forsake; (sich v. auf) depend on, rely on.

verlas'sen, adj. abandoned, deserted, forlorn.

verläß'lich, adj. dependable.

Verlauf', n.m. course, lapse.

verlau'fen*, vb. pass, elapse; (sich v.) get lost.

verle'ben, vb. pass.

verlebt', adj. dissipated.

verle'gen, vb. move, shift; block; misplace; publish.

verle'gen, adj. embarrassed.

Verle'ger, -, n.m. publisher.

Verle'gung, -en, n.f. transfer, removal.

verlei'hen*, vb. lend; confer, bestow.

Verlei'hung, -en, n.f. bestowal.

verlei'ten, vb. lead astray, inveigle.

verler'nen, vb. forget.

verletz'bar, adj. vulnerable.

verlet'zen, vb. hurt, offend; violate, infringe.

Verlet'zung, -en, n.f. injury; violation.

verleug'nen, vb. deny, disown.

verleum'den, vb. slander.

verleum'derisch, adj. libelous.

Verleum'dung, -en, n.f. libel, slander.

verlie'ben, vb. (sich v.) fall in love.

verliebt', adj. in love.

verlie'ren*, vb. lose.

verlo'ben, vb. affiance, betroth; (sich v.) get engaged.

verlobt', adj. engaged.

Verlobt'-, n.m. fiancé.

Verlobt'-, n.f. fiancée.

Verlo'bung, -en, n.f. engagement.

verlo'cken, vb. entice, lure.

verlö'schen*, vb. go out, be extinguished.

Verlust', -e, n.m. loss; (pl.) casualties.

verma'chen, vb. bequeath.

Vermächt'nis, -se, n.nt. bequest, legacy.

vermäh'len, vb. espouse.

Vermäh'lung, -en, n.f. espousal.

vermeh'ren, vb. augment, multiply, increase.

vermeid'bar, adj. avoidable.

vermei'den*, vb. avoid.

vermeint'lich, adj. supposed.

vermen'gen, vb. blend; mix up.

Vermerk', -e, n.m. note; entry.

vermer'ken, vb. note down.

vermes'sen*, vb. measure, survey; (sich v.) have the audacity.

Vermes'senheit, n.f. presumptuousness.

Vermes'sung, -en, n.f. survey.

vermie'ten, vb. rent (to someone).

vermin'dern, vb. diminish.

vermis'sen, vb. miss.

vermit'teln, vb. mediate, negotiate, arrange.

Vermitt'ler, -, n.m. mediator.

vermö'ge, prep. by virtue of.

vermö'gen*, vb. be able.

Vermö'gen, -, n.nt. fortune, wealth, estate; ability, power.

vermö'gend, adj. wealthy, well-to-do.

vermu'ten, vb. presume.

vermut'lich, adj. presumable.

Vermu'tung, -en, n.f. surmise.

vernach'lässigen, vb. neglect.

Vernach'lässigung, -en, n.f. neglect.

verneh'men*, vb. perceive, hear, learn; examine.

vernehm'lich, adj. perceptible.

Verneh'mung, -en, n.f. hearing.

vernei'gen, vb. (sich v.) bow.

vernei'nen, vb. deny.

vernei'nend, adj. negative.

Vernei'nung, -en, n.f. denial.

vernich'ten, vb. annihilate, destroy.

vernich'tend, adj. devastating.

Vernich'tung, -en, n.f. annihilation, destruction.

Vernunft', n.f. reason.

vernunft'gemäß, adj. rational, according to reason.

vernünf'tig, adj. reasonable, sensible.

veröf'fentlichen, vb. publish.

Veröf'fentlichung, -en, n.f. publication.

verord'nen, vb. decree, order.

Verord'nung, -en, n.f. decree, ordinance, edict.

verpa'cken, vb. pack up, wrap up.

verpas'sen, vb. miss.

verpes'ten, vb. infect.

verpfän'den, vb. pawn, pledge.

verpfle'gen, *vb.* care for; feed.

Verpfle'gung, -en, *n.f.* food, board.

verpflich'ten, *vb.* oblige; (sich v.) commit oneself.

Verpflich'tung, -en, *n.f.* obligation.

Verrat', *n.m.* treason, betrayal.

verra'ten*, *vb.* betray.

Verräter, -, *n.m.* traitor.

verrä'terisch, *adj.* treacherous.

verrech'nen, *vb.* reckon up; (sich v.) make a mistake in figuring, miscalculate.

verrei'sen, *vb.* go away on a trip.

verreist', *adj.* away on a trip.

verren'ken, *vb.* sprain.

verrich'ten, *vb.* do, perform, carry out.

verrin'gern, *vb.* decrease.

verros'ten, *vb.* rust.

verrucht', *adj.* infamous, wicked.

verrückt', *adj.* mad, crazy.

Verruf', *n.m.* disrepute, notoriety.

verru'fen, *adj.* disreputable, notorious.

Vers, -e, *n.m.* verse.

versa'gen, *vb.* refuse; fail.

Versa'gen, *n.nt.* failure.

Versa'ger, -, *n.m.* failure, flop.

versam'meln, *vb.* assemble.

Versamm'lung, -en, *n.f.* assembly, gathering, meeting.

Versand', *n.m.* dispatch.

versäu'men, *vb.* neglect, miss.

Versäum'nis, -se, *n.nt.* omission.

verschaf'fen, *vb.* procure.

verschämt', *adj.* bashful, coy.

verschan'zen, *vb.* entrench.

verschär'fen, *vb.* intensify.

verschei'den, *vb.* expire.

verschen'ken, *vb.* give away.

verscher'zen, *vb.* throw away, lose frivolously.

verscheu'chen, *vb.* scare away.

verschi'cken, *vb.* send off.

verschie'ben*, *vb.* shift, displace; postpone.

Verschie'bung, -en, *n.f.* shift; postponement.

verschie'den, *adj.* different, distinct; various, assorted, separate.

verschie'denartig, *adj.* various; heterogeneous.

verschie'ßen*, *vb.* fire off; fade.

verschla'fen*, **1.** *vb.* miss by sleeping too long; sleep off; (sich v.) oversleep. **2.** *adj.* sleepy.

Verschlag', -̈e, *n.m.* partition, compartment.

verschla'gen*, **1.** *vb.* drive away; (es verschlägt mir den Atem) it takes my breath away. **2.** *adj.* sly.

verschlech'tern, *vb.* make worse, impair; (sich v.) become worse, deteriorate.

Verschlech'terung, -en, *n.f.* deterioration.

verschlei'ern, *vb.* veil.

verschlep'pen, *vb.* delay; abduct.

verschleu'dern, *vb.* squander.

verschlie'ßen*, *vb.* close, lock.

verschlim'mern, *vb.* make worse, aggravate; (sich v.) become worse, deteriorate.

verschlin'gen*, *vb.* devour.

verschlis'sen, *adj.* worn out, frayed.

verschlos'sen, *adj.* closed, locked; reserved, taciturn.

verschlu'cken, *vb.* swallow; (sich v.) swallow the wrong way, choke.

Verschluß', -̈sse, *n.m.* closure; lock, plug, stopper; fastening, fastener; (camera) shutter.

verschmach'ten, *vb.* languish.

verschmel'zen*, *vb.* fuse, merge.

Verschmel'zung, -en, *n.f.* fusion.

verschneit', *adj.* covered with snow.

Verschnitt', *n.m.* adulteration; watered spirits.

verschnupft', *adj.* having a cold.

verschol'len, *adj.* missing, never heard of again.

verscho'nen, *vb.* spare.

verschö'nern, *vb.* beautify.

verschrei'ben*, *vb.* prescribe.

verschü'chtern, *vb.* intimidate.

verschul'det, *adj.* indebted.

verschüt'ten, *vb.* spill.

verschwei'gen*, *vb.* keep quiet about.

verschwen'den, *vb.* squander, waste, dissipate.

Verschwen'der, -, *n.m.* spendthrift.

verschwen'derisch, *adj.* wasteful, extravagant, prodigal.

Verschwen'dung, -en, *n.f.* extravagance, wastefulness.

verschwie'gen, *adj.* silent, discreet, reticent.

verschwin'den*, *vb.* disappear.

Verschwin'den, *n.nt.* disappearance.

verschwommen, *adj.* blurred.

verschwö'ren*, *vb.* renounce; (sich v.) conspire.

Verschwö'rer, -, *n.m.* conspirator.

Verschwö'rung, -en, *n.f.* conspiracy.

verse'hen*, *vb.* provide; perform; (sich v.) make a mistake.

Verse'hen, -, *n.nt.* oversight, error; (aus V.) by mistake.

versen'den*, *vb.* send off.

versen'gen, *vb.* singe, scorch.

versen'ken, *vb.* sink.

verset'zen, *vb.* move, transfer; (school) promote; pawn, hock; reply.

versi'chern, *vb.* insure, assure; affirm, assert.

Versi'cherung, -en, *n.f.* insurance, assurance.

versie'geln, *vb.* seal.

versie'gen, *vb.* dry up.

versin'ken*, *vb.* sink.

versinn'bildlichen, *vb.* symbolize.

Version', -en, *n.f.* version.

versöh'nen, *vb.* reconcile.

versöh'nend, *adj.* conciliation.

versöhn'lich, *adj.* conciliatory.

Versöh'nung, -en, *n.f.* reconciliation.

versor'gen, *vb.* provide, supply.

Versor'gung, *n.f.* supply, maintenance.

verspä'ten, *vb.* (sich v.) be late.

verspä'tet, *adj.* late.

Verspä'tung, -en, *n.f.* lateness.

versper'ren, *vb.* bar, obstruct.

verspie'len, *vb.* gamble away; (sich v.) misplay.

verspielt', *adj.* playful.

verspot'ten, *vb.* mock, deride.

verspre'chen*, *vb.* promise; (sich v.) make a slip of the tongue.

Verspre'chen, -, *n.nt.* promise.

verstaat'lichen, *vb.* nationalize.

Verstand', *n.m.* mind, intellect, brains.

verstän'dig, *adj.* sensible, intelligent.

verstän'digen, *vb.* inform; (sich v.) make oneself understood, make an agreement.

Verstän'digung, -en, *n.f.* agreement, understanding.

verständ'lich, *adj.* understandable.

Verständ'nis, *n.nt.* understanding.

verständ'nisvoll, *adj.* understanding.

verstär'ken, *vb.* strengthen, reinforce, intensify, amplify.

Verstär'ker, -, *n.m.* amplifier.

Verstär'kung, -en, *n.f.* reinforcement.

verstau'ben, *vb.* get covered with dust.

verstäu'ben, *vb.* atomize.

verstau'chen, *vb.* sprain.

Versteck', -e, *n.nt.* hiding place; ambush; (V. spielen) play hide-and-go-seek.

verste'cken, *vb.* hide.

versteckt', *adj.* hidden; veiled, oblique, ulterior.

verste'hen*, *vb.* understand.

Verstei'gerung, -en, *n.f.* auction.

verstell'bar, *adj.* adjustable.

verstel'len, *vb.* adjust; change, disguise.

Verstel'lung, -en, *n.f.* adjustment; disguise, sham, hypocrisy.

versteu'ern, *vb.* pay tax on.

verstim'men, *vb.* annoy, upset.

verstimmt', *adj.* annoyed, cross; *(music)* out of tune.

verstockt', adj. obdurate; impenitent.

verstoh'len, adj. stealthy, surreptitious.

verstop'fen, vb. stop up, clog.

Verstop'fung, -en, n.f. obstruction, jam; (med.) constipation.

verstor'ben, adj. deceased.

verstört', adj. distracted, bewildered.

Verstoß, -e, n.m. violation, offence.

versto'ßen*, vb. expel, disown; (v. gegen) infringe on, offend.

verstrei'chen*, vb. elapse.

verstri'cken, vb. ensnare, enmesh.

verstüm'meln, vb. mutilate.

Verstüm'melung, -en, n.f. mutilation.

verstum'men, vb. become silent.

Versuch', -e, n.m. attempt; test, trial, experiment; effort.

versu'chen, vb. attempt, try, test; strive; entice, tempt.

versuchs'weise, adv. experimentally.

Versu'chung, -en, n.f. temptation.

versün'digen, vb. (sich v.) sin against.

versun'ken, adj. sunken; (v. sein*) be absorbed, be lost.

versü'ßen, vb. sweeten.

verta'gen, vb. adjourn.

Verta'gung, -en, n.f. adjournment.

vertau'schen, vb. exchange for; mistake for; substitute.

vertei'digen, vb. defend, advocate.

Vertei'diger, -, n.m. defender; (jur.) counsel for the defense.

Vertei'digung, -en, n.f. defense.

vertei'len, vb. distribute, disperse, divide.

Vertei'ler, -, n.m. distributor.

Vertei'lung, -en, n.f. distribution; dispersal, division.

vertie'fen, vb. deepen; (sich v.) deepen, become engrossed.

vertieft', adj. absorbed.

vertil'gen, vb. consume; exterminate.

Vertrag', -e, n.m. contract, treaty, pact.

vertra'gen*, vb. endure, tolerate, stand; (sich v.) agree, get along.

vertrag'lich, adj. contractual.

verträg'lich, adj. compatible, good-natured.

vertrau'en, vb. trust; confide in; rely on.

Vertrau'en, n.f. trust, confidence, faith.

vertrau'ensvoll, adj. confident, reliant.

Vertrau'ensvotum, n.nt. vote of confidence.

vertrau'lich, adj. confidential.

Vertrau'lichkeit, -en, n.f. familiarity, intimacy; (in aller V.) in strict confidence.

vertraut', adj. acquainted, familiar; intimate.

Vertraut', -, n.m.&f. confidant(e).

Vertraut'heit, -en, n.f. familiarity; intimacy.

vertrei'ben*, vb. drive away, expel.

Vertrei'bung, -en, n.f. expulsion.

vertre'ten*, vb. represent; act as substitute; advocate.

Vertre'ter, -, n.m. representative, agent; deputy, substitute.

Vertre'tung, -en, n.f. representation, agency; substitution.

Vertrieb', -e, n.m. sale, market.

Vertrie'ben-, n.m.&f. expellee, refugee.

Vertriebs'stelle, -n, n.f. distributor.

vertu'schen, vb. hush up.

verü'beln, vb. take amiss.

verü'ben, vb. commit.

verun'glücken, vb. meet with an accident; fail.

verun'reinigen, vb. pollute.

verun'stalten, vb. disfigure.

verun'zieren, vb. mar.

verur'sachen, vb. cause, bring about; result in.

verur'teilen, vb. condemn; (jur.) sentence.

Verur'teilung, n.f. condemnation; (jur.) sentence.

verviel'fachen, vb. multiply.

verviel'fältigen, vb. multiply; mimeograph; (sich v.) multiply.

vervoll'kommnen, vb. perfect.

Vervoll'kommnung, n.f. perfection.

vervoll'ständigen, vb. complete.

verwach'sen*, vb. grow together; become deformed.

Verwach'sung, -en, n.f. deformity.

verwah'ren, vb. keep, hold in safe-keeping.

verwahr'losen, vb. neglect.

Verwah'rung, n.f. custody.

verwal'ten, vb. administer, manage.

Verwal'ter, -, n.m. administrator.

Verwal'tung, -en, n.f. administration, management.

verwan'deln, vb. change, transform.

Verwand'lung, -en, n.f. change, transformation; metamorphosis.

verwandt', adj. related.

Verwandt'-, n.m.&f. relation, relative.

Verwandt'schaft, -en, n.f. relationship, affinity.

verwech'seln, vb. mistake for, confuse.

Verwechs'lung, -en, n.f. mistake, mix-up.

verwe'gen, adj. daring, bold.

verweh'ren, vb. prevent from; refuse.

verwei'gern, vb. refuse.

Verwei'gerung, -en, n.f. refusal.

verwei'len, vb. linger.

Verweis', -e, n.m. reprimand; (einen V. erteilen) reprimand.

verwei'sen*, vb. banish; (v. auf) refer to.

verwend'bar, adj. usable, applicable.

Verwend'barkeit, n.f. usability, applicability.

verwen'den(*), vb. use, supply; expend.

Verwen'dung, -en, n.f. use, application.

verwer'fen*, vb. reject.

verwe'sen, vb. putrify, decay.

verwi'ckeln, vb. entangle, involve, implicate.

verwi'ckelt, adj. involved, intricate, complicated.

Verwick'lung, -en, n.f. entanglement, implication; complication.

verwin'den*, vb. get over, overcome.

verwir'ken, vb. forfeit.

verwirk'lichen, vb. realize, materialize.

Verwirk'lichung, -en, n.f. realization.

verwir'ren, vb. confuse, bewilder, confound, puzzle, mystify.

Verwir'rung, -en, n.f. confusion, bewilderment, perplexity.

verwi'schen, vb. wipe out; smudge.

verwit'wet, adj. widowed.

verwor'fen, adj. depraved.

verwor'ren, adj. confused.

verwun'den, vb. wound.

verwun'dern, vb. astonish.

Verwun'dung, -en, n.f. wound, injury.

verwun'schen, adj. enchanted.

verwün'schen, vb. curse; bewitch.

verwüs'ten, vb. devastate.

verza'gen, vb. despair.

verzagt', adj. depondent.

verzäh'len, vb. (sich v.) miscount.

verzär'teln, vb. pamper.

verzau'bern, vb. bewitch.

verzeh'ren, vb. consume.

verzeich'nen, vb. register, list.

Verzeich'nis, -se, n.nt. list, index.

verzei'hen*, vb. pardon, forgive.

Verzei'hung, -en, n.f. pardon, forgiveness; (ich bitte um V.) I beg your pardon.

verzer'ren, vb. distort.

Verzicht', -e, n.m. renunciation; (V. leisten) renounce.

verzich'ten, vb. renounce, forego, waive.

verzie´hen*, *vb.* pull out of shape; (child) spoil; **(sich v.)** withdraw; vanish, disperse; (wood) warp.

verzie´ren, *vb.* embellish.

Verzie´rung, -en, *n.f.* ornament, embellishment.

verzin´sen, *vb.* pay interest; **(sich v.)** bear interest.

Verzin´sung, -en, *n.f.* interest return; payment of interest; interest rate.

verzo´gen, *adj.* moved away; (child) spoiled.

verzö´gern, *vb.* delay.

Verzö´gerung, -en, *n.f.* delay.

verzol´len, *vb.* pay duty on.

verzückt´, *adj.* enraptured.

Verzug´, -e, *n.m.* delay; default.

verzwei´feln, *vb.* despair.

verzwei´felt, *adj.* desperate.

Verzweif´lung, -en, *n.f.* desperation.

verzwickt´, *adj.* complicated.

Vesper, -n, *n.f.* vespers.

Veterinär´, -e, *n.m.* veterinary.

Vetter, -n, *n.m.* cousin.

Viadukt´, -e, *n.m.* viaduct.

Vibration´, -en, *n.f.* vibration.

vibrie´ren, *vb.* vibrate.

Vieh, *n.nt.* cattle.

viehisch, *adj.* brutal.

Viehzucht, *n.f.* cattle breeding.

viel, *adj.* much; *(pl.)* many.

vielbedeutend, *adj.* significant.

vieldeutig, *adj.* ambiguous.

Vieleck, -e, *n.nt.* polygon.

vielerlei, *adj.* various, many.

vielfach, *adj.* manifold.

vielfältig, *adj.* multiple.

Vielfältigkeit, *n.f.* multiplicity.

vielfarbig, *adj.* multicolored.

Vielfraß, -e, *n.m.* glutton.

Vielheit, -en, *n.f.* multiplicity.

vielleicht´, *adv.* perhaps.

vielmals, *adv.* many times.

vielmehr, *adv.* rather.

vielsagend, *adj.* significant, highly suggestive.

vielseitig, *adj.* many-sided; versatile.

vielverheißend, *adj.* very promising.

vielversprechend, *adj.* very promising.

vier, *num.* four.

Viereck, -e, *n.nt.* square.

viereckig, *adj.* square.

vierfach, *adj.* fourfold.

Vierfüßler, -, *n.m.* quadruped.

vierschrötig, *adj.* thick-set.

viert-, *adj.* fourth.

vierteilen, *vb.* quarter.

Viertel, -, *n.nt.* fourth part, quarter; **(ein v.)** one-fourth.

vierzehn, *num.* fourteen.

vierzig, *num.* forty.

vierzigst-, *adj.* fortieth.

Vierzigstel, -, *n.nt.* fortieth part; **(ein v.)** one-fortieth.

violett´, *adj.* violet.

Violi´ne, -n, *n.f.* violin.

Violinist´, -en, -en, *n.m.* violinist.

Virtuo´se, -n, -n, *n.m.* virtuoso.

Visier´, -e, *n.nt.* visor; (gun) sight.

visuell´, *adj.* visual.

Visum, -sa, *n.nt.* visa.

Vitalität´, *n.f.* vitality.

Vize-, *cpds.* vice-.

Vogel, -, *n.m.* bird.

vogelartig, *adj.* birdlike.

Vogelbauer, -, *n.nt.* bird cage.

Vogelscheuche, -n, *n.f.* scarecrow.

Vogt, -e, *n.m.* overseer.

Vokal´, -e, *n.m.* vowel.

Volant´, -s, *n.m.* flounce.

Volk, -er, *n.nt.* people, nation.

Völkerbund, *n.m.* League of Nations.

Völkerkunde, *n.f.* ethnology; (school) social studies.

Völkermord, *n.m.* genocide.

Völkerrecht, *n.nt.* international law.

Volksabstimmung, -en, *n.f.* plebiscite, referendum.

Volkscharakter, *n.m.* national character.

Volksentscheid, *n.m.* plebiscite, referendum.

Volksgenosse, -n, -n, *n.m.* fellow countryman.

Volkskunde, *n.f.* folklore.

Volkslied, -er, *n.nt.* folksong.

Volksmenge, -n, *n.f.* crowd, mob.

Volksschule, -n, *n.f.* elementary school.

Volkstanz, -e, *n.m.* folk-dance.

volkstümlich, *adj.* popular.

Volkszählung, -en, *n.f.* census.

voll, *adj.* full.

Vollblut, *n.nt.* thoroughbred.

vollblütig, *adj.* full-blooded.

vollbrin´gen*, *vb.* accomplish, fulfill.

vollen´den, *vb.* finish, complete.

vollen´det, *adj.* accomplished.

vollends, *adv.* completely.

Völlerei´, *n.f.* gluttony.

vollfüh´ren, *vb.* accomplish.

Vollgas, *n.nt.* full throttle.

völlig, *adj.* complete, entire.

volljährig, *adj.* of age.

vollkom´men, *adj.* perfect.

Vollkom´menheit, *n.f.* perfection.

Vollmacht, -e, *n.f.* authority, warrant, proxy, power of attorney.

vollständig, *adj.* complete.

voll·stopfen, *vb.* cram, stuff.

vollstre´cken, *vb.* execute, carry out.

Vollversammlung, *n.f.* (U.N.) General Assembly.

vollzählig, *adj.* complete.

vollzie´hen*, *vb.* execute, carry out; consummate; **(sich v.)** take place.

Volontär´, -e, *n.m.* volunteer.

Volontär´arzt, -e, *n.m.* intern.

Volt, -, -, *n.nt.* volt.

Volu´men, -, *n.nt.* volume.

von, *prep.* before; in front of; ago.

vor, *prep.* before; in front of; ago.

Vorabend, -e, *n.m.* eve.

Vorahnung, -en, *n.f.* premonition, foreboding.

voran´, *adv.* in front of, ahead; onward.

voran´gehen*, *vb.* precede.

voran´kommen*, *vb.* get ahead.

Voranmeldung, -en, *n.f.* (telephone) **(mit V.)** person-to-person call.

Voranschlag, -e, *n.m.* estimate.

Vorarbeit, -en, *n.f.* preparatory work.

Vorarbeiter, -, *n.m.* foreman.

vorauf´, *adv.* before, ahead.

voraus´, *adv.* in advance, ahead; **(im v.)** in advance.

voraus´bedingen*, *vb.* precede.

voraus´bestellen, *vb.* order ahead, make reservations.

voraus´gehen*, *vb.* precede.

voraus´gesetzt, *adv.* **(v. daß)** provided that.

voraus´nehmen*, *vb.* state now, anticipate.

Voraus´sage, -n, *n.f.* prediction, forecast.

voraus´sagen, *vb.* predict, forecast.

voraus´setzen, *vb.* presume, presuppose.

Voraus´setzung, -en, *n.f.* supposition, assumption; prerequisite.

Voraus´sicht, *n.f.* foresight.

voraus´sichtlich, 1. *adj.* probable, prospective. **2.** *adv.* presumably.

voraus´zahlen, *vb.* pay in advance, advance.

Vorbedacht, *n.m.* forethought.

Vorbedeutung, -en, *n.f.* omen.

Vorbedingung, -en, *n.f.* prerequisite.

Vorbehalt, -e, *n.m.* reservation.

vor·behalten*, *vb.* reserve.

vorbei´, *adv.* over, past.

vorbelastet, *adj.* having a questionable record; *(jur.)* having a criminal record.

vor·bereiten, *vb.* prepare.

vor·bestellen, *vb.* order in advance, make reservations.

vor·beugen, *vb.* prevent.

vorbeugend, *adj.* preventive.

Vorbild, -er, *n.nt.* model.

vorbildlich, *adj.* exemplary.

vor·bringen*, *vb.* state; propose.

vorder-, *adj.* front, anterior.

Vorderfront, -en, *n.f.* frontage; *(fig.)* forefront.

Vordergrund, *n.m.* foreground.

vorderhand, *adv.* for the time being; right now.

Vordermann, -er, *n.m.* person ahead of one.

Vorderseite, -n, *n.f.* front.

Vorderteil, -e, *n.nt.* front part.

vor·drängen, *vb.* **(sich v.)** elbow one's way forward.

vor·dringen*, vb. press forward, advance.

Vordruck, -̈e, n.m. form, blank.

voreilig, adj. rash, hasty.

voreingenommen, adj. prejudiced.

Voreingenommenheit, n.f. partiality.

vor·enthalten*, vb. withhold.

vorerst, adv. first of all.

Vorfahr, -en, -en, n.m. ancestor.

vor·fahren*, vb. drive up; (v. lassen*) let pass.

Vorfahrtsrecht, -e, n.nt. right of way.

Vorfall, -̈e, n.m. incident.

vor·fallen*, vb. occur.

vor·finden*, vb. find.

vor·führen, vb. show, demonstrate, produce.

Vorführung, -en, n.f. demonstration, show, production.

Vorgang, -̈e, n.m. occurrence, process, procedure.

Vorgänger, -, n.m. predecessor.

vor·geben*, vb. pretend, feign.

Vorgefühl, -e, n.nt. presentiment, hunch.

vor·gehen*, vb. advance; come first, precede.

Vorgehen, n.nt. procedure, policy.

Vorgericht, -e, n.nt. appetizer; first course.

Vorgeschichte, n.f. prehistory; history, background.

vorgeschrieben, adj. prescribed.

vorgesehen, adj. planned, scheduled.

Vorgesetzt-, n.m.&f. superior.

vorgestern, adv. the day before yesterday.

vorgetäuscht, adj. make-believe.

vor·greifen*, vb. anticipate.

vor·haben*, vb. plan, intention.

Vorhaben, n.nt. plan, intention.

Vorhalle, -n, n.f. lounge.

vor·halten*, vb. (fig.) reproach.

Vorhand, n.f. forehand.

vorhan'den, adj. existing, present, available.

Vorhang, -̈e, n.m. curtain, drapery.

vorher, adv. before, beforehand, previously.

vorher'gehend, adj. previous.

vor·herrschen, vb. prevail.

Vorherrschaft, n.f. predominance.

vorherrschend, adj. prevalent, predominant.

Vorher'sage, -n, n.f. prediction.

vorher'·sagen, vb. foretell.

vorher'·sehen*, vb. foresee.

Vorhut, n.f. vanguard.

vorig, adj. previous, last.

Vorjahr, -e, n.nt. preceding year.

Vorkämpfer, -, n.m. pioneer, champion.

Vorkenntnis, -se, n.f. preliminary knowledge; rudiments.

Vorkommen, n.nt. occurrence.

vor·kommen*, vb. occur.

Vorkommnis, -se, n.nt. occurrence.

Vorkriegs-, cpds. prewar.

vor·laden*, vb. summon.

Vorladung, -en, n.f. summons.

vor·lassen*, vb. let pass; admit.

Vorlassung, -en, n.f. admittance.

vorläufig, 1. adj. preliminary, tentative; temporary. **2.** adv. for the time being.

vorlaut, adj. flippant, fresh.

vor·legen, vb. show, submit, produce.

vor·lesen*, vb. read out loud.

Vorlesung, -en, n.f. reading; lecture.

Vorlesungsverzeichnis, -se, n.nt. university catalogue.

vorletzt, adj. last but one.

Vorliebe, n.f. preference, fondness.

vorlieb'·nehmen*, vb. be satisfied with.

vor·liegen*, vb. exist.

vorliegend, adj. present, at hand, in question.

vor·machen, vb. show how to do; (einem etwas v.) deceive, fool.

Vormachtstellung, -en, n.f. predominance.

vormalig, adj. former.

vormals, adv. heretofore.

Vormann, -̈er, n.m. foreman.

Vormarsch, -̈e, n.m. advance.

vor·merken, vb. make a note of; reserve.

Vormittag, -e, n.m. forenoon.

Vormund, -e, n.m. guardian.

vorn, adv. in front.

Vorname(n), -, -n, n.m. first name.

vornehm, adj. noble, distinguished.

vor·nehmen*, vb. (sich v.) undertake, consider, take up, resolve.

vornehmlich, adv. chiefly.

Vorort, -e, n.m. suburb.

Vorortzug, -̈e, n.m. local (train).

Vorplatz, -̈e, n.m. hall; court.

Vorrang, -, n.m. priority, precedence.

Vorrat, -̈e, n.m. supply, provision, stock, stockpile.

vorrätig, adj. in stock.

Vorratskammer, -n, n.f. storeroom; pantry.

Vorrecht, -e, n.nt. privilege, prerogative.

Vorrede, -n, n.f. preface.

Vorrichtung, -en, n.f. arrangement; contrivance, device, fixture.

vor·rücken, vb. move forward, advance.

Vorsatz, -̈e, n.m. purpose, intention; (jur.) premeditation.

vorsätzlich, adj. willful, intentional; (jur.) premeditated.

Vorschein, n.m. (zum V. kommen*) appear.

Vorschlag, -̈e, n.m. proposal, proposition, suggestion.

vor·schlagen*, vb. propose, suggest.

vorschnell, adj. rash.

vor·schreiben*, vb. prescribe.

Vorschrift, -en, n.f. regulation.

vorschriftsmäßig, adj. as prescribed, regulation.

Vorschub, n.m. assistance.

Vorschule, -n, n.f. elementary school.

Vorschuß, -̈sse, n.m. advance payment.

vor·schützen, vb. pretend, plead.

vor·sehen*, vb. earmark, plan, schedule; (sich v.) be careful.

Vorsehung, n.f. providence.

Vorsicht, -en, n.f. caution.

vorsichtig, adj. careful, cautious.

vorsichtshalber, adv. as a precaution.

Vorsichtsmaßregel, -n, n.f. precaution.

Vorsilbe, -n, n.f. prefix.

Vorsitz, -e, n.m. chairmanship, presidency; (den V. führen) preside.

Vorsitzend-, n.m.&f. chairperson.

Vorsitzende(r), -n, n.m.&f. chairman; chairwoman.

Vorsorge, n.f. providence, foresight; (V. treffen*) take precautions.

vorsorglich, adv. as a precaution.

Vorspeise, -n, n.f. appetizer.

vor·spiegeln, vb. deceive, delude.

Vorspiel, -e, n.nt. prelude.

vor·springen*, vb. project.

Vorsprung, -̈e, n.m. advantage; head start; (arch.) ledge.

Vorstadt, -̈e, n.f. suburb, outskirts.

vorstellbar, adj. conceivable.

vor·stellen, vb. present, introduce; (clock) set ahead; (sich v.) imagine, picture.

Vorstellung, -en, n.f. presentation, introduction; imagination, idea, notion; (theater) performance, show.

Vorstoß, -̈e, n.m. attack.

vor·stoßen*, vb. push forward.

vor·strecken, vb. stretch forward; (money) advance.

vor·täuschen, vb. make-believe, simulate.

Vorteil, -e, n.m. advantage.

vorteilhaft, adj. advantageous, profitable.

Vortrag, -̈e, n.m. lecture, talk.

vor·tragen*, vb. lecture, recite, report.

Vortragend-, n.m.&f. lecturer.

vortreff'lich, adj. excellent.

Vortritt, -e, n.m. precedence.

vorü'ber, adv. past, gone.

vorü'ber·gehen*, vb. pass.

vorü'bergehend, *adj.* temporary.

Vorurteil, -e, *n.nt.* prejudice.

Vorväter, *n.pl.* forefathers.

Vorwahl, -en, *n.f.* primary election.

Vorwahlnummer, -n, *n.f.* area code (telephone).

Vorwand, ̈e, *n.m.* pretense, pretext.

Vorwarnung, -en, *n.f.* forewarning.

vorwärts, *adv.* forward.

vorwärts·kommen*, *vb.* get ahead, make headway.

vorweg'nehmen*, *vb.* anticipate; forestall.

vor·werfen*, *vb.* reproach.

Vorwort, -e, *n.nt.* preface.

Vorwurf, ̈e, *n.m.* reproach.

vorzeigen, *vb.* show, produce.

vorzeitig, *adj.* premature.

vorziehen*, *vb.* prefer.

Vorzimmer, -, *n.nt.* antechamber, anteroom.

Vorzug, ̈e, *n.m.* preference; advantage.

vorzüg'lich, 1. *adj.* excellent, exquisite. **2.** *adv.* especially.

Vorzüg'lichkeit, -en, *n.f.* excellence.

vorzugsweise, *adv.* preferably.

vulgär, *adj.* vulgar.

Vulkan', -e, *n.m.* volcano.

W

Waage, -n, *n.f.* scales.

waagerecht, *adj.* horizontal.

Waagschale, -n, *n.f.* scale.

Wabe, -n, *n.f.* honeycomb.

wach, *adj.* awake.

Wache, -n, *n.f.* watch, guard.

wachen, *vb.* be awake, stay awake; watch over.

wachhabend, *adj.* on duty.

Wachlokal, -e, *n.nt.* guardhouse, police station.

Wachposten, -, *n.m.* sentry.

Wachs, -e, *n.nt.* wax.

wachsam, *adj.* watchful, vigilant.

Wachsamkeit, *n.f.* vigilance.

wachsen*, *vb.* grow, increase.

wachsen, *vb.* wax.

Wachskerze, -n, *n.f.* candle.

Wachstum, *n.nt.* growth.

Wacht, *n.f.* guard, watch.

Wächter, -, *n.m.* watchman; keeper.

Wachtmeister, -, *n.m.* (police) sergeant.

wackelig, *adj.* shaky, wobbly.

wackeln, *vb.* shake, wobble.

wacker, *adj.* staunch, brave, stouthearted.

Wade, -n, *n.f.* calf (of the leg).

Waffe, -n, *n.f.* weapon, arm.

Waffel, -n, *n.f.* waffle.

Waffenfabrik, -en, *n.f.* arms factory.

Waffengattung, -en, *n.f.* arm; branch of the army.

waffenlos, *adj.* unarmed, defenseless.

Waffenstill'stand, ̈e, *n.m.* armistice, truce.

waffnen, *vb.* arm.

wagemutig, *adj.* venturesome.

wagen, *vb.* dare, risk, venture.

Wagen, -, *n.m.* carriage, coach, wagon, car.

wägen(*), *vb.* consider.

Wagenheber, -, *n.m.* auto jack.

Waggon', -s, *n.m.* railroad car.

Waggon'ladung, -en, *n.f.* carload.

waghalsig, *adj.* rash, risky.

Wagnis, -se, *n.nt.* venture.

Wahl, -en, *n.f.* choice, election, vote, ballot.

wählbar, *adj.* eligible; **(nicht w.)** ineligible.

wahlberechtigt, *adj.* eligible to vote.

Wahlbezirk, -e, *n.m.* constituency.

wählen, *vb.* choose; elect, vote; (telephone) dial.

Wähler, -, *n.m.* constituent, voter.

wählerisch, *adj.* choosy, fastidious.

Wählerschaft, *n.f.* electorate.

Wahlgang, ̈e, *n.m.* ballot.

Wahlkampf, ̈e, *n.m.* election campaign.

Wahlliste, -n, *n.f.* ticket, slate.

Wahlrecht, -e, *n.nt.* franchise; suffrage; **(W. erteilen)** enfranchise; **(W. entziehen*)** disenfranchise.

Wählscheibe, -n, *n.f.* dial (on a telephone).

Wahlspruch, ̈e, *n.m.* slogan, motto.

Wahlstimme, -n, *n.f.* vote.

Wahn, -, *n.m.* delusion.

Wahnsinn, *n.m.* insanity.

wahnsinnig, *adj.* insane, delirious.

wahr, *adj.* true, truthful, real; **(nicht w.?)** isn't that so?

wahren, *vb.* keep, preserve.

währen, *vb.* continue, last.

während, 1. *prep.* during. **2.** *conj.* while.

wahrhaftig, *adj.* true, sincere.

Wahrheit, -en, *n.f.* truth.

wahrnehmbar, *adj.* perceptible.

wahr·nehmen*, *vb.* perceive.

Wahrnehmung, -en, *n.f.* perception.

wahr·sagen, *vb.* prophesy, tell fortunes.

Wahrsager, -, *n.m.* fortuneteller.

wahrschein'lich, *adj.* probable, likely.

Währung, -en, *n.f.* currency.

Wahrzeichen, -, *n.nt.* distinctive mark, landmark.

Waise, -n, *n.f.* orphan.

Waisenhaus, ̈er, *n.nt.* orphanage.

Wald, ̈er, *n.m.* wood, forest.

Walfisch, -e, *n.m.* whale.

Wall, ̈e, *n.m.* rampart.

wallen, *vb.* undulate; bubble.

Wallfahrer, -, *n.m.* pilgrim.

Wallfahrt, -en, *n.f.* pilgrimage.

Walnuß, ̈sse, *n.f.* walnut.

Walroß, -sse, *n.nt.* walrus.

walten, *vb.* rule.

Walze, -n, *n.f.* roll, roller.

walzen, *vb.* roll.

wälzen, *vb.* roll.

Walzer, -, *n.m.* waltz.

Wand, ̈e, *n.f.* wall.

Wandel, *n.m.* change.

wandelbar, *adj.* changeable.

Wandelhalle, -n, *n.f.* lobby.

wandeln, *vb.* change; go, wander.

wandern, *vb.* hike, wander, roam.

Wanderschaft, *n.f.* travels.

Wanderung, -en, *n.f.* hike, wandering; migration.

Wandgemälde, -, *n.nt.* mural.

Wandlung, -en, *n.f.* change, transformation.

Wandschrank, ̈e, *n.m.* **(eingebauter W.)** closet.

Wandtafel, -n, *n.f.* blackboard.

Wandteppich, -e, *n.m.* tapestry.

Wandverkleidung, -en, *n.f.* wallcovering.

Wange, -n, *n.f.* cheek.

wankelmütig, *adj.* fickle.

wanken, *vb.* stagger, sway.

wann, 1. *conj.* when. **2.** *adv.* when.

Wanne, -n, *n.f.* tub.

Wanze, -n, *n.f.* bedbug.

Wappen, -, *n.nt.* coat of arms.

Ware, -n, *n.f.* article, commodity, merchandise, ware; *(pl.)* goods.

Warenhandel, *n.m.* trade, commerce.

Warenhaus, ̈er, *n.nt.* department store.

Warenrechnung, -en, *n.f.* invoice.

warm (̈), *adj.* warm.

Wärme, *n.f.* warmth, heat.

wärmen, *vb.* warm.

Wärmflasche, -n, *n.f.* hot water bottle.

warnen, *vb.* warn, caution.

Warnung, -en, *n.f.* warning.

Warte, -n, *n.f.* watch-tower, lookout.

warten, *vb.* wait.

Wärter, -, *n.m.* keeper, guard.

Warteraum, ̈e, *n.m.* waiting room.

Wartezeit, -en, *n.f.* wait.

Wartezimmer, -, *n.nt.* waiting room.

warum', *adv.&conj.* why.

Warze, -n, *n.f.* wart.

was, *pron.* what.

Waschanstalt, -en, *n.f.* laundry.

waschbar, *adj.* washable.

Waschbecken, -, *n.nt.* washbasin.

Wäsche, *n.f.* laundry, linen.

waschecht, *adj.* colorfast; *(fig.)* dyed in the wool.

waschen*, vb. wash, launder.
Wäscherei', -en, n.f. laundry.
Wäscheschrank, ⁓e, n.m. linen closet.
Waschfrau, -en, n.f. laundress.
Waschlappen, -, n.m. face cloth.
Waschleder, n.nt. chamois.
Waschmaschine, -n, n.f. washing machine.
Waschpulver, n.nt. soap powder.
Waschraum, ⁓e, n.m. washroom.
Waschseife, -n, n.f. laundry soap.
Waschtisch, -e, n.m. washstand, washbowl.
Waschzettel, -, n.m. laundry list; (book) blurb; memo.
Wasser, -, n.nt. water.
wasserdicht, adj. watertight, waterproof.
Wasserfall, ⁓e, n.m. waterfall.
Wasserflugzeug, -e, n.nt. hydroplane.
Wasserhahn, ⁓e, n.m. faucet.
wässerig, adj. watery, aqueous.
Wasserleitung, -en, n.f. water main; aqueduct.
wässern, vb. water.
Wasserrinne, -n, n.f. gully, gutter.
Wasserstoff, n.m. hydrogen.
Wasserstoffbombe, -n, n.f. hydrogen bomb.
Wasserstoffsu'peroxyd, n.nt. hydrogen peroxide.
Wassersucht, n.f. dropsy.
waten, vb. wade.
watscheln, vb. waddle.
weben(*), vb. weave.
Webeschiffchen, -, n.nt. shuttle.
Webstuhl, ⁓e, n.m. loom.
Wechsel, -, n.m. change, shift, rotation; (comm.) draft.
Wechselgeld, n.nt. change.
Wechseljahre, n.pl. menopause.
Wechselkurs, -e, n.m. rate of exchange.
wechseln, vb. change, exchange.
wechselnd, adj. intermittent.
Wechselstrom, ⁓e, n.m. alternating current.
wecken, vb. wake, awaken.
Wecker, -, n.m. alarm clock.
wedeln, vb. wag.
weder, adj. (w. . . . noch) neither . . . nor.
weg, adv. away; gone.
Weg, -e, n.m. way, path, route.
wegen, prep. because of.
weg-fahren*, vb. drive away, leave.
weg-fallen*, vb. be omitted; not take place.
weg-gehen*, vb. go away, leave.
weg-kommen*, vb. get away; get off.
weg-lassen*, vb. leave out.
weg-nehmen*, vb. take away.

weg-räumen, vb. remove.
weg-schicken, vb. send off.
Wegweiser, -, n.m. guidepost, signpost.
Wegzehrung, -en, n.f. provisions for a journey.
Weh, n.nt. woe, pain, ache.
weh, adj. sore; (w. tun*) hurt, be sore.
wehen, vb. (wind) blow; (flag) wave.
Wehen, n.pl. labor pains.
Wehklage, -n, n.f. lament, lamentation.
wehklagen, vb. wail, lament.
Wehmut, n.f. sadness.
wehmütig, adj. sad, melancholy.
Wehr, -e, n.nt. dam.
Wehr, -en, n.f. defense, resistance.
Wehrdienst, n.nt. military service.
wehren, vb. (sich w.) defend oneself, fight.
wehrfähig, adj. fit to serve (in the army).
wehrlos, adj. defenseless.
Wehrmacht, n.f. armed forces; (specifically, German army to 1945).
Wehrpflicht, n.f. duty to serve in armed forces; (allgemeine W.) compulsory military service.
weh-tun*, vb. hurt, be sore.
Weib, -er, n.nt. woman.
Weibchen, -, n.nt. (zool.) female.
Weibersache, -n, n.f. women's affair.
weiblich, adj. female, feminine.
weich, adj. soft.
Weiche, -n, n.f. switch.
weichen*, vb. give way, yield.
weichen, vb. soften.
weichlich, adj. soft; effeminate.
Weide, -n, n.f. pasture; willow.
weiden, vb. graze; (sich w.) feast one's eyes, gloat.
weidlich, adv. thoroughly.
weigern, vb. (sich w.) refuse.
Weihe, -n, n.f. consecration.
weihen, vb. consecrate.
Weiher, -, n.m. pond.
weihevoll, adj. solemn.
Weihnachten, -, n.nt. Christmas.
Weihnachtslied, -er, n.nt. Christmas carol.
Weihnachtsmann, ⁓er, n.m. Santa Claus.
Weihrauch, n.m. incense.
Weihung, -en, n.f. consecration.
weil, conj. because, since.
Weile, n.f. while.
weilen, vb. stay.
Weiler, -, n.m. hamlet.
Wein, -e, n.m. wine.
Weinbauer, -, n.m. wine grower.
Weinberg, -e, n.m. vineyard.

Weinbrand, -e, n.m. brandy.
weinen, vb. cry, weep.
Weingarten, ⁓, n.m. vineyard.
Weinlese, n.f. vintage.
Weinrebe, -n, n.f. grapevine.
Weinstock, ⁓e, n.m. grapevine.
Weinstube, -n, n.f. tap room.
Weintraube, -n, n.f. grape.
weise, adj. wise.
Weise, -n, n.f. manner, way, method.
weisen*, vb. show; (von sich w.) reject.
Weisheit, -en, n.f. wisdom.
weis-machen, vb. make someone believe, fool.
weiß, adj. white.
weissagen, vb. prophesy, tell fortunes.
Weissager, -, n.m. fortune teller.
Weißwaren, n.pl. linen goods.
Weisung, -en, n.f. order, direction.
weit, adj. far; wide, large.
weitab', adv. far away.
weitaus', adv. by far.
Weite, -n, n.f. width, largeness, expanse; size.
weiter, adv. farther; further; (und so w.) and so forth.
weiterhin, adv. furthermore.
weitgehend, adj. far-reaching.
weither', adv. from afar.
weitläufig, adj. lengthy, elaborate, complex.
weitreichend, adj. far-reaching.
weitsichtig, adj. far-sighted.
weittragend, adj. far-reaching.
weitverbreitet, adj. widespread.
weitverstreut, adj. far-flung.
Weizen, n.m. wheat.
welcher, -es, -e, pron.&adj. which, what.
welchergestalt, adv. in what manner.
welk, adj. wilted.
welken, vb. wilt.
Welle, -n, n.f. wave; (tech.) shaft.
wellen, vb. wave; (tech.) corrugate.
Wellenlänge, -n, n.f. wave length.
wellig, adj. wavy.
Welt, -en, n.f. world.
Weltall, n.nt. universe.
Weltanschauung, -en, n.f. philosophy of life.
Weltbürger, -, n.m. cosmopolite.
weltgeschichtlich, adj. historical.
weltgewandt, adj. sophisticated.
weltklug (⁓), adj. worldly-wise.
Weltkrieg, -e, n.m. world war.
Weltkugel, -n, n.f. globe.
weltlich, adj. worldly, secular.
Weltmeister, -, n.m. world's champion.
Weltmeisterschaft, -en, n.f. world's championship.

weltnah, *adj.* worldly, realistic.

Weltraum, *n.m.* outer space.

Weltreich, **-e**, *n.nt.* empire.

Weltschmerz, *n.m.* world-weariness.

Weltstadt, ⸗e, *n.f.* metropolis.

weltweit, *adj.* world-wide.

Wende, **-n**, *n.f.* turn, bend.

Wendekreis, **-e** *n.m.* tropic; **(W. des Krebses)** tropic of Cancer; **(W. des Steinbocks)** tropic of Capricorn.

wenden*, *vb.* turn; **(sich w. an)** appeal to.

wendig, *adj.* versatile, resourceful.

Wendung, **-en**, *n.f.* turn.

wenig, *adj.* few, little.

weniger, *adj.* fewer, less; minus.

Wenigkeit, **-e**, *n.f.* trifle; **(meine W.)** yours truly.

wenigstens, *adv.* at least.

wenn, *conj.* when, if.

wer, *pron.* who.

werben*, *vb.* recruit, enlist, advertise; woo.

Werbeplakat, **-e**, *n.nt.* poster.

Werber, **-**, *n.m.* suitor.

Werbung, **-en**, *n.f.* recruiting, advertising; courting.

Werdegang, ⸗e, *n.m.* development; career.

werden*, *vb.* become, get, grow.

werfen*, *vb.* throw, cast; **(über den Haufen w.)** upset.

Werft, **-en**, *n.f.* dockyard, shipyard.

Werk, **-e**, *n.nt.* work, labor, deed; factory, plant.

werken, *vb.* work, operate.

Werkstatt, ⸗en, *n.f.* plant, shop.

Werktag, **-e**, *n.m.* work day, weekday.

werktags, *adv.* weekdays.

Werkzeug, **-e**, *n.nt.* tool, instrument.

Wermut, *n.m.* vermouth.

Wert, **-e**, *n.m.* value, worth, merit.

wert, *adj.* worth, valued, esteemed.

Wertarbeit, **-en**, *n.f.* workmanship.

Wertbrief, **-e**, *n.m.* registered insured letter.

wertlos, *adj.* worthless, useless.

Wertlosigkeit, **-en**, *n.f.* worthlessness, uselessness.

Wertpapier, **-e**, *n.nt.* security, bond, stock.

Wertschätzung, **-en**, *n.f.* esteem, value.

Werturteil, **-e**, *n.nt.* value judgement.

Wertverminderung, **-en**, *n.f.* depreciation.

wertvoll, *adj.* valuable.

Wesen, **-**, *n.nt.* being, creature; nature, character; essence, substance.

Wesenheit, *n.f.* entity.

wesenlos, *adj.* unreal.

Wesenszug, ⸗e, *n.m.* characteristic.

wesentlich, *adj.* essential, material; substantial, vital.

weshalb, 1. *conj.* for which reason. **2.** *adv.* why.

Wespe, **-n**, *n.f.* wasp.

wessen, *pron.* whose.

West, Westen, *n.m.* west.

Weste, **-n**, *n.f.* vest, waistcoat.

westlich, *adj.* western; to the west.

westwärts, *adv.* westward.

Wettbewerb, **-e**, *n.m.* competition.

Wettbewerber, **-**, *n.m.* competitor, contestant.

Wette, **-n**, *n.f.* wager, bet.

wetteifern, *vb.* compete, rival.

wetten, *vb.* wager, bet.

Wetter, *n.nt.* weather.

Wetterfahne, **-n**, *n.f.* weather vane.

Wettermeldung, **-en**, *n.f.* weather report.

Wetterverhältnisse, *n.pl.* weather conditions.

Wettkampf, ⸗e, *n.m.* match, contest; competition.

Wettlauf, ⸗e, *n.m.* race (on foot).

Wettläufer, **-**, *n.m.* runner.

Wettrennen, **-**, *n.nt.* race.

Wettrüsten, *n.nt.* armament race.

Wettspiel, **-e**, *n.nt.* match, tournament.

Wettstreit, **-e**, *n.m.* contest, competition; match, race.

wetzen, *vb.* hone, sharpen.

Whisky, **-s**, *n.m.* whiskey.

wichsen, *vb.* shine; thrash.

Wicht, **-e**, *n.m.* little fellow.

wichtig, *adj.* important.

Wichtigkeit, *n.f.* importance.

Wichtigtuer, **-**, *n.m.* busybody, pompous fellow.

Wickel, **-**, *n.m.* wrapping, compress; curler.

wickeln, *vb.* wind, reel; wrap; curl.

wider, *prep.* against, contrary to.

widerfahren*, *vb.* happen to.

Widerhall, **-e**, *n.m.* reverberation.

wider-hallen, *vb.* resound, reverberate.

Widerhalt, *n.m.* support.

widerlegen, *vb.* refute, disprove.

Widerlegung, **-en**, *n.f.* refutation, disproof, rebuttal.

widerlich, *adj.* distasteful, repulsive.

widernatürlich, *adj.* perverse.

widerraten*, *vb.* dissuade.

widerrechtlich, *adj.* illegal.

Widerrede, **-n**, *n.f.* contradiction.

Widerruf, **-e**, *n.m.* revocation; cancellation.

widerrufen*, *vb.* revoke, repeal; retract; cancel.

Widersacher, **-**, *n.m.* antagonist.

Widerschein, *n.m.* reflection.

widersetzen, *vb.* **(sich w.)** oppose.

Widersinn, *n.m.* absurdity.

widersinnig, *adj.* absurd, preposterous.

widerspenstig, *adj.* recalcitrant, contrary.

wider-spiegeln, *vb.* reflect.

widersprechen*, *vb.* contradict.

widersprechend, *adj.* contradictory.

Widerspruch, ⸗e, *n.m.* contradiction, disagreement.

Widerstand, ⸗e, *n.m.* resistance.

widerstandsfähig, *adj.* resistant, tough.

Widerstandskraft, ⸗e, *n.f.* power of resistance, resilience.

widerstandslos, *adj.* without resistance.

widerstehen*, *vb.* resist, withstand.

widerstreben, *vb.* resist, be repugnant.

Widerstreben, *n.nt.* reluctance.

widerstrebend, *adj.* reluctant.

Widerstreit, **-e**, *n.m.* antagonism, conflict.

widerstreiten*, *vb.* resist, conflict with.

widerwärtig, *adj.* repugnant, repulsive.

Widerwille(n), *n.m.* distaste.

widerwillig, *adj.* unwilling, reluctant.

widmen, *vb.* dedicate, devote.

Widmung, **-en**, *n.f.* dedication.

widrig, *adj.* contrary.

widrigenfalls, *adv.* failing which, otherwise.

wie, 1. *conj.* how; as. **2.** *adv.* how.

wieder, *adv.* again; back, in return.

Wiederaufbau, *n.m.* reconstruction.

wieder aufbereiten, *vb.* recycle.

Wiederauferstehung, *n.f.* resurrection.

Wiederaufrüstung, **-en**, *n.f.* armament.

Wiederaufwertung, **-en**, *n.f.* revaluation.

Wiederbelebung, **-en**, *n.f.* revival.

wiedereinsetzen, *vb.* reinstate.

wiedereinstellen, *vb.* reinstate.

wiedererkennen*, *vb.* recognize.

Wiedererkennung, **-en**, *n.f.* recognition.

wiedererlangen, *vb.* retrieve.

wiedererstatten, *vb.* reimburse, refund.

wiederfinden*, *vb.* recover.

Wiedergabe, -n, *n.f.* return; rendition, reproduction.

wieder-geben*, *vb.* return, restore.

wiedergeboren, *adj.* born-again.

Wiedergeburt, *n.f.* rebirth.

wieder-gewinnen*, *vb.* recover, regain.

Wiedergewinnung, -en, *n.f.* recovery.

wiedergut'-machen, *vb.* redress, make amends for.

Wiedergut'machung, -en, *n.f.* restitution, redress.

wiederher'-stellen, *vb.* restore.

Wiederher'stellung, -en, *n.f.* restoration.

wiederho'len, *vb.* repeat.

Wiederho'lung, -en, *n.f.* repetition.

Wiederhören, *n.nt.* hearing again; (auf W.) good-bye (at the end of a telephone call).

Wiederinstand'setzung, -en, *n.f.* reconditioning.

Wiederkehr, *n.f.* return, recurrence.

wieder-kehren, *vb.* return.

Wiedersehen, *n.nt.* seeing again; (auf W.) good-bye.

Wiedervereinigung, *n.f.* reunification.

wieder-verheiraten, *vb.* (sich w.) remarry.

wieder-versöhnen, *vb.* reconcile.

Wiederversöhnung, -en, *n.f.* reconciliation.

Wiege, -n, *n.f.* cradle.

wiegen, *vb.* rock.

wiegen*, *vb.* weigh.

Wiegenlied, -er, *n.nt.* lullaby.

wiehern, *vb.* neigh.

Wiese, -n, *n.f.* meadow.

wieso', *adv.* how so, why.

wild, *adj.* wild, ferocious, savage.

Wild, *n.nt.* game.

Wild-, *n.m.* savage.

Wildbret, *n.nt.* game.

Wildfang, ⸚e, *n.m.* tomboy.

Wildheit, *n.f.* ferocity, fierceness.

Wildleder, -, *n.nt.* chamois, suede.

Wildnis, -se, *n.f.* wilderness.

Wille(n), *n.m.* will.

willenlos, *adj.* irresolute, passive, shifting.

Willenskraft, *n.f.* willpower.

willensstark (⸚), *adj.* strong-willed, resolute.

willfah'ren*, *vb.* comply with, gratify.

willfährig, *adj.* complaisant.

willig, *adj.* willing, ready.

Willkom'men, *n.nt.* welcome.

Willkür, *n.f.* arbitrariness, choice.

willkürlich, *adj.* arbitrary.

wimmeln, *vb.* swarm.

wimmern, *vb.* moan.

Wimper, -n, *n.f.* eyelash.

Wind, -e, *n.m.* wind.

Winde, -n, *n.f.* reel.

Windel, -n, *n.f.* diaper.

winden*, *vb.* wind, coil; (sich w.) squirm.

Windhund, -e, *n.m.* greyhound.

windig, *adj.* windy.

Windmühle, -n, *n.f.* windmill.

Windpocken, *n.pl.* chickenpox.

Windschutzscheibe, -n, *n.f.* windshield.

windstill, *adj.* calm.

Windstoß, ⸚e, *n.m.* gust.

Windzug, *n.m.* draft.

Wink, -e, *n.m.* sign, wave; (fig.) hint, tip.

Winkel, -, *n.m.* angle, corner.

Winkelzug, ⸚e, *n.m.* dodge, subterfuge.

winken, *vb.* wave, beckon.

winseln, *vb.* whimper, wail.

Winter, -, *n.m.* winter.

Winterfrische, *n.f.* winter resort.

Wintergarten, ⸚, *n.m.* conservatory.

winterlich, *adj.* wintry.

Winzer, -, *n.m.* wine-grower.

winzig, *adj.* tiny, minute.

Wippe, -n, *n.f.* seesaw.

wir, *pron.* we.

Wirbel, -, *n.m.* whirl, whirlpool; cowlick; vertebra.

wirbeln, *vb.* whirl.

Wirbelsäule, -n, *n.f.* vertebral column, spine.

Wirbelsturm, ⸚e, *n.m.* cyclone.

Wirbeltier, -e, *n.nt.* vertebrate.

wirken, *vb.* work, effect; (w. auf) effect.

wirklich, *adj.* real, actual.

Wirklichkeit, *n.f.* reality.

Wirklichkeitsflucht, *n.f.* escapism.

wirklichkeitsnah, *adj.* realistic.

wirksam, *adj.* effective.

Wirksamkeit, *n.f.* effectiveness, validity; (in W. treten*), take effect.

Wirkung, -en, *n.f.* effect.

Wirkungskraft, *n.f.* effect, efficacy.

wirkungslos, *adj.* ineffectual.

wirkungsvoll, *adj.* effective.

wirr, *adj.* confused.

Wirrnis, -se, *n.f.* tangle, confusion.

Wirrwarr, *n.nt.* confusion, maze.

Wirt, -e, *n.m.* host; landlord; proprietor.

Wirtin, -nen, *n.f.* hostess; landlady.

Wirtschaft, -en, *n.f.* inn, tavern; household; economy.

wirtschaften, *vb.* manage; keep house.

Wirtschafterin, -nen, *n.f.* housekeeper.

wirtschaftlich, *adj.* economic(al).

Wirtschaftlichkeit, *n.f.* economy.

Wirtschaftsabkommen, -, *n.nt.* trade agreement.

Wirtschaftsprüfer, -, *n.m.* certified public accountant.

Wirtschaftswissenschaft, *n.f.* economics.

Wirtshaus, ⸚er, *n.nt.* inn.

Wisch, -e, *n.m.* scrap.

wischen, *vb.* wipe.

Wischlappen, -, *n.m.* cleaning rag.

wispern, *vb.* whisper.

Wißbegier, *n.f.* desire for knowledge; curiosity.

wissen*, *vb.* know.

Wissen, *n.nt.* learning, knowledge.

Wissenschaft, -en, *n.f.* learning, knowledge, science, scholarship.

wissenschaftlich, *adj.* scientific, scholarly.

wissenswert, *adj.* worth knowing.

wissentlich, *adv.* knowingly.

wittern, *vb.* smell; suspect.

Witterung, *n.f.* weather.

Witterungsverhältnisse, *n.pl.* weather conditions.

Witwe, -n, *n.f.* widow.

Witwer, -, *n.m.* widower.

Witz, -e, *n.m.* joke, pun, gag.

Witzbold, -e, *n.m.* joker, wise guy.

witzeln, *vb.* quip.

witzig, *adj.* witty, humorous.

witzlos, *adj.* pointless, fatuous.

wo, *adv.* where, in what place.

woan'ders, *adv.* elsewhere.

wobei', *adv.* whereby.

Woche, -n, *n.f.* week.

Wochenblatt, ⸚er, *n.nt.* weekly paper.

Wochenende, -n, *n.nt.* weekend.

Wochenschau, *n.f.* newsreel.

Wochentag, -e, *n.m.* weekday.

wöchentlich, *adj.* weekly.

wodurch', *adv.* through what; whereby.

wofern', *conj.* in so far as.

Woge, -n, *n.f.* wave, billow.

wogen, *vb.* wave, heave.

woher', *adv.* whence, from where.

wohl, *adv.* well; presumably, I suppose.

Wohl, *n.nt.* well-being, good health; (zum W.) here's to you.

wohlbedacht, *adj.* well-considered.

Wohlbehagen, *n.nt.* comfort.

Wohlergehen, *n.nt.* welfare.

wohlerzogen, *adj.* well brought up.

Wohlfahrt, *n.f.* welfare.

Wohlfahrtsstaat, -en, *n.m.* welfare state.

Wohlgefallen, *n.nt.* pleasure.

wohlgefällig, *adj.* pleasant, agreeable.

wohlgemerkt, *adv.* nota bene.

wohlgemut, *adj.* cheerful.

wohlgeneigt, *adj.* affectionate.

Wohlgeruch, ⸚e, *n.m.* fragrance.

wohlhabend, *adj.* prosperous, well-to-do.

wohlig, *adj.* comfortable.

wohlklingend, *adj.* melodious.

wohlriechend, *adj.* fragrant.

wohlschmeckend, *adj.* tasty.

Wohlsein, *n.nt.* good health; (zum W.) your health.

Wohlstand, *n.m.* prosperity.

Wohltat, -en, *n.f.* benefit; pleasure.

Wohltäter, -, *n.m.* benefactor.

wohltätig, *adj.* charitable.

Wohltätigkeit, -en, *n.f.* charity.

wohltuend, *adj.* beneficial, pleasant, soothing.

wohlweislich, *adv.* wisely, prudently.

Wohlwollen, *n.nt.* benevolence, good will.

wohlwollend, *adj.* benevolent.

wohnen, *vb.* reside, live, dwell.

wohnhaft, *adj.* resident.

wohnlich, *adj.* comfortable, cozy.

Wohnort, -e, *n.m.* domicile, place of residence.

Wohnsitz, -e, *n.m.* residence.

Wohnung, -en, *n.f.* apartment, place of living.

Wohnwagen, -, *n.m.* trailer.

wölben, *vb.* (sich w.) arch over.

Wolf, -e, *n.m.* wolf.

Wolke, -n, *n.f.* cloud.

Wolkenbruch, ⁻e, *n.m.* cloudburst.

wolkenlos, *adj.* cloudless.

Wolle, -n, *n.f.* wool.

wollen, *adj.* woolen.

wollen*, *vb.* want, be willing, intend.

wollig, *adj.* fluffy, fleecy.

Wollust, *n.f.* voluptuousness, lust.

wollüstig, *adj.* lascivious.

womöglich, *adv.* if possible.

Wonne, -n, *n.f.* delight.

wonnig, *adj.* charming, delightful.

Wort, -e *or* ⁻er, *n.nt.* word.

Wortart, -en, *n.f.* part of speech.

Wörterbuch, ⁻er, *n.nt.* dictionary.

Wörterverzeichnis, -se, *n.nt.* vocabulary.

Wortführer, -, *n.m.* spokesman.

wortgetreu, *adj.* literal, vebatim.

wortkarg, *adj.* taciturn.

Wortlaut, -e, *n.m.* wording, text.

wörtlich, *adj.* literal.

wortlos, *adj.* speechless.

wortreich, *adj.* wordy, verbose.

Wortschatz, ⁻e, *n.m.* vocabulary.

Wortspiel, -e, *n.nt.* pun.

Wortwechsel, -, *n.m.* altercation.

Wrack, -s, *n.nt.* wreck.

wringer*, *vb.* wring.

Wucher, *n.m.* usury.

wucherisch, *adj.* usurious.

Wuchs, *n.m.* growth, figure, height.

Wucht, *n.f.* weight; momentum.

wühlen, *vb.* burrow, rummage; (*fig.*) agitate.

wühlerisch, *adj.* inflammatory, subversive.

wulstig, *adj.* thick.

wund, *adj.* sore, wounded.

Wunde, -n, *n.f.* wound.

Wunder, -, *n.nt.* miracle, wonder.

wunderbar, *adj.* wonderful, miraculous.

Wunderdoktor, -en, *n.m.* quack.

Wunderkind, -er, *n.nt.* child prodigy.

wunderlich, *adj.* strange.

wundern, *vb.* surprise; (sich w.) be surprised.

wundersam, *adj.* wondrous.

wunderschön, *adj.* lovely, exquisite.

wundervoll, *adj.* wonderful.

Wundmal, -e, *n.nt.* scar; (*pl.*) stigmata.

Wunsch, ⁻e, *n.m.* wish, desire.

wünschen, *vb.* wish, desire, want.

wünschenswert, *adj.* desirable.

Würde, -n, *n.f.* dignity.

Würdenträger, -, *n.m.* dignitary.

würdig, *adj.* worthy, dignified.

würdigen, *vb.* honor, appreciate.

Wurf, ⁻e, *n.m.* throw; litter, brood.

Würfel, -, *n.m.* cube; (*pl.*) dice.

Würfelzucker, *n.m.* lump sugar.

Wurfpfeil, -e, *n.m.* dart.

würgen, *vb.* choke, retch; strangle.

Wurm, ⁻er, *n.m.* worm.

wurmen, *vb.* annoy, rankle.

wurmstichig, *adj.* wormy.

Wurst, ⁻e, *n.f.* sausage.

Würstchen, -, *n.nt.* (heißes W.) frankfurter.

Würze, -n, *n.f.* seasoning, flavor.

Wurzel, -n, *n.f.* root.

würzen, *vb.* season, spice.

würzig, *adj.* aromatic, spicy.

wüst, *adj.* waste, desolate; unkempt; wild; vulgar.

Wüste, -n, *n.f.* desert.

Wut, *n.f.* rage, fury.

wüten, *vb.* rage.

wütend, *adj.* furious.

X

X-beinig, *adj.* knock-kneed.

x-beliebig, *adj.* any old, any . . . at all; (jeder x-beliebige) every Tom, Dick, and Harry.

X-Strahlen, *n.pl.* x-rays.

Xylophon', -e, *n.nt.* xylophone.

Y

Yacht, -en, *n.f.* yacht.

Z

Zacke, -n, *n.f.* jag; spike; (fork) prong; (dress) edging.

zacken, *vb.* indent, notch.

zackig, *adj.* jagged; notched; snappy.

zag, *adj.* faint-hearted.

zagen, *vb.* hesitate.

zaghaft, *adj.* timid.

zäh, *adj.* tough, tenacious.

zähflüssig, *adj.* viscous.

Zähigkeit, *n.f.* tenacity, perseverance.

Zahl, -en, *n.f.* number, figure.

zahlen, *vb.* pay; (Herr Ober, bitte z.) waiter, the check please.

zählen, *vb.* count.

Zahlenangaben, *n.pl.* figures.

zahlenmäßig, *adj.* numerical.

Zähler, -, *n.m.* meter.

Zahlkarte, -n, *n.f.* money order.

zahllos, *adj.* countless.

zahlreich, *adj.* numerous.

Zahltag, -e, *n.m.* payday.

Zahlung, -en, *n.f.* payment.

zahlungsfähig, *adj.* solvent.

Zahlungsmittel, -, *n.nt.* tender, currency.

zahlungsunfähig, *adj.* insolvent.

Zahlwort, ⁻er, *n.nt.* numeral.

zahm, *adj.* tame.

zähmen, *vb.* tame, domesticate.

Zahn, ⁻e, *n.m.* tooth; (*tech.*) cog.

Zahnarzt, ⁻e, *n.m.* dentist.

Zahnbürste, -n, *n.f.* toothbrush.

zahnen, *vb.* teethe.

Zahnfleisch, *n.nt.* gum.

Zahnheilkunde, *n.f.* dentistry.

Zahnpaste, -n, *n.f.* toothpaste.

Zahnplombe, -n, *n.f.* filling.

Zahnputzmittel, -, *n.nt.* dentifrice.

Zahnradbahn, -en, *n.f.* cog railroad.

Zahnschmerzen, *n.pl.* toothache.

Zahnstein, *n.m.* tartar.

Zahnstocher, -, *n.m.* toothpick.

Zahnweh, *n.nt.* toothache.

Zange, -n, *n.f.* pliers; forceps.

Zank, *n.m.* quarrel.

zanken, *vb.* (sich z.) quarrel, bicker.

zapfen, *vb.* tap.

Zapfen, -, *n.m.* peg, plug.

Zapfenstreich, *n.m.* tattoo, retreat to quarters.

zappelig, *adj.* fidgety.

zappeln, *vb.* flounder, fidget.

Zar, -en, -en, *n.m.* czar.

zart, *adj.* tender, dainty.

Zartheit, -en, *n.f.* tenderness, daintiness.

zärtlich, *adj.* tender, affectionate.

Zauber, -, *n.m.* enchantment, spell, charm, fascination.

Zauberei, *n.f.* sorcery, magic.

Zauberer, -, *n.m.* magician, wizard.

zauberhaft, *adj.* enchanting.

Zauberkraft, ⸚e, *n.f.* magic power.

Zauberkunst, ⸚e, *n.f.* magic.

Zauberspruch, ⸚e, *n.m.* incantation, charm.

zaudern, *vb.* hesitate.

Zaum, -e, *n.m.* bridle.

zäumen, *vb.* bridle.

Zaun, ⸚e, *n.m.* fence.

zausen, *vb.* tousle.

Zebra, -s, *n.nt.* zebra.

Zeche, -n, *n.f.* bill for drinks; mine, colliery.

zechen, *vb.* drink, carouse.

Zeder, -, *n.f.* cedar.

Zeh, -en, *n.m.* toe.

Zehe, -n, *n.f.* toe.

Zehenspitze, -n, *n.f.* tip of the toe; **(auf Z.n gehen)** tiptoe.

zehn, *num.* ten.

zehnt-, *adj.* tenth.

Zehntel, -, *n.nt.* tenth part; **(ein z.)** one-tenth.

zehren, *vb.* **(z. an)** wear out, consume; **(z. von)** live on.

Zeichen, -, *n.nt.* sign, mark, token.

Zeichenfilm, -e, *n.m.* animated cartoon.

zeichnen, *vb.* draw; initial; *(comm.)* subscribe.

Zeichner, -, *n.m.* draftsman.

Zeichnung, -en, *n.f.* drawing, *(comm.)* subscription.

Zeigefinger, -, *n.m.* forefinger.

zeigen, *vb.* show, indicate, point; demonstrate; exhibit.

Zeiger, -, *n.m.* (clock) hand.

Zeile, -n, *n.f.* line.

Zeit, -en, *n.f.* time.

Zeitalter, -, *n.nt.* age, era.

Zeitaufnahme, -n, *n.f.* time exposure.

Zeitdauer, *n.f.* period of time.

Zeitgeist, *n.m.* spirit of the times.

zeitgemäß, *adj.* timely.

Zeitgenosse, -n, -n, *n.m.* contemporary.

zeitgenössisch, *adj.* contemporary.

zeitig, *adj.* early.

zeitlich, 1. *adj.* temporal. **2.** *adv.* in time.

zeitlos, *adj.* timeless, ageless.

Zeitmangel, *n.m.* lack of time.

Zeitpunkt, -e, *n.m.* time, moment.

zeitraubend, *adj.* time-consuming.

Zeitraum, -e, *n.m.* period.

Zeitschrift, -en, *n.f.* magazine, journal, periodical.

Zeitspanne, -n, *n.f.* period of time.

Zeitung, -en, *n.f.* newspaper.

Zeitungsanzeige, -n, *n.f.* ad, announcement.

Zeitungsausschnitt, -e, *n.m.* newspaper clipping.

Zeitungshändler, -, *n.m.* newsdealer.

Zeitungsjunge, -n, -n, *n.m.* paper-boy.

Zeitungsnotiz, -en, *n.f.* press item.

Zeitvertreib, *n.m.* pastime.

zeitweilig, *adj.* temporary.

Zeitwort, ⸚er, *n.nt.* verb.

Zelle, -n, *n.f.* cell.

zellig, *adj.* cellular.

Zellophan', *n.nt.* cellophane.

Zellstoff, -e, *n.m.* cellulose.

Zelluloid', *n.nt.* celluloid.

Zellulo'se, *n.f.* cellulose.

Zelt, -e, *n.nt.* tent.

zelten, *vb.* live in a tent, camp.

Zelter, -, *n.m.* camper.

Zement', -e, *n.m.* cement, concrete.

zensie'ren, *vb.* censor; (school) grade, mark.

Zensor, -'oren, *n.m.* censor.

Zensur', -en, *n.f.* censorship; (school) grade, mark.

Zensus, *n.m.* census.

Zentime'ter, -, *n.nt.* centimeter.

Zentner, -, *n.m.* 100 German pounds.

zentral', *adj.* central.

Zentral'heizung, *n.f.* central heating.

zentralisie'ren, *vb.* centralize.

Zentrum, -tren, *n.nt.* center.

zerbre'chen*, *vb.* break to pieces, shatter.

zerbrech'lich, *adj.* fragile, frail.

zerbrö'ckeln, *vb.* crumble.

zerdrü'cken, *vb.* crush.

Zeremonie', -i'en, *n.f.* ceremony.

zeremoniell', *adj.* ceremonial.

zerfah'ren, *adj.* absentminded, scatter-brained.

Zerfall', *n.m.* ruin, decay.

zerfal'len*, *vb.* fall into ruin, disintegrate; **(in Teile z.)** be divided.

zerfet'zen, *vb.* tear into shreds.

zerflei'schen, *vb.* mangle.

zerfres'sen*, *vb.* erode, corrode.

zerge'hen*, *vb.* dissolve, melt.

zerglie'dern, *vb.* dismember, dissect.

zerklei'nern, *vb.* reduce to small pieces; crush; (wood) chop.

zerknaut'schen, *vb.* crumple.

zerknirscht', *adj.* contrite.

zerknül'len, *vb.* crumple.

zerlas'sen*, *vb.* dissolve, melt.

zerle'gen, *vb.* separate, cut up, carve.

zerlumpt', *adj.* ragged.

zermal'men, *vb.* crunch.

zermar'tern, *vb.* torture; **(den Kopf z.)** rack one's brain.

zermür'ben, *vb.* wear down.

Zermür'bung, -en, *n.f.* attrition.

zerpflü'cken, *vb.* pick to pieces.

zerquet'schen, *vb.* squash.

Zerrbild, -er, *n.nt.* distorted picture, caricature.

zerrei'ßen*, *vb.* tear up, rend.

zerren, *vb.* tug, pull.

zerrin'nen*, *vb.* disappear, melt away.

zerrüt'ten, *vb.* ruin.

Zerrüt'tung, -en, *n.f.* ruin.

zerschla'gen*, *vb.* smash, shatter.

zerschmei'ßen*, *vb.* smash.

zerset'zen, *vb.* decompose.

zerset'zend, *adj.* subversive.

Zerset'zung, -en, *n.f.* decomposition; subversion.

zersprin'gen*, *vb.* burst.

zerstäu'ben, *vb.* pulverize; atomize; scatter.

zerstö'ren, *vb.* destroy, demolish.

zerstö'rend, *adj.* destructive.

Zerstö'rung, -en, *n.f.* destruction, demolition.

zerstreu'en, *vb.* scatter; divert, amuse.

zerstreut', *adj.* absent-minded.

Zerstreu'ung, -en, *n.f.* scattering; relaxation, amusement.

zertei'len, *vb.* cut up; separate, divide.

zertren'nen, *vb.* sever; (dress) cut up.

zertre'ten*, *vb.* trample.

zertrüm'mern, *vb.* wreck, demolish.

Zerwürf'nis, -se, *n.nt.* discord, quarrel.

zerzau'sen, *vb.* tousle, rumple.

Zettel, -, -n, *n.m.* slip of paper, note, sticker, bill.

Zeug, -e, *n.nt.* stuff, material, cloth.

Zeuge, -n, -n, *n.m.* witness.

zeugen, *vb.* testify, give evidence; beget, create, produce.

Zeugenaussage, -n, *n.f.* testimony.

Zeugnis, -se, *n.nt.* testimony, evidence; reference (for a job); (school) report card.

Zicho'rie, -n, *n.f.* chickory.

Zickzack, -e, *n.m.* zigzag.

Ziege, -n, *n.f.* (she-)goat.

ziegel, -, *n.m.* tile.

Ziegelstein, -e, *n.m.* brick.

Ziegenbock, ⸚e, *n.m.* billygoat.

Ziegenpeter, *n.m.* mumps.

ziehen*, *vb.* *(intr.)* move, go, draw, be drafty; *(tr.)* pull, drag, draw, tug; cultivate.

Ziehharmonika, -s, *n.f.* accordion.

Ziehung, -en, *n.f.* drawing.

Ziel, -e, *n.nt.* goal, target, end, objective.

zielbewußt, *adj.* with a clear goal, resolute.

zielen, *vb.* aim.

ziellos, *adj.* aimless, erratic.

Zielscheibe, -n, n.f. target.

ziemen, vb. be fitting for; (sich z.) be proper.

ziemlich, 1. adj. suitable, fitting; pretty much of. 2. adv. pretty, rather, quite.

Zier, n.f. ornament(ation).

Zierat, -e, n.m., or -en, n.f. ornament, decoration.

Zierde, -n, n.f. ornament; honor.

zieren, vb. adorn, ornament.

zierlich, adj. dainty.

Ziffer, -n, n.f. figure, numeral.

Zifferblatt, ̈-er, n.nt. dial, face (of a clock).

Zigaret'te, -n, n.f. cigarette.

Zigar're, -n, n.f. cigar.

Zigeu'ner, -, n.m. gypsy.

Zimbel, -n, n.f. cymbal.

Zimmer, -, n.nt. room.

Zimmerdecke, -n, n.f. ceiling.

Zimmermädchen, -, n.nt. chambermaid.

Zimmermann, -leute, n.m. carpenter.

zimperlich, adj. finicky, prim.

Zimt, n.m. cinnamon.

Zinke, -n, n.f. prong.

Zinn, n.nt. tin, pewter.

Zins, -en, n.m. interest.

Zinseszins, -en, n.m. compound interest.

Zinssatz, ̈-e, n.m. rate of interest.

Zipfel, -, n.m. tip.

Zirkel, -, n.m. compass (for making a circle).

zirkulie'ren, vb. circulate.

zirkulie'rend, adj. circulatory.

Zirkus, -se, n.m. circus.

zirpen, vb. chirp.

zischen, vb. hiss, sizzle; whiz.

ziselie'ren, vb. engrave, chase.

Zitadel'le, -n, n.f. citadel.

Zitat', -e, n.nt. quotation.

zitie'ren, vb. quote, cite.

Zitro'ne, -n, n.f. lemon.

zittern, vb. quiver, shiver, tremble.

zivil', adj. civil; reasonable.

Zivil', n.nt. civilians; civilian clothes.

Zivil'bevölkerung, -en, n.f. civilian population.

Zivilisation', -en, n.f. civilization.

zivilisie'ren, vb. civilize.

Zivilist', -en, -en, n.m. civilian.

Zobel, n.m. sable.

zögern, vb. hesitate.

Zögern, n.nt. hesitation.

zögernd, adj. hesitant.

Zölibat', n.m. or nt. celibacy.

Zoll, -, n.m. inch.

Zoll, ̈-e, n.m. tariff, duty, toll.

Zollamt, ̈-er, n.nt. custom house.

Zollbeamt-, n.m. customs officer.

zollfrei, adj. duty free.

Zöllner, -, n.m. customs collector; (Bible) publican.

zollpflichtig, adj. subject to duty.

Zolltarif, -e, n.m. tariff.

Zollverein, -e, n.m. customs union.

Zollverschluß, n.m. customs seal; (unter Z.) under bond.

Zone, -, n.f. zone.

Zoo, -s, n.m. zoo.

Zoologie', n.f. zoology.

zoolo'gisch, adj. zoological.

Zorn, n.m. ire, wrath, anger.

zornig, adj. angry.

zottig, adj. shaggy.

zu, adv. too; closed.

zu, prep. to.

Zubehör, n.nt. accessories, appurtenances, trimmings.

zu-bereiten, vb. prepare.

Zubereitung, -en, n.f. preparation.

zu-bringen*, vb. bring to; pass, spend.

Zucht, -en, n.f. breed(ing), rearing, education, training, decency.

züchten, vb. breed, raise.

Züchter, -, n.m. breeder.

Zuchthaus, ̈-er, n.nt. penitentiary.

züchtig, adj. chaste, demure.

züchtigen, vb. chasten, chastise.

zucken, vb. twitch, jerk, flash.

Zucker, n.m. sugar.

Zuckerbäcker, -, n.m. confectioner.

Zuckerguß, ̈-sse, n.m. icing.

Zuckerkrankheit, n.f. diabetes.

Zuckerwerk, n.nt. confectionery.

Zuckung, -en, n.f. twitch, convulsion.

zu-decken, vb. cover up.

zudem', adv. in addition.

zudringlich, adj. intruding, obtrusive.

Zueignung, -en, n.f. dedication.

zueinan'der, adv. to one another.

zu-erkennen*, vb. award.

zuerst', adv. first, at first.

Zufall, ̈-e, n.m. chance, coincidence.

zufällig, 1. adj. chance, fortuitous. 2. adv. by chance.

Zuflucht, n.f. refuge; recourse.

Zufluchtsort, -e, n.m. place of refuge.

Zufluß, ̈-sse, n.m. flowing in, influx.

zufol'ge, prep. as a result of; according to.

zufrie'den, adj. content, satisfied.

zufrie'den-stellen, vb. satisfy.

zu-frieren*, vb. freeze over, freeze up.

zu-fügen, vb. inflict.

Zufuhr, -en, n.f. bringing in, importation, supply.

zu-führen, vb. bring to, import, supply.

Zug, ̈-e, n.m. pull, drawing, draft; stroke; feature, trait;

move; train; procession; trend; flight; (mil.) squad.

Zugabe, -n, n.f. bonus, premium, encore.

Zugang, ̈-e, n.m. access, approach.

zugänglich, adj. accessible, approachable.

zu-geben*, vb. give in addition; admit.

zugegebenerma'ßen, adv. admittedly.

zuge'gen, adv. present.

zugehörig, adj. belonging to, pertinent.

Zügel, -, n.m. rein; restraint.

zügellos, adj. unbridled, unrestrained.

zügeln, vb. bridle, curb, check.

zugestandenerma'ßen, adv. avowedly.

Zugeständnis, -se, n.nt. confession; concession.

zu-gestehen*, vb. confess, concede.

zugetan, adj. devoted to, fond of.

zugig, adj. drafty.

Zugkraft, n.f. pull, thrust.

zugleich', adv. at the same time.

zu-greifen*, vb. lend a hand; help oneself.

zugrun'de, adv. at the bottom, as a basis; (z. gehen*) go to ruin, perish; (z. richten) ruin, destroy.

zugun'sten, adv.&prep. for the benefit of, in favor of.

zugu'te, adv. for the benefit of.

zu-haken, vb. hook.

zu-halten*, vb. keep shut.

zuhan'den, adv. at hand.

zu-hören, vb. listen to.

Zuhörer, -, n.m. listener, auditor; (pl.) audience.

Zuhörerraum, ̈-e, n.m. auditorium.

Zuhörerschaft, -en, n.f. audience.

zu-kleben, vb. paste together.

zu-knallen, vb. slam.

zu-knöpfen, vb. button up.

zu-knüpfen, vb. tie, knot, fasten.

zu-kommen*, vb. be one's due; be proper for.

Zukunft, n.f. future.

zukünftig, adj. future.

Zulage, -n, n.f. extra pay, pay raise.

zu-langen, vb. help oneself.

zulänglich, adj. adequate.

zu-lassen*, vb. leave closed; admit; permit.

zulässig, adj. permissible, admissible.

Zulauf, n.m. run; (Z. haben*) be popular.

zu-laufen*, vb. run up to.

zu-legen, vb. add; (sich etwas z.) acquire.

zulei'de, adv. (z. tun*) hurt, harm.

zu·leiten, vb. lead to, direct to.

zuletzt', adv. at last, finally.

zulie'be, adv. for the sake of.

zu·machen, vb. shut.

zumal', 1. adv. especially; together. 2. conj. especially; because.

zu·mauern, vb. wall up.

zumeist', adv. for the most part.

zu·messen*, vb. allot.

zumin'dest, adv. at least.

zumu'te, adv. (z. sein*) feel, be in a mood.

zu·muten, vb. expect, demand.

Zumutung, -en, n.f. imposition.

zunächst', adv. first of all.

Zunahme, -n, n.f. increase.

Zuname(n), -, n.m. surname, last name.

zünden, vb. ignite; (fig.) inflame.

zündend, adj. inflammatory.

Zünder, -, n.m. fuse.

Zündholz, ¨er, n.nt. match.

Zündkerze, -n, n.f. spark plug.

Zündschlüssel, -, n.m. ignition key.

Zündstoff, -e, n.m. fuel.

Zündung, n.f. ignition; detonation.

zu·nehmen*, vb. grow, increase; (moon) wax; put on weight.

zu·neigen, vb. incline.

Zuneigung, -en, n.f. inclination; affection.

Zunft, ¨e, n.f. guild.

Zunge, -n, n.f. tongue.

zungenfertig, adj. glib.

zunich'te, adv. to nothing, ruined; (z. machen) ruin, frustrate.

zunut'ze, adv. (z. machen) profit by, utilize.

zuo'berst, adv. at the top.

zu'packen, vb. (fig.) get to work.

zupfen, vb. pull, (wool) pick.

zu·raten*, vb. advise in favor of.

zurechnungsfähig, adj. accountable.

zurecht', adv. right, in good order.

zurecht'·finden*, vb. (sich z.) find one's way.

zurecht'·machen, vb. prepare.

zu·reden, vb. urge, encourage.

zureichend, adj. sufficient.

zu·richten, vb. prepare; (übel z.) maul.

zürnen, vb. be angry.

Zurschau'stellung, -en, n.f. display.

zurück', adv. back, behind.

zurück'·behalten*, vb. keep back.

zurück'·bleiben*, vb. lag behind.

zurück·bringen*, vb. return.

zurück'·drängen*, vb. drive back.

zurück'·erstatten, vb. reimburse.

zurück'·fahren*, vb. drive back; recoil.

zurück'·fallen*, vb. fall back; relapse.

zurück'·führen, vb. lead back; trace back, attribute.

zurück'·geben*, vb. return.

zurück'geblieben, adj. backward.

Zurück'gebliebenheit, n.f. backwardness.

zurück'·gehen*, vb. go back; decline.

zurück'gesetzt, adj. (prices) reduced.

zurück'gezogen, adj. secluded.

Zurück'gezogenheit, n.f. seclusion.

zurück'·halten*, vb. retain; restrain; withhold.

zurück'haltend, adj. reticent.

Zurück'haltung, n.f. restraint.

zurück'·kehren, vb. return, revert.

zurück'·kommen*, vb. return.

zurück'·lassen*, vb. leave behind.

zurück'·legen, vb. lay aside; accomplish.

zurück'·lehnen, vb. (sich z.) lean back, recline.

zurück'·liegen*, vb. lie in the past.

zurück'·nehmen*, vb. take back; retract.

zurück'·prallen*, vb. recoil, rebound.

zurück'·rufen*, vb. recall.

zurück'·schauen, vb. look back.

zurück'·schlagen*, vb. hit back, repulse.

zurück'·schrecken, vb. be startled; shrink (from).

zurück'·sehen*, vb. look back on; reflect.

zurück'·sehnen, vb. (sich z.) long to return.

zurück'·setzen, vb. put back; set aside; reduce.

zurück'·stehen*, vb. stand back; (fig.) be inferior.

zurück'·stellen, vb. set back; set aside; (mil.) defer.

zurück'·stoßen*, vb. repulse.

zurück'·strahlen, vb. reflect.

zurück'·treiben*, vb. repel.

zurück'·treten*, vb. resign.

zurück'·verfolgen, vb. trace.

zurück'·versetzen, vb. put back; (sich z.) go back to a time.

zurück'·weichen*, vb. retreat.

zurück'·weisen*, vb. send back; reject.

Zurück'weisung, -en, n.f. rebuff.

zurück'·zahlen, vb. refund, repay.

zurück'·ziehen*, vb. pull back, withdraw; (sich z.) withdraw, back out.

Zuruf, -e, n.m. call, shout; acclamation.

Zusage, -n, n.f. acceptance.

zu·sagen, vb. accept; (es sagt mir zu) it pleases me, it agrees with me.

zusam'men, adv. together.

Zusam'menarbeit, n.f. cooperation, collaboration.

zusam'men·arbeiten, vb. cooperate, collaborate.

Zusam'menbau, n.m. assemblage.

zusam'men·brauen, vb. concoct.

zusam'men·brechen*, vb. collapse.

Zusam'menbruch, ¨e, n.m. collapse.

zusam'men·drängen, vb. (sich z.) crowd together; huddle.

zusam'men·fahren*, vb. ride together; crash; be startled, wince.

zusam'men·fassen, vb. summarize, recapitulate.

zusam'menfassend, adj. comprehensive; summary.

Zusam'menfassung, -en, n.f. summary, condensation.

zusam'men·fügen, vb. join together.

zusam'men·gehören, vb. belong together.

zusam'men·geraten*, vb. collide.

zusam'mengesetzt, adj. composed; compound.

Zusam'menhang, ¨e, n.m. connection, relation; context; association.

zusam'men·hängen*, vb. hang together, be connected, cohere.

zusam'menhängend, adj. coherent.

zusam'menhangslos, adj. disconnected, incoherent.

zusam'men·häufen, vb. pile up.

zusam'men·kauern, vb. huddle.

zusam'men·kommen*, vb. get together, convene.

Zusam'menkunft, ¨e, n.f. meeting.

zusam'men·laufen*, vb. converge.

zusam'men·legen, vb. combine, pool, merge.

zusam'men·nehmen*, vb. (sich z.) pull oneself together.

zusam'men·passen, vb. go well together.

Zusam'menprall, -e, n.m. collision, impact.

zusam'men·pressen, vb. compress.

zusam'men·rechnen, vb. add up.

zusam'men·reißen*, vb. (sich z.) pull oneself together.

zusam'men·rotten, vb. (sich z.) band together.

zusam'men·rufen*, vb. summon, convene.

zusam'men·scharen, vb. scrape together; (sich z.) band together, cluster.

zusam'men·schließen*, vb. join together; (sich z.) close ranks.

Zusam'menschluß, ·̈sse, n.m. federation, merger.

zusam'men·schrumpfen, vb. shrink, dwindle.

zusam'men·setzen, vb. combine, compound; (sich z.) consist, be composed.

Zusam'mensetzung, -en, n.f. combination, composition.

zusam'men·stehen*, vb. stand together, stick together.

zusam'men·stellen, vb. make up, compile.

Zusam'menstellung, -en, n.f. composition, arrangement.

Zusam'menstoß, ·̈e, n.m. collision, clash.

zusam'men·stoßen*, vb. get together; collide, clash, crash.

zusam'men·strömen, vb. flow together, flock together.

zusam'men·stürzen, vb. collapse.

zusam'men·tragen*, vb. compile.

zusam'men·treffen*, vb. meet, encounter; coincide.

Zusam'mentreffen, -, n.nt. encounter; coincide.

zusam'men·treten*, vb. convene.

zusam'men·tun*, vb. put together; (sich z.) unite.

zusam'men·wirken*, vb. act together, collaborate.

zusam'men·zählen, vb. sum up.

zusam'men·ziehen*, vb. draw together; (sich z.) contract, constrict.

Zusam'menziehung, -en, n.f. contraction.

Zusatz, ·̈e, n.m. addition.

zusätzlich, adj. additional, supplementary.

zuschan'den·machen, vb. ruin.

zu·schauen, vb. look on, watch.

Zuschauer, -, n.m. spectator.

zu·schicken, vb. send to, forward.

zu·schieben*, vb. shove towards; (die Schuld z.) put the blame on.

zu·schießen*, vb. contribute.

Zuschlag, ·̈e, n.m. increase; additional charge.

zu·schlagen*, vb. strike; bang shut.

zu·schließen*, vb. lock.

zu·schneiden*, vb. cut out.

zu·schreiben*, vb. ascribe, attribute, impute.

Zuschrift, -en, n.f. communication.

Zuschuß, ·̈sse, n.m. subsidy.

zu·sehen*, vb. look on, watch.

zusehends, adv. visibly.

zu·senden*, vb. send, forward.

zu·sichern, vb. assure, promise.

Zustand, ·̈e, n.m. state, condition; situation.

zustan'de·bringen*, vb. bring about, achieve, accomplish.

zustan'de·kommen*, vb. come about, be accomplished.

zuständig, adj. competent, qualified.

Zuständigkeit, -en, n.f. competence; jurisdiction.

zustat'ten·kommen*, vb. be useful.

zu·stehen*, vb. be due to; become, suit; behoove.

zu·stellen, vb. deliver.

Zustellung, -en, n.f. delivery.

zu·stimmen, vb. agree, consent.

Zustimmung, -en, n.f. agreement, consent, approval.

zu·stopfen, vb. plug.

zu·stoßen*, vb. slam tight, meet with, befall.

Zustrom, n.m. influx.

Zutat, -en, n.f. ingredient.

zu·teilen, vb. allot, assign, allocate.

zu·trauen, vb. believe someone capable of doing.

Zutrauen, n.nt. confidence.

zu·treffen*, vb. prove right, apply.

zutreffend, adj. correct, applicable.

Zutritt, -e, n.m. admittance, admission.

Zutun, n.nt. assistance.

zuverlässig, adj. reliable, trustworthy.

Zuversicht, n.f. confidence, trust.

zuversichtlich, adj. confident, sure.

zuviel', adv. too much.

zuvor', adv. beforehand.

zuvor'derst, adv. up front.

zuvör'derst, adv. first of all.

zuvor'·kommen*, vb. anticipate, forestall.

zuvor'kommend, adj. obliging, polite.

Zuvor'kommenheit, n.f. civility.

Zuwachs, n.m. increase, rise, growth.

zu·wandern, vb. immigrate.

zuwe'ge·bringen*, vb. bring about, achieve.

zuwei'len, adv. at times.

zu·weisen*, vb. assign, apportion, allot.

Zuweisung, -en, n.f. assignment, allocation.

zu·wenden*, vb. turn towards; bestow upon.

Zuwendung, -en, n.f. donation.

zuwi'der, 1. adj. abhorrent, repugnant. 2. prep. contrary to.

zuwi'der·handeln, vb. act contrary to, disobey.

zu·zahlen, vb. pay extra.

zu·ziehen*, vb. pull closed; (sich etwas z.) contract, incur.

Zuzug, n.m. move, influx.

zuzüglich, adv. plus.

Zwang, n.m. compulsion, coercion, duress; constraint.

zwanglos, adj. unrestrained, informal, casual.

Zwangsarbeit, n.f. forced labor; hard labor.

zwangsläufig, adv. necessarily.

zwangsräumen, vb. evict.

Zwangsverschleppt·, n.m.&f. displaced person.

zwangsweise, adv. forcibly.

Zwangswirtschaft, n.f. controlled economy.

zwanzig, num. twenty.

zwanzigst·, adj. twentieth.

Zwanzigstel, -, n.nt. twentieth part; (ein z.) one-twentieth.

zwar, adv. to be sure (means that a but is coming); (und z.) namely, to give further details.

Zweck, -e, n.m. purpose, end, aim.

zweckdienlich, adj. expedient.

Zwecke, -n, n.f. tack.

zweckmäßig, adj. expedient.

zwecks, prep. for the purpose of.

zwei, num. two.

zweideutig, adj. ambiguous.

Zweideutigkeit, -en, n.f. ambiguity.

zweierlei, adj. of two kinds.

zweifach, adj. twofold.

zweifältig, adj. twofold, double.

Zweifel, -, n.m. doubt.

zweifelhaft, adj. doubtful.

zweifellos, adj. doubtless.

zweifeln, vb. doubt.

Zweifler, -, n.m. doubter, sceptic.

Zweig, -e, n.m. branch, bough, twig.

Zweikampf, ·̈e, n.m. duel.

zweimal, adv. twice.

zweimalig, adj. repeated, done twice.

zweimonatlich, adj. bimonthly.

Zweirad, ·̈er, n.nt. bicycle.

zweiseitig, adj. two-sided, bilateral.

Zweisitzer, -, n.m. two-seater, roadster.

zweit·, adj. second.

zweitbest·, adj. second-best.

zweiteilig, adj. two-piece; bipartite.

zweitens, adv. in the second place, secondly.

zweitklassig, adj. second-class.

Zwerchfell, -e, n.nt. diaphragm.

Zwerg, -e, n.m. dwarf; midget.

zwergenhaft, adj. dwarfish, diminutive.

Zwetschge, -n, n.f. plum.

zwicken, vb. pinch.

Zwickmühle, -n, n.f. dilemma, jam.

Zwieback, ·̈e or -e, n.m. zwieback, rusk.

Zwiebel, -n, n.f. onion.

zwiefach, adj. double.

Zwiegespräch, -e, n.nt. dialogue.

Zwielicht, n.nt. twilight.

zwielichtig, adj. shady.

Zwiespalt, -e, *n.m.* discrepancy; discord; schism.

zwiespältig, *adj.* discrepant, conflicting.

Zwilling, -e, *n.m.* twin.

zwingen*, *vb.* force, compel.

zwingend, *adj.* compelling.

Zwinger, -, *n.m.* cage; (dog) kennel.

zwinkern, *vb.* wink.

Zwirn, -e, *n.m.* thread; twine.

Zwirnfaden, ⁻, *n.m.* thread.

zwischen, *prep.* between, among.

Zwischenakt, -e, *n.m.* entr'acte; interval.

Zwischenbemerkung, -en, *n.f.* incidental remark, interruption.

Zwischendeck, -e, *n.nt.* steerage.

Zwischending, -e, *n.nt.* something halfway between, mixture, cross.

zwischendurch′, *adv.* in between; now and then.

Zwischenfall, ⁻e, *n.m.* incident.

Zwischenhändler, -, *n.m.* jobber.

Zwischenlandung, -en, *n.f.* stopover.

Zwischenraum, ⁻e, *n.m.* space in between; interval.

Zwischenruf, -e, *n.m.* interjection, interruption.

Zwischenspiel, -e, *n.nt.* interlude, intermezzo.

Zwischenstock, ⁻e, *n.m.* mezzanine.

Zwischenzeit, *n.f.* interval, interim.

Zwist, -e, *n.m.* quarrel, discord.

zwitschern, *vb.* twitter, chirp.

Zwitter, -, *n.m.* hybrid.

zwo, *num.* two (used especially on the telephone to avoid having *zwei* misunderstood as *drei*).

zwölf, *num.* twelve.

Zwölffin′gerdarm, ⁻e, *n.m.* duodenum.

zwölft-, *adj.* twelfth.

Zwölftel, -, *n.nt.* twelfth part; (ein z.) one-twelfth.

zwot-, *adj.* second.

Zyklamat′, -e, *n.nt.* cyclamate.

Zyklon′, -e, *n.m.* cyclone.

Zyklotron′, -e, *n.nt.* cyclotron.

Zyklus, -klen, *n.m.* cycle.

Zylin′der, -, *n.m.* cylinder; top hat.

Zyniker, -, *n.m.* cynic.

zynisch, *adj.* cynical.

Zypres′se, -n, *n.f.* cypress.

Zyste, -n, *n.f.* cyst.

English-German

A

a, *art.* ein, -, -e.
abandon, *vb.* verlas'sen*.
abandoned, *adj.* verlas'sen; *(depraved)* verwor'fen.
abandonment, *n.* Aufgeben *nt.*
abash, *vb.* beschä'men.
abate, *vb.* nach-lassen*.
abatement, *n.* Vermin'derung, -en *f.*
abbess, *n.* Äbtis'sin, -nen *f.*
abbey, *n.* Abtei', -en *f.*, Klo-ster, ‑ *nt.*
abbot, *n.* Abt, ‑e *m.*
abbreviate, *vb.* ab-kürzen.
abbreviation, *n.* Abkürzung, -en *f.*
abdicate, *vb.* ab-danken.
abdication, *n.* Abdankung, -en *f.*
abdomen, *n.* Unterleib, -er *m.*
abdominal, *adj.* Leib- *(cpds.).*
abduct, *vb.* entführ'ren.
abduction, *n.* Entführ'rung, -en *f.*
abductor, *n.* Entführ'rer, - *m.*
aberration, *n.* Abweichung, -en *f.*
abet, *vb.* an-treiben*, helfen*.
abetment, *n.* Beistand, -e *m.*
abettor, *n.* Helfershelfer, - *m.*
abeyance, *n.* Schwebezustand, ‑e *m.*
abhor, *vb.* verab'scheuen.
abhorrence, *n.* Abscheu, -e *m.*
abhorrent, *adj.* zuwi'der.
abide, *vb. (dwell)* wohnen; *(remain)* bleiben*; *(tolerate)* lei-den*.
abiding, *adj.* dauernd.
ability, *n.* Fähigkeit, -en *f.*
abject, *adj.* elend, niedrig, un-terwür'fig.
abjure, *vb.* ab-schwören*, ent-sa'gen.
ablative, *n.* Ablativ, -e *m.*
ablaze, *adj.* in Flammen.
able, *adj.* fähig, tüchtig; *(to be a.)* können*.
able-bodied, *adj.* kräftig.
ablution, *n.* Abwaschung, -en *f.*
ably, *adv.* fähig, tüchtig.
abnormal, *adj.* ungewöhnlich, abnorm'.
abnormality, *n.* Mißbildung, -en *f.*, Abnormität', -en *f.*
aboard, *adv.* an Bord.
abode, *n.* Wohnsitz, -e *m.*, Wohnung, -en *f.*
abolish, *vb.* ab-schaffen.
abolition, *n.* Aufhebung, -en *f.*
abominable, *adj.* abscheu'lich.
abominate, *vb.* verab'scheuen.
abomination, *n.* Abscheu, -e *m.*
aboriginal, *adj.* ursprüng'lich, Ur- *(cpds.).*
aborigine, *n.* Ureinwohner, - *m.*

abort, *vb.* fehl-gebären*, ab--treiben*.
abortion, *n.* Fehlgeburt, -en *f.*, Abtreibung, -en *f.*
abortive, *adj.* mißglückt'.
abound, *vb.* im Überfluß vor-handen sein.
about, **1.** *adv. (approximately)* etwa, ungefähr'; *(around)* herum', umher'; *(be a. to)* im Begriff sein*. **2.** *prep. (around)* um; *(concerning)* über.
about-face, *n.* Kehrtwendung -f.
above, **1.** *adj.* obig. **2.** *adv.* oben. **3.** *prep.* über.
aboveboard, *adj.* offen, unver-hoh'len.
abrasion, *n.* Abschaben *nt.*, Abschleifen *nt.*
abrasive, **1.** *n.* Schleifmittel, - *nt.* **2.** *adj.* abschaben, ab-schleifend.
abreast, *adv.* nebeneinan'der, Seite an Seite.
abridge, *vb.* ab-kürzen.
abridgment, *n.* Abkürzung, -en *f.*
abroad, *adv.* im Ausland.
abrupt, *adj.* schroff.
abruptness, *n.* Schroffheit, -en *f.*
abscess, *n.* Eitergeschwulst, -e *f.*
abscond, *vb.* durch-brennen*.
absence, *n.* Abwesenheit, -en *f.*
absent, *adj.* abwesend.
absentee, *n.* Abwesend- *m.*
absent-minded, *adj.* zerstreut'.
absinthe, *n.* Absinth', -e *m.*
absolute, *adj.* absolut', unbe-dingt'.
absoluteness, *n.* Unbedingt'-heit, -en *f.*
absolution, *n.* Absolution', -en *f.*
absolve, *vb.* frei-sprechen*, entla'sten.
absorb, *vb.* auf-saugen, absor-bie'ren.
absorbed, *adj. (fig.)* vertieft'.
absorbent, **1.** *n.* Absorbie'-rungsmittel, - *nt.* **2.** *adj.* aufs-augend.
absorbing, *adj.* aufsaugend; *(interesting)* packend.
absorption, *n.* Absorption', -en *f.*
abstain, *vb.* sich enthal'ten*.
abstemious, *adj.* enthalt'sam.
abstinence, *n.* Enthalt'samkeit, -en *f.*
abstract, **1.** *n. (book, article)* Auszug, ‑e *m.* **2.** *adj.* ab-strakt'. **3.** *vb.* abstrahie'ren.
abstraction, *n.* Abstraktion', -en *f.*
abstruse, *adj.* abstrus'.
absurd, *adj.* unsinnig.
absurdity, *n.* Unsinnigkeit, -en *f.*

abundance, *n.* Überfluß, ‑sse *m.*
abundant, *adj.* Überreich.
abuse, **1.** *vb.* mißbrau'chen; **2.** *n.* Mißbrauch, ‑e *m.*
abusive, *adj.* mißbräuchlich, beschimp'fend.
abut, *vb.* an-grenzen.
abutment, *n.* Angrenzung, -en *f.*
abyss, *n.* Abgrund, ‑e *m.*
academic, *adj.* akade'misch.
academy, *n.* Akademie', -mi'en *f.*, Hochschule, -n *f.*
acanthus, *n.* Akan'thus, -se *m.*
accede, *vb.* ein-willigen.
accelerate, *vb.* beschleu'nigen.
acceleration, *n.* Beschleu'ni-gung, -en *f.*
accelerator, *n.* Gashebel, - *m.*
accent, **1.** *n.* Akzent', -e *m.* **2.** *vb.* beto'nen.
accept, *vb.* an-nehmen*.
acceptability, *n.* Annehmbar-keit, -en *f.*
acceptable, *adj.* annehmbar.
acceptance, *n.* Annahme, -n *f.*
access, *n.* Zugang, ‑e *m.*
accessible, *adj.* zugänglich.
accessory, **1.** *n. (person)* Mit-helfer, - *m.*; *(thing)* Zubehör *nt.* **2.** *adj.* zusätzlich.
accident, *n.* Unfall, ‑e *m.*; *(chance)* Zufall, ‑e *m.*
accidental, *adj.* zufällig.
acclaim, **1.** *n.* Beifall, ‑e *m.* **2.** *vb.* Beifall rufen*.
acclamation, *n.* Zuruf, ‑e *m.*, Beifall, ‑e *m.*
acclimate, *vb.* akklamatisie'-ren.
accommodate, *vb.* an-passen, *(lodge)* unter-bringen*.
accommodating, *adj.* entge'-genkommend.
accommodation, *n.* Anpas-sung, -en *f.*, *(lodging)* Unter-kunft, ‑e *f.*
accompaniment, *n.* Beglei'-tung, -en *f.*
accompanist, *n.* Beglei'ter, - *m.*
accompany, *vb.* beglei'ten.
accomplice, *n.* Mittäter, - *m.*
accomplish, *vb.* leisten.
accomplished, *adj.* vollen'det.
accomplishment, *n.* Leistung, -en *f.*
accord, *n.* Einvernehmen, - *nt.*
accordance, *n.* Überein'stim-mung, -en *f.*
accordingly, *adv.* demgemäß.
according to, *prep.* laut, gemäß.
accordion, *n.* Ziehharmonika, - s *f.*
accost, *vb.* an-sprechen*.
account, *n. (comm.)* Konto, -ten *nt.*, *(narrative)* Bericht', - e *m.*

accountable, *adj.* verant'wort-lich.

accountant, *n.* Buchhalter, - *m.*

accounting, *n.* Buchführung, - en *f.*

accredit, *vb.* akkredit'ren, beglau'bigen.

accrual, *n.* Zuwachs *m.*

accrue, *vb.* an·wachsen*.

accumulate, *vb.* (sich) an·häufen.

accumulation, *n.* Anhäufung, - en *f.*

accumulator, *n.* Ansammler, - *m.*, Akkumula'tor, -to'ren *m.*

accuracy, *n.* Genau'igkeit, -en *f.*

accurate, *adj.* genau'.

accursed, *adj.* verflucht'.

accusation, *n.* Anklage, -n *f.*

accusative, 1. *n.* Akkusativ, -e *m.* **2.** *adj.* anklagend.

accuse, *vb.* an·klagen.

accused, *n.* Angeklagt- *m.&f.*

accuser, *n.* Anklāger, - *m.*

accustom, *vb.* gewöhn'nen.

accustomed, *adj.* gewohnt', gewöhnt'; **(become a. to)** sich gewöh'nen an.

ace, *n.* As, -se *nt.*

acetate, *n.* Acetat', -e *nt.*

acetic, *adj.* ace'tisch.

acetylene, *n.* Acetylen' *nt.*

ache, 1. *n.* Schmerz, -en *m.* **2.** *vb.* weh tun*, schmerzen.

achieve, *vb.* errei'chen.

achievement, *n.* Leistung, -en *f.*

acid, 1. *n.* Säure, -n *f.* **2.** *adj.* sauer.

acidify, *vb.* in Säure verwandeln.

acidity, *n.* Säuerlichkeit, -en *f.*

acknowledge, *vb.* an·erken-nen*, bestä'tigen.

acme, *n.* Höhepunkt, -e *m.*

acne, *n.* Akne, -n *f.*

acolyte, *n.* Altar'diener, - *m.*

acorn, *n.* Eichel, -n *f.*

acoustics, *n.* Aku'stik *f.*

acquaint, *vb.* bekannt'machen.

acquaintance, *n.* Bekannt'-schaft, -en *f.*

acquainted, *adj.* bekannt', vertraut'.

acquiesce, *vb.* ein·willigen, ruhig hin·nehmen*.

acquiescence, *n.* Einwilligung, -en *f.*

acquire, *vb.* erwer'ben*.

acquisition, *n.* Erwer'bung, -en *f.*

acquisitive, *adj.* gewinn'süchtig.

acquit, *vb.* frei·sprechen*.

acquittal, *n.* Freispruch, -e *m.*

acre, *n.* Morgen, - *m.*

acreage, *n.* Flächeninhalt nach Morgen.

acrimonious, *adj.* scharf, bitter.

acrimony, *n.* Bitterkeit, -en *f.*

acrobat, *n.* Akrobat', -en, -en *m.*

across, 1. *prep.* über. **2.** *adv.* hinü'ber, herü'ber.

act, 1. *n. (deed)* Tat, -en *f.; (drama)* Akt, -e *m.; (law)* Gesetz', -e *nt.* **2.** *vb.* handeln; *(stage)* spielen; *(behave)* sich beneh'men*.

acting, 1. *n. (stage)* Schauspielkunst, -e *f.* **2.** *adj.* stellvertretend.

action, *n.* Handlung, -en *f.*

activate, *vb.* aktivie'ren.

activation, *n.* Aktivie'rung, -en *f.*

active, *adj.* tätig, aktiv'.

activity, *n.* Tätigkeit, -en *f.*

actor, *n.* Schauspieler, - *m.*

actress, *n.* Schauspielerin, -nen *f.*

actual, *adj.* tatsächlich.

actuality, *n.* Wirklichkeit, -en *f.*

actually, *adv.* wirklich.

actuary, *n.* Gerichts'schreiber, - *m.*; Versi'cherungsmathe-ma'tiker, - *m.*

acumen, *n.* Scharfsinn *m.*

acupuncture, *n.* Akupunktur', -en, *f.*

acute, *adj.* scharf, scharfsinnig, akut'; *(angle)* spitz.

acuteness, *n.* Schärfe, -n *f.,* Scharfsinnigkeit *f.*

adage, *n.* Sprichwort, -e *nt.*

adamant, *adj.* hartnäckig.

adapt, *vb.* an·passen, bear'bei-ten.

adaptability, *n.* Anpassungsfä-higkeit, -en *f.*

adaptable, *adj.* anpassungsfä-hig.

adaptation, *n.* Anwendung, -en *f.,* Bear'beitung, -en *f.*

adapter, *n.* Bear'beiter, - *m.*

add, *vb.* hinzu'·fügen, addie'ren.

adder, *n.* Natter, -n *f.*

addict, *n.* **(drug a.)** Rauschgift-süchtig- *m.&f.;* **(alcohol a.)** Alkoholsüchtig- *m.&f.*

addition, *n.* Zusatz, -e *m.*

additional, *adj.* zusätzlich.

address, 1. *n. (on letters, etc.)* Adres'se, -n *f.; (speech)* An-sprache, -n *f.* **2.** *vb. (a letter)* adressie'ren; *(a person)* an·sprechen*.

addressee, *n.* Empfäng'er, - *m.*

adenoid, *n.* Nasenwucherung *f.; (pl.)* Poly'pen *pl.*

adept, *adj.* erfah'ren, geschickt'.

adequacy, *n.* Angemessenheit, -en *f.*

adequate, *adj.* angemessen.

adhere, *vb.* haften, fest·hal-ten*.

adherence, *n.* Festhalten *nt.*

adherent, *n.* Anhänger, - *m.*

adhesive, 1. *n.* Klebemittel, - *nt.* **2.** *adj.* anhaftend; **(a. tape)** Leukoplast' *n.nt.*

adieu, *interj.* lebewohl'!, ade'!

adjacent, *adj.* angrenzend.

adjective, *n.* Eigenschaftswort, -er *nt.,* Adjektiv, -e *nt.*

adjoin, *vb.* an·grenzen.

adjourn, *vb.* verta'gen.

adjournment, *n.* Verta'gung, - en *f.*

adjunct, 1. *n.* Zusatz, -e *m.* **2.** *adj.* zusätzlich.

adjust, *vb.* passend machen, berich'tigen, aus·gleichen*.

adjuster, *n.* Ausgleicher, - *m.*

adjustment, *n.* Ausgleichung, - en *f.*

adjutant, *n.* Adjutant', -en, -en *m.*

administer, *vb.* verwal'ten; ertei'len.

administration, *n.* Verwal'tung, -en *f.*

administrative, *adj.* Verwal'-tungs- *(cpds.).*

administrator, *n.* Verwal'ter, - *m.*

admirable, *adj.* bewun'derns-wert.

admiral, *n.* Admiral', -e *m.*

admiralty, *n.* Admiralitāt', -en *f.*

admiration, *n.* Bewun'derung *f.*

admire, *vb.* bewun'dern.

admirer, *n.* Vereh'rer, - *m.*

admissible, *adj.* zulässig.

admission, *n. (entrance)* Ein-tritt, -e *m.; (confession)* Zugeständnis, -se *nt.*

admit, *vb. (permit)* zu·lassen*; *(concede)* zu·gestehen*.

admittance, *n.* Zutritt, -e *m.*

admittedly, *adv.* zugegebener-ma'ßen.

admixture, *n.* Beimischung, -en *f.*

admonish, *vb.* ermah'nen.

admonition, *n.* Ermah'nung, - en *f.*

adolescence, *n.* das heran'-wachsende Alter, Jugendzeit, -en *f.*

adolescent, 1. *n.* der heran'-wachsende Junge, das heran'-wachsende Mädchen. **2.** *adj.* jugendlich.

adopt, *vb.* adoptie'ren, an·nehmen*.

adoption, *n.* Adoption', -en *f.*

adorable, *adj.* reizend, entzück'end.

adoration, *n.* Vereh'rung *f.,* Anbetung *f.*

adore, *vb.* vereh'ren, an·beten.

adorn, *vb.* schmücken, zieren.

adornment, *n.* Verzie'rung, -en *f.*

adrift, *adv.* treibend, Wind und Wellen preisgegeben.

adroit, *adj.* geschickt'.

adulation, *n.* Schmeichelei', -en *f.*

adult, 1. *n.* Erwach'sen- *m.&f.* **2.** *adj.* erwach'sen.

adulterate, *vb.* verfäl'schen.

adultery, *n.* Ehebruch, -e *m.*

advance, 1. *n.* Fortschritt, -e *m.; (mil.)* Vormarsch, -e *m.; (pay)* Vorschuß, -sse; **(in a.)**

im voraus'. **2.** *vb.* Fortschritte machen; *(mil.)* vor•rücken; *(pay)* voraus'•zahlen; *(promote)* beför'dern.

advanced, *adj.* fortgeschritten, modern'.

advancement, *n.* Förderung, -en *f.*, Beför'derung, -en *f.*

advantage, *n.* Vorteil, -e *m.*

advantageous, *adj.* vorteilhaft.

advent, *n.* Ankunft, ̃e *f.*; *(eccl.)* Advent' *m.*

adventure, *n.* Abenteuer, - *nt.*

adventurer, *n.* Abenteurer, - *m.*

adventurous, *adj.* abenteuerlich.

adverb, *n.* Abverb', -en *nt.*, Umstandswort, ̃er *nt.*

adverbial, *adj.* adverbial'.

adversary, *n.* Gegner, -m.

adverse, *adj.* ungünstig, nachteilig.

adversity, *n.* Mißgeschick, -e *nt.*

advertise, *vb.* an•zeigen, annoncie'ren, Rekla'me machen.

advertisement, *n.* Annon'ce, -n *f.*, Inserat, -e *nt.*, Rekla'me, -n *f.*

advertiser, *n.* Inserent', -en, - en *m.*, Anzeiger, -m.

advertising, *n.* Rekla'me, -n *f.*

advice, *n.* Rat *m.*

advisability, *n.* Ratsamkeit *f.*

advisable, *adj.* ratsam.

advise, *vb.* raten*, bera'ten*.

advisedly, *adv.* absichtlich.

adviser, *n.* Bera'ter, -m.

advocacy, *n.* Befür'wortung *f.*

advocate, 1. *n.* Anwalt, ̃e *m.* **2.** *vb.* vertei'digen, befür'worten.

aerate, *vb.* mit Luft vermen'gen.

aerial, 1. *n.* Anten'ne, -n *f.* **2.** *adj.* Luft- *(cpds.).*

aeronautics, *n.* Aeronau'tik *f.*

aesthetic, *adj.* ästhe'tisch.

aesthetics, *n.* Ästhe'tik *f.*

afar, *adv.* von ferne.

affability, *n.* Freundlichkeit *f.*

affable, *adj.* freundlich.

affair, *n.* Angelegenheit, -en *f.*; Affä're, -n *f.*

affect, 1. *n.* Affekt', -e *m.* **2.** *vb.* wirken auf.

affectation, *n.* Affektiert'heit, - en *f.*

affected, *adj.* betrof'fen; *(unnatural)* affektiert'.

affection, *n.* Zuneigung, -en *f.*, Liebe, -n *f.*

affectionately, *adv. (letter)* mit herzlichen Grüßen.

affidavit, *n.* eidesstattliche Erklä'rung, -en *f.*

affiliate, *vb.* an•gliedern.

affiliation, *n.* Angliederung, - en *f.*

affinity, *n.* Verwandt'schaft, - en *f.*

affirm, *vb. (declare)* erklä'ren;

(confirm) bestä'tigen; *(say yes to)* beja'hen.

affirmation, *n.* Bestä'tigung, - en *f.*; Beja'hung, -en *f.*

affirmative, *adj.* beja'hend.

affix, 1. *n. (gram.)* Affix, -e *nt.* **2.** *vb.* an•heften; *(add on)* bei•fügen.

afflict, *vb.* plagen.

affliction, *n.* Plage, -n *f.*, Leid *nt.*

affluence, *n.* Reichtum, ̃er *m.*

affluent, *adj.* reich.

afford, *vb.* gewäh'ren; *(have the means to)* sich leisten.

affront, 1. *n.* Belei'digung, -en *f.* **2.** *vb.* belei'digen.

afield, *adv.* (far a.) weit entfernt'.

afire, *adv.* in Flammen.

afraid, *adj.* bange; **(be a. of)** sich fürchten vor.

Africa, *n.* Afrika, *nt.*

African, 1. *n.* Afrika'ner, - *m.* **2.** *adj.* afrika'nisch.

aft, *adv.* achtern.

after, 1. *prep.* nach, hinter. **2.** *conj.* nachdem'.

aftermath, *n.* Nachernte, -n *f.*

afternoon, *n.* Nachmittage, -e *m.*

afterward(s), *adv.* hinterher', nachher.

again, *adv.* wieder, noch einmal.

against, *prep.* gegen.

age, 1. *n.* Alter, - *nt.*; *(era)* Zeitalter, - *nt.* **2.** *vb.* altern.

aged, *adj.* bejahrt'.

ageism, *n.* Vorurteil gegen, Benachteiligung von älteren Menschen.

ageless, *adj.* zeitlos.

agency, *n.* Vertre'tung, -en *f.*, Agentur', -en *f.*

agenda, *n.* Tagesordnung, -en *f.*

agent, *n.* Vertre'ter, -m.

aggrandizement, *n.* Machterweiterung, -en *f.*

aggravate, *vb.* verschlim'mern, erschwe'ren.

aggravation, *n.* Verschlim'merung, -en *f.*

aggregate, 1. *n.* Aggregat', -e *nt.* **2.** *adj.* Gesamt- *(cpds.).*

aggregation, *n.* Anhäufung, - en *f.*

aggression, *n.* Angriff, -e *m.*, Aggression', -en *f.*

aggressive, *adj.* aggresiv'.

aggressiveness, *n.* Angriffslust *f.*

aggressor, *n.* Angreifer, - *m.*

aghast, *adj.* entsetzt'.

agile, *adj.* flink, behen'd(e).

agility, *n.* Behen'digkeit *f.*

agitate, *vb.* bewe'gen, beun'ruhigen.

agitation, *n.* Bewe'gung, -en *f.*, Beun'ruhigung, -en *f.*

agitator, *n.* Hetzredner, -m.

agnostic, 1. *n.* Agno'stiker, - *m.* **2.** *adj.* agno'stisch.

ago, *adv.* vor.

agony, *n.* Qual, -en *f.*

agree, *vb.* überein'•stimmen.

agreeable, *adj.* angenehm.

agreement, *n.* Überein'stimmung, -en *f.*

agricultural, *adj.* landwirtschaftlich.

agriculture, *n.* Landwirtschaft *f.*

ahead, *adv.* voraus'; **(straight a.)** gera'de aus.

aid, *n.* Hilfe, -n *f.* **2.** *vb.* helfen*.

aide, *n.* Adjutant', -en, -en *m.*

ail, *vb.* kranken.

ailment, *n.* Krankheit, -en *f.*

aim, 1. *n. (goal)* Ziel, -e *nt.*; *(purpose)* Zweck, -e *m.* **2.** *vb.* zielen.

aimless, *adj.* ziellos.

air, 1. *n.* Luft, ̃e *f.* **2.** *vb.* lüften.

airbag, (automobile) Luftsack, ̃e *m.*

air base, *n.* Luftstützpunkt, -e *m.*

airborne, *adj.* in der Luft; **(a. troops)** Luftlandetruppen *pl.*

air-condition, *vb.* klimatisie'ren, mit Klima-Anlage verse'hen*.

air-conditioned, *adj.* klimatisiert', mit Klima-Anlage verse'hen.

air-conditioning, *n.* Klima-Anlage, -n *f.*

aircraft, *n.* Flugzeug, -e *nt.*

aircraft carrier, *n.* Flugzeugträger, -, *m.*, Flugzeugmut'terschiff, -e *nt.*

air line, *n.* Luftlinie, -n *f.*

air liner, *n.* Verkehrs'flugzeug, -e *nt.*

air mail, *n.* Luftpost *f.*

airplane, *n.* Flugzeug, -e *nt.*

air pollution, *n.* Luftverpestung, *f.*

airport, *n.* Flughafen, ̃ *m.*

air pressure, *n.* Luftdruck, -e *m.*

air raid, *n.* Luftangriff, -e *m.*

airsick, *adj.* luftkrank (̃).

airtight, *adj.* luftdicht.

airy, *adj.* luftig.

aisle, *n.* Gang, ̃e *m.*; *(church)* Chorgang, ̃e *m.*

ajar, *adj.* angelehnt, halb offen.

akin, *adj.* verwandt'.

alarm, 1. *n.* Alarm', -e *m.* **2.** *vb.* alarmie'ren, beun'ruhigen.

albino, *n.* Albi'no, -s *m.*

album, *n.* Album, -ben *nt.*

albumen, *n.* Eiweißstoff, -e *m.*, Albu'men *nt.*

alcohol, *n.* Alkohol, -e *m.*

alcoholic, 1. *n.* Alkoho'liker, - *m.* **2.** *adj.* alkoho'lisch.

alcove, *n.* Alko'ven, - *m.*

ale, *n.* englisches Bier, Ale *nt.*

alert, 1. *n.* Alarm', -e *m.*, Vorwarnung, -en *f.* **2.** *adj.* aufmerksam. **3.** *vb.* alarmie'ren.

alfalfa, *n.* Alfal'fa *f.*

algebra, *n.* Algebra *f.*

algebraic, *adj.* algebra'isch.

alias, *adv.* alias.

alibi, *n.* Alibi, -s *nt.*

alien, 1. *n.* Ausländer, - *m.* **2.** *adj.* fremd, ausländisch.

alienate, *vb.* entfrem'den.

alight, *vb.* sich nieder-lassen*; (dismount)* ab-steigen*.

align, *vb.* aus-richten; *(ally)* zusam'men-tun*.

alike, *adj.* gleich.

alive, *adj.* leben'dig; **(be a.)** leben.

alkali, *n.* Alka'li *nt.*

alkaline, *adj.* alka'lisch.

all, *adj.* aller, -es, -e; **(above a.)** vor allem; **(a. at once)** auf einmal; **(a. the same)** gleich; **(a. of you)** Sie alle; **(not at a.)** gar nicht.

allay, *vb.* beru'higen, stillen.

allegation, *n.* Behaup'tung, -en *f.*

allege, *vb.* an-führen, behaupten.

allegiance, *n.* Treue *f.,* Gehor'sam *m.*

allegory, *n.* Allegorie', -i'en *f.;* Sinnbild, -er *nt.*

allergy, *n.* Allergie', -i'en *f.*

alleviate, *vb.* erleich'tern, lindern.

alley, *n.* Gasse, -n *f.;* Durchgang, -e *m.;* **(blind a.)** Sackgasse, -n *f.*

alliance, *n.* Bündnis, -se *nt.;* Allianz', -en *f.*

allied, *adj.* verbün'det; *(related)* verwandt'.

alligator, *n.* Alliga'tor, -to'ren *m.*

allocate, *vb.* zu-teilen.

allot, *vb.* zu-weisen*; zu-teilen.

allotment, *n.* Zuweisung, -en *f.*

allow, *vb.* erlau'ben, gestat'ten.

allowance, *n.* *(money)* Taschengeld, -er *nt.;* *(permission)* Erlaub'nis, -se *f.;* **(make a.s for)** Rücksicht nehmenauf*.

alloy, 1. *n.* Legie'rung, -en *f.* **2.** *vb.* legie'ren.

all right, *interj.* gut, schön, in Ordnung.

allude, *vb.* hin-weisen*, anspielen.

allure, 1. *n.* Charme *m.* **2.** *vb.* verlock'en.

allusion, *n.* Anspielung, -en *f.*

ally, 1. *n.* Verbün'det- *m.,* Alliiert'- *m.* **2.** *vb.* verbün'den.

almanac, *n.* Almanach, -e *m.*

almighty, *adj.* allmäch'tig.

almond, *n.* Mandel, -n *f.*

almost, *adv.* beinahe, fast.

alms, *n.* Almosen, - *nt.*

aloft, *adv.* hochoben; empor'.

alone, *adv.* allein'; **(leave a.)** in Ruhe lassen*.

along, 1. *adv.* entlang'; **(come a.)** mit-kommen*. **2.** *prep.* entlang', längs.

alongside, *prep.* neben.

aloof, 1. *adj.* gleichgültig. **2.** *adv.* abseits.

aloud, *adv.* laut.

alpaca, *n.* Alpa'ka, -s *nt.*

alphabet, *n.* Alphabet', -e *nt.*

alphabetical, *adj.* alphabe'tisch.

alphabetize, *vb.* alphabetisie'ren.

Alps, *n.pl.* Alpen *pl.*

already, *adv.* schon.

also, *adv.* auch.

altar, *n.* Altar', -e *m.*

alter, *vb.* ändern.

alteration, *n.* Änderung, -en *f.*

alternate, 1. *n.* Stellvertreter, - *m.* **2.** *adj.* alternativ'. **3.** *vb.* ab-wechseln.

alternating current, *n.* Wechselstrom, -e *m.*

alternative, 1. *n.* Alternati've, -n *f.* **2.** *adj.* alternativ'.

although, *conj.* obwohl', obgleich'.

altitude, *n.* Höhe, -n *f.*

alto, *n.* Altstimme, -n *f.*

altogether, *adv.* völlig, ganz und gar; alles in allem.

altruism, *n.* Altruis'mus *m.*

alum, *n.* Alaun', -e *m.*

aluminum, *n.* Alumi'nium *nt.*

always, *adv.* immer.

amalgamate, *vb.* amalgamie'ren.

amass, *vb.* an-sammeln.

amateur, *n.* Amateur', -e *m.*

amaze, *vb.* erstau'nen.

amazement, *n.* Erstau'nen *nt.*

amazing, *adj.* erstaun'lich.

ambassador, *n.* Botschafter, - *m.,* Gesandt'- *m.*

amber, *n.* Bernstein, -e *m.*

ambiguity, *n.* Zweideutigkeit, -en *f.*

ambiguous, *adj.* zweideutig.

ambition, *n.* Ehrgeiz *m.,* Ambition', -en *f.*

ambitious, *adj.* ehrgeizig.

ambulance, *n.* Krankenwagen, - *m.,* Krankenauto, -s *nt.*

ambush, 1. *n.* Hinterhalt *m.* **2.** *vb.* aus dem Hinterhalt überfallen*.

ameliorate, *vb.* verbes'sern.

amenable, *adj.* zugänglich.

amend, *vb.* verbes'sern, ergänzen.

amendment, *n.* Gesetz'abänderung, -en *f.,* Verfas'sungszusatz, -e *m.*

amenity, *n.* Annehmlichkeit, -en *f.*

America, *n.* Ame'rika *nt.*

American, 1. *n.* Amerika'ner, - *m.* **2.** *adj.* amerika'nisch.

amethyst, *n.* Amethyst', -e *m.*

amiable, *adj.* liebenswürdig.

amicable, *adj.* freundschaftlich.

amid, *prep.* inmit'ten.

amidships, *adv.* mittschiffs.

amiss, *adj.* los, schief; **(take a.)** übel-nehmen*.

amity, *n.* Freundschaft, -en *f.*

ammonia, *n.* Ammoniak *nt.;* **(household a.)** Salmiak'geist *m.*

ammunition, *n.* Munition', -en *f.*

amnesia, *n.* Amnesie' *f.*

amnesty, *n.* Amnestie', -i'en *f.*

amniocentesis, *n.* Amniokent'e'se *f.*

amoeba, *n.* Amö'be, -n *f.*

among, *prep.* unter, zwischen, bei.

amorous, *adj.* verliebt'.

amortize, *vb.* tilgen, amortisie'ren.

amount, 1. *n.* *(sum)* Betrag', -e *m.;* **(large a.)** Menge, -n *f.* **2.** *vb.* **(a. to)** betra'gen*.

ampere, *n.* Ampere, - *(pron.* Ampär') *nt.*

amphibian, 1. *n.* Amphi'bie, -n *f.* **2.** *adj.* amphi'bisch.

amphibious, *adj.* amphi'bisch.

amphitheater, *n.* Amphi'theater, - *nt.*

ample, *adj.* reichlich.

amplify, *vb.* *(enlarge)* erweitern; *(make louder)* verstärken; *(state more fully)* ausführ'licher dar-stellen.

amputate, *vb.* amputie'ren.

amuse, *vb.* belus'tigen, amüsie'ren.

amusement, *n.* Unterhal'tung, -en *f.;* Belus'tigung, -en *f.*

an, *art.* ein, -, -e.

anachronism, *n.* Anachronis'mus, -men *m.*

analogical, *adj.* analo'gisch.

analogous, *adj.* analog'.

analogy, *n.* Analogie', -i'en *f.*

analysis, *n.* Analy'se, -n *f.*

analyst, *n.* Analy'tiker, - *m.*

analytic, *adj.* analy'tisch.

analyze, *vb.* analysie'ren.

anarchy, *n.* Anarchie', -i'en *f.*

anatomy, *n.* Anatomie', -i'en *f.*

ancestor, *n.* Vorfahr, -en, *m.*

ancestral, *adj.* Stamm- *(cpds.).*

ancestry, *n.* Abstammung, -en *f.*

anchor, 1. *n.* Anker, - *m.* **2.** *vb.* veran'kern.

anchovy, *n.* Sardel'le, -n *f.*

ancient, *adj.* alt, uralt.

and, *conj.* und.

anecdote, *n.* Anekdo'te, -n *f.*

anemia, *n.* Blutarmut *f.*

anemic, *adj.* blutarm.

anesthesia, *n.* Anästhesie' *f.*

anesthetic, 1. *n.* Narko'se, -n *f.,* Betäu'bungsmittel, - *nt.* **2.** *adj.* betäu'bend, narko'tisch.

anew, *adv.* aufs neue, von neuem.

angel, *n.* Engel, - *m.*

anger, *n.* Zorn *m.,* Ärger *m.*

angle, 1. *n.* *(geom.)* Winkel, - *m.;* *(point of view)* Gesichtspunkt, -e *m.* **2.** *vb. (fish)* angeln.

angry, *adj.* böse, ärgerlich; **(be a.)** sich ärgern.

anguish, *n.* Qual, -en *f.*

angular, *adj.* eckig.

animal, 1. *n.* Tier, -e *nt.* **2.** *adj.* tierisch.

animate, *vb.* bele'ben.

animated, *adj.* lebhaft.

animated cartoon, n. Trickfilm, -e m.

animation, n. Lebhaftigkeit, -en f.

animosity, n. Erbit'terung, -en f.

ankle, n. Fessel, -n f.; Fessel-gelenk, -e nt.

annals, n.pl. Anna'len pl.

annex, 1. n. Anhang, ⸗e m.; (building) Nebengebäude, - nt. 2. vb. annektie'ren.

annexation, n. Annektie'rung, -en f.

annihilate, vb. vernich'ten.

anniversary, n. Jahrestag, -e m.

annotate, vb. mit Anmer-kungen verse'hen*, annotie'-ren.

announce, vb. an-kündigen, be-kannt'geben*.

announcement, n. Bekannt'-machung, -en f.

announcer, n. Ansager, - m.

annoy, vb. beläs'tigen, ärgern.

annoyance, n. Ärger m.; Belä-s'tigung, -en f.

annual, 1. n. Jahrbuch, ⸗er nt. 2. adj. jährlich.

annuity, n. jährliche Rente, -n f.

annul, vb. annullie'ren.

anoint, vb. salben.

anomaly, n. Anomalie', -i'en f.

anonymous, adj. anonym'.

another, adj. (different) ein an-der-; (additional) noch ein; (one a.) sich, einan'der.

answer, 1. n. Antwort, -en f. 2. vb. antworten, beant'worten.

answerable, adj. beant'wort-bar; verant'wortlich.

ant, n. Ameise, -n f.

antagonism, Widerstreit, -e m.

antagonist, n. Widersacher, - m., Gegner, - m.

antagonistic, adj. widerstrei'-tend.

antagonize, vb. vor den Kopf stoßen*.

antarctic, 1. n. Antark'tis, f. 2. adj. antark'tisch.

antecedent, 1. n. (gram.) Be-zie'hungswort, ⸗er nt. 2. adj. vorher'gehend.

antelope, n. Antilo'pe, -n f.

antenna, n. (radio) Anten'ne, -n f.; (insect) Fühler, - m.

anterior, adj. vorder-.

anteroom, n. Vorzimmer, - nt.

anthem, Hymne, -n f.; (na-tional a.) National'hymne, -n f.

anthology, n. Anthologie', -i'en f.

anthracite, n. Anthrazit' nt.

anthropologist, n. Anthropo-lo'ge, -n, -n m.

anthropology, n. Anthropolo-gie' -i'en f.

antiaircraft, adj. Flak (cpds.).

antibody, n. Antikörper, - m.

antic, n. Posse, -n f.; Mätz-chen, - nt.

anticipate, vb. vorweg'-neh-men*; erwar'ten.

anticipation, n. Erwar'tung, -en f.

anticlimax, n. enttäu'schende Wendung, -en f.

antidote, n. Gegengift, -e nt.

antinuclear, adj. antinuklear'.

antiquated, adj. veral'tet.

antique, adj. antik'.

antiquity, n. Anti'ke f.; Alter-tum, ⸗er nt.

antiseptic, 1. n. antisep'tisches Mittel nt. 2. adj. antisep'tisch.

antisocial, adj. antisozial'.

antitoxin, n. Gegengift, -e nt.

antlers, n.pl. Geweih', -e nt.

anvil, n. Amboß, -sse m.

anxiety, n. Angst, ⸗e f.; Be-sorg'nis, -se f.

anxious, adj. besorgt'; ängst-lich.

any, adj. irgendein, -, -e; ir-gendwelcher, -es, -e; jeder, -, es, -e; (not a.) kein, -, -e.

anybody, pron. jemand, ir-gendjemand; (not . . . a.) nie-mand.

anyhow, adv. sowieso'.

anyone, pron. jemand, irgend-jemand; (not . . . a.) niemand.

anything, pron. etwas, irgend-etwas; (not . . . a.) nichts.

anyway, adv. sowieso'.

anywhere, adv (location) ir-gendwo; (direction) irgend-wohin.

apart, adv. abseits, beisei'te; (a. from) abgesehen von; (take a.) auseinan'der-neh-men*.

apartheid, n. Apart'heid f.

apartment, n. Mietswohnung, -en f.

ape, 1. n. Affe, -n, -n m. 2. vb. nach-affen.

aperture, n. Öffnung, -en f.

apex, n. Gipfel, - m.

aphorism, n. Aphoris'mus, -men m.

apiece, adv. (ten dollars a.) je zehn Dollar.

apologetic, adj. entschul'di-gend.

apologize, vb. sich entschul'di-gen.

apology, n. Entschul'digung, -en f.

apoplexy, n. Schlaganfall, ⸗e m.

apostle, n. Apos'tel, - m.

appall, vb. entset'zen.

apparatus, n. Apparat', -e m.; Ausrüstung, -en f.

apparel, n. Kleidung, -en f.

apparent, adj. (visible) sicht-bar; (clear) klar; (obvious) of-fensichtlich; (probable) scheinbar.

apparition, n. Erschei'nung, -en f.; Gespenst', -er, nt.

appeal, 1. n. (request) Bitte, -n f.; (charm) Reiz, -e m.; (law) Beru'fung, -en f. 2. vb. (law) Beru'fung ein-legen, ap-

pellie'ren; (a. to, turn to) sich wenden* an; (a. to, please) gefal'len*.

appear, vb. (seem) scheinen*; (come into view) erschei'nen*.

appearance, n. Erschei'nung, -en f., Anschein, -e m.

appease, vb. beschwich'tigen.

appeasement, n. Beschwich'ti-gung, -en f.

appendage, n. Anhang, ⸗e m.

appendectomy, n. Blinddarm-operation -en f.

appendicitis, n. Blinddarment-zündung, -en f.

appendix, n. Anhang, ⸗e m.; (med.) Blinddarm, ⸗e m.

appetite, n. Appetit' m.

appetizer, n. Vorgericht, -e nt.

appetizing, adj. appetit'lich; lecker.

applaud, vb. applaudie'ren, Beifall klatschen.

applause, n. Beifall, ⸗e m.

apple, n. Apfel, ⸗ m.

applesauce, n. Apfelmus nt.

appliance, n. Gerät', -e nt.

applicable, adj. anwendbar.

applicant, n. Bewer'ber, - m.

application, n. (request) Be-wer'bung, -en f.; (use) An-wendung, -en f.

appliqué, adj. (a. work) Appli-kations'stickerei, -en f.

apply, vb. (make use of) an-wenden*; (request) sich be-wer'ben*.

appoint, vb. ernen'nen*.

appointment, n. (to a position) Ernen'nung, -en f.; (doctor's) Anmeldung, -en f.; (date) Verab'redung, -en f.

apportion, vb. proportional'-vertei'len; zu-teilen.

appraisal, n. Abschätzung, -en f.

appraise, vb. ab-schätzen.

appreciable, adj. beträcht'lich.

appreciate, vb. schätzen; an-er-kennen*.

appreciation, n. Anerkennung, -en f.

apprehend, vb. (grasp) erfas'-sen; (arrest) verhaf'ten; (fear) befürch'ten.

apprehension, n. (worry) Be-sorg'nis, -se f.; (arrest) Ver-haf'tung, -en f.

apprehensive, adj. besorgt'.

apprentice, n. Lehrling, -e m.

apprise, vb. benach'richtigen.

approach, 1. n. (nearing) Annä-herung, -en f.; (access) Zu-gang, ⸗e m. 2. vb. (come nearer) sich nähern; (turn to) sich wenden* an.

approachable, adj. zugänglich.

approbation, n. Geneh'migung, -en f.

appropriate, 1. adj. angemes-sen, passend. 2. vb. (seize) sich an-eignen; (vote funds) bewilligen.

appropriation, n. (seizure) An-

eignung, -en f.; (approval) Be-
wil'ligung, -en f.

approval, n. Zustimmung,
-en f., Einwilligung, -en f.

approve, vb. zu·stimmen, geneh'migen.

approximate, 1. vb. sich nähern. **2.** adj. annähernd.

approximately, adv. ungefähr,
etwa.

approximation, n. Annäherung, -en f.

apricot, n. Apriko'se, -n f.

April, n. April' m.

apron, n. Schürze, -n f.

apropos, 1. adj. treffend. **2.**
prep. hinsichtlich.

apt, adj. (fitting) passend;
(likely) geneigt'; (able) fähig.

aptitude, n. Fähigkeit, -en f.

aquarium, n. Aqua'rium,
-ien nt.

aquatic, adj. Wasser- (cpds.).

aqueduct, n. Wasserleitung, -
en f.

Arab, 1. n. Araber, -n m. **2.** adj.
ara'bisch.

Arabian, adj. ara'bisch.

Arabic, adj. ara'bisch.

arable, adj. bestell'bar.

arbiter, n. Schlichter, - m.

arbitrary, adj. willkürlich.

arbitrate, vb. schlichten.

arbitration, n. Schlichtung,
-en f.

arbitrator, n. Schlichter, - m.

arbor, n. Laube, -n f.

arc, n. Bogen, ·· m.

arcade, n. Arka'de, -n f.

arch, n. Bogen, (··) m.; (instep)
Spann, -e m.

archaeology, n. Altertumskunde f., Archäologie' f.

archaic, adj. archa'isch, altertümlich.

archbishop, n. Erzbischof, ··e
m.

archdiocese, n. Erzdiözese,
-n f.

archduke, n. Erzherzog, ··e m.

archer, n. Bogenschütze, -n, -n
m.

archery, n. Bogenschießen nt.

architect, n. Architekt', -en, -
en m.

architectural, adj. architekto'-
nisch.

architecture, n. Architektur',
-en f.

archives, n. Archiv', e nt.

archway, n. Torbogen, ··m.

arctic, 1. n. Arktis f. **2.** adj.
arktisch.

ardent, adj. eifrig, inbrünstig.

ardor, n. Eifer m., Inbrunst f.

arduous, adj. mühsam.

area, n. Fläche, -n f., Gebiet',
-e nt.

area code, n. (phone) Vorwahlnummer, -n f.

arena, n. Are'na, -nen f.

Argentina, n. Argenti'nien nt.

argue, vb. argumentie'ren;
(quarrel) sich streiten*.

argument, n. Argument', -e nt.

argumentative, adj. streitsüchtig.

aria, n. Arie, -n f.

arid, adj. dürr, trocken.

arise, vb. auf·stehen*, sich erhe'ben*; (come into being)
entste'hen*.

aristocracy, n. Aristokratie', -
i'en f.

aristocrat, n. Aristokrat', -en,
-en m.

aristocratic, adj. aristokra'-
tisch.

arithmetic, n. Rechnen nt.,
Arithmetik' f.

ark, n. Arche, -n f.; (Noah's a.)
Arche Noah.

arm, 1. n. Arm, -e m.; (weapon)
Waffe, -n f. **2.** v. bewaff'nen,
rüsten.

armament, n. Bewaff'nung, -
en f.; (weapons) Waffen pl.

armchair, n. Lehnstuhl, ··e m.

armful, n. Menge, -n f.

armhole, n. Armloch, ··er nt.

armistice, n. Waffenstill'stand
m.

armor, Rüstung, -en f., Panzer,
- m.

armored, adj. gepan'zert; Pan-
zer- (cpds.).

armory, n. Exerzier'halle, -n f.;
Waffenfabrik, -en f.

armpit, n. Achselhöhle, -n f.

arms, n.pl. Waffen pl.

army, n. Heer, -e nt., Armee',
-me'en f.

aroma, n. Aro'ma, -s nt.

aromatic, adj. würzig.

around, 1. adv. herum'; (approximately) etwa, ungefähr.
2. prep. um.

arouse, vb. (excite) erre'gen;
(waken) wecken.

arraign, vb. richterlich vor·
führen.

arrange, vb. arrangie'ren, ein·
richten; (agree) verein'baren.

arrangement, n. Anordnung, -
en f.

array, 1. n. Anordnung, -en f.;
(fig.) Menge, -n f. **2.** vb. ordnen.

arrears, n.pl. Schulden pl.; (in
a.) in Rückstand.

arrest, 1. n. (law) Verhaf'tung,
-en f. **2.** vb. (law) verhaf'ten;
(stop) an·halten*.

arrival, n. Ankunft, ··e f.

arrive, vb. an·kommen*.

arrogance, n. Anmaßung,
-en f., Arroganz, -en f.

arrogant, adj. anmaßend, arrogant'.

arrow, n. Pfeil, -e m.

arsenal, n. Waffenlager, - nt.

arsenic, n. Arsen' nt.

arson, n. Brandstiftung, -en f.

art, n. Kunst, ··e f.

arterial, adj. Arte'rien- (cpds.);
(a. highway) Hauptverkehrs'-
straße, -n f.

arteriosclerosis, n. Arte'rien-
verkalkung, -en f.

artful, adj. kunstvoll; (sly)
schlau.

arthritis, n. Arthri'tis f.

artichoke, n. Artischock'e,
-n f.

article, n. Arti'kel, - m.

articulate, 1. vb. (utter) artikulie'ren; (join) zusam'men·
fügen. **2.** adj. deutlich.

articulation, n. Artikulie'rung,
-en f.

artifice, n. List, -en f.

artificial, adj. künstlich.

artificiality, n. Künstlichkeit, -
en f.

artillery, n. Artillerie', -i'en f.

artisan, n. Handwerker, - m.

artist, n. Künstler, - m.

artistic, adj. künstlerisch.

artistry, n. Künstlertum nt.

artless, adj. kunstlos.

as, conj.&adv. (when) wie, als;
(because) da; (a. if) als ob;
(with X a. Hamlet) mit X als
Hamlet; (a. big a.) so groß
wie; (just a. big a.) ebenso
groß wie; (he a. well a. I) er
sowohl wie ich.

asbestos, n. Asbest', -e m.

ascend, vb. (intr.) steigen*; (tr.)
bestei'gen*.

ascent, n. Aufstieg, -e m.

ascertain, vb. fest·stellen.

ascetic, 1. n. Asket', -en, -en m.
2. adj. aske'tisch.

ascribe, vb. zu·schreiben*.

ash, n. Asche, -n f.; (tree)
Esche, -n f.

ashamed, adj. beschämt'; (be
a.) sich schämen.

ashen, adj. aschgrau.

ashes, n.pl. Asche f.

ashore, adv. an Land.

ash tray, n. Aschenbecher,
- m., Aschbecher, - m.

Asia, n. Asien nt.

Asian, 1. n. Asiat', -en, -en m.
2. adj. asia'tisch.

aside, adv. beisei'te; (a. from)
außer.

ask, vb. (question) fragen; (request) bitten*; (demand) ver-
langen.

asleep, adj. schlafend; (be a.)
schlafen*.

asparagus, n. Spargel, - m.

aspect, n. Anblick, -e m.; (fig.)
Gesichts'punkt, -e m.

aspersion, n. Verleum'dung, -
en f.

asphalt, n. Asphalt', -e m.

asphyxiate, vb. ersticˈk'en.

aspirant, Anwärter, - m.

aspirate, 1. n. Hauchlaut, -e
m., **2.** adj. aspiriert'. **3.** vb.
aspirie'ren.

aspiration, n. Aspiration',
-en f., Bestre'bung, -en f.

aspire, vb. streben.

aspirin, n. Aspirin' nt.

ass, n. Esel, - m.

assail, vb. an·greifen*.

assailable, adj. angreifbar.

assailant, n. Angreifer, - m

assassin, n. Attentä'ter, - m., Mörder, - m.

assassinate, vb. ermor'den.

assassination, n. Ermor'dung, -en f., Attentat', -e nt.

assault, 1. n. Angriff, -e m.; (law) tätliche Belei'digung, -en f. **2.** vb. an·greifen*.

assay, 1. n. Probe, -n f. **2.** vb. prüfen.

assemblage, n. Versamm'lung, -en f.

assemble, vb. versam'meln; (tech.) montie'ren.

assembly, n. Versamm'lung, -en f.; (tech.) Monta'ge, -n f.

assent, 1. n. Zustimmung, -en f. **2.** vb. zu·stimmen.

assert, vb. behaup'ten.

assertion, n. Behaup'tung, -en f.

assertive, adj. bestimmt'.

assess, vb. ein·schätzen*.

assessor, n. Steuerabschätzer, - m.

asset, n. Vorzug, -e m.; (comm.) Guthaben, - nt.

asseverate, vb. beteu'ern.

assiduous, adj. emsig.

assign, vb. zu·teilen, zu·weisen*; (homework) auf·geben*.

assignable, bestimm'bar.

assignation, n. Anweisung, -en f.; (tryst) Stelldichein, - nt.

assignment, n. Anweisung, -en f.; (homework) Aufgabe, - n f.

assimilate, vb. an·gleichen*, assimilie'ren.

assimilation, n. Angleichung, -en f., Assimilie'rung, -en f.

assimilative, adj. angleichend.

assist, vb. unterstüt'zen, helfen*.

assistance, n. Unterstüt'zung, -en f., Hilfe, -n f.

assistant, 1. n. Gehil'fe, -n, -n m., Assistent', -en, -en m. **2.** adj. Hilfs- (cpds.) stellvertretend.

associate, 1. n. Partner, - m. **2.** vb. verkeh'ren, assoziie'ren.

association, n. Verbin'dung, -en f., Verei'nigung, -en f.

assonance, n. Assonanz', -en f.

assort, vb. sortie'ren.

assorted, adj. verschie'den.

assortment, n. Auswahl, -en f.

assuage, vb. beschwich'tigen.

assume, vb. an·nehmen*; (arrogate) sich an·maßen.

assuming adj. anmaßend; (a. that) angenommen, daß.

assumption, n. Annahme, -n f.; (eccles.) Himmelfahrt f.

assurance, n. Versi'cherung, -en f., Zusicherung, -en f.

assure, vb. versi'chern, zu·sichern.

assured, adj. sicher, zuversichtlich.

aster, n. Aster, -n f.

asterisk, n. Sternchen, - nt.

asthma, n. Asthma nt.

astigmatism, n. Astigmatis'mus, -men m.

astonish, vb. erstau'nen; (be astonished) staunen.

astonishment, n. Erstau'nen, - nt.

astound, vb. erstau'nen.

astray, adj. irre; (go a.) sich verir'ren, auf Abwege gera'ten*.

astringent, adj. gefäß'spannend, hautstraffend, adstringie'rend.

astrology, n. Astrologie', -i'en f.

astronaut, n. Astronaut', -en, -en m.

astronomy, n. Astronomie', -i'en f.

astute, adj. scharf (-), schlau.

asylum, n. (refuge) Asyl', -e nt.; (institution) Anstalt, -en f.

at, prep. an; (at home) zu Hause.

atheist, n. Atheist', -en, -en m.

athlete, n. Athlet', -en, -en m., Sportler, - m.

athletic, adj. athle'tisch, sportlich.

athletics, n. Sport, -e m.

Atlantic, 1. n. Atlan'tik m. **2.** adj. atlan'tisch.

Atlantic Ocean, n. Atlan'tik m.

atlas, n. Atlas, -lan'ten m.

atmosphere, n. Atmosphä're, - n f.

atmospheric, adj. atmosphä'risch.

atoll, n. Atoll', -e nt.

atom, n. Atom', -e nt.

atomic, adj. atomar'; Atom'- (cpds.).

atomize, vb. atomisie'ren.

atone, vb. büßen, sühnen.

atonement, n. Buße, -n f., Sühne, -n f.

atrocious, adj. entsetz'lich, grausam.

atrocity, n. Grausamkeit, -en f.

atrophy, n. Atrophie', -i'en f.

attach, vb. an·heften, beifügen; (attribute) bei·messen*.

attaché, n. Attaché, -s m.

attachment, n. Beifügung, -en f.; (device) Vorrichtung, -en f., Zubehör nt.; (liking) Zuniegung, -en f.

attack, 1. n. Angriff, -e m. **2.** vb. an·greifen*.

attain, vb. errei'chen.

attainable, adj. erreich'bar.

attainment, n. Errun'genschaft, -en f.

attempt, 1. n. Versuch', -e m. **2.** vb. versu'chen.

attend, vb. (meeting) bei·wohnen; (lecture) besu'chen, hören; (patient) behan'deln; (person) beglei'ten.

attendance, n. Anwesenheit, -en f., Besuch', -e m.

attendant, 1. n. Beglei'ter,

- m. **2.** adj. beglei'tend, anwesend.

attention, n. Aufmerksamkeit, -en f.; (a.!) Achtung!; (pay a.) auf·passen.

attentive, adj. aufmerksam.

attenuate, vb. verdün'nen, vermin'dern; (jur.) mildern.

attest, vb. bezeu'gen.

attic, n. Dachboden, -= m., Boden, -= m.

attire, 1. n. Kleidung, -en f. **2.** vb. kleiden.

attitude, n. n. Haltung, -en f.

attorney, n. Anwalt, -=e m.

attract, vb. an·ziehen*.

attraction, n. Anziehungskraft, -=e f.

attractive, adj. anziehend.

attribute, 1. n. Eigenschaft, -en f. **2.** vb. zu·schreiben*.

attribution, n. Beimessung, -en f.

auction, n. Verstei'gerung, -en f.

auctioneer, n. Verstei'gerer, - m., Auktiona'tor, -to'ren m.

audacious, adj. kühn.

audacity, n. Kühnheit, -en f.

audible, adj. hörbar.

audience, n. Zuhörerschaft, - en f., Publikum, -ka nt.; (of a king) Audienz', -en f.

audiovisual, adj. audiovisuell'.

audit, 1. n. Rechnungsprüfung, -en f. **2.** vb. prüfen.

audition, n. Vorführungsprobe, -n f.

auditor, n. Hörer, - m; (comm.) Rechnungsprüfer, - m.

auditorium, n. Zuhörerraum, -= e m., Auditorium, -rien nt.

augment, vb. vermeh'ren.

augur, 1. n. Augur', -en, -en m. **2.** vb. weissagen.

August, n. August' m.

aunt, n. Tante, -n f.

auspices, n.pl. Auspi'zien.

auspicious, adj. günstig.

austere, adj. streng.

austerity, n. Enthalt'samkeit, - en f.

Austria, n. Österreich nt.

Austrian, 1. n. Österreicher, - m. **2.** adj. österreichisch.

authentic, adj. authen'tisch.

authenticate, vb. beglau'bigen.

authenticity, n. Echtheit, -en f.

author, n. Verfas'ser – m.

authoritarian, adj. autoritär'.

authoritative, adj. maßgebend.

authority, n. Autorität', -en f.

authorization, n. Vollmacht, -=e f.

authorize, vb. bevoll'mächtigen.

auto, n. Auto, -s nt.

autobiography, n. Selbstbiographie, -i'en f.

autocracy, n. Autokratie', i'en f.

autocrat, n. Autokrat', -en, -en m.

autograph, n. Autogramm', -e nt.

automatic, *adj.* automa'tisch.

automation, *n.* Automation' *f.*

automaton, *n.* Automat', en, -en *m.*

automobile, *n.* Kraftwagen, - *m.*

automotive, *adj.* Auto (cpds.).

autonomous, *adj.* autonom'.

autonomy, *n.* Autonomie', -i'en *f.*

autopsy, *n.* Leichenöffnung, -en *f.*

autumn, *n.* Herbst, -e *m.*

auxiliary, *adj.* Hilfs- (cpds.).

avail, 1. *n.* Nutzen *m.* **2.** *vb.* nützen; **(a. oneself of)** benut'-zen.

available, *adj.* vorhan'den.

avalanche, *n.* Lawi'ne, -n *f.*

avarice, *n.* Geiz, -e *m.*

avaricious, *adj.* geizig.

avenge, *vb.* rächen.

avenue, *n.* Allee', -e'en *f.*

average, 1. *n.* Durchschnitt, -e *m.* **2.** *adj.* durchschnittlich; Durchschnitts- (cpds.).

averse, *adj.* abgeneigt.

aversion, *n.* Abneigung, -en *f.*

aviation, *n.* Luftfahrt *f.*

aviator, *n.* Flieger, - *m.*

aviatrix, *n.* Fliegerin, -nen *f.*

avid, *adj.* begie'rig.

avocation, *n.* Nebenberuf, -e *m.*

avoid, *vb.* vermei'den*.

avoidable, *adj.* vermeid'lich.

avoidance, *n.* Vermei'dung, -en *f.*

avow, *vb.* geste'hen*.

avowal, *n.* Gestädnis, -se *nt.*

await, *vb.* erwar'ten.

awake, *adj.* wach.

awaken, *vb.* (tr.) wecken, (intr.) erwach'en.

award, 1. *n.* Preis, -e *m.;* (jur.) Urteil, -e *nt.* **2.** *vb.* zu-erken-nen*.

aware, *adj.* bewußt'.

away, *adv.* weg, fort.

awe, *n.* Ehrfurcht *f.*

awful, *adj.* schrecklich.

awhile, *adv.* eine Weile.

awkward, *adj.* (clumsy) unge-schickt; (embarrassing) pein-lich.

awning, *n.* Marki'se, -n *f.*

awry, *adj.* schief.

axe, *n.* Axt, -*e f.*

axiom, *n.* Axiom', -e *nt.*

axis, *n.* Achse, -n *f.*

axle, *n.* Achse, -n *f.*

ayatollah, *n.* Ajatol'lah, -s *m.*

azure, *adj.* azur'blau.

B

babble, 1. *n.* Geschwätz' *nt.* **2.** *vb.* schwatzen.

baboon, *n.* Pavian, -e *m.*

baby, *n.* Baby, -s *nt.,* Säugling, -e *m.*

bachelor, *n.* Junggeselle, -n, -n *m.*

---

back, 1. *n.* Rücken, - *m.,* Kreuz, -e *nt.;* (chair) Lehne, -n *f.* **2.** *vb.* rückwärts-fahren*; (support) unterstüt'zen. **3.** *adj.* hinter-. **4.** *adv.* zurück'.

backbone, *n.* Rückgrat, -e *nt.*

backfire, *n.* Fehlzündung, -en *f.*

background, *n.* Hintergrund, -e *m.*

backing, *n.* Unterstüt'zung, -en *f.*

backlash, *n.* Rückprall *m;* Be-wir'kung des Gegenteils *f.*

backpack, *vb.* mit Rucksack wandern.

backward, 1. *adj.* zurück'ge-blieben, rückständig. **2.** *adv.* rückwärts.

backwards, *adv.* rückwärts; (wrongly) verkehrt'.

bacon, *n.* Speck *m.*

bacterium, *n.* Bakte'rium, -rien *nt.*

bad, *adj.* (not good) schlecht; (serious) schlimm; (too b.) schade.

bag, *n.* Sack, -e *m.;* (paper) Tüte, -n *f.;* (luggage) Koffer, - *m.;* (woman's purse) Tasche, -n *f.*

baggage, *n.* Gepäck' *nt.*

baggage cart, *n.* (airport) Kof-ferkuli, -s *m.*

baggy, *adj.* bauschig.

bail, *n.* Kaution', -en *f.,* Bürg-schaft, -en *f.*

bail out, *vb* (set free) Kaution' stellen für; (empty out water) schöpfen, aus-schöpfen; (make a parachute jump) ab-springen*.

bake, *vb.* backen*.

baking, *n.* Backen *nt.*

baking soda, *n.* doppelkohlen-saures Natron.

balance, 1. *n.* (equilibrium) Gleichgewicht *nt.;* (remain-der) Rest, -e *m;* (trade) Bi-lanz', -en *f.* **2.** *vb.* balancie'ren; (make come out equal) aus-gleichen*.

balcony, *n.* Balkon', -s *or* -e *m.*

bald, *adj.* kahl; **(b. head)** Glatzkopf, -e *m.;* **(b. spot)** Glatze, -n *f.*

balk, *vb.* (hinder) verhin'dern; **(b. at nothing)** vor nichts zu-rück'-scheuen.

ball, *n.* (for throwing, game, dance) Ball, -e *m.;* (spherical object, bullet) Kugel, -n *f.*

ballerina, *n.* Balleri'na, -nen *f.*

ballot, *n.* (paper) Stimmzettel, - *m.;* (voting) Wahl, -en *f.*

ballroom, *n.* Tanzsaal, -säle *m.*

balm, *n.* Balsam, -e *m.*

balmy, *adj.* sanft.

balsam, *n.* Balsam, -e *m.*

Baltic Sea, *n.* Ostsee *f.*

bamboo, *n.* Bambus, -se *m.*

ban, 1. *n.* Bann, -e *m.* **2.** *vb.* bannen, verbie'ten*.

banal, *adj.* banal'.

banana, *n.* Bana'ne, -n *f.*

---

band, *n.* Band, -er *nt.;* (gang) Bande, -n *f.;* (music) Musik'-kapelle, -n *f.*

bandage, 1. *n.* Verband', -e *m.* **2.** *vb.* verbin'den*.

bandanna, *n.* Kopftuch, -er *nt.,* Halstuch, -er *nt.*

bandit, *n.* Bandit', -en, -en *m.*

baneful, *adj.* giftig, verder b'lich.

bang, 1. *n.* Knall, -e *m.* **2.** *vb.* knallen.

banish, *vb.* verban'nen.

banishment, *n.* Verban'nung, -en *f.*

banister, *n.* Treppengeländer, - *nt.*

bank, *n.* Bank, -en *f.;* (river) Ufer, - *nt.;* (slope) Böschung, -en *f.*

bankbook, *n.* Kontobuch, -er *nt.*

banker, *n.* Bankier', -s *m.*

banking, *n.* Bankgeschäft, -e *nt.*

bank note, *n.* Banknote, -n, *f.*

bankrupt, *adj.* bankrott'.

bankruptcy, *n.* Konkurs', -e *m.*

banner, *n.* Banner, - *nt.*

banquet, *n.* Festessen, - *nt.*

banter, 1. *n.* Scherz, -e *m.* **2.** *vb.* scherzen.

baptism, *n.* Taufe, -n *f.*

baptismal, *adj.* Tauf- (cpds.).

Baptist, *n.* Baptist', -en, -en *m.*

baptistery, *n.* Taufkapelle, -n *f.,* Taufstein, -e *m.*

baptize, *vb.* taufen.

bar, 1. *n.* Stange, -n *f.;* (for drinks) Bar, -s *f.;* (jur.) Ge-richt', -e *nt.* **2.** *vb.* aus-schließen*.

barb, *n.* Widerhaken, - *m.*

barbarian, 1. *n.* Barbar', -en, -en *m.* **2.** *adj.* barba'risch.

barbarism, *n.* Barbarei', -en *f.*

barbarous, *adj.* barba'risch.

barber, *n.* Herrenfriseur, -e *m.*

barbiturate, *n.* Barbitur'säure-präparat, -e *nt.*

bare, 1. *adj.* bloß, nackt. **2.** *vb.* entblö'ßen.

barefoot, *adj.* barfuß.

barely, *adv.* kaum.

bargain, 1. *n.* Gele'genheits-kauf, -e *m.* **2.** *vb.* feilschen, handeln.

barge, 1. *n.* Schleppkahn, -e *m.,* Leichter, - *m.* **2.** *vb.* stür-men.

baritone, *n.* Bariton, -e *m.*

barium, *n.* Barium *nt.*

bark, 1. *n.* (tree) Rinde, -n *f.;* (boat) Barke, -n *f.;* (dog) Bel-len *nt.* **2.** *vb.* bellen.

barley, *n.* Gerste, -n *f.,* Grau-pen *pl.*

barn, *n.* (hay, grain) Scheune, -n *f.;* (animals) Stall, -e *m.*

barnacle, *n.* Entenmuschel, -n *f.*

barnyard, *n.* Bauernhof, -e *m.*

barometer, *n.* Barome'ter, - *nt.*

barometric, *adj.* barome'trisch.

baron, *n.* Baron', -e *m.*

baroness, *n.* Barones'se, -n *f.*

baroque, 1. *n.* Barock', *nt.* 2. *adj.* barock'.

barracks, *n.* Kaser'ne, -n *f.*

barrage, *n.* Sperre, -n *f.; (mil.)* Sperrfeuer, - *nt.*

barrel, *n.* Faß, ̈sser *nt.*

barren, *adj.* unfruchtbar, dürr.

barricade, 1. *n.* Barrika'de, -n *f.* 2. *vb.* verbarrikadie'ren.

barrier, *n.* Schranke, -n *f.*

barroom, *n.* Schankstube, -n *f.*

bartender, *n.* Barmixer, - *m.*

barter, 1. *n.* Tauschhandel *m.* 2. *vb.* tauschen.

base, 1. *n.* der unterste Teil, -e *m.; (geom.)* Grundlinie, -n *f.; (mil.)* Stützpunkt, -e *m.* 2. *vb.* basie'ren. 3. *adj.* niederträchtig.

baseball, *n.* Baseball, ̈e *m.*

baseboard, *n.* Waschleiste, -n *f.*

basement, *n.* Keller, - *m.*

baseness, *n.* Niederträchtigkeit, -en *f.*

bashful, *adj.* schüchtern.

bashfulness, *n.* Schüchternheit, -en *f.*

basic, *adj.* grundlegend.

basin, *n.* Becken, - *nt.*

basis, *n.* Grundlage, -n *f.*, Basis, -sen *f.*

basket, *n.* Korb, ̈e *m.*

bass, *n. (singer)* Baß, ̈sse *m.; (fish)* Barsch, -e *m.*

bassinet, *n.* Korbwiege, -n *f.*

bassoon, *n.* Fagott', -e *nt.*

bastard, *n.* uneheliches Kind *nt.*, Bastard, -e *m.*

baste, *vb. (thread)* heften; *(roast)* begie'ßen*.

bat, *n.* Fledermaus, ̈e *f.; (sport)* Schlagholz, ̈er *nt.*

batch, *n.* Schub, ̈e *m.*

bath, *n.* Bad, ̈er *nt.*

bathe, *vb.* baden.

bather, *n.* Badend- *m.&f.*

bathrobe, *n.* Bademantel, ̈ *m.*

bathroom, *n.* Badezimmer, - *nt.*

bathtub, *n.* Badewanne, -n *f.*

baton, *n.* Taktstock, ̈e *m.*

battalion, *n.* Bataillon', -e *nt.*

batter, 1. *n. (one who bats)* Schläger, - *m.; (cooking)* Teig, -e *m.* 2. *vb.* schlagen*.

battery, *n.* Batterie', -i'en *f.*

battle, 1. *n.* Schlacht, -en *f.* 2. *vb.* kämpfen.

battlefield, *n.* Schlachtfeld, -er *nt.*

battleship, *n.* Schlachtschiff, -e *nt.*

bawl, *vb.* brüllen.

bay, 1. *n. (geography)* Bucht, -en *f.; (plant)* Lorbeer, -en *m.; (at b.)* in Schach. 2. *adj. (color)* rotbraun. 3. *vb.* bellen.

bayonet, *n.* Bajonett', -e *nt.*

bazaar, *n.* Bazar', -e *m.*

be, *vb.* sein*.

beach, *n.* Strand, -e *m.*

beachhead, *n.* Landekopf, ̈e *m.*

beacon, *n.* Leuchtfeuer, - *nt.*

bead, *n.* Perle, -n *f.; (drop)* Tropfen, - *m.*

beading, *n.* Perlstickerei, -en *f.*

beak, *n.* Schnabel, ̈ *m.*

beaker, *n.* Becher, - *m.*

beam, 1. *n. (construction)* Balken, - *m.; (light)* Strahl, -en *m.* 2. *vb.* strahlen, glänzen.

beaming, *adj.* strahlend.

bean, *n.* Bohne, -n *f.*

bear, 1. *n. (animal)* Bär, -en, -en *m.* 2. *vb. (carry)* tragen*; *(endure)* ertra'gen*; *(give birth to)* gebä'ren*.

bearable, *adj.* erträg'lich.

beard, *n.* Bart, ̈e *m.*

bearer, *n.* Überbrin'ger, - *m.*

bearing, *n. (behavior)* Haltung, -en *f.; (affect)* Bezug', -e *m.; (machinery)* Lager, - *nt.*

beast, *n.* Vieh *nt.*, Tier, -e *nt.*, Bestie - *f.*

beat, 1. *n.* Schlag, ̈e *m.; (music)* Takt, -e *m.* 2. *vb.* schlagen*.

beaten, *adj.* geschla'gen.

beatify, *vb.* selig-sprechen*.

beating, *n. (punishment)* Prügel *pl.*, Schläge *pl.; (defeat)* Niederlage, -n *f.*

beatitudes, *n.pl. (biblical)* Seligpreisungen *pl.*

beau, *n.* Vereh'rer, - *m.*

beautiful, *adj.* schön.

beautify, *vb.* verschö'nern.

beauty, *n.* Schönheit, -en *f.*

beauty parlor, *n.* Schönheitssalon, -s *m.*, Frisier'salon, -s *m.*

beaver, *n.* Biber, - *m.*

because, *conj.* weil; **(b. of)** wegen.

beckon, *vb.* winken.

become, *vb.* werden*.

becoming, *adj.* kleidsam.

bed, *n.* Bett, -en *nt.; (garden)* Beet, -e *nt.*

bedbug, *n.* Wanze, -n *f.*

bedding, *n.* Bettzeug *nt.*

bedroom, *n.* Schlafzimmer, - *nt.*

bedspread, *n.* Bettdecke, -n *f.*

bee, *n.* Biene, -n *f.*

beef, *n.* Rindfleisch *nt.*

beefsteak, *n.* Beefsteak, -s *nt.*

beehive, *n.* Bienenstock, ̈e *m.*

beer, *n.* Bier, -e *nt.*

beet, *n.* Bete, -n *f.*, Runkelrübe, -n *f.*, rote Rübe, -n *f.*

beetle, *n.* Käfer, - *m.*

befall, *vb.* zu-stoßen*.

befit, *vb.* gezie'men.

befitting, *adj.* schicklich; **(be b.)** sich schicken.

before, 1. *adv. (time)* vorher; *(place)* voran'. 2. *prep.* vor. 3. *conj.* ehe, bevor'.

beforehand, *adv.* vorher.

befriend, *vb.* sich an-freunden mit.

befuddle, *vb.* verwir'ren.

beg, *vb.* betteln; *(implore)* bitten*.

beggar, *n.* Bettler, - *m.*

begin, *vb.* an-fangen*, begin'nen*.

beginner, *n.* Anfänger, - *m.*

beginning, *n.* Anfang, ̈e *m.*

begrudge, *vb.* mißgön'nen.

beguile, *vb.* bestrick'en.

behalf, *n.* **(on b. of)** zugun'sten von, im Namen von.

behave, *vb.* sich beneh'men*.

behavior, *n.* Beneh'men, *nt.*

behead, *vb.* enthaup'ten.

behind, 1. *adv.* hinten, zurück. 2. *prep.* hinter.

behold, 1. *vb.* sehen*. 2. *interj.* sieh(e) da.

beige, *adj.* beigefarben.

being, *n.* Sein *nt.*, Wesen, - *nt.*

belated, *adj.* verspä'tet.

belch, *vb.* rülpsen.

belfry, *n.* Glockenturm, ̈e *m.*

Belgian, 1. *n.* Belgier, - *m.* 2. *adj.* belgisch.

Belgium, *n.* Belgien *nt.*

belie, *vb.* Lügen strafen.

belief, *n.* Glaube(n), - *m.*

believable, *adj.* glaubhaft.

believe, *vb.* glauben.

believer, *n.* Gläubig- *m.&f.*

belittle, *vb.* bagatellisie'ren.

bell, *n. (small)* Klingel, -n *f.; (large)* Glocke, -n *f.*

bellboy, *n.* Hotel'boy, -s *m.*

belligerence, *n.* Kriegslust, ̈e *f.; Kriegszustand, ̈e *m.*

belligerent, *adj.* kriegerisch, kriegsführend.

bellow, *vb.* brüllen.

bellows, *n.* Blasebalg, ̈e *m.*

belly, *n.* Bauch, ̈e *m.*

belong, *vb.* gehö'ren.

belongings, *n.pl.*, Habseligkeiten *pl.*

beloved, *adj.* geliebt'.

below, 1. *adv.* unten. 2. *prep.* unter.

belt, *n.* Gürtel, - *m.*

bench, *n.* Bank, ̈e *f.*

bend, *vb.* biegen*.

beneath, 1. *adv.* unten. 2. *prep.* unter.

benediction, *n.* Segen, - *m.*

benefactor, *n.* Wohltäter, - *m.*

benefactress, *n.* Wohltäterin, -nen *f.*

beneficent, *adj.* wohltätig.

beneficial, *adj.* wohltuend, nützlich.

beneficiary, *n.* Begün'stigt- *m.&f.;* Nutznießer, - *m.*

benefit, 1. *n.* Wohltat, -en *f.; (advantage)* Nutzen, - *m.*, Vorteil, -e *m.* 2. *vb.* nützen; **(b. from)** Nutzen ziehen* aus.

benevolence, *n.* Wohlwollen *nt.*

benevolent, *adj.* wohlwollend.

benign, *adj.* gütig.

bent, *adj.* gebeugt'; *(out of shape)* verbo'gen.

benzine, *n.* Benzin' *nt.*

bequeath, vb. verma'chen.
bequest, n. Vermächt'nis, -se nt. Legat', -e nt.
berate, vb. aus·schelten*.
bereave, vb. berau'ben.
bereavement, n. Verlust durch Tod.
berry, n. Beere, -n f.
berth, n. Bettplatz, ⸗e m.
beseech, vb. an·flehen.
beset, vb. bedrän'gen.
beside, prep. neben; (b. oneself) außer sich.
besides, 1. adv. außerdem. 2. prep. außer.
besiege, vb. bela'gern.
best, 1. adj. best-. 2. vb. übertref'fen*.
bestial, adj. bestia'lisch, tierisch.
bestow, vb. verlei'hen*.
bestowal, n. Verlei'hung, -en f.
bet, 1. n. Wette, -n f. 2. vb. wetten.
betake oneself, vb. sich auf·machen.
betoken, vb. bezeich'nen.
betray, vb. verra'ten*.
betrayal, n. Verrat' m.
betroth, vb. verlo'ben; (be b.ed) sich verlo'ben.
betrothal, n. Verlo'bung, -en f.
better, 1. adj. besser. 2. vb. verbes'sern.
between, prep. zwischen.
bevel, 1. n. schräger Anschnitt, -e m. 2. vb. schräg ab·schneiden*.
beverage, n. Getränk', -e nt.
bewail, vb. bekla'gen.
beware, vb. sich hüten.
bewilder, vb. verwir'ren.
bewilderment, n. Verwir'rung, -en f.
bewitch, vb. bezau'bern; verzau'bern.
beyond, 1. adv. jenseits. 2. prep. jenseits, über.
biannual, adj. halbjährlich.
bias, n. Vorurteil, -e nt.
bib, n. Lätzchen, - nt.
Bible, n. Bibel, -n f.
Biblical, adj. biblisch.
bibliography, n. Bibliographie', -i'en f.
bicarbonate, n. (of soda) doppelkohlensaures Natron nt.
biceps, n. Bizeps, - m.
bicker, vb. sich zanken.
bicycle, n. Fahrrad, ⸗er nt.
bicyclist, n. Radfahrer, - m.
bid, 1. n. Angebot, -e nt. 2. vb. bieten*.
bide, vb. ab·warten.
biennial, adj. zweijährlich.
bier, n. Bahre, -n f.
bifocal, adj. bifokal'.
big, adj. groß (größer, größt-).
bigamist, n. Bigamist', -en, -en m.
bigamous, adj. biga'misch.
bigamy, n. Bigamie', -i'en f.
bigot, n. Frömmler, - m.
bigoted, adj. bigott'.

bigotry, n. Frömmelei', -en f.
bilateral, adj. zweiseitig.
bile, n. Galle, -n f.
bilingual, adj. zweisprachig.
bilious, adj. gallig.
bill, n. (bird) Schnabel ⸗ m.; (banknote) Geldschein, -e m.; (sum owed) Rechnung, -en f.; (legislative) Geset'zesvorlage, -n f.
billboard, n. Rekla'meschild, -er nt.
billet, 1. n. Quartier', -e nt. 2. vb. ein·quartieren.
billfold, n. Brieftasche, -n f.
billiards, n. Billard nt.
billion, n. Billion', -en f.
bill of fare, n. Speisekarte, -n f.
bill of health, n. Gesund'heitsattest, -e nt.
bill of lading, n. Frachtbrief, -e m.
bill of sale, n. Kaufkontrakt, -e m.
billow, 1. n. Woge, -n f. 2. vb. wogen.
bimonthly, adj. zweimo'natlich.
bin, n. Kasten, ⸗ m.
bind, vb. binden*; verbin'den*.
bindery, n. Buchbinderei' -en f.
binding, 1. n. (book) Einband, ⸗e m.; (ski) Bindung, -en f. 2. adj. bindend.
binocular, n. Fernglas, ⸗er nt.
biochemistry, n. Biochemie' f.
biodegradable, adj. orga'nisch abbaubar.
biofeedback, n. Biosignalrückgabe, -n f.
biographer, n. Biograph' -en, -en m.
biographical, adj. biogra'phisch.
biography, n. Biographie', -i'en f.
biological, adj. biolo'gisch.
biology, n. Biologie', -i'en f.
bipartisan, adj. die Regierungs- und die Oppositionspartei vertretend.
bird, n. Vogel, ⸗ m.
birth, n. Geburt', -en f.
birth control, n. Gebur'tenkontrolle f.
birthday, n. Geburts'tag, -e m.
birthmark, n. Muttermal, -e nt.
birthplace, n. Geburts'ort, -e m.
birth rate, n. Gebur'tenziffer, -n f.
birthright, n. Erstgeburtsrecht, -e nt.; angestammtes Recht nt.
biscuit, n. Biskuit', -e nt.; Keks, -e m.
bisect, vb. halbie'ren.
bishop, n. Bischof, ⸗e m.
bismuth, n. Wismut nt.
bison, n. Bison, -s m.
bit, n. (piece) Bißchen, - nt.; (a b. of) ein bißchen; (harness)

Gebiß, -sse nt.; (computer) Bit, - nt.
bitch, n. Hündin, -nen f.
bite, 1. n. Bissen, - m. 2. vb. beißen*.
biting, adj. beißend.
bitter, adj. bitter.
bitterness, n. Bitterkeit, -en f.
biweekly, adj. zweiwöchentlich.
black, 1. adj. schwarz (-). 2. n. (person) Schwarz- m.&f.
blackberry, n. Brombeere, -n f.
blackbird, n. Amsel, -n f.
blackboard, n. Wandtafel, -n f.
blacken, vb. schwärzen.
blackmail, 1. n. Erpres'sung, -en f. 2. vb. erpres'sen.
black market, n. Schwarzmarkt, ⸗e m.
blackout, n. Verdun'kelung, -en f.
blacksmith, n. Schmied, -e m.
bladder, n. Blase, -n f.
blade, n. (knife) Klinge, -n f.; (grass) Halm, -e m.
blame, 1. n. Schuld, -en f. 2. vb. beschul'digen.
blanch, vb. bleichen; bleich werden*.
bland, adj. mild.
blank, 1. n. (form) Formular', -e nt. 2. adj. unbeschrieben, leer.
blanket, n. Decke, -n f., Wolldecke, -n f.
blaspheme, vb. lästern.
blasphemer, n. Gotteslästerer, - m.
blasphemous, adj. gotteslästerlich.
blasphemy, n. Gotteslästerung, -en f., Blasphemie', -i'en f.
blast, 1. n. (of wind) Windstoß, ⸗e m.; (explosion) Explosion', -en f. 2. vb. sprengen.
blatant, adj. laut, aufdring'lich.
blaze, 1. n. Flamme, -n f. 2. vb. lodern, leuchten.
bleach, vb. bleichen.
bleak, adj. öde.
bleed, vb. bluten.
blemish, n. Makel, - m.
blend, 1. n. Mischung, -en f. 2. vb. mischen.
bless, vb. segnen.
blessed, adj. gese'gnet, selig.
blessing, n. Segen, - m.
blight, 1. n. (bot.) Brand, ⸗e m. 2. (fig.) verei'teln.
blind, 1. adj. blind. 2. vb. blenden.
blindfold, 1. n. Augenbinde -n f. 2. vb. die Augen verbin'den*.
blindness, n. Blindheit, -en f.
blink, vb. blinken, blinzeln.
blinker, n. Scheuklappe, -n f.; (signal) Blinklicht, -er nt.
bliss, n. Glückseligkeit, -en f.
blissful, adj. glückselig.
blister, n. Blase, -n f.
blithe, adj. fröhlich.
blizzard, n. Schneesturm, ⸗e m.
bloat, vb. blähen.

bloc, n. Block, -e m.

block, 1. n. (wood) Holzblock, -e m.; (city) Häuserblock, -e m. 2. vb. sperren.

blockade, n. Blocka'de, -n f.

blond, adj. blond.

blood, n. Blut nt.

bloodhound, n. Bluthund, -e m.

blood plasma, n. Plasma, -men nt.

blood poisoning, n. Blutvergiftung, -en f.

blood pressure, n. Blutdruck, m.

bloodshed, n. Blutvergießen, nt.

bloodshot, adj. blutunterlaufen.

bloody, adj. blutig.

bloom, 1. n. Blüte, -n f. 2. vb. blühen.

blossom, n. Blüte, -n f.

blot, 1. n. Fleck, -e m. 2. vb. beflecken, (ink) löschen.

blotter, n. Löschpapier, -e nt.

blouse, n. Bluse, -n f.

blow, 1. n. Schlag, -e m., Stoß, -e, m. 2. vb. blasen*.

blowout, n. Reifenpanne, -n f.

blubber, 1. n. Walfischspeck m. 2. vb. flennen.

blue, adj. blau.

bluebird, n. Blaukehlchen, - nt.

blue jeans, n.pl. Jeans, Bluejeans.

blueprint, n. Blaudruck, -e m.; (fig.) Plan, -e m.

bluff, 1. n. (cliff) Klippe, -n f., schroffer Felsen, - m.; (cards) Bluff, -s m. 2. adj. schroff. 3. vb. bluffen.

bluffer, n. Bluffer, - m.

bluing, n. Waschblau nt.

blunder, 1. n. Fehler, - m. 2. vb. Fehler machen.

blunderer, n. Tölpel, - m.

blunt, adj. stumpf; (fig.) unverblümt.

blur, 1. n. Verschwom'menheit f. 2. vb. (intr.) verschwim'men*; (tr.) trüben.

blurred, adj. verschwommen.

blush, 1. n. Erröten nt. 2. vb. erröten.

bluster, vb. toben; (swagger) prahlen.

boar, n. Eber, - m.

board, 1. n. (plank) Brett, -er nt., Bord, -e nt.; (food) Verpfle'gung, -en f.; (committee) Ausschuß, -sse m.; (council) Behör'de, -n f.; (ship) Bord, - e m. 2. vb. an Bord gehen*.

boarder, n. Kostgänger, - m.

boarding house, n. Pension', - en f.

boast, 1. n. Angeberei', -en f. 2. vb. prahlen, an'geben*.

boaster, n. Angeber, - m.

boastful, adj. angeberisch.

boastfulness, n. Angeberei', - en f.

boat, n. Boot, -e nt., Schiff, -e nt.

bob, 1. n. (hair) Bubikopf m. 2. vb. baumeln; (hair) kurz schneiden*.

bobby pin, n. Haarklammer, -n f.

bodice, n. Oberteil, -e nt.

bodily, adj. leiblich.

body, n. Körper, - m., Leib, -er m.

bodyguard, n. Leibwache, -n f.

bog, 1. n. Sumpf, -e m. 2. vb. (b. down) stecken bleiben*.

Bohemian, 1. n. Böhme, -n, -n m. 2. adj. böhmisch.

boil, 1. n. (med.) Furun'kel, -n f. 2. vb. kochen.

boiler, n. Kessel, - m.

boisterous, adj. ungestüm.

bold, adj. kühn.

boldface, n. Fettdruck, -e m.

boldness, n. Kühnheit, -en f.

Bolivian, 1. n. Bolivia'ner, - m. 2. adj. bolivia'nisch.

bolster, 1. n. Polster, - nt. 2. vb. (support) unterstüt'zen.

bolster up, vb. stärken.

bolt, 1. n. (lock) Riegel, - m.; (screw with nut) Schraube, -n f.; (lightning) Blitz, -e m. 2. vb. (lock) verrie'geln; (dash, of persons) davon'stürzen, (of horses) durch'gehen*.

bomb, 1. n. Bombe, -n f. 2. vb. bomben.

bombard, vb. bombardie'ren.

bombardier, n. Bombardier', - m.

bombardment, n. Beschie'ßung, -en f.

bomber, n. Bombenflugzeug, - e nt.

bombproof, adj. bombensicher.

bombshell, n. Bombe, -n f.

bombsight, n. Bombenziel'vorrichtung, -en f.

bonbon, n. Fondant', -s m.

bond, n. Band, -e nt., Fessel, -n f.; (law) Bürgschaft, -en f.; (stock exchange) Obligation'- en f.

bondage, n. Knechtschaft, -en f.

bone, n. Knochen, - m.; (fish) Gräte, -n f.

bonfire, n. Freudenfeurer, - nt.

bonnet, n. Damenhut, -e m.

bonus, n. Extrazahlung, -en f.; Tantie'me, -n f.

bony, adj. knochig.

book, 1. n. Buch, -er nt. 2. vb. buchen.

bookcase, n. Bücherschrank, -e m.

bookkeeper, n. Buchhalter, - m.

bookkeeping, n. Buchführung, -en f.

booklet, n. Broschü're, -n f.

bookseller, n. Buchhändler, - m.

bookstore, n. Buchhandlung, -en f.

boom, 1. n. Baum, -e m.; (econ.) Hochkonjunktur, -

-en f. 2. vb. brummen, dröhnen.

boon, n. Geschenk', -e nt.; (fig.) Segen, - m.

boor, n. Grobian, -e m.

boorish, adj. grob (-).

boost, 1. n. (increase) Aufschwung, -e m.; (push) Antrieb, -e m. 2. vb. (increase) steigern; (push) nachhelfen*.

boot, n. Stiefel, - m.

bootblack, n. Schuhputzer, - m.

booth, n. Bude, -n f.; (telephone) Fernsprechzelle, -n f.

border, 1. n. Grenze, -n f. 2. vb. grenzen an.

borderline, n. Grenze, -n f.

bore, 1. n. (hole) Bohrloch, -er nt.; (cylinder) Bohrung, -en f.; (person) langweiliger Mensch, -en, -en m. 2. vb. bohren; (annoy) langweilen.

boredom, n. Langeweile f.

boric, adj. Bor- (cpds.).

boring, adj. langweilig.

born, adj. gebo'ren.

born-again, adj. wiedergeboren.

borough, n. Stadtteil, -e m.

borrow, vb. borgen, leihen*.

bosom, n. Busen, - m.

boss, n. Chef, -s m.

bossy, adj. herrschsüchtig.

botanical, adj. bota'nisch.

botany, n. Bota'nik f.

both, adj.&pron. beide.

bother, 1. n. Verdruß' m. 2. vb. belästigen; (disturb) stören.

bothersome, adj. lästig.

bottle, n. Flasche, -n f.

bottom, n. Grund, -e m.

bottomless, adj. bodenlos.

boudoir, n. Boudoir', -s nt.

bough, n. Ast, -e m., Zweig, -e m.

bouillon, n. Kraftbrühe, -n f.

boulder, n. Felsblock, -e m.

boulevard, n. Boulevard', -s m.

bounce, vb. springen*.

bound, 1. n. (jump) Sprung. -e m.; (b.s.) Grenzen pl. 2. vb. (jump) springen*; (limit) begren'zen. 3. adj. (obl.) gebun'den; (duty b.) verpflich'tet; (b. for) unterwegs' nach.

boundary, n. Grenze, -n f.

bound for, adj. unterwegs' nach.

boundless, adj. grenzenlos.

bounty, n. Freigebigkeit, -en f.

bouquet, n. Blumenstrauß, -e m.

bourgeois, adj. bürgerlich.

bout, n. (boxing) Boxkampf, -e m.

bovine, adj. Rinder- (cpds.).

bow, 1. n. (for arrows, violin) Bogen, - f.; (greeting) Verbeu'gung, -en f.; (hair, dress) Schleife, -n f.; (of boats) Bug, -e m. 2. vb. sich verbeu'gen

bowels, n.pl. Eingeweide pl.

bowl, 1. n. Schüssel -n f., Schale, -n f. 2. vb. kegeln.

bowlegged, adj. o-beinig.

bowler, n. Kegelspieler, - m.; (hat) Melo'ne, -n f.

bowling, n. Kegeln nt.

box, 1. n. (small) Schachtel, -n f.; (large) Kasten. ≃ m.; (theater) Loge, -n f.; (letter b.) Briefkasten, ≃ m. **2.** vb. (sport) boxen.

boxcar, n. Güterwagen, - m.

boxer, n. Boxer, - m.

boxing, n. Boxen nt.

box office, n. Thea'terkasse, -n, f.

boy, n. Junge, -n, -n m., Bube, -n, -n m.

Boycott, 1. n. boykott', -e m. **2.** vb. boykottie'ren.

boyhood, n. Jugend, -en f.

boyish, adj. jungenhaft, jung.

brace, 1. n. Klammer, -n f., Stütze, -n f. **2.** vb. abstei'fen.

bracelet, n. Armband, ≃er nt.

bracket, n. Klammer, -n f.; (typography) Klammer, -n f.; (group) Gruppe, -n f.

brag, vb. prahlen, an'geben*.

braggart, n. Angeber, - m.

braid, 1. n. Flechte, -n f. **2.** vb. flechten*.

brain, n. Gehirn', -e nt.

brake, 1. n. Bremse, -n f. **2.** vb. bremsen.

bran, n. Kleie, -n f.

branch, n. Ast, ≃e m., Zweig, -e m.

brand, 1. n. (sort) Sorte, -n f.; (mark) Marke, -n f. **2.** vb. brandmarken.

brandish, vb. schwingen*.

brandy, n. Weinbrand, ≃e m., Kognak, -s m.

brash, adj. dreist.

brass, n. Messing m.

brassiere, n. Büstenhalter, - m.

brat, n. Balg, ≃e nt.

bravado, n. Bravour' f., Schneid m.

brave, adj. tapfer.

bravery, n. Tapferkeit, -en f.

brawl, n. Rauferei', -en f.

brawn, n. Muskelkraft, ≃e f.

bray, 1. n. Eselsgeschrei' nt. **2.** vb. schreien*.

brazen, adj. ehern; (insolent) unverschämt.

Brazil, n. Brasi'lien nt.

Brazilian, 1. n. Brasilia'ner, - m. **2.** adj. brasilia'nisch.

breach, n. Bruch, ≃e m.

bread, n. Brot, -e nt.

breadth, n. Breite, -n f.

break, 1. n. Bruch, ≃e m.; Pause, -n f. **2.** vb. brechen*.

breakable, adj. zerbrech'lich.

breakfast, n. Frühstück, -e nt.

breakneck, adj. halsbrecherisch.

breakwater, n. Mole, -n f.

breast, n. Brust, ≃e f.

breath, n. Atem, - m.

breathe, vb. atmen.

breathing, n. Atmen nt.

breathless, adj. atemlos.

breeches, n. Kniehose -n f.

breed, 1. n. Zucht, -en f. **2.** vb. (beget) erzeu'gen; (raise) züchten; (educate) erzie'hen*.

breeder, n. Züchter, - m.

breeding, n. Erzie'hung, -en f.

breeze, n. Brise, -n f.

breezy, adj. luftig.

brevity, n. Kürze, -n f.

brew, 1. n. Gebräu, -e nt. **2.** vb. brauen.

brewer, n. Brauer, - m.

brewery, n. Brauerei', -en f.

briar, n. Dornbusch, ≃e m.; Bruyèreholz nt.

bribe, vb. beste'chen*.

briber, n. Beste'cher, - m.

bribery, n. Beste'chung, -en f.

brick, n. Backstein, -e m.; Ziegelstein, -e m.

bricklayer, n. Maurer, - m.

bridal, adj. Hochzeits- (cpds.).

bride, n. Braut, ≃e f.

bridegroom, n. Bräutigam, -e m.

bridesmaid, n. Brautjungfer, -n f.

bridge, 1. n. Brücke, -n f.; (game) Bridge nt. **2.** vb. überbrü'cken.

bridle, n. Zaum, ≃e m.

brief, adj. kurz (-).

brief case, n. Aktenmappe, -n f.

bright, adj. hell; (smart) gescheit'.

brighten, vb. erhel'len.

brightness, n. Klarheit, -en f.

brilliance, n. Glanz, -e m.

brilliant, adj. glänzend; (smart) hochbegabt.

brim, n. (cup) Rand, ≃er m.; (hat) Krempe, -n f.

brine, n. Salzwasser, - nt., Sole, -n f.

bring, vb. bringen*.

brink, n. Rand, ≃er m.

briny, adj. salzig.

brisk, adj. lebhaft.

brisket, n. (meat) Bruststück, -e nt.

briskness, n. Lebhaftigkeit, -en f.

bristle, 1. n. Borste, -n f. **2.** vb. sich sträuben.

Britain, n. Britan'nien nt.

British, adj. britisch.

Briton, n. Brite, -n, -n m.

brittle, adj. brüchig, spröde.

broad, adj. breit, weit.

broadcast, 1. n. Rundfunksendung, -en f., Übertra'gung, -en f. **2.** vb. senden, im Radio übertra'gen*.

broadcaster, n. Rundfunksprecher, - m.

broadcloth, n. feiner Wäschestoff m.

broaden, vb. erwei'tern.

broadly, adv. allgemein'.

broadminded, adj. großzügig, tolerant'.

brocade, n. Brokat', -e m.

broil, vb. grillen.

broiler, n. Bratrost, -e m.

broke, adj. pleite.

broken, adj. gebro'chen; kaputt'.

broker, n. Makler, - m.

brokerage, n. (business) Maklergeschäft, -e nt.; (charge) Maklergebühr, -en f.

bronchial, adj. bronchial'.

bronchitis, n. Bronchi'tis f.

bronze, n. Bronze, -n f.

brooch, n. Brosche, -n f.

brood, 1. n. Brut, -en f. **2.** vb. brüten.

brook, n. Bach, ≃e m.

broom, n. Besen, - m.

broomstick, n. Besenstiel, -e m.

broth, n. Brühe, -n f.

brothel, n. Bordell', -e nt.

brother, n. Bruder, ≃ m.

brotherhood, n. Brüderschaft, -en f.

brother-in-law, n. Schwager, ≃ m.

brotherly, adj. brüderlich.

brow, n. Stirn, -en f.

brown, adj. braun.

browse, vb. schmökern.

bruise, 1. n. Quetschung, -en f.; **2.** vb. quetschen, stoßen*.

brunette, n. Brünet'te, -n f.

brunt, n. (bear the b.) die Hauptlast tragen*.

brush, 1. n. Bürste, -n f.; (artist's) Pinsel, - m. **2.** vb. bürsten.

brusque, adj. brüsk.

brutal, adj. brutal'.

brutality, n. Brutalität', -en f.

brutalize, vb. verro'hen.

brute, n. Unmensch, -en, -en m.

bubble, 1. n. Luftblase, -n f. **2.** vb. sprudeln.

buck, 1. n. Bock, ≃e m. **2.** vb. bocken; (fig.) sich gegen etwas auf'bäumen.

bucket, n. Eimer, - m.

buckle, 1. n. Schnalle, - f. **2.** vb. (fasten) schnallen; (bend) sich krümmen, sich biegen*.

buckwheat, n. Buchweizen m.

bud, 1. n. Knospe, -n f. **2.** vb. knospen.

budge, vb. sich rühren.

budget, n. Etat', -s m.

buffalo, n. Büffel, - m.

buffer, n. Puffer, - m.; (b. state) Pufferstaat, -en m.

buffet, 1. n. Büfett', -e, Buffet', -s nt. **2.** vb. schlagen*.

bug, n. Käfer, - m.

bugle, n. Signal'horn, ≃er nt.

build, vb. bauen.

builder, n. Baumeister, - m.

building, n. Gebäu'de, - nt.

bulb, n. Knolle, -n f.; (electric) Glühbirne, -n f.

bulge, 1. n. Ausbuchtung, -en f. **2.** vb. sich aus'buchten.

bulk, n. Umfang m., Hauptteil, -e m.

bulky, adj. umfangreich.

bull, n. Bulle, -n, -n m.

bulldog, n. Bulldogge, -n f.

bullet, n. Kugel, -n f.

bulletin, *n.* Bericht', -e *m.*

bully, 1. *n.* Kraftmeier, - *m.* 2. *vb.* kraftmeiern.

bulwark, *n.* Bollwerk, -e *nt.*

bum, 1. *n. (fam.)* Lump, -en, -en *m.* 2. *vb. (fam.)* pumpen.

bumblebee, *n.* Hummel, -n *f.*

bump, 1. *n.* Stoß, ¨e *m.* 2. *vb.* stoßen*.

bumper, *n.* Stoßstange, -n *f.*

bun, *n.* Brötchen, - *nt.*

bunch, *n.* Büschel, - *nt.*

bundle, *n.* Bündel, - *nt.*

bungle, *vb.* pfuschen.

bunion, *n.* Enzün'dung am großen Zeh.

bunny, *n.* Kanin'chen, - *nt.*

buoy, *n.* Boje, -n *f.*

buoyant, *adj.* schwimmend, tragfähig; *(fig.)* lebhaft.

burden, 1. *n.* Last, -en *f.* 2. *vb.* belas'ten.

burdensome, *adj.* beschwer'lich.

bureau, *n.* Büro', -s *nt.; (furniture)* Kommo'de, -n *f.*

burglar, *n.* Einbrecher, - *m.*

burglary, *n.* Einbruch, ¨e *m.*

burial, *n.* Begräb'nis, -se *nt.*

burlap, *n.* grobe Leinwand *f.*

burly, *adj.* stämmig.

burn, 1. *n.* Verbren'nung, -en *f.* 2. *vb. (intr.)* brennen*, *(tr.)* verbren'nen*.

burner, *n.* Brenner, - *m.*

burrow, 1. *n. (of an animal)* Bau, -e *m.* 2. *vb.* sich eingraben*.

burst, 1. *n.* Krach, -e *m.;* Explosion', -en *f.* 2. *vb. (intr.)* platzen; *(tr.)* sprengen.

bury, *vb.* begra'ben*; eingraben*.

bus, *n.* Bus, -se *m.*

bush, *n.* Busch, ¨e *m.*

bushel, *n.* Scheffel, - *m.*

bushy, *adj.* buschig.

business, *n.* Geschäft', -e *nt.*

businesslike, *adj.* geschäftsmäßig.

businessman, *n.* Geschäfts'mann, ¨er *or* -leute *m.*

businesswoman, *n.* Geschäfts'frau, -en *f.*

bust, 1. *n.* Büste, -n *f.* 2. *vb. (fam.)* kaputt' machen.

bustle, *n.* Geschäf'tigkeit, -en *f.*

busy, *adj.* beschäf'tigt; geschäf'tig.

but, 1, *prep.* außer., 2. *conj.* aber.

butcher, *n.* Fleischer, - *m.,* Metzger, - *m.,* Schlächter, - *m.,* Schlachter, - *m.*

butler, *n.* Diener, - *m.*

butt, 1, *n. (gun)* Kolben, - *m.; (aim)* Ziel, -e *nt.* 2. *vb.* mit dem Kopf stoßen*.

butter, *n.* Butter *f.*

butterfly, *n.* Schmetterling, -e *m.*

buttermilk, *n.* Buttermilch *f.*

buttocks, *n.pl.* Gesäß', -e *nt.*

button, *n.* Knopf, ¨e *m.*

buttonhole, *n.* Knopfloch, ¨er *nt.*

buttress, 1. *n.* Stütze, -n *f.; (arch.)* Strebepfeiler, - *m.* 2. *vb.* stützen.

buxom, *adj.* drall.

buy, *vb.* kaufen.

buyer, *n.* Käufer, - *m.*

buzz, *vb.* summen.

buzzard, *n.* Bussard, -e *m.*

buzzer, *n.* Klingel, -n *f.*

by, *prep.* von; *(through)* durch; *(near)* bei.

by-and-by, *adv.* später.

bygone, *adj.* vergan'gen.

by-pass, *n.* Umge'hungsstraße, -n *f.*

by-product, *n.* Nebenprodukt, -e *nt.*

bystander, *n.* Zuschauer, - *m.*

byte, *n.* Byte, -s *nt.*

byway, *n.* Nebenweg, -e *m.*

C

cab, *n. (taxi)* Taxe, -n *f.,* Taxi, -s *nt.; (locomotive)* Führerstand, -e *m.*

cabaret, *n.* Kabarett' -e *nt.*

cabbage, *n.* Kohl *m.*

cabin, *n.* Kabi'ne, -n *f.*

cabinet, *n.* Kabinett', -e *nt.*

cabinetmaker, *n.* Kunsttischler, - *m.*

cable, 1. *n.* Kabel, - *nt.* 2. *vb.* kabeln.

cablegram, *n.* Kabel, - *nt.*

cache, *n.* Versteck', -e *nt.*

cackle, *vb.* gackern.

cactus, *n.* Kaktus, -te'en *m.*

cad, *n.* Schuft, -e *m.*

cadaver, *n.* Leichnam, -e *m.*

cadet, *n.* Kadett', -en, -en *m.*

cadence, *n.* Tonfall, ¨e *m.;* Kadenz', -en *f.*

cadmium, *n.* Kadmium *nt.*

café, *n.* Cafe', -s *nt.;* Konditorei', -en *f.*

caffeine, *n.* Koffein', -e *nt.*

cage, *n.* Käfig, -e *m.*

cajole, *vb.* beschwat'zen.

cake, *n.* Kuchen, - *m.*

calamity, *n.* Unglück, -e *nt.*

calcium, *n.* Kalzium *nt.*

calculable, *adj.* bere'chenbar.

calculate, *vb.* berech'nen.

calculating machine, *n.* Rechenmaschine, -n *f.*

calculation, *n.* Berech'nung, -en *f.*

calculus, *n.* Differential'rechnung, -en *f.*

caldron, *n.* Kessel, - *m.*

calendar, *n.* Kalen'der, - *m.*

calf, *n.* Kalb, ¨er *nt.*

calfskin, *n.* Kalbleder, - *nt.*

caliber, *n.* Kali'ber, - *nt.*

calico, *n.* Kattun', -e *m.*

calipers, *n.pl.* Greifzirkel, - *m.*

calisthenics, *n.pl.* Leibesübungen *pl.*

call, 1. *n.* Ruf, -e *m.; (telephone)* Anruf, -e *m.* 2. *vb.* rufen*.

calling card, *n.* Visi'tenkarte, -n *f.*

callous, *adj.* schwielig; *(unfeeling)* gefühl'los.

callus, *n.* Schwiele, -n *f.*

calm, 1. *adj.* ruhig. 2. *vb.* beru'higen.

calmness, *n.* Ruhe *f.*

caloric, *adj.* kalo'risch.

calorie, *n.* Kalorie', -i'en *f.*

Calvary, *n.* Kalva'rienberg *m.*

calve, *vb.* kalben.

cambric, *n.* Batist', -e *m.*

camel, *n.* Kamel', -e *nt.*

cameo, *n.* Kame'e, -n *f.*

camera, *n.* Kamera, -s *f.;* Photoapparat, -e *m.*

camouflage, 1. *n.* Tarnung, -en *f.; (natural c.)* Mimikry *f.* Schutzfarbe, -n *f.* 2. *vb.* tarnen.

camp, 1. *n.* Lager, - *nt.* 2. *vb.* lagern.

campaign, 1. *n.* Feldzug, ¨e *m.;* Kampag'ne, -n *f.* 2. *vb. (political)* Wahlreden halten*.

camper, *n.* Zelter, - *m.*

camphor, *n.* Kampfer *m.*

camping, *n.* Zelten *nt.*

campus, *n.* Universitäts'gelände, - *nt.,* College-Gelände, - *nt.*

can, 1. *n. (tin)* Büchse, -n *f.; (large)* Kanne, -n *f.* 2. *vb. (preserve)* ein·machen; *(be able)* können*.

Canada, *n.* Kanada *nt.*

Canadian, 1. *n.* Kana'dier, - *m.* 2. *adj.* kana'disch.

canal, *n.* Kanal', -e *m.*

canapé, *n.* Cocktailgebäck *nt.*

canary, *n.* Kana'rienvogel, ¨ *m.*

cancel, *vb.* entwer'ten, rückgängig machen, auf·heben*.

cancellation, *n.* Aufhebung, -en *f.,* Entwer'tung, -en *f.*

cancer, *n.* Krebs, -e *m.*

candelabrum, *n.* Armleuchter, - *m.*

candid, *adj.* offen, ehrlich.

candidacy, *n.* Kandidatur', -en *f.*

candidate, *n.* Kandidat', -en, -en *m.*

candied, *adj.* kandiert'.

candle, *n.* Kerze, -n *f.*

candlestick, *n.* Leuchter, - *m.*

candor, *n.* Offenheit, -en *f.*

cane, *n.* Stock, ¨e *m; (sugar)* Rohr, -e *nt.*

canine, *adj.* Hunde- *(cpds.).*

canister, *n.* Blechbüchse, -n *f.*

canker, *n.* Krebs, -e *m.*

canned, *adj.* eingemacht; Büchsen- *(cpds.).*

cannibal, *n.* Kanniba'le, -n, -n *m.*

canning, *n.* Einmachen *nt.*

cannon, *n.* Kano'ne, -n *f.*

cannot, *vb.* nicht können*.

canny, *adj.* schlau, umsichtig.

canoe, *n.* Kanu´, -s *nt.*

canon, *n.* *(rule, song)* Kanon, -s *m.;* *(person)* Domherr, -n, -en *m.*

canonical, *adj.* kano´nisch.

canonize, *vb.* kanonisie´ren.

can opener, *n.* Büchsenöffner, - *m.*

canopy, *n.* Baldachin, -e *m.*

cant, *n.* Heuchelei´, -en *f.*

cantaloupe, *n.* Melo´ne, -n *f.*

canteen, *n.* Kanti´ne, -n *f.*

canvas, *n.* *(material)* Segeltuch *nt.; (painter's)* Leinwand *f.*

canvass, 1. *n.* Stimmenprüfung, -en *f.* **2.** *vb.* untersu´chen, prüfen.

canyon, *n.* Schlucht, -en *f.*

cap, *n.* Mütze, -n *f.*

capability, *n.* Fähigkeit, -en *f.*

capable, *adj.* fähig.

capacious, *adj.* geräu´mig.

capacity, *n.* *(content)* Inhalt *m.; (ability)* Fähigkeit, -en *f.; (quality)* Eigenschaft, -en *f.*

cape, *n.* *(clothing)* Umhang, ⸚e *m.; (geogr.)* Kap, -s *nt.*

caper, 1. *n.* Luftsprung, ⸚e *m.* **2.** *vb.* Luftsprünge machen.

capital, 1. *n.* *(money)* Kapital´, -ien *nt.; (city)* Hauptstadt, ⸚e *f.* **2.** *adj.* kapital´.

capitalism, *n.* Kapitalis´mus *m.*

capitalist, *n.* Kapitalist´, -en, - en *m.*

capitalistic, *adj.* kapitalistisch.

capitalization, *n.* Kapitalisie´rung, -en *f.*

capitalize, *vb.* kapitalisie´ren.

capitulate, *vb.* kapitulie´ren.

capon, *n.* Kapaun´, -e *m.*

caprice, *n.* Laune, -n *f.*

capricious, *adj.* launenhaft.

capsize, *vb.* kentern.

capsule, *n.* Kapsel, -n *f.*

captain, *n.* Kapitän´, -e *m.; (army)* Hauptmann, -leute *m.*

caption, *n.* Überschrift, -en *f.*

captious, *adj.* verfäng´lich.

captivate, *vb.* fesseln.

captive, 1. *n.* Gefan´gen, - *m.&f.* **2.** *adj.* gefan´gen.

captivity, *n.* Gefan´genschaft, - en *f.*

captor, *n.* Fänger, - *m.*

capture, 1. *n.* Gefan´gennahme, -n *f.* **2.** *vb.* *(person)* fangen*; *(city)* ero´bern.

car, *n.* Wagen, - *m.;* Auto, -s *nt.*

carafe, *n.* Karaf´fe, -n *f.*

caramel, *n.* Karamel´ *nt.*

carat, *n.* Karat´, -e *nt.*

caravan, *n.* Karawa´ne, -n *f.*

caraway, *n.* Kümmel *m.*

carbide, *n.* Karbid´ *nt.*

carbine, *n.* Karabi´ner, - *m.*

carbohydrate, *n.* Kohlehydrat, -e *nt.*

carbon, *n.* Kohlenstoff, -e *m.*

carbon dioxide, *n.* Kohlendioxyd *nt.*

carbon monoxide, *n.* Kohleoxyd´ *nt.*

carbon paper, *n.* Kohlepapier, -e *nt.*

carbuncle, *n.* Karbun´kel, - *m.; (gem)* Karfun´kel, - *m.*

carburetor, *n.* Verga´ser, - *m.*

carcass, *n.* Kada´ver, - *m.*

carcinogenic, *adj.* krebserregend.

card, *n.* Karte, -n *f.*

cardboard, *n.* Pappe, -n *f.*

cardiac, *adj.* Herz- *(cpds.).*

cardinal, 1. *n.* Kardinal´, -e *m.* **2.** *adj.* hauptsächlich.

care, 1. *n.* *(worry)* Sorge, -n *f.; (prudence)* Vorsicht *f.; (accuracy)* Sorgfalt *f.; (take c. of)* sorgen für. **2.** *vb.* *(attend)* sorgen für; (c. for, like) gern mögen*; **(c. about)** sich kümmern um.

careen, *vb.* wild fahren*.

career, *n.* Karrie´re, -n *f.*

carefree, *adj.* sorglos.

careful, *adj.* *(prudent)* vorsichtig; *(accurate)* sorgfältig.

carefulness, *n.* *(prudence)* Vorsicht *f.; (accuracy)* Sorgfalt *f.*

careless, *adj.* *(imprudent)* unvorsichtig; *(inaccurate)* unsorgfältig, nachlässig.

carelessness, *n.* *(imprudence)* Unvorsichtigkeit, -en *f.; (inaccuracy)* Nachlässigkeit, -en *f.*

caress, 1. *n.* Liebkosung, -en *f.* **2.** *vb.* liebkosen, streicheln.

caretaker, *n.* Verwal´ter, - *m.*

cargo, *n.* Ladung, -en *f.,* Fracht, -en *f.*

caricature, 1. *n.* Karikatur´, -en *f.* **2.** *vb.* karikie´ren.

caries, *n.* Karies *f.*

carload, *n.* Waggon´ladung, -en *f.*

carnal, *adj.* fleischlich.

carnation, *n.* Nelke, -n *f.*

carnival, *n.* Karneval, -s *m.*

carnivorous, *adj.* fleischfressend.

carol, 1. *n.* Weihnachtslied, -er *nt.* **2.** *vb.* singen*.

carouse, *vb.* zechen.

carousel, *n.* Karussell´, -s *nt.*

carpenter, *n.* *(construction)* Zimmermann, -leute *m; (finer work)* Tischler, - *m.*

carpet, *n.* Teppich, -e *m.*

car pool, *n.* Mitnehmen von anderen im Auto zwecks Benzin-und Zeitersparnis *nt.*

carriage, *n.* *(vehicle)* Wagen, - *m.; (posture)* Haltung, -en *f.*

carrier, *n.* Träger, - *m.*

carrot, *n.* Mohr´rübe, -n *f.*

carry, *vb.* tragen*; (c. on, intr.) fort·fahren*; (c. on, tr.) fortsetzen; (c. out) aus·führen; (c. through) durch·führen.

cart, *n.* Karren, - *m.*

cartage, *n.* Transport´, -e *m.*

cartel, *n.* Kartell´, -e *nt.*

cartilage, *n.* Knorpel, - *m.*

carton, *n.* Karton´, -s *m.*

cartoon, *n.* Karikatur´, -en *f.*

cartridge, *n.* Patro´en, -n *f.*

carve, *vb.* schneiden*; *(wood)* schnitzen; *(meat)* zerle´gen, tranchie´ren.

carving, *n.* Schnitzerk, -e *nt.*

case, 1. *n.* Fall, ⸚e *m.*

cash, 1. *n.* Bargeld, -er *nt.* **2.** *vb.* ein·lösen. **3.** *adj.* bar.

cashier, *n.* Kassie´rer, - *m.*

cashmere, *n.* Kaschmir, -e *m.*

casing, *n.* Hülle, -n *f.*

casino, *n.* Kasi´no, -s *nt.*

cask, *n.* Tonne, -n *f.,* Faß, ⸚sser *nt.*

casket, *n.* Sarg, ⸚e *m.*

casserole, *n.* Schmorpfanne, -n *f.*

cassette, *n.* Kaset´te, -n *f.*

cast, 1. *n.* *(theater)* Rollenverteilung, -en *f.* **2.** *vb.* *(throw)* werfen*; *(metal)* gießen*.

caste, *n.* Kaste, -n *f.*

castigate, *vb.* züchtigen.

castle, *n.* Schloß, ⸚sser, *nt.*

castoff, *adj.* abgelegt.

castor oil, *n.* Rizinusöl, -e *nt.*

casual, *adj.* *(accidental)* zufällig; *(nonchalant)* zwanglos.

casualness, *n.* Zwanglosigkeit, -en *f.*

casualty, *n.* Opfer, - *nt.; (casualties)* Verlus´te *pl.*

cat, *n.* Katze, -n *f.; (tomcat)* Kater, - *m.*

cataclysm, *n.* Sündflut, -en *f.*

catacomb, *n.* Katakom´be, -n *f.*

catalogue, *n.* Katalog´, -e *m.*

catapult, *n.* Katapult´, -e *m.*

cataract, *n.* *(eye)* Katarakt´, -e *m.,* grauer Star, -e *m.*

catarrh, *n.* Katarrh´, -e *m.*

catastrophe, *n.* Katastro´phe, - *f.*

catch, *vb.* fangen*; *(sickness, train)* bekom´men*.

catcher, *n.* Fänger, - *m.*

catechism, *n.* Katechis´mus, -men *m.*

categorical, *adj.* katego´risch.

category, *n.* Kategorie´, -i´en *f.*

cater, *vb.* versor´gen.

caterpillar, *n.* Raupe, -n *f.*

cathartic, 1. *n.* Abführmittel, - *nt.* **2.** *adj.* abführend.

cathedral, *n.* Kathedra´le, -n *f.;* Dom, -e *m.*

cathode, *n.* Katho´de, -n *f.*

Catholic, 1. *n.* Katholik´, -en, -en *m.* **2.** *adj.* katho´lisch.

Catholicism, *n.* Katholizis´mus, -men *m.*

catsup, *n.* Ketchup *m.*

cattle, *n.* Vieh *nt.*

cauliflower, *n.* Blumenkohl, - *m.*

cause, 1. *n.* *(origin)* Ursache, - *f.; (idea)* Sache, -n *f.* **2.** *vb.* verur´sachen.

caustic, *adj.* beißend.

cauterize, *vb.* aus·brennen*.

cautery, *n.* Ausbrennen *nt.*

caution, 1. *n.* Vorsicht, -en *f.* **2.** *vb.* warnen.

cautious, *adj.* vorsichtig.

cavalcade, *n.* Kavalka'de, -n *f.*

cavalier, *n.* Kavalier', -e *m.*

cavalry, *n.* Kavallerie', -i'en *f.*

cave, *n.* Höhle, -n *f.*

cavern, *n.* Höhle, -n *f.*

caviar, *n.* Kaviar *m.*

cavity, *n.* Loch, ⁼er *nt.*, Höhle, -n *f.*

cease, *vb.* *(intr.)* auf•hören, *(tr.)* ein•stellen.

cedar, *n.* Zeder, -n *f.*

cede, *vb.* ab•treten*.

ceiling, *n.* Zimmerdecke, -n *f.; (fig.)* Höchstgrenze, -n *f.*

celebrate, *vb.* feiern.

celebrated, *adj.* berühmt'.

celebration, *n.* Feier, -n *f.*

celebrity, *n.* Berühmt'heit, -en *f.*

celery, *n.* Sellerie *m.*

celestial, *adj.* himmlisch.

celibacy, *n.* Zölibat', *nt.*, Ehelosigkeit *f.*

celibate, *adj.* ehelos.

cell, *n.* Zelle, -n *f.*

cellar, *n.* Keller, - *m.*

cellist, *n.* Cellist', -en, -en *m.*

cello, *n.* Cello, -s *nt.*

cellophane, *n.* Cellophan' *nt.*

celluloid, *n.* Zelluloid' *nt.*

cellulose, *n.* Zellstoff, -e *m.*

Celtic, *adj.* keltisch.

cement, 1. *n.* Zement', -e *m.* 2. *vb.* zementie'ren.

cemetery, *n.* Friedhof, ⁼e *m.*

censor, 1. *n.* Zensor, -o'ren *m.* 2. *vb.* zensie'ren.

censorship, *n.* Zensur', -en *f.*

censure, *n.* Tadel, - *m.*, Verweis', -e *m.*

census, *n.* Volkszählung, -en *f.*, Zensus, - *m.*

cent, *n.* Cent, -s *m.*

centenary, *n.* Hundertjahr'feier, -n *f.*

centennial, 1. *n.* Hundertjahr'feier, -n *f.* 2. *adj.* hundertjährig.

center, *n.* Mitte, -n *f.;* Mittelpunkt, -e *m.;* Zentrum, -tren *nt.*

centerfold, *n.* Mittelfaltblatt, ⁼er *nt.*

centigrade, *n.* (c. thermometer) Celsiusthermometer, - *nt.;* (10 degrees c.) 10 Grad Celsius.

central, *adj.* zentral'.

centralize, *vb.* zentralisie'ren.

century, *n.* Jahrhun'dert, -e *nt.*

ceramic, *adj.* kera'misch.

ceramics, *n.* Kera'mik, -en *f.*

cereal, *n.* Getrei'de, - *nt.*, Getrei'despeise, - n *f.*

cerebral, *adj.* Gehirn- *(cpds.).*

ceremonial, *adj.* zeremoniell'.

ceremonious, *adj.* feierlich.

ceremony, *n.* Zeremonie', -i'en *f.;* Feierlichkeit, -en *f.*

certain, *adj.* sicher.

certainty, *n.* Gewißheit, -en *f.*

certificate, *n.* Beschei'nigung, -en *f.;* Urkunde, -n *f.*

certification, *n.* Beschei'nigung, -en *f.*

certify, *vb.* beschei'nigen, beglau'bigen, bezeu'gen.

cervix, *n.* Gebär'mutterhals *m.*

cessation, *n.* Aufhören *nt.*

cesspool, *n.* Senkgrube, -n *f.*

chafe, *vb.* reiben*.

chagrin, *n.* Kummer, - *m.*

chain, 1. *n.* Kette, -n *f.* 2. *vb.* an•ketten, fesseln.

chain reaction, *n.* Kettenreaktion, -en *f.*

chair, *n.* Stuhl, ⁼e *m.*

chairman, *n.* Vorsitzend- *m.*

chairperson, *n.* Vorsitzend- *m. & f.*

chalice, *n.* Kelch, -e *m.*

chalk, *n.* Kreide, -n *f.*

chalky, *adj.* kreidig.

challenge, 1. *n.* Heraus'forderung, -en *f.* 2. *vb.* heraus•fordern, auf•fordern.

challenger, *n.* Heraus'forderer, - *m.*

chamber, *n.* Kammer, -n *f.; (pol.)* Haus, ⁼er *nt.*

chambermaid, *n.* Zimmermädchen, - *nt.*

chamber music, *n.* Kammermusik *f.*

chamois, *n.* (animal) Gemse, -n *f.;* (leather) Wildleder *nt.*

champagne, *n.* Sekt, -e *m.*, Champag'ner, - *m.*

champion, *n.* Kämpfer, - *m.;* (sport) Meister, - *m.*

championship, *n.* Meisterschaft, -en *f.*

chance, 1. *n.* Zufall, ⁼e *m.; (expectation)* Aussicht, -en *f.; (occasion)* Gele'genheit, -en *f.* 2. *vb.* wagen. 3. *adj.* zufällig.

chancel, *n.* Altar'platz, ⁼e *m.*

chancellery, *n.* Kanzlei', -en *f.*

chancellor, *n.* Kanzler, - *m.*

chandelier, *n.* Kronleuchter, - *m.*

change, 1. *n.* Verän'derung, -en *f.; (alteration)* Änderung, -en *f.; (variety)* Abwechslung, -en *f.; (small coins)* Kleingeld *nt.; (money due)* Rest *m.* 2. *vb.* verändern; (alter) ändern; (money) wechseln.

changeability, *n.* Unbeständigkeit, -en *f.*

changeable, *adj.* unbeständig.

channel, *n.* Fahrwasser *nt.*, Kanal', ⁼e *m.;* (radio) Frequenz'band, Fer *nt.*

chant, 1. *n.* Gesang', ⁼e *m.* 2. *vb.* singen*.

chaos, *n.* Chaos, *nt.*

chaotic, *adj.* chao'tisch.

chap, 1. *n.* Bursche, -n, -n *m.*, Kerl, -e *m.* 2. *vb.* (become chapped) auf•springen*.

chapel, *n.* Kapel'le, -n *f.*

chaplain, *n.* Geistlich- *m.;* (mil.) Feldgeistlich- *m.*

chapter, *n.* Kapi'tel, - *nt.*

char, *vb.* verkoh'len.

character, *n.* Charak'ter, -te're *m.*

characteristic, *adj.* charakteri'stisch.

characterization, *n.* Charakterisie'rung, -en *f.*

characterize, *vb.* charakterisie'ren.

charcoal, *n.* Holzkohle, -n *f.*

charge, 1. *n.* (load) Ladung, -en *f.; (attack)* Angriff, -e *m.; (price)* Preis, -e *m.; (custody)* Obhut, -en *f.* 2. *vb.* (load) laden*; (set a price) berech'nen; (put on one's account) an•schreiben* lassen*.

chariot, *n.* Wagen, - *m.*

charisma, *n.* Charis'ma *nt.*

charitable, *adj.* wohltätig, nachsichtig.

charity, *n.* Wohltätigkeit, -en *f.*, Nächstenliebe *f.*

charlatan, *n.* Scharlatan, -e *m.*

charm, 1. *n.* Charme *m.;* Liebreiz, -e *m.; (magic saying)* Zauberspruch, ⁼e *m.* 2. *vb.* bezau'bern.

charming, *adj.* bezau'bernd, reizend.

chart, *n.* (map) Karte, -n *f.;* (graph) Tabel'le, -n *f.*

charter, *n.* Urkunde, -n *f.*

charter flight, *n.* Charterflug, ⁼e *m.*

charwoman, *n.* Putzfrau, -en *f.*

chase, 1. *n.* Jagd, -en *f.* 2. *vb.* jagen.

chasm, *n.* Abgrund, ⁼e *m.*

chassis, *n.* Fahrgestell, -e *nt.*

chaste, *adj.* züchtig, keusch.

chasten, *vb.* züchtigen.

chastise, *vb.* züchtigen.

chastity, *n.* Keuschheit *f.*

chat, 1. *n.* Plauderei', -en *f.* 2. *vb.* plaudern.

chateau, *n.* Chateau', -s *nt.*

chatter, 1. *n.* Geschwätz' *nt.* 2. *vb.* schwatzen; (teeth) klappern.

chauffeur, *n.* Fahrer, - *m.*, Chauffeur', -e *m.*

cheap, *adj.* billig, (fig.) ordinär'.

cheapen, *vb.* im Wert herab'setzen.

cheapness, *n.* Billigkeit, -en *f.*

cheat, *vb.* betrü'gen*; (harmless) schummeln.

check, 1. *n.* (restraint) Hemmnis, -se *nt.; (verification)* Kontrol'le, - n *f.,* Überprü'fung, -en *f.; (clothes, luggage)* Kontroll'marke, -n *f.; (bank)* Scheck, -s *m.; (bill)* Rechnung, -en *f.* 2. *vb.* (verify) kontrollie'ren, überprü'fen; (luggage) auf•geben*, ab•geben*; (mark) ab•hacken.

checkerboard, *n.* Damebrett, - er *nt.*

checkers, *n.* Damespiel *nt.*

cheek, *n.* Backe, -n *f.*, Wange, - n *f.*

cheer, 1. *n.* Beifallsruf, -e *m.* 2. *vb.* Beifall rufen*; (c. up) auf•muntern.

cheerful, *adj.* fröhlich.

cheerfulness, n. Fröhlichkeit f.

cheery, adj. heiter.

cheese, n. Käse m.

cheesecloth, n. grobe Gaze, -n f.

chef, n. Küchenchef, -s m.

chemical, 1. chemisches Präparat', -e nt.; (c. s) Chemikal'ien pl. 2. adj. chemisch.

chemist, n. Chemiker, -m.

chemistry, n. Chemie' f.

chemotherapy, n. Chemotherapie' f.

chenille, n. Chenille', -n f.

cherish, vb. schätzen.

cherry, n. Kirsche, -n f.

cherub, n. Cherub, -s or -im or -i'nen m.

chess, n. Schach nt., Schachspiel nt.

chessboard, n. Schachbrett, -er nt.

chessman, n. Schachfigur, -en f.

chest, n. (box) Kiste, -n f., Truhe, -n f.; (body) Brust f.

chestnut, n. Kasta'nie, -n f.

chevron, n. Dienstgradabzeichen, - nt.

chew, vb. kauen.

chic, adj. schick; elegant'.

chick, n. Küken, - nt.

chicken, n. Huhn, -er nt.

chicken pox, n. Windpocken pl.

chicory, n. Zicho'rie, -n f.

chide, vb. schelten*.

chief, 1. n. Oberhaupt, -er nt. 2. adj. hauptsächlich; Haupt- (cpds.).

chieftain, n. Häuptling, -e m.

chiffon, n. Chiffon', -s m.

child, n. Kind, -er nt.

childbirth, n. Niederkunft f.

childhood, n. Kindheit, -en f.

childish, adj. kindisch.

childishness, n. Kindhaftigkeit, -en f.

childless, adj. kinderlos.

childlike, adj. kindlich.

chill, 1. n. Frost, -e m.; (fever) Schauer, - m. 2. vb. auf Eis stellen.

chilliness, n. Kühle f.

chilly, adj. kühl.

chime, 1. n. (chimes) Glockenspiel, -e nt. 2. vb. läuten.

chimney, n. Schornstein, -e m.

chimpanzee, n. Schimpan'se, -n, -n m.

chin, n. Kinn, -e nt.

china, n. Porzellan', -e nt.

China, n. China nt.

chinchilla, n. Chinchil'la, -s m.

Chinese, 1. n. Chine'se, -n, -n m.; Chine'sin, -nen f. 2. adj. chine'sisch.

chintz, n. Chintz, -e m.

chip, 1. n. Splitter, - m. 2. vb. ab•brechen*; ab•splittern.

chiroposdist, n. Fußpfleger, - m.

chiropractor, n. Chiroprak'tiker, - m.

chirp, 1. n. Gezirp' nt. 2. vb. zirpen.

chisel, 1. n. (stone, metal) Meißel, - m.; (wood) Beitel, - m. 2. vb. meißeln.

chivalrous, adj. ritterlich.

chivalry, n. Ritterlichkeit, -en f.

chive, n. Schnittlauch, m.

chloride, n. Chlorid', -e nt.

chlorine, n. Chlor, -s nt.

chloroform, n. Chloroform' nt.

chocolate, n. Schokola'de, -n f.

choice, n. Wahl, -en f.; (selection) Auswahl, -en f.

choir, n. Chor, -e m.

choke, vb. erwür'gen, erstick'en.

choker, n. Halsband, -er nt.

cholera, n. Cholera f.

choose, vb. wählen.

chop, 1. n. (meat) Kotelett', -s nt. 2. vb. hacken.

choppy, adj. (sea) unruhig.

choral, adj. Chor- (cpds.).

chord, n. (string) Saite, -n f.; (harmony) Akkord', -e m.

chore, n. Alltagsarbeit, -en f.

choreographer, n. Choreograph', -en, -en m.

choreography, n. Choreographie', -i'en f.

chorus, n. Chor, -e m.; Refrain', -s m.

Christ, n. Christus m.

christen, vb. taufen.

Christendom, n. Christenheit f.

christening, n. Taufe, -n f.

Christian, 1. n. Christ, -en, -en m. 2. adj. christlich.

Christianity, n. Christentum nt.

Christmas, n. Weihnachten nt.

chrome, chromium, n. Chrom nt.

chronic, adj. chronisch.

chronicle, n. Chronik, -en f.

chronological, adj. chronologisch.

chronology, n. Chronologie', -i'en f.

chrysanthemum, n. Chrysanthe'me, -n f.

chubby, adj. dicklich.

chuckle, vb. vergnügt'lachen.

chug, vb. daher'•keuchen.

chunk, n. Stück, -e m.

church, n. Kirche, -n f.

churchyard, n. Kirchhof, -e m.

churn, 1. n. Butterfaß, -sser nt. 2. vb. buttern; (fig.) auf•wühlen.

chute, n. (mail) Postschacht, -e m.; (laundry) Wäscheschacht, -e m.

cider, n. Apfelwein, -e m.

cigar, n. Zigar're, -n f.

cigarette, n. Zigaret'te, -n f.

cinch, n. Sattelgurt, -e m; (fam.) Kleinigkeit, -en f.

cinder, n. Asche, -n f.

cinema, n. Kino, -s nt.

cinnamon, n. Zimt m.

cipher, n. (number) Ziffer, -n

f.; (zero) Null, -en f.; (code) Chiffre, -n f.

circle, n. Kreis, -en m.

circuit, n. (course) Umkreis, -e m.; (elec.) Stromkreis, -e m.; (short c.) Kurzschluß, -sse m.

circuitous, adj. umwegig.

circular, 1. n. Rundschreiben, - nt. 2. adj. kreisförmig.

circulate, vb. zirkulie'ren.

circulation, n. (blood) Kreislauf, -e m.; (paper) Auflage, -n f.; (money) Umlauf, -e m.

circulatory, adj. zirkulie'rend.

circumcise, vb. beschnei'den*.

circumcision, n. Beschneidung, -en f.

circumference, n. Umfang, -e m.

circumlocution, n. Umschreibung, -en f.

circumscribe, vb. (geom.) umschrei'ben*; (delimit) begren'zen.

circumspect, adj. umsichtig.

circumstance, n. Umstand, -e m.; (pl.) Verhält'nisse pl.

circumstantial, adj. eingehend; (c. evidence) Indi'zienbeweis, -e m.

circumvent, vb. umge'hen*.

circumvention, n. Umge'hung, -en f.

circus, n. Zirkus, -se m.

cirrhosis, n. Zirrho'se, -n f.

cistern, n. Zister'ne, -n f.

citadel, n. Zitadel'le, -n f.

citation, n. Auszeichnung, -en f.; (law) Vorladung, -en f.

cite, vb. an•führen, zitie'ren; (law) vor•laden*.

citizen, n. Bürger, - m.

citizenship, n. Staatsangehörigkeit, -en f.

city, n. Stadt, -e f.

civic, adj. Bürger- (cpds.).

civil, adj. bürgerlich; (law) zivil'rechtlich; (polite) höflich.

civilian, 1. n. Zivilist', -en, -en m. 2. adj. bürgerlich.

civility, n. Höflichkeit, -en f.

civilization, n. Zivilisation', -en f.

civilize, vb. zivilisie'ren.

civilized, adj. zivilisiert'.

clad, adj. gekleidet.

claim, 1. n. Anspruch, -e m. 2. vb. bean'spruchen, fordern.

claimant, n. Bean'spruchende m.&f.

clairvoyance, n. Hellsehen f.

clairvoyant, 1. n. Hellseher, - m. 2. adj. hellseherisch.

clammy, adj. feuchtkalt.

clamor, 1. n. Geschrei' nt. 2. vb. schreien*.

clamp, 1. n. Klammer, -n f. 2. vb. fest•klammern.

clandestine, adj. heimlich.

clap, vb. klatschen.

claret, n. Rotwein, -e m.

clarification, n. Klarstellung, -en f.

clarify, vb. klar•stellen.

clarinet, *n.* Klarinet'te, -n *f.*

clarity, *n.* Klarheit, -en *f.*

clash, 1. *n.* Zusam'menstoß, = *m.* 2. *vb.* zusam'men·stoßen*; *(fig.)* sich nicht vertra'gen*.

clasp, 1. *n.* Schnalle, -n *f.;* *(hands)* Händedruck *m.* 2. *vb.* fest·schnallen; *(grasp)* umfas'sen; *(embrace)* umar'men.

class, *n.* Klasse, -n *f.; (period of instruction)* Stunde, -n *f.*

classic, classical, *adj.* klassisch.

classicism, *n.* Klassizis'mus, -men *m.*

classification, *n.* Klassifizie'rung, -en *f.*

classify, *vb.* klassifizie'ren.

classmate, *n.* Klassenkamerad, -en, -en *m.*

classroom, *n.* Klassenzimmer, - *nt.*

clatter, 1. *n.* Geklap'per *nt.* 2. *vb.* klappern.

clause, *n.* Satzteil, -e *m.;* **(main c.)** Hauptsatz, =e *m.;* **(subordinate c.)** Nebensatz, =e *m.;* *(law)* Klausel, -n *f.*

claw, 1. *n.* Kralle, -n *f.,* Klaue, -n *f.* 2. *vb.* krallen.

clay, *n.* Ton, -e *m.,* Lehm, -e *m.*

clean, 1. *vb.* sauber machen, reinigen. 2. *adj.* sauber.

clean-cut, *adj.* sauber.

cleaner, *n.* **(the c.s)** Reinigung, -en *f.*

cleanliness, cleanness, *n.* Sauberkeit *f.*

cleanse, *vb.* reinigen.

clear, 1. *vb.* klären; *(profit)* rein verdie'nen; *(weather)* sich auf·klären. 2. *adj.* klar.

clearance, *n. (enough space)* Raum *m.; (sale)* Räumung, -en *f.; (approval)* Gutheißung *f.*

clearing, *n.* Lichtung, -en *f.*

clearness, *n.* Klarheit, -en *f.*

cleat, *n. (naut.)* Klampe, -n *f.; (on boots)* Krampe, -n *f.*

cleavage, *n.* Spaltung, -en *f.*

cleave, *vb.* spalten*.

cleaver, *n.* Fleischerbeil, -e *nt.*

clef, *n.* Notenschlüssel, - *m.*

cleft, 1. *n.* Spalte, -n *f.* 2. *adj.* gespal'ten.

clemency, *n.* Milde *f.*

clench, *vb.* zusam'men·pressen; *(fist)* ballen.

clergy, *n.* Geistlichkeit *f.*

clergyman, *n.* Geistlich, -n *m.*

clerical, *adj. (eccles.)* geistlich, klerikal'; *(writing)* Schreib- *(cpds.).*

clerk, *n.* Schreiber, - *m.; (salesc.)* Verkäu'fer, - *m.,* Verkäu'ferin, -nen *f.*

clever, *adj.* klug (-), geschickt', schlau.

cleverness, *n.* Klugheit, -en *f.,* Geschick'lichkeit, -en *f.*

clew, *n. (object)* Knäuel, - *nt.; (fact)* Anhaltspunkt, -e *m.,* Schlüssel, - *m.*

cliché, *n.* Klischee', -s *nt.*

click, 1. *n.* Klicken *nt.; (lan-*

---

guage) Schnalzlaut, -e *m.* 2. *vb.* klicken, knacken.

client, *n.* Kunde, -n, -n *m.,* Klient', -en, -en *m.*

clientele, *n.* Kundschaft, -en *f.*

cliff, *n.* Klippe, -n *f.*

climate, *n.* Klima, -s *or* a'te *nt.*

climatic, *adj.* klima'tisch.

climax, *n.* Höhepunkt, -e *m.*

climb, *vb. (intr.)* steigen*, klettern; *(tr.)* erstei'gen*.

climber, *n.* Kletterer, - *m.*

clinch, *vb.* fest·machen; *(fig.)* den Ausschlag geben*.

cling, *vb.* sich an·klammern.

clinic, *n.* Klinik, -en *f.*

clinical, *adj.* klinisch.

clip, 1. *n.* Klammer, -n *f.; (jewelry)* Schmucknadel, -n *f.* 2. *vb.* beschnei'den*.

clippers, *n.pl.* Schere, -n *f.; (barber)* Haarschneidemaschine, -n, *f.*

clipping, *n. (newspaper)* Zeitungsausschnitt, -e *m.*

clique, *n.* Clique, -n *f.*

cloak, *n.* Mantel, =m.

cloakroom, *n.* Gardero'be, -n *f.*

clock, *n.* Uhr, -en *f.*

clod, *n.* Klumpen, - *m.*

clog, 1. *n.* Holzschuh, -e *m.* 2. *vb.* verstop'fen.

cloister, *n.* Kloster, = *nt.; (arch.)* Kreuzgang, =e *m.*

clone, *n.* Klon, -e *f.*

close, 1. *adj. (narrow)* eng. knapp; *(near)* nah (-). 2. *vb.* schließen*, zu·machen.

closeness, *n.* Enge, -n *f.,* Nähe, -n *f.*

closet, *n.* Wandschrank, =e *m.*

clot, 1. *n.* Klumpen, - *m.* 2. *vb.* gerin'nen*.

cloth, *n.* Tuch, =er *nt.,* Stoff, -e *m.*

clothe, *vb.* kleiden.

clothes, *n.pl.* Kleider *pl.*

clothing, *n.* Kleidung, -en *f.*

cloud, *n.* Wolke, -n *f.*

cloudburst, *n.* Wolkenbruch, =e *m.*

cloudiness, *n.* Bewölkt'heit *f.*

cloudy, *adj.* bewölkt', trübe.

clove, *n.* Gewürz'nelke, -n *f.*

clover, *n.* Klee *m.*

clown, *n.* Clown, -s *m.*

cloy, *vb.* übersät'tigen.

club, *n. (group)* Klub, -s *m.; (stick)* Keule, -n *f.*

clubs, *n. (cards)* Treff *nt.*

clue, *n.* Anhaltspunkt, -e *m.,* Schlüssel, - *m.*

clump, *n.* Klumpen, - *m.*

clumsiness, *n.* Ungeschicklichkeit, -en *f.*

clumsy, *adj.* ungeschickt.

cluster, 1. *n.* Büschel, - *m.* 2. *vb.* sich zusam'men·scharen.

clutch, 1. *n. (auto)* Kuppelung, -en *f.* 2. *vb.* packen.

clutter, *vb.* umher·streuen.

coach, 1. *n.* Kutsche, -n *f.; (train)* Eisenbahnwagen, - *m.; (sports)* Trainer, - *m.;*

(tutor) Privat'lehrer, - *m.* 2, *vb. (sports)* trainie'ren; *(tutor)* Privat'stunden geben*.

coagulate, *vb.* gerin'nen*.

coagulation, *n.* Gerin'nen *nt.*

coal, *n.* Kohle, -n *f.*

coalesce, *vb.* verschmel'zen*.

coalition, *n.* Koalition', -en *f.*

coarse, *adj.* grob (-).

coarsen, *vb.* vergrö'bern.

coarseness, *n.* Grobheit, -en *f.*

coast, *n.* Küste, -n *f.*

coastal, *adj.* Küsten- *(cpds.).*

coaster, *n.* Küstenfahrer, - *m.*

coat, *n. (suit)* Jacke, -n *f.; (overcoat)* Mantel, = *m.*

coating, *n.* Überzug, = *m.*

coat of arms, *n.* Wappen, - *nt.*

coax, *vb.* überre'den.

cobalt, *n.* Kobalt *m.*

cobblestone, *n.* Kopfstein, -e *m.*

cobweb, *n.* Spinngewebe, - *nt.*

cocaine, *n.* Kokain' *nt.*

cock, 1. *n.* Hahn, =e *m.* 2. *vb. (gun)* spannen.

cockeyed, *adj.* schielend; *(crazy)* verrückt'.

cockpit, *n.* Führersitz, -e *m.*

cockroach, *n.* Küchenschabe, -n *f.*

cocktail, *n.* Cocktail, -s *m.*

cocky, *adj.* frech.

cocoa, *n.* Kaka'o, -s *m.*

coconut, *n.* Kokosnuß, =sse *f.*

cocoon, *n.* Kokon', -s *m.*

cod, *n.* Kabeljau, -s *m.*

C. O. D., *adv.* per Nachnahme.

coddle, *vb.* verpäp'peln.

code, *n. (law)* Kodex, -dizes *m.; (secret)* Kode, -s *m.*

codeine, *n.* Kodein' *nt.*

codfish, *n.* Kabeljau, -s *m.*

codify, *vb.* kodifizie'ren.

cod-liver oil, *n.* Lebertran *m.*

coeducation, *n.* Koedukation' *f.*

coerce, *vb.* zwingen*.

coercion, *n.* Zwang *m.*

coexist, *vb.* koexistie'ren.

coffee, *n.* Kaffee *m.*

coffin, *n.* Sarg, =e *m.*

cog, *n.* Zahn, =e *m.; (c. railway)* Zahnradbahn, -en *f.*

cogent, *adj.* zwingend.

cogitate, *vb.* nach·denken*.

cognizance, *n.* Kenntnis, -se *f.*

cognizant, *adj.* bewußt'.

cogwheel, *n.* Zahnrad, =er *nt.*

cohere, *vb.* zusam'men·hängen*.

coherent, *adj.* zusam'menhängend.

cohesion, *n.* Kohäsion' *f.*

cohesive, *adj.* kohärent'.

cohort, *n.* Kohor'te, -n *f.*

coiffure, *n.* Frisur', -en *f.*

coil, 1. *n.* Rolle, -n *f.; (elec.)* Spule, -n *f.* 2. *vb.* auf·rollen; *(rope)* auf·schießen.

coin, 1. *n.* Münze, -n *f.* 2. *vb.* prägen.

coinage, n. Prägung, -en f.

coincide, vb. zusam'men·treffen*.

coincidence, n. Zufall, -̈e m.

coincident, adj. gleichzeitig.

coincidental, adj. zufällig.

cold, 1. n. Kälte, -n f.; (med.) Erkäl'tung, -en f. 2. adj. kalt (-̈).

cold-blooded, adj. kaltblütig.

collaborate, vb. zusam'men·arbeiten, mit·arbeiten.

collaboration, n. Mitarbeit f.

collaborator, n. Mitarbeiter, - m.

collapse, 1. n. Zusam'menbruch -̈e m. 2. vb. zusam'men·brechen*.

collar, n. Krage, - m.

collarbone, n. Schlüsselbein, -e nt.

collate, vb. verglei'chen*.

collateral, 1. n. (econ.) Deckung f. 2. adj. kollateral'.

colleague, n. Kolle'ge, -n, -n m.

collect, vb. sammeln; (money) ein·kassieren.

collection, n. Sammlung, -en f.; (church) Kollek'te, -n f.

collective, adj. kollektiv'.

collector, n. (art.) Sammler, - m.; (tickets) Schaffner, - m.; (tax) Steuereinnehmer, - m.

college, n. College, -s nt.

collegiate, adj. College- (cpds.).

collide, vb. zusam'men·stoßen*.

collision, n. Zusam'menstoß,-̈e m.

colloquial, adj. umgangssprachlich.

colloquialism, n. umgangssprachlicher Ausdruck, -̈e m.

collusion, n. Kollusion', -en f.

Cologne, n. Köln nt.

colon, n. (typogr.) Doppelpunkt, -e m., Kolon, -s or Kola nt.; (med.) Dickdarm, -̈e m., Kolon, -s or Kola nt.

colonel, n. Oberst, -en, -en m.

colonial, adj. kolonial'.

colonist, n. Siedler, - m., Kolonist', -en, -en m.

colonization, n. Kolonisation', -en f.

colonize, vb. kolonisie'ren.

colony, n. Kolonie', -i'en f.

color, 1. n. Farbe, -n f. 2. vb. färben.

colored, adj. farbig.

colorful, adj. farbenreich.

coloring, n. Färbung, -en f.

colorless, adj. farblos.

colossal, adj. kolossal'.

colt, n. Fohlen, - nt.

column, n. (arch.) Säule, -n f.; (typogr.) Spalte, -n f.; (mil.) Kolon'ne, -n f.

columnist, n. Zeitungsartikelschreiber, - m.

coma, n. Koma nt.

comb, 1. n. Kamm, -̈e m. 2. vb. kämmen.

combat, 1. n. Kampf, -̈e m. 2. vb. bekäm'pfen.

combatant, n. Kämpfer, - m.

combination, n. Kombination', -en f.

combine, vb. verbin'den*, verei'nigen, zusam'men·setzen, kombinie'ren.

combustible, adj. (ver)brenn'bar.

combustion, n. Verbren'nung f.

come, vb. kommen*.

comedian, n. Komiker, - m.

comedienne, n. Komikerin, -nen f.

comedy, n. Komö'die, -n f.

come in, interj. herein'!

comely, adj. hübsch.

comet, n. Komet', -en, -en m.

comfort, 1. n. Behag'lichkeit, -en f., Bequem'lichkeit, -en f. 2. vb. trösten.

comfortable, adj. behag'lich, bequem'.

comforter, n. Steppdecke, -n f.

comic, comical, adj. komisch.

comma, n. Komma, -s or -ta nt.

command, 1. n. Befehl', -e m. 2. vb. befeh'len*.

commandeer, vb. requirie'ren.

commander, n. Befehls'haber, - m.; (navy) Fregat'tenkapitän, -e m.

commander in chief, n. Oberbefehlshaber, - m.

commandment, n. Gebot', -e nt.

commemorate, vb. geden'ken*.

commemoration, n. Gedächt'nisfeier, -n f.

commemorative, adj. Gedächt'nis- (cpds.).

commence, vb. begin'nen*.

commencement, n. Anfang, -̈e m.; (college) akade'mische Abschlußfeier, -n f.

commend, vb. (praise) loben; (recommend) empfeh'len*.

commendable, adj. lobenswert.

commendation, n. Lob nt., Auszeichnung, -en f.

commensurate, adj. angemessen.

comment, 1. n. Bemerkung, -en f. 2. vb. bemer'ken.

commentary, n. Kommentar', -e m.

commentator, n. Kommenta'tor, -o'ren m.

commerce, n. Handel m.

commercial, adj. kommerziell', kaufmännisch; (cpds.) Handels-.

commercialism, n. Handelsgeist m.

commercialize, vb. in den Handel bringen*.

commiserate, vb. bemit'leiden.

commissary, n. Kommissar', -e m.; (store) Militärversor'gungsstelle, -n f.

commission, 1. n. (committee) Kommission', -en f.; (percentage) Provision', -en f.; (assignment) Auftrag, -̈e m. 2.

vb. beauf'tragen; (mil.) das Offiziers'patent verlei'hen*.

commissioner, n. Beauf'tragt· m.

commit, vb. (give over) an·vertrauen; (crime) bege'hen*; (oneself) sich verpflich'ten.

commitment, n. Verpflich'tung, -en f.

committee, n. Ausschuß, -̈sse m.

commodity, n. Ware, -n f.

common, adj. allgemein', gewöhn'lich; (vulgar) ordinär'.

Common Market, n. EG f.; Europä'ische Gemein'schaft f.

commonness, n. Häufigkeit f.

commonplace, 1. n. Gemeinplatz, -̈e m. 2. adj. abgedroschen.

commonwealth, n. Commonwealth nt.

commotion, n. Aufruhr m.

communal, adj. Gemein'de- (cpds.).

commune, 1. n. Gemein'de, -n f. 2. vb. Kommunizie'ren.

communicable, adj. mitteilbar; (med.) ansteckbar.

communicant, n. Kommunikant', -en, -en m.

communicate, vb. mit·teilen.

communication, n. Mitteilung, -en f.

communicative, adj. mitteilsam.

communion, n. Gemein'schaft f.; (eccl.) Abendmahl nt.; (Catholic) Kommunion', -en f.

communiqué, n. Kommuniqué' -s nt.

communism, n. Kommunis'mus m.

communist, 1. n. Kommunist', -en, -en m. 2. adj. kommuni'stisch.

communistic, adj. kommuni'stisch.

community, n. Gemein'de, -n f., Gemein'schaft, -en f.

commutation, n. Austausch m.; (law) Milderung f.

commute, vb. täglich von der Vorstadt in die Stadt fahren und zurück; (law) herab·setzen.

commuter, n. Pendler m.

compact, 1. n. (cosmetics) Puderdose, -n f. 2. adj. kompakt'.

compactness, n. Kompakt'heit f.

companion, n. Beglei'ter m.

companionable, adj. gesel'lig.

companionship, n. Kamerad'schaft, -en f.

company, n. Gesell'schaft, -en f., Firma, -men f.

comparable, adj. vergleich'bar.

comparative, 1. n. (gram.) Komparativ, -e m. 2. adj. verhält'nismäßig.

compare, vb. verglei'chen*.

comparison, n. Vergleich', -e m.

compartment, n. Abtei'lung, -en f., Fach, =er nt.; (train) Abteil, -e nt.

compass, n. (naut.) Kompaß, -sse m.; (geom.) Zirkel, - m.

compassion, n. Mitleid nt., Erbar'men nt.

compassionate, adj. mitleidig.

compatible, adj. verträg'lich.

compatriot, n. Landsmann, -leute m.

compel, vb. zwingen*.

compensate, vb. entschä'digen, kompensie'ren.

compensation, n. Entschä'digung, -en f., Kompensation', -en f.

compete, vb. wetteifern, konkurrie'ren.

competence, n. (ability) Fähigkeit, -en f.; (field of responsibility) Zuständigkeit, -en f.

competent, adj. (able) fähig; (responsible) zuständig.

competition, n. Wettbewerb, -e m., Konkurrenz', -en f.

competitive, adj. auf Konkurrenz' eingestellt.

competitor, n. Mitbewerber, - m., Konkurrent', -en, -en m.

compile, vb. zusam'mentragen*.

complacency, n. Selbstzufriedenheit f.

complacent, adj. selbstzufrieden.

complain, vb. sich bekla'gen, sich beschwe'ren.

complaint, n. Klage, -n f., Beschwer'de, -n f.

complement, 1. n. Ergän'zung, -en f. 2. vb. ergän'zen.

complete, 1. vb. vollen'den. 2. adj. vollständig, fertig.

completely, adv. völlig.

completion, n. Vollen'dung, -en f.

complex, 1. n. Komplex, -e m. 2. adj. komplex', weitläufig.

complexion, n. (type) Natur' f.; (skin) Teint, -s m.

complexity, n. Weitläufigkeit, -en f.

compliance, n. Bereit'willigkeit f., Einwilligen nt.

compliant, adj. bereit'willig, nachgiebig.

complicate, vb. (make more complex) verwi'ckeln; (make harder) erschwe'ren.

complicated, adj. kompliziert', verwi'ckelt.

complication, n. Komplikation', -en f.

compliment, 1. n. Kompliment', -e nt. 2. vb. beglück'wünschen.

complimentary, adj. schmeichelhaft; (free) Frei- (cpds.).

comply, vb. ein'willigen, sich fügen.

component, n. Bestand'teil, -e m.

compose, vb. zusam'mensetzen; (music) komponie'ren.

composer, n. Komponist', -en, -en m.

composite, adj. zusam'mengesetzt.

composition, n. Zusam'mensetzung, -en f.; (school) Aufsatz, =e m.; (mus.) Komposition', -en f.

composure, n. Fassung f.

compote, n. Kompott', -e nt.

compound, 1. n. Mischung, -en f.; (gram.) Kompo'situm, -ta nt.; (chem.) Verbin'dung, -en f.; (mil.) eingezäunte Lagerabteilung, -en f. 2. adj. zusam'mengesetzt; (c. interest) Zinszins m. 3. vb. zusam'mensetzen.

comprehend, vb. verste'hen*, begrei'fen*.

comprehensible, adj. verständ'lich.

comprehension, n. Fassungsvermögen, - nt.

comprehensive, adj. umfas'send.

compress, 1. n. Kompres'se, -n f. 2 vb. zusam'menpressen.

compressed, adj. Press- (cpds.).

compression, n. Kompression', -en f.

comprise, vb. umfas'sen, enthal'ten*.

compromise, 1. n. Kompromiß', -sse m. 2. vb. einen Kompromiß schließen*; (embarrass) kompromittie'ren.

compulsion, n. Zwang m.

compulsive, adj. Zwangs- (cpds.).

compulsory, adj. obligato'risch.

compunction, n. Beden'ken, - nt.

computation, n. Berech'nung, -en f.

compute, vb. rechnen, berech'nen.

computer, n. Komputer, - m.; Elektro'nenrechner, -e m.

computerize, vb. auf Komputer umstellen.

computer science, n. Kompu'terwissenschaft f.

comrade, n. Kamerad', -en, -en m.

concave, adj. konkav'.

conceal, vb. verste'cken, verheim'lichen.

concealment, n. Versteck', -e nt., Verheim'lichung, -en f.

concede, vb. zu·gestehen*.

conceit, n. Einbildung, -en f.

conceited, adj. eingebildet.

conceivable, adj. vorstellbar.

conceivably, adv. unter Umständen.

conceive, vb. begrei'fen*, sich vor·stellen; (child) empfan'gen*.

concentrate, vb. konzentrie'ren.

concentration camp, n. Konzentra'tionslager, - nt.

concept, n. Begriff', -e m.

concern, 1. n. (affair) Angelegenheit, -en f.; (interest) Interes'se, -n nt.; (firm) Konzern', -e m.; (worry) Sorge, -n f. 2. vb. an·gehen*.

concerning, prep. hinsichtlich.

concert, n. Konzert', -e nt.

concession, n. Konzession', -en f.

concierge, n. Portier', -s m.

conciliate, vb. versöh'nen, schlichten.

conciliation, n. Versöh'nung, -en f., Schlichtung, -en f.

conciliator, n. Schlichter, - m.

conciliatory, adj. versöh'nend.

concise, adj. knapp, gedrängt'.

conciseness, n. Gedrängt'heit f.

conclude, vb. schließen*.

conclusion, n. Abschluß, =sse m., Schluß, =sse m.

conclusive, adj. entschei'dend.

concoct, vb. zusam'menbrauen.

concoction, n. Gebräu', -e nt.

concomitant, adj. beglei'tend.

concord, n. Eintracht f.

concourse, n. Sammelplatz, -e m.

concrete, 1. n. Zement' m. 2. adj. konkret'.

concubine, n. Konkubi'ne, -n f.

concur, vb. überein'·stimmen.

concurrence, n. Zustimmung, -en f.

concurrent, adj. (simultaneous) gleichzeitig; (agreeing) überein'stimmend.

concussion, n. Erschüt'terung, -en f.; (brain) Gehirn'erschüt'terung, -en f.

condemn, vb. verur'teilen; (disapprove) mißbil'ligen.

condemnable, adj. strafbar; nichtswürdig.

condemnation, n. Verur'teilung f.; Mißbilligung f.

condensation, n. Kondensation', -en f.; (summary) Zusam'menfassung, -en f.

condense, vb. kondensie'ren; (summarize) zusam'menfassen.

condenser, n. Kondensa'tor, -o'ren m.

condescend, vb. sich herab'·lassen*.

condescending, adj. herab'lassend.

condescension, n. Herab'lassung, -en f.

condiment, n. Gewürz', -e nt.

condition, 1. n. (stipulation) Bedin'gung, -en f.; (state) Zustand, =e m. 2. vb. bedin'gen; (training) in Form bringen*.

conditional, adj. abhängig.

conditionally, *adv.* unter gewissen Bedingungen.

condolence, *n.* Beileid *nt.*

condominium, *n.* Eigentumswohnung, -en *f.*

condone, *vb.* entschul'digen.

conducive, *adj.* förderlich.

conduct, 1. *n.* Betra'gen *nt.* **2.** *vb.* leiten; *(behave)* sich betra'gen*; (music)* dirigie'ren.

conductor, *n.* Leiter, - *m.; (train)* Schaffner - *m.; (music)* Dirigent', -en, -en *m.*

conduit, *n.* Leitungsrohr, -e *nt.*

cone, *n.* Kegel, - *m.; (pine)* Tannenzapfen, - *m.*

confection, *n.* Konfekt', -e *nt.*

confectioner, *n.* Zuckerbäcker, - *m.*

confectionery, *n.* Zuckerwerk *nt.*

confederacy, *n.* Bündnis, -se *nt.; (conspiracy)* Verschwö'rung, -en *f.*

confederate, 1. *n.* Helfershelfer, - *m.* **2.** *adj.* verbün'det.

confederation, *n.* Staatenbund, -̈e *m.*

confer, *vb. (bestow)* verlei'hen*; (counsel)* berat'schlagen.

conference, *n.* Bespre'chung, - en *f.,* Konferenz', -en *f.*

confess, *vb.* zu·gestehen*; (eccles.)* beichten.

confession, *n.* Geständ'nis, -se *nt.; (eccles.)* Beichte, -n *f.*

confessional, *n.* Beichtstuhl, -̈e *m.*

confessor, *n.* Beken'ner, - *m.; (father c.)* Beichtvater, -̈ *m.*

confidant, *n.* Vertraut'- *m.*

confidante, *n.* Vertraut'- *f.*

confide, *vb.* vertrau'en; sich an·vertrauen.

confidence, *n. (trust)* Vertrau'en *nt.; (assurance)* Zuversicht *f.*

confident, *adj.* zuversichtlich.

confidential, *adj.* vertrau'lich.

confidentially, *adv.* unter uns.

confine, *vb.* beschrän'ken; *(imprison)* ein·sperren.

confirm, *vb.* bestä'tigen; *(church)* konfirmie'ren.

confirmation, *n.* Bestä'tigung, - en *f.; (church)* Konfirmation', -en *f.*

confiscate, *vb.* beschlag'nahmen, konfiszie'ren.

confiscation, *n.* Beschlag'nahme, -n *f.*

conflagration, *n.* Brand, -̈e *m.,* Feuersbrunst *f.*

conflict, 1. *n.* Konflikt', -e *m.* **2.** *vb.* in Widerspruch stehen*, nicht überein'·stimmen.

conform, *vb.* sich an·passen.

conformation, *n.* Anpassung, - en *f.; (shape)* Gestal'tung, -en *f.*

conformer, conformist, *n.* Mitmacher, - *m.*

conformity, *n.* Überein'stimmung, -en *f.*

confound, *vb. (make confused)* verwir'ren; **(c. A with B)** A mit B verwech'seln; **(c. it!)** zum Donnerwetter!

confront, *vb.* gegenü'ber·stellen, konfrontie'ren.

confuse, *vb. (make confused)* verwir'ren; **(c. A with B)** A mit B verwech'seln.

confusion, *n.* Verwir'rung, -en *f.; Durcheinan'der nt.;* Verwechs'lung, -en *f.*

congeal, *vb.* erstar'ren.

congenial, *adj.* sympa'thisch.

congenital, *adj.* angeboren.

congestion, *n.* Stauung, -en *f.*

conglomerate, 1. *n.* Anhäufung, -en *f.* **2.** *vb.* zusam'men·ballen.

conglomeration, *n.* Anhäufung, -en *f.*

congratulate, *vb.* gratulie'ren, beglück'wünschen.

congratulation, *n.* Glückwunsch, -̈e *m.*

congratulatory, *adj.* Glückwunsch- *(cpds.).*

congregate, *vb.* sich versam'meln.

congregation, *n. (church)* Gemein'de, -n *f.*

congress, *n.* Kongreß', -sse *m.*

congressional, *adj.* Kon-greß'- *(cpds.).*

conjecture, 1. *n.* Mutmaßung, - en *f.* **2.** *vb.* mutmaßen.

conjugal, *adj.* ehelich.

conjugate, *vb.* konjugie'ren.

conjugation, *n.* Konjugation', - en *f.*

conjunction, *n.* Zusam'men·treffen, - *nt.; (gram.)* Bindewort, -̈er *nt.,* Konjunktion', - en *f.*

conjunctive, *adj.* verbin'dend.

conjunctivitis, *n.* Bindehautentzündung, -en *f.*

conjure, *vb.* zaubern.

connect, *vb.* verbin'den*.

connection, *n.* Verbin'dung, - en *f.*

connive, *vb.* in heimlichem Einverständnis stehen*.

connoisseur, *n.* Kenner, - *m.*

connotation, *n.* Nebenbedeutung, -en *f.,* Beiklang, -̈e *m.*

connote, *vb.* in sich schließen*.

conquer, *vb.* ero'bern.

conqueror, *n.* Ero'berer, - *m.*

conquest, *n.* Ero'berung, -en *f.*

conscience, *n.* Gewis'sen, - *nt.*

conscientious, *adj.* gewis'senhaft.

conscious, *adj.* bewußt, **bei Bewußtsein.

consciousness, *n.* Bewußtsein *nt.*

conscript, *n.* Dienstpflichtig-*m.*

conscription, *n.* Militär'dienstpflicht *f.*

consecrate, *vb.* weihen.

consecration, *n.* Weihung, -en *f.*

consecutive, *adj.* aufeinan'der·folgend.

consensus, *n.* allgemeine Meinung, -en *f.*

consent, 1. *n.* Zustimmung, -en *f.* **2.** *vb.* zu·stimmen.

consequence, *n.* Folge, -n *f.*

consequent, *adj.* folgend.

consequential, *adj.* folgenreich.

consequently, *adv.* folglich.

conservation, *n.* Bewah'rung, - en *f.;* Konservie'rung, -en *f.*

conservatism, *n.* Konservatis'mus *m.*

conservative, *adj.* konservativ'.

conservatory, *n. (music)* Konservato'rium, -rien *nt.; (plants)* Treibhaus, -̈er *nt.*

conserve, *vb.* bewah'ren.

consider, *vb.* betrach'ten; *(take into account)* berück'sichtigen.

considerable, *adj.* beträcht'lich.

considerate, *adj.* rücksichtsvoll.

consideration, *n. (thought)* Erwä'gung, -en *f.; (kindness)* Rücksicht, -en *f.;* **(in c. of)** in Anbetracht.

consign, *vb.* übersen'den*.

consignment, *n.* Übersen'dung, -en *f.*

consist, *vb.* beste'hen*.

consistency, *n.* Folgerichtigkeit *f.; (substance)* Konsistenz' *f.*

consistent, *adj.* folgerichtig, konsequent'.

consolation, *n.* Trost *m.*

console, *vb.* trösten.

consolidate, *vb.* festigen, konsolidie'ren.

consommé, *n.* Bouillon', -s *f.*

consonant, *n.* Konsonant', -en, -en *m.*

consort, 1. *n.* Gemahl', -e *m.;* Gemah'lin, -nen *f.* **2.** *vb.* verkeh'ren.

conspicuous, *adj.* auffällig.

conspiracy, *n.* Verschwö'rung, -en *f.*

conspirator, *n.* Verschwö'rer, - *m.*

conspire, *vb.* sich verschwö'ren*.

constancy, *n.* Standhaftigkeit *f.*

constant, *adj.* bestän'dig, konstant'.

constantly, *adv.* dauernd.

constellation, *n.* Konstellation', -en *f.*

consternation, *n.* Bestür'zung, -en *f.*

constipated, *adj.* verstopft*.

constipation, *n.* Verstop'fung, - en *f.*

constituency, *n. (people)* Wählerschaft, -en *f.; (place)* Wahlbezirk, -e *m.*

constituent, *n.* Bestand'teil, -e *m.; (voter)* Wähler, - *m.*

constitute, vb. (make up) ausmachen; (found) gründen.
constitution, n. Konstitution', -en f.; (government) Verfas'sung, -en f.
constitutional, adj. konstitutionell'.
constrain, vb. zwingen*.
constrict, vb. zusam'menziehen*.
construct, vb. konstruie'ren.
construction, n. Konstruktion', -en f.
constructive, adj. positiv.
construe, vb. aus'legen.
consul, n. Konsul, -n, m.
consular, adj. konsula'risch.
consulate, n. Konsulat', -e nt.
consult, vb. zu Rate ziehen*; konsultie'ren.
consultant, n. Bera'ter, - m.
consultation, n. Konferenz', -en f.; (med.) Konsultation', -en f.
consume, vb. verzeh'ren, verbrau'chen.
consumer, n. Verbrau'cher, - m.
consummate, 1. vb. vollen'den. 2. adj. vollen'det.
consummation, n. Vollzie'hung, -en f.
consumption, n. Verbrauch' m.; (med.) Schwindsucht f.
consumptive, adj. schwindsüchtig.
contact, 1. n. Kontakt', -e m. 2. vb. sich in Verbin'dung setzen mit.
contagion, n. Ansteckung, -en f.
contagious, adj. ansteckend.
contain, vb. enthal'ten*.
container, n. Behäl'ter, - m.
contaminate, vb. verum'reinigen.
contemplate, vb. betrach'ten.
contemplation, n. Betrach'tung, -en f.
contemplative, adj. nachdenklich.
contemporary, 1. n. Zeitgenosse, -n, -n, m. 2. adj. zeitgenössisch.
contempt, n. Verach'tung, -en f.
contemptible, adj. verach'tenswert.
contemptuous, adj. veräch'tlich.
contend, vb. (assert) behaup'ten; (fight) streiten*.
contender, n. Streiter, - m.
content, 1. n. Inhalt m. 2. adj. zufrie'den.
contented, adj. zufrie'den.
contention, n. (assertion) Behaup'tung, -en f.; (fight) Streit, -e m.
contentment, n. Zufrie'denheit f.
contest, 1. n. Wettstreit, -e m.; (advertising) Preisausschreiben, - nt. 2. vb. bestrei'ten*.

contestant, n. Bewer'ber, - m.
context, n. Zusam'menhang, -e m.
continent, 1. n. Kontinent, -e m. 2. adj. enthalt'sam.
continental, adj. kontinental'.
contingency, n. Eventualität', -en f.
continual, adj. dauernd.
continuation, n. Fortsetzung, -en f.
continue, vb. (tr.) fort'setzen; (intr.) fort'fahren*.
continuity, n. Fortdauer f.
continuous, adj. fortdauernd.
contort, vb. verdre'hen.
contortion, n. Verdre'hung, -en f.
contour, n. Umriß, -sse m.
contraband, n. Schmuggelware, -n f.
contraception, n. Schwangerschaftsverhütung f.
contraceptive device, n. Verhütungsmittel, - nt.
contract, 1. n. Vertrag', -e m. 2. vb. vertrag'lich abschließen*; (disease) sich zuziehen*.
contraction, n. Zusam'menziehung, -en f.
contractor, n. Bauunternehmer, - m.
contradict, vb. weidersprechen*.
contradiction, n. Widerspruch, -e m.
contradictory, adj. widersprechend.
contralto, n. Altstimme, -n f.
contraption, n. Vorrichtung, -en f.
contrary, 1. n. Gegenteil, -e nt. 2. adj. (opposite) entge'gengesetzt; (obstinate) widerspenstig.
contrast, 1. n. Gegensatz, -e m. 2. vb. entge'gen·setzen.
contribute, vb. bei'tragen*.
contribution, n. Beitrag, -e m.
contributor, n. Beiträger, - m.
contributory, adj. mitwirkend.
contrite, adj. zerknirscht'.
contrivance, n. Vorrichtung, -en f.
contrive, vb. fertig bringen*, erfin'den*.
control, 1. n. Kontrol'le, -n f. 2. vb. beherr'schen.
controllable, adj. kontrollier'bar.
controller, n. Überprü'fer, - m.
controversial, adj. strittig.
controversy, n. Streitfrage, -n f.
contusion, n. Quetschung, -en f.
convalesce, vb. gene'sen*.
convalescence, n. Konvaleszenz' f.
convalescent, adj. gene'send.

convene, vb. zusam'men·kommen*.
convenience, n. Annehmlichkeit, -en f.
convenient, adj. bequem', geeig'net.
convent, n. Nonnenkloster, ·· nt.
convention, n. Versamm'lung, -en f., Tagung, -en f.; (contract) Abkommen, - nt.; (tradition) Konvention', -en f.
conventional, adj. konventionell'.
converge, vb. zusam'men·laufen*.
convergence, n. Konvergenz', -en f.
convergent, adj. konvergie'rend.
conversant with, adj. bewan'dert in.
conversational, adj. Gesprächs'- (cpds.).
converse, 1. n. Kehrseite, -n f. 2. vb. sich unterhal'ten*. 3. adj. umgekehrt.
convert, 1. n. Konvertit', -en, -en m. 2. vb. (belief, goods, money) konvertie'ren; (missionary) bekeh'ren.
converter, n. Bekeh'rer, - m.; (elec.) Transforma'tor, -o'ren m.
convertible, 1. n. (auto) Kabriolett', -s nt. 2. adj. konvertier'bar.
convex, adj. konvex'.
convey, vb. beför'dern, übermit'teln.
conveyance, n. (vehicle) Beför'derungsmittel, - nt.; Übermitt'lung, -en f.
conveyor, n. Beför'derer, - m.
convict, 1. n. Sträfling, -e m. 2. vb. überführ'en.
conviction, n. Schuldigsprechung, -en f.; (belief) Überzeu'gung, -en f.
convince, vb. überzeu'gen.
convincing, adj. überzeu'gend.
convivial, adj. gesel'lig.
convocation, n. Versamm'lung, -en f.
convoy, 1. n. Geleit'zug, -e m. 2. vb. gelei'ten.
convulse, vb. in Zuckungen versetzen; (be c.d) sich krümmen.
convulsion, n. Krampf, -e m.
convulsive, adj. krampfhaft.
cook, 1. n. Koch, -e m.; Köchin, -nen f. 2. vb. kochen.
cookbook, n. Kochbuch, -er nt.
cookie, n. Keks, -e m.
cool, 1. adj. kühl. 2. vb. ab·kühlen.
coolness, n. Kühle, f.
coop, n. Hühnerkorb, -e m.
cooperate, vb. zusam'men·arbeiten.
cooperation, n. Zusam'menarbeit, -en f.

cooperative, 1. n. Konsum've-rein, -e m. **2.** adj. hilfsbereit.

coordinate, 1. adj. beigeordnet, koordiniert'. **2.** vb. bei·orden, koordinie'ren.

coordination, n. Beiordnung, - en f.; Koordination', -en f.

coordinator, n. Organisations'-planer, - m.

cop, n. Schupo, -s m.

cope, vb. sich ab·mühen.

copier, n. Kopier'maschine, -n f.

copious, adj. reichlich.

copper, n. Kupfer nt.

copy, 1. n. Abschrift, -en f., Kopie', -i'en f.; (book) Exem-plar', -e nt. **2.** vb. ab·schrei-ben*, kopie'ren.

copyright, n. Urheberrecht, -e nt.

coquette, 1. n. Koket'te, -n f. **2.** adj. kokett'.

coral, n. Koral'le, -n f.

cord, n. Schnur, -e f.

cordial, adj. herzlich.

cordiality, n. Herzlichkeit f.

cordovan, n. Korduanleder, - nt.

core, n. (fruit) Kernhaus, -er nt.; (heart) Kern, -e m.

cork, n. (material) Kork m.; (stopper) Korken, - m.

corkscrew, n. Korkenzieher, - m.

corn, n. (grain) Getrei'de nt.; (maize) Mais m.; (foot) Hüh-nerauge, -n nt.

cornea, n. Hornhaut, -e f.

corner, n. Ecke, -n f.

cornet, n. Kornett', -e nt.

cornice, n. Gesims', -e nt.

corn-plaster, n. Hühneraugen-pflaster, - nt.

cornstarch, n. Maize'na nt.

coronation, n. Krönung, -en f.

coronet, n. Adelskrone, -n f.

corporal, 1. n. (mil.) Gefreit-m. **2.** adj. körperlich.

corporate, adj. körperschaft-lich.

corporation, n. Körperschaft, -en f.; (comm.) Aktiengesell-schaft, -en f.

corps, n. Korps, - nt.

corpse, n. Leichnam, -e m.

corpulent, adj. korpulent'.

corpuscle, n. Körperchen, - nt.

correct, 1. adj. richtig, kor-rekt'. **2.** vb. verbes'sern, be-rich'tigen, korrigie'ren.

correction, n. Verbes'serung, -en f., Berich'tigung, -en f.

corrective, adj. korrektiv'.

correctness, n. Korrekt'heit, - en f.

correlate, vb. aufeinan'der be-zie'hen*.

correlation, n. Korrelation', -en f.

correspond, vb. entspre'chen*; (agree) überein'stimmen; (letters) korrespondie'ren.

correspondence, n. Entspre'-chung, -en f.; (agreement) Überein'stimmung, -en f.; (letters) Korrespondenz, -en f.

correspondent, n. Korrespon-dent', -en, -en m.

corridor, n. Korridor, -e m.

corroborate, vb. bestä'tigen.

corroboration, n. Bestä'tigung, -en f.

corrode, vb. korrodie'ren.

corrosion, n. Korrosion', -en f.

corrugate, vb. wellen.

corrupt, 1. vb. korrumpie'ren. **2.** adj. korrupt'.

corrupter, n. Verfüh'rer, m.

corruptible, adj. verführ'bar.

corruption, n. Korruption', -en f.

corsage, n. Blume or Blumen zum Anstecken.

corset, n. Korsett', -s nt.

cortège, n. Leichenzug, -e m.

cosmetic, 1. n. kosme'tisches Mittel, - nt. **2.** adj. kosme'-tisch.

cosmic, adj. kosmisch.

cosmopolitan, adj. kosmopoli'-tisch.

cosmos, n. Kosmos m.

cost, 1. n. Preis, -e m.; Kosten pl. **2.** vb. kosten.

costliness, n. Kostspieligkeit, - en f.

costly, adj. kostspielig.

costume, n. (fancy) Kostüm, -e nt.; (native) Tracht, -en f.

cot, n. Feldbett, -en nt.

cottage, n. Häuschen, - nt.; Landhaus, -er nt.

cotton, n. Baumwolle f.

couch, n. Couch, -es f.

cough, 1. n. Husten m. **2.** vb. husten.

could, v. (was able) konnte; (would be able) könnte.

council, n. Rat, -e m.

counsel, 1. n. Rat, -e m.; (law-yer) Anwalt, -e m. **2.** vb. be-ra'ten*, raten*.

counselor, n. Bera'ter, - m.

count, 1. n. (sum) Zusam'menzahl, -en f.; (noble) Graf, -en, -en m. **2.** vb. zählen.

countenance, n. Gesicht', -er nt.

counter, 1. n. Zähler, - m.; (store) Ladentisch, -e m. **2.** adv. (c. to) entge'gen.

counteract, vb. entge'gen·ar-beiten.

counterattack, 1. n. Gegenan-griff, -e m. **2.** vb. einen Ge-genangriff machen.

counterbalance, 1. n. Gegenge-wicht, -e nt. **2.** vb. auf·wiegen*.

counterfeit, 1. n. Falschgeld, -er nt. **2.** adj. gefälscht'. **3.** vb. fälschen.

countermand, vb. widerru'fen*.

counteroffensive, n. Gegenof-fensive, -n f.

counterpart, n. Gegenstück, -e nt.

countess, n. Gräfin, -nen f.

countless, adj. zahllos.

country, n. Land, -er nt.

countryman, n. Landsmann, -leute m.

countryside, n. Landschaft, -en f.

county, n. Grafschaft, -en f.

coupé, n. geschlossenes Zwei-sitzer-Auto, -s nt.

couple, 1. n. Paar, -e nt. **2.** vb. koppeln.

coupon, n. Coupon', -s m.

courage, n. Mut m.

courageous, adj. mutig.

courier, n. Kurier', -e m.

course, n. Lauf, -e m.; (race) Rennbahn, -en f.; (nautical) Kurs, -e m.; (school) Kursus, Kurse m.; (food) Gang, -e m.; (of c.) natür'lich.

court, 1. n. Hof, -e m. **2.** vb. den Hof machen.

courteous, adj. höflich.

courtesan, n. Kurtisa'ne, -n f.

courtesy, n. Höflichkeit, -en f.

courthouse, n. Gerichts'ge-bäude, - nt.

courtier, n. Höfling, -e m.

courtly, adj. höfisch.

court-martial, n. Kriegsgericht, -e nt.

courtroom, n. Gerichts'saal, -säle m.

courtship, n. Freien nt.

courtyard, n. Hof, -e m.

cousin, n. Vetter, -n m.; Cou-si'ne, -n f.

covenant, n. Vertrag', -e m.

cover, 1. n. Deckel, - m. **2.** vb. bede'cken; (c. up) zu·decken.

covering, n. Bede'ckung, -en f.

covet, vb. begeh'ren.

covetous, adj. begie'rig.

cow, n. Kuh, -e f.

coward, n. Feigling, -e m.

cowardice, n. Feigheit, -en f.

cowardly, adj. feige.

cowboy, n. Cowboy, -s m.

cower, vb. kauern.

cowhide, n. Rindsleder, - nt.

coy, adj. spröde.

cozy, adj. behag'lich.

crab, n. Taschenkrebs, -e m.

crack, 1. n. Spalt, -e m.; Sprung, -e m., Riß, -sse m. **2.** vb. brechen*, springen*.

cracker, n. Salzkeks, -e m.

cradle, n. Wiege, -n f.

craft, n. Kunstfertigkeit, -en f.; (ship) Schiff, -e nt.

craftsman, n. Handwerker, - m.

craftsmanship, n. Kunstfertig-keit, -en f.

crafty, adj. gewiegt'.

cram, vb. voll·stopfen; (exam) pauken.

cramp, n. Krampf, -e m.

crane, n. Kran, -e m.; (bird) Kranich, -e m.

crank, 1. n. (handle) Kurbel, -n f.; (crackpot) Sonderling, -e m. **2.** vb. an·kurbeln.

cranky, adj. mißvergnügt.

cranny, n. Ritze, -n f.

crash, 1. n. Krach m.; (collision) Zusam'menstoß, -e m.; (plane) Absturz, ⁻e m. 2. vb. krachen; zusam'men·stoßen*; ab·stürzen.

crate, n. Kiste, -n f.

crater, n. Krater, - m.

crave, vb. verlan'gen nach.

craving, adj. gieriges Verlan'gen, - nt.

crawl, vb. kriechen*; (swimming) kraulen.

crayon, n. Buntstift, -e m.

crazed, adj. wahnsinnig.

crazy, adj. verrückt'.

creak, vb. knarren.

cream, n. Sahne f., Rahm m; (cosmetic) Creme, -s f., Krem, -s m.

creamery, n. Molkerei', -en f.

creamy, adj. sahnig.

crease, 1. n. Falte, -n f. 2. vb. falten.

create, vb. schaffen*, erschaf'fen*; erzeu'gen.

creation, n. Erschaf'fung, -en f.; Schöpfung, -en f.

creative, adj. schöpferisch.

creator, n. Schöpfer, - m.

creature, n. Geschöpf', -e nt.; Wesen, - nt.

credentials, n.pl. Beglau'bigungsschreiben, - nt.

credibility, n. Glaubwürdigkeit f.

credible, adj. glaubwürdig.

credit, 1. n. Verdienst', nt.; (comm.) Kredit', -e m. 2. vb. gut·schreiben*.

creditable, adj. anerkennenswert.

credit card, n. Kredit'karte, -n f.

creditor, n. Gläubig - m.

credo, n. Glaubensbekenntnnis, -se nt.

credulity, n. Leichtgläubigkeit f.

credulous, adj. leichtgläubig.

creed, n. Glaubensbekenntnis, -se nt.

creek, n. Bach, ⁻e m.

creep, vb. kriechen*.

cremate, vb. ein·äschern.

cremation, n. Einäscherung, -en f.

crematory, n. Kremato'rium, -rien nt.

crepe, n. Krepp m.

crescent, n. Mondsichel, -n f.

crest, n. Kamm, ⁻e m.

crestfallen, adj. geknickt'.

cretonne, n. Kretonn'e, -s m.

crevasse, n. Gletscherspalte, -n f.

crevice, n. Riß, -sse m.

crew, n. Mannschaft, -en f.

crib, n. Krippe, -n f.; (bed) Kinderbett, -en nt.

cricket, n. Grille, -n f.

crime, n. Verbre'chen, - nt.

criminal, 1. n. Verbre'cher, - m. 2. adj. verbre'cherisch.

criminology, n. Kriminalis'tik f.

crimson, adj. karmin'rot.

cringe, vb. sich krümmen.

cripple, 1. n. Krüppel, - m. 2. vb. zum Krüppel machen; lähmen.

crippled, adj. verkrüp'pelt, gelähmt'.

crisis, n. Krise, -n f.

crisp, adj. (weather, vegetables) frisch; (bread, etc.) knusprig.

criterion, n. Krite'rium, -rien nt.

critic, n. Kritiker, - m.

critical, adj. kritisch.

criticism, n. Kritik', -en f.

criticize, vb. kritisie'ren.

croak, vb. krächzen.

crochet, vb. häkeln.

crock, n. Steintopf, ⁻e m.

crockery, n. Steingut nt.

crocodile, n. Korkodil', -e nt.

crook, n. (bend) Biegung, -en f.; (cheater) Schwindler, - m.

crooked, adj. (not straight) krumm, schief; (dishonest) unehrlich, betrü'gerisch.

croon, vb. summen; (jazz) Schlager singen*.

crop, n. Ernte, -n f.; (riding) Peitsche, -n f.

croquet, n. Kroket'spiel nt.

croquette, n. Kroket'te, -n f.

cross, 1. n. Kreuz, -e nt.; (mixture) Kreuzung, -en f. 2. vb. kreuzen.

cross-eyed, adj. (be c.) schielen.

crossing, n. Kreuzung, -en f.

crossroads, n.pl. Scheideweg, - e m.; Kreuzung, -en f.

cross section, n. Querschnitt, -e m.

crossword puzzle, n. Kreuzworträtsel, - nt.

crotch, n. (trousers) Schritt, -e m.; (tree) Gabelung, -en f.

crouch, vb. kauern.

croup, n. Krupp m.

crouton, n. Crouton', -s m.

crow, 1. n. Krähe, -n f. 2. vb. krähen.

crowd, 1. n. Menge, -n f. 2. vb. drängeln.

crown, 1. n. Krone, -n f. 2. vb. krönen.

crucial, adj. entschei'dend.

crucible, n. Schmelztiegel, - m.

crucifix, n. Kruzifix, -e nt.

crucifixion, n. Kreuzigung, -en f.

crucify, vb. kreuzigen.

crude, adj. roh, grob (⁻).

crudeness, n. Grobheit, -en f., Unfeinheit, -en f.

crudity, n. Roheit, -en f., Unfeinheit, -en f.

cruel, adj. grausam.

cruelty, n. Grausamkeit, -en f.

cruise, 1. n. Seereise, -n f. 2. vb. kreuzen.

cruiser, n. Kreuzer, - m.

crumb, n. Krümel, - m.

crumble, vb. zerbrö'ckeln.

crumple, vb. zerknül'len.

crusade, n. Kreuzzug, ⁻e m.

crusader, n. Kreuzzügler, - m.

crush, 1. n. (crowd) Gedrän'ge nt. 2. vb. zerdrü'cken.

crust, n. Kruste, -n f.

crustacean, n. Krustentier, -e nt.

crusty, adj. knusprig.

crutch, n. Krücke, -n f.

cry, 1. n. Schrei, -e m. 2. vb. schreien*; (weep) weinen.

crying, adj. (urgent) dringend.

cryosurgery, n. Kryochirurgie' f.

cryptic, adj. geheim'.

cryptography, n. Geheim'schrift, -en f.

crystal, 1. n. Kristall', -e nt. 2. adj. kristal'len.

crystalline, adj. kristal'len.

crystallize, vb. kristallisie'ren.

cub, n. Jung - nt.

cube, n. Würfel, - m.

cubic, adj. würfelförmig, kubisch; Kubik'- (cpds.).

cubicle, n. kleiner Schlafraum, ⁻e m.

cuckoo, n. Kuckuck, -e m.

cucumber, n. Gurke, -n f.

cud, n. Widergekäut- nt.; (chew the c.) wieder·käuen.

cuddle, vb. herzen.

cudgel, n. Keule, -n f.

cue, n. Stichwort, ⁻er nt.

cuff, n. (sleeve) Manschet'te, -n f.; (trousers) Hosenaufschlag, - m.

cuisine, n. Küche, -e f.

culinary, adj. kulina'risch.

cull, vb. pflücken.

culminate, vb. gipfeln.

culmination, n. Höhepunkt, -e m.

culpable, adj. schuldhaft.

culprit, n. Täter, - m.

cult, n. Kult, -e m.

cultivate, vb. kultivie'ren.

cultivated, adj. kultiviert'.

cultivation, n. Kultivie'rung f.

cultural, adj. kulturell'.

culture, n. Kultur', -ren f.

cultured, adj. kultiviert'.

cumbersome, adj. schwerfällig.

cumulative, adj. kumulativ'.

cunning, 1. n. List, -en f. 2. adj. listig; (sweet) goldig.

cup, n. Tasse, -n f.

cupboard, n. Schrank, ⁻e m.

cupidity, n. Begier'de, -n f.

cupola, n. Kuppel, -n f.

curable, adj. heilbar.

curator, n. Kura'tor, -o'ren m.

curb, 1. n. (sidewalk) Bordstein, -e m.; (harness) Zügel, - m. 2. vb. zügeln.

curdle, vb. gerin'nen*.

cure, 1. n. Kur, -en f.; (medicine) Heilmittel, - nt. 2. vb. heilen.

curfew, n. Polizei'stunde, -n f.

curio, n. Kuriosität', -en f.

curiosity, *n.* Neugierde *f.*

curious, *adj.* neugierig.

curl, 1. *n.* Locke, -n *f.* **2.** *vb.* locken, kräuseln.

curly, *adj.* lockig, kraus.

currant, *n.* Johan'nisbeere, -n *f.; (dried)* Korin'the, -n *f.*

currency, *n.* Währung, -en *f.*

current, 1. *n.* Strom, -̈e *m.* **2.** *adj.* laufend.

currently, *adv.* zur Zeit.

curriculum, *n.* Lehrplan, -̈e *m.*

curry, *n.* Curry *nt.*

curse, 1. *n.* Fluch, -̈e *m.* **2.** *vb. (intr.)* fluchen, *(tr.)* verflu'-chen.

cursed, *adj.* verflucht'.

curse-word, *n.* Schimpfwort, -̈ er *nt.*

cursory, *adj.* flüchtig.

curt, *adj.* kurz angebunden.

curtail, *vb.* ein·schränken.

curtain, *n.* Gardi'ne, -n *f.; (drapes)* Vorhang, -̈e *m.*

curtsy, *n.* Knicks, -e *m.*

curvature, *n.* Krümmung, -en *f.*

curve, *n.* Kurve, -n *f.*

cushion, *n.* Kissen, - *nt.*

custard, *n.* Eierpudding, -s *m.*

custodian, *n.* Hausmeister, - *m.*

custody, *n.* Verwah'rung *f.*

custom, *n.* Sitte, -n *f.,* Brauch, -̈ e *m.; (habit)* Gewohn'heit, - en *f.*

customary, *adj.* gebräuch'lich.

customer, *n.* Kunde, -n, -n *m.*

custom house, *n.* Zollamt, -̈er *nt.*

customs, *n.* Zoll, -̈e *m.*

customs officer, *n.* Zollbeamt-*m.*

cut, 1. *n.* Schnitt, -e *m.; (wound)* Schnittwunde, -n *f.; (salary)* Kürzung, -en *f.; (taxes)* Senkung, -en *f.* **2.** *vb.* schneiden*; kürzen; senken; *(class)* schwänzen.

cute, *adj.* niedlich, süß, goldig.

cut glass, *n.* geschlif'fenes Glas *nt.*

cuticle, *n.* Nagelhaut, -̈e *f.*

cutlery, *n.* Stahlwaren *pl.*

cutlet, *n.* Kotelett', -s *nt.*

cutter, *n.* Zuschneider, - *m.; (boat)* Kutter, - *m.*

cyclamate, *n.* Zyklamat', -e *nt.*

cycle, 1. *n.* Kreislauf, -̈e *m.,* Zyklus, -klen *m.* **2.** *vb.* radeln.

cyclist, *n.* Radfahrer, - *m.*

cyclone, *n.* Wirbelsturm, -̈e *m.*

cyclotron, *n.* Zyklotron', -e *nt.*

cylinder, *n.* Zylin'der, - *m.*

cylindrical, *adj.* zylin'drisch.

cymbal, *n.* Zimbel, -n *f.*

cynic, *n.* Zyniker, - *m.*

cynical, *adj.* zynisch.

cynicism, *n.* Zynis'mus, -men *m.*

cypress, *n.* Zypres'se, -n *f.*

cyst, *n.* Zyste, -n *f.*

D

dab, *vb.* tupfen.

dabble, *vb.* sich dilettan'ten-haft mit einer Sache ab·ge-ben*.

daffodil, *n.* Narzis'se, -n *f.*

dagger, *n.* Dolch, -e *m.*

dahlia, *n.* Dahlie, -n *f.*

daily, 1. *n. (newspaper)* Tages-zeitung, -en *f.* **2.** *adj.* täglich.

daintiness, *n.* Zartheit, -en *f.*

dainty, *adj.* zart, delikat', zier-lich.

dairy, *n.* Milchwirtschaft, -en *f.,* Molkerei' -en *f.*

dairyman, *m.* Milchhändler, - *m.*

dais, *n.* Podium, -ien *nt.*

daisy, *n.* Margeri'te, -n *f.*

dale, *n.* Tal, -̈er *nt.*

dally, *vb.* tändeln; *(dawdle)* trö-deln.

dam, 1. *n.* Damm, -̈e *m.* **2.** *vb.* ein·dämmen.

damage, 1. *n.* Schaden, -̈ *m.; (damages, law)* Schadenersatz *m.* **2.** *vb.* schädigen; beschä'-digen.

damask, *n.* Damast, -e *m.*

damn, *vb.* verdam'men; *(curse)* verflu'chen.

damnation, *n.* Verdam'mung, -en *f.*

damp, *adj.* feucht.

dampen, *vb. (moisten)* ein·feuchten; *(quiet)* dämpfen; *(fig.)* nieder·schlagen*.

dampness, *n.* Feuchtigkeit, -en *f.*

dance, 1. *n.* Tanz, -̈e *m.* **2.** *vb.* tanzen.

dancer, *n.* Tänzer, - *m.*

dancing, *n.* Tanzen *nt.*

dandelion, *n.* Löwenzahn *m.*

dandruff, *n.* Kopfschuppen *pl.*

dandy, 1. *n.* Geck, -en, -en *m.* **2.** *adj.* prima.

Dane, *n.* Däne, -n, -n *m.*

danger, *n.* Gefahr', -en *f.*

dangerous, *adj.* gefähr'lich.

dangle, *vb.* baumeln; baumeln lassen*.

Danish, *adj.* dänisch.

dapper, *adj.* klein und elegant'.

dare, *vb.* wagen.

daredevil, *n.* Draufgänger, - *m.*

daring, *adj.* gewagt'.

dark, 1. *n.* Dunkel *nt.; Dunkel-heit, -en *f.* **2.** *adj.* dunkel.

darken, *vb.* verdun'keln.

darkness, *n.* Dunkel *nt.; Dun-kelheit, -en *f.*

darling, 1. *n.* Liebling, -e *m.* **2.** *adj.* goldig.

darn, *vb. (socks)* stopfen.

dart, 1. *n.* Wurfpfeil, -e *m.* **2.** *vb.* fliezen*.

dash, 1. *n. (pen)* Strich, -e *m; (sport)* Lauf, -̈e *m.* **2.** *vb. (intr.)* sich stürzen; *(tr.)* stoßen*, schleudern.

dashboard, *n.* Armatu'renbrett, -er *nt.*

dashing, *adj.* schneidig.

data, *n.pl.* Angaben *pl.*

data processing, *n.* Datenver-arbeitung, -en *f.*

date, 1. *n.* Datum, -ten *nt.; (ap-pointment)* Verab'redung, -en *f.; (fruit)* Dattel, -n *f.* **2.** *vb.* datie'ren; aus·gehen* mit.

daub, *vb.* schmieren.

daughter, *n.* Tochter, -̈ *f.*

daughter-in-law, *n.* Schwieger-tochter, -̈ *f.*

daunt, *vb.* entmu'tigen.

dauntless, *adj.* kühn.

dawdle, *vb.* trödeln.

dawn, 1. *n.* Morgendämme-rung, -en *f.* **2.** *vb.* dämmern.

day, *n.* Tag, -e *m.*

daybreak, *n.* Tagesanbruch *m.*

daydream, 1. *n.* Träumerei', - en *f.* **2.** *vb.* vor sich hin träu-men; sinnie'ren.

daylight, *n.* Tageslicht *nt.*

daze, 1. *n.* Benom'menheit *f.* **2.** *vb.* betäu'ben.

dazzle, *vb.* blenden.

deacon, *n.* Diakon', -e *m.*

dead, *adj.* tot.

deaden, *vb.* dämpfen.

dead end, *n.* Sackgasse, -n *f.*

deadline, *n.* Termin', -e *m.*

deadlock, *n.* Stockung, -en *f.*

deadly, *adj.* tötlich.

deaf, *adj.* taub.

deafen, *vb.* betäu'ben.

deafness, *n.* Taubheit *f.*

deal, 1. *n.* Anzahl *f.; (business)* Geschäft', -e *nt.* **2.** *vb. (cards)* geben*; *(d. with)* behan'deln; *(d. in)* handeln mit.

dealer, *n.* Händler, - *m.; (cards)* Geber, - *m.*

dean, *n.* Dekan', -e *m.*

dear, *adj.* lieb, teuer.

dearly, *adv.* sehr.

dearth, *n.* Mangel, -̈ *m.*

death, *n.* Tod *m.;* Todesfall, -̈e *m.*

deathless, *adj.* unsterblich.

debase, *vb.* ernie'drigen.

debatable, *adj.* bestreit'bar.

debate, 1. *n.* Debat'te, -n *f.* **2.** *vb.* debattie'ren.

debauch, 1. *n.* Orgie, -n *f.* **2.** *vb.* verfüh'ren.

debenture, *n.* Obligation', -en *f.*

debilitate, *vb.* entkräf'ten.

debit, *n.* Debet, -s *nt.*

debonair, *adj.* zuvor'kom-mend; heiter und sorglos.

debris, *n.* Trümmer *pl.*

debt, *n.* Schuld, -en *f.*

debtor, *n.* Schuldner, - *m.*

debunk, *vb.* mit etwas auf-räumen, den Nimbus rauben.

debut, *n.* Debüt', -s *nt.*

debutante, *n.* Debütan'tin, -nen *f.*

decade, *n.* Jahrzehnt', -e *nt.*

decadence, *n.* Dekadenz' *f.*

decadent, *adj.* dekadent'.

decaffeinated, *adj.* koffein'frei.
decanter, *n.* Karaf'fe, -n *f.*
decapitate, *vb.* enthaup'ten.
decay, 1. *n.* Verfall' *m.;* Verwe'sung, -en *f.* **2.** *vb.* verfal'len*; verwe'sen.
deceased, *adj.* verstor'ben.
deceit, *n.* Täuschung, -en *f.;* Betrug', ⸚e *m.*
deceitful, *adj.* falsch; betrü'gerisch.
deceive, *vb.* täuschen; betrü'gen*.
December, *n.* Dezem'ber *m.*
decency, *n.* Anständigkeit, -en *f.*
decent, *adj.* anständig.
decentralization, *n.* Dezentralisation', -en *f.*
decentralize, *vb.* dezentralisie'ren.
deception, *n.* Täuschung, -en *f.*
deceptive, *adj.* irreführend, täuschend.
decibel, *n.* Dezi'bel, -n *f.*
decide, *vb.* entschei'den*; sich entschlie'ßen*.
decimal, 1. *n.* Dezimal'bruch, ⸚e *m.* **2.** *adj.* Dezimal'- *(cpds.).*
decimate, *vb.* dezimie'ren.
decipher, *vb.* entzif'fern.
decision, *n.* Entschei'dung, -en *f.;* Beschluß', ⸚sse *m.*
decisive, *adj.* entschei'dend.
deck, *n.* *(ship)* Deck, -s *nt.;* *(cards)* Spiel, -e *nt.*
declaration, *n.* Erklä'rung, -en *f.*
declarative, *adj.* erklä'rend; **(d. sentence)** Aussagesatz, ⸚e *m.*
declare, *vb.* erklä'ren, behaup'ten; *(customs)* deklarie'ren.
declension, *n.* Deklination', -en *f.*
decline, 1. *n.* Niedergang *m.* **2.** *vb.* neigen; *(refuse)* ab•lehnen; *(gram.)* deklinie'ren.
décolleté, *n.* Dekolleté', -s *nt.*
decompose, *vb.* *(tr.)* zerset'zen; *(intr.)* verwe'sen.
decomposition, *n.* Zerset'zung, -en *f.;* Verwe'sung, -en *f.*
decongestant, *n.* schleimlösendes Mittel *nt.*
décor, *n.* Ausstattung, -en *f.*
decorate, *vb.* schmücken, dekorie'ren.
decoration, *n.* Dekoration', -en *f.*
decorative, *adj.* dekorativ'.
decorator, *n.* Dekorateur', -e *m.;* **(interior d.)** Innenarchitekt, -en, -en *m.*
decorous, *adj.* schicklich.
decorum, *n.* Schicklichkeit *f.*
decoy, 1. *n.* Lockvogel, ⸚ *m.* **2.** *vb.* locken.
decrease, 1. *n.* Abnahme, -n *f.* **2.** *vb.* *(tr.)* verrin'gern; *(intr.)* ab•nehmen*.
decree, 1. *n.* Erlaß', -sse *m.* **2.** *vb.* verord'nen.
decrepit, *adj.* gebrech'lich, klapprig.
decry, *vb.* mißbil'ligen, tadeln.
dedicate, *vb.* widmen.
dedication, *n.* Widmung, -en *f.*
deduce, *vb.* folgern.
deduct, *vb.* ab•ziehen*.
deduction, *n.* Abzug, ⸚e *m.;* *(logic)* Folgerung, -en *f.*
deductive, *adj.* deduktiv'.
deed, *n.* Tat, -en *f.;* *(document)* Urkunde, -n *f.*
deem, *vb.* denken*; halten* für.
deep, *adj.* tief.
deepen, *vb.* vertie'fen.
deep freeze, *n.* Tiefkühltruhe, -n *f.*
deer, *n.* Reh, -e *nt.;* Hirsch, -e *m.*
deerskin, *n.* Rehleder, - *nt.;* Hirschleder, - *nt.*
deface, *vb.* entstel'len.
defamation, *n.* Verleum'dung, -en *f.*
defame, *vb.* in schlechten Ruf bringen*.
default, 1. *n.* Versäum'nis, -se *nt.;* Unterlas'sung, -en *f.* **2.** *vb.* im Verzug' sein*.
defeat, 1. *n.* Niederlage, -n *f.* **2.** *vb.* besie'gen.
defect, 1. *n.* Fehler, - *m.,* Defekt', -e *m.* **2.** *vb.* über•laufen*.
defection, *n.* Versa'gen *nt.;* Treubruch, ⸚e *m.*
defective, *adj.* fehlerhaft.
defend, *vb.* vertei'digen.
defendant, *n.* Angeklagt- *m.&f.*
defender, *n.* Vertei'diger, - *m.,* Beschüt'zer, - *m.*
defense, *n.* Vertei'digung, -en *f.*
defenseless, *adj.* wehrlos.
defensible, *adj.* verfecht'bar, zu vertei'digen.
defensive, 1. *n.* Defensi've, -n *f.* **2.** *adj.* defensiv'.
defer, *vb.* *(put off)* auf•schieben*; *(yield)* nach•geben*.
deference, *n.* Achtung *f.*
deferential, *adj.* ehrerbietig.
defiance, *n.* Heraus'forderung, -en *f.;* Trotz *m.*
defiant, *adj.* trotzig, heraus'fordernd.
deficiency, *n.* Mangel, ⸚ *m.*
deficient, *adj.* unzureichend.
deficit, *n.* Defizit, -e *nt.*
defile, 1. *n.* Engpaß, ⸚sse *m.* **2.** *vb.* *(march)* defilie'ren; *(soil)* besu'deln.
definite, *adj.* bestimmt'.
definition, *n.* Definition', -en *f.*
definitive, *adj.* definitiv'.
deflate, *vb.* die Luft heraus'•lassen*.
deflation, *n.* Deflation', -en *f.*
deflect, *vb.* ab•wenden*.
deform, *vb.* entstel'len.
deformity, *n.* Verwachs'ung, -en *f.*
defraud, *vb.* betrü'gen*.
defray, *vb.* bestrei'ten*.
defrost, *vb.* entfros'ten.
deft, *adj.* geschickt'.
defy, *vb.* trotzen.
degenerate, 1. *adj.* degeneriert'. **2.** *vb.* entar'ten.
degeneration, *n.* Degeneration' *f.*
degradation, *n.* Ernie'drigung, -en *f.*
degrade, *vb.* ernie'drigen.
degree, *n.* Grad, -e *m.*
deify, *vb.* vergött'lichen.
deign, *vb.* geru'hen.
deity, *n.* Gottheit, -en *f.*
dejected, *adj.* niedergeschlagen.
dejection, *n.* Trübsinn *m.*
delay, 1. *n.* Verzö'gerung, -en *f.* **2.** *vb.* auf•schieben*, verzö'gern.
delectable, *adj.* ergötz'lich.
delegate, 1. *n.* Delegiert'- *m.&f.* **2.** *vb.* delegie'ren.
delegation, *n.* Abordnung, -en *f.,* Delegation', -en *f.*
delete, *vb.* aus•streichen*.
deliberate, 1. *vb.* erwä'gen*. **2.** *adj.* bedäch'tig; *(on purpose)* absichtlich.
deliberation, *n.* Überle'gung, -en *f.,* Erwä'gung, -en *f.*
delicacy, *n.* *(food)* Delikates'se, -n *f.;* *(fig.)* Feinheit, -en *f.*
delicate, *adj.* delikat'.
delicious, *adj.* köstlich.
delight, 1. *n.* Entzü,'cken, - *nt.* **2.** *vb.* entzü'cken.
delightful, *adj.* entzü'ckend.
delineate, *vb.* dar•stellen.
delinquency, *n.* Verge'hen, - *nt.;* Unterlas'sung, -en *f.*
delinquent, 1. *n.* Kriminell' - *m.&f.;* **(juvenile d.)** Jugendverbrecher, - *m.* **2.** *adj.* verbre'cherisch, kriminell'; *(in default)* säumig.
delirious, *adj.* im Fieberwahnsinn; wahnsinnig.
delirium, *n.* Deli'rium, -rien *nt.*
deliver, *vb.* *(set free)* erlö'sen; *(hand over)* überge'ben*, ab•liefern.
deliverance, *n.* Erlö'sung, -en *f.,* Befrei'ung, -en *f.*
delivery, *n.* Lieferung, -en *f.;* *(childbirth)* Entbin'dung, -en *f.*
delude, *vb.* täuschen, verlei'ten.
deluge, 1. *n.* Überschwem'mung, -en *f.;* *(Bible)* Sintflut *f.* **2.** *vb.* überflu'ten.
delusion, *n.* Täuschung, -en *f.,* Wahn *m.*
de luxe, *adj.* Luxus- *(cpds.)*
delve, *vb.* graben*; *(fig.)* sich vertie'fen.
demand, 1. *n.* Forderung, -en *f.;* *(claim)* Anspruch, ⸚e *m.;* *(econ.)* Nachfrage *f.* **2.** *vb.* fordern, verlan'gen; fragen.
demean (oneself), *vb.* sich entwür'digen.
demeanor, *n.* Betra'gen *nt.*

demerit, n. (school) Tadel, - m.

demilitarize, vb. entmilitarisie´ren.

demobilization, n. Demobilisie´rung, -en f.

demobilize, vb. demobilisie´ren.

democracy, n. Demokratie´, -n f.

democrat, n. Demokrat´, -en, -en m.

democratic, adj. demokra´tisch.

demolish, vb. ab·rei´ßen*, zerstö´ren.

demolition, n. Zerstö´rung, -en f.

demon, n. Dämon, -o´nen m.

demonstrable, adj. nachweisbar.

demonstrate, vb. zeigen, vorführen, demonstrie´ren.

demonstration, n. Beweis´ -e m., Darlegung, -en f.; Kundgebung, -en f.

demonstrative, adj. demonstrativ´.

demonstrator, n. Demonstrie´rend- m.&f.

demoralize, vb. demoralisie´ren.

demote, vb. degradie´ren.

demur, vb. Einwendungen ma-chen.

demure, adj. züchtig.

den, n. Höhle, -n f.

denaturalize, vb. denaturalisie´ren.

denial, n. Vernei´nung, -en f.

denim, n. Jeansstoff, -e m.

Denmark, n. Dänemark nt.

denomination, n. (money) Nennwert, -e m.; (church) Sekte, -n f.

denominator, n. Nenner, - m.

denote, vb. kennzeichnen.

dense, adj. dicht.

density, n. Dichte f.

dent, n. Einbuchtung, -en f.

dental, adj. Zahn- (cpds.).

dentifrice, n. Zahnputzmittel, - nt.

dentist, n. Zahnarzt, -e m.

dentistry, n. Zahnheilkunde f.

denture, n. künstliches Gebiß´, -sse nt.

denunciation, n. Denunzie´rung, -en f.

deny, vb. leugnen, vernei´nen.

deodorant, n. Desodorisie´rungsmittel, - nt.

depart, vb. ab·fah´ren*; (deviate) ab·wei´chen*.

department, n. Abtei´lung, -en f.; (government) Ministe´rium, -rien nt.

departmental, adj. Abtei´lungs- (cpds.).

departure, n. Abfahrt, -en, - f.; (deviation) Abweichung, -en f.

depend, vb. ab·hän´gen*; (rely) sich verlas´sen*.

dependability, n. Verläß´lichkeit f.

dependable, adj. zuverlässig.

dependence, n. Abhängigkeit f.

dependent, 1. n. Angehörig- m.&f. **2.** adj. abhängig.

depict, vb. dar·stellen.

depiction, n. Darstellung, -en f.

deplete, vb. erschöp´fen.

deplorable, adj. bekla´genswert.

deplore, vb. bekla´gen.

deport, vb. deportie´ren.

deportation, n. Deportation´, -en f.

deportment, n. Betra´gen nt.

depose, vb. ab·setzen.

deposit, 1. n. Anzahlung, -en f.; (bank) Einzahlung, -en f.; (ore, etc.) Lager, - nt. **2.** vb. ein·zahlen; hinterle´gen.

deposition, n. (eidesstattliche) schriftliche Aussage, -n f.

depositor, n. Einzahler, - m., Bankkunde, -n, -n m.

depot, n. Lager, - nt.; Depot´, -s nt.; (railroad) Kleinbahnhof, -e m.

depravity, n. Verwor´fenheit f.

deprecate, vb. mißbilligen.

depreciate, vb. (tr.) entwer´ten, den Wert mindern; (intr.) im Wert sinken*.

depreciation, n. Wertminderung f.

depress, vb. deprimie´ren.

depression, n. Depression´, -en f.

deprivation, n. Berau´bung, -en f.

deprive, vb. berau´ben.

depth, n. Tiefe, -n f.

deputy, n. (substitute) Stellvertreter, - m.; (parliament) Abgeordnet- m.&f.

derail, vb. entglei´sen lassen*; (be d.ed) entglei´sen.

deranged, adj. geistesgestört.

derelict, 1. n. Wrack, -s or -e nt. **2.** adj. nachlässig.

dereliction, n. Vernach´lässigung, -en f.

deride, vb. verspot´ten.

derision, n. Hohn m.

derisive, adj. spöttisch.

derivation, n. Ableitung, -en f.

derivative, adj. abgeleitet.

derive, vb. ab·leiten.

derogatory, adj. abfällig.

derrick, n. Ladebaum, -e m.; (oil) Bohrturm, -e m.

descend, vb. herab´steigen*; (ancestry) ab·stammen.

descendant, n. Nachkomme, -n, -n m.

descent, n. Abstieg, -e m.

describe, vb. beschrei´ben*.

description, n. Beschrei´bung, -en f.

descriptive, adj. beschrei´bend.

desecrate, vb. entwei´hen.

desert, 1. n. Wüste, -n f.; (merit) Verdienst´, -e nt. **2.** vb. verlas´sen*.

deserter, n. Fahnenflüchtig- m.&f., Deserteur´, -e m.

desertion, n. (law) böswilliges Verlas´sen nt.; (army) Desertion´, -en f.; Fahnenflucht f.

deserve, vb. verdie´nen.

deserving, adj. verdienst´voll.

design, 1. n. Entwurf´, -e m., Muster, - nt.; (aim) Absicht, -en f. **2.** vb. entwer´fen*; beab´sichtigen.

designate, vb. bezeich´nen, bestim´men.

designation, n. Bezeich´nung, -en f., Bestim´mung, -en f.

designer, n. Konstrukteur´, -e m.; (fashion) Modeschöpfer, - m.

desirability, n. Erwünscht´heit, -en f.

desirable, adj. wünschenswert.

desire, 1. n. Verlan´gen, - nt., Wunsch, -e m. **2.** vb. verlan´gen, wünschen.

desirous, adj. begie´rig.

desist, vb. ab·lassen*.

desk, n. Schreibtisch, -e m.

desolate, 1. adj. trostlos. **2.** vb. verhee´ren.

desolation, n. Verwüs´tung, -en f.; Trostlosigkeit f.

despair, 1. n. Verzweif´lung, -en f. **2.** vb. verzwei´feln.

despatch, 1. n. Absendung, -en f. **2.** vb. ab·senden*, eilig weg·schicken.

desperado, n. Bandit´, -en, -en m., Despera´do, -s m.

desperate, adj. verzwei´felt.

desperation, n. Verzweif´lung, -en f.

despicable, adj. verach´tenswert, gemein´.

despise, vb. verach´ten.

despite, prep. trotz.

despondent, adj. verzagt´.

despot, n. Despot´, -en, -en m.

despotic, adj. despo´tisch.

despotism, n. Gewalt´herrschaft f.

dessert, n. Nachtisch, -e m.

destination, n. Bestim´mung f.; Bestim´mungsort, -e m.

destine, vb. bestim´men.

destiny, n. Schicksal, -e nt.

destitute, adj. mittellos.

destitution, n. Armut f., Not, -e f.

destroy, vb. zerstö´ren.

destroyer, n. Zerstö´rer, - m.

destruction, n. Zerstö´rung, -en f.

destructive, adj. zerstö´rend.

desultory, adj. flüchtig.

detach, vb. ab·trennen; (mil.) ab·kommandieren.

detachment, n. (mil.) Abtei´lung, -en f.; Objektivität´ f.

detail, n. Einzelheit, -en f.

detain, vb. ab·halten*; festhalten*; auf·halten*.

detect, vb. entde´cken, ermit´teln.

detection, n. Entde´cken nt., Ermitt´lung, -en f.

detective, *n.* Detektiv' -e *m.*

détente, *n.* Entspan'nung *f.*

detention, *n.* Haft *f.*

deter, *v.* ab·halten*, hindern.

detergent, *n.* chemisches Seifenmittel, -*nt.*

deteriorate, *vb.* sich verschlech'tern.

deterioration, *n.* Verschlech'terung, -en *f.*

determination, *n.* Bestim'mung, -en *f.; (resolve)* Entschlos'senheit *f.*

determine, *vb.* bestim'men.

determined, *adj.* entschlos'sen.

deterrence *n.* Abschreckung *f.*

detest, *vb.* verab'scheuen.

detonate, *vb.* explodie'ren.

detonation, *n.* Explosion', -en *f.*

detour, *n.* Umweg, -e *m.; (traffic)* Umleitung, -en *f.*

detract, *vb.* ab·ziehen*; **(d. from)** schmälern.

detriment, *n.* Nachteil, -e *m.*, Schaden, ˉ *m.*

detrimental, *adj.* nachteilig.

devaluate, *vb.* ab·werten.

devastate, *vb.* verwüs'ten.

devastation, *n.* Verwüs'tung, -en *f.*

develop, *vb.* entwi'ckeln.

developer, *n.* Entwick'ler, - *m.*

developing nation, *n.* Entwick'lungsland, ˉer *nt.*

development, *n.* Entwick'lung, -en *f.*

deviate, *vb.* ab·weichen*.

deviation, *n.* Abweichung, -en *f.*

device, *n.* Vorrichtung, -en *f.*

devil, *n.* Teufel, - *m.*

devilish, *adj.* teuflisch.

devious, *adj.* abweichend.

devise, *vb.* ersin'nen*.

devoid, *adj.* **(d. of)** leer an, ohne.

devote, *vb.* widmen.

devoted, *adj.* erge'ben.

devotee, *n.* Verfech'ter, - *m.*

devotion, *n.* Hingebung *f.; (religious)* Andacht, -en *f.*

devour, *vb.* verschlin'gen*.

devout, *adj.* andächtig, fromm.

dew, *n.* Tau *m.*

dewy, *adj.* betaut'.

dexterity, *n.* Gewandt'heit, -en *f.*

dexterous, *adj.* gewandt'.

diabetes, *n.* Zuckerkrankheit *f.*

diabolic, *adj.* teuflisch.

diadem, *n.* Diadem', -e *nt.*

diagnose, *vb.* diagnostizie'ren.

diagnosis, *n.* Diagno'se, -n *f.*

diagnostic, *adj.* diagnos'tisch.

diagonal, 1. *n.* Diagona'le, -n *f.* **2.** *adj.* diagonal', schräg.

diagram, *n.* graphische Darstellung, -en *f.*

dial, 1. *n.* Zifferblatt, ˉer *nt.; (telephone)* Wählscheibe, -n *f.* **2.** *vb. (telephone)* wählen.

dialect, *n.* Dialekt', -e *m.*, Mundart, -en *f.*

dialogue, *n.* Dialog', -e *m.*

diameter, *n.* Durchmesser, -*m.*

diametrical, *adj.* diametral'.

diamond, *n.* Diamant', -en, -en *m.; (cards)* Karo *nt.*

diaper, *n.* Windel, -n *f.*

diaphragm, *n.* Zwerchfell, -e *nt.*

diarrhea, *n.* Durchfall *m.*

diary, *n.* Tagebuch, ˉer *nt.*

diathermy, *n.* Diathermie' *f.*

diatribe, *n.* Schmähschrift, -en *f.*

dice, *n.pl.* Würfel, - *m.*

dicker, *vb.* feilschen.

dictate, *vb.* diktie'ren.

dictation, *n.* Diktat', -e *nt.*

dictator, *n.* Dikta'tor, -o'ren *m.*

dictatorial, *adj.* diktato'risch.

dictatorship, *n.* Diktatur', -en *f.*

diction, *n.* Aussprache, -n *f.*

dictionary, *n.* Wörterbuch, ˉer *nt.*, Lexikon, -ka *nt.*

didactic, *adj.* didak'tisch.

die, 1. *n. (gaming cube)* Würfel, - *m.; (stamper)* Prägestempel, - *m.* **2.** *vb.* sterben*.

diet, *n.* Diät' -en *f.; (government)* Parlament', -e *nt.*

dietary, *adj.* diät'gemäß.

dietetic, *adj.* diäte'tisch.

dietitian, *n.* Diät'planer, - *m.*

differ, *vb.* sich unterschei'den*, ab·weichen*, verschiedener Meinung sein*.

difference, *n.* Unterschied, -e *m.*

different, *adj.* verschie'den, ander-.

differential, 1. *n.* Unterschied, - *m.; (d. gear)* Differential, -e *nt.*, Ausgleichsgetriebe, - *nt.* **2.** *adj.* differential'.

differentiate, *vb.* unterschei'den*.

difficult, *adj.* schwer, mühsam, schwierig.

difficulty, *n.* Schwierigkeit, -en *f.*

diffident, *adj.* zurück'haltend, schüchtern.

diffuse, 1. *adj.* weitverbreitet, diffus'. **2.** *vb.* verbrei'ten.

diffusion, *n.* Diffusion', -en *f.*

dig, *vb.* graben*.

digest, *vb.* verdau'en.

digestible, *adj.* verdau'lich.

digestion, *n.* Verdau'ung *f.*

digestive, *adj.* Verdau'ungs-*(cpds.).*

digital, *adj.* digital'.

digitalis, *n.* Digita'lis *nt.*

dignified, *adj.* würdig.

dignify, *vb.* ehren, aus·zeichnen.

dignitary, *n.* Würdenträger, - *m.*

dignity, *n.* Würde *f.*

digress, *vb.* ab·schweifen.

digression, *n.* Abschweifung, -en *f.*

dike, *n.* Deich, -e *m.*

dilapidated, *adj.* baufällig.

dilate, *vb.* aus·dehnen.

dilemma, *n.* Dilem'ma, -s *nt.*

dilettante, *n.* Dilettant', -en, -en *m.*

diligence, *n.* Fleiß *m.*

diligent, *adj.* fleißig.

dill, *n.* Dill *m.*

dilute, *vb.* verdün'nen.

dilution, *n.* Verdün'nung, -en *f.*

dim, 1. *adj.* trübe, dunkel. **2,** *vb.* trüben; *(auto lights)* ab·blenden.

dimension, *n.* Ausmaß, -e *nt.*, Dimension', -en *f.*

diminish, *vb.* vermin'dern.

diminution, *n.* Vermin'derung, -en *f.*

diminutive, 1. *n.* Diminutiv', -e *nt.* **2.** *adj.* winzig.

dimness, *n.* Dunkelheit *f.*

dimple, *n.* Grübchen, - *nt.*

din, *n.* Lärm *m.*

dine, *vb.* speisen.

diner, dining-car, *n.* Speisewagen, - *m.*

dingy, *adj.* schäbig.

dinner, *n. (noon)* Mittagessen, - *nt.; (evening)* Abendessen, - *nt.*

dinosaur, *n.* Dinosau'rier, - *m.*

diocese, *n.* Diöze'se, -n *f.*

dip, *vb.* tauchen, ein·tauchen; sich senken.

diphtheria, *n.* Diphtherie' *f.*

diploma, *n.* Diplom', -e *nt.*

diplomacy, *n.* Diplomatie', -en *f.*

diplomat, *n.* Diplomat', -en, -en *m.*

diplomatic, *adj.* diploma'tisch.

dipper, *n.* Schöpflöffel, - *m.*, Schöpfkelle, -n *f.;* **(Big D.)** Großer Bär *m.;* **(Little D.)** Kleiner Bär *m.*

dire, *adj.* gräßlich.

direct, 1. *adj.* direkt'. **2.** *vb.* führen; an·weisen*; leiten.

direct current, *n.* Gleichstrom, ˉe *m.*

direction, *n. (leadership)* Leitung, -en *f.*, Führung, -en *f.; (instruction)* Anweisung, -en *f.; (course)* Richtung, -en *f.*

directional, *adj.* Leitungs-, Richtungs- *(cpds.).*

directive, 1. *adj.* leitend; Richtung gebend. **2.** *n.* Direkti've, -n *f.*

directness, *n.* Gerad'heit *f.*, Offenheit *f.*

director, *n.* Leiter, - *m.*, Direk'tor, -o'ren *m.*

directory, *n. (addresses)* Adreß'buch, ˉer *nt.;* **(telephone d.)** Telephon'buch, ˉer *nt.*

dirigible, *n.* Luftschiff, -e *nt.*

dirt, *n.* Schmutz *m.*

dirty, *adj.* schmutzig.

disability, *n.* Unfähigkeit *f.;* Körperbehinderung, -en *f.*

disable, *vb.* untauglich machen.

disabled, *adj.* untauglich; kriegsversehrt.

disadvantage, *n.* Nachteil, -e *m.*

disagree, *vb.* anderer Meinung sein*; *(food)* nicht bekommen*.

disagreeable, *adj.* unangenehm.

disagreement, *n.* Uneinigkeit, -en *f.,* Widerspruch, -̈e *m.*

disappear, *vb.* verschwin'den*.

disappearance, *n.* Verschwin'den *nt.*

disappoint, *vb.* enttäu'schen.

disappointment, *n.* Enttäu'-schung, -en *f.*

disapproval, *n.* Mißbilligung, -en *f.*

disapprove, *vb.* mißbilligen.

disarm, *vb.* entwaff'nen, ab·rü-sten.

disarmament, *n.* Abrüstung, -en *f.*

disarray, *n.* Unordnung *f.*

disaster, *n.* Unglück, -e *nt.,* Katastro'phe, -n *f.*

disastrous, *adj.* verhee'rend.

disavow, *vb.* ab·leugnen.

disband, *vb.* auf·lösen.

disburse, *vb.* aus·zahlen.

discard, *vb.* ab·legen.

discern, *vb.* unterschei'den*.

discerning, *adj.* scharfsinnig.

discernment, *n.* Scharfsinn *m.,* Einsicht *f.*

discharge, 1. *n.* Entlas'sung, -en *f.; (medicine)* Ausschei-dung, -en *f.* **2.** *vb.* entlas'sen*, aus·scheiden*; *(gun)* ab·feu-ern.

disciple, *n.* Jünger, - *m.*

disciplinary, *adj.* maßregelnd.

discipline, 1. *n.* Disziplin' *f.* **2.** *vb.* schulen, disziplinie'ren.

disclaim, *vb.* ab·leugnen; ver-zich'ten.

disclose, *vb.* enthül'len.

disclosure, *n.* Enthül'lung, -en *f.*

discomfort, *n.* Unbehagen *nt.*

disconcert, *vb.* in Verwir'rung bringen*.

disconnect, *vb.* los·lösen; *(elec.)* aus·schalten.

discontent, 1. *n.* Unzufrieden-heit *f.* **2.** *adj.* unzufrieden.

discontinue, *vb.* ein·stellen.

discord, *n.* Mißklang -̈e *m.; (fig.)* Uneinigkeit, -en *f.*

discotheque, *n.* Diskothek', -en *f.*

discount, 1. *n.* Rabatt' *m.* **2.** *vb.* ab·ziehen*.

discourage, *vb.* entmu'tigen.

discouragement, *n.* Entmu'ti-gung, -en *f.*

discourse, *n.* Gespräch', -e *nt.;* Abhandlung, -en *f.* **2.** *vb.* sprechen*.

discourteous, *adj.* unhöflich.

discourtesy, *n.* Unhöflichkeit, -en *f.*

discover, *vb.* entde'cken.

discovery, *n.* Entde'ckung, -en *f.*

discredit, 1. *n.* Nichtachtung *f.* **2.** *vb.* nicht glauben; in schlechten Ruf bringen*.

discreet, *adj.* diskret'.

discrepancy, *n.* Zwiespalt, -e *m.*

discretion, *n.* Diskretion' *f.;* Beson'nenheit *f.*

discriminate, *vb.* unterschei'-den*; diskriminie'ren.

discrimination, *n.* Diskrimi-nie'rung, -en *f.*

disdain, *vb.* verach'ten.

disdainful, *adj.* verächt'lich.

disease, *n.* Krankheit, -en *f.*

disembark, *vb.* landen.

disembarkation, *n.* Landung, -en *f.*

disenchantment, *n.* Enttäu'-schung, -en *f.,* Ernüch'terung *f.*

disengage, *vb.* los·lösen.

disentangle, *vb.* entwir'ren.

disfavor, *n.* Mißfallen *nt.;* Ungnade *f.*

disfigure, *vb.* entstel'len.

disgrace, 1. *n.* Schande, -n *f.,* Unehre *f.* **2.** *vb.* schänden, blamie'ren.

disgraceful, *adj.* schändlich.

disgruntled, *adj.* mürrisch.

disguise, 1. *n.* Verklei'dung, -en *f.* **2.** *vb.* verklei'den.

disgust, 1. *n.* Ekel *m.* **2.** *vb.* an-ekeln.

disgusting, *adj.* ekelhaft, wi-derlich.

dish, *n.* Schüssel, -n *f.; (food)* Gericht', -e *nt.*

dishcloth, *n.* Abwaschtuch, -̈er *nt.*

dishearten, *vb.* entmu'tigen.

dishonest, *adj.* unehrlich.

dishonesty, *n.* Unehrlichkeit, -en *f.*

dishonor, 1. *n.* Schande, -n *f.* **2.** *vb.* enteh'ren.

dishonorable, *adj.* unehren-haft.

dishtowel, *n.* Geschirr'hand-tuch, -̈er *nt.*

disillusion, 1. *n.* Enttäu'-schung, -en *f.* **2.** *vb.* enttäu'-schen.

disinfect, *vb.* desinfizie'ren.

disinfectant, *n.* Desinfizie'-rungsmittel, - *nt.*

disinherit, *vb.* enter'ben.

disintegrate, *vb.* zerfal'len*.

disinterested, *adj.* gleichgültig.

disjointed, *adj.* unzusammen-hängend.

disk, *n.* Scheibe, -n *f.*

dislike, 1. *n.* Abneigung, -en *f.* **2.** *vb.* nicht mögen*.

dislocate, *vb.* aus·renken.

dislodge, *vb.* los·reißen*, ver-trei'ben*.

disloyal, *adj.* treulos.

disloyalty, *n.* Untreue, -n *f.*

dismal, *adj.* jämmerlich.

dismantle, *vb.* demontie'ren.

dismay, 1. *n.* Bestür'zung, -en *f.* **2.** *vb.* erschre'cken.

dismember, *vb.* zerstü'ckeln.

dismiss, *vb.* entlas'sen*; fallen lassen*.

dismissal, *n.* Entlas'sung, -en *f.*

dismount, *vb.* ab·steigen*.

disobedience, *n.* Ungehorsam *m.*

disobedient, *adj.* ungehorsam.

disobey, *vb.* nicht gehor'chen.

disorder, *n.* Unordnung *f.*

disorderly, *adj.* unordentlich, liederlich.

disorganize, *vb.* in Unordnung bringen*.

disown, *vb.* verleug'nen.

disparage, *vb.* herab'setzen.

disparity, *n.* Ungleichheit, -en *f.*

dispassionate, *adj.* leiden-schaftslos.

dispatch, 1. *n.* Absendung, -en *f.* **2.** *vb.* ab·senden*, eilig weg·schicken.

dispatcher, *n.* Absender, - *m.*

dispel, *vb.* vertrei'ben*.

dispensable, *adj.* entbehr'lich.

dispensary, *n.* Arznei'ausgabe-stelle, -n *f.*

dispensation, *n.* Befrei'ung, -en *f.*

dispense, *vb.* aus·geben*; **(d. with)** verzich'ten auf.

dispersal, *n.* Vertei'lung, -en *f.*

disperse, *vb.* vertei'len.

displace, *vb.* verdrän'gen.

displaced person, *n.* Zwangs-verschleppt- *m.&f.*

display, 1. *n.* Aufwand *m.; (window)* Schaufensterausla-ge, -n *f.* **2.** *vb.* entfal'ten, zeigen.

displease, *vb.* mißfal'len*.

displeasure, *n.* Mißfallen *nt.*

disposable, *adj.* verfüg'bar.

disposal, *n.* Verfü'gung, -en *f.*

dispose, *vb.* bestim'men.

disposition, *n.* Verfü'gung, -en *f.; (character)* Anlage *f.*

dispossess, *vb.* enteig'nen.

disproof, *n.* Widerle'gung, -en *f.*

disproportion, *n.* Mißverhält-nis, -se *nt.*

disproportionate, *adj.* unver-hältnismäßig.

disprove, *vb.* widerle'gen.

disputable, *adj.* bestreit'bar.

dispute, 1. *n.* Streit, -e *m.* **2.** *vb.* bestrei'ten*.

disqualification, *n.* Disqualifi-zie'rung, -en *f.*

disqualify, *vb.* disqualifizie'ren.

disregard, 1. *n.* Nichtbe-achtung *f.* **2.** *vb.* nicht beach'-ten.

disrepair, *n.* Verfall' *m.*

disreputable, *adj.* verru'fen.

disrespect, *n.* Nichtachtung *f.,* Mißachtung *f.*

disrespectful, *adj.* unehrerbietig, unhöflich.

disrobe, *vb.* entklei′den.

disrupt, *vb.* auseinan′der-reißen*.

dissatisfaction, *n.* Unzufriedenheit, -en *f.*

dissatisfy, *vb.* nicht befrie′digen.

dissect, *vb.* zerglie′dern; *(med.)* sezie′ren.

disseminate, *vb.* verbrei′ten.

dissension, *n.* Uneinigkeit, -en *f.*

dissent, 1. *n.* Meinungsverschiedenheit, -en *f.* 2. *vb.* anderer Meinung sein*.

dissertation, *n.* Dissertation′, -en *f.*

dissimilar, *adj.* unähnlich.

dissipated, *adj.* ausschweifend, verlebt′.

dissipation, *n.* Ausschweifung, -en *f.*

dissociate, *vb.* trennen.

dissolute, *adj.* verkom′men.

dissolution, *n.* Auflösung, -en *f.*

dissolve, *vb.* auf·lösen.

dissonance, *n.* Dissonanz′, -en *f.*

dissonant, *adj.* dissonant′.

dissuade, *vb.* ab·raten*.

distance, *n.* Entfer′nung, -en *f.*, Abstand, ∸e *m.*

distant, *adj.* entfernt′; *(fig.)* zurück′haltend.

distaste, *n.* Widerwille(n), - *m.*, Abneigung, -en *f.*

distasteful, *adj.* widerwärtig, widerlich.

distemper, *n. (dog)* Staupe *f.*

distend, *vb.* aus·dehnen.

distill, *vb.* destillie′ren.

distillation, *n.* Destillation′, -en *f.*

distiller, *n.* Destillateur′, -e *m.*

distillery, *n.* Branntweinbrennerei, -en *f.*

distinct, *adj.* deutlich; *(different)* verschie′den.

distinction, *n. (difference)* Unterschied, -e *m.; (elegance)* Vornehmheit *f.; (honor)* Auszeichnung, -en *f.*

distinctive, *adj.* kennzeichnend.

distinctness, *n.* Deutlichkeit *f.*

distinguish, *vb. (differentiate)* unterschei′den*; *(honor)* aus·zeichnen.

distinguished, *adj. (famous)* berühmt′; *(elegant)* vornehm.

distort, *vb.* verzer′ren.

distract, *vb.* ab·lenken.

distraction, *n.* Ablenkung, -en *f.*

distress, 1. *n.* Not, ∸e *f.* 2. *vb.* betrü′ben.

distribute, *vb.* vertei′len.

distribution, *n.* Vertei′lung, -en *f.*

distributor, *n.* Vertei′ler, - *m.; (agent)* Vertriebs′stelle, -n *f.*

district, *n.* Bezirk′, -e *m.*

distrust, 1. *n.* Mißtrauen *nt.* 2. *vb.* mißtrau′en.

distrustful, *adj.* mißtrauisch.

disturb, *vb.* stören, beun′ruhigen.

disturbance, *n.* Störung, -en *f.*, Unruhe, -n *f.*

ditch, *n.* Graben, ∸ *m.*

diva, *n.* Diva, -s *f.*

divan, *n.* Diwan, -e *m.*

dive, 1. *n.* Kopfsprung, ∸e *m.* 2. *vb.* tauchen.

diver, *n.* Taucher, - *m.*

diverge, *vb.* auseinan′der-gehen*.

divergence, *n.* Divergenz′, -en *f.*

divergent, *adj.* divergie′rend.

diverse, *adj.* verschie′den.

diversion, *n.* Ablenkung, -en *f.; (pastime)* Zeitvertreib, -e *m.*

diversity, *n.* Mannigfaltigkeit, -en *f.*

divert, *vb.* ab·lenken, um·leiten.

divest, *vb.* entklei′den.

divide, *vb.* teilen.

dividend, *n.* Dividen′de, -n *f.*

divine, *adj.* göttlich.

divinity, *n.* Gottheit, -en *f.; (study)* Theologie′, -i′en *f.*

divisible, *adj.* teilbar.

division, *n.* Teilung, -en *f.; (mil.)* Division′, -en *f.*

divorce, 1. *n.* Scheidung, -en *f.* 2. *vb.* **(get d.d)** sich scheiden lassen*; **(d. a person)** sich von einem Menschen scheiden lassen*.

divorcée, *n.* geschie′dene Frau, -en *f.*

divulge, *vb.* enthül′len.

dizziness, *n.* Schwindel *m.*

dizzy, *adj.* schwindlig.

do, *vb.* tun*, machen.

docile, *adj.* fügsam.

dock, *n.* Dock, -s *nt.*

docket, *n.* Gerichts′kalender, - *m.; Geschäfts′ordnung, -en *f.*

doctor, *n.* Doktor, -o′ren *m.; (physician)* Arzt, ∸e *m.*

doctorate, *n.* Doktorat′, -e *nt.*

doctrine, *n.* Lehre, -n *f.; Grundsatz, ∸e *m.*

document, *n.* Urkunde, -n *f.;* Dokument′, -e *nt.*

documentary, *adj.* urkundlich, dokumenta′risch.

documentation, *n.* Dokumentation′, -en *f.*

dodge, *vb.* aus·weichen*.

doe, *n.* Reh, -e *nt.*

doeskin, *n.* Rehleder *nt.*

dog, *n.* Hund, -e *m.*

dogma, *n.* Dogma, -men *nt.*

dogmatic, *adj.* dogma′tisch.

dogmatism, *n.* Dogma′tik *f.*

dole, 1. *n.* Arbeitslosenunterstützung, -en *f.;* **(be on the d.)** stempeln gehen*. 2. *vb.* **(d. out)** vertei′len.

doleful, *adj.* kummervoll.

doll, *n.* Puppe, -n *f.*

dollar, *n.* Dollar, -s *m.*

domain, *n.* Bereich′, -e *m.*

dome, *n.* Dom, -e *m.*, Kuppel, -n *f.*

domestic, *adj.* häuslich; **(d. policy)** Innenpolitik *f.*

domesticate, *vb.* zähmen.

domicile, *n.* Wohnort, -e *m.*

dominance, *n.* Herrschaft, -en *f.*

dominant, *adj.* vorherrschend.

dominate, *vb.* beherr′schen.

domination, *n.* Herrschaft, -en *f.*

domineer, *vb.* tyrannisie′ren.

dominion, *n.* Domi′nion, -s *nt.*

domino, *n.* Domino, -s *m.*

don, *vb.* an·ziehen*; *(hat)* auf·setzen.

donate, *vb.* stiften.

donation, *n.* Gabe, -n *f.*, Schenkung, -en *f.*

done, *adj. (food)* gar.

donkey, *n.* Esel, - *m.*

doom, *n.* Verder′ben *nt.*

door, *n.* Tür, -en *f.*

doorman, *n.* Portier′, -s *m.*

doorway, *n.* Türeingang, ∸e *m.*

dope, *n. (drug)* Rauschgift, -e *nt.; (fool)* Trottel, - *m.*

dormant, *adj.* ruhend, latent′.

dormitory, *n. (room)* Schlafsaal, -säle *m.; (building)* Studentenheim, -e *nt.*

dosage, *n.* Dosie′rung, -en *f.*

dose, *n.* Dosis, -dosen *f.*

dossier, *n.* Akte, -n *f.*

dot, *n.* Punkt, -e *m.*

double, 1. *n.* Doppelgänger, - *m.* 2. *adj.* doppelt.

double-breasted, *adj.* zweireihig.

double-cross, *vb.* hintergehen*.

doubt, 1. *n.* Zweifel, - *m.* 2. *vb.* zweifeln, bezwei′feln.

doubtful, *adj.* zweifelhaft.

doubtless, *adj.* zweifellos.

dough, *n.* Teig, -e *m.*

douse, *vb.* begie′ßen; *(fire)* löschen.

dove, *n.* Taube, -n *f.*

dowdy, *adj.* schlampig.

down, 1. *n.* Flaum *m.; (material)* Daune, -n *f.* 2. *vb.* nieder-werfen*, *(fig.)* besie′gen. 3. *adv.* unten, nieder, ab; hin-, herun′ter; hin-, herab′

downcast, *adj.* niedergeschlagen.

downfall, *n.* Untergang, ∸e *m.*

downhearted, *adj.* betrübt′.

downhill, *adv.* bergab′.

down payment, *n.* Anzahlung, -en *f.*

downpour, *n.* Regenguß, ∸sse *m.*

downstairs, *adv.* unten.

downtown, 1. *n.* Geschäfts′viertel, - *nt.* 2. *adv. (direction)* in die Stadt; *(location)* in der Stadt.

downward, *adv.* nach unten.

dowry, *n.* Mitgift, -en *f.*

doze, *vb.* dösen.

dozen, *n.* Dutzend, -e *nt.*

drab, *adj.* (*color*) bräunlich gelb; (*dull*) farblos.

draft, 1. *n.* (*plan*) Entwurf', ⁼e *m.;* (*money*) Wechsel, - *m.;* (*air*) Zug, ⁼e *m.;* (*military service*) militä'rische Dienstpflicht *f.* **2.** *vb.* entwer'fen*; (*mil.*) ein-ziehen*.

draftee, *n.* Rekrut', -en, -en *m.*

draftsman, *n.* Zeichner, - *m.*

drafty, *adj.* zugig.

drag, *vb.* schleppen, schleifen.

dragon, *n.* Drache, -n, -n *m.*

drain, 1. *n.* Abfluß, ⁼sse *m.* **2.** *vb.* ab-laufen lassen*; entwäs'sern.

drainage, *n.* Abfluß, ⁼sse *m.;* Entwäs'serung, -en *f.*

dram, *n.* Drachme, -n *f.*

drama, *n.* Drama, -men *nt.;* Schauspiel, -e *nt.*

dramatic, *adj.* drama'tisch.

dramatics, *n.* Thea'terwissenschaft, -en *f.*

dramatist, *n.* Drama'tiker, - *m.*

dramatize, *vb.* dramatisie'-ren.

drape, 1. *n.* Vorhang, ⁼e *m.* **2.** *vb.* drapie'ren.

drapery, *n.* Vorhang, ⁼e *m.;* Behang', ⁼e *m.*

drastic, *adj.* drastisch.

draught, see draft.

draw, *vb.* (*pull*) ziehen*; (*picture*) zeichnen; (**d. up**) ab-fassen.

drawback, *n.* Nachteil, -e *m.;* Schattenseite, -n *f.*

drawbridge, *n.* Zugbrücke, -n *f.*

drawer, *n.* Schublade, -n *f.*

drawing, *n.* (*picture*) Zeichnung, -en *f.;* (*lottery*) Ziehung, -en *f.*

drawl, *vb.* langsam und ausgedehnt sprechen*.

dread, 1. *n.* Furcht *f.*, Angst, ⁼e *f.* **2.** *vb.* fürchten.

dreadful, *adj.* furchtbar.

dream, 1. *n.* Traum, ⁼e *m.* **2.** *vb.* träumen.

dreamy, *adj.* träumerisch, verträumt'.

dreary, *adj.* trostlos.

dredge, 1. *n.* Bagger, - *m.* **2.** *vb.* baggern.

dregs, *n.pl.* Bodensatz, ⁼e *m.;* (*fig.*) Abschaum, ⁼e *m.*

drench, *vb.* durchnäs'sen.

dress, 1. *n.* Kleid, -er *nt.* **2.** *vb.* an-ziehen*, kleiden.

dresser, *n.* Kommo'de, -n *f.*

dressing, *n.* (*food*) Soße, -n *f.;* (*med.*) Verband', ⁼e *m.*

dressing gown, *n.* Schlafrock, ⁼e *m.*, Morgenrock, ⁼e *m.*

dressmaker, *n.* Schneiderin, -nen *f.*

drier, *n.* (*hair*) Trockenhaube, -n *f.;* (*clothes*) Trockenautomat, -en, -en *m.*

drift, 1. *n.* (*snow*) Schneewehe, -n *f.;* (*tendency*) Richtung, -en *f.*, Strömung, -en *f.* **2.** *vb.* treiben*.

drill, 1. *n.* (*tool*) Drillbohrer, - *m.;* (*practice*) Schulung, -en *f.;* (*mil.*) Exerzie'ren *nt.* **2.** *vb.* bohren; schulen; exerzie'-ren.

drink, 1. *n.* Getränk', -e *nt.* **2.** *vb.* trinken*.

drinkable, *adj.* trinkbar.

drip, *vb.* tropfen.

drive, 1. *n.* (*ride*) Spazier'fahrt, -en *f.;* (*energy*) Schwungkraft *f.* **2.** *vb.* treiben*; (*auto*) fahren*.

driver, *n.* Fahrer, - *m.*

driveway, *n.* Auffahrt, -en *f.*

drizzle, 1. *n.* Sprühregen, - *m.* **2.** *vb.* nieseln.

drone, 1. *n.* (*bee*) Drohne, -n *f.;* (*hum*) Gesum'me *nt.* **2.** *vb.* summen.

droop, *vb.* herab'-hängen*.

drop, 1. *n.* Tropfen, - *m.* **2.** *vb.* (*fall*) fallen*; (*let fall*) fallen* lassen*.

dropout, *n.* jemand, der absichtlich seine ordnungsgemäße Tätigkeit, Ausbildung, Lebensart, aufgibt.

dropper, *n.* Tropfer, - *m.*

dropsy, *n.* Wassersucht *f.*

drought, *n.* Dürre, -n *f.*, Trockenheit, -en *f.*

drown, *vb.* (*intr.*) ertrin'ken*; (*tr.*) erträn'ken.

drowsiness, *n.* Schläfrigkeit *f.*

drowsy, *adj.* schläfrig.

drudgery, *n.* Plackerei', -en *f.*

drug, *n.* Droge, -n *f.*, Medikament', -e *nt.*

druggist, *n.* Drogist', -en, -en *m.*, Apothe'ker, - *m.*

drug store, *n.* Drogerie', -i'en *f.*, Apothe'ke, -n *f.*

drum, *n.* Trommel, -n *f.*

drummer, *n.* Trommler, *m.*

drumstick, *n.* Trommelschlegel, - *m.;* (*fowl*) Geflü'gelschlegel, - *m.*

drunk, *adj.* betrun'ken; (**get d.**) sich betrin'ken*.

drunkard, *n.* Trinker, - *m.;* Trunkenbold, -e *m.*

drunken, *adj.* betrun'ken.

drunkenness, *n.* Trunkenheit *f.*

dry, 1. *adj.* trocken. **2.** *vb.* trocknen.

dry cell, *n.* Trockenelement, -e *nt.*

dry-cleaner, *n.* Reinigung, -en *f.*

dry-cleaning, *n.* chemische Reinigung, -en *f.*

dry goods, *n.pl.* Texti'lien *pl.*

dryness, *n.* Trockenheit, -en *f.*

dual, *adj.* Doppel- (*cpds.*).

dubious, *adj.* zweifelhaft.

duchess, *n.* Herzogin, -nen *f.*

duchy, *n.* Herzogtum, -er *nt.*

duck, 1. *n.* Ente, -n *f.* **2.** *vb.* sich ducken.

duct, *n.* Rohr, -e *nt.;* Kanal', ⁼e *m.*

due, *adj.* schuldig; fällig.

duel, *n.* Duell', -e *nt.*

dues, *n.pl.* Gebüh'ren *pl.*, Beitrag, ⁼e *m.*

duet, *n.* Duett', -e *nt.*

duffle bag, *n.* Seesack, ⁼e *m.*

duke, *n.* Herzog, ⁼e *m.*

dull, *adj.* (*not sharp*) stumpf; (*boring*) langweilig.

dullness, *n.* Stumpfheit *f.;* Langweiligkeit *f.*

duly, *adv.* gebüh'rend.

dumb, *adj.* stumm; (*stupid*) dumm (⁼), blöde.

dumbwaiter, *n.* Drehaufzug, ⁼e *m.*

dumfound, *vb.* verblüf'fen.

dummy, *n.* (*posing as someone*) Strohmann, ⁼er *m.;* (*window-display*) Schaufensterpuppe, -n *f.;* (*bridge*) Tisch *m.;* (*theater*) Statist', -en, -en *m.*

dump, 1. *n.* Abladeplatz, ⁼e *m.;* (*refuse*) Schuttablade, -n *f.* **2.** *vb.* ab-laden*.

dumpling, *n.* Kloß, ⁼e *m.*

dun, *1. adj.* graubraun. **2.** *vb.* zur Zahlung mahnen.

dunce, *n.* Schafskopf, ⁼e *m.*, Dummkopf, ⁼e *m.*

dune, *n.* Düne, -n *f.*

dung, *n.* Dung *m.*

dungarees, *n.pl.* Arbeitshose, -n *f.*

dungeon, *n.* Kerker, - *m.*

dunk, *vb.* tunken.

dupe, 1. *n.* düpie'ren. **2.** *n.* Düpiert'- *m.&f.*

duplex, *adj.* Doppelt- (*cpds.*).

duplicate, *vb.* verdop'peln, kopie'ren.

duplication, *n.* Verdop'pelung, -en *f.*

duplicity, *n.* Duplizität', -en *f.*

durability, *n.* Dauerhaftigkeit *f.*

durable, *adj.* dauerhaft.

duration, *n.* Dauer *f.*

duress, *n.* Zwang *m.*

during, *prep.* während.

dusk, *n.* Abenddämmerung, -en *f.*

dust, 1. *n.* Staub *m.* **2.** *vb.* ab-stauben.

dusty, *adj.* staubig.

Dutch, *adj.* holländisch.

Dutchman, *n.* Holländer, - *m.*

dutiful, *adj.* pflichtgetreu.

duty, *n.* Pflicht, -en *f.;* (*tax*) Zoll, ⁼e *m.*

duty-free, *adj.* zollfrei.

dwarf, *n.* Zwerg, -e *m.*

dwell, *vb.* wohnen.

dweller, *n.* Bewoh'ner, - *m.*

dwelling, *n.* Wohnung, -en *f.;* Wohnsitz, -e *m.*

dwindle, *vb.* schrumpfen.

dye, 1. *n.* Farbe, -n *f.;* Farbstoff, -e *m.* **2.** *vb.* färben.

dyer, *n.* Färber, - *m.*

dyestuff, *n.* Farbstoff, -e *m.*

dynamic, *adj.* dyna'misch.

dynamite, *n.* Dynamit' *nt.*

dynamo, *n.* Dyna'mo, -s *m.*

dynasty, *n.* Dynastie', -i'en *f.*

dysentery, *n.* Ruhr *f.*

dyslexia, n. Dysle'xia f.
dyspepsia, n. Dyspepsie' f.

E

each, adj. jeder, -es, -e.
each other, pron. einan'der.
eager, adj. eifrig.
eagerness, n. Eifer m.
eagle, n. Adler, - m.
ear, n. Ohr, -en nt.
earache, n. Ohrenschmerzen pl.
eardrum, n. Trommelfell, -e nt.
earl, n. Graf, -en, -en m.
early, adj. früh.
earmark, 1. n. Anzeichen, - nt. 2. vb. bestim'men; (be e.ed) vorgesehen sein*.
earn, vb. verdie'nen.
earnest, adj. ernst.
earnestness, n. Ernst m.
earnings, n.pl. Einnahmen pl.
earring, n. Ohrring, -e m.
earth, n. Erde, -n f.
earthenware, n. Steingut nt.
earthly, adj. irdisch.
earthquake, n. Erdbeben, - nt.
earthy, adj. erdig; (fig.) derb.
ease, 1. n. Leichtigkeit, -en f.; (comfort) Behag'lichkeit, -en f. 2. vb. erleich'tern, lindern.
easel, n. Staffelei', -en f.
easiness, n. Leichtigkeit, -en f.
east, 1. n. Osten m., Orient m. 2. adj. östlich; Ost (cpds.).
Easter, n. Ostern nt.
easterly, adj. östlich.
eastern, adj. östlich.
eastward, adv. ostwärts.
easy, adj. leicht.
easygoing, adj. gutmütig, ungezwungen.
eat, vb. essen*.
eatable, adj. eßbar.
eaves, n.pl. Dachrinne, -n f.
ebb, 1. n. Ebbe, -n f. 2. vb. abnehmen*.
ebony, n. Ebenholz, -er nt.
eccentric, adj. exzen'trisch.
eccentricity, n. Exzentrizität', -en f.
ecclesiastic, adj. kirchlich, geistlich.
ecclesiastical, adj. kirchlich, geistlich.
echelon, n. Staffel, -n f.
echo, 1. n. Echo, -s nt. 2. vb. widerhallen.
eclipse, n. Finsternis, -se f.
ecological, adj. ökolo'gisch.
ecology, n. Ökologie' f.
economic, adj. wirtschaftlich.
economical, adj. sparsam.
economics, n. Volkswirtschaft f., National'ökonomie f.
economist, n. Volkswirtschaftler, - m.
economize, vb. haushalten*.
economy, n. Wirtschaft f.; Sparsamkeit f.
ecstasy, n. Verzü'ckung, -en f.

ecumenical, adj. ökume'nisch.
eczema, n. Ekzem', -e nt.
eddy, n. Strudel, - m.
edge, n. Rand, -er m.; (knife, etc.) Schneide, -n f.
edible, adj. eßbar.
edict, n. Verord'nung, -en f., Edikt', -e nt.
edifice, n. Gebäu'de, - nt.
edify, vb. erbau'en.
edit, vb. heraus'geben*.
edition, n. Ausgabe, -n f., Auflage, -n f.
editor, n. Heraus'geber, - m.
editorial, 1. n. Leitartikel, - m. 2. adj. Redaktions'- (cpds.).
educate, vb. (bring up) erzie'hen*; (train) aus'bilden.
education, n. (upbringing) Erzie'hung f.; (training) Aus'bildung f.; (culture) Bildung f.
educational, adj. erzie'herisch.
educator, n. Erzie'her, - m.; Pädago'ge, -n, -n m.
eel, n. Aal, -e m.
effect, n. Wirkung, -en f.
effective, adj. wirkungsvoll.
effectiveness, n. Wirksamkeit f.
effectual, adj. wirksam.
effeminate, adj. verweich'licht.
effervescence, n. Sprudeln m.
effete, adj. entkräf'tet.
efficiency, n. Leistungsfähigkeit f., Tüchtigkeit f., Wirksamkeit f.
efficient, adj. leistungsfähig, tüchtig, wirksam.
effigy, n. Abbild, -er nt.
effort, n. Mühe, -n f.; (exertion) Anstrengung, -en f.; (attempt) Versuch, -e m.
effrontery, n. Frechheit, -en f.
effusive, adj. überschwenglich.
egg, n. Ei, -er nt.
eggplant, n. Aubergi'ne, -n f.
ego, n. Ich nt.
egoism, n. Egois'mus m.
egotism, n. Egotis'mus m.
egotist, n. Egoist', -en, -en m.
Egypt, n. Ägyp'ten nt.
Egyptian, 1. n. Ägyp'ter, - m. 2. adj. ägyp'tisch.
eight, num. acht.
eighteen, num. achtzehn.
eighteenth, 1. adj. achtzehnt-. 2. n. Achzehntel, -nt.
eighth, 1. adj. acht-. 2. n. Achtel, - nt.
eightieth, 1. adj. achtzigst-. 2. n. Achtzigstel, - nt.
eighty, num. achtzig.
either, 1. pron.&adj. jeder, -es, -e; beides, pl. beide. 2. conj. (e. . . . or) entweder . . . oder. 3. adv. (not . . . e.) auch nicht, auch kein, -, -e.
ejaculation, n. Ausruf, -e m.
eject, vb. hinaus'-werfen*; vertrei'ben*.
ejection, n. Hinaus'werfen nt.
eke out, vb. sich durch-helfen*.
elaborate, 1. adj. weitläufig;

kunstvoll. 2. vb. ins einzelne gehen*.
elapse, vb. verge'hen*.
elastic, 1. n. Gummiband, -er nt. 2. adj. elas'tisch.
elasticity, n. Elastizität' f.
elate, vb. erfreu'en.
elated, adj. hocherfreut.
elation, n. Freude, -n f.
elbow, n. Ellbogen, - m.
elder, 1. n. (tree) Holun'der, - m.; (church) Ältest- m. 2. adj. älter.
elderly, adj. ältlich.
eldest, adj. ältest-.
elect, vb. wählen.
election, n. Wahl, -en f.
elective, adj. Wahl- (cpds.).
electorate, n. Wählerschaft, -en f.
electric, electrical, adj. elek'trisch.
electrician, n. Elek'triker, - m.
electricity, n. Elektrizität' f.
electrocardiogram, n. EKG, -s nt.; Elektrokardiogramm', -e nt.
electrocution, n. Tötung durch elektrischen Strom; Hinrichtung auf dem elektrischen Stuhl.
electrode, n. Elektro'de, -n f.
electrolysis, n. Elektroly'se f.
electron, n. Elektron, -o'nen nt.
electronic, adj. Elektro'nen- (cpds.).
electronics, n. Elektro'nenwissenschaft f.
elegance, n. Eleganz' f.
elegant, adj. elegant'.
elegy, n. Elegie', -i'en f.
element, n. Element', -e nt.
elemental, elementary, adj. elementar'.
elephant, n. Elefant', -en, -en m.
elephantine, adj. elefan'tenartig.
elevate, vb. erhö'hen.
elevation, n. Erhö'hung, -en f.; Höhe, -n f.
elevator, n. Fahrstuhl, -e m.
eleven, num. elf.
eleventh, 1. adj. elft-. 2. n. Elftel, - nt.
elf, n. Kobold, -e m.
elfin, adj. koboldartig.
elicit, vb. heraus'-holen, erwirken.
eligibility, n. Qualifiziert'heit f.
eligible, adj. qualifiziert'.
eliminate, vb. besei'tigen, ausscheiden*.
elimination, n. Besei'tigung, -en f.; Ausscheidung, -en f.
elixir, n. Elixier', -e nt.
elk, n. Elch, -e m.
elm, n. Ulme, -n f.
elocution, n. Redekunst, -e f.
elongate, vb. verlän'gern.
elope, vb. mit einem Mädchen oder einem Jungen durchbrennen*.

eloquence, *n.* Bered'samkeit *f.*

eloquent, *adj.* redegewandt.

else, *adv.* anders, sonst.

elsewhere, *adv.* anderswo.

elucidate, *vb.* erläu'tern.

elude, *vb.* entge'hen*.

elusive, *adj.* nicht greifbar; aalglatt.

emaciated, *adj.* abgezehrt.

emanate, *vb.* aus•strömen.

emancipate, *vb.* emanzipie'ren.

emancipation, *n.* Emanzipa- tion', -en *f.*

emancipator, *n.* Befrei'er, - *m.*

emasculate, *vb.* entman'nen.

embalm, *vb.* ein•balsamieren.

embankment, *n.* Uferanlage, -n *f.*

embargo, *n.* Embar'go, -s *nt.*

embark, *vb.* ein•schiffen.

embarrass, *vb.* in Verle'genheit bringen*.

embarrassed, *adj.* verle'gen.

embarrassment, *n.* Verle'gen- heit, -en *f.*

embassy, *n.* Botschaft, -en *f.*

embellish, *vb.* aus•schmücken.

embellishment, *n.* Aus- schmückung, -en *f.*

embezzle, *vb.* unterschla'gen*.

embitter, *vb.* verbit'tern.

emblem, *n.* Wahrzeichen, - *nt.* , Emblem', -e *nt.*

embody, *vb.* verkör'pern.

embrace, *vb.* umar'men.

embroider, *vb.* sticken.

embroidery, *n.* Stickerei', -en *f.*

embroil, *vb.* verwi'ckeln.

embryo, *n.* Embryo, -s *m.*

emerald, *n.* Smaragd', -e *m.*

emerge, *vb.* hervor•'treten*, auf•tauchen.

emery, *n.* Schmirgel *m.*

emetic, *n.* Brechmittel, - *nt.*

emigrant, *n.* Auswanderer, - *m.*

emigrate, *vb.* aus•wandern.

emigration, *n.* Auswanderung, -en *f.*

eminence, *n.* (hill) Anhöhe, -n *f.; (distinction)* Auszeich- nung, -en *f.; (title)* Eminenz', -en *f.*

eminent, *adj.* erha'ben.

emissary, *n.* Gesandt' - *m.&f.*

emission controls, *n.pl.* Abgas- bestimmungen *f.pl.*

emit, *vb.* von sich geben*.

emotion, *n.* Gefühl', -e *nt.;* Er- re'gung, -en *f.*

emotional, *adj.* gefühls'mäßig; erreg'bar.

emperor, *n.* Kaiser, - *m.*

emphasis, *n.* Nachdruck *m.*

emphasize, *vb.* beto'nen, her- vor'•heben*.

emphatic, *adj.* nachdrücklich.

empire, *n.* Kaiserreich, -e *nt.*

empirical, *adj.* empi'risch.

employ, *vb.* an•stellen, be- schäf'tigen.

employee, *n.* Arbeitnehmer, - *m.,* Angestellt- *m.&f.*

employer, *n.* Arbeitgeber, - *m.*

employment, *n.* Anstellung, - en *f.;* Beschäf'tigung, -en *f.*

empower, *vb.* ermäch'tigen.

empress, *n.* Kaiserin, -nen *f.*

emptiness, *n.* leere *f.*

empty, **1.** *vb.* leeren. **2.** *adj.* leer.

emulate, *vb.* nach•eifern.

emulsion, *n.* Emulsion', -en *f.*

enable, *vb.* ermög'lichen; **(en- abling act)** Ermäch'tigungs- gesetz, -e *nt.*

enact, *vb.* (law) erlas'sen; *(role)* spielen.

enactment, *n.* Verord'nung, - en *f.*

enamel, *n.* Emai'lle *f.*

enamor, *vb.* **(be e.ed of)** in je- mand verliebt' sein*; **(be- come e.ed of)** sich in jemand verlie'ben.

encamp, *vb.* sich lagern.

encampment, *n.* Lager, - *nt.*

encephalitis, *n.* Gehirn'entzün- dung, -en *f.*

enchant, *vb.* entzü'cken; be- zau'bern.

enchantment, *n.* Bezau'berung *f.;* Zauber *m.*

encircle, *vb.* umrin'gen.

enclose, *vb.* ein•schließen*; *(letter)* bei•fügen.

enclosure, *n.* Einzäunung, -en *f.; (letter)* Beilage, -n *f.*

encompass, *vb.* umschlie'ßen*, ein•schließen*.

encounter, *vb.* treffen*, begeg'- nen.

encourage, *vb.* ermu'tigen.

encouragement, *n.* Ermu'ti- gung, -en *f.*

encroach upon, *vb.* sich ein• drängen.

encyclical, *n.* Enzy'klika, -ken *f.*

encyclopedia, *n.* Konversa- tions'lexikon, -ka *nt.;* Enzyklopädie', -i'en *f.*

end, **1.** *n.* Ende, -n *nt.; (pur- pose)* Zweck, -e *m.; (goal)* Ziel, -e *nt.* **2.** *vb.* been'den, vollen'den, been'digen.

endanger, *vb.* gefähr'den.

endear, *vb.* lieb, teuer, wert machen.

endearment, *n.* Zärtlichkeit, - en *f.*

endeavor, *vb.* sich bemü'hen, streben.

ending, *n.* Ende, -n *nt.,* Schluß, ¬sse *m.*

endless, *adj.* endlos.

endocrine, *adj.* endokrin'.

endorse, *vb.* gut•heißen*; *(check)* girie'ren.

endorsement, *n.* Billigung, -en *f.; (check)* Giro *nt.*

endow, *vb.* aus•statten; stiften.

endowment, *n.* Ausstattung, - en *f.;* Stiftung, -en *f.*

endurance, *n.* Ausdauer *f.*

endure, *vb.* (last) dauern; *(bear)* ertra'gen*.

enema, *n.* Klistier', -e *nt.*

enemy, *n.* Feind, -e *m.*

energetic, *adj.* tatkräftig.

energy, *n.* Tatdrft, ¬e *f.,* Ener- gie', -n *f.*

enfold, *vb.* ein•hüllen.

enforce, *vb.* durch•setzen; auf•- swingen*.

enforcement, *n.* Durchführung -en *f.,* Durchsetzung, -en *f.*

engage, *vb.* (hire) an•stellen; *(affiance)* verlo'ben; *(rent)* mieten.

engaged, *adj.* (busy) beschäf'- tigt; *(affianced)* verlobt'.

engagement, *n.* (date) Verab'- redung, -en *f.; (betrothal)* Verlo'bung, -en *f.*

engaging, *adj.* anziehend.

engender, *vb.* hervor'•brin- gen*.

engine, *n.* Maschi'ne, - *f.;* Mo- tor, -o'ren, *m.;* Lokomoti've, -n *f.*

engineer, *n.* Ingenieur', -e *m; (locomotive)* Lokomotiv'füh- rer, - *m.; (mil.)* Pionier', -e *m.*

engineering, *n.* Ingenieur'- wesen *nt.*

England, *n.* England *nt.*

English, *adj.* englisch.

Englishman, *n.* Engländer, - *m.*

Englishwoman, *n.* Englän- derin, -en *f.*

engrave, *vb.* gravie'ren.

engraver, *n.* Graveur', -e *m.*

engraving, *n.* Kupferstich, -e *m.*

engross, *vb.* in Anspruch neh- men*.

enhance, *vb.* erhö'hen.

enigma, *n.* Rätsel, - *nt.*

enigmatic, *adj.* rätselhaft, dun- kel.

enjoin, *vb.* (command) befeh'- len*; *(forbid)* verbie'ten*.

enjoy, *vb.* genie'ßen*, sich er- freu'en.

enjoyable, *adj.* erfreu'lich, an- genehm, nett.

enjoyment, *n.* Freude, -n *f.,* Genuß', ¬sse *m.*

enlarge, *vb.* vergrö'ßern.

enlargement, *n.* Vergrö'ße- rung, -en *f.*

enlarger, *n.* Vergrö'ßerungsap- parat, -e *m.*

enlighten, *vb.* auf•klären.

enlightenment, *n.* Aufklärung *f.*

enlist, *vb.* ein•spannen; *(mil.)* sich freiwillig melden.

enlisted man, *n.* Soldat', -en, - en *m.*

enlistment, *n.* freiwillige Mel- dung zum Militärdienst.

enliven, *vb.* bele'ben.

enmity, *n.* Feindschaft, -en *f.*

ennui, *n.* Langeweile *f.*

enormity, *n.* Ungeheuerlich- keit, -en *f.*

enormous, *adj.* ungeheuer, enorm'.

enough, *adv.* genug', genü'gend.

enrage, *vb.* rasend machen.

enrapture, *vb.* entzü'cken.

enrich, *vb.* berei'chern.

enroll, *vb.* als Mitglied eintragen.*

enrollment, *n.* Eintragung (f.) als Mitglied; Mitgliederzahl,.-en *f.*

ensemble, *n.* Ensem'ble, -s *nt.*

enshrine, *vb.* als Heiligtum verwah'ren.

ensign, *n.* *(rank)* Fähnrich, -e *m.; (flag)* Fahne, -n *f.*

enslave, *vb.* verskla'ven, knechten.

ensnare, *vb.* verstri'cken.

ensue, *vb.* folgen.

entail, *vb.* ein·schließen*.

entangle, *vb.* verwi'ckeln.

enter, *vb.* ein·treten*, eindringen*.

enterprise, *n.* Unterneh'men, - *nt.*

enterprising, *adj.* unternehmend.

entertain, *vb.* unterhal'ten*.

entertainment, *n.* Unterhal'tung, -en *f.*

enthrall, *vb.* bezau'bern.

enthusiasm, *n.* Begeis'terung, *f.*

enthusiastic, *adj.* begeis'tert.

entice, *vb.* verlo'cken.

entire, *adj.* ganz, gesamt'.

entirety, *n.* Ganz- *nt.*, Ganzheit *f.*, Gesamt'heit *f.*

entitle, *vb.* berech'tigen; *(name)* beti'teln.

entity, *n.* Wesenheit *f.*

entrails, *n.pl.* Eingeweide *pl.*

entrain, *vb.* den Zug bestei'gen*.

entrance, *n.* Eingang, -e *m.*

entrant, *n.* Teilnehmer, - *m.*

entrap, *vb.* in einer Falle fangen*; verstri'cken.

entreat, *vb.* an·flehen.

entreaty, *n.* Gesuch', -e *nt.*

entrench, *vb.* verschan'zen.

entrepreneur, *n.* Unterneh'mer, - *m.*

entrust, *vb.* an·vertrauen.

entry, *n.* Eintritt, -e *m.; (writing)* Eintragung, -en *f.*

enumerate, *vb.* auf·zählen.

enumeration, *n.* Aufzählung, -en *f.*

enunciate, *vb.* aus·sprechen*.

enunciation, *n.* Aussprache, -n *f.*

envelop, *vb.* ein·hüllen.

envelope, *n.* Umschlag, -e *m.*, Kuvert', -s *nt.*

enviable, *adj.* benei'denswert.

envious, *adj.* neidisch.

environment, *n.* Umge'bung, -en *f.*, Umwelt *f.*

environmentalist, *n.* Umweltschützler, *n.*

environmental protection, *n.* Umweltschutz *m.*

environs, *n.* Umge'bung, -en *f.*

envisage, *vb.* vergegenwär'tigen.

envoy, *n.* Gesandt'- *m.*

envy, *n.* Neid *m.*

eon, *n.* Äon', -en *m.*

ephemeral, *adj.* vergäng'lich.

epic, **1.** *n.* Epos, -pen *nt.* **2.** *adj.* episch.

epicure, *n.* Feinschmecker, - *m.*

epidemic, **1.** *n.* Epidemie', i'en *f.* **2.** *adj.* epide'misch.

epidermis, *n.* Epider'mis *f.*

epigram, *n.* Epigramm', -e *nt.*

epilepsy, *n.* Epilepsie' *f.*

episode, *n.* Episo'de, -n *f.*

epistle, *n.* Schreiben, - *nt.*

epitaph, *n.* Epitaph', -e *nt.*

epithet, *n.* Beiwort, -er *nt.*

epitome, *n.* Kurzfassung, -en *f.; (fig.)* Verkör'perung, -en *f.*

epitomize, *vb.* zusam'menfassen; bezeich'nend sein* für.

epoch, *n.* Epo'che, -n *f.*

equal, **1.** *adj.* gleich. **2.** *vb.* gleichen*.

equality, *n.* Gleichheit *f.*

equalize, *vb.* gleich·machen; aus·gleichen*.

equanimity, *n.* Gleichmut *m.*

equate, *vb.* gleich·setzen.

equation, *n.* Gleichung, -en *f.*

equator, *n.* Äqua'tor *m.*

equatorial, *adj.* äquatorial'.

equestrian, *n.* Reiter, - *m.*

equilateral, *adj.* gleichseitig.

equilibrium, *n.* Gleichgewicht *nt.*

equinox, *n.* Tag- und Nachtgleiche, -n *f.*

equip, *vb.* aus·rüsten.

equipment, *n.* Ausrüstung, -en *f.*

equitable, *adj.* gerecht', billig.

equity, *n.* Billigkeit *f.;* Billigkeitsrecht *nt.; (mortgage, etc.)* Rückkaufswert, -e *m.*

equivalent, *adj.* gleichwertig.

equivocal, *adj.* zweideutig.

equivocate, *vb.* zweideutig sein*.

era, *n.* Zeitalter, - *nt.*

eradicate, *vb.* aus·rotten.

erase, *vb.* aus·radieren.

erasure, *n.* Ausradierung, -en *f.*

erect, **1.** *adj.* gera'de. **2.** *vb.* errich'ten.

erection, *n.* Errich'tung, -en *f.*

erectness, *n.* Gerad'heit *f.*

ermine, *n.* Hermelin' *m.*

erode, *vb.* erodie'ren, zerfres'sen*.

erosion, *n.* Erosion', -en *f.*

erotic, *adj.* ero'tisch.

err, *vb.* irren.

errand, *n.* Besor'gung, -en *f.*

errant, *adj.* wandernd; abwegig.

erratic, *adj.* verirrt'; ziellos.

erroneous, *adj.* irrtümlich.

error, *n.* Fehler, - *m.;* Irrtum, - *m.*

erudite, *adj.* gelehrt'.

erudition, *n.* Gelehr'samkeit *f.*

erupt, *vb.* hervor'·brechen*, aus·brechen*.

eruption, *n.* Ausbruch, -e *m.*

escalate, *vb.* steigern.

escalator, *n.* Rolltreppe, -n *f.*

escapade, *n.* Streich, -e *m.*

escape, **1.** *n.* Flucht *f.* **2.** *vb.* entkom'men*, entge'hen*.

escapism, *n.* Wirklichkeitsflucht *f.*

escort, **1.** *n.* Beglei'ter, - *m.* **2.** *vb.* beglei'ten.

escutcheon, *n.* Wappenschild, -er *nt.*

esophagus, *n.* Speiseröhre, -n *f.*

esoteric, *adj.* esote'risch.

especial, *adj.* beson'der-.

especially, *adv.* beson'ders.

espionage, *n.* Spiona'ge *f.*

espousal, *n.* Vermäh'lung, -en *f.; (e. of)* Eintreten für *nt.*

espouse, *vb.* vermäh'len; **(e. a cause)** ein·treten* für.

essay, **1.** *n.* Essay, -s *m.* **2.** *vb.* versu'chen.

essence, *nt.* Wesen *nt.*, Wesentlich- *nt.*

essential, *adj.* wesentlich.

establish, *vb.* fest·setzen; errich'ten; ein·richten.

establishment, *n.* Einrichtung, -en *f.;* Betrieb', -e *m.*

estate, *n.* *(inheritance)* Nachlaß, -sse *m.; (possessions)* Vermö'gen *nt.; (condition)* Zustand, -e *m.*, Stand, -e *m.*

esteem, **1.** *n.* Achtung *f.* **2.** *vb.* achten, schätzen.

estimable, *adj.* schätzenswert.

estimate, **1.** *n.* Kostenanschlag, -e *m.* **2.** *vb.* schätzen.

estimation, *n.* Achtung *f.; (view)* Ansicht, -en *f.*

estrange, *vb.* entfrem'den.

etch, *vb.* ätzen.

etching, *n.* Radie'rung, -en *f.*

eternal, *adj.* ewig.

eternity, *n.* Ewigkeit, -en *f.*

ether, *n.* Äther *m.*

ethereal, *adj.* äthe'risch.

ethical, *adj.* ethisch, sittlich, mora'lisch.

ethics, *n.* Ethik *f.*

ethnic, *adj.* ethnisch.

etiquette, *n.* Etiket'te *f.*

etymology, *n.* Etymologie', -i'en *f.*

eucalyptus, *n.* Eukalyp'tus, -ten *m.*

eugenic, *adj.* euge'nisch.

eugenics, *n.* Eugene'tik *f.*

eulogize, *vb.* lobpreisen*.

eulogy, *n.* Lobrede, -n *f.*

eunuch, *n.* Eunuch', -en, -en *m.*

euphonious, *adj.* wohlklingend.

Europe, *n.* Euro'pa *nt.*

European, **1.** *n.* Europä'er, - *m.* **2.** *adj.* europä'isch.

euthanasia, *n.* Gnadentod *m.*, Euthanasie' *f.*

evacuate, vb. evakuie'ren.

evade, vb. aus·weichen*, vermei'den*.

evaluate, vb. ab·schätzen, den Wert berech'nen.

evaluation, n. Abschätzung, -en f., Wertbestimmung, -en f.

evangelist, n. Evangelist', -en, -en m.

evaporate, vb. verdam'pfen.

evaporation, n. Verdam'pfung f.

evasion, n. Umge'hen, - nt.

evasive, adj. ausweichend.

eve, n. Vorabend, -e m.

even, 1. adj. gleich, gera'de, eben. **2.** adv. eben, sogar', selbst.

evening, n. Abend, -e m.

evenness, n. Ebenheit, -en f.; Gleichheit, -en f.; Gleichmut m.

event, n. Ereig'nis, -se nt.

eventful, adj. ereig'nisreich.

eventual, adj. (approximate) etwaig; (final) schließlich.

ever, adv. je, jemals.

evergreen, adj. immergrün.

everlasting, adj. ewig.

every, adj. jeder, -es, -e.

everybody, pron. jeder m.; alle pl.

everyday, adj. Alltags (cpds.).

everyone, pron. jeder m.; alle pl.

everything, pron. alles.

everywhere, adv. überall'.

evict, vb. aus·weisen*; zwangsräumen.

eviction, n. Ausweisung, -en f.; Zwangsräumung, -en f.

evidence, n. Beweis', -e m.; Augenschein, m.; (law) Beweis'material, -ien nt.; (give e.) aus·sagen.

evident, adj. klar, deutlich.

evidently, adv. offenbar.

evil, 1. n. Bös- nt. **2.** adj. böse, übel.

evince, vb. offenba'ren.

evoke, vb. hervor'·rufen*.

evolution, n. Evolution', -en f.

evolve, vb. entwi'ckeln.

ewe, n. Mutterschaf, -e nt.

exact, 1. adj. genau'. **2.** vb. erzwin'gen*.

exaggerate, vb. übertrei'ben*.

exaggeration, n. Übertrei'bung, -en f.

exalt, vb. erhö'hen, verherr'lichen.

exaltation, n. Erhö'hung f.; Erre'gung, -en f.

examination, n. Prüfung, -en f., Exa'men, - nt.; Untersu'chung, -en f.

examine, vb. prüfen; untersu'chen.

example, n. Beispiel, -e nt.

exasperate, vb. reizen, verär'gern.

exasperation, n. Gereizt'heit f.

excavate, vb. aus·graben*.

excavation, n. Ausgrabung, -en f.; Aushöhlung, -en f.

exceed, vb. übertref'fen*.

exceedingly, adv. außerordentlich.

excel, vb. sich aus·zeichnen.

excellence, n. Vorzüg'lichkeit, -en f.

Excellency, n. Excellenz', -en f.

excellent, adj. ausgezeich'net.

except, 1. vb. aus·schließen*. **2.** prep. außer, ausgenommen; (e. for) außer.

exception, n. Ausnahme, -n f.

exceptional, adj. außergewöhnlich.

excerpt, n. Auszug, ⸗e m.

excess, n. Übermaß nt.

excessive, adj. übermäßig.

exchange, 1. n. Tausch m.; (rate of e.) Wechselkurs m.; (foreign e.) Valu'ta f.; (student e.) Austausch m.; (stock e.) Börse, -n f. **2.** vb. tauschen; wechseln; aus·tauschen; (goods) um·tauschen.

exchangeable, adj. austauschbar; umtauschbar.

excise, n. Verbrauchs'steuer, -n f. **2.** vb. heraus'·schneiden*.

excite, vb. auf·regen, erre'gen; (get e.d) sich auf·regen.

excitement, n. Erre'gung, -en f.; Aufregung, -en f.

exclaim, vb. aus·rufen*.

exclamation, n. Ausruf, -e m.

exclamation point or **mark,** n. Ausrufungszeichen, - nt.

exclude, vb. aus·schließen*.

exclusion, n. Ausschluß, ⸗sse m.

exclusive, adj. ausschließlich; (e. of) abgesehen von; (select) exklusiv'.

excommunicate, vb. exkommunizie'ren.

excommunication, n. Exkommunikation', -en f.

excrement, n. Exkrement', -e nt.

excruciating, adj. qualvoll.

excursion, n. Ausflug, ⸗e m.

excusable, adj. entschuld'bar.

excuse, vb. entschul'digen, verzei'hen*.

execute, vb. aus·führen; (legal killing) hin·richten.

execution, n. Ausführung, -en f.; (legal killing) Hinrichtung, -en f.

executioner, n. Scharfrichter, - m.

executive, 1. n. Mann in leitender Stellung; (gov't.) Exekuti've f. **2.** adj. vollzie'hend, ausübend.

executor, n. Testaments'vollstrecker, - m.

exemplary, adj. musterhaft.

exemplify, vb. als Beispiel dienen.

exempt, 1. adj. befreit'. **2.** vb. befrei'en.

exercise, 1. n. Übung, -en f.; (carrying out) Ausübung, -en f.; (physical) Bewe'gung, -en f. **2.** vb. üben; aus·üben; bewe'gen.

exert, vb. aus·üben; (e. oneself) sich an·strengen.

exertion, n. Anstrengung, -en f.

exhale, vb. aus·atmen.

exhaust, 1. n. (auto.) Auspuff, -e m. **2.** vb. erschöp'fen.

exhaustion, n. Erschöp'fung, -en f.

exhaustive, adj. erschöp'fend.

exhibit, 1. n. Ausstellung, -en f. **2.** vb. aus·stellen; zeigen.

exhibition, n. Ausstellung, -en f.

exhibitionism, n. Exhibitionis'mus m.

exhilarate, vb. auf·heitern.

exhort, vb. ermah'nen.

exhortation, n. Ermah'nung, -en f.

exhume, vb. aus·graben*.

exigency, n. Dringlichkeit, -en f.

exile, 1. n. Verban'nung, -en f. **2.** vb. verban'nen.

exist, vb. beste'hen*, existie'ren.

exodus, n. Auszug, ⸗e m.; Auswanderung, -en f.

exonerate, vb. entlas'ten.

exorbitant, adj. übermäßig.

exotic, adj. exo'tisch.

expand, vb. aus·dehnen, aus·breiten, erwei'tern.

expanse, n. Ausdehnung, -en f., Weite, -n f.

expansion, n. Ausdehnung, -en f., Ausbreitung, -en f.; Expansion' f.

expansive, adj. umfas'send.

expatriate, n. Emigrant', -en, -en m.

expect, vb. erwar'ten.

expectancy, n. Erwar'tung, -en f.

expectation, n. Erwar'tung, -en f.

expectorate, vb. (aus·)spuken.

expediency, n. Zweckmäßigkeit, -en f.

expedient, adj. zweckmäßig.

expedite, vb. beschleu'nigen.

expedition, n. Expedition', -en f.

expel, vb. vertrei'ben*.

expend, vb. (money) aus·geben*; (energy) auf·wenden*.

expenditure, n. Ausgabe, -n f., Aufwand m.

expense, n. Ausgabe, -n f.; Kosten pl., Unkosten pl.; (on an e. account) auf Spesen.

expensive, adj. teuer, kostspielig.

experience, 1. n. Erfah'rung, -en f. **2.** vb. erfah'ren*.

experienced, adj. erfah'ren.

experiment, 1. n. Versuch' -e

m., Experiment', -e nt. 2. vb. experimentie'ren.

experimental, adj. Versuchs'- (cpds.).

experimentally, adv. versuchs'- weise.

expert, 1. n. Sachverständig- m., Exper'te, -n, -n m. 2. adj. erfah'ren.

expiate, vb. büßen.

expiration, n. (breath) Ausat- mung, -en f.; (end) Ablauf m.

expire, vb. (breathe out) aus-at- men; (die) verschei'den; (end) ab-laufen*.

explain, vb. erklä'ren.

explanation, n. Erklä'rung, -en f.

explanatory, adj. erklä'rend.

expletive, 1. n. Füllwort, "er nt.; Ausruf, -e m. 2. adj. aus- füllend.

explicit, adj. ausdrücklich.

explode, vb. explodie'ren.

exploit, vb. aus-beuten, aus- nutzen.

exploitation, n. Ausbeutung, - en f., Ausnutzung, -en f.

exploration, n. Erfor'schung, - en f.

exploratory, adj. untersu'- chend, erkun'dend.

explore, vb. erfor'schen, unter- su'chen.

explorer, n. Forscher, - m., Forschungsreisend- m.

explosion, n. Explosion', -en f.

explosive, 1. n. Sprengstoff, -e m. 2. adj. explosiv'.

exponent, n. Exponent', -en, - en m.

export, 1. n. Export', -e m., Ausfuhr f. 2. vb. exportie'- ren, aus-führen.

exportation, n. Ausfuhr f.

expose, vb. aus-setzen; (photo) belich'ten; (disclose) enthül'- len.

exposé, n. Darlegung, -en f.; (disclosure) Enthül'lung, -en f.

exposition, n. Darlegung, -en f.; (exhibit) Ausstellung, - en f.

expository, adj. erklä'rend.

exposure, n. Aussetzung, -en f.; (photo) Belich'tung, -en f.; Bloßstellung, -en f.

expound, vb. aus-legen, erklä'- ren.

express, 1. n. (train) Schnell- zug, -e m. 2. vb. aus-drücken. 3. adj. ausdrücklich.

expression, n. Ausdruck, "e m.

expressive, adj. ausdrucksvoll.

expropriate, vb. enteig'nen.

expulsion, n. Vertrei'bung, -en f., Entlas'sung, -en f.

expurgate, vb. reinigen.

exquisite, adj. vorzüg'lich.

extant, adj. vorhan'den.

extemporaneous, adj. aus dem Stegreif.

extend, vb. (intr.) sich er-

stre'cken, reichen; (tr.) aus- dehnen.

extension, n. Ausdehnung, -en f.; Verlän'gerung, -en f.

extensive, adj. umfangreich.

extent, n. Umfang, "e m.

exterior, adj. äußer-, äußer- lich.

exterminate, vb. aus-rotten, vernich'ten.

extermination, n. Ausrottung, -en f., Vernich'tung, -en f.

external, adj. ärußer-; auswär- tig.

extinct, adj. ausgestorben.

extinction, n. Aussterben nt.

extinguish, vb. aus-löschen.

extol, vb. loben, preisen*.

extort, vb. ab-zwingen*.

extortion, n. Erpres'sung, -en f.

extra, adj. extra, beson'der-.

extra-, (cpds.) außer-.

extract, 1. n. Auszug, "e m., Extrakt', -e m. 2. vb. heraus'- ziehen*, heraus'-holen.

extraction, n. Ausziehen nt.; (ethnic) Herkunft, "e f., Ab- stammung, -en f.

extradite, vb. aus-liefern.

extradition, n. Auslieferung, - en f.

extraneous, adj. fremd.

extraordinary, adj. außerge- wöhnlich.

extravagance, n. Verschwen'- dung, -en f., Extravaganz', - en f.

extravagant, adj. verschwen'- derisch; übertrie'ben.

extravaganza, n. phanta- s'tische, überspann'te Kom- position', -en f.

extreme, adj. äußerst-.

extremely, adv. äußerst, höchst.

extremity, n. Äußerst- nt.; (limbs) Gliedmaßen pl.

extricate, vb. heraus'-winden*.

exuberant, adj. überschweng- lich.

exult, vb. frohlo'cken.

exultant, adj. frohlo'ckend.

eye, n. Auge, -n nt.

eyeball, n. Augapfel, " m.

eyebrow, n. Augenbraue, -n f.

eyeglasses, n.pl. Brille, -n f.

eyelash, n. Augenwimper, -n f.

eyelet, n. Öse, -n f.

eyelid, n. Augenlid -er nt.

eyesight, n. Augensicht f.; Au- gen pl.

F

fable, n. Fabel, -n f.

fabric, n. Stoff, -e m.

fabricate, vb. her-stellen; (lie) erdich'ten.

fabrication, n. Herstellung, -en f.; (lie) Erdich'tung, -en f.

fabulous, adj. sagenhaft.

façade, n. Fassa'de, -n f.

face, 1. n. Gesicht', -er nt.; (surface) Oberflä'che, -n f. 2. vb. ins Gesicht' sehen*; (be opposite) gegenü'ber-liegen*.

facet, n. Facet'te, -n f.

facetious, adj. scherzhaft.

face value, n. Nennwert, -e m.

facial, 1. n. Gesichts'massage, - n f. 2. adj. Gesichts'- (cpds.).

facile, adj. gewandt'.

facilitate, vb. erleich'tern.

facility, n. (ease) Leichtigkeit f.; (skill) Geschick'lichkeit f.; (possibility) Möglichkeit, -en f.

facing, n. (clothing) Besatz' m.

facsimile, n. Faksi'mile, -s nt.

fact, n. Tatsache, -n f.

faction, n. Gruppe, -n f.

factor, n. Faktor, -o'ren m.

factory, n. Fabrik', -en f.

factual, adj. auf Tatsachen be- schränkt'; Tatsachen- (cpds.).

faculty, n. Fähigkeit, -en f., Gabe, -n f.; (college) Fakul- tät', -en f.

fad, n. Mode, -n f.

fade, vb. verblas'sen.

fail, vb. versa'gen; (school) durch-fallen*; (f. to do) nicht tun*.

failure, n. Versa'gen nt., Mißerfolg, -e m.; (bank- ruptcy) Bankrott', -e m.

faint, 1. adj. schwach. 2. vb. in Ohnmacht fallen*.

fair, 1. n. Messe, -n f., Jahr- markt, "e m. 2. adj. (weather) heiter; (blond) blond; (just) gerecht'.

fairness, n. Gerech'tigkeit, -en f.

fairy, n. Fee, Fe'en f.

fairy tale, n. Märchen, - nt.

faith, n. (trust) Vertrau'en nt.; (belief) Glaube(n), - m.

faithful, adj. treu.

faithfulness, n. Treue f.

faithless, adj. treulos.

fake, 1. adj. falsch. 2. vb. vor- täuschen.

faker, n. Schwindler, - m.

falcon, n. Falke, -n, -n m.

fall, 1. n. Fall, "e m., Sturz "e m.; (autumn) Herbst, -e m. 2. vb. fallen*.

fallacious, adj. trügerisch.

fallacy, n. Trugschluß, "sse m.

fallible, adj. fehlbar.

fallout, n. (radioaktiver) Nie- derschlag, "e m.

fallow, adj. brach.

false, adj. falsch.

falsehood, n. Lüge, -n f.

falseness, n. Falschheit, -en f.

falsetto, n. Falsett', -e nt.

falsification, n. Verfäl'schung, -en f.

falsify, vb. verfäl'schen.

falter, vb. straucheln, stocken.

fame, n. Ruhm m.

famed, adj. berühmt'.

familiar, adj. vertraut'.

familiarity, n. Vertraut'heit, -

en *f.;* Vertrau'lichkeit, -en *f.*

familiarize, *vb.* vertraut'machen.

family, *n.* Fami'lie, -n *f.*

famine, *n.* Hungersnot, ⁼e *f.*

famished, *adj.* ausgehungert.

famous, *adj.* berühmt'.

fan, 1. *n.* Fächer, - *m.;* Ventila'tor, -'o'ren *m.; (enthusiast)* Vereh'rer, - *m.,* Anhänger, - *m.* **2.** *vb.* fächern.

fanatic, 1. *n.* Fana'tiker, - *m.* **2.** *adj.* fana'tisch.

fanatical, *adj.* fana'tisch.

fanaticism, *n.* Fanatis'mus *m.*

fanciful, *adj.* phantas'tisch.

fancy, 1. *n. (imagination)* Einbildung, -en *f.; (mood)* Laune, -n *f.; (liking)* Vorliebe *f.* **2.** *adj.* apart', ausgefallen; Luxus- *(cpds.).* **3.** *vb.* sich ein·bilden.

fanfare, *n.* Fanfa're, -n *f.; (fig.)* Getu'e *nt.*

fang, *n.* Fang, ⁼e, phantas'tisch.

fantastic, *adj.* phantas'tisch.

fantasy, *n.* Phantasie', -i'en *f.*

far, *adj.* weit, fern.

faraway, *adj.* entfernt'; *(fig.)* träumerisch.

farce, *n.* Farce, -n *f.*

fare, 1. *n. (passenger)* Fahrgeld, -er *nt.; (price)* Fahrpreis, -e *m.; (food)* Kost *f.* **2.** *vb.* gehen*.

farewell, 1. *n.* Abschied, -e *m.;* Abschieds- *(cpds.).* **2.** *interj.* lebe wohl! leben Sie wohl!

far-fetched, *adj.* gesucht'.

farina, *n.* Griessmehl *nt.*

farm, 1. *n.* landwirtschaftlicher Betrieb', -e *m.,* Farm, -en *f.* **2.** *vb.* Landwirtschaft betrei'ben*, Landwirt sein*.

farmer, *n.* Landwirt, -e *m.,* Farmer, - *m.,* Bauer, (-n), -n *m.*

farmhouse, *n.* Farmhaus, ⁼er *nt.;* Bauernhaus, ⁼er *nt.*

farming, *n.* Landwirtschaft *f.;* Ackerbau *m.*

farmyard, *n.* Bauernhof, ⁼e *m.*

far-sighted, *adj.* weitsichtig.

farther, *adj.* weiter.

farthest, *adj.* weitest-.

fascinate, *vb.* faszinie'ren, bezau'bern.

fascination, *n.* Faszination *f.,* Zauber *m.*

fascism, *n.* Faschis'mus *m.*

fascist, 1. *n.* Faschist', -en, -en *m.* **2.** *adj.* faschis'tisch.

fashion, *n.* Mode, -n *f.; (manner)* Art, -en *f.*

fashionable, *adj.* modern', schick.

fast, 1. *n.* Fasten *nt.* **2.** *adj. (speedy)* schnell; **(be f.,** of a clock)* vor·gehen*; *(firm)* fest. **3.** *vb.* fasten.

fasten, *vb.* fest·machen.

fastener, fastening, *n.* Verschluß', ⁼sse *m.*

fastidious, *adj.* wählerisch; eigen.

fat, 1. *n.* Fett, -e *nt.* **2.** *adj.* fett, dick.

fatal, *adj.* tötlich; verhäng'nisvoll.

fatality, *n.* Verhäng'nis, -se *nt.;* Todesfall, ⁼e *m.*

fate, *n.* Schicksal, -e *nt.*

fateful, *adj.* schicksalsschwer; verhäng'nisvoll.

father, *n.* Vater, ⁼ *m.*

fatherhood, *n.* Vaterschaft, -en *f.*

father-in-law, *n.* Schwiegervater, ⁼ *m.*

fatherland, *n.* Vaterland *nt.*

fatherless, *adj.* vaterlos.

fatherly, *adj.* väterlich.

fathom, 1. *n.* Klafter, -n *f.* **2.** *vb.* loten; *(fig.)* ergrün'den.

fatigue, 1. *n.* Ermü'dung *f.* **2.** *vb.* ermü'den.

fatten, *vb.* mästen.

fatty, *adj.* fettig.

faucet, *n.* Wasserhahn, ⁼e *m.*

fault, *n.* Fehler, - *m.; (it's my f.)* es ist meine Schuld.

faultless, *adj.* fehlerlos, makellos.

faulty, *adj.* fehlerhaft.

favor, 1. *n.* Gunst, -en *f.; (do a f.)* einen Gefallen tun*. **2.** *vb.* begün'stigen, bevor'zugen; *(a sore limb)* schonen.

favorable, *adj.* günstig.

favorite, 1. *n.* Liebling, -e *m.; (sport)* Favorit', -en, -en *m.* **2.** *adj.* Lieblings- *(cpds.).*

favoritism, *n.* Begün'stigung *f.*

fawn, *n.* Rehkalb, -er *nt.*

faze, *vb.* in Verle'genheit bringen*.

fear, 1. *n.* Furcht *f.,* Angst, ⁼e *f.* **2.** *vb.* fürchten.

fearful, *adj. (afraid)* furchtsam; *(terrible)* furchtbar.

fearless, *adj.* furchtlos.

fearlessness, *n.* Furchtlosigkeit *f.*

feasible, *adj.* durchführbar.

feast, *n.* Fest, -e *nt.,* Festmahl, -e *nt.*

feat, *n.* Tat, -en *f.;* Kunststück, -e *nt.*

feather, *n.* Feder, -n *f.*

feature, *n. (quality)* Eigenschaft, -en *f.; (face)* Gesichtszug, ⁼e *m.; (distinguishing mark)* Kennzeichen, - *nt.*

February, *n.* Februar *m.*

feces, *n.pl.* Exkremen'te *pl.*

federal, *adj.* bundesstaatlich; Bundes- *(cpds.).*

federation, *n.* Staatenbund, -e *m.,* Föderation', -en *f.;* Bundesstaat, -en *m.*

fee, *n.* Gebühr', -en *f.*

feeble, *adj.* schwach (⁼).

feeble-minded, *adj.* schwachsinnig.

feebleness, *n.* Schwäche, -n *f.*

feed, 1. *n.* Futter, - *nt.* **2.** *vb.* füttern.

feedback, *n.* Feedback *m.,* Rückkopplung *f.*

feel, *vb.* fühlen.

feeling, *n.* Gefühl', -e *nt.*

feign, *vb.* vor·geben*, heucheln.

felicitate, *vb.* beglück'wünschen.

felicity, *n.* Glück *nt.*

fell, *vb.* fällen.

fellow, *n.* Kerl, -e *m.,* Bursche, -n, -n *m.; (member)* Mitglied, -er *nt.*

fellowship, *n.* Gemein'schaft, -en *f.*

felony, *n.* Gewalt'verbrechen, - *nt.*

felt, *n.* Filz, -e *m.*

female, 1. *n. (human)* Frau, -en *f.; (animal)* Weibchen, - *nt.* **2.** *adj.* weiblich.

feminine, *adj.* weiblich, feminin'.

femininity, *n.* Weiblichkeit *f.*

fence, 1. *n.* Zaun, ⁼e *m.* **2.** *vb.* ein·zäunen; *(sport)* fechten*.

fencing, *n.* Fechten *nt.*

fender, *n. (auto)* Kotflügel, - *m.*

ferment, *vb.* gären*.

fermentation, *n.* Gärung, -en *f.*

fern, *n.* Farnkraut, ⁼er *nt.*

ferocious, *adj.* wild.

ferocity, *n.* Wildheit *f.*

ferry, *n.* Fähre, -n *f.*

fertile, *adj.* fruchtbar.

fertility, *n.* Fruchtbarkeit *f.*

fertilization, *n.* Befruch'tung, -en *f.*

fertilize, *vb.* befruch'ten; düngen.

fertilizer, *n.* Dünger *m.,* Kunstdünger *m.*

fervent, *adj.* inbrünstig.

fervid, *adj.* brennend.

fervor, *n.* Inbrunst *f.,* Eifer *m.*

fester, *vb.* eitern.

festival, *n.* Fest, -e *nt.*

festive, *adj.* festlich.

festivity, *n.* Festlichkeit, -en *f.*

festoon, *n.* Girlan'de, -n *f.*

fetch, *vb.* holen.

fetching, *adj.* reizend.

fête, *n.* Fest, -e *nt.*

fetid, *adj.* stinkend.

fetish, *n.* Fetisch, -e *m.*

fetters, *n.pl.* Fesseln *pl.*

fetus, *n.* Foetus, -se *m.*

feud, *n.* Feindschaft, -en *f.; (historical)* Fehde, -n *f.*

feudal, *adj.* feudal'.

feudalism, *n.* Feudalis'mus *m.*

fever, *n.* Fieber, - *nt.*

feverish, *adj.* fieberhaft.

few, *adj.* wenig; **(a f.)** ein paar.

fiancé, *n.* Verlobt'- *m.*

fiancée, *n.* Verlobt'- *f.*

fiasco, *n.* Fias'ko, -s *nt.*

fib, *n.* Lüge, -n *f.*

fiber, *n.* Faser, -n *f.*

fickle, *adj.* wankelmütig.

fickleness, *n.* Wankelmütigkeit *f.*

fiction, *n.* Erdich'tung, -; *f.;*

(novel writing) Prosadichtung, -en *f.*

fictional, *adj.* erdich'tet.

fictitious, *adj.* fingiert'.

fiddle, 1. *n.* Geige, -n *f.* **2.** *vb.* geigen.

fidelity, *n.* Treue *f.*

fidget, *vb.* zappeln.

field, *n.* Feld, -er *nt.*

fiend, *n.* Teufel, - *m.*

fiendish, *adj.* teuflisch.

fierce, *adj.* wild.

fiery, *adj.* feurig.

fife, *n.* Querpfeife, -n *f.*

fifteen, *num.* fünfzehn.

fifteenth, 1. *adj.* fünfzehnt-. **2.** *n.* Fünfzehntel, - *nt.*

fifth, 1. *adj.* fünft-. **2.** *n.* Fünftel, - *nt.*

fiftieth, 1. *adj.* fünfzigst-. **2.** *n.* Fünfzigstel, - *nt.*

fifty, *num.* fünfzig.

fig, *n.* Feige, -n *f.*

fight, 1. *n.* Kampf, ⸚e *m.; (brawl)* Schlägerei', -en *f.; (quarrel)* Streit, -e *m.* **2.** *vb.* kämpfen; bekämp'fen.

fighter, *n.* Kämpfer, - *m.*

figment, *n.* Fiktion', -en *f.*

figurative, *adj.* bildlich; **(f. meaning)** übertra'gene Bedeu'tung, -en *f.*

figure, 1. *n.* Figur', -en *f.,* Gestalt', -en *f.; (number)* Zahl, -en *f.* **2.** *vb.* rechnen; berech'nen.

figurehead, *n.* Galionsfigur, -en *f.; (fig.)* Repräsentations'figur, -en *f.*

figure of speech, *n.* Redewendung, -en *f.*

figurine, *n.* Porzellan'figur, -en *f.*

filament, *n.* Faser, -n *f.,* Faden, ⸚ *m.*

file, 1. *n. (tool)* Feile, -n *f.; (row)* Reihe, -n *f.; (papers, etc.)* Akte, -n *f.; (cards)* Kartothek', -en *f.* **2.** *vb. (tool)* feilen; *(papers)* ein·ordnen.

filigree, *n.* Filigran', -e *nt.*

fill, *vb.* füllen.

fillet, *n.* Filet', -s *nt.*

filling, *n. (tooth)* Plombe, -n *f.*

filling station, *n.* Tankstelle, -n *f.*

film, 1. *n.* Film, -e *m.* **2.** *vb.* filmen.

filmy, *adj.* mit einem Häutchen bedeckt; duftig.

filter, 1. *n.* Filter, - *m.* **2.** *vb.* filtrie'ren.

filth, *n.* Dreck *m.*

filthy, *adj.* dreckig; *(fig.)* unanständig.

fin, *n.* Flosse, -n *f.*

final, *adj.* endgültig.

finale, *n.* Fina'le, -s *nt.*

finalist, *n.* Teilnehmer (-, *m.*) in der Schlußrunde.

finality, *n.* Endgültigkeit *f.*

finance, 1. *n.* Finanz', -en *f.; (study)* Finanz'wesen *nt.; (f.s.)* Finan'zen *pl.* **2.** *vb.* finanzie'ren.

financial, *adj.* finanziell'.

financier, *n.* Finanz'mann, ⸚er *m.*

find, *vb.* finden*.

findings, *n.pl.* Tatbestand, ⸚e *m.*

fine, 1. *n.* Geldstrafe, -n *f.* **2.** *adj.* fein. **3.** *vb.* zu einer Geldstrafe verur'teilen.

fine arts, *n.* Kunstwissenschaft *f.*

finery, *n.* Putz *m.*

finesse, *n.* Fines'se, -n *f.*

finger, *n.* Finger, - *m.*

fingernail, *n.* Fingernagel, *m.*

fingerprint, *n.* Fingerabdruck, ⸚e *m.*

finicky, *adj.* zimperlich.

finish, 1. *n.* Ende, -n *nt.;* Abschluß, ⸚sse *m.* **2.** *vb.* beenden, vollen'den.

finite, *adj.* endlich.

fir, *n.* Fichte, -n *f.*

fire, 1. *n.* Feuer, - *nt.* **2.** *vb. (shoot)* feuern; *(dismiss)* entlas'sen*.

fire alarm, *n.* Feueralarm *m.*

fire-alarm box, *n.* Feuermelder, - *m.*

firearm, *n.* Feuerwaffe, -n *f.*

fire engine, *n.* Feuerspritze, -n *f.*

fire escape, *n.* Feuerleiter, -n *f.*

fire extinguisher, *n.* Feuerlöscher, - *m.*

fireman, *n.* Feuerwehrmann, ⸚er *m.*

fireplace, *n.* Kamin', -e *m.*

fireproof, *adj.* feuerfest.

fireworks, *n.* Feuerwerk, -e *nt.*

firm, 1. *n.* Firma, -men *f.* **2.** *adj.* fest.

firmness, *n.* Festigkeit *f.*

first, 1. *adj.* erst. **2.** *adv.* zuerst'.

first aid, *n.* erste Hilfe *f.*

first-class, *adj.* erstklassig, erster Klasse.

fiscal, *adj.* fiska'lisch.

fish, 1. *n.* Fisch, -e *m.* **2.** *vb.* fischen, angeln.

fisherman, *n.* Fischer, - *m.,* Angler, - *m.*

fishing, *n.* Angeln *nt.*

fission, *n.* Spaltung, -en *f.; (nuclear f.)* Kernspaltung *f.*

fissure, *n.* Spalt, -e *m.*

fist, *n.* Faust, ⸚e *f.*

fit, 1. *(attack)* Anfall, ⸚e *m.* **2.** *adj.* in Form. **3.** *vb.* passen; *(adapt)* an·passen.

fitful, *adj.* unregelmäßig.

fitness, *n.* Tauglichkeit *f.;* Gesund'heit *f.*

fitting, 1. *n.* Anprobe, -n *f.* **2.** *adj.* passend.

five, *num.* fünf.

fix, 1. *n. (predicament)* Verle'genheit, -en *f.* **2.** *vb.* fest·setzen; *(prepare)* zubereiten; *(repair)* reparie'ren.

fixation, *n.* Fixie'rung, -en *f.*

fixed, *adj. (repaired)* heil; *(set)* fest.

fixture, *n.* Vorrichtung, -en *f.;* Zubehör *nt.*

flabby, *adj.* schlaff.

flag, *n.* Fahne, -n *f.,* Flagge, -n *f.*

flagpole, *n.* Fahnenstange, -n *f.*

flagrant, *adj.* schreiend.

flagship, *n.* Flaggschiff, -e *nt.*

flair, *n.* Flair *nt.*

flake, *n.* Flocke, -n *f.*

flamboyant, *adj.* flammend; *(fig.)* überla'den.

flame, 1. *n.* Flamme, -n *f.* **2.** *vb.* flammen.

flank, 1. *n.* Flanke, -n *f.* **2.** *vb.* flankie'ren.

flannel, *n.* Flanell', -e *m.*

flap, 1. *n.* Klappe, -n *f.; (wings)* Flügelschlag, ⸚e *m.* **2.** *vb.* flattern.

flare, 1. *n.* Leuchtsignal, -e *nt.* **2.** *vb.* flackern.

flash, 1. *n.* Lichtstrahl, -en *m.* **2.** *vb.* auf·flammen.

flashcube, *n.* Blitzwürfel, - *m.*

flashlight, *n.* Taschenlampe, -n *f.*

flashy, *adj.* auffällig; *(clothes, etc.)* laut.

flask, *n.* Flasche, -n *f.*

flat, 1. *n.* Mietswohnung, -en *f.* **2.** *adj.* flach, platt.

flatcar, *n.* offener Güterwagen, - *m.*

flatness, *n.* Flachheit, -en *f.*

flatten, *vb.* flach machen.

flatter, *vb.* schmeicheln.

flattering, *adj.* schmeichelhaft.

flattery, *n.* Schmeichelei', -en *f.*

flaunt, *vb.* zur Schau stellen.

flavor, 1. *n. (taste)* Geschmack', ⸚e *m.; (odor)* Geruch', ⸚e *m.* **2.** *vb.* würzen.

flavoring, *n.* Geschmack', -e *m.;* Essenz', -en *f.*

flavorless, *adj.* fade.

flaw, *n.* Fehler, - *m.,* Makel, - *m.*

flawless, *adj.* fehlerfrei, makellos.

flax, *n.* Flachs *m.*

flay, *vb.* schinden*.

flea, *n.* Floh, ⸚e *m.*

fleck, *n.* Fleck, -e *m.*

flee, *vb.* fliehen*, flüchten.

fleece, *n.* Vlies, -e *nt.*

fleecy, *adj.* wollig.

fleet, *n.* Flotte, -n *f.*

fleeting, *adj.* flüchtig.

Fleming, *n.* Flame, -n, -n *m.*

Flemish, *adj.* flämisch.

flesh, *n.* Fleisch *nt.*

fleshy, *adj.* fleischig.

flex, *vb.* biegen*; beugen.

flexibility, *n.* Biegsamkeit *f.*

flexible, *adj.* biegsam, flexi'bel.

flicker, *vb.* flackern.

flier, *n.* Flieger, - *m.*

flight, *n.* Flug, ⸚e *m.; (escape)* Flucht, -en *f.*

flight attendants, *n.pl.* Flugpersonal *nt.*

flimsy, *adj.* dünn; lose.

flinch, *vb.* zurück'·zucken.

fling, vb. schleudern.

flint, n. Feuerstein, -e m.

flip, vb. schnellen.

flippant, adj. vorlaut.

flirt, 1. n. Flirt, -s m. **2.** vb. flirten, kokettie'ren.

flirtation, n. Flirt, -s m.

float, 1. n. Floß, ̈e nt. **2.** vb. treiben; schwimmen*.

flock, n. Herde, - f., Schar, -en f.

flog, vb. peitschen.

flood, 1. n. Flut, -en f.; Überschwem'mung, -en f. **2.** vb. überschwem'men.

floodlight, n. Scheinwerfer, - m.

floor, n. Fußboden, ̈ m.; (story) Stockwerk, -e nt.

floorwalker, n. Abteilungsaufseher (, - m.) in einem Warenhaus.

flop, 1. n. (thud) Plumps m.; (failure) Reinfall, ̈e m. **2.** vb. plumpsen: rein-gallen*.

floral, adj. Blumen- (cpds.).

florid, adj. gerö'tet.

florist, n. Blumenhändler, - m.

flounce, 1. n. Volant', -s m. **2.** vb. tänzeln.

flounder, 1. n. Flunder, -n f. **2.** vb. taumeln.

flour, n. Mehl nt.

flourish, vb. (grow) gedei'hen*, blühen; (shake) schwenken.

flow, vb. fließen*.

flower, 1. n. Blume, -n f. **2.** vb. blühen.

flowerpot, n. Blumentopf, ̈e m.

flowery, adj. blumig.

fluctuate, vb. schwanken.

fluctuation, n. Schwankung, -en f.

flue, n. Rauchfang, ̈e m.

fluency, n. Geläu'figkeit f.

fluent, adj. fließend.

fluffy, adj. flaumig, wollig.

fluid, 1. n. Flüssigkeit, -en f. **2.** adj. flüssig.

fluidity, n. flüssiger Aggregat'zustand m.; Flüssigsein nt.

fluorescent, adj. fluoreszie'rend.

fluoroscope, n. Leuchtschirm, -e m., Fluroskop', -e nt.

flurry, n. Wirbel, - m.

flush, 1. n. Röte f.; (fig.) Flut f. **2.** vb. errö'ten; (wash out) aus-spülen; (toilet) aufzie-hen*.

flute, n. Flöte, -n f.

flutter, vb. flattern.

flux, n. Fluss m.; Strömen m.

fly, 1. n. Fliege, -n f. **2.** vb. fliegen*.

foam, 1. n. Schaum, ̈e m. **2.** vb. schäumen.

focal, adj. fokal'.

focus, 1. n. Brennpunkt, -e m. **2.** vb. (scharf, richtig) ein-stellen.

fodder, n. Futter nt.

foe, n. Feind, -e m.

fog, n. Nebel m.

foggy, adj. neblig.

foil, 1. n. Rapier', -e nt. **2.** vb. verei'teln.

foist, vb. unterschie'ben*.

fold, 1. n. Falte, -n f. **2.** vb. falten.

folder, n. (for papers) Mappe, -n f.; Hefter, - m.; (brochure) Broschü're, -n f., Prospekt', -e m.

foliage, n. Laub nt.

folio, n. Folio, -lien nt.

folk, n. Volk, ̈er nt.

folklore, n. Volkskunde f.

folks, n.npl. Leute pl.

follow, vb. folgen.

follower, n. Anhänger, - m.

folly, n. Torheit, -en f.

foment, vb. schüren.

fond, adj. (be f. of) gern haben*.

fondle, vb. liebkosen.

fondness, n. Vorliebe f.

food, n. Nahrung, - f., Essen nt.

foodstuffs, n. Nahrungsmittel pl.

fool, 1. n. Narr, -en, -en m. **2.** vb. täuschen, zum Narren halten*.

foolhardiness, n. Tollkühnheit, -en f.

foolhardy, adj. tollkühn.

foolish, adj. dumm, närrisch.

foolproof, adj. narrensicher.

foot, n. Fuss, ̈e m.

footage, n. Länge in Fuß gemessen.

football, n. Fußball, ̈e m.

foothills, n.npl. Vorgebirge nt.

foothold, n. Halt m.

footing, n. Stand m.; Boden m.

footlights, n.npl. Rampenlicht, -er nt.

footnote, n. Fußnote, -n f.

footprint, n. Fußstapfe, -n f.

footstep, n. Fußstapfe, -n f.

for, 1. prep. für. **2.** conj. denn.

forage, 1. n. Futter nt. **2.** vb. furagie'ren.

foray, n. Überfall, ̈e m.

forbearance, n. Enthal'tung f.; Nachsicht f.

forbid, vb. verbie'ten*.

forbidding, adj. abschreckend.

force, 1. n. Kraft, ̈e f., Gewalt', -en f. **2.** vb. zwingen*.

forceful, adj. kräftig, wirkungsvoll.

forcefulness, n. Überzeu'gungskraft f.

forceps, n. Zange, -n f.

forcible, adj. kräftig, heftig, mit Gewalt'.

ford, n. Furt, -en f.

fore, adv. vorn.

forearm, n. Unterarm, -e m.

forebears, n.pl. Vorfahren pl.

foreboding, n. Vorahnung, -en f.

forecast, 1. n. Voraus'sage, -n f. **2.** vb. voraus'sagen.

forecaster, n. Wetterprophet', -en, -en m.

foreclosure, n. Zwangsvollstreckung, -en f.

forefather, n. Vorfahr, -en, -en m.

forefinger, n. Zeigefinger, - m.

forefront, n. Vordergrund m.

foreground, n. Vordergrund m.

forehead, n. Stirn, -en f.

foreign, adj. fremd, ausländisch.

foreign aid, n. Entwick'lungshilfe f.

foreigner, n. Ausländer, - m.

foreman, n. Vorarbeiter, - m.

foremost, adj. vorderst-.

forenoon, n. Vormittag, -e m.

forerunner, n. Vorläufer, - m.

foresee, vb. vorher'sehen*.

foreshadow, vb. ahnen lassen*.

foresight, n. Voraus'sicht f.

forest, n. Wald, ̈er m.

forestall, vb. verhin'dern, vorweg'nehmen*.

forester, n. Förster, - m.

forestry, n. Forstwirtschaft f.

foretaste, n. Vorgeschmack, ̈e m.

foretell, vb. vorher'sagen, prophezei'en.

forever, adv. ewig.

forevermore, adv. für, auf immer und ewig.

forewarn, vb. vorher warnen.

foreword, n. Vorwort, -e nt.

forfeit, vb. verwir'ken, ein-büßen.

forfeiture, n. Verwir'kung f., Einbuße f.

forgather, vb. sich versam'meln.

forge, 1. n. Schmiede, -n f. **2.** vb. schmieden; (falsify) fälschen.

forger, n. Fälscher, - m.

forgery, n. Fälschung, -en f.

forget, vb. verges'sen*.

forgetful, adj. vergeß'lich.

forgive, vb. verge'ben*, verzei'hen*.

forgiveness, n. Verge'bung f.

forgo, vb. verzich'ten auf.

fork, n. Gabel, -n f.

forlorn, adj. verlas'sen.

form, 1. n. Form, -en f.; (blank) Formular', -e nt. **2.** vb. bilden, formen.

formal, adj. formell'; offiziell'.

formaldehyde, n. Formaldehyd', -e nt.

formality, n. Formalität', -en f.; Förmlichkeit, -en f.

format, n. Format', -e nt.

formation, n. Gestal'tung, -en f.; (mil.) Formation', -en f.

former, adj. ehemalig, früher; (the f.) jener, -es, -e.

formerly, adv. früher.

formidable, adj. beacht'lich.

formless, adj. formlos.

formula, n. Formel, -n f.

formulate, vb. formulie'ren.

formulation, n. Formulie'rung, -en f.

forsake, vb. verlas'sen*.

fort, n. Feste, -n f.

forte, n. Stärke, -n f.

forth, adv. fort; **(and so f.)** und so weiter.

forthcoming, adj. angekündigt.

forthright, adj. offen, ehrlich.

fortieth, 1. adj. vierzigst-. **2.** n. Vierzigstel, - nt.

fortification, n. Befes'tigungswerk, -e nt.

fortify, vb. stärken, befes'tigen.

fortissimo, adj. fortis'simo.

fortitude, n. seelische Stärke f., Mut m.

fortnight, n. vierzehn Tage pl.

fortress, n. Festung, -en f.

fortuitous, adj. zufällig.

fortunate, adj. glücklich.

fortune, n. Glück nt.; (money) Vermö'gen, - nt.

fortune-teller, n. Wahrsager, - m.

forty, adj. vierzig.

forum, n. Forum, -ra nt.

forward, adv. vorwärts.

forwardness, n. Dreistigkeit f.

fossil, n. Fossil', -ien nt.

foster, vb. (nourish) nähren; (raise) auf'ziehen*; Pflege- (cpds.).

foul, adj. schmutzig.

found, vb. gründen.

foundation, n. (building) Fundament', -e nt.; (fund) Stiftung, -en f.

founder, n. Gründer, - m.

foundling, n. Findling, -e m.

foundry, n. Gießerei', -en f.

fountain, n. Springbrunnen, - m.

fountainhead, n. Urquell, -e m.

fountain pen, n. Füllfederhalter, - m.

four, num. vier.

fourteen, num. vierzehn.

fourteenth, 1. adj. vierzehnt- **2.** n. Vierzehntel, - nt.

fourth, 1. adj. viert-. **2.** n. Viertel, - nt.

fowl, n. Geflü'gel nt.; Huhn, ⸗er nt.

fox, n. Fuchs, ⸗e m.

foxglove, n. Fingerhut, ⸗e m.

foxhole, n. Schüt'zenloch, ⸗er nt.

foxy, adj. schlau.

foyer, n. Foyer', -s f.

fracas, n. Keilerei', -en f.

fraction, n. (number) Bruchstück, -e nt.; (part) Bruchteil, -e m.; (f.s.) Bruchrechnung f.

fracture, n. Bruch, ⸗e m. **2.** vb. brechen*.

fragile, adj. zerbrech'lich.

fragment, n. Bruchstück, -e nt.

fragmentary, adj. fragmenta'risch.

fragrance, n. Duft, ⸗e m.

fragrant, adj. wohlriechend.

frail, adj. zerbrech'lich, schwach (⸗).

frailty, n. Schwachheit, -en f.

frame, 1. n. Rahmen, - m. **2.** vb. (shape) formen; (enclose) ein'rahmen.

framework, n. Rahmen, - m.

France, n. Frankreich nt.

franchise, n. Wahlrecht, -e nt.

frank, adj. frei, offen.

frankfurter, n. Frankfurter Würstchen, - nt.

frankly, adv. ehrlich gesagt'.

frankness, n. Offenheit f.

frantic, adj. wahnsinnig.

fraternal, adj. brüderlich.

fraternity, n. Brüderlichkeit f.; (students) Studen'tenverbindung, -en f.

fraternize, vb. fraternisie'ren.

fraud, n. Betrug' m.

fraudulent, adj. betrügerisch.

fraught, adj. voll.

fray, n. Tumult', -e m.; Schlägerei', -en f.

freak, 1. n. Mißgeburt, -en f.; Kurio'sum, -sa nt. **2.** adj. monströs', bizarr'.

freckle, n. Sommersprosse, -n f.

freckled, adj. sommersprossig.

free, 1. adj. frei; kostenlos. **2.** vb. befrei'en; frei'lassen*.

freedom, n. Freiheit, -en f.

freeze, vb. (be cold) frieren*; (turn to ice) (intr.) gefrie'ren*, (tr.) gefrie'ren lassen*; (food) tief kühlen; (wages) stoppen (Löhne).

freezer, n. Tiefkühler, - m.; (in refrigerator) Gefrier'fach, ⸗er nt.

freezing, adj. eisig.

freight, n. Fracht, -en f.; Frachtgut nt.

freightage, n. Frachtspesen pl.

freighter, n. Frachter, - m.

French, adj. franzö'sisch.

Frenchman, n. Franzo'se, -n, - n m.

Frenchwoman, n. Franzö'sin, -nen f.

frenzied, adj. rasend.

frenzy, n. Raserie', -en f.

frequency, n. Häufigkeit, -en f.; (physics) Frequenz', -en f.

frequent, adj. häufig.

fresh, adj. frisch; (impudent) frech.

freshen, vb. erfri'schen.

freshman, n. Student' im ersten College-Jahr.

freshness, n. Frische f.

fresh water, n. Süßwasser nt.

fret, n. nervös' sein*, nervös' werden*.

fretful, adj. nervös', unruhig.

fretfulness, n. Reizbarkeit, f.

friar, n. Bettelmönch, -e m.

fricassee, n. Frikassee', -s nt.

friction, n. Reibung, -en f.

Friday, n. Freitag, -e m.

friend, n. Freund, -e m.; Freundin, -nen f.

friendless, adj. freundlos.

friendliness, n. Freundlichkeit, -en f.

friendly, adj. freundlich.

friendship, n. Freundschaft, -en f.

frigate, n. Fregat'te, -n f.

fright, n. Angst, ⸗e f., Schreck m.

frighten, vb. ängstigen, erschre'cken; **(be f.ed)** erschre'cken*.

frightful, adj. schrecklich.

frigid, adj. kalt (⸗); (sexual) frigid'.

frill, n. Krause, -n f.

fringe, n. Franse, -n f.; Rand, ⸗er m.

frisky, adj. lebhaft.

fritter, n. eine Art Pfannkuchen.

frivolity, n. Frivolität', -en f.

frivolous, adj. leichtsinnig, frivol'.

frivolousness, n. Leichtsinnigkeit, -en f.

frock, n. Kleid, -er nt.; (monk) Kutte, -n f.

frog, n. Frosch, ⸗e m.

frolic, vb. ausgelassen sein*.

from, prep. von, aus.

front, n. Vorderseite, -n f.; (mil.) Front, -en f.; **(in f.)** vorn; **(in f. of)** vor.

frontage, n. Vorderfront, -en f.

frontal, adj. frontal'.

frontier, n. Grenze, -n f.

frost, n. Frost, ⸗e m.

frostbite, n. Frostbeule, -n f.

frosting, n. Kuchenglasur, -en f.

frosty, adj. frostig.

froth, n. Schaum, ⸗e m.

frown, vb. die Stirn runzeln.

frugal, adv. sparsam, frugal'.

frugality, n. Sparsamkeit f.

fruit, n. Frucht, ⸗e f., Obst nt.

fruitful, adj. fruchtbar.

fruition, n. Reife f.

fruitless, adj. unfruchtbar; (fig.) vergeb'lich.

frustrate, vb. verdrän'gen; (nullify) verei'teln.

frustration, n. Verdrän'gung, -en f.; Verei'telung, -en f.

fry, vb. braten*.

fryer, n. junges Brathuhn, ⸗er nt.

frying pan, n. Bratpfanne, -n f.

fuchsia, n. Fuchsie, -n f.

fuel, n. Brennstoff, -e m.

fugitive, n. Flüchtling, -e m.

fugue, n. Fuge, -n f.

fulcrum, n. Drehpunkt, -e m.

fulfill, vb. erfül'len.

fulfillment, n. Erfül'lung, -en f.

full, adj. voll.

full dress, n. Frack, ⸗e m.; Gala-Uniform, -en f.

fullness, n. Fülle f.

fully, adv. völlig.

fumble, vb. umher'-tappen.

fume, 1. n. Dampf, ⸗e m., Dunst, ⸗e m. **2.** vb. dampfen, dunsten; (fig.) wüten.

fumigate, vb. aus'räuchern.

fumigator, n. Räucherapparat, -e m.

fun, n. Vergnü'gen nt., Spaß m., Jux m.

function, 1. n. Funktion', -en f. 2. vb. funktionie'ren.

functional, adj. sachlich.

fund, n. Fond, -s m.

fundamental, adj. grundlegend.

funeral, n. Begräb'nis, -se nt., Beer'digung, -en f.

funereal, adj. düster.

fungicide, n. Pilzvernichtungsmittel, - nt.

fungus, n. Fungus, - m.

funnel, n. Trichter, - m.; (smoke-stack) Schornstein, -e m.

funny, adj. komisch, drollig.

fur, n. Pelz, -e m.

furious, adj. wütend.

furlough, n. Urlaub, -e m.

furnace, n. Ofen, = m.

furnish, vb. möblie'ren.

furnishings, n.pl. Ausstattung, -en f.

furniture, n. Möbel pl.

furor, n. Aufsehen nt.

furrier, n. Pelzhändler, - m.

furrow, n. Furche, -n f.

furry, adj. pelzartig.

further, 1. vb. fördern. 2. adj. weiter, ferner.

furtherance, n. Förderung, -en f.

furthermore, adv. ausserdem, überdies'.

fury, n. Wut f.; Zorn m.; (mythology) Furie, -n f.

fuse, 1. n. (elec.) Sicherung, -en f.; (explosives) Zünder, - m. 2. vb. verschmel'zen*.

fuselage, n. Rumpf, =e m.

fusillade, n. Gewehr'feurer nt.

fusion, n. Verschmel'zung, -en f.; Fusion', -en f.

fuss, n. Aufheben nt, Umstand, =e m.

fussy, adj. umständlich, genau', betu'lich.

futile, adj. vergeb'lich, nutzlos.

futility, n. Nutzlosigkeit f.

future, 1. n. Zukunft f. 2. adj. zukünftig.

futurity, n. Zukunft f.

futurology, n. Futurologie' f.

fuzz, n. Flaum m.

fuzzy, adj. flaumig.

G

gab, vb. schwatzen.

gabardine, n. Gabardine m.

gable, n. Giebel, - m.

gadget, n. Vorrichtung, -en f.

gag, 1. n. Knebel, - m.; (joke) Witz, -e m. 2. vb. knebeln.

gaiety, n. Ausgelassenheit f.

gain, 1. n. Gewinn', -e m. 2. vb. gewin'nen*.

gainful, adj. einträglich.

gait, n. Gang, =e m.

gala, adj. festlich.

galaxy, n. Milchstrasse, -n f.

gale, n. Sturm, =e m.

gall, 1. n. (bile) Galle, -n f.; (insolence) Unverschämtheit, -en f. 2. vb. ärgern.

gallant, adj. aufmerksam, galant'.

gallantry, n. Höflichkeit, -en f., Galanterie', -i'en f.

gall bladder, n. Gallenblase, -n f.

gallery, n. Galerie', -i'en f.

galley, n. (ship) Galee're, -n f.; (kitchen) Kombü'se, -n f.; (typogr.) Setzschiff, -e nt.

Gallic, adj. gallisch.

gallivant, vb. bummeln.

gallon, n. Gallo'ne, -n f.

gallop, 1. n. Galopp', -s m. 2. vb. galoppie'ren.

gallows, n.pl. Galgen, - m.

gallstone, n. Gallenstein, -e m.

galore, adv. in Hülle und Fülle.

galosh, n. Überschuh, -e m.

gamble, 1. n. (game) Glücksspiel, -e nt.; (risk) Risiko, -s nt. 2. vb. um Geld spielen; riskie'ren.

gambler, n. Glücksspieler,- m.

gambling, n. Glücksspiel, -e nt.

game, 1. n. Spiel, -e nt.; (hunting) Wild m., Wildbret nt. 2. adj. beherzt'; (lame) lahm.

gander, n. Gänserich, -e m.

gang, n. Bande, -n f.

gangplank, n. Laufplanke, -n f.

gangrene, n. Gangrän', -e nt.

gangrenous, adj. gangränös', brandig.

gangster, n. Gangster, - m.

gangway, n. Laufplanke, -n f.

gap, n. Lücke, -n f.; Spalte, -n f.

gape, vb. gaffen.

garage, n. Gara'ge, -n f.

garb, n. Gewand', =er m.

garbage, n. Abfall, =e m., Müll m.

garble, vb. entstel'len, verzer'ren.

garden, n. Garten, = m.

gardener, n. Gärtner, - m.

gardenia, n. Garde'nia, -ien f.

gargle, vb. gurgeln.

gargoyle, n. Wasserspeier, - m.

garish, adj. grell.

garland, n. Girlan'de, -n f.

garlic, n. Knoblauch m.

garment, n. Kleidungsstück, -e nt.

garner, vb. auf·speichern.

garnet, n. Granat', -e m.

garnish, vb. garnie'ren.

garret, n. Dachstube, -n f.

garrison, n. Garnison', -en f.

garrulous, adj. schwatzhaft.

garter, n. Strumpfband, =er nt.; Hosenband, =er nt.; Sockenhalter, - m.

gas, n. Gas, -e nt.; (gasoline) Benzin' nt.

gaseous, adj. gasförmig.

gash, 1. n. klaffende Wunde, -

n f. 2. vb. eine tiefe Wunde schlagen*.

gasket, n. Dichtung f.

gas mask, n. Gasmaske, -n f.

gasohol, n. Benzin-Alkohol-Gemisch' nt.

gasoline, n. Benzin' nt.

gasp, vb. keuchen; nach Luft schnappen.

gastric, adj. gastrisch.

gastritis, n. Magenschleimhautentzündung, -en f.

gastronomical, adj. gastrono'misch.

gate, n. Tor, -e nt., Pforte, -n f.

gateway, n. Einfahrt, -en f., Tor, -e nt.

gather, vb. sammeln, pflücken; (infer) schließen*.

gathering, n. Versamm'lung, -en f.

gaudiness, n. auffälliger Protz m.

gaudy, adj. protzig.

gauge, 1. n. (measurement) Maß, -e nt.; (instrument) Messer, - m.; Zeiger, - m.; (railway) Spurweite, -n f. 2. vb. ab·messen*.

gaunt, adj. hager.

gauntlet, n. Handschuh, -e m.

gauze, n. Gaze, -n f.

gavel, n. Hammer, = m.

gawky, adj. linkisch.

gay, adj. fröhlich, heiter; (homosexual) homosexuell, schwul.

gaze, vb. starren.

gazelle, n. Gazel'le, -n f.

gazette, n. Zeitung, -en f.

gazetteer, n. geogra'phisches Namensverzeichnis, -se nt.

gear, n. Zahnrad, =er nt.; (auto) Gang, =e m.; (equipment) Zeug nt.

gearing, n. Getrie'be, - nt.

gearshift, n. Schalthebel, - m.

gelatin, n. Gelati'ne, -n f.

gelatinous, adj. gallertartig.

geld, vb. kastrie'ren.

gelding, n. Wallach, -e m.

gem, n. Edelstein, -e m.

gender, n. Geschlecht', -er nt., Genus, -nera nt.

gene, n. Gen, -e nt.

genealogical, adj. genealo'gisch.

genealogy, n. Genealogie', -i'en f.

general, 1. n. General', =e m. 2. adj. allgemein.

generality, n. Allgemein'heit, -en f.

generalization, n. Verallgemei'nerung, -en f.

generalize, vb. verallgemei'nern.

generally, adv. (in general) im allgemei'nen; (usually) gewöhn'lich, meistens.

generate, vb. erzeu'gen.

generation, n. Generation', -en f.

generator, n. Genera'tor, -o'ren m.

generic, *adj.* Gattungs- *(cpds.).*

generosity, *n.* Großzügigkeit *f.*

generous, *adj.* großzügig, freigebig.

genetic, *adj.* gene'tisch.

genetics, *n.* Verer'bungslehre *f.*

Geneva, *n.* Genf *nt.*

genial, *adj.* freundlich, froh.

geniality, *n.* Freundlichkeit *f.*

genital, *adj.* genital'.

genitals, *n.* Geschlechts'organe *pl.*

genitive, *n.* Genitiv, -e *m.*

genius, *n.* Genie', -s *nt.*

genocide, *n.* Völkermord *m.*

genre, *n.* Genre, -s *nt.*

genteel, *adj.* vornehm.

gentile, 1. *n.* Nichtjude, -n, -n *m.* 2. *adj.* nichtjüdisch.

gentility, *n.* Vornehmheit *f.*

gentle, *adj.* sanft, mild.

gentleman, *n.* Gentleman, -men *m.*

gentleness, *n.* Sanftheit *f.*

gentry, *n.* niederer Adel *m.*

genuflect, *vb.* das Knie beugen.

genuine, *adj.* echt.

genuineness, *n.* Echtheit *f.*

genus, *n.* Geschlecht', -er *nt.*, Gattung, -en *f.*

geographer, *n.* Geograph', -en, -en *m.*

geographical, *adj.* geogra'phisch.

geography, *n.* Geographie' *f.*, Erdkunde *f.*

geometric, *adj.* geome'trisch.

geometry, *n.* Geometrie' *f.*

geopolitics, *n.* Geopolitik' *f.*

geranium, *n.* Gera'nie, -n *f.*

germ, *n.* Keim, -e *m.*; Bakte'rie, -n *f.*

German, 1. *n.* Deutsch- *m.&f.* 2. *adj.* deutsch.

germane, *adj.* zur Sache gehö'rig.

Germanic, *adj.* germa'nisch.

German measles, *n.* Röteln *pl.*

Germany, *n.* Deutschland *nt.*; (West G.) Bundesrepublik' *f.* Westdeutschland *nt.*; (East G.) Deutsche Demokratische Republik *f.*; Ostdeutschland *nt.*

germicide, *n.* keimtötendes Mittel, - *nt.*

germinal, *adj.* Keim- *(cpds.).*

germinate, *vb.* keimen.

gestate, *vb.* aus'tragen*.

gestation, *n.* Gestation', -en *f.*

gesticulate, *vb.* gestikulie'ren.

gesticulation, *n.* Gebär'de, -n *f.*

gesture, *n.* Gebär'de, -n *f.*, Geste, -n *f.*

get, *vb.* (receive) bekom'men*, kriegen; (fetch) holen; (become) werden*; (arrive) ankommen*; (g. to) hin'kommen*; (g. up) auf'stehen*; (g. in) ein'steigen*; (g. out) aus'steigen*.

geyser, *n.* Geiser, - *m.*

ghastly, *adj.* grauenhaft.

ghost, *n.* Geist, -er *m.*, Gespenst', -er *nt.*

giant, 1. *n.* Riese, -n, -n *m.* 2. *adj.* riesenhaft.

gibberish, *n.* Kauderwelsch *nt.*

gibbon, *n.* Gibbon, -s *m.*

giblets, *n.* Geflü'gelklein *nt.*

giddy, *adj.* schwindlig.

gift, *n.* Gabe, -n *f.*, Geschenk', -e *nt.*

gifted, *adj.* begabt'.

gigantic, *adj.* riesenhaft.

giggle, *vb.* kichern.

gigolo, *n.* Eintänzer, - *m.*

gild, *vb.* vergol'den.

gill, *n.* Kieme, -n *f.*

gilt, *n.* Vergol'dung, -en *f.*

gimlet, *n.* Handbohrer, - *m.*

gin, *n.* Gin, -s *m.*; *(cotton)* Entker'nungsmaschine, -n *f.*

ginger, *n.* Ingwer *m.*

gingerly, *adv.* sachte.

gingham, *n.* Kattun', -e *m.*

giraffe, *n.* Giraf'fe, -n *f.*

gird, *vb.* gürten.

girder, *n.* Träger, - *m.*

girdle, *n.* Gürtel, - *m.*; Strumpfbandgürtel, - *m.*

girl, *n.* Mädchen, - *nt.*

girlish, *adj.* mädchenhaft.

girth, *n.* Umfang, -̈e *m.*

gist, *n.* Kern, -e *m.*

give, *vb.* geben*.

given name, *n.* Vorname(n), - *m.*

gizzard, *n.* Geflü'gelmagen, -̈ *m.*

glacé, *adj.* glaciert'.

glacial, *adj.* Eis- *(cpds.).*

glad, *adj.* froh.

gladden, *vb.* erfreu'en.

gladiolus, *n.* Schwertlilie, -n *f.*

gladly, *adv.* gern.

gladness, *n.* Freude, -n *f.*

glamor, *n.* äußerer Glanz *m.*; beste'chende Schönheit *f.*

glamorous, *adj.* äußerlich beste'chend, blendend.

glance, 1. *n.* Blick, -e *m.* 2. *vb.* blicken.

gland, *n.* Drüse, -n *f.*

glandular, *adj.* Drüsen- *(cpds.).*

glare, 1. *n.* blendendes Licht *nt.* 2. *vb.* blenden: *(look)* starren; (g. at) an'starren.

glaring, *adj.* grell.

glass, *n.* Glas, -̈er *nt.*

glasses, *n.pl.* Brille, -n *f.*

glassware, *n.* Glasware, -n *f.*

glassy, *adj.* glasig.

glaucoma, *n.* Glaukom', -e *nt.*

glaze, 1. *n.* Glasur', -en *f.* 2. *vb.* glasie'ren.

glazier, *n.* Glaser, - *m.*

gleam, 1. *n.* Lichtstrahl, -en *m.* 2. *vb.* strahlen, glänzen.

glee, *n.* Freude, -n *f.*

gleeful, *adj.* fröhlich.

glen, *n.* enges Tal, -̈er *nt.*

glib, *adj.* zungenfertig.

glide, 1. *n.* Gleitflug, -̈e *m.* 2. *vb.* gleiten*.

glider, *n.* Segelflugzeug, -e *nt.*

glimmer, 1. *n.* Schimmer, - *m.* 2. *vb.* schimmern.

glimpse, *n.* flüchtiger Blick, -e *m.*

glint, *n.* Lichtschimmer, - *m.*

glisten, *vb.* glänzen.

glitter, 1. *n.* Glanz *m.* 2. *vb.* glitzern.

gloat, *vb.* sich weiden; schadenfroh sein*.

global, *adj.* global'.

globe, *n.* Erdkugel, -n *f.*; Globus, -se *m.*

globular, *adj.* kugelförmig.

globule, *n.* Kügelchen, - *nt.*

gloom, *n.* Düsterheit *f.*; *(fig.)* Trübsinn *m.*

gloomy, *adj.* düster; trübsinnig.

glorification, *n.* Verherr'lichung *f.*

glorify, *vb.* verherr'lichen.

glorious, *adj.* ruhmvoll, glorreich.

glory, *n.* Ruhm *m.*; Herrlichkeit *f.*

gloss, *n.* Glanz *m.*

glossary, *n.* Glossar', -e *nt.*

glossy, *adj.* glänzend.

glove, *n.* Handschuh, - *m.*

glow, 1. *n.* Glühen *nt.* 2. *vb.* glühen.

glucose, *n.* Traubenzucker *m.*

glue, 1. *n.* Leim *m.* 2. *vb.* leimen.

glum, *adj.* mürrisch.

glumness, *n.* Mürrischkeit *f.*

glut, 1. *n.* Überfluß *m.* 2. *vb.* übersät'tigen.

glutinous, *adj.* leimig.

glutton, *n.* Vielfraß, -e *m.*

gluttonous, *adj.* gefrä'ßig.

glycerine, *n.* Glyzerin' *nt.*

gnarled, *adj.* knorrig.

gnash, *vb.* knirschen.

gnat, *n.* Schnake, -n *f.*

gnaw, *vb.* knabbern.

go, *vb.* gehen*; *(become)* werden*; (g. without) entbeh'ren.

goad, 1. *n.* Treibstock, -̈e *m.* 2. *vb.* an'stacheln.

goal, *n.* Ziel, -e *nt.*; *(soccer)* Tor, -e *nt.*

goal-keeper, *n.* Torwart, -er *m.*

goat, *n.* Ziege, -n *f.*; Geiß, -en *f.*; (billy g.) Ziegenbock, -̈e *m.*

goatee, *n.* Spitzbart, -̈e *m.*

goatskin, *n.* Ziegenleder *nt.*

gobble, *vb.* verschlin'gen*.

go-between, *n.* Vermitt'ler, - *m.*

goblet, *n.* Kelchglas, -̈er *nt.*

goblin, *n.* Kobold, - *m.*

god, *n.* Gott, -̈er *m.*

godchild, *n.* Patenkind, -er *nt.*

goddess, *n.* Göttin, -nen *f.*

godfather, *n.* Patenonkel, *m.*

godless, *adj.* gottlos.

godlike, *adj.* gottähnlich.

godly, *adj.* göttlich.

godmother, *n.* Patentante, -n *f.*

godsend, *n.* Gottesgabe, -n *f.*

Godspeed, *n.* Lebewohl' *nt.*

go-getter, *n.* Draufgänger, - *m.*

goiter, *n.* Kropf, -̈e *m.*

gold, n. Gold nt.
golden, adj. golden.
goldfinch, n. Stieglitz, -e m.
goldfish, n. Goldfisch, -e m.
goldsmith, n. Goldschmied, -e m.
golf, n. Golf nt.
gondola, n. Gondel, -n f.
gondolier, n. Gondelführer, - m.
gone, adv. weg.
gong, n. Gong, -s m.
gonorrhea, n. Tripper m.
good, adj. gut (besser, best-).
good-by, interj. auf Wiedersehen.
Good Friday, n. Karfrei'tag m.
good-hearted, adj. gutherzig.
good-humored, adj. gutmütig.
good-looking, adj. gutaussehend.
good-natured, adj. gutmütig.
goodness, n. Güte f.
goods, n.pl. Waren pl.
good will, n. Wohlwollen nt.
goose, n. Gans, ⁻e f.
gooseberry, n. Stachelbeere, -n f.
gooseneck, n. Gänsehals, ⁻e m.
goose step, n. Stechschritt m.
gore, 1. n. Blut nt. **2.** vb. aufspießen.
gorge, n. (anatomical) Gurgel, -n f.; (ravine) Schlucht, -en f.
gorgeous, adj. prachtvoll.
gorilla, n. Goril'la, -s m.
gory, adj. blutig.
gospel, n. Evange'lium, -ien nt.
gossamer, 1. n. hauchdünner Stoff m. **2.** adj. hauchdünn.
gossip, 1. n. Klatsch m. **2.** vb. klatschen.
Gothic, 1. n. Gotik f. **2.** adj. gotisch.
gouge, 1. n. Hohleisen, - nt. **2.** vb. aus⁻höhlen.
gourd, n. Kürbis, -se m.
gourmand, n. Vielfraß, -e m.
gourmet, n. Feinschmecker, - m.
govern, vb. regie'ren.
governess, n. Erzie'herin, -nen f.
government, n. Regie'rung, -en f.
governmental, adj. Regie'rungs- (cpds.)
governor, n. Gouverneur', -e m.
governorship, n. Gouverneurs'amt, ⁻er nt.
gown, n. Kleid, -er nt.
grab, vb. greifen*.
grace, n. Anmut f.; (mercy) Gnade f.
graceful, adj. anmutig.
graceless, adj. unbeholfen.
gracious, adj. gnädig, gütig.
grade, 1. n. Grad, -e m., Rang, ⁻e m.; (mark) Zensur', -en f.; (class) Klasse, -n f.; (rise) Steigung, -en f. **2.** vb. bewer'ten; (smooth) ebnen.

grade crossing, n. Bahnübergang, -e m.
gradual, adj. allmäh'lich.
graduate, vb. graduie'ren.
graft, 1. n. Beste'chung, -en f., Korruption' f. **2.** vb. (bot.) propfen.
grail, n. Gral m.
grain, n. Körnchen, - nt; (wheat, etc.) Getrei'de nt.; (wood) Maserung, -en f.
gram, n. Gramm, - nt.
grammar, n. Gramma'tik, -en f.
grammar school, n. Grundschule, -n f.
grammatical, adj. gramma'tisch.
gramophone, n. Grammophon', -e nt.
granary, n. Kornspeicher, - m.
grand, adj. großartig.
grandchild, n. Enkelkind, -er nt.
granddaughter, n. Enkelin, -nen f.
grandeur, n. Erha'benheit f.
grandfather, n. Großvater, ⁻ m.
grandiloquent, adj. schwülstig.
grandiose, adj. grandios'.
grandmother, n. Großmutter, ⁻ f.
grandparents, n.pl. Großeltern pl.
grandson, n. Enkel, - m.
grandstand, n. Tribü'ne, -n f.
granite, n. Granit' m.
grant, 1. n. finanziel'le Beihilfe, -n f.; Stipen'dium, -en nt. **2.** vb. gewäh'ren.
granular, adj. körnig.
granulated sugar, n. Streuzucker m.
granulation, n. Körnung f.
granule, n. Körnchen, - nt.
grape, n. Weintraube, -n f.
grapefruit, n. Pampelmu'se, -n f.
grapevine, n. Weinstock, ⁻e m.; (rumor) Amtstratsch m.
graph, n. graphische Darstellung, -en f., Diagramm', -e nt.
graphic, adj. graphisch.
graphite, n. Graphit', -e m.
graphology, n. Graphologie' f.
grapple, 1. n. Enterhaken, - m. **2.** vb. packen; ringen*.
grasp, 1. n. Griff, -e m.; (mental) Fassungsvermögen nt. **2.** vb. ergrei'fen*.
grasping, adj. habgierig.
grass, n. Gras, ⁻er nt.; (lawn) Rasen, - m; (marijuana) Hasch m.
grasshopper, n. Heuschrecke, -n f.
grassy, adj. grasartig.
grate, 1. n. Rost m. **2.** vb. (cheese, etc.) reiben*, (irritate) irritie'ren.
grateful, adj. dankbar.
grater, n. Reibe, -n f.
gratify, vb. befrie'digen.

grating, n. Gitter, - nt.
gratis, adj. gratis.
gratitude, n. Dankbarkeit, -en f.
gratuitous, adj. unentgeltlich.
gratuity, n. Geschenk', -e nt.; (tip) Trinkgeld, -er nt.
grave, 1. n. Grab, ⁻er nt. **2.** adj. schwerwiegend.
gravel, n. Kies m.
graveyard, n. Friedhof, ⁻e m.
gravitate, vb. angezogen werden*; gravitie'ren.
gravity, n. Schwerkraft f.; Ernst m.
gravure, n. Gravü're, -n f.
gravy, n. Soße, -n f.
gray, adj. grau.
graze, vb. grasen, weiden.
grease, 1. n. Fett, -e nt. **2.** vb. fetten; schmieren.
greasy, adj. fettig, schmierig.
great, adj. groß (größer, größt-).
greatness, n. Größe, -n f.
Greece, n. Griechenland nt.
greed, n. Gier f., Habsucht f.
greediness, n. Gier f., Habsucht f.
greedy, adj. gierig, habsüchtig.
Greek, 1. n. Grieche, -n, -n m. **2.** adj. griechisch.
green, adj. grün.
greenery, n. Grün nt.
greenhouse, n. Gewächs'haus, ⁻er nt., Treibhaus, ⁻er nt.
greet, vb. begrü'ßen.
greeting, n. Gruß, ⁻e m.
gregarious, adj. gesel'lig.
grenade, n. Grana'te, -n f.
grenadine, n. Granat'apfellikör m.
greyhound, n. Windhund, -e m.
grid, n. Gitter, - nt.; (elec.) Stromnetz, -e nt.
griddle, n. Bratpfanne, -n f.
grief, n. Kummer m.
grievance, n. Beschwer'de, -n f.
grieve, vb. (intr.) trauern; (tr.) betrü'ben.
grievous, adj. schmerzlich; (serious) schwerwiegend.
grill, n. Grill, -s m.
grim, adj. grimmig.
grimace, n. Grimas'se, -n f., Fratze, -n f.
grime, n. Ruß m.
grimy, adj. schmutzig.
grin, 1. n. Grinsen nt. **2.** vb. grinsen.
grind, vb. mahlen*.
grindstone, n. Schleifstein, -e m.
grip, 1. n. Griff, -e m.; (suitcase) Koffer, - m. **2.** vb. fassen.
gripe, 1. n. (complaint) Ärgernis, -se nt. **2.** vb. (complain) nörgeln.
grippe, n. Grippe, -n f.
gristle, n. Knorpel, - m.
grit, 1. n. Kies m.; (courage) Mut m. **2.** vb. (g. one's teeth)

die Zähne zusam'men·beis-
sen*.
grizzled, adj. grau.
groan, 1. n. Stöhnen nt. 2. vb.
stöhnen.
grocer, n. Kolonial'warenhändler, - m.
groceries, n.pl. Kolonial'waren
pl.
grocery store, n. Kolonial'wa-
rengeschäft, -e nt., Lebensmittelgeschäft, -e nt.
grog, n. Grog, -s m.
groggy, adj. benom'men; (be
g.) taumeln.
groin, n. Leistengegend f.
groom, n. Reitknecht, -e m.;
(footman) Diener, - m.;
(bridegroom) Bräutigam -e m.
groove, n. Rinne, -n f.
grope, vb. tappen.
gross, 1. n. Gros, -se nt. 2. adj.
grob (ö); (weight) brutto.
grossness, n. Kraßheit, -en f.
grotesque, adj. grotesk'.
grotto, n. Grotte, -n f.
grouch, 1. n. Griesgram, -e m.
2. vb. verdrieß'lich sein*.
ground, 1. n. Grund, ÷e m., Boden m.; Gebiet', -e nt.;
(elec.) erden.
groundless, adj. grundlos.
groundwork, n. Grundlage,
-n f.
group, 1. n. Gruppe, -n f. 2. vb.
gruppie'ren.
groupie, n. Mitläufer im Ge-
folge Prominenter, besonders
Rockmusikstars.
grouse, n. schottisches Schnee-
huhn, ÷er nt.
grove, Hain, -e m.
grovel, vb. kriechen*, speichel-
leckerisch sein*.
growl, vb. knurren.
grown, adj. erwach'sen.
grown-up, 1. n. Erwach'sen-
m.&f. 2. adj. erwach'sen.
growth, n. Wachstum nt.;
(med.) Gewächs', -e nt.
grub, 1. n. Larve, -n f.; (food)
Fressa'lien pl. 2. vb. wühlen.
grudge, n. Groll m.
gruel, n. dünne Hafergrütze f.
gruesome, adj. schauerlich.
gruff, adj. bärbeißig.
grumble, vb. murren.
grumpy, adj. mürrisch.
grunt, 1. n. Grunzen, - nt. 2.
vb. grunzen.
guarantee, 1. n. Garantie',
-i'en f. 2. vb. garantie'ren.
guarantor, n. Bürge, -n, -n m.
guaranty, n. Sicherheit, -en f.;
Bürgschaft, -en f.
guard, 1. n. Wache, -n f.; 2. vb.
bewa'chen.
guarded, adj. vorsichtig.
guardian, n. Vormund, -e m.
guerrilla, n. Partisan', (-en,) -
en m.
guess, vb. raten*.

guesswork, n. Raterei' f.
guest, n. Gast, ÷e m.
guidance, n. Leitung f., Führung f.
guide, 1. n. Führer, - m. 2. vb.
führen, leiten.
guidebook, n. Reiseführer,
- m.
guidepost, n. Wegweiser,
- m.
guild, n. Gilde, -n f.
guile, n. Arglist f.
guillotine, n. Guilloti'ne, -n f.
guilt, n. Schuld f.
guiltless, adj. schuldlos.
guilty, adj. schuldig.
guinea fowl, n. Perlhuhn, ÷er
nt.
guinea pig, n. Meerschwein-
chen, - nt.
guise, n. Art, -en f.; (clothes)
Aussehen nt.
guitar, n. Gitar're, -n f.
gulf, n. Golf, -e m.
gull, n. Möwe, -n f.
gullet, n. Kehle, -n f.
gullible, adj. leichtgläubig.
gully, n. Wasserrinne, -n f.
gulp, vb. schlucken.
gum, n. Gummi, -s nt.; (teeth)
Zahnfleisch nt.; (chewing g.)
Kaugummi, -s nt.
gummy, adj. gummiartig, klebrig.
gun, n. (small) Gewehr', -e nt.;
(large) Geschütz', -e nt.
gunboat, n. Kano'nenboot,
-e nt.
gunner, n. Kanonier', -e m.
gunpowder, n. Schießpulver nt.
gunshot, n. Schuß, ÷sse m.
gurgle, vb. gluckern.
guru, n. Guru, -s m.
gush, vb. hervor'quellen*.
gusher, n. sprudelnde Petrole-
umquelle, -n f.
gusset, n. Zwickel, - m.
gust, n. Windstoß, ÷e m.
gustatory, adj. Geschmacks'-
(cpds.).
gusto, n. Schwung m.
gusty, adj. windig.
guts, n. Eingeweide pl.; (courage) Mumm m.
gutter, n. (street) Rinnstein, -e
m., Gosse, -n f.; (house)
Dachtraufe, -n f.
guttural, adj. guttural'.
guy, n. Kerl, -e m.
guzzle, vb. saufen*.
gymnasium, n. Turnhalle, -n f.
gymnast, n. Turner, - m.
gymnastic, adj. gymnas'tisch.
gymnastics, n. Gymnas'tik f.
gynecologist, n. Frauenarzt, ÷e
m., Gynäkolo'ge, -n, -n m.
gynecology, n. Gynäkologie' f.
gypsum, n. Gips m.
gypsy, n. Zigeu'ner, - m.
gyrate, vb. kreiseln.
gyroscope, n. Kreiselkompaß,
-sse m.

H

haberdashery, n. Geschäft' für
Herrenartikel.
habit, n. Gewohn'heit, -en f.;
Kleidung, -en f.
habitable, adj. bewohn'bar.
habitat, n. Wohnbereich, -e m.
habitual, adj. gewöhn'lich; Gewohn'heits- (cpds.).
habitué, n. Stammgast, ÷e m.
hack, 1. n. Droschke, -n f.;
(horse) Klepper, - m. 2. vb.
hacken.
hacksaw, n. Metall'säge, -n f.
hag, n. Vettel, -n f.
haggard, adj. abgehärmt.
haggle, vb. feilschen.
Hague, n. Den Haag m.
hail, 1. n. Hagel m. 2. vb. ha-
geln; (greet) begrü'ßen. 3.
interj. heil!
hailstone, n. Hagelkorn, ÷er nt.
hailstorm, n. Hagelwetter,
- nt.
hair, n. Haar, -e nt.
haircut, n. Haarschnitt, -e m.;
(get a h.) sich die Haare
schneiden lassen*.
hairdo, n. Frisur', -en f.
hairdresser, n. Friseur', - m.,
Friseu'se, -n f.
hairline, n. Haaransatz, ÷e m.;
Haarstrich, -e m.
hairpin, n. Haarnadel, -n f.
hair-raising, adj. haarsträubend.
hairspray, n. Haarspray m.
hairy, adj. haarig.
hale, adj. kräftig.
half, 1. n. Hälfte, -n f. 2. adj.
halb.
half-breed, n. Mischling, -e m.
half-brother, n. Stiefbruder, ÷
m.
half-hearted, adj. lauwarm.
half-mast, n. Halbmast m.
halfway, adv. halbwegs.
half-wit, n. Narr, -en, -en m.
halibut, n. Heilbutt, -e m.
hall, n. (auditorium) Halle,
-n f.; (large room) Saal, Säle
m.; (corridor) Gang, ÷e
m., Korridor, -e m.; (front h.)
Diele, -n f.
hallmark, n. Stempel der Echtheit m.
hallow, vb. heiligen.
Halloween, n. Abend (m.) vor
Allerhei'ligen.
hallucination, n. Wahnvorstel-
lung, -en f., Halluzination', -
en f.
hallway, n. Gang, ÷e m., Korridor, -e m.
halo, n. Heiligenschein, -e m.
halt, 1. n. Halt, -e m.; (fig.)
Stillstand m. 2. vb. an·hal-
ten*. 3. interj. halt!
halter, n. (horse) Halfter,
- nt.; (female clothing) Oberteil eines Bade- oder Luftan-
zuges.

halve, vb. halbie'ren.

ham, n. Schinken, - m.

Hamburg, n. Hamburg nt.

hamlet, n. Flecken, - m.

hammer, 1. n. Hammer, ⁻ m. **2.** vb. hämmern.

hammock, n. Hängematte, -n f.

hamper, 1. n. Korb, ⁻e m. **2.** vb. hemmen.

hamstring, vb. lähmen.

hand, 1. n. Hand, ⁻e f. **2.** vb. reichen.

handbag, n. Handtasche, -n f.

handbook, n. Handbuch, ⁻er nt.

handcuffs, n.pl. Handschellen pl.

handful, n. Handvoll f.

handicap 1. n. Handikap, -s nt.; Hindernis, -se nt. **2.** vb. hemmen.

handicraft, n. Handwerk nt.

handiwork, n. Handarbeit, -en f., Handwerk nt.

handkerchief, n. Taschentuch, ⁻er nt.

handle, 1. n. Henkel, - m., Griff, -e m. **2.** vb. handhaben.

hand-made, adj. handgearbeitet.

handout, n. Almosen, - nt.

hand-rail, n. Gelän'der, - nt.

handsome, adj. gutaussehend; ansehnlich.

handwriting, n. Handschritt, -en f.

handy, adj. handlich; (skilled) geschickt'.

handy man, n. Fakto'tum, -s nt.

hangar, n. Schuppen, - m.

hanger, n. Aufhänger, - m.; (clothes) Kleiderbügel, - m.

hanger-on, n. Schmarot'zer, -s m.

hang glider, n. Drachenflieger, - m.

hanging, n. Hinrichtung (-en f.) durch Hängen.

hangman, n. Henker, - m.

hangnail, n. Niednagel, ⁻ m.

hangout, n. Stammlokal, -e nt.

hang-over, n. Kater, - m., Katzenjammer m.

hangup, n. (to have a h.) mit etwas nicht fertig werden, einen Komplex haben, verklemmt sein.

haphazardly, adv. aufs Geratewohl'.

happen, vb. sich ereig'nen, geschehen*, passie'ren.

happening, n. Ereig'nis, -se nt.

happiness, n. Glück nt.

happy, adj. glücklich.

happy-go-lucky, adj. sorglos.

harangue, 1. n. marktschreierische Ansprache, -n f. **2.** vb. eine marktschreierische Ansprache halten*.

harass, vb. plagen.

harbinger, n. Vorbote, -n, -n m.

harbor, n. Hafen, ⁻ m.

hard, adj. (not soft) hart (⁻); (not easy) schwer, schwierig.

hard-boiled, adj. hartgekocht; (fig.) abgebrüht.

hard coal, n. Anthrazit', -e m.

harden, vb. (intr.) hart werden*; (tr.) ab'härten.

hard-headed, adj. praktisch, realis'tisch.

hard-hearted, adj. hartherzig.

hardiness, n. Rüstigkeit f.

hardly, adv. kaum.

hardness, n. Härte, -n f.

hardship, n. Not, -e f.; (exertion) Anstrengung, -en f.

hardware, n. Eisenwaren pl.

hardwood, n. Hartholz nt.

hardy, adj. rüstig.

hare, n. Hase, -n, -n m.

harem, n. Harem, -s m.

hark, vb. horchen.

Harlequin, n. Harlekin, -e m.

harm, 1. n. Schaden, ⁻ m.; Unrecht, -e nt. **2.** vb. schaden; Unrecht zu'fügen.

harmful, adj. schädlich.

harmless, adj. harmlos.

harmonic, adj. harmo'nisch.

harmonica, n. Harmo'nika, -s f.

harmonious, adj. harmo'nisch.

harmonize, vb. harmonisie'ren.

harmony, n. Harmonie', -i'en f.; (fig.) Eintracht f.

harness, 1. n. Geschirr', -e nt. **2.** vb. ein'spannen.

harp, n. Harfe, -n f.

harpoon, 1. n. Harpu'ne, -n f. **2.** vb. harpunie'ren.

harpsichord, n. Spinett', -e nt.

harrow, 1. n. Egge, -n f. **2.** vb. eggen.

harry, vb. plündern; plagen.

harsh, adj. rauh; streng.

harshness, n. Rauheit f.; Strenge f.

harvest, 1. n. Ernte, -n f. **2.** vb. ernten.

hassle, n. Hetze f.

hassock, n. gepolsterter Hocker, - m.

haste, n. Eile f.

hasten, vb. eilen; sich beei'len.

hat, n. Hut, ⁻e m.

hatch, 1. n. Luke, -n f. **2.** vb. aus'brüten.

hatchet, n. Beil, -e nt.

hate, 1. n. Haß m. **2.** vb. hassen.

hateful, adj. verhaßt'; widerlich.

hatred, n. Haß m.

haughtiness, n. Hochmut m.

haughty, adj. hochmütig.

haul, vb. schleppen.

haunch, n. Keule, -n f.

haunt, vb. verfol'gen.

have, vb. haben*; (I h. it made) ich lasse* es machen; (I h. him make it) ich lasse* ihn es machen.

haven, n. Hafen, ⁻ m.; Zufluchtsort, -e m.

havoc, n. Verwüs'tung, -en f.

hawk, n. Habicht, -e m.

hawser, n. Trosse, -n f.

hay, n. Heu nt.

hay fever, n. Heuschnupfen, - m.

hayloft, n. Heuboden, ⁻ m.

haystack, n. Heuhaufen, - m.

hazard, 1. n. Risiko, -s nt. **2.** vb. riskie'ren.

hazardous, adj. gewagt'.

haze, n. Dunst, ⁻e m.

hazel, adj. haselnußbraun.

hazelnut, n. Haselnuß, ⁻sse f.

hazy, adj. dunstig, unklar.

he, pron. er.

head, n. Kopf, ⁻e m., Haupt, ⁻er nt.

headache, n. Kopfschmerzen pl.

headfirst, adv. Hals über Kopf.

headgear, n. Kopfbedeckung, -en f.

heading, n. Überschrift, -en f., Rubrik', -en f.

headlight, n. Scheinwerfer, - m.

headline, n. Überschrift -en f.; (newspaper) Schlagzeile, -n f.

headlong, adj. überstürzt'.

headmaster, n. Schuldirektor, -en m.

head-on, adv. direkt von vorn.

headquarters, n.pl. Hauptquartier, -e nt.

headstone, n. (grave) Grabstein, -e m.; (arch.) Eckstein, -e m.

headstrong, adj. dickköpfig.

headwaters, n.pl. Quelle, -n f.

headway, n. (make h.) vorwärts kommen*.

heal, vb. heilen.

health, n. Gesund'heit, -en f.

healthful, adj. gesund' (⁻).

healthy, adj. gesund'(⁻).

heap, 1. n. Haufen, - m. **2.** vb. häufen.

hear, vb. hören.

hearing, n. Gehör' nt.; (jur.) Verhör', -e nt.

hearsay, n. Hörensagen nt.

hearse, n. Leichenwagen, - m.

heart, n. Herz(en), - nt.

heartache, n. Herzenskummer m.

heart-breaking, adj. herzzerbrechend.

heartbroken, adv. tieftraurig.

heartburn, n. Sodbrennen, - nt.

heartfelt, adj. aufrichtig.

hearth, n. Kamin', -e m.

heartless, adj. herzlos.

heart-rending, adj. herzzerreißend.

heart-sick, adj. niedergeschlagen.

heart-to-heart, adj. freimütig.

hearty, adj. herzhaft.

heat, 1. n. Hitze f., Wärme f.; (house) Heizung f. **2.** vb. heiß machen, erhit'zen; (house) heizen.

heated, adj. geheizt'; (fig.) hitzig.

heater, *n.* Heizvorrichtung, -en *f.*

heathen, 1. *n.* Heide, -n, -n *m.* **2.** *adj.* heidnisch.

heather, *n.* Heidekraut *nt.*

heat-stroke, *n.* Hitzschlag, ⁼e *m.*

heat wave, *n.* Hitzewelle, -n *f.*

heave, *vb.* heben*; wogen; (utter)* aus·stoßen*.

heaven, *n.* Himmel, - *m.*

heavenly, *adj.* himmlisch.

heavy, *adj.* schwer; *(fig.)* heftig.

heavyweight, *n.* Schwergewicht *nt.*

Hebrew, 1. *n.* Hebrä'er, - *m.* **2.** *adj.* hebrä'isch.

heckle, *vb.* hecheln.

hectic, *adj.* hektisch.

hedge, *n.* Hecke, -n *f.*

hedgehog, *n.* Igel, - *m.*

hedge-hop, *vb. (mil.)* im Tiefflug an·fliegen*.

hedgerow, *n.* Baumhecke, -n *f.*

hedonism, *n.* Hedonis'mus *m.*

heed, *vb.* beach'ten.

heedless, *adj.* achtlos.

heel, *n. (shoes)* Absatz, ⁼e *m.; (foot)* Ferse, -n *f.; (scoundrel)* Schuft, -e *m.*

heifer, *n.* junge Kuh, ⁼e *f.*

height, *n.* Höhe, -n *f.; (person)* Größe -n *f.*

heighten, *vb.* erhö'hen.

heinous, *adj.* abscheu'lich, verrucht'.

heir, *n.* Erbe, -n, -n *m.*

heirloom, *n.* Erbstück, -e *nt.*

helicopter, *n.* Hubschrauber, - *m.*

heliotrope, *n.* Heliotrop', -e *nt.*

helium, *n.* Helium *nt.*

hell, *n.* Hölle, -n *f.*

Hellenic, *adj.* helle'nisch.

Hellenism, *n.* Hellenis'mus *m.*

hello, *interj.* guten Tag (Morgen, Abend); *(call for attention)* hallo.

helm, *n.* Steuerruder, - *nt.*

helmet, *n.* Helm, -e *m.*

helmsman, *n.* Steuermann, ⁼er *m.*

help, 1. *n.* Hilfe *f.* **2.** *vb.* helfen*.

helper, *n.* Helfer, - *m.*

helpful, *adj.* hilfreich, hilfsbereit.

helpfulness, *n.* Hilfsbereitschaft *f.*

helping, *n.* Portion', -en *f.*

helpless, *adj.* hilflos.

helter-skelter, *adv.* hol'terdiepol'ter.

hem, 1. *n.* Saum, ⁼e *m.* **2.** *vb.* säumen.

hematite, *n.* Hematit', -e *nt.*

hemisphere, *n.* Halbkugel, -n *f.*

hemlock, *n.* Schierling *m.*

hemoglobin, *n.* Hämoglobin' *nt.*

hemophilia, *n.* Bluterkrankheit *f.*

hemorrhage, *n.* Bluterguß, ⁼sse *m.*

hemorrhoid, *n.* Hämorrhoi'de, -n *f.*

hemp, *n.* Hanf *m.*

hemstitch, *n.* Hohlsaum, ⁼e *m.*

hen, *n.* Henne, -n *f.*

hence, *adv. (time)* von nun an; *(place)* von hier aus; *(therefore)* daher, deshalb, deswegen, also.

henceforth, *adv.* von nun an.

henchman, *n.* Trabant', -en, -en *m.*

henna, *n.* Henna *f.*

henpecked, *adj.* unter dem Pantof'fel stehend.

hepatic, *adj.* Leber- *(cpds.).*

hepatica, *n.* Hepa'tika, -ken *f.*

her, 1. *pron.* sie, ihr. **2.** *adj.* ihr, -, -e.

heraldic, *adj.* heral'disch.

heraldry, *n.* Wappenkunde *f.*

herb, *n.* Kraut, ⁼er *n.,* Gewürz'kraut, ⁼er *nt.*

herculean, *adj.* herku'lisch.

herd, *n.* Herde, -n *f.*

here, *adv. (in this place)* hier; *(to this place)* hierher'; *(from h.)* hierhin'.

hereabout, *adv.* hier.

hereafter, 1. *n.* Leben *(nt.)* nach dem Tode. **2.** *adv.* in Zukunft.

hereby, *adv.* hiermit.

hereditary, *adj.* erblich.

heredity, *n.* Erblichkeit *f.;* Verer'bung, -en *f.*

herein, *adv.* hierbei, hiermit.

heresy, *n.* Ketzerei', -en *f.*

heretic, 1. *n.* Ketzer, - *m.* **2.** *adj.* ketzerisch.

heritage, *n.* Erbe *nt.*

hermetic, *adj.* herme'tisch.

hermit, *n.* Einsiedler, - *m.*

hernia, *n.* Bruch, ⁼e *m.*

hero, *n.* Held, -en, -en *m.*

heroic, *adj.* heldenhaft.

heroin, *n.* Heroin' *nt.*

heroine, *n.* Heldin, -nen *f.*

heroism, *n.* Heldenmut *m.*

heron, *n.* Reiher, - *m.*

herring, *n.* Hering, -e *m.*

herringbone, *n.* Heringsgräte, -n *f.*

hers, *pron.* ihrer, -es, -e.

hertz, *n.* Hertz *nt.*

hesitancy, *n.* Zögern *nt.*

hesitant, *adj.* zögernd.

hesitate, *vb.* zögern.

hesitation, *n.* Zögern *nt.*

heterodox, *adj.* heterodox'.

heterogeneous, *adj.* heterogen'.

heterosexual, *adj.* heterosexuell'.

hew, *vb.* hauen*.

hexagon, *n.* Sechseck, -e *nt.*

heyday, *n.* Blütezeit, -en *f.*

hi, *interj.* hallo.

hibernate, *vb.* überwin'tern.

hibernation, *n.* Überwin'terung, -en *f.*

hibiscus, *n.* Hibis'kus, -ken *m.*

hiccup, *n.* Schluckauf *m.*

hickory, *n.* Hickoryholz, ⁼er *nt.*

hide, 1. *n.* Haut, ⁼e *f.;* Fell, -e *nt.* **2.** *vb.* verber'gen*, verste'cken; verheim'lichen.

hideous, *adj.* gräßlich.

hide-out, *n.* Schlupfwinkel, - *m.*

hierarchy, *n.* Rangordnung, -en *f.,* Hierarchie', -i'en *f.*

hieroglyphic, *adj.* hierogly'phisch.

high, *adj.* hoch, hoh- (höher, höchst); *(tipsy)* beschwipst'.

highbrow, *adj.* intellektuell'.

high fidelity, *n.* Hifi *nt.*

high-handed, *adj.* anmaßend.

highland, *n.* Hochland, ⁼er *nt.*

highlight, *n.* Höhepunkt, -e *m.*

highly, *adv.* höchst.

high-minded, *adj.* edelmütig.

Highness, *n.* Hoheit, -en *f.*

high school, *n.* höhere Schule, -n *f.*

high seas, *n.* hohe See *f.*

high-strung, *adj.* nervös, kribbelig.

high tide, *n.* Flut, -en *f.*

highway, *n.* Landstraße, -n *f.,* Chaussee', -n *f.*

hijacker, *n.* Flugzeugentführer, - *m;* Luftpirat, -en, -en *m.*

hike, 1. *n.* Wanderung, -en *f.* **2.** *vb.* wandern.

hilarious, *adj.* ausgelassen.

hilarity, *n.* Ausgelassenheit *f.*

hill, *n.* Hügel, - *m.*

hilt, *n.* Heft, -e *nt.*

him, *pron.* ihn; ihm.

hind, *adj.* hinter-.

hinder, *vb.* hindern; verhin'dern.

hindmost, *adj.* letzt-, hinterst-.

hindrance, *n.* Hindernis, -se *nt.; (disadvantage)* Nachteil, -e *m.*

hinge, *n.* Scharnier, -e *nt.*

hint, 1. *n.* Wink, -e *m.* **2.** *vb.* an·deuten.

hinterland, *n.* Hinterland *nt.*

hip, *n.* Hüfte, -n *f.*

hippopotamus, *n.* Nilpferd, -e *nt.*

hire, *vb.* mieten; *(persons)* an·stellen.

his, 1. *adj.* sein, -, -e. **2.** *pron.* seiner, -es, -e.

Hispanic, *n.* erste oder zweite Generation Amerikaner spanisch sprechender Herkunft.

hiss, *vb.* zischen.

historian, *n.* Histo'riker, - *m.*

historic, historical, *adj.* histo'risch.

history, *n.* Geschich'te, -en *f.*

hit, 1. *n.* Stoß, ⁼e *m.,* Schlag, ⁼e *m.; (success)* Treffer, - *m.* **2.** *vb.* stoßen*, schlagen*, treffen*.

hitch, 1. *n. (knot)* Knoten, - *m.; (obstacle)* Hindernis, -se *nt.* **2.** *vb.* fest·machen.

hitchhike, *vb.* per Anhalter fahren*.

hive, *n.* Bienenstock, ⁼e *m.*

hives, *n.* Nesselsucht *f.*

hoard, 1. *n.* Vorrat, ¨e *m.* **2.** *vb.* hamstern.

hoarse, *adj.* heiser.

hoax, *n.* Schabernack, -e *m.*

hobble, *vb.* humpeln.

hobby, *n.* Liebhaberei', -en *f.*

hobgoblin, *n.* Kobold, -e *m.*

hobnob with, *vb.* mit jemand auf vertrau'tem Füße stehen*.

hobo, *n.* Landstreicher, - *m.*

hockey, *n.* Hockey *nt.*

hocus-pocus, *n.* Ho'kuspo'kus *m.*

hod, *n.* Traggestell, -e *nt.*

hodgepodge, *n.* Mischmasch, - e *m.*

hoe, 1. *n.* Hacke, -n *f.* **2.** *vb.* hacken.

hog, *n.* Schwein, -e *nt.*

hogshead, *n.* Oxhoft, -e *nt.*

hoist, *vb.* hoch·ziehen*, hissen.

hold, 1. *n.* Halt *m.;* *(ship)* Laderaum, ¨e *m.* **2.** *vb.* halten*; *(contain)* enthal'ten*; **(h. up)** auf·halten*.

holder, *n.* Halter, - *m.*

holdup, *n.* Überfall, ¨e *m.*

hole, *n.* Loch, ¨er *nt.*

holiday, *n.* Feiertag, -e *m.,* Festtag, -e *m.*

holiness, *n.* Heiligkeit *f.*

Holland, *n.* Holland *nt.*

hollow, *adj.* hohl.

holly, *n.* Stechpalme, -n *f.*

hollyhock, *n.* Malve, -n *f.*

holocaust, *n.* Brandopfer, - *nt.,* Großfeuer, - *nt.*

hologram, *n.* Hologramm', -e *nt.*

holography, *n.* Holografie' *f.*

holster, *n.* Pisto'lenhalter, - *m.*

holy, *adj.* heilig.

holy day, *n.* Kirchenfeiertag, -e *m.*

Holy See, *n.* der Heilige Stuhl *m.*

Holy Spirit, *n.* der Heilige Geist *m.*

Holy Week, *n.* Karwoche *f.*

homage, *n.* Huldigung, -en *f.*

home, 1. *n.* Heim, -e *nt.;* **(h. town)** Heimat, -en *f.;* *(place of residence)* Wohnort, -e *m.;* *(house)* Haus, ¨er *nt.;* *(institution)* Heim, -e *nt.* **2.** *adv.* *(location)* zu Hause, daheim'; *(direction)* nach Hause, heim.

homeland, *n.* Heimatland, ¨er *nt.*

homeless, *adj.* heimatlos; obdachlos.

homelike, *adj.* behag'lich.

homely, *adj.* häßlich.

home-made, *adj.* selbstgefertigt.

home rule, *n.* Selbstverwaltung *f.*

homesick, be, *vb.* Heimweh haben*.

homesickness, *n.* Heimweh *n.*

homestead, *n.* Fami'liensitz, -e *m.*

homeward, *adv.* heimwärts.

homework, *n.* Hausaufgabe, -n *f.,* Schularbeiten *pl.*

homicide, *n.* Mord, -e *m.*

homogeneous, *adj.* homogen'.

homogenize, *vb.* homogenisie'ren.

homonym, *n.* Homonym', -e *nt.*

homosexual, *adj.* homosexuell'.

hone, *n.* Wetzstein, -e *m.*

honest, *adj.* ehrlich, aufrichtig.

honesty, *n.* Ehrlichkeit, -en *f.*

honey, *n.* Honig *m.*

honey-bee, *n.* Honigbiene, -n *f.*

honeycomb, *n.* Honigwabe, -n *f.*

honeymoon, *n.* Hochzeitsreise, -n *f.,* Flitterwochen *pl.*

honeysuckle, *n.* Geißblatt *nt.*

honor, 1. *n.* Ehre, -n *f.* **2.** *vb.* ehren; honorie'ren.

honorable, *adj.* ehrbar, ehrenvoll.

honorary, *adj.* Ehren- *(cpds.).*

hood, *n.* Haube, -n *f.,* *(monk)* Kapu'ze, -n *f.*

hoodlum, *n.* Rowdy, -s *m.*

hoodwink, *vb.* übertöl'peln.

hoof, *n.* Huf, -e *nt.*

hook, 1. *n.* Haken, - *m.* **2.** *vb.* zu·haken; *(catch)* fangen*.

hoop, *n.* Reifen, - *m.*

hoot, *vb.* schreien*.

hop, 1. *n.* *(plant)* Hopfen *m.;* *(jump)* Sprung, ¨e *m.* **2.** *vb.* hüpfen, springen*.

hope, 1. *n.* Hoffnung, -en *f.* **2.** *vb.* hoffen.

hopeful, *adj.* hoffnungsvoll.

hopeless, *adj.* hoffnungslos.

hopelessness, *n.* Hoffnungslosigkeit *f.*

horde, *n.* Horde, -n *f.*

horizon, *n.* Horizont', -e *m.*

horizontal, *adj.* waagerecht, horizontal'.

hormone, *n.* Hormon', -e *nt.*

horn, *n.* Horn, ¨er *nt.*

hornet, *n.* Hornis'se, -n *f.*

horny, *adj.* hornig, hörnern.

horoscope, *n.* Horoskop', -e *nt.*

horrible, *adj.* grauenhaft.

horrid, *adj.* gräßlich.

horrify, *vb.* entset'zen.

horror, *n.* Grauen *nt.*

horse, *n.* Pferd, -e *nt.*

horseback, on, *adv.* zu Pferde.

horsehair, *n.* Roßhaar, -e *nt.*

horseman, *n.* Reiter, - *m.*

horsemanship, *n.* Reitkunst *f.*

horse-power, *n.* Pferdestärke, - n *f.*

horseradish, *n.* Meerrettich, -e *m.*

horseshoe, *n.* Hufeisen, - *nt.*

horticulture, *n.* Gartenbau *m.*

hose, *n.* *(tube)* Schlauch, ¨e *m.;* *(stocking)* Strumpf, ¨e *m.*

hosiery, *n.* Strumpfwaren *pl.*

hospitable, *adj.* gastfreundlich, gastfrei.

hospital, *n.* Krankenhaus, ¨er *nt.*

hospitality, *n.* Gastfreundschaft, Gastfreiheit *f.*

hospitalization, *n.* Krankenhausaufenthalt *m.*

hospitalize, *vb.* ins Krankenhaus stecken; **(be h.d)** im Krankenhaus liegen müssen*.

host, *n.* Gastgeber, - *m.;* *(innkeeper)* Wirt, -e *m.;* *(crowd)* Menge, -n *f.;* *(Eucharist)* Hostie *f.*

hostage, *n.* Geisel, -n *m.*

hostel, *n.* Herberge, -n *f.;* **(youth h.)** Jugendherberge, -n *f.*

hostess, *n.* Gastgeberin, -nen *f.*

hostile, *adj.* feindlich.

hostility, *n.* Feindseligkeit, -en *f.,* Krieg, -e *m.*

hot, *adj.* heiß.

hotbed, *n.* Mistbeet, -e *nt.;* *(fig.)* Brutstätte, -n *f.*

hot dog, *n.* Bockwurst, ¨e *f.*

hotel, *n.* Hotel', -s *nt.*

hothouse, *n.* Treibhaus, ¨er *nt.*

hound, *n.* Hund, -e *m.*

hour, *n.* Stunde, -n *f.*

hourglass, *n.* Stundenglas, ¨er *nt.*

hourly, *adj.* stündlich.

house, *n.* Haus, ¨er *nt.*

housefly, *n.* Stubenfliege, -n *f.*

household, *n.* Haushalt, -e *m.*

housekeeper, *n.* Haushälterin, -nen *f.*

housekeeping, *n.* Haushaltung *f.*

housemaid, *n.* Hausmädchen, - *nt.*

housewife, *n.* Hausfrau, -en *f.*

housework, *n.* Hausarbeit, -en *f.*

hovel, *n.* Hütte, -n *f.*

hover, *vb.* schweben.

hovercraft, *n.* Hovercraft *m.* & *nt.;* Luftkissenboot, -e *nt.*

how, *adv.* wie.

however, 1. *conj.* aber, doch, jedoch'. **2.** *adv.* wie . . . auch.

howitzer, *n.* Haubit'ze, -n *f.*

howl, 1. *n.* Gebrüll' *nt.* **2.** *vb.* brüllen.

hub, *n.* Nabe, -n *f.;* *(fig.)* Mittelpunkt, -e *m.*

hubbub, *n.* Tumult', -e *m.*

huckleberry, *n.* Heidelbeere, -n *f.*

huddle, *vb.* zusam'men·kauern, sich zusam'men·drängen

hue, *n.* Färbung, -en *f.*

hug, 1. *n.* Umar'mung, -en *f.* **2.** *vb.* umar'men.

huge, *adj.* sehr groß, ungeheuer.

hull, *n.* Hülse, -n *f.;* *(fruit)* Schale, -n *f.;* *(ship)* Rumpf, ¨e *m.*

hum, 1. *n.* *(people)* Gemur'mel *nt.;* *(insects)* Summen *nt.* **2.** *vb.* murmeln; summen.

human, *adj.* menschlich.

humane, *adj.* human', menschlich.

humanism, n. Humanis'mus m.

humanitarian, adj. menschen-freundlich.

humanity, n. (mankind) Menschheit f.; (humaneness) Menschlichkeit f.

humble, adj. demütig, beschei'den.

humbug, n. Schwindel m., Quatsch m.

humdrum, adj. langweilig, eintönig.

humid, adj. feucht.

humidity, n. Feuchtigkeit f.

humidor, n. Tabakstopf, ¨e m.

humiliate, vb. demütigen.

humiliation, n. Demütigung, -en f.

humility, n. Demut f.

humor, n. Humor' m.; (mood) Laune, -n f.

humorist, n. Humorist', -en, -en m.

humorous, adj. humor'voll, witzig.

hump, n. Buckel,- m., Höcker, - m.

hunch, 1. n. Höcker, - m., Buckel, - m.; (suspicion) Ahnung, -en f., Riecher, - m. **2.** vb. krümmen.

hunchback, 1. n. Buckel, - m.; (person) Bucklig- m.&f. **2.** adj. bucklig.

hundred, num. hundert.

hundredth, 1. adj. hundertst-. **2.** n. Hundertstel, - nt.

Hungarian, 1. n. Ungar, -n, -n m. **2.** adj. ungarisch.

Hungary, n. Ungarn nt.

hunger, n. Hunger m.

hungry, adj. hungrig.

hunt, 1. n. Jagd, -en f. **2.** vb. jagen.

hunter, n. Jäger, - m.

hunting, n. Jagd, -en f.

hurdle, 1. n. Hürde, -n f. **2.** vb. hinü'ber-springen*.

hurl, vb. schleudern.

hurrah, interj. (h. for him) er lebe hoch!

hurricane, n. Orkan', -e m.

hurry, vb. eilen, sich beei'len.

hurt, vb. weh tun*, verlet'zen.

hurtful, adj. schädlich.

husband, n. Mann, ¨er m., Gatte, -n, -n m.

husbandry, n. Landwirtschaft f.; (management) Wirtschaften nt.

hush, 1. n. Stille f. **2.** vb. zum Schweigen bringen*. **3.** interj. still!

husk, 1. n. Hülse, -n f. **2.** vb. enthül'sen.

husky, adj. (hoarse) rauh; (strong) stark (¨).

hustle, vb. rührig sein*.

hut, n. Hütte, -n f.

hyacinth, n. Hyazin'the, -n f.

hybrid, adj. hybrid'.

hydrangea, n. Horten'sie, -n f.

hydrant, n. Hydrant', -en, -en m.

hydraulic, adj. hydrau'lisch.

hydrochloric acid, n. Salzsäure f.

hydroelectric, adj. hydroelek'trisch.

hydrogen, n. Wasserstoff m.

hydrogen bomb, n. Wasserstoffbombe, -n f.

hydrophobia, n. krankhafte Wasserscheu f.

hydroplane, n. Wasserflugzeug, -e nt.

hydrotherapy, n. Hydrotherapie' f.

hyena, n. Hyä'ne, -n f.

hygiene, n. Hygie'ne f.

hygienic, adj. hygie'nisch.

hymn, n. Hymne -n f., Choral', ¨e m., Kirchenlied, -er nt.

hymnal, n. Gesang'buch, ¨er nt.

hyperacidity, n. Hyperacidität', f.

hyperbole, n. Hyper'bel, -n f.

hypercritical, adj. überkritisch.

hypersensitive, adj. überempfindlich.

hypertension, n. übernormaler Blutdruck m.

hyphen, n. Bindestrich, -e m.

hyphenate, vb. trennen.

hypnosis, n. Hypno'se, -n f.

hypnotic, adj. hypno'tisch.

hypnotism, n. Hypnotis'mus m.

hypnotize, vb. hypnotisie'ren.

hypochondria, n. Schwermut f.

hypochondriac, 1. n. Hypochon'der, - m. **2.** adj. schwermütig.

hypocrisy, n. Heuchelei', -en f.

hypocrite, n. Heuchler, - m.

hypocritical, adj. heuchlerisch.

hypodermic, n. Spritze, -n f.

hypothesis, n. Hypothe'se, -n f.

hypothetical, adj. hypothe'tisch.

hysterectomy, n. Hysterek'tomie f.

hysteria, hysterics, n. Hysterie' f.

hysterical, adj. hyste'risch.

I

I, pron. ich.

ice, n. Eis nt.

iceberg, n. Eisberg, -e m.

ice-box, n. Eisschrank, ¨e m.

ice cream, n. Eis nt., Sahneneis nt.

ice skate, 1. n. Schlittschuh, -e m. 2. vb. Schlittschuh laufen*.

icing, n. Zuckerguß, ¨sse m.

icon, n. Iko'ne, -n f.

icy, adj. eisig.

idea, n. Idee', -de'en f., Gedan'ke(n), - m.

ideal, 1. n. Ideal', -e nt. **2.** adj. ideal'.

idealism, n. Idealis'mus m.

idealist, n. Idealist', -en, -en m.

idealistic, adj. idealis'tisch.

idealize, vb. idealisie'ren.

identical, adj. iden'tisch.

identifiable, adj. identifizier'bar.

identification, n. Identifizie'rung, -en f.; (card) Ausweis, -e m.

identify, vb. identifizie'ren.

identity, n. Identität', -en f.

ideology, n. Ideologie', -i'en f.

idiocy, n. Blödsinn m.

idiom, n. Idiom', -e nt.

idiot, n. Idiot', -en, -en m.

idiotic, adj. idio'tisch, blödsinnig.

idle, adj. müßig; arbeitslos.

idleness, n. Müßigkeit f.

idol, n. Götzenbild, -er nt.

idolatry, n. Abgötterrei', -en f.

idolize, vb. vergöt'tern.

if, conj. wenn; (as if) als ob.

ignite, vb. an-zünden.

ignition, n. Zündung f.

ignition key, n. Zündschlüssel, - m.

ignominious, adj. schmachvoll.

ignoramus, n. Nichtswisser, - m.

ignorance, n. Unwissenheit f.

ignorant, adj. unwissend.

ignore, vb. überse'hen*, unbeachtet lassen*.

ill, adj. krank (¨).

illegal, adj. illegal, ungesetzlich.

illegible, adj. unleserlich.

illegitimate, adj. ungesetzlich; (unmarried) unehelich.

illicit, adj. unerlaubt.

illiteracy, n. Analphabe'tentum, nt.

illiterate, 1. n. Analphabet', -en, -en m. **2.** adj. des Lesens und Schreibens unkundig.

illness, n. Krankheit, -en f.

illogical, adj. unlogisch.

illuminate, vb. beleuch'ten, erleuch'ten.

illumination, n. Beleuch'tung, -en f.

illusion, n. Illusion', -en f.

illusive, illusory, adj. trügerisch, illuso'risch.

illustrate, vb. erläu'tern; (with pictures) illustrie'ren.

illustration, n. Erläu'terung, -en f.; (picture) Illustration', -en f.

illustrative, adj. erläu'ternd.

illustrious, adj. berühmt'.

image, n. Abbild, -er nt.

imaginable, adj. denkbar.

imaginary, adj. scheinbar, imaginär'.

imagination, n. Einbildung, -en f., Vorstellung, -en f.

imaginative, adj. phantasievoll.

imagine, vb. sich ein-bilden, sich vor-stellen.

imam, n. Imam, -e m.

imbecile, adj. schwachsinnig.

imitate, vb. nach-ahmen, imitie'ren.

imititation, n. Nachahmung, -en f., Imitation', -en f.

immaculate, adj. unbeflekt, makellos, blitzsauber; **(i. conception)** unbeflekte Empfäng'nis f.

immaterial, adj. unwesentlich.

immature, adj. unreif.

immediate, adj. ummittelbar.

immediately, adv. sofort'.

immense, adj. unermeßlich.

immerse, vb. unter•tauchen, versen'ken.

immigrant, n. Einwanderer, - m.

immigrate, vb. ein•wandern.

imminent, adj. bevor'stehend.

immobile, adj. unbeweglich.

immobilize, vb. unbeweglich machen.

immoderate, adj. unbescheiden.

immodest, adj. unbescheiden, anstößig.

immoral, adj. unsittlich, unmoralisch.

immorality, n. Unsittlichkeit, - en f.

immortal, adj. unsterblich.

immortality, n. Unsterblichkeit f.

immortalize, vb. unsterblich machen.

immune, adj. immun'.

immunity, n. Immunität', -en f.

immunize, vb. immunisie'ren.

impact, n. Zusam'menprall m.; (fig.) Auswirkung, -en f.

impair, vb. verrin'gern, verschlechtern.

impart, vb. zu•kommen lassen*.

impartial, adj. unparteiisch.

impatience, n. Ungeduld f.

impatient, adj. ungeduldig.

impeach, vb. an•klagen, beschul'digen.

impeachment, n. Anklage, -n f.; Beschul'digung, -en f.; (U.S.) Verhandlung gegen einen Beamten vor dem Kongress.

impede, vb. behin'dern.

impediment, n. Behin'derung, - en f. **(speech i.)** Sprachfehler, - m.

impel, vb. an•treiben*, zwingen*.

impenetrable, adj. undurchdringlich.

imperative, 1. n. Imperativ, -e m. **2.** adj. zwingend.

imperceptible, adj. unmerklich, unwahrnehmbar.

imperfect, 1. n. Imperfekt, -e nt. **2.** adj. unvollkommen, fehlerhaft.

imperfection, n. Unvollkommenheit, -en f., Fehler, - m.

imperial, adj. kaiserlich.

imperialism, n. Imperialis'mus m.

impersonal, adj. unpersönlich.

impersonate, vb. verkör'pern; (theater) dar•stellen.

impersonation, n. Verkör'perung, -en f.; (theater) Darstellung, -en f.

impersonator, n. Imita'tor, -o'ren m.; (swindler) Hochstapler, - m.

impertinence, n. Frechheit, -en f., Unverschämtheit, -en f.

impertinent, adj. frech, unverschämt.

impervious, adj. unzugänglich; (fig.) gefühl'los.

impetuous, adj. ungestüm.

impetus, n. Anstoß m., Antrieb m.

implement, 1. n. Werkzeug, -e nt. **2.** vb. durch•führen.

implicate, vb. verwi'ckeln.

implication, n. implizier'ter Gedan'ke(n), - m.; Verwick'lung, -en f.; **(by i.)** impli'cite.

implicit, adj. inbegriffen, stillschweigend.

implied, adj. miteinbegriffen.

implore, vb. an•flehen.

imply, vb. in sich schliessen*, impli'cite sagen, an•deuten.

impolite, adj. unhöflich.

import, 1. n. Einfuhr f., Import', -e m.; (meaning) Bedeu'tung, -en f. **2.** vb. ein•führen, importie'ren.

importance, n. Wichtigkeit f.

important, adj. wichtig, bedeu'tend.

importation, n. Einfuhr f.

impose, vb. auf•erlegen.

imposition, n. Belas'tung, -en f.

impossibility, n. Unmöglichkeit, -en f.

impossible, adj. unmöglich.

impotence, n. Unfähigkeit, -en f.; (med.) Impotenz, -en f.

impotent, adj. unfähig; (med.) impotent.

impoverish, vb. arm machen; (fig.) aus•saugen.

impregnable, adj. uneinnehmbar.

impregnate, vb. durchdrin'gen*; (make pregnant) schwängern.

impresario, n. Impresa'rio, -s m.

impress, vb. (imprint) prägen, ein•prägen; (affect) beein'drucken.

impression, n. Druck, -e m.; (copy) Abdruck, -e m.; (fig.) Eindruck, -̈e m.

impressive, adj. eindrucksvoll.

imprison, vb. ein•sperren.

imprisonment, n. Haft f.

improbable, adj. unwahrscheinlich.

impromptu, adv. aus dem Stegreif.

improper, adj. unrichtig; unschicklich.

improve, vb. verbes'sern.

improvement, n. Verbes'serung, -en f.; Besserung f.

improvise, vb. improvisie'ren.

impudent, adj. frech.

impulse, n. Impuls', -e m.

impulsive, adj. impulsiv'.

impunity, n. **(with i.)** ungestraft.

impure, adj. unrein.

impurity, n. Unreinheit, -en f.

in, prep. in.

inadvertent, adj. achtlos, unaufmerksam.

inalienable, adj. unveräußerlich.

inane, adj. leer, geistlos.

inaugural, adj. Antritts- (cpds.).

inaugurate, vb. ins Amt einführen.

inauguration, n. Einweihung, -en f.; Amtseinführung, -en f.

incandescence, n. Glühen nt.

incandescent, adj. glühend; Glüh- (cpds.).

incantation, n. Beschwö'rung f., Zauberspruch, -̈e m.

incapacitate, vb. unfähig machen.

incapacity, n. Unfähigkeit, -en f.

incarcerate, vb. ein•kerkern.

incarnate, adj. verkör'pert, fleischgeworden.

incarnation, n. Verkör'perung, -en f., Fleischwerdung f.

incendiary, adj. Brand- (cpds.); aufwieglerisch.

incense, n. Weihrauch m.

incentive, n. Anreiz, -e m., Antrieb, -e m.

inception, n. Begin'nen nt.

incessant, adj. unaufhörlich.

incest, n. Blutschande f.

inch, n. Zoll, - m.

incidence, n. Vorkommen nt.

incident, n. Vorfall, -̈e m.

incidental, adj. zufällig.

incidentally, adv. übrigens.

incision, n. Einschnitt, -e m.

incisor, n. Schneidezahn, -̈e m.

incite, vb. an•regen, an•stacheln.

inclination, n. Neigung, -en f.

incline, vb. neigen; **(be i.d)** geneigt sein*.

inclose, vb. ein•schließen*.

include, vb. ein•schließen*.

including, prep. einschließlich.

inclusive, adj. einschließlich.

incognito, adv. inkog'nito.

income, n. Einkommen, - nt.

incomparable, adj. unvergleichlich.

inconsiderate, adj. unüberlegt, rücksichtslos.

inconvenience, n. Mühe, -n f., Belas'tung, -en f.

inconvenient, adj. mühsam, ungelegen.

incorporate, vb. verei'nigen; auf•nehmen*.

incorrigible, adj. unverbesserlich.

increase, 1. n. Zunahme, -n f.

2. *vb.* zu'nehmen*, wachsen*.
incredible, *adj.* unglaublich.
incredulity, *n.* Zweifel, - *m.*
incredulous, *adj.* zweifelnd.
increment, *n.* Zunahme, -n *f.*
incriminate, *vb.* belas'ten, be-schul'digen.
incrimination, *n.* Beschul'di-gung, -en *f.*, Belas'tung, -en *f.*
incrust, *vb.* überkrus'ten.
incubator, *n.* Brutapparat, -e *m.*
incumbent, 1. *n.* Amtsinhaber, - *m.* **2.** *adj.* verpflich'tend.
incur, *vb.* auf sich laden*.
incurable, *adj.* unheilbar.
indebted, *adj.* verschul'det.
indeed, *adv.* in der Tat.
indefatigable, *adj.* unermüd-lich.
indefinite, *adj.* unbestimmt.
indefinitely, *adv.* endlos.
indelible, *adj.* unauslöschlich.
indemnify, *vb.* sicher∙stellen; entschä'digen.
indemnity, *n.* Sicherstellung, -en *f.*; Entschä'digung, -en *f.*
indent, *vb.* zacken; *(paragraph)* ein'rücken; *(damage)* ver-beu'len.
indentation, *n.* Einkerbung, -en *f.*; *(paragraph)* Ein-rückung, -en *f.*; *(damage)* Verbeu'lung, -en *f.*
independence, *n.* Unabhängig-keit *f.*
independent, *adj.* unabhängig.
in-depth, *adj.* gründlich, Tie-fen- *(cpds.)*
index, *n.* Verzeich'nis, -se *nt.*, Regis'ter, - *nt.*; **(i. finger)** Zei-gefinger, - *m.*
India, *n.* Indien *nt.*
Indian, 1. *n.* Inder, - *m.*; **(American I.)** India'ner, - *m.* **2.** *adj.* indisch; india'-nisch.
indicate, *vb.* zeigen, an∙deuten.
indication, *n.* Hinweis, -e *m.*, Anzeichen, - *nt.*
indicative, 1. *n.* Indikativ, -e *m.* **2.** *adj.* bezeich'nend.
indicator, *n.* Zeiger, - *m.*, Indi-ka'tor, -o'ren *m.*; *(sign)* Zei-chen, - *nt.*
indict, *vb.* an∙klagen.
indictment, *n.* Anklage, -n *f.*
indifference, *n.* Gleichgültig-keit.
indifferent, *adj.* gleichgültig.
indigestion, *n.* Verdau'ungs-störung, -en *f.*
indignant, *adj.* entrüs'tet.
indignation, *n.* Entrüs'tung, - en *f.*
indignity, *n.* Unwürdigkeit, -en *f.*; *(insult)* Belei'digung, -en *f.*
indirect, *adj.* indirekt.
indiscreet, *adj.* indiskret.
indiscretion, *n.* Indiskretion', -en *f.*
indispensable, *adj.* unab-kömmlich.

indisposed, *adj.* unpäßlich; *(disinclined)* abgeneigt.
indisposition, *n.* Unpäßlich-keit, -en *f.*; Abneigung, -en *f.*
individual, 1. *n.* Einzeln- *m.*, Indivi'duum, -duen *nt.* **2.** *adj.* einzeln, individuell'.
individually, *n.* Individualität', -en *f.*
indivisible, *adj.* unteilbar.
indoctrinate, *vb.* schulen.
indolent, *adj.* träge.
Indonesia, *n.* Indone'sien *nt.*
indoor, *adj.* Haus-, Zimmer- *(cpds.)*
indoors, *adv.* zu Hause, drin-nen.
indorse, *vb.* gut∙heißen*; *(check)* girie'ren.
induce, *vb.* veran'lassen; *(elec.)* induzie'ren.
induct, *vb.* ein'führen; *(physics)* induzie'ren; *(mil.)* verei'di-gen.
induction, *n.* Einführung, -en *f.*; *(physics)* Induktion', -en *f.*; *(mil.)* Verei'digung, -en *f.*
inductive, *adj.* induktiv'.
indulge, *vb.* nach∙sehen*; frö-nen.
indulgence, *n.* Nachsicht, -en *f.*, Langmut *m.*, Frönen *nt.*; *(eccles.)* Ablaß, ¨sse *m.*
indulgent, *adj.* nachsichtig, langmütig, kommend.
industrial, *adj.* industriell', In-dustrie'- *(cpds.)*
industrialist, *n.* Industriell'- *m.*
industrious, *adj.* fleißig.
industry, *n.* Industrie', -i'en *f.*; *(hard work)* Fleiß *m.*
ineligible, *adj.* nicht wählbar; nicht in Frage kommend.
inept, *adj.* ungeschickt, unfä-hig.
inert, *adj.* träge.
inertia, *n.* Trägheit, -en *f.*
inevitable, *adj.* unvermeidlich.
infallible, *adj.* unfehlbar.
infamous, *adj.* berüch'tigt.
infamy, *n.* Niedertracht, -en *f.*, Schande, -n *f.*
infancy, *n.* Kindheit, -en *f.*; *(fig.)* Anfang, ¨e *m.*
infant, *n.* Säugling, -e *m.*
infantile, *adj.* kindlich, kin-disch.
infantry, *n.* Infanterie', -i'en *f.*
infantryman, *n.* Infantorist', - en, -en *m.*
infatuate, *vb.* betö'ren, hin-reißen*.
infect, *vb.* an∙stecken.
infected, *adj.* entzün'det.
infection, *n.* Entzün'dung, -en *f.*
infectious, *adj.* ansteckend.
infer, *vb.* folgern, an∙nehmen*.
inference, *n.* Folgerung, -en *f.*, Annahme, -n *f.*
inferior, *adj.* minderwertig, un-terle'gen.
inferiority, *n.* Minderwertig-

keit, -en *f.*, Unterle'genheit *f.*
infernal, *adj.* höllisch.
inferno, *n.* Hölle *f.*; Fegefeuer *nt.*
infest, *vb.* heim∙suchen.
infidel, *n.* Ungläubig- *m.&f.*
infidelity, *n.* Untreue *f.*
infiltrate, *vb.* ein∙dringen*, in-filtrie'ren.
infinite, *adj.* unendlich.
infinitesimal, *adj.* unendlich klein; winzig.
infinitive, *n.* Infinitiv, -e *m.*
infinity, *n.* Unendlichkeit, -en *f.*
infirm, *adj.* schwach (¨).
infirmary, *n.* Schul- oder Stu-den'tenkrankenhaus, ¨er *nt.*
infirmity, *n.* Schwachheit, -en *f.*
inflame, *vb.* entzün'den.
inflammable, *adj.* entzünd'bar, feuergefährlich.
inflammation, *n.* Entzün'dung, -en *f.*
inflate, *vb.* auf∙blasen*; *(tires)* auf∙pumpen.
inflation, *n.* Inflation', -en *f.*
inflection, *n.* Biegung, -en *f.*; *(voice)* Tonfall, ¨e *m.*; *(gram.)* Beugung, -en *f.*
inflict, *vb.* zu∙fügen.
infliction, *n.* Last, -en *f.*
influence, 1. *n.* Einfluß, ¨sse *m.* **2.** *vb.* beein'flussen.
influential, *adj.* einflußreich.
influenza, *n.* Grippe, -n *f.*
inform, *vb.* benach'richtigen, mit∙teilen; **(i. on)** denunzie'-ren.
informal, *adj.* zwanglos, nicht formell'.
information, *n.* Auskunft, ¨e *f.*
infringe, *vb.* übertre'ten*; *(jur.)* verlet'zen.
infuriate, *vb.* wütend machen, rasend machen, erbo'sen.
ingenious, *adj.* erfin'derisch, genial'.
ingenuity, *n.* Findigkeit *f.*, Ge-nialität' *f.*
ingredient, *n.* Bestand'teil, -e *m.*; *(cooking)* Zutat, -en *f.*
inhabit, *vb.* bewoh'nen.
inhabitant, *n.* Bewoh'ner, - *m.*, Einwohner, - *m.*
inhale, *vb.* ein∙atmen.
inherent, *adj.* angeboren, ei-gen.
inherit, *vb.* erben.
inheritance, *n.* Erbe *nt.*; Erb-schaft, -en *f.*
inhibit, *vb.* hindern, ab∙hal-ten*.
inhibition, *n.* Hemmung, -en *f.*
inhuman, *adj.* unmenschlich.
inimitable, *adj.* unnachahm-lich.
iniquity, *n.* Ungerechtigkeit, - en *f.*; Schändlichkeit, ¨en *f.*
initial, 1. *n.* Anf¨ stabe, -n, -n *m* fänglich; Anf¨

initiate, vb. ein·führen, ein··weihen.

initiation, n. Einführung, -en f., Einweihung, -en f.

initiative, n. Initiati've, -n f.

inject, vb. ein·spritzen.

injection, n. Einspritzung, -en f.

injunction, n. gerichtlicher Unterlas'sungsbefehl, -e m.

injure, vb. verlet'zen.

injurious, adj. schädlich; (fig.) nachteilig.

injury, n. Verlet'zung, -en f.; Schaden, ∹ m.

injustice, n. Ungerechtigkeit, -en f.

ink, n. Tinte, -n f.

inland, 1. n. Binnenland, ∹er nt. **2.** adj. inländisch.

inlet, n. kleine Bucht, -en f.

inmate, n. Insasse, -n, -n m.

inn, n. Gasthaus, ∹er nt., Wirtshaus, ∹er nt.

inner, adj. inner-.

innermost, adj. innerst-.

innocence, n. Unschuld f.

innocent, adj. unschuldig.

innovation, n. Neuerung, -en f.

innuendo, n. Unterstel'lung, -en f.

innumerable, adj. zahllos.

inoculate, vb. ein·impfen.

inoculation, n. Einimpfung, - f.

input, n. Input, -s m.; Eingabe, -n f.

inquest, n. gerichtliche Untersuchung, -en f.

inquire, vb. fragen, sich erkun'digen.

inquiry, n. Nachfrage, -n f.; Erkun'digung, -en f.

inquisition, n. Untersu'chung, -en f.; (eccles.) Inquisition', -en f.

inquisitive, adj. neugierig.

insane, adj. wahnsinnig.

insanity, n. Wahnsinn m.

inscribe, vb. ein·zeichnen, ein·schreiben*.

inscription, n. Inschrift, -en f.

insect, n. Insekt', -en nt.

insecticide, n. Insek'tenpulver, - nt.

insensible, adj. gefühl'los.

insensitive, adj. unempfindlich.

inseparable, adj. unzertrennlich.

insert, 1. n. Beilage, -n f. **2.** vb. ein·fügen, ein·setzen.

insertion, n. Einsatz, ∹e m.

inside, 1. n. Innenseite, -n f., Inner- nt. **2.** adj. inner-. **3.** adv. innen, drinnen.

insidious, adj. hinterlistig.

insight, n. Einsicht, -en f.

insignia, n.pl. Abzeichen, - nt.; Insig'nien pl.

insignificance, n. Bedeu'tungslosigkeit f.

insignificant, adj. bedeu'tungslos.

insinuate, vb. an·spielen auf;

(i. oneself) sich ein·schmeicheln.

insinuation, n. Anspielung, -en f.

insipid, adj. fade.

insist, vb. beste'hen*, behar'ren.

insistence, n. Beste'hen nt., Behar'ren nt.

insistent, adj. beharr'lich, hartnäckig.

insolence, n. Unverschämtheit, -en f.

insolent, adj. unverschämt.

insomnia, n. Schlaflosigkeit f.

inspect, vb. besich'tigen.

inspection, n. Besich'tigung, -en f.

inspector, n. Inspek'tor, -o'ren m.

inspiration, n. Eingebung, -en f., Inspiration', -en f.

inspire, vb. an·feuern, begeis'tern.

install, vb. ein·bauen; (fig.) ein·führen.

installation, n. Installation', -en f.

installment, n. Rate, -n f.; (i. plan) Ratenzahlung, -en f.

instance, n. (case) Fall, ∹e m.; (example) Beispiel, -e nt.; (law) Instanz', -en f.; (for i.) zum Beispiel.

instant, 1. n. Augenblick, -e m. **2.** adj. augenblicklich.

instantaneous, adj. sofor'tig.

instantly, adv. sofort', auf der Stelle.

instead, adv. statt dessen, dafür; (i. of) statt, anstatt'.

instigate, vb. veran'lassen, an·stacheln.

instill, vb. ein·flößen.

instinct, n. Instinkt', -e m.

instinctive, adj. unwillkürlich, instinktiv'.

institute, 1. n. Institut', -e nt. **2.** vb. ein·leiten, an·ordnen.

institution, n. Einrichtung, -en f.; Institut' -e nt., Anstalt, -en f.

instruct, vb. unterrich'ten, an·weisen*.

instruction, n. Anweisung, -en f.; (school) Unterricht m.

instructive, adj. lehrreich.

instructor, n. Lehrer, - m.

instructress, n. Lehrerin, -nen f.

instrument, n. Werkzeug, -e nt., Instrument', -e nt.

instrumental, adj. behilf'lich; (music) Instrumental'- (cpds.).

insufferable, adj. unerträglich.

insufficient, adj. ungenügend.

insulate, vb. insolie'ren.

insulation, n. Isolie'rung, -en f.

insulator, n. Isola'tor, -o'ren m.

insulin, n. Insulin' f.

insult, 1. n. Belei'digung, -en f. **2.** vb. belei'digen.

insurance, n. Versi'cherung, -en f.

insure, vb. versi'chern.

insurgent, 1. n. Aufständisch - m. **2.** adj. aufständisch.

insurrection, n. Aufstand, ∹e m.

intact, adj. intakt'.

intangible, adj. nicht greifbar.

integral, 1. n. (math.) Integral', -e nt. **2.** adj. unerläßlich.

integrate, vb. integrie'ren.

integrity, n. Unbescholtenheit f.

intellect, n. Verstand' m., Intellekt' m.

intellectual, 1. n. Intellektuell- m.&f. **2.** adj. intellektuell'.

intelligence, n. Intelligenz' f.

intelligent, adj. intelligent'.

intelligentsia, n. geistige Oberschicht f.

intelligible, adj. verständ'lich.

intend, vb. beab'sichtigen.

intense, adj. angespannt, intensiv'.

intensify, vb. verstär'ken.

intensive, adj. intensiv'.

intent, 1. n. Absicht, -en f. **2.** adj. erpicht'.

intention, n. Absicht, -en f.

intentional, adj. absichtlich.

inter, vb. beer'digen.

intercede, vb. dazwi'schen·treten*.

intercept, vb. ab·fangen*.

intercourse, n. Verkehr' m., Umgang m.

interest, 1. n. Interes'se, -n nt.; (comm.) Zins, -en m. **2.** vb. interessie'ren.

interesting, adj. interessant'.

interface, n. Schnittstelle, -n f.

interfere, vb. sich ein·mischen; ein·greifen*.

interference, n. Einmischung, -en f.; (radio) Störung, -en f.

interim, 1. n. Zwischenzeit, -en f. **2.** adj. Interims- (cpds.).

interior, 1. n. Inner- nt. **2.** adj. inner-; Innen- (cpds.).

interject, vb. dazwi'schen·werfen*.

interjection, n. Ausruf, -e m.; (gram.) Interjektion', -en f.

interlude, n. Zwischenspiel, -e nt.

intermarry, vb. untereinander heiraten.

intermediary, 1. n. Vermitt'ler, - m. **2.** adj. Zwischen- (cpds.).

intermediate, adj. Zwischen- (cpds.).

interment, n. Begräb'nis, -se nt.

intermission, n. Unterbre'chung, -en f.; (theater) Pause, -n f.

intermittent, adj. wechselnd, perio'disch.

intern, vb. internie'ren.

internal, adj. inner-, innerlich.

international, adj. international'.

internationalism, n. Internationa'lis'mus m.

interne, n. Volontär'arzt, -e m.
interpose, vb. ein·fügen.
interpret, vb. interpretie'ren; (language) dolmetschen.
interpretation, n. Interpreta'tion', -en f., Auslegung, -en f.
interpreter, n. Dolmetscher, - m.
interrogate, vb. aus·fragen; (law) verneh'men*, verhö'ren.
interrogation, n. Verhör', -e nt.
interrogative, 1. n. Fragewort, ¨er nt. 2. adj. fragend, Frage- (cpds.).
interrupt, vb. unterbre'chen*.
interruption, n. Unterbre'chung, -en f.
intersect, vb. (intr.) sich schneiden*, sich kreuzen; (tr.) durchschnei'den, durch·kreu'zen.
intersection, n. Kreuzung, -en f.
intersperse, vb. durchset'zen.
interval, n. Abstand, ¨e m.
intervene, vb. dazwi'schen·kommen*, sich ein·mischen.
intervention, n. Dazwi'schentreten nt., Einmischung, -en f.
interview, 1. n. Interview' -s nt. 2. vb. interview'en.
intestine, n. Darm, ¨e m.
intimacy, n. Vertrau'lichkeit, -en f.
intimate, adj. vertraut', innig.
intimidate, vb. ein·schüchtern.
intimidation, n. Einschüchterung, -en f.
into, prep. in.
intolerant, adj. intolerant.
intonation, n. Tonfall, ¨e m.
intoxicate, vb. berau'schen.
intoxication, n. Rausch, ¨e m.
intravenous, adj. intravenös'.
intrepid, adj. furchtlos.
intricacy, n. Kompliziert'heit, -en f.
intricate, adj. verwi'ckelt; kompliziert'.
intrigue, 1. n. Intri'ge, -n f. 2. vb. intrigie'ren.
intrinsic, adj. innerlich; wahr.
introduce, vb. ein·führen, ein·leiten; (persons) vor·stellen.
introduction, n. Einführung, -en f., Einleitung, -en f.; Vorstellung, -en f.
introductory, adj. einleitend.
introvert, n. nach innen gekehr'ter Mensch, -en, -en m.
intrude, vb. ein·dringen*.
intruder, n. Eindringling, -e m.
intuition, n. Intuition', -en f.
inundate, vb. überschwem'men.
invade, vb. ein·dringen*, ein·fallen*.
invader, n. Angreifer, - m.
invalid, 1. n. Invali'de, -n, -n m. 2. adj. ungültig.
invariable, adj. unveränderlich.
invasion, n. Invasion', -en f.
inveigle, vb. verlei'ten.
invent, vb. erfin'den*.

invention, n. Erfin'dung, -en f.
inventive, adj. erfin'derisch.
inventor, n. Erfin'der, - m.
inventory, n. Inventar', -e nt.; Inventur', -en f.
inverse, adj. umgekehrt.
invertebrate, adj. ohne Wirbelsäule.
invest, vb. investie'ren, an·legen.
investigate, vb. untersu'chen.
investigation, n. Untersu'chung, -en f.
investment, n. Kapitals'anlage, -n f.
inveterate, adj. eingefleischt.
invigorate, vb. bele'ben, erfri'schen.
invincible, adj. unbesiegbar.
invisible, adj. unsichtbar.
invitation, n. Einladung, -en f., Aufforderung, -en f.
invite, vb. ein·laden*, auf·fordern.
invocation, n. Anrufung, -en f.; (eccles.) Bittgebet, -e nt.
invoice, n. Warenrechnung, -en f.
invoke, vb. an·rufen*; erbit'ten.
involuntary, adj. unfreiwillig.
involve, vb. ein·schließen*; verwi'ckeln.
involved, adj. verwi'ckelt.
invulnerable, adj. unverletzlich; uneinnehmbar.
inward, adj. inner-, innerlich.
inwardly, adv. innerlich.
iodine, n. Jod nt.
Iran, n. Iran' nt.
Iraq, n. Irak' m.
irate, adj. zornig.
Ireland, n. Irland nt.
iridium, n. Iri'dium nt.
iris, n. Iris f.; (flower) Schwertlilie, -n f.
Irish, adj. irisch.
Irishman, n. Irländer,- m., Ire, -n, -n m.
Irishwoman, n. Irländerin, -nen f.
irk, vb. ärgern.
iron, 1. n. Eisen nt.; (flati.) Bügeleisen, - nt. 2. adj. eisern. 3. vb. bügeln.
ironical, adj. spöttisch, iro'nisch.
irony, n. Spott m., Ironie' f.
irrational, adj. irrational'.
irrefutable, adj. unwiderlegbar.
irregular, adj. unregelmäßig.
irregularity, n. Unregelmäßigkeit, -en f.
irrelevant, adj. belang'los; unanwendbar.
irresistible, adj. unwiderstehlich.
irresponsible, adj. unverantwortlich.
irreverent, adj. unehrerbietig.
irrevocable, adj. unwiderruflich.
irrigate, vb. bewäs'sern.
irrigation, n. Bewäs'serung, -en f.

irritability, n. Reizbarkeit f.
irritable, adj. reizbar.
irritant, n. Reizfaktor, -en m.
irritate, vb. reizen, irritie'ren.
irritation, n. Reizung, -en f.; Ärger m.
island, n. Insel, -n f.
isolate, vb. isolie'ren.
isolation, n. Isolie'rung, -en f.
isolationist, n. Isolationist', -en, -en m.
Israel, n. Israel nt.
Israeli, 1. n. Israe'li, -s m. 2. adj. israe'lisch.
Israelite, 1. n. Israelit', -en, -en m. 2. adj. israeli'tisch.
issuance, n. Ausgabe, -n f.
issue, 1. n. Ausgabe, -n f.; Problem', -e nt.; (result) Erbeg'nis, -se nt. 2. vb. aus·geben*, aus·stellen.
isthmus, n. Isthmus, -men nt.
it, pron. es.
Italian, 1. n. Italie'ner, - m. 2. adj. italie'nisch.
Italic, adj. ita'lisch.
italics, n. Kursiv'schrift f.
Italy, n. Ita'lien nt.
itch, 1. n. Jucken nt. 2. vb. jucken.
item, n. Arti'kel, - m., Posten, - m.
itemize, vb. auf·zählen.
itinerary, n. Reiseroute, -n f.
ivory, n. Elfenbein nt.
ivy, n. Efeu m.

J

jab, 1. n. Stoß, ¨e m., Stich, -e m. 2. vb. stoßen*, stechen*.
jack, n. (auto) Wagenheber, - m.; (card) Bube, -n, -n m.
jackal, n. Schakal', -e m.
jackass, n. Esel, - m.
jacket, n. Jacke, -n f.
jack-knife, n. Klappmesser, - nt.
jack-of-all-trades, n. Hans Dampf in allen Gassen m.
jade, n. Jade m.
jaded, adj. ermat'tet.
jagged, adj. zackig.
jail, n. Gefäng'nis, -se nt.
jailer, n. Gefäng'niswärter, - m.
jam, 1. n. Marmela'de, -n f., Konfitüre, -n f.; (trouble) Klemme, -n f. 2. vb. klemmen.
jangle, vb. rasseln.
janitor, n. Pförtner, - m., Hausmeister, - m.
January, n. Januar m.
Japan, n. Japan nt.
Japanese, 1. n. Japa'ner, - m. 2. adj. japa'nisch.
jar, 1. n. Krug, ¨e m., Glas, ¨er nt. 2. vb. rütteln.
jargon, n. Jargon', -s m.
jasmine, n. Jasmin', -e m.
jaundice, n. Gelbsucht f.
jaunt, n. kurze Reise, -n f.

javelin, n. Speer, -e m.

jaw, n. Kiefer, - m.

jay, n. Eichelhäher, - m.

jaywalk, vb. quer über eine Straßenkreuzung gehen*.

jazz, n. Jazz m.

jealous, adj. eifersüchtig.

jealousy, n. Eifersucht f.

jeans, n. Jeans pl.

jeer, vb. spotten.

jelly, n. Gelee', -s nt.

jeopardize, vb. gefähr'den.

jeopardy, n. Gefahr', -en f.

jerk, 1. n. Ruck, -e m. 2. vb. ruckartig bewe'gen.

jerky, adj. ruckartig.

jersey, n. Jersey, -s m.

Jerusalem, n. Jeru'salem nt.

jest, 1. n. Scherz, -e m. 2. vb. scherzen.

jester, n. Spaßmacher, - m.; (court f.) Hofnarr, -en, -en m.

Jesuit, 1. n. Jesuit', -en, -en m. 2. adj. jesui'tisch; Jesui'ten- (cpds.)

Jesus Christ, n. Jesus Christus m.

jet, n. Strahl, -en m.; (tech.) Düse, -n f.; (plane) Düsenflugzeug, -e nt.; (mineral) Pechkohle, -n f.

jet lag, n. Jet-lag m.; körperliches Unbehagen durch Zeitverschiebung.

jetsam, n. Strandgut nt.; über Bord gewor'fenes Gut nt.

jetty, n. Mole, -n f.

Jew, n. Jude, -n, -n m.

jewel, n. Juwel', -en nt., Edelstein, -e m.

jeweler, n. Juwelier', -e m.

jewelry, n. Schmucksachen pl., Schmuck m.

Jewish, adj. jüdisch.

jib, n. Klüver, - m.

jibe, vb. (sailing) halsen; (agree) sich decken.

jiffy, n. Nu m.

jig, n. Gigue f.

jilt, vb. sitzen lassen*.

jingle, vb. klingeln.

job, n. Stellung, -en f.; Aufgabe, -n f.

jobber, n. Zwischenhändler, - m.

jockey, n. Jockey, -s m.

jocular, adj. scherzhaft.

jog, vb. schubsen.

joggle, vb. (tr.) stubsen; (intr.) wackeln.

join, vb. verbin'den*; (club, etc.) bei·treten*.

joint, 1. n. Gelenk', -e nt. 2. adj. gemein'sam.

joist, n. Querbalken, - m.

joke, 1. n. Witz, -e m., Scherz, - e m., Spaß, -̈e m. 2. vb. einen Witz machen, scherzen.

joker, n. Witzbold, -e m.; (cards) Joker, - m.

jolly, adj. heiter.

jolt, 1. n. Stoß, -̈e m. 2. vb. rütteln.

jonquil, n. gelbe Narzis'se, -n f.

jostle, vb. stoßen*.

journal, n. Journal', -e nt.; (diary) Tagebuch, -̈er nt.; (newspaper) Zeitung, -en f.; (periodical) Zeitschrift, -en f.

journalism, n. Zeitungswesen nt.

journalist, n. Journalist', -en, -en m.

journey, n. Reise, -n f.

journeyman, n. Gesel'le, -n, -n m.

jovial, adj. jovial'.

jowl, n. Backe, -n f.

joy, n. Freude, -n f.

joyful, adj. freudig.

joyous, adj. freudig.

jubilant, adj. frohlockend.

jubilee, n. Jubilä'um, -ä'en nt.

Judaism, n. Judentum nt.

judge, 1. n. Kenner, - m.; (law) Richter, - m. 2. vb. beur'teilen; (law) richten, Recht sprechen*.

judgment, n. Urteil, -e nt.; (law also:) Rechtsspruch, -̈e m.

judicial, adj. richterlich; Gerichts'- (cpds.)

judiciary, 1. n. Justiz'gewalt f.; Richterstand m. 2. adj. richterlich.

judicious, adj. weise, klug.

jug, n. Krug, -̈e m.

juggle, vb. jonglie'ren.

juggler, n. Jongleur', -e m.

juice, n. Saft, -̈e m.

juicy, adj. saftig.

July, n. Juli m.

jumble, n. Durcheinan'der nt.

jump, 1. n. Sprung, -̈e m. 2. vb. springen*.

junction, n. Verbin'dung, -en f.; (railroad) Knotenpunkt, -e m.

juncture, n. Zusam'mentreffen, - nt.

June, n. Juni m.

jungle, n. Dschungel, - m. or nt. (or -n f.).

junior, adj. jünger.

juniper, n. Wachol'der, - m.

junk, n. Altwaren pl.; (fig.) Kram m.

junket, n. (food) Milchpudding m.; (trip) Reise, -n f.

jurisdiction, n. Rechtsprechung, -en f.; Gerichts'barkeit f.; Zuständigkeit f.

jurisprudence, n. Rechtswissenschaft f.

jurist, n. Rechtsgelehrt- m.

juror, n. Geschwo'ren- m.&f.

jury, n. Geschwo'ren- pl.

just, 1. adj. gerecht'. 2. adv. gera'de, eben.

justice, n. Gerech'tigkeit f.

justifiable, adj. berech'tigt.

justification, n. Rechtfertigung, -en f., Berech'tigung, -en f.

justify, vb. rechtfertigen.

jut, vb. hervor'stehen*.

jute, n. Jute f.

juvenile, adj. jugendlich.

K

kale, n. Grünkohl m.

kaleidoscope, n. Kaleidoskop', -e nt.

kangaroo, n. Känguruh', -s nt.

karat, n. Karat', -e nt.

karate, n. Kara'te nt.

keel, n. Kiel, -e m.

keen, adj. scharf; (fig.) eifrig.

keep, 1. n. (lodging) Unterhalt m. 2. vb. behal'ten*, bewah'ren; (animals, etc.) halten*; (k. doing something) etwas immer wieder tun*; (k. on doing something) etwas weiter tun*.

keeper, n. Wärter, - m., Wächter, - m.

keepsake, n. Andenken, - nt.

keg, n. Faß, -̈sser nt.

kennel, n. Hundezwinger, - m.

kerchief, n. Halstuch, -̈er nt.; Kopftuch, -̈er nt.

kernel, n. Kern. -e m.; (grain) Korn, -̈er nt.

kerosene, n. Kerosin' nt.

ketchup, n. Ketchup nt.

kettle, n. Kessel, - m.

kettledrum, n. Kesselpauke, -n f.

key, n. Schlüssel, - m.; (piano) Taste, -n f.; (musical structure) Tonart, -en f.

keyhole, n. Schlüsselloch, -̈er nt.

khaki, n. Khaki nt.

kick, 1. n. Stoß, -̈e m., Tritt, -e m. 2. vb. stoßen*, treten*.

kid, 1. n. (goat) Zicklein, - nt.; (child) Kind, -er nt. 2. vb. necken, rein·legen.

kidnap, vb. gewalt'sam entfüh'ren.

kidnaper, n. Kinderräuber, - m.

kidnaping, n. Kinderraub m.

kidney, n. Niere, -n f.

kidney bean, n. Schminkbohne, -n f.

kill, vb. töten, um·bringen*.

killer, n. Mörder, - m.

kiln, n. Brennofen, - m.

kilocycle, n. Kilohertz, - nt.

kilogram, n. Kilo, - nt.

kilohertz, n. Kilohertz nt.

kilometer, n. Kilome'ter, - nt.

kilowatt, n. Kilowatt, - nt.

kilt, n. Kilt, -s m.

kimono, n. Kimo'no, -s m.

kin, n. Verwandt'schaft, -en f.

kind, 1. n. Art, -en f., Sorte, -n f. 2. adj. gütig, freundlich.

kindergarten, n. Kindergarten, - m.

kindle, vb. an·zünden, entzün'den.

kindly, adj. freundlich.

kindness, n. Güte f., Freundlichkeit f.

kindred, adj. verwandt'.

king, *n.* König, -e *m.*

kingdom, *n.* Königreich, -e *nt.*

kink, *n.* Knoten, - *m.*

kiosk, *n.* Kiosk, -e *m.*

kiss, 1. *n.* Kuß, ̈sse *m.* **2.** *vb.* küssen.

kitchen, *n.* Küche, -n *f.*

kite, *n.* Drachen, - *m.; (bird)* Milan, -e *m.*

kitten, *n.* Kätzchen, - *nt.*

kleptomaniac, *n.* Kleptoma'ne, -n, -n *m.*

knack, *n.* Talent', -e *nt.*

knapsack, *n.* Rucksack, ̈e *m.*

knead, *vb.* kneten.

knee, *n.* Knie, Kni'e *nt.*

kneel, *vb.* knien.

knickers, *n.pl.* Kniehose, -n *f.*

knife, *n.* Messer, - *nt.*

knight, 1. *nn.* Ritter, - *m.; (chess)* Springer, - *m.*

knit, *vb.* stricken; *(fig.)* verknüp'fen.

knock, 1. *n.* Klopfen *nt.* **2.** *vb.* klopfen.

knot, 1. *n.* Knoten, - *m.; (wood)* Knorren, - *m.* **2.** *vb.* knoten.

knotty, *adj.* knotig; *(wood)* knorrig; *(fig.)* schwierig.

know, *vb. (facts)* wissen*; *(people, places, things)* kennen*.

knowledge, *n.* Kenntnis, -se *f.;* Wissen *nt.*

knuckle, *n.* Knöchel, - *m.*

Korea, *n.* Kore'a *nt.*

L

label, *n.* Etiket'te, -n *f.*

labor, 1. *n.* Arbeit, -en *f.; (workers)* Arbeiterschaft *f.; (birth)* Wehen *pl.* **2.** *vb.* arbeiten.

laboratory, *n.* Laborato'rium, -rien *nt.*

laborer, *n.* Arbeiter, - *m.*

laborious, *adj.* arbeitsam, mühselig.

labor union, *n.* Gewerk'schaft, -en *f.*

labyrinth, *n.* Labyrinth', -e *nt.*

lace, *n.* Spitze, -n *f.*

lacerate, *vb.* auf•reißen*.

laceration, *n.* Riß, -sse *m.*

lack, 1. *n.* Mangel, ̈ *m.* **2.** *vb.* Mangel leiden* an; **(I 1. something)** es fehlt, mangelt mir an etwas.

lackadaisical, *adj.* schwunglos, unlustig.

laconic, *adj.* lako'nisch.

lacquer, 1. *n.* Lack, -e *m.* **2.** *vb.* lackie'ren.

lacy, *adj.* spitzenartig; Spitzen- *(cpds.).*

lad, *n.* Knabe, -n, -n *m.*

ladder, *n.* Leiter, -n *f.*

ladle, *n.* Schöpflöffel, - *m.*

lady, *n.* Dame, -n *f.*

ladybug, *n.* Mari'enkäfer, - *m.*

lag, *n.* Verzö'gerung, -en *f.*

lag behind, *vb.* zurück'•bleiben*.

lagoon, *n.* Lagu'ne, -n *f.*

laid-back, *adj.* entspannt, unverkrampft, die Dinge auf sich zukommen lassend.

lair, *n.* Lagerstatt, ̈e *f.;* Höhle, -n *f.*

laity, *n.* Laienstand *m.,* Laien *pl.*

lake, *n.* See, Se'en *m.*

lamb, *n.* Lamm, ̈er *nt.*

lame, *adj.* lahm.

lament, 1. *n.* Wehklage, -n *f.* **2.** *vb.* bekla'gen.

lamentable, *adj.* bekla'genswert.

lamentation, *n.* Wehklage, -n *f.*

laminate, *vb. (metal)* aus•walzen, plattie'ren; **(l.d wood)** Furnier'holz nt.

lamp, *n.* Lampe, -n *f.*

lance, 1. *n.* Lanze, -n *f.* **2.** *vb.* durchsto'ßen*; *(med.)* mit der Lanzet'te öffnen.

land, 1. *n. (country)* Land, ̈er *nt.; (ground)* Grund und Boden *m.* **2.** *vb.* landen.

landing, *n.* Landung, -en *f.; (stairs)* Treppenabsatz, ̈e *m.*

landlady, *n.* Wirtin, -nen *f.;* Hausbesitzerin, -nen *f.*

landlord, *n.* Wirt, -e *m.;* Hausbesitzer, - *m.*

landmark, *n.* Markstein, -e *m.*

landscape, *n.* Landschaft, -en *f.*

landslide, *n.* Erdrutsch, -e *m.; (election)* überwäl'tigender Wahlsieg, -e *m.*

lane, *n.* Pfad, -e *m.; (boat)* Fahrrinne, -n *f.; (auto)* Fahrbahn, -en *f.*

language, *n.* Sprache, -n *f.*

languid, *adj.* energie'los, schlaff.

languish, *vb.* schmachten.

lanky, *adj.* baumlang.

lanolin, *n.* Lanolin' *nt.*

lantern, *n.* Later'ne, -n *f.*

lap, 1. *n.* Schloß, ̈e *m.; (sport)* Runde, -n *f.* **2.** *vb.* übereinan'der•legen.

lapel, *n.* Revers', - *m.*

lapin, *n.* Kanin'chenpelz *m.*

lapse, 1. *n. (error)* Lapsus - *m.,* Verse'hen, - *nt.; (time)* Zwischenzeit, -en *f.* **2.** *vb.* verstrei'chen*.

larceny, *n.* Diebstahl, ̈e *m.*

lard, *n.* Schweinefett *nt.*

large, *adj.* groß (größer, größt-); weit; umfangreich.

largely, *adv.* größtenteils.

largo, *adj.* Largo, -s *nt.*

lariat, *n.* Lasso, -s *nt.*

lark, *n.* Lerche, -n *f.; (fun)* Vergnü'gen *nt.*

larkspur, *n.* Rittersporn *m.*

larva, *n.* Larve, -n *f.*

laryngitis, *n.* Kehlkopfentzündung, -en *f.*

larynx, *n.* Kehlkopf, ̈e *m.*

lascivious, *adj.* wollüstig.

laser, *n.* Laser *m.*

lash, 1. *n.* Peitsche, -n *f.;* Peitschenhieb, -e *m.; (eye)* Wimper, -n *f.* **2.** *vb.* peitschen.

lass, *n.* Mädchen, - *nt.*

lasso, *n.* Lasso, -s *nt.*

last, 1. *n.* Leisten, - *m.* **2.** *adj.* letzt-. **3.** *vb.* dauern.

lasting, *adj.* dauernd, anhaltend, bestän'dig.

latch, 1. *n.* Klinke, -n *f.* **2.** *vb.* ein•klinken.

late, *adj.* spät, verspä'tet; *(dead)* verstor'ben.

lately, *adv.* in letzter Zeit.

latent, *adj.* latent.

lateral, *adj.* seitlich.

lath, *n.* Latte, -n *f.*

lathe, *n.* Drehbank, ̈e *f.*

lather, *n.* Schaum *m.*

Latin, 1. *n. (language)* Latein' *nt.; (person)* Roma'ne, -n, -n *m.* **2.** *adj.* latei'nisch; roma'nisch.

latitude, *n.* Breite, -n *f.*

latrine, *n.* Latri'ne, -n *f.*

latter, 1. *adj.* letzter-. **2.** *pron.* **(the l.)** dieser, -es, -e.

lattice, *n.* Gitterwerk *nt.*

laud, *vb.* loben, preisen*.

laudable, *adj.* lobenswert.

laudanum, *n.* Laudanum *nt.*

laudatory, *adj.* Lob- *(cpds.).*

laugh, 1. *n.* Lachen *nt.* **2.** *vb.* lachen.

laughable, *adj.* lächerlich.

laughter, *n.* Geläch'ter *nt.*

launch, 1. *n.* Barkas'se, -n *f.* **2.** *vb. (throw)* schleudern; *(boat)* vom Stapel lassen*.

launching, *n.* Stapellauf, ̈e *m.*

launder, *vb.* waschen*.

laundress, *n.* Waschfrau, -en *f.*

laundry, *n. (clothes)* Wäsche *f.; (establishment)* Wäscherei', -en *f.*

laundryman, *n.* Wäscherei'angestellt- *m.*

laurel, *n.* Lorbeer, -en *m.*

lava, *n.* Lava *f.*

lavatory, *n.* Waschraum, ̈e *m.*

lavender, *n.* Laven'del *m.*

lavish, *adj.* üppig.

law, *n. (individual)* Gesetz' -e *nt.; (system)* Recht *nt.*

lawful, *adj.* gesetz'lich, rechtmäßig.

lawless, *adj.* gesetz'los; *(fig.)* zügellos.

lawn, *n.* Rasen *m.*

lawsuit, *n.* Prozeß', -sse *m.*

lawyer, *n.* Rechtsanwalt, ̈e *m.;* Jurist', -en, -en *m.*

lax, *adj.* lax.

laxative, *n.* Abführmittel, - *nt.*

laxity, *n.* Laxheit *f.*

lay 1. *adj.* Laien- *(cpds.).* **2.** *vb.* legen.

layer, *n.* Schicht, -en *f.*

layman, *n.* Laie, -n, -n *m.*

lazy, *adj.* faul.

lead, 1. *n.* Führung *f.,* Leitung *f.; (metal)* Blei *nt.* **2.** *vb.* führen, leiten.

leaden, *adj.* bleiern.

leader, *n.* Führer, - *m.;* Leiter, - *m.*

leadership, *n.* Führung *f.*

lead pencil, *n.* Bleistift, -e *m.*

leaf, *n.* Blatt, ¨er *nt.*

leaflet, *n.* Broschü're, -n *f.;* Flugblatt, ¨er *nt.*

league, *n.* Bund, ¨e *m.,* Bünd'nis, -se *nt.*

League of Nations, *n.* Völkerbund *m.*

leak, 1. *n.* Leck, -e *nt.* **2.** *vb.* lecken.

leakage, *n.* Durchsickern *nt.*

leaky, *adj.* leck, undicht.

lean, 1. *adj.* mager. **2.** *vb.* lehnen.

leap, 1. *n.* Sprung, ¨e *m.* **2.** *vb.* springen*.

leap year, *n.* Schaltjahr, -e *nt.*

learn, *vb.* lernen; erfah'ren*.

learned, *adj.* gelehrt'.

learning, *n.* Wissen *nt.,* Bildung *f.*

lease, 1. *n.* Mietvertrag, ¨e *m.,* Pacht, -en *f.* **2.** *vb.* mieten, pachten.

leash, *n.* Leine, -n *f.*

least, *adj. (slightest)* geringst'-; *(smallest)* kleinst-; **(at l.,** *in any case)* wenigstens; **(at l.,** *surely this much)* mindestens, zum mindesten.

leather, 1. *n.* Leder, – *nt.* **2.** *adj.* ledern.

leathery, *adj.* ledern.

leave, 1. *n. (farewell)* Abschied, -e *m.; (permission)* Erlaub'nis, -e *f.; (furlough)* Urlaub, - e *m.* **2.** *vb. (depart)* ab-fah'ren*; *(go away)* fort-gehen*; *(abandon)* verlas'sen*; *(let)* lassen*.

leaven, *n.* Sauerteig, -e *m.*

lecherous, *adj.* lüstern.

lecture, 1. *n.* Vortrag, ¨e *m.; (academic)* Vorlesung, -en *f.* **2.** *vb.* einen Vortrag halten*; eine Vorlesung halten*.

lecturer, *n.* Vortragend- *m.*

ledge, *n.* Felsvorsprung, ¨e *m.;* Sims, -e *m.*

ledger, *n.* Hauptbuch, ¨er *nt.*

lee, *n.* Lee *f.*

leech, *n.* Blutegel, - *m.*

leek, *n.* Lauch, -e *m.*

leer, *vb.* begehr'lich schielen.

leeward, *adv.* leewärts.

left, 1. *n. (pol.)* Link- *f.* **2.** *adj.* link-; **(l. over)** übriggeblieben. **3.** *adv.* links.

leftist, *adj.* links orientiert'.

left-over, *n.* Überbleibsel, - *nt.,* Rest, -e *m.*

leg, *n.* Bein, -e *nt.*

legacy, *n.* Vermächt'nis, -se *nt.,* Erbschaft, -en *f.*

legal, *adj.* gesetz'lich, gesetz'mäßig.

legalize, *vb.* legalisie'ren.

legation, *n.* Gesandt'schaft, - en *f.*

legend, *n.* Legen'de, -n *f.*

legendary, *adj.* legendär'.

legible, *adj.* leserlich.

legion, *n.* Legion', -e *f.*

legislate, *vb.* Gesetze geben*.

legislation, *n.* Gesetz'gebung *f.*

legislator, *n.* Gesetz'geber, - *m.*

legislature, *n.* gesetz'gebende Gewalt' *f.;* gesetz'gebende Versamm'lung, -en *f.*

legitimate, *adj.* legitim'.

leisure, *n.* Muße *f.*

leisurely, *adj.* gemäch'lich.

lemon, *n.* Zitro'ne, -n *f.*

lemonade, *n.* Limona'de, -n *f.*

lend, *vb.* leihen*.

length, *n.* Länge, -n *f.; (time)* Dauer *f.*

lengthen, *vb.* verlän'gern.

lengthwise, *adv.* der Länge nach.

lengthy, *adj.* langwierig.

lenient, *adj.* mild, nachsichtig.

lens, *n.* Linse, -n *f.; (photo)* Objectiv', -e *nt.*

Lent, *n.* Fastenzeit *f.*

Lenten, *adj.* Fasten- *(cpds.).*

lentil, *n.* Linse, -n *f.*

leopard, *n.* Leopard', -en, -en *m.*

leper, *n.* Aussätzig- *m.&f.*

leprosy, *n.* Aussatz *m.*

lesbian, *adj.* lesbisch.

lesion, *n.* Verlet'zung, -en *f.*

less, *adj.* weniger.

lessen, *vb. (tr.)* vermin'dern; *(intr.)* nach-lassen*.

lesser, *adj. (size)* kleiner; *(degree)* gerin'ger.

lesson, *n.* Lehre, -n *f.; (school)* Lehrstunde, -n *f.; (assignment)* Aufgabe, -n *f.*

lest, *conj.* damit' . . . nicht.

let, *vb. (allow)* lassen*; *(lease)* vermie'ten.

letdown, *n.* Enttäu'schung, -en *f.*

lethal, *adj.* tödlich.

lethargic, *adj.* teilnahmslos, lethar'gisch.

lethargy, *n.* Teilnahmslosigkeit *f.,* Lethargie' *f.*

letter, *n. (alphabet)* Buchstabe(n), - *(or -n, -n) m.; (communication)* Brief, -e *m.*

letterhead, *n.* Briefkopf, ¨e *m.*

lettuce, *n.* Kopfsalat, -e *m.*

leukemia, *n.* Leukämie' *f.*

levee, *n.* Damm, ¨e *m.*

level, 1. *n.* Stand, ¨e *m.,* Niveau', -s *nt.* **2.** *adj.* eben, gera'de; flach. **3.** *vb.* ebnen; gleich-machen.

lever, *n.* Hebel, - *m.*

levity, *n.* Leichtsinn *m.*

levy, 1. *n.* Abgabe, -n *f.,* Steuer, -n *f.*

lewd, *adj.* unzüchtig.

lexicon, *n.* Lexikon, -ka *nt.*

liability, *n.* Verant'wortlichkeit, -en *f.;* Verpflich'tung, - en *f.*

liable, *adj.* verant'wortlich; *(law)* haftbar.

liaison, *n.* Verbin'dung, -en *f.;* Liaison', -s *f.*

liar, *n.* Lügner, - *m.*

libel, *n.* Verleum'dung, -en *f.*

libelous, *adj.* verleum'derisch.

liberal, 1. *n.* Liberal'- *m.* **2.** *adj.* liberal'.

liberalism, *n.* Liberalis'mus *m.*

liberality, *n.* Freigebigkeit *f.;* Freisinnigkeit *f.*

liberate, *vb.* befrei'en.

liberation, *n.* Befrei'ung, -en *f.*

libertine, *n.* Lüstling, -e *m.*

liberty, *n.* Freiheit, -en *f.*

libido, *n.* Libido *f.*

librarian, *n.* Bibliothekar', - *m.;* Bibliotheka'rin, -nen *f.*

library, *n.* Bibliothek', -en *f.,* Bücherei, -en *f.*

libretto, *n.* Libret'to, -s *nt.*

license, *n.* Erlaub'nis, -se *f.; (driver's l.)* Führerschein, -e *m.*

lick, *n.* lecken.

licorice, *n.* Lakrit'ze, -n *f.*

lid, *n.* Deckel, - *m.; (eye)* Lid, - er *nt.*

lie, 1. *n.* Lüge, -n *f.* **2.** *vb. (tell untruths)* lügen*; *(recline)* liegen*; **(l. down)** sich (hin·)-legen.

lien, *n.* dinglich gesi'chertes Anrecht *nt.*

lieutenant, *n.* Leutnant, -s *m.*

life, *n.* Leben, - *nt.*

lifeboat, *n.* Rettungsboot, -e *nt.*

lifeguard, *n.* Bademeister, - *m.*

life insurance, *n.* Lebensversicherung, -en *f.*

lifeless, *adj.* leblos.

life preserver, *n.* Rettungsring, -e *m.; (vest)* Schwimmweste, - n *f.*

life style, *n.* Lebensstil *m.*

lifetime, *n.* Lebenszeit, -en *f.*

lift, 1. *n.* Fahrstuhl, ¨e *m.* **2.** *vb.* heben*.

ligament, *n.* Sehne, -n *f.*

ligature, *n.* Ligatur', -en *f.*

light, 1. *n.* Licht, -er *nt.* **2.** *adj. (color)* hell; *(weight)* leicht. **3.** *vb. (fire)* an'zünden; *(illuminate)* beleuch'ten.

lighten, *vb.* leichter machen; *(fig.)* erleich'tern; *(lightning)* blitzen.

lighter, *n. (cigar, cigarette)* Feuerzeug, -e *nt.*

lighthouse, *n.* Leuchtturm, -¨e *m.*

lightness, *n. (color)* Helligkeit *f.; (ease)* Leichtfertigkeit *f.*

lightning, *n.* Blitz, -e *m.*

like, 1. *adj.* gleich. **2.** *vb.* gern haben*, (gern) mögen*; **(I l. it)** es gefällt' mir; **(I l. to do it)** ich tue(*) es gern, ich mag es gern; **(l. this, l. that)** so.

likeable, *adj.* angenehm, liebenswert.

likelihood, *n.* Wahrschein'lichkeit, -en *f.*

likely, *adj.* wahrschein'lich.

liken, vb. verglei'chen*.

likeness, n. Ähnlichkeit, -en f.

likewise, adv. ebenso.

lilac, n. Flieder m.

lilt, n. wiegender Rhythmus m.

lily, n. Lilie, -n f.

lily of the valley, n. Maiglöckchen, - nt.

limb, n. Glied, -er nt.

limber, adj. biegsam.

limbo, n. Vorhölle f.

lime, n. Kalk m.; (fruit) Limo'ne, -n f.

limelight, n. Rampenlicht, -er nt.

limestone, n. Kalkstein m.

limit, 1. n. Grenze, -n f.; Höchstgrenze, -n f. 2. vb. begren'zen, beschrän'ken.

limitation, n. Begren'zung, -en f., Beschrän'kung, -en f.

limited, adj. begrenzt', beschränkt'.

limitless, adj. unbegrenzt.

limousine, n. Limousi'ne -n f.

limp, 1. adj. schlaff. 2. vb. hinken.

linden, n. Linde, -n f.

line, n. Linie, -n f.; (mark) Strich, -e m. (row) Reihe, -n f.; (writing) Zeile, -n f.; (rope) Leine, -n f.

lineage, n. Geschlecht', -er nt.

lineal, adj. in gerader Linie.

linear, adj. linear'.

linen, 1. n. Leinen (n.; (household) Wäsche f. 2. adj. leinen.

liner, n. (boat) Ozeandampfer, - m.

linger, vb. verwei'len.

lingerie, n. Damenunterwäsche f.

linguist, n. Sprachwissenschaftler, - m., Linguist', -en, -en m.

linguistic, adj. sprachlich; sprachwissenschaftlich, lingu'istisch.

linguistics, n. Sprachwissenschaft, -en f.; Linguis'tik f.

liniment, n. Einreibemittel, - nt.

lining, n. Futter, - nt.

link, 1. n. (bond) Band, -e nt.; (chain) Glied, -er nt. 2. vb. verbin'den*; verket'ten.

linoleum, n. Lino'leum nt.

linseed oil, n. Leinöl nt.

lint, n. Fussel, -n f.

lion, n. Löwe, -n, -n m.

lip, n. Lippe, -n f.

lip-stick, n. Lippenstift, -e m.

liquefy, vb. flüssig machen.

liqueur, n. Likör', -e m.

liquid, 1. n. Flüssigkeit, -en f. 2. adj. flüssig.

liquidate, vb. liquidie'ren.

liquidation, n. Liquidation', -en f.

liquor, n. Alkohol m., Spiritu'o'sen pl.

lira, n. Lira, -re f.

lisp, vb. lispeln.

lisle, n. Baumwollfaden m.

list, 1. n. Liste, -n f., Verzeich'nis, -se nt.; (ship) Schlagseite f. 2. vb. verzeich'nen.

listen, vb. zu·hören, horchen.

listless, adj. lustlos.

litany, n. Litanei' f.

liter, n. Liter, - nt.

literacy, n. Lesen und Schreiben Können nt.

literal, adj. buchstäblich, wörtlich.

literary, adj. litera'risch.

literate, adj. des Lesens und Schreibens kundig.

literature, n. Literatur', -en f.

lithe, adj. geschmei'dig.

lithograph, 1. n. Lithographie', -i'en f. 2. vb. lit'hgraphie'ren.

litigant, n. Rechtsstreitführer, - m.

litigation, n. Rechtsstreit, -e m.

litter, 1. n. (rubbish) Abfall, (e m.; (stretcher) Tragbahre, -n f.; (puppies, kittens, etc.) Wurf, (e m. 2. vb. Sachen herum'·liegen lassen*.

little, adj. (size) klein; (amount) wenig; (a l.) ein bißchen, ein wenig.

liturgical, adj. litur'gisch.

liturgy, n. Liturgie', -i'en f.

live, 1. adj. leben'dig. 2. vb. (be alive) leben; (dwell) wohnen.

livelihood, n. Lebensunterhalt m.

lively, adj. lebhaft.

liver, n. Leber, -n f.

livery, n. Livree', -s f.

livestock, n. Viehbestand m.

livid, adj. aschfahl.

living, 1. n. Leben nt.; Lebensweise f. 2. adj. lebend.

lizard, n. Eidechse, -n f.

lo, interj. siehe!

load, 1. n. Ladung, -en f., (burden) Last, -en f. 2. vb. laden*.

loaf, 1. n. Laib, -e m. 2. vb. faulenzen.

loafer, n. Faulenzer, - m.

loam, n. Lehm m.

loan, 1. n. Anleihe, -n f. 2. vb. leihen*.

loath, adj. abgeneigt.

loathe, vb. verab'scheuen.

loathing, n. Abscheu f.

loathsome, adj. widerlich, ekelhaft.

lobby, n. Wandelhalle, -n f.; (political) Interes'sengruppe, -n f.

lobe, n. Lappen, - m.

lobster, n. Hummer, - m.

local, 1. n. (train) Vorortzug, (e m. 2. adj. örtlich, lokal'.

locale, n. Schauplatz, (e m.

locality, n. Ort, -e m.

localize, vb. lokalisie'ren.

locate, vb. finden*; (be l.d) liegen*.

location, n. Lage, -n f.

lock, 1. n. Schloß, (er nt.; (canal) Schleuse, -n f.; (hair) Locke, -n f. 2. vb. ab·schließen*.

locker, n. Schrank, (e m.; (baggage) Schließfach, (er nt.

lockjaw, n. Kieferkrampf.

locksmith, n. Schlosser, - m.

locomotion, n. Fortbewegung, -en f.

locomotive, n. Lokomoti've, -n f.

locust, n. Heuschrecke, -n f.

lode, n. Erzader, -n f.

lodge, 1. n. Häuschen, - nt.; (fraternal) Loge -n f. 2. vb. (intr.) logie'ren; (tr.) beherbergen.

lodger, n. Untermieter, - m.

lodging, n. Unterkunft, (e f.

loft, n. Boden, (= m.; (warehouse) Speicher, - m.

lofty, adj. erha'ben.

log, n. Holzklotz, (e m.; (tree trunk) Baumstamm, (e m.; (ship's l.) Logbuch, (er nt.

loge, n. Loge, -n f.

logic, n. Logik f.

logical, adj. logisch.

loin, n. Lende, -n f.

loiter, vb. herum'·stehen*.

London, n. London nt.

lone, lonely, lonesome, adj. einsam.

loneliness, n. Einsamkeit f.

long, 1. adj. lang (-). 2. vb. sich sehnen.

longevity, n. Langlebigkeit f.

longing, 1. n. Sehnsucht f. 2. adj. sehnsüchtig.

longitude, n. Länge f.

longitudinal, adj. Längen-(cpds.).

long-lived, adj. langlebig.

long playing record, n. Langspielplatte, -n f.

look, 1. n. Blick, -e m.; (appearance, l.s) Aussehen nt. 2. vb. sehen*, schauen, blicken, gucken; (l. at) an·sehen*, ·schauen, ·blicken, ·gucken; (l. good, etc.) gut (etc.) aus·sehen*; (l. out, be careful) auf·passen.

looking glass, n. Spiegel, - m.

loom, n. Webstuhl, (e m.

loop, n. Schlaufe, -n f.

loophole, n. Schlupfloch, (er nt.

loose, adj. lose, locker.

loosen, vb. lockern.

loot, 1. n. Beute f. 2. vb. plündern.

lop off, vb. ab·schlagen*.

lopsided, adj. schief.

loquacious, adj. schwatzhaft.

lord, n. Herr, -n, -en m.; (title) Lord, -s m.

lordship, n. Herrschaft, -en f.

lose, vb. verlie'ren*.

loss, n. Verlust', -e m.

lot, n. Los, -e nt.; (quantity) Menge, -n f.; (ground) Grundstück, -e nt.

lotion, n. Lotion', -en f.

lottery, n. Lotterie', -i'en f.

lotus, n. Lotosblume, -n f.

loud, *adj.* laut; *(color)* grell.

loud-speaker, *n.* Lautsprecher, - *m.*

lounge, 1. *n.* Vorhalle, -n *f.* **2.** *vb.* herum'lungern.

louse, *n.* Laus, ⁼e *f.*

lout, *n.* Lümmel, - *m.*

louver, *n.* Lattenfenster, - *nt.*

lovable, *adj.* liebenswert.

love, 1. *n.* Liebe, -n *f.* **2.** *vb.* lieben; **(fall in l.)** sich verlie'ben.

lovely, *adj.* lieblich, reizend.

lover, *n.* Liebhaber, - *m.*

low, *adj.* niedrig, tief; *(nasty)* gemein'.

lowbrow, *adj.* unintellektuell, ungeistig.

lower, 1. *adj.* tiefer, niedriger; gemei'ner. **2.** *vb.* herun'terlassen*; herab'setzen, senken.

lowly, *adj.* beschei'den.

loyal, *adj.* treu.

loyalist, *n.* Regie'rungstreu, - *m.*

loyalty, *n.* Treue *f.,* Loyalität' *f.*

lozenge, *n.* Pastil'le, -n *f.*

lubricant, *n.* Schmiermittel, - *nt.*

lubricate, *vb.* schmieren.

lucid, *adj.* klar.

luck, *n.* Glück *nt.,* Zufall, ⁼e *m.*

lucky, *adj.* glücklich; **(be l.)** Glück haben*.

lucrative, *adj.* gewinn'bringend.

ludicrous, *adj.* lächerlich.

lug, *vb.* schleppen.

luggage, *n.* Gepäck' *nt.*

lukewarm, *adj.* lauwarm.

lull, 1. *n.* Pause, -n *f.* **2.** *vb.* beru'higen; **(l. to sleep)** ein·schläfern.

lullaby, *n.* Wigenlied, -er *nt.*

lumbago, *n.* Hexenschuß *m.*

lumber, *n.* Holz *nt.*

luminous, *adj.* leuchtend.

lump, *n.* Klumpen, - *m.,* *(skin)* Beule, -n *f.*

lumpy, *adj.* klumpig.

lunacy, *n.* Irrsinn *m.*

lunar, *adj.* Mond- *(cpds.).*

lunatic, 1. *n.* Irrsinnig- *m.* **2.** *adj.* irrsinnig.

lunch, *n.* leichtes Mittagessen, - *nt.* **2.** *vb.* zu Mittag essen*.

luncheon, *n.* leichtes Mittagessen, - *nt.*

lung, *n.* Lunge, -n *f.*

lunge, *vb.* vor·stoßen*.

lurch, *vb.* torkeln; **(leave in the l.)** sitzen lassen*.

lure, *vb.* locken.

lurid, *adj.* grell; *(fig.)* grausig.

lurk, *vb.* lauren.

luscious, *adj.* saftig, lecker.

lush, *adj.* saftig, üppig.

lust, 1. *n.* Wollust *f.* **2.** *vb.* gelü'sten.

luster, *n.* Glanz *m.*

lustful, *adj.* lüstern.

lustrous, *adj.* glänzend.

lusty, *adj.* munter; kräftig.

lute, *n.* Laute, -n *f.*

Lutheran, 1. *n.* Luthera'ner, - *m.* **2.** *adj.* luthe'risch.

luxuriant, *adj.* üppig.

luxurious, *adj.* verschwen'derisch.

luxury, *n.* Luxus *m.*

lying, *adn.* lügnerisch.

lymph, *n.* Lymphe, -n *f.*

lynch, *vb.* lynchen.

lyre, *n.* Leier, -n *f.*

lyric, *adj.* lyrisch.

lyricism, *n.* Lyrik *f.*

M

macabre, *adj.* maka'ber.

macaroni, *n.* Makkaro'ni *pl.*

machine, *n.* Maschi'ne, -n *f.*

machine gun, *n.* Maschi'nengewehr, - *nt.*

machinery, *n.* Mechanis'mus *m.;* Maschi'nen *pl.*

machinist, *n.* Maschinist', -en, -en *m.*

machismo, *n.* Männlichkeit, Virilität' *f.*

macho, *adj.* protzig männlich.

mackerel, *n.* Makre'le, -n *f.*

mackinaw, *n.* kurzer wollener Mantel, ⁼ *m.*

mad, *adj.* verrückt'; *(angry)* böse.

madam, *n.* gnädige Frau *f.*

madden, *vb.* verrückt' machen.

mafia, *n.* Mafia *f.*

magazine, *n.* Magazin', -e *nt.,* Zeitschrift, -en *f.*

magic, 1. *n.* Zauberkunst, ⁼e *f.* **2.** *adj.* magisch.

magician, *n.* Zauberer, - *m.*

magistrate, *n.* Polizei'richter, - *m.*

magnanimous, *adj.* großzügig.

magnate, *n.* Magnat', -en, -en *m.*

magnesium, *n.* Magne'sium *nt.*

magnet, *n.* Magnet', (-en), -en *m.*

magnetic, *adj.* magne'tisch.

magnificence, *n.* Herrlichkeit *f.,* Pracht *f.*

magnificent, *adj.* großartig, prächtig.

magnify, *vb.* vergrö'ßern.

magnitude, *n.* Größe, -n *f.*

mahogany, *n.* Mahago'ni *nt.*

maid, *n.* Dienstmädchen, - *nt.;* **(old m.)** alte Jungfer, -n *f.*

maiden, *adj.* Jungfern- *(cpds.);* **(m. name)** Mädchenname(n), - *m.*

mail, 1. *n.* Post *f.* **2.** *vb.* mit der Post schicken; zur Post bringen*.

mail-box, *n.* Briefkasten, ⁼ *m.*

mailman, *n.* Postbote, -n, -n *m.,* Briefträger, - *m.*

maim, *vb.* verstüm'meln.

main, *adj.* hauptsächlich.

mainland, *n.* Festland *nt.*

mainspring, *n.* Triebfeder, -n *f.*

maintain, *vb.* aufrecht·erhalten*; *(assert)* behaup'ten.

maintenance, *n.* Aufrechterhaltung *f.,* Instand'haltung *f.*

mainframe, *n.* Großrechenanlage, -n *f.*

maize, *n.* Mais *m.*

majestic, *adj.* majestä'tisch.

majesty, *n.* Majestät', -en *f.*

major, 1. *n.* Major', -e *m.* **2.** *adj.* größer; Haupt- *(cpds.);* *(music)* Dur *nt.,* **(A-major)** A-dur.

majority, *n.* Mehrzahl, -en *f.,* Mehrheit, -en *f.,* Majorität, - en *f.*

make, *vb.* machen; *(manufacture)* her·stellen; *(compel)* zwingen*.

make-believe, 1. *n.* Vorspiegelung, -en *f.* **2.** *adj.* vorgetäuscht. **3.** *vb.* vor·täuschen.

maker, *n.* Hersteller, - *m.*

makeshift, *n.* Notbehelf *m.*

make-up, *n.* Struktur', -en *f.;* Aufmachung, -en *f.;* *(face)* Schminke *f.,* Make-up *nt.*

malady, *n.* Krankheit, -en *f.*

malaria, *n.* Mala'ria *f.*

male, 1. *n.* *(human)* Mann, ⁼er *m.;* *(animal)* Männchen, - *nt.* **2.** *adj.* männlich.

malevolent, *adj.* böswillig.

malice, *n.* Bosheit, -en *f.*

malicious, *adj.* boshaft.

malignant, *adj.* bösartig.

malnutrition, *n.* Unterernährung *f.*

malt, *n.* Malz *nt.*

maltreat, *vb.* mißhan'deln.

mammal, *n.* Säugetier, -e *nt.*

man, 1. *n.* Mann, ⁼er *m.;* *(human being)* Mensch, -en, -en *m.*

manage, *n.* handhaben; *(administer)* verwal'ten; *(direct)* leiten.

management, *n.* Verwal'tung, -en *f.;* Leitung, -en *f.*

manager, *n.* Leiter, - *m.;* Unterneh'mer, - *m.*

mandate, *n.* Mandat', -e *nt.*

mandatory, *adj.* unerläßlich.

mandolin, *n.* Mandoli'ne, -n *f.*

mane, *n.* Mähne, -n *f.*

maneuver, 1. *n.* Manö'ver, - *nt.* **2.** *vb.* manövrie'ren.

manganese, *n.* Mangan' *nt.*

manger, *n.* Krippe, -n *f.*

mangle, *vb.* zerflei'schen; *(laundry)* mangeln.

manhood, *n.* Mannesalter *nt.;* Mannhaftigkeit *f.*

mania, *n.* Manie', -i'en *f.*

maniac, *n.* Wahnsinnig- *m.*

manicure, 1. *n.* Maniku're, -n *f.* **2.** *vb.* maniku'ren.

manifest, 1. *adj.* offenkundig. **2.** *vb.* bekun'den.

manifesto, *n.* Manifest', -e *nt.*

manifold, *adj.* mannigfaltig.

manipulate, *vb.* manipulie'ren.

mankind, *n.* Menschheit *f.*

manly, *adj.* mannhaft.

manner, *n.* Art, -en *f.,* Weise, -n *f.;* Manier', -en *f.*

mannerism, *n.* Manieris'mus *m.*

mansion, *n.* Haus, ⸗er *nt.*

manslaughter, *n.* Totschlag, ⸗e *m.*

mantelpiece, *n.* Kamin'sims, -e *m.*

mantle, *n.* Mantel, - *m.*

manual, 1. *n.* Handbuch, ⸗er *nt.* **2.** *adj.* Hand- *(cpds.).*

manufacture, 1. *n.* Herstellung, -en *f.* **2.** *vb.* her·stellen.

manufacturer, *n.* Fabrikant', -en, -en *m.*

manure, *n.* Mist *m.*

manuscript, *n.* Handschrift, -en *f.,* Manuskript', -e *nt.*

many, *adj.* viele.

map, *n.* Landkarte, -n *f.; (of a small area)* Plan, ⸗e *m.*

maple, *n.* Ahorn, -e *m.*

mar, *vb.* verun'zieren.

marble, *n.* Marmor, -e *m.*

march, 1. *n.* Marsch, ⸗e *m.* **2.** *vb.* marschie'ren.

March, *n.* März *m.*

mare, *n.* Stute, -n *f.*

margarine, *n.* Margari'ne *f.*

margin, *n. (edge)* Rand, ⸗er *m.; (latitude)* Spielraum, ⸗e *m.*

marginal, *adj.* Rand- *(cpds.).*

marijuana, *n.* Marihua'na *nt.*

marinate, *vb.* marinie'ren.

marine, *adj.* Meeres-, See- *(cpds.).*

mariner, *n.* Seemann, -leute *m.*

marionette, *n.* Marionet'te, -n *f.*

marital, *adj.* ehelich.

maritime, *adj.* Schiffahrts-, Seemanns- *(cpds.).*

mark, 1. *n.* Zeichen, - *nt.; (school)* Zensur', -en *f.,* Note, -n *f.* **2.** *vb.* kennzeichnen.

market, *n.* Markt, ⸗e *m.*

market place, Marktplatz, ⸗e *m.*

marmalade, *n.* Oran'genmarmelade, -n *f.*

maroon, 1. *adj.* rotbraun. **2.** *vb.* aus·setzen.

marquee, *n.* Überda'chung, -en *f.*

marquis, *n.* Marquis', - *m.*

marriage, *n.* Heirat, -en *f.; (ceremony)* Trauung, -en *f.; (institution)* Ehe, -n *f., (matrimony)* Ehestand *f.*

marrow, *n.* Mark *nt.*

marry, *vb.* heiraten; *(join in marriage)* trauen; **(get married)** heiraten, sich verhei'raten; **(m. off)** verhei'raten.

marsh, *n.* Marsch, -en *f.*

marshal, *n.* Marschall, ⸗e *m.*

martial, *adj.* kriegerisch; Kriegs- *(cpds.).*

martyr, *n.* Märtyrer, - *m.*

martyrdom, *n.* Märtyrertum *nt.*

marvel, 1. *n.* Wunder, - *nt.* **2.** *vb.* **(m. at)** bewun'dern.

marvelous, *adj.* wunderbar.

---

mascara, *n.* Augenwimperntusche *f.*

mascot, *n.* Maskot'te, -n *f.*

masculine, *adj.* männlich, maskulin.

mash, 1. *n.* Brei, -e *m.* **2.** *vb.* zerstoΒen*.

mask, 1. *n.* Maske, -n *f.* **2.** *vb.* maskie'ren.

mason, *n.* Maurer, - *m.*

masquerade, *n.* Maskera'de, -n *f.*

mass, *n.* Masse, -n *f., (church)* Messe, -n *f.*

massacre, 1. *n.* Gemet'zel, - *nt.* **2.** *vb.* nieder·metzeln.

massage, 1. *n.* Massa'ge, -n *f.* **2.** *vb.* massie'ren.

masseur, *n.* Masseur', -e *m.*

massive, *adj.* massiv'.

mass meeting, *n.* Massenversammlung, -en *f.*

mast, *n.* Mast, -en *m.*

master, 1. *n.* Meister, - *m.;* Herr, -n, -en *m.* **2.** *vb.* beherr'schen.

masterpiece, *n.* Meisterstück, -e *nt.*

mastery, *n.* Beherr'schung *f.;* Herrschaft *f.*

mat, *n.* Matte, -n *f.*

match, 1. *n. (light)* Streichholz, ⸗er *nt.; (contest)* Wettkampf, ⸗e *m.; (marriage)* Heirat, -en *f.,* Partie', -i'en *f.* **2.** *vb.* passen zu; sich messen* mit.

mate, 1. *n. (spouse)* Ehemann, ⸗er *m.;* Ehefrau, -en *f.; (naut.)* Maat, -e *m.* **2.** *vb.* sich paaren.

material, 1. *n.* Material', -ien *nt.; (cloth)* Stoff, -e *m.* **2.** *adj.* materiell'; wesentlich.

materialism, *n.* Materialis'mus *m.*

materialize, *vb.* sich verwirk'lichen.

maternal, *adj.* mütterlich.

maternity, *n.* Mutterschaft *f.*

mathematical, *adj.* mathema'tisch.

mathematics, *n.* Mathematik' *f.*

matinée, *n.* Nachmittagsvorstellung, -en *f.*

matrimony, *n.* Ehestand *m.*

matron, *n.* Matro'ne, -n *f.*

matter, 1. *n.* Stoff, -e *m.,* Mate'rie, -n *f.; (fig.)* Sache, -n *f.,* Angelegenheit, -en *f.* **2.** *vb.* von Bedeu'tung sein*; ausmachen;* **(it doesn't m.)** es macht nichts.

mattress, *n.* Matrat'ze, -n *f.*

mature, 1. *adj.* reif. **2.** *vb.* reifen; *(fall due)* fällig werden*.

maturity, *n.* Reife *f.;* Fälligkeit *f.*

maul, *vb.* übel zu·richten.

mausoleum, *n.* Mausole'um, -le'en *nt.*

maxim, *n.* Grundsatz, ⸗e *m.*

maximum, 1. *n.* Maximum, -ma *nt.* **2.** *adj.* höchst- *(cpds.).*

may, *vb. (be permitted)* dür-

---

fen*; **(he m. come)** er wird vielleicht kommen*; **(that m. be)** das kann *or* mag sein*.

May, *n.* Mai *m.*

maybe, *adv.* vielleicht'.

mayhem, *n.* Mord und Totschlag *m.*

mayonnaise, *n.* Mayonnai'se, -n *f.*

mayor, *n.* Bürgermeister, - *m.*

maze, *n.* Wirrwarr *nt.*

me, *pron.* mir; mich.

meadow, *n.* Wiese, -n *f.*

meager, *adj.* dürftig.

meal, *n.* Mahlzeit, -en *f.; (flour)* Mehl *nt.*

mean, 1. *n. (average)* Durchschnitt, -e *m.* **2.** *adj.* mittler-, durchschnittlich; Mittel-, Durchschnitts- *(cpds.); (nasty)* gemein'. **3.** *vb. (signify)* bedeu'ten; *(intend to say)* meinen.

meaning, *n.* Bedeu'tung, -en *f., (sense)* Sinn, -e *m.*

means, *n.* Mittel *pl.*

meantime, meanwhile, *n.* Zwischenzeit *f.;* **(in the m.)** inzwi'schen, unterdes'sen.

measles, *n.* Masern *pl.*

measure, 1. *n.* Maß -e *nt.; (fig.)* Maßnahme, -n *f.* **2.** *vb.* messen*.

measurement, *n.* Maß, -e *nt.*

measuring, *n.* Messen *nt.*

meat, *n.* Fleisch *nt.*

mechanic, *n.* Mecha'niker, - *m.*

mechanical, *adj.* mecha'nisch.

mechanism, *n.* Mechanis'mus, -men *m.*

mechanize, *vb.* mechanisie'ren.

medal, *n.* Orden, - *m.*

meddle, *vb.* sich ein·mischen.

mediaeval, *adj.* mittelalterlich.

median, *n.* Mittelwert, -e *m.*

mediate, *vb.* vermit'teln.

mediator, *n.* Vermitt'ler, - *m.*

medical, *adj.* ärztlich, medizi'nisch.

medicate, *vb.* medizi'nisch behan'deln.

medicine, *n.* Medizin', -en *f.*

mediocre, *adj.* mittelmäßig.

mediocrity, *n.* Mittelmäßigkeit *f.*

meditate, *vb.* nach·denken*.

meditation, *n.* Nachdenken *nt.*

Mediterranean, *adj.* Mittelmeer- *(cpds.).*

Mediterranean Sea, *n.* Mittelmeer *nt.*

medium, 1. *n.* Mittel, - *nt.;* Medium, -ien *nt.* **2.** *adj.* mittler-.

medley, *n. (music)* Potpourri, -s *nt.*

meek, *adj.* sanft.

meekness, *n.* Sanftmut *f.*

meet, *vb.* treffen*; sich treffen*; begeg'nen.

meeting, *n.* Versamm'lung, -en *f.,* Zusam'menkunft, ⸗e *f.;* Tagung, -en *f.; (encounter)* Begeg'nung, -en *f.*

melancholy, 1. *n.* Schwermut *f.*, Melancholie' *f.* **2.** *adj.* schwermütig, melancho'lisch.

megahertz, *n.* Megahertz *nt.*

mellow, *adj.* gereift'.

melodious, *adj.* wohlklingend, melo'disch.

melodrama, *n.* Melodrama, -men *nt.*

melody, *n.* Melodie', -i'en *f.*

melon, *n.* Melo'ne, -n *f.*

melt, *vb.* schmelzen*.

meltdown, *n. (Atomkraftwerk)* Zerschmel'zen *nt.*

member, *n.* Mitglied, -er *nt.*

membership, *n.* Mitgliedschaft *f.*

membrane, *n.* Membra'ne, -n *f.*

memento, *n.* Andenken, - *nt.*

memoirs, *n.pl.* Memoi'ren *pl.*

memorable, *adj.* denkwürdig.

memorandum, *n.* Memoran'-dum, -den *nt.*

memorial, 1. *n.* Denkmal, -er *nt.;* Andenken, - *nt.* **2.** *adj.* Gedenk- *(cpds.).*

memorize, *vb.* auswendig lernen.

memory, *n. (retentiveness)* Gedächt'nis, -se *nt.; (remembrance)* Erin'nerung, -en *f.*

menace, 1. *n.* drohende Gefahr', -en *f.* **2.** *vb.* drohen, bedro'hen.

menagerie, *n.* Menagerie', -i'en *f.*

mend, *vb.* aus'bessern.

menial, *adj.* niedrig.

menopause, *n.* Wechseljahre *pl.*

menstruation, *n.* Regel *f.*, Menstruation' *f.*

menswear, *n.* Herrenkleidung *f.*

mental, *adj.* geistig.

mentality, *n.* Mentalität', -en *f.*

menthol, *n.* Menthol *nt.*

mention, 1. *n.* Erwäh'nung, -en *f.* **2.** *vb.* erwäh'nen.

menu, *n.* Menü', -s *nt.;* Speisekarte, -n *f.*

mercantile, *adj.* kaufmännisch.

mercenary, *adj.* gewinnsüchtig.

merchandise, *n.* Ware, -n *f.*

merchant, *n.* Kaufmann, -leute *m.;* Geschäfts'mann, -leute *m.*

merchant marine, *n.* Handelsmarine, -n *f.*

merciful, *adj.* barmher'zig, gütig, gnädig.

merciless, *adj.* unbarmherzig, schonungslos.

mercury, *n.* Quecksilber *nt.*

mercy, *n.* Gnade *f.*, Mitleid *nt.* Erbar'men *nt.*

mere, *adj.* bloß, nichts als.

merely, *adv.* nur, bloß.

merge, *vb.* verschmel'zen*.

merger, *n.* Zusam'menschluß, -sse *m.;* Fusion', -en *f.*

meringue, *n.* Baiser', -s *nt.*

merit, 1. *n.* Verdienst', -e *nt.;* Wert, -e *m.;* Vorzug, -e *m.* **2.** *vb.* verdie'nen.

meritorious, *adj.* verdienst'lich.

mermaid, *n.* Nixe, -n *f.*

merriment, *n.* Fröhlichkeit, -en *f.*

merry, *adj.* fröhlich, lustig.

merry-go-round, *n.* Karussell', -s *nt.*

mesh, *n.* Netz, -e *nt.*

mess, *n.* Durcheinan'der *nt.;* Unordnung *f.;* Schlamas'sel *nt.; (mil.)* Eßsaal, -säle *m.*

message, *n.* Botschaft, -en *f.*, Nachricht, -en *f.*

messenger, *n.* Bote, -n, -n *m.*

messy, *adj.* unordentlich, schlampig.

metabolism, *n.* Stoffwechsel *m.*

metal, *n.* Metall', -e *nt.*

metallic, *adj.* metal'len.

metamorphosis, *n.* Metamorpho'se, -n *f.*

metaphysics, *n.* Metaphysik' *f.*

meteor, *n.* Meteor', -e *m.*

meteorite, *n.* Meteorit', -e *m.*

meteorology, *n.* Meteorologie' *f.*

meter, *n. (unit of measure)* Meter, - *nt.* or *m.; (recording device)* Zähler, - *m.*

method, *n.* Metho'de, -n *f.*

meticulous, *adj.* sorgfältig.

metric, *adj.* metrisch.

metropolis, *n.* Großstadt, -e *f.*

metropolitan, *adj.* zur Großstadt gehö'rend.

mettle, *n.* Mut *m.*

Mexican, 1. *n.* Mexika'ner, - *m.* **2.** *adj.* mexika'nisch.

Mexico, *n.* Mexiko *nt.*

mezzanine, *n.* Zwischenstock *m.*

microbe, *n.* Mikro'be, -n *f.*

microfiche, *n.* Mikrofiche *m.*

microfilm, *n.* Mikrofilm, -e *m.*

microform, *n.* Mikroform *f.*

microphone, *n.* Mikrophon', -e *nt.*

microscope, *n.* Mikroskop', -e *nt.*

mid, *adj.* Mittel- *(cpds.);* **(in m. air)** mitten in der Luft.

middle, 1. *n.* Mitte, -n *f.* **2.** *adj.* mittler-.

middle-aged, *adj.* in mittlerem Alter.

Middle Ages, *n.* Mittelalter *nt.*

middle class, *n.* Mittelstand, -e *m.*

Middle East, *n.* Mittler-Osten *m.;* Nahost- *(cpds.)*

midget, *n.* Lilliputa'ner, - *m.*

midnight, *n.* Mitternacht *f.*

midwife, *n.* Hebamme, -n *f.*

mien, *n.* Miene, -n *f.*

might, *n.* Macht, -e *f.*

mighty, *adj.* mächtig.

migraine, *n.* Migrä'ne *f.*

migrate, *vb.* wandern.

migration, *n.* Wanderung *f.*

migratory, *adj.* wandernd, Zug- *(cpds.).*

mildew, *n.* Schimmel *m.*

mildness, *n.* Milde *f.*

mile, *n.* Meile, -n *f.*

mileage, *n.* Meilenzahl *f.*

militant, *adj.* kriegerisch.

militarism, *n.* Militaris'mus *m.*

military, 1. *n.* Militär', -s *nt.* **2.** *adj.* militä'risch.

militia, *n.* Miliz', -en *f.*

milk, 1. *n.* Milch *f.* **2.** *vb.* melken*.

milkman, *n.* Milchmann, -er *m.*

milky, *adj.* milchig.

mill, 1. *n.* Mühle, -n *f.; (factory)* Fabrik', -en *f.* **2.** *vb.* mahlen*.

miller, *n.* Müller, - *m.*

millimeter, *n.* Millime'ter, - *nt.*

millinery, *n.* Putzwaren *pl.*

million, *n.* Million', -en *f.*

millionaire, *n.* Millionär', -e *m.*

mimic, 1. *n.* Schauspieler, - *m.* **2.** *vb.* nach'ahmen.

mince, *vb.* klein schneiden*; **(he doesn't m. his words)** er nimmt kein Blatt vor den Mund.

mind, 1. *n.* Geist *m.*, Verstand' *m.*, Sinn *m.* **2.** *vb. (obey)* gehor'chen; *(watch over)* auf'passen auf; **(never m.)** das macht nichts.

mindful, *adj.* eingedenk.

mine, 1. *n.* Bergwerk, -e *nt.; (mil.)* Mine, -n *f.* **2.** *pron.* meiner, -es, -e. **3.** *vb.* ab'bauen; *(mil.)* Minen legen.

miner, *n.* Bergarbeiter, - *m.*

mineral, 1. *n.* Mineral', -e *nt.* **2.** *adj.* minera'lisch.

mingle, *vb.* mischen.

miniature, *n.* Miniatur', -en *f.*

miniaturize, *vb.* miniaturisie'ren.

minimal, *adj.* minimal'; Mindest-, Minimal'- *(cpds.).*

minimize, *vb.* herab'setzen.

minimum, *n.* Minimum, -ma *nt.*

mining, *n.* Bergbau *m.*

minister, *n. (government)* Mini'ster, - *m.; (church)* Pfarrer, - *m.*, Pastor, -o'ren *m.*, Geistlich- *m.*

ministry, *n. (government)* Ministe'rium, -rien *nt.; (church)* Geistlicher Stand *m.*

mink, *n.* Nerz, -e *m.*

minnow, *n.* Elritze, -n *f.*

minor, 1. *n.* Minderjährig *m.&f.* **2.** *adj.* gering'; minderjährig; *(music)* Moll *nt.*, **(A-minor)** a-Moll.

minority, *n.* Minderzahl, -en *f.*, Minderheit, -en *f.*, Minorität', -en *f.*

minstrel, *n.* Spielmann, -leute *m.*

mint, 1. *n. (plant)* Minze, -n *f.; (coin factory)* Münze, -n *f.* **2.** *vb.* münzen.

minus, *prep.* minus, weniger.

minute, 1. *n.* Minu'te, -n *f.* **2.** *adj.* winzig.

miracle, *n.* Wunder, - *nt.*

miraculous, *adj.* wie ein Wunder.

mirage, *n.* Luftspiegelung, -en *f.*

mire, *n.* Sumpf, -̈e *m.;* Schlamm *m.*

mirror, *n.* Spiegel, - *m.*

mirth, *n.* Fröhlichkeit *f.*

misappropriate, *vb.* verun'treuen.

misbehave, *vb.* sich schlecht beneh'men*.

miscellaneous, *adj.* divers'.

mischief, *n.* Unfug *m.*

mischievous, *adj.* schelmisch.

misconstrue, *vb.* mißdeu'ten.

misdemeanor, *n.* Verge'hen, -*nt.*

miser, *n.* Geizhals, -̈e *m.*

miserable, *adj.* jämmerlich, kläglich.

miserly, *adj.* geizig.

misery, *n.* Elend *nt.,* Jammer *m.*

misfit, *n.* Blindgänger, - *m.*

misfortune, *n.* Unglück, -e *nt.,* Pech *nt.*

misgiving, *n.* Beden'ken, - *nt.*

mishap, *n.* Unglück, -e *nt.*

mislay, *vb.* verle'gen.

mislead, *vb.* irre'führen.

misplace, *vb.* verle'gen.

mispronounce, *vb.* falsch aussprechen*.

miss, 1. *n.* Fehlschlag, -̈e *m.* 2. *vb.* verfeh'len; *(feel the lack of)* vermis'sen; *(fail to obtain)* verpas'sen.

Miss, *n.* Fräulein, - *nt.*

missile, *n.* Wurfgeschoß, -sse *nt.;* **(guided m.)** ferngesteuertes Rake'tengeschoß, -sse *nt.*

mission, *n.* Mission', -en *f.*

missionary, 1. *n.* Missionar', -e *m.* 2. *adj.* Missionars'- *(cpds.).*

misspell, *vb.* falsch buchstabie'ren.

mist, *n.* *(fog)* Nebel, - *m.;* *(haze)* Dunst, -̈e *m.*

mistake, 1. *n.* Feh'ler, - *m.,* Irrtum, -̈er *m.* 2. *vb.* verken'nen*.

mistaken, *adj.* falsch; irrig; **(be m.)** sich irren.

mister, *n.* Herr, -n, -en *m.*

mistletoe, *n.* Mistel, -n *f.*

mistreat, *vb.* mißhan'deln.

mistress, *n.* Herrin, -nen *f.; (of the house)* Hausfrau, -en *f.; (of a pet)* Frauchen, - *nt.; (lover)* Geliebt'- *f.*

mistrust, 1. *n.* Mißtrauen *nt.* 2. *vb.* mißtrau'en.

misty, *adj.* neblig; dunstig.

misunderstand, *vb.* mißverstehen*.

misuse, 1. *n.* Mißbrauch, -̈e *m.* 2. *vb.* mißbrau'chen.

mite. *n.* Bißchen *nt.; (bug)* Milbe, -n *f.*

mitigate, *vb.* mildern.

mitten, *n.* Fausthandschuh, -e *m.*

mix, *vb.* mischen.

mixture, *n.* Mischung, -en *f.*

mix-up, *n.* Verwir'rung, -en *f.;* Verwechs'lung, -en *f.*

moan, *n.* stöhnen.

mob, *n.* Menschenmenge, -n *f.;* Pöbel *m.*

mobile, *adj.* beweg'lich; mobilisiert'.

mobilization, *n.* Mobil'machung, -en *f.*

mobilize, *vb.* mobilisie'ren.

mock, *vb.* *(tr.)* verspot'ten; *(intr.)* spotten.

mockery, *n.* Spott *m.,* Hohn *m.*

mod, *adj.* auffällig modern in Kleidung, Benehmen.

mode, *n.* *(way)* Art und Weise *f.; (fashion)* Mode, -n *f.*

model, 1. *n.* Vorbild, -er *nt.,* Muster, - *nt.;* Modell', -e *nt.* 2. *vb.* modellie'ren.

moderate, 1. *adj.* mäßig, gemä'ßigt. 2. *vb.* mäßigen; vermit'teln.

moderation, *n.* Mäßigung *f.*

modern, *adj.* modern'.

modernize, *vb.* modernisie'ren.

modest, *adj.* bescheiden.

modesty, *n.* Beschei'denheit *f.*

modify, *vb.* modifizie'ren.

modish, *adj.* modisch.

modulate, *vb.* modulie'ren.

moist, *adj.* feucht.

moisten, *vb.* befeuch'ten.

moisture, *n.* Feuchtigkeit *f.*

molar, *n.* Backenzahn -̈e *m.*

molasses, *n.* Melas'se *f.;* Sirup *m.*

mold, 1. *n.* Form, -en *f.; (mildew)* Schimmel *m.* 2. *vb.* formen; schimmelig werden*.

moldy, *adj.* schimmelig.

mole, *n.* *(animal)* Maulwurf, -̈e *m.; (mark)* Muttermal, -e *nt.*

molecule, *n.* Molekül', -e *nt.*

molest, *vb.* belas'tigen.

molten, *adj.* flüssig.

moment, *n.* Augenblick, -e *m.,* Moment', -e *m.; (factor)* Moment', -e *nt.*

momentary, *adj.* augenblick'lich, momentan'.

momentous, *adj.* folgenschwer.

monarch, *n.* Monarch', -en, -en *m.*

monarchy, *n.* Monarchie', -i'en *f.*

monastery, *n.* Kloster, -̈ *nt.*

Monday, *n.* Montag, -e *m.*

monetary, *adj.* Geld- *(cpds.).*

money, *n.* Geld, -er *nt.*

money changer, *n.* Geldwechsler, - *m.*

money order, *n.* Postanweisung, -en *f.*

mongrel, *n.* Bastard, -e *m.*

monitor, *n.* *(man)* Abhörer, - *m.; (apparatus)* Kontroll'gerät, -e *nt.*

monk, *n.* Mönch, -e *m.*

monkey, *n.* Affe, -n, -n *m.*

monocle, *n.* Mono'kel, - *nt.*

monologue, *n.* Monolog', -e *m.*

monopolize, *vb.* monopolizie'ren.

monopoly, *n.* Monopol', -e *nt.*

monotone, *n.* einförmiger Ton, -̈e *m.*

monotonous, *adj.* eintönig, monoton'.

monotony, *n.* Eintönigkeit *f.,* Monotonie' *f.*

monster, *n.* Ungeheuer, - *nt.*

monstrosity, *n.* Ungeheuerlichkeit, -en *f.*

monstrous, *adj.* ungeheuerlich, haarsträubend.

month, *n.* Monat, -e *m.*

monthly, 1. *n.* Monatsschrift, -en *f.* 2. *adj.* monatlich.

monument, *n.* Denkmal, -̈er *nt.*

monumental, *adj.* monumental'.

mood, *n.* Stimmung, -en *f.;* Laune, -n *f.*

moody, *adj.* launisch; schwermütig.

moon, *n.* Mond, -e *m.*

moonlight, *n.* Mondschein *m.*

moor, 1. *n.* Moor, -e *nt.* 2. *vb.* veran'kern.

mooring, *n.* Ankerplatz, -̈e *m.*

moot, *adj.* strittig.

mop, *n.* Mop, -s *m.*

moped, *n.* Mofa, -s *nt.*

moral, 1. *n.* Moral', -en *f.* 2. *adj.* sittlich, mora'lisch.

morale, *n.* Stimmung, -en *f.,* Moral' *f.*

moralist, *n.* Moralist', -en, -en *m.*

morality, *n.* Sittlichkeit *f.,* Moral' *f.;* Sittenlehre *f.*

morbid, *adj.* morbid'.

more, *adv.* mehr.

moreover, *adv.* außerdem.

morgue, *n.* Leichenhaus, -̈er *nt.*

morning, *n.* Morgen, - *m.,* Vormittag, -e *m.*

moron, *n.* Schwachsinnige *&f.*

morose, *adj.* verdrieß'lich.

morphine, *n.* Morphium *nt.*

morsel, *n.* Bissen, - *m.*

mortal, *adj.* sterblich; tödlich.

mortality, *n.* Sterblichkeit *f.*

mortar, *n.* *(vessel)* Mörser, - *m.; (building material)* Mörtel *m.*

mortgage, *n.* Hypothek', -en *f.*

mortician, *n.* Leichenbestatter, - *m.*

mortify, *vb.* kastei'en; demütigen.

mortuary, *n.* Leichenhalle, -n *f.*

mosaic, *n.* Mosaik', -e *nt.*

mosquito, *n.* Mücke, -n *f.*

moss, *n.* Moos, -e *nt.*

most, *adj.* meist-.

mostly, *adv.* meistens, hauptsächlich.

moth, *n.* Motte, -n *f.*

mother, *n.* Mutter, -̈ *f.*

mother-in-law, *n.* Schwiegermutter, -̈ *f.*

motif, *n.* Motiv', -e *nt.*

motion, *n.* Bewe'gung, -en *f.;* (parliament) Antrag, ː̈e *m.*
motionless, *adj.* bewe'gungslos.
motion picture, *n.* Film, -e *m.*
motivate, *vb.* veran'lassen, motivie'ren.
motivation, *n.* Motivie'rung, -en *f.*
motive, *n.* Beweg'grund, ː̈e *m.*
motor, *n.* Motor, -o'ren *m.*
motorboat, *n.* Motorboot, -e *nt.*
motorcycle, *n.* Motorrad, ː̈er *nt.*
motorist, *n.* Kraftfahrer, - *m.*
motto, *n.* Motto, -s *nt.*
mound, *n.* Erdhügel, - *m.*
mount, *vb.* (get on) bestei'gen*; (put on) montie'ren.
mountain, *n.* Berg, -e *m.*
mountaineer, *n.* Bergbewohner, - *m.;* Bergsteiger, - *m.*
mountainous, *adj.* bergig, gebir'gig.
mourn, *vb.* (intr.) trauern; (tr.) betrau'ern.
mournful, *adj.* trauervoll.
mourning, *n.* Trauer *f.*
mouse, *n.* Maus, ː̈e *f.*
mouth, *n.* Mund, ː̈er *m.;* (river) Mündung, -en *f.*
mouthpiece, *n.* (instrument) Mundstück, -e *nt.;* (spokesman) Wortführer, - *m.*
movable, *adj.* beweg'lich.
move, 1. *n.* (household goods) Umzug, ː̈e *m.;* (motion) Bewe'gung, -en *f.;* (games) Zug, ː̈e *m.* 2. *vb.* um·ziehen*; bewe'gen, sich bewe'gen; ziehen*; (parliamentary) bean'tragen.
movement, *n.* Bewe'gung, -en *f.;* (music) Satz, ː̈e *m.*
movie, *n.* Kino, -s *nt;* Film, -e *m.*
moving, 1. *n.* Umzug, ː̈e *m.* 2. *adj.* ergrei'fend.
mow, *vb.* mähen.
Mr., *n.* Herr *m.*
Mrs., *n.* Frau *f.*
much, *adj.* viel.
mucilage, *n.* Klebstoff, -e *m.*
muck, *n.* Schlamm *m.*
mucous, *adj.* schleimig.
mucus, *n.* Nasenschleim *m.*
mud, *n.* Schlamm *m.,* Dreck *m.*
muddy, *adj.* schlammig, trübe.
muff, 1. *n.* Muff, -e *m.* 2. *vb.* vermas'seln.
muffle, *vb.* (wrap up) ein·hüllen; (silence) dämpfen.
muffler, *n.* (scarf) Schal, -s *m.;* (auto) Auspufftopf, ː̈e *m.*
mug, *n.* Krug, ː̈e *m.*
mulatto, *n.* Mulat'te, -n, -n *m.*
mule, *n.* Esel, - *m.*
mullah, *n.* Mullah, -s *m.*
multinational, *adj.* multinatio-nal'.
multiple, *adj.* vielfältig.
multiplication, *n.* Multiplikation', -en *f.*

multiply, *vb.* (math.) multipli-zie'ren; (increase) verviel'fältigen.
multitude, *n.* Menge, -n *f.*
mummy, *n.* Mumie, -n *f.*
mumps, *n.* Ziegenpeter *m.*
Munich, *n.* München *nt.*
municipal, *adj.* städtisch.
munificent, *adj.* freigebig.
munition, *n.* Munition', -en *f.*
mural, *n.* Wandgemälde, - *nt.*
murder, 1. *n.* Mord, -e *m.* 2. *vb.* morden, ermor'den.
murderer, *n.* Mörder, - *m.*
murmur, 1. *n.* Gemur'mel, - *nt.* 2. *vb.* murmeln.
muscle, *n.* Muskel, -n *m.*
muscular, *adj.* muskulös; Muskel- (cpds.).
muse, 1. *n.* Muse, -n *f.* 2. *vb.* nach·denken*.
museum, *n.* Muse'um, -se'en *nt.*
mushroom, *n.* Pilz, -e *m.*
music, *n.* Musik' *f.*
musical, *adj.* musika'lisch.
musical comedy, *n.* Operet'te, -n *f.*
musician, *n.* Musiker, - *m.*
muslin, *n.* Musselin', -e *m.*
must, *vb.* müssen*.
mustache, *n.* Schnurrbart, ː̈e *m.*
mustard, *n.* Senf *m.,* Mostrich *m.*
muster, 1. *n.* Musterung, -en *f.* 2. *vb.* mustern.
musty, *adj.* muffig.
mutation, *n.* Mutation', -en *f.*
mute, *adj.* stumm.
mutilate, *vb.* verstüm'meln.
mutiny, 1. *n.* Meuterei', -en *f.* 2. *vb.* meutern.
mutter, *vb.* murmeln.
mutton, *n.* Hammelfleisch *nt.*
mutual, *adj.* gegenseitig, gemein'sam.
muzzle, *n.* (gun) Mündung, -en *f.;* (animal's mouth) Maul, ː̈er *nt.;* (mouth covering) Maulkorb, ː̈e *m.*
my, *adj.* mein, -, -e.
myopia, *n.* Kurzsichtigkeit *f.*
myriad, 1. *n.* Myria'de, -n *f.;* (fig.) Unzahl, -en *f.* 2. *adj.* unzählig.
myrtle, *n.* Myrte, -n *f.*
mysterious, *adj.* geheim'nisvoll.
mystery, *n.* Geheim'nis, -se *nt.;* Rätsel, - *nt.*
mystic, 1. *n.* Mystiker, - *m.* 2. *adj.* mystisch; Geheim'- (cpds.).
mystify, *vb.* verwir'ren; verdun'keln.
myth, *n.* Sage, -n *f.;* Mythus, -then *m.*
mythical, *adj.* sagenhaft, mythisch.
mythology, *n.* Mythologie', -i'en *f.*

N

nag, 1. *n.* Gaul, ː̈e *m.* 2. *vb.* herum'nörgeln; keifen.
nail, 1. *n.* Nagel, ː̈ *m.* 2. *vb.* na-geln.
naïve, *adj.* naiv', unbefangen.
naked, *adj.* nackt.
name, 1. *n.* Name(n), - *m.* 2. *vb.* nennen*.
namely, *adv.* nämlich.
namesake, *n.* Namensvetter, -n *m.*
nap, 1. *n.* (sleep) Nickerchen, - *nt.,* Nachmittagsschläfchen, - *nt.;* (cloth) Noppe, -n *f.* 2. *vb.* ein·nicken.
naphtha, *n.* Naphtha *nt.*
napkin, *n.* Serviet'te, -n *f.;* (sanitary n.) Binde, -n *f.*
narcissus, *n.* Narzis'se, -n *f.*
narcotic, 1. *n.* Rauschgift, -e *nt.* 2. *adj.* narko'tisch.
narrate, *vb.* erzäh'len.
narration, *n.* Erzäh'lung, -en *f.*
narrative, 1. *n.* Erzäh'lung, -en *f.* 2. *adj.* erzäh'lend.
narrow, *adj.* (tight, confined) eng; (not broad) schmal (ː̈, -).
nasal, *adj.* nasal'.
nasty, *adj.* häßlich.
natal, *adj.* Geburts'- (cpds.).
nation, *n.* Nation', -en *f.,* Volk, ː̈er *nt.*
national, 1. *n.* Staatsangehörig-*m.&f.* 2. *adj.* national'.
nationalism, *n.* Nationalis'mus *m.*
nationality, *n.* Staatsangehörigkeit, -en *f.,* Nationalität', -en *f.*
nationalization, *n.* Verstaat'lichung, -en *f.*
nationalize, *vb.* verstaat'lichen.
native, 1. *n.* Eingeborene-*m.&f.,* Einheimisch- *m.&f.* 2. *adj.* gebür'tig, einheimisch.
nativity, *n.* Geburt', -en *f.*
natural, *adj.* natür'lich.
naturalist, *n.* Natur'forscher, - *m.,* Naturalist', -en, -en *m.*
naturalize, *vb.* naturalisie'ren.
naturalness, *n.* Natür'lichkeit *f.*
nature, *n.* Natur', -en *f.;* (essence) Wesen *nt.*
naughty, *adj.* unartig.
nausea, *n.* Übelkeit *f.*
nauseating, *adj.* ekelerregend.
nautical, *adj.* nautisch.
naval, *adj.* See-, Schiffs-, Mari'ne- (cpds.).
nave, *n.* Kirchenschiff, -e *nt.*
navel, *n.* Nabel, - *m.*
navigable, *adj.* schiffbar.
navigate, *vb.* schiffen, steuern.
navigation, *n.* Schiffahrt *f.,* Navigation' *f.*
navigator, *n.* Seefahrer, - *m.;* (airplane) Orter, - *m.*
navy, *n.* Mari'ne *f.;* Flotte, -n *f.*

navy yard, n. Mari'newerft, -en f.

near, 1. prep. in der Nähe von. **2.** adj. nahe (näher, nächst-).

nearby, 1. adj. naheliegend, nahe gele'gen. **2.** adv. in der Nähe.

nearly, adv. beinahe, fast.

near-sighted, adj. kurzsichtig.

neat, adj. sauber.

neatness, n. Sauberkeit f.

nebula, n. Nebelfleck, -e m.

nebulous, adj. nebelhaft.

necessary, adj. nötig, notwendig.

necessity, n. Notwendigkeit, -en f.

neck, n. Hals, -̈e m.

necklace, n. Halskette, -n f.

necktie, n. Schlips, -e m., Krawat'te, -n f.

nectar, n. Nektar m.

need, 1. n. Not, -̈e f.; Bedürf'nis, -se nt. **2.** vb. benö'tigen, brauchen.

needful, adj. notwendig.

needle, n. Nadel, -n f.

needless, adj. unnötig.

needy, adj. notleidend.

negative, 1. n. (photo) Negativ, -e nt. **2.** adj. vernei'nend, negativ.

neglect, 1. n. Vernach'lässigung, -en f. **2.** vb. vernach'lässigen.

negligee, n. Negligé', -s nt.

negligent, adj. nachlässig, fahrlässig.

negligible, adj. gering'fügig.

negotiate, vb. verhan'deln.

negotiation, n. Verhand'lung, -en f.

Negro, n. Neger, - m.

neighbor, n. Nachbar, (-n,) -n m.

neighborhood, n. Nachbar-schaft, -en f.

neither, 1. pron. keiner, -es, -e (von beiden). **2.** conj. (n. . . nor) weder . . . noch.

neon, n. Neon nt.

nephew, n. Neffe, -n, -n m.

nepotism, n. Nepotis'mus m.

nerve, n. Nerv, -en m.; (effrontery) Dreistigkeit f.

nervous, adj. nervös'.

nest, n. Nest, -er nt.

nestle, vb. nisten; (fig.) sich an'schmiegen.

net, 1. n. Netz, -e nt. **2.** adj. netto.

network, n. Netz, -e nt.

neuralgia, n. Neuralgie' f.

neurology, n. Neurologie' f.

neurotic, adj. neuro'tisch.

neutral, adj. neutral', unparteiisch.

neutrality, n. Neutralität' f.

neutron, n. Neutron, -o'nen nt.

neutron bomb, n. Neutro'nenbombe, -n f.

never, adv. nie, niemals.

nevertheless, adv. dennoch, trotzdem.

new, adj. neu.

news, n. Nachrichten pl.; (item of n.) Nachricht, -en f.

newsboy, n. Zeitungsjunge, -n, -n m.

newscast, n. Nachrichtensendung, -en f.

newspaper, n. Zeitung, -en f.

newsreel, n. Wochenschau f.

next, adj. nächst-.

nibble, vb. knabbern.

nice, adj. nett, hübsch.

nick, n. Kerbe, -n f.

nickel, n. Nickel nt.

nickname, n. Spitzname(n), -m.

nicotine, n. Nikotin' nt.

niece, n. Nichte, -n f.

niggardly, adj. knauserig.

night, n. Nacht, -̈e f.

night club, n. Nachtlokal, -e nt.

nightgown, n. Nachthemd, -en nt.

nightingale, n. Nachtigall, -en f.

nightly, adj. nächtlich, jede Nacht.

nightmare, n. böser Traum, -̈e m., Alpdruck m.

nimble, adj. flink.

nine, num. neun.

nineteen, num. neunzehn.

nineteenth, 1. adj. neunzehnt-. **2.** n. Neunzehntel-, nt.

ninetieth, 1. adj. neunzigst-. **2.** n. Neunzigstel-, nt.

ninety, num. neunzig.

ninth, 1. adj. neunt-. **2.** n. Neuntel-, nt.

nip, 1. n. Zwick, -e m.; (drink) Schlückchen, - nt. **2.** vb. zwicken.

nipple, n. Brustwarze, -n f.; (baby's bottle) Sauger, - m.

nitrate, n. Nitrat', -e nt.

nitrogen, n. Stickstoff m.

no, 1. adj. kein, -, -e. **2.** interj. nein.

nobility, n. Adel m.

noble, adj. (rank) adlig; (character) edel.

nobleman, n. Adlig- m.

nobody, pron. niemand, keiner.

nocturnal, adj. nächtlich.

nocturne, n. Noktur'ne, -n f.

nod, vb. nicken.

no-frills, adj. einfach, ohne Verschönerung.

noise, n. Geräusch', -e nt.; Lärm m.

noiseless, adj. geräusch'los.

noisy, adj. laut.

nomad, n. Noma'de, -n, -n m.

nominal, adj. nominal'.

nominate, vb. ernen'nen*; (candidate) auf'stellen.

nomination, n. Ernen'nung, -en f.; Kandidatur', -en f.

nominee, n. Kandidat', -en, -en m.

non-aligned, adj. blockfrei.

nonchalant, adj. zwanglos, nonchalant'.

noncombatant, n. Nichtkämpfer, - m.

non-commissioned officer, n. Unteroffizier, -e m.

noncommittal, adj. nichtverpflich'tend.

nondescript, adj. unbestimmbar.

none, pron. keiner, -es, -e.

nonpartisan, adj. unparteiisch.

nonsense, n. Unsinn m.

nonstop, adj. durchgehend.

noodle, n. Nudel, -n f.

nook, n. Ecke, -n f., Winkel, -m.

noon, n. Mittag m.

noose, n. Schlinge, -n f.

nor, conj. noch.

normal, adj. normal', gewöhn'lich.

north, 1. n. Norden m. **2.** adj. nördlich; Nord- (cpds.).

northeast, 1. n. Nordos'ten m. **2.** adj. nordöst'lich; Nordost- (cpds.).

northeastern, adj. nordöst'lich.

northern, adj. nördlich.

North Pole, n. Nordpol m.

northwest, 1. n. Nordwes'ten m. **2.** adj. nordwest'lich; Nordwest- (cpds.).

Norway, n. Norwegen nt.

Norwegian, 1. n. Norweger, -m. **2.** adj. norwegisch.

nose, n. Nase, -n f.

nosebleed, n. Nasenbluten nt.

nose dive, n. Sturz, -̈e m.; (airplane) Sturzflug, -̈e m.

nostalgia, n. Heimweh nt.; Sehnsucht f.

nostril, n. Nasenloch, -̈er nt., Nüster, -n f.

not, adv. nicht; (n. a, n. any) kein, -, -e.

notable, adj. bemer'kenswert.

notary, n. Notar', -e m.

notation, n. Aufzeichnung, -en f.

notch, 1. n. Kerbe, -n f. **2.** vb. ein'kerben.

note, 1. n. Notiz', -en f.; (comment) Anmerkung, -en f.; (music) Note, -n f.; (letter) kurzer Brief, -e m. **2.** vb. bemer'ken.

note-book, n. Notiz'buch, -̈er nt., Heft, -e nt.

noted, adj. bekannt'.

notepaper, n. Notiz'block, -̈e m.; Schreibblock, -̈e m.

noteworthy, adj. beach'tenswert.

nothing, pron. nichts.

notice, 1. n. (attention) Beach'tung, -en f.; (poster) Bekannt'machung, -en f.; (announcement) Anzeige, -n f.; (give n.) kündigen. **2.** vb. beach'ten; bemer'ken.

noticeable, adj. bemer'kenswert; (conspicuous) auffällig.

notification, n. Benach'richtigung, -en f.

notify, vb. benach'richtigen.

notion, n. Vorstellung, -en f., Idee', -de'en f.; (n.s, articles) Kurzwaren pl.

notoriety, n. Verruf' m., Ver-ru'fenheit f.

notorious, adj. berüch'tigt.

notwithstanding, 1. prep. ungeachtet, trotz. **2.** adv. nichtsdestoweniger.

noun, n. Hauptwort, -̈er nt., Substantiv, -e nt.

nourish, vb. nähren; ernäh'ren.

nourishment, n. Nahrung, -en f.

novel, 1. n. Roman', -e m. **2.** adj. neu.

novelist, n. Roman'schriftsteller, - m.

novelty, n. Neuheit, -en f.

November, n. Novem'ber m.

novena, n. Nove'ne, -n f.

novice, n. Neuling, -e m.

novocaine, n. Novocain' nt.

now, adv. jetzt, nun.

nowhere, adv. nirgends.

nozzle, n. Düse, -n f.; (gun) Mündung, -en f.

nuance, n. Nuan'ce, -n f.

nuclear, adj. Kern- (cpds.); nukleaf.

nuclear warhead, n. nuklea'rer Sprengkopf m.

nuclear waste, n. Atom'müll m.

nucleus, n. Kern, -e m.

nude, adj. nackt.

nugget, n. Klumpen, - m.

nuisance, n. Ärgernis, -se nt.; **(be a n.)** ärgerlich, lästig sein*.

nuke, n. Rakete mit nuklearem Sprengkopf.

nullify, vb. annullie'ren, aufheben*.

number, 1. n. Zahl, -en f.; (figure) Ziffer, -n f.; (magazine, telephone, house) Nummer, -n f.; (amount) Anzahl, -en f. **2.** vb. numerie'ren; (amount to) sich belau'fen auf.

numerical, adj. zahlenmäßig.

numerous, adj. zahlreich.

nun, n. Nonne, -n f.

nuptial, adj. Hochzeits-, Ehe- (cpds.).

nurse, 1. n. Krankenschwester, -n f. **2.** vb. pflegen; (suckle) stillen.

nursery, n. Kinderzimmer, - nt.; (plants) Pflanzschule, -n f.

nurture, vb. ernäh'ren, nähren; (fig.) hegen.

nut, n. Nuß, -̈sse f.

nutcracker, n. Nußknacker, - m.

nutrition, n. Ernäh'rung f.

nutritious, adj. nahrhaft.

nylon, n. Nylon nt.

nymph, n. Nymphe, -n f.

O

oak, n. Eiche, -n f.

oar, n. Ruder, - nt.

oasis, n. Oa'se, -n f.

oath, n. (pledge) Eid, -e m., Schwur, -̈e m.; (curse) Fluch, -̈e m.

oatmeal, n. Hafergrütze f.

oats, n. Hafer m.; Haferflocken pl.

obedience, n. Gehor'sam m.

obedient, adj. gehor'sam.

obeisance, n. Ehrerbietung, -en f.

obese, adj. fettleibig.

obey, vb. gehor'chen, befol'gen.

obituary, n. Nachruf, -e m.

object, 1. n. Gegenstand, -̈e m.; (aim) Ziel, -e nt.; (purpose) Zweck, -e m.; (gram.) Objekt', -e nt. **2.** vb. einwenden*, Einspruch erheben*.

objection, n. Einwand, -̈e m., Einspruch, -̈e m.

objectionable, adj. widerwärtig.

objective, 1. n. Ziel, -e nt.; (photo) Objektiv', -e nt. **2.** adj. sachlich, objektiv'.

obligation, n. Verpflich'tung, -en f.

obligatory, adj. obligato'risch.

oblige, vb. verpflich'ten; jemandem gefäl'lig sein*.

obliging, adj. gefäl'lig.

oblique, adj. schief, schräg.

obliterate, vb. aus·radieren, vernich'ten.

oblivion, n. Verges'senheit f.

oblong, adj. länglich; rechteckig.

obnoxious, adj. widerlich.

obscene, adj. unanständig, obszön'.

obscure, adj. dunkel.

obsequious, adj. unterwür'tig.

observance, n. Beach'tung, -en f.; (celebration) Feier f.

observation, n. Beob'achtung, -en f.

observatory, n. Sternwarte, -n f.

observe, vb. beob'achten; befol'gen.

observer, n. Beob'achter, - m.

obsession, n. fixe Idee', -de'en f.

obsolete, adj. veral'tet, überholt'.

obstacle, n. Hindernis, -se nt.

obstetrical, adj. geburts'hilflich.

obstetrician, n. Geburts'helfer, - m.

obstinate, adj. hartnäckig.

obstreperous, adj. lautmäulig.

obstruct, vb. versper'ren, hindern.

obstruction, n. Hindernis, -se nt.

obtain, vb. erhal'ten*, bekom'men*.

obviate, vb. besei'tigen.

obvious, adj. selbstverständlich, offensichtlich.

occasion, n. Gele'genheit, -en f.

occasional, adj. gele'gentlich.

Occident, n. Abendland nt.

occidental, adj. abendländisch.

occult, adj. verbor'gen, okkult'.

occupant, n. Inhaber, - m., Insasse, -n, -n m., Bewoh'ner, - m.

occupation, n. (profession) Beruf', -e m.; (mil.) Beset'zung, -en f.; (o. forces) Besat'zung, -en f.

occupy, vb. (take up) einnehmen*; (keep busy) beschäf'tigen; (mil.) beset'zen.

occur, vb. vor'kommen*, gesche'hen*, passie'ren.

occurrence, n. Ereig'nis, -se nt.

ocean, n. Ozean, -e m.

o'clock, n. Uhr f.

octagon, n. Achteck, -e nt.

octave, n. Okta've, -n f.

October, n. Okto'ber m.

octopus, n. Tintenfisch, -e m.

ocular, adj. Augen- (cpds.).

oculist, n. Augenarzt, -̈e m.

odd, adj. (numbers) ungerade; (queer) merkwürdig.

oddity, n. Merkwürdigkeit, -en f.

odds, n.pl. Chance, -n f.; (probability) Wahrschein'lichkeit, -en f.; (advantage) Vorteil, -e m.

odious, adj. verhaßt'.

odor, n. Geruch', -̈e m.

of, prep. von.

off, adv. ab.

offend, vb. verlet'zen, belei'digen.

offender, n. Missetäter, - m.

offense, n. (crime) Verge'hen, - nt.; (offensive) Offensi've, -n f.; (insult) Kränkung, -en f.

offensive, 1. n. Offensi've, -n f. 2. adj. anstößig.

offer, 1. n. Angebot, -e nt. **2.** vb. an·bieten*.

offering, n. Opfer, - nt., Spende, -n f.

offhand, adj. beiläufig.

office, n. Amt, -̈er nt.; (room) Büro', -s nt.; (doctor's, dentist's o.) Praxis f.

officer, n. Offizier', -e m.; (police) Polizist', -en, -en m.

official, 1. n. Beamt'- m. **2.** adj. amtlich, offiziell'.

officiate, vb. amtie'ren.

offspring, n. Abkömmling, -e m.

often, adv. oft, häufig.

oil, 1. n. Öl, -e nt.; Petro'leum nt. **2.** vb. ölen.

oily, adj. ölig, fettig.

ointment, n. Salbe, -n f.

okay, adv. okay.

old, adj. alt (-̈).

old-fashioned, adj. altmodisch.

olive, n. Oli've, -n f.

ombudsman, n. Ombudsmann, -̈er m.

omelet, n. Omelett', -e nt.

omen, n. Omen nt.

ominous, adj. unheilvoll.

omission, n. Versäum'nis, -se nt., Überse'hen, - nt.

omit, vb. aus·lassen*, unter·las'sen*.

omnibus, n. Omnibus, -se m.

omnipotent, adj. allmäch'tig.

on, prep. auf, an.

once, adv. einmal.

one, 1. pron. man; einer, -es, -e. 2. adj. ein, -, -e. 3. num. eins.

one-sided, adj. einseitig.

one-way, adj. Einbahn- (cpds.).

onion, n. Zwiebel, -n f.

only, 1. adj. einzig. 2. adv. nur.

onslaught, n. Angriff, -e m.

onward, adv. vorwärts.

ooze, vb. hervor'·quellen*.

opacity, n. Undurchsichtigkeit f.

opal, n. Opal', -e m.

opaque, adj. undurchsichtig.

open, 1. adj. offen. 2. adv. offen, auf. 3. vb. öffnen, auf·machen; (inaugurate) eröff'nen.

opening, n. 1. n. (hole) Öffnung, -en f.; (inauguration) Eröff'nung, -en f. 2. adj. eröff'nend.

opera, n. Oper, -n f.

opera-glasses, n.-pl. Opernglas, -er nt.

operate, vb. operie'ren.

operatic, adj. Opern- (cpds.).

operation, n. Verfah'ren, - nt.; Unterneh'men, - nt.; (med.) Operation', -en f.

operator, n.(of a machine) Bedie'ner, - m.; (telephone) Telefon'fräulein, - nt., Vermitt'lung f.; (manager) Manager, - m.

operetta, n. Operet'te, -n f.

ophthalmic, adj. Augen- (cpds.).

opinion, n. Meinung, -en f., Ansicht, -en f.

opponent, n. Gegner, - m.

opportunism, n. Opportunis'mus m.

opportunity, n. günstige Gelegenheit, -en f., Chance, -n f.

oppose, vb. sich widerset'zen.

opposite, 1. n. Gegenteil, -e nt.; (contrast) Gegensatz, -e m. 2. adj. entge'gengesetzt. 3. adv. gegenü'ber.

opposition, n. Opposition', -en f.

oppress, vb. unterdrü'cken.

oppression, n. Unterdrü'ckung, -en f.

oppressive, adj. tyran'nisch; bedrü'ckend, drü'ckend.

oppressor, n. Unterdrü'cker, - m.

optic, adj. optisch.

optician, n. Optiker, - m.

optics, n. Optik f.

optimism, n. Optimis'mus m.

optimistic, adj. optimis'tisch.

option, n. Wahl, -en f.; (privi-

lege of buying) Vorkaufsrecht, -e nt.

optional, adj. freigestellt, fakultativ'.

optometry, n. praktische Augenheilkunde f.

opulence, n. Üppigkeit f.

opulent, adj. üppig.

or, conj. oder.

oracle, n. Ora'kel, - nt.

oral, adj. mündlich.

orange, 1. n. Apfelsi'ne, -n f., Oran'ge, -n f. 2. adj. orangefarbig; (pred. adj. only) orange'.

oration, n. Rede, -n f.

orator, n. Redner, - m.

oratory, n. Redekunst f.

orbit, n. Bahn, -en f.; Gestirns-, Plane'tenbahn, -en f.

orchard, n. Obstgarten, -̈ m.

orchestra, n. (large) Orches'ter, - nt.; (small) Kapel'le, -n f.

orchid, n. Orchide'e, -n f.

ordain, vb. in den geistlichen Stand auf·nehmen*.

ordeal, n. Qual, -en f.

order, n. 1. n. (command) Befehl', -e m.; (neatness) Ordnung f.; (decree) Erlaß, -sse m., Verord'nung, -en f.; (fraternity, medal) Orden, - m. 2. vb. (command) befeh'len*; (put in o.) ordnen; (decree) verord'nen.

orderly, adj. ordentlich; geord'net.

ordinance, n. Verord'nung, -en f.

ordinary, adj. gewöhn'lich.

ore, n. Erz, -e nt.

organ, n. Organ', -e nt.; (music) Orgel, -n f.

organdy, n. Organ'dy m.

organic, adj. orga'nisch.

organism, n. Organis'mus, -men m.

organist, n. Organist', -en, -en m.

organization, n. Organisation', -en f.

organize, vb. organisie'ren.

orgy, n. Orgie, -n f.

orient, vb. orientie'ren.

Orient, n. Orient m.

Oriental, adj. orienta'lisch.

orientation, n. Orientie'rung, -en f.

origin, n. Ursprung, -̈e m.

original, adj. ursprünglich; (novel) originell'.

originality, n. Originalität', -en f.

ornament, n. 1. n. Verzie'rung, -en f., Schmuck m. 2. vb. verzie'ren, schmücken.

ornamental, adj. dekorativ'.

ornate, adj. überla'den.

ornithology, n. Vogelkunde f.

orphan, n. Waise, -n f.

orphanage, n. Waisenhaus, -̈er nt.

orthodox, adj. orthodox'.

orthography, n. Rechtschrei-

bung, -en f., Orthographie', -i'en f.

orthopedic, adj. orthopä'disch.

oscillate, vb. schwingen*.

osmosis, n. Osmo'se f.

ostensible, adj. augenscheinlich.

ostentation, n. Schaustellung f.

ostentatious, adj. ostentativ'.

ostracize, vb. ächten.

ostrich, n. Strauß, -e m.

other, adj. ander-.

otherwise, adv. sonst.

ouch, interj. au!

ought, vb. sollte; (o. to have) hätte . . . sollen.

ounce, n. Unze, -n f.

our, adj. unser, -, -e.

ours, pron. unserer, -es, -e.

oust, vb. enthe'ben* (eines Amtes).

out, adv. aus, hin-, heraus'.

outbreak, n. Ausbruch, -̈e m.

outburst, n. Ausbruck, -̈e m.

outcast, n. Ausgestoßen- m.&f.

outcome, n. Ergeb'nis, -se nt.

outdoors, adv. draußen, im Freien.

outer, adj. äußer-.

outfit, 1. n. Ausrüstung. -en f.; (mil.) Einheit, -en f. 2. vb. aus·rüsten.

outgrowth, n. Folge, -n f.

outing, n. Ausflug, -̈e m.

outlandish, adj. bizarr'.

outlaw, 1. n. Gesetz'los- m. 2. vb. verbie'ten*.

outlet, n. Abfluß, -̈sse m.; (fig.) Ventil', -e nt.; (elec.) Steckdose, -n f.

outline, 1. n. Umriß, -sse m., Kontur', -en f.; (summary) Übersicht, -en f. 2. vb. um·rei'ßen*.

outlive, vb. überle'ben, überdau'ern.

out of, prep. aus.

out-of-date, adj. veral'tet, überholt'.

outpost, n. Vorposten, - m.

output, n. Leistung, -en f., Produktion', -en f.; (computer) Output, -s m.; Ausgabe, -n f.

outrage, n. Frevel, - m.

outrageous, adj. unerhört.

outrank, vb. einen höheren Rang bekleiden.

outright, adj. uneingeschränkt.

outrun, vb. hinter sich lassen*.

outside, 1. n. Außenseite, -n f.; Außenwelt f. 2. adj. äußer-. 3. adv. draußen. 4. prep. außer, außerhalb.

outskirts, n. Außenbezirke pl.

outward, adj. äußerlich.

oval, adj. oval'.

ovary, n. Eierstock, -̈e m.

ovation, n. Huldigung, -en f.

oven, n. Ofen, -̈ m.

over, 1. prep. über. 2. adv. über; hin-, herü'ber; (past) vorbei'.

overbearing, adj. anmaßend.

overcoat, n. Mantel, -̈ m., Überzieher, - m.

overcome, vb. überwin'den*.

overdue, adj. überfällig.

overflow, 1. n. Überfluß, -sse m. **2.** vb. über-fließen*.

overhaul, vb. überho'len.

overhead, 1. n. laufende Unkosten pl. **2.** adv. oben.

overkill, n. Overkill nt.; übertriebenes Vernichtungsvermögen nt.

overlook, vb. überse'hen*.

overnight, adv. über Nacht.

overpass, n. Unterfüh'rung, -en f.

overpower, vb. überwäl'tigen.

overrule, vb. überstim'men.

overrun, vb. überlau'fen*, (flood) überflu'ten.

oversee, vb. beauf'sichtigen.

oversight, 1. n. Überse'hen, - nt.

overt, adj. offen.

overtake, vb. ein-holen.

overthrow, 1. n. Sturz m. **2.** vb. stürzen; um-werfen*.

overtime, n. Überstunden pl.

overture, n. (music) Ouvertü're, -n f.; Annäherung, -en f.

overturn, vb. um-stürzen.

overview, n. Übersicht f.

overweight, n. Übergewicht nt.

overwhelm, vb. überwäl'tigen.

overwork, vb. überar'beiten.

owe, vb. schulden.

owing, adj. schuldig; (o. to) dank.

owl, n. Eule, -n f.

own, 1. adj. eigen. **2.** vb. besit'zen*.

owner, n. Besitz'er,- m., Eigentümer, - m., Inhaber, - m.

ox, n. Ochse, -n, -n m.

oxygen, n. Sauerstoff m.

oyster, n. Auster, -n f.

P

pace, n. Schritt, -e m.; (fig.) Tempo, -pi nt.

pacific, adj. friedlich.

Pacific Ocean, n. Stiller Ozean m.

pacifier, n. (baby's) Schnuller, - m.

pacifism, n. Pazifis'mus m.

pacifist, n. Pazifist', -en, -en m.

pacify, vb. beschwich'tigen.

pack, 1. n. Bündel, - nt.; (gang) Bande, -n f.; (cards) Kartenspiel, -e nt.; (animals) Rudel, - nt. **2.** vb. packen.

package, n. Paket, -e nt.

packing, n. Dichtung, -en f.

pact, n. Pakt, -e m.

pad, 1. n. Polster, - nt.; (paper) Block, -s m. **2.** vb. polstern.

padding, n. Polsterung, -en f.

paddle, 1. n. Paddel, - nt. **2.** vb. paddeln.

padlock, n. Vorlegeschloß, ¨-sser nt.

pagan, adj. heidnisch.

page, 1. n. (book) Seite, -n f.; (servant) Page, -n, -n m. **2.** vb. suchen lassen.

pageant, n. prunkvoller Aufzug, ¨-e m.

pail, n. Eimer, - m.

pain, 1. n. Schmerz, -en m. **2.** vb. schmerzen.

painful, adj. schmerzlich, schmerzhaft.

painstaking, adj. sorgfältig.

paint, 1. n. Farbe, -n f. **2.** vb. malen.

painter, n. Maler, - m.

painting, n. Bild, -er nt., Malerei', -en f.

pair, n. Paar, -e nt.

palace, n. Schloß, ¨-sser nt., Palast', ¨-e m.

palatable, adj. schmackhaft.

palate, n. Gaumen, - m.

palatial, adj. palast'artig.

pale, adj. blaß (-, -).

paleness, n. Blässe f.

palette, n. Palet'te, -n f.

pall, vb. schal werden*.

pallbearer, n. Sargträger, - m.

palm, n. (tree) Palme, -n f.; (hand) Handfläche, -n f.

palpitate, vb. klopfen.

paltry, adj. armselig.

pamper, vb. verzär'teln.

pamphlet, n. Broschü're, -n f.

pan, n. Pfanne, -n f. **2.** vb. herun'ter-machen.

panacea, n. Universal'mittel, - nt.

pancake, n. Pfannkuchen, - m.

pane, n. Glasscheibe, -n f.

panel, n. (wood) Einsatzstück, - e nt., Täfelung f.; (group of men) Diskussionsgruppe, -n f.; (dashboard) Armatu'renbrett, -er nt.

pang, n. plötzlicher Schmerz, - en m

panic, n. Panik f.

panorama, n. Panora'ma, -men nt.

pant, vb. keuchen, schnaufen.

panther, n. Panther, - m.

pantomime, n. Pantomi'me, -n f.

pantry, n. Speisekammer, -n f.

pants, n. Hose, -n f.

pantyhose, n. Strumpfhose, -n f.

papal, adj. päpstlich.

paper, 1. n. Papier', -e nt.; (news) Zeitung, -en f. **2.** adj. papieren; Papier'- (cpds.).

paperback, n. Taschenausgabe, -n f.

paper-hanger, n. Tapezie'rer, - m.

par, n. Pari nt.

parachute, n. Fallschirm, -e m.

parade, n. Para'de, -n f.

paradise, n. Paradies' nt.

paradox, n. Paradox', -e nt.

paraffin, n. Paraffin', -e nt.

paragraph, n. Paragraph', -en m.; (typing) Absatz, ¨-e m.

parallel, 1. n. Paralle'le, -n f. **2.** adj. parallel'.

paralysis, n. Lähmung, -en f.

paralyze, vb. lähmen.

paramedic, n. jemand, der Erste Hilfe bei Unglücksfällen leistet.

parameter, n. Para'meter, - m.

paramount, adj. oberst-.

paraphrase, vb. umschrei'ben*.

parasite, n. Schmarot'zer, - m.

parcel, n. Päckchen, - nt.; Paket', -e nt.

parch, vb. dörren.

parchment, n. Pergament', -e nt.

pardon, 1. n. Verzei'hung, -en f.; (legal) Begna'digung, -en f. **2.** vb. verzei'hen*; begna'digen.

pare, vb. schälen.

parentage, n. Herkunft. ¨-e f.

parenthesis, n. Klammer, -n f.

parents, n.pl. Eltern pl.

Paris, n. Paris' nt.

parish, n. Kirchspiel, -e nt., Gemein'de, -n f.

Parisian, 1. n. Pari'ser, - m. **2.** adj. pari'sisch.

park, 1. n. Park, -s m. **2.** vb. parken.

parking meter, n. Parkuhr, -en f.

parkway, n. Ausfallstrasse, -n f.

parliament, n. Parlament', -e nt.

parliamentary, adj. parlamenta'risch.

parlor, n. gute Stube, -n f., Salon', -s m.

parochial, adj. Pfarr-, Gemein'de- (cpds.); (fig.) beschränkt'.

parody, n. Parodie', -i'en f.

parrot, n. Papagei', -en m.

parsimony, n. Geiz m.

parsley, n. Petersi'lie f.

parson, n. Geistlich-m.

part, 1. n. Teil, -e.m.; (hair) Scheitel, - m.; (theater) Rolle -n f. **2.** vb. trennen.

partake, vb. teil-nehmen*.

partial, adj. Teil- (cpds.); partei'isch.

partiality, n. Voreingenommenheit f.

participant, n. Teilnehmer, - m.

participate, vb. teil-nehmen*.

participation, n. Teilnahme f.

participle, n. Partizip', -ien nt.

particle, n. Teilchen, - nt.

particular, adj. beson'der-.

parting, n. Abschied, -e m.

partisan, 1. n. Anhänger, - m., Partisan', (-en), -en m **2.** adj. partei'isch.

partition, n. Teilung, -en f.; (wall) Scheidewand, ¨-e f.

partly, adv. teilweise, teils.

partner, n. Teilhaber, - m., (games) Partner, - m.

part of speech, n. Redeteil, -e m., Wortart, -en f.

party, n. (pol.) Partei', -en f.; (social) Gesell'schaft, -en f.

pass, 1. n. (mountain) Paß, -sse m.; (identification) Ausweis, -e m. **2.** vb. vorü'ber-gehen*; (car) überho'len; (exam) beste'hen*; (to hand) reichen.

passable, adj. (roads) befahr'bar; (fig.) erträg'lich, passa'bel.

passage, n. Durchgang, -e m., Durchfahrt, -en f.; (steamer) Überfahrt, -en f.; (law) Annahme, -n f.

passenger, n. Passagier', -e m.

passer-by, n. Passant', -en, -en m.

passion, n. Leidenschaft, -en f.; (Christ) Passion' f.

passionate, adj. leidenschaftlich.

passive, 1. n. Passiv nt. **2.** adj. passiv.

passport, n. Paß, -sse m.

past, 1. n. Vergan'genheit f. **2.** adj. vergan'gen, früher. **3.** adv. vorbei', vorü'ber.

paste, 1. n. Paste, -n f.; (mucilage) Klebstoff, -e m. **2.** vb. kleben.

pasteurize, vb. pasteurisie'ren.

pastime, n. Zeitvertreib m.

pastor, n. Pfarrer, - m.

pastry, n. Gebäck' nt.

pastry shop, n. Bäckerei', -en f.

pasture, n. Weide, -n f.

pat, 1. n. Klaps, -e m. **2.** vb. einen leichten Schlag geben*.

patch, 1. n. Flicken, - m. **2.** vb. flicken.

patchwork, n. Flickwerk nt.

patent, n. Patent', -e nt.

patent leather, n. Lackleder nt.

paternal, adj. väterlich.

path, n. Weg, -e m., Pfad, -e m.

pathetic, adj. rührend, armselig.

pathology, n. Pathologie' f.

patience, n. Geduld' f.

patient, 1. n. Patient', -en, -en m. **2.** adj. gedul'dig.

patio, n. Patio, -s m.

patriarch, n. Patriarch', -en, -en m.

patriot, n. Patriot', -en, -en m.

patriotic, adj. patrio'tisch.

patriotism, n. Patriotis'mus m.

patrol, 1. n. Streife, -n f. **2.** vb. patrouillie'ren.

patrolman, n. Polizist', -en, -en m.

patron, n. Schutzherr, -, -en m.; (client) Kunde, -n, -n m.

patronage, n. Schirmherrschaft f.

patronize, vb. begün'stigen.

pattern, n. Muster, - nt.; (sewing) Schnittmuster, - nt.

pauper, n. Arm- m.&f.

pause, n. Pause, -n f.

pave, vb. pflastern.

pavement, n. Pflaster, - nt.

pavillion, n. Pavillon, -s m.

paw, n. Pfote, -n f.

pawn, 1. n. Pfand, -er m.; (chess) Bauer, (-n,) -n m. **2.** vb. pfänden.

pay, 1. n. Bezah'lung f., Gehalt', -er nt. **2.** vb. bezah'len.

payment, n. Bezah'lung f.; (installment) Rate, -n f.

pea, n. Erbse, -n f.

peace, n. Friede(n), - m.

peaceful, adj. friedlich.

peach, n. Pfirsich, -e m.

peacock, n. Pfau, -e m.

peak, n. Gipfel, - m.

peal, vb. läuten, dröhnen.

peanut, n. Erdnuß, -sse f.

pear, n. Birne, -n f.

pearl, n. Perle, -n f.

peasant, n. Bauer, (-n,) -n m.

pebble, n. Kieselstein, -e m.

peck, vb. picken.

peculiar, adj. merkwürdig, beson'der-.

peculiarity, n. Beson'derheit, - en f.

pedal, n. Pedal', -e nt.

pedant, n. Pedant', -en, -en m.

peddler, n. Hausie'rer, - m.

pedestal, n. Sockel, - m.

pedestrian, n. Fußgänger, - m.

pediatrician, n. Kinderarzt, -e m.

pedigree, n. Stammbaum, -e m.

peek, vb. gucken.

peel, 1. n. Schale, -n f. **2.** vb. schälen.

peep, vb. (look) lugen; (chirp) piepsen.

peer, n. Ebenbürtig- m.

peg, n. Pflock, -e m.; Stift, -e m.

pelt, 1. n. Fell, -e nt. **2.** vb. bewer'fen*; nieder-prasseln.

pelvis, n. Becken, - nt.

pen, 1. n. Feder, -n f.; (sty) Stall, -e m. **2.** vb. schreiben*.

penalty, n. Strafe, -n f.

penchant, n. Hang m.

pencil, n. Bleistift, -e m.

pendant, n. Anhänger, - m.

penetrate, vb. (tr.) durchdrin'gen*; (intr.) ein-dringen*.

penetration, n. Eindringen nt., Durchdrin'gung f.

penicillin, n. Penicillin' nt.

peninsula, n. Halbinsel, -n f.

penitent, adj. reuig.

penitentiary, n. Zuchthaus, -er nt.

pen-knife, n. Federmesser, - nt.

penniless, adj. mittellos.

penny, n. Pfennig, -e m.

pension, n. Pension', -en f.

pensive, adj. nachdenklich.

people, n. Leute pl., Menschen pl.; (nation) Volk, -er nt.

pepper, n. Pfeffer m.

per, prep. pro.

perambulator, n. Kinderwagen, - m.

perceive, vb. wahr-nehmen*.

percent, n. Prozent', -e nt.

percentage, n. Prozent'satz, -e m.; Provision', -en f.

perceptible, adj. wahrnehmbar.

perception, n. Wahrnehmung, -en f.

perch, 1. n. (fish) Barsch, -e m.; (pole) Stange, -n f. **2.** vb. sich nieder-setzen.

peremptory, adj. endgültig, diktato'risch.

perennial, 1. n. (plant) Staude, -n f. **2.** adj. alljähr'lich.

perfect, 1. n. (gram.) Perfekt, -e nt. **2.** adj. vollkom'men, perfekt'. **3.** vb. vervoll'kommnen.

perfection, n. Vollkom'menheit f.

perforate, vb. durchlö'chern.

perforation, n. Durchlö'cherung, -en f.

perform, vb. aus-führen; (drama) auf-führen.

performance, n. Ausführung, - en f.; (accomplishment) Leistung, -en f.; (drama) Aufführung, -en f., Vorstellung, -en f.

perfume, n. Parfüm', -s nt.

perfunctory, adj. oberflächlich, mecha'nisch.

perhaps, adv. vielleicht'.

peril, n. Gefahr', -en f.

perimeter, n. Umfang, -e m.

period, n. Zeitraum, -e m., Perio'de, -n f.; (punctuation) Punkt, -e m.

periodic, adj. perio'disch.

periphery, n. Umkreis, -e m., Peripherie', -i'en f.

perish, vb. unter-gehen*; verder'ben*.

perishable, adj. verderb'lich.

perjure oneself, vb. Meineid bege'hen*.

perjury, n. Meineid, -e m.

permanent, 1. n. (hair) Dauerwelle, -n f. **2.** adj. bestän'dig.

permissible, adj. zulässig.

permission, n. Erlaub'nis, -se f.

permit, 1. n. Erlaub'nisschein, -e m. **2.** vb. erlau'ben, zu-lassen*.

perpendicular, adj. senkrecht.

perpetrate, vb. bege'hen*.

perpetual, adj. ewig.

perplex, vb. verwir'ren.

perplexity, n. Verwir'rung, -en f.

persecute, vb. verfol'gen.

persecution, n. Verfol'gung, - en f.

perseverance, n. Beharr'lichkeit f.

persevere, vb. behar'ren.

persist, n. behar'ren, beste'hen*.

persistent, adj. beharr'lich.

person, n. Mensch, -en, -en m., Person', -en f.

personal, adj. persön'lich.

personality, *n.* Persön'lichkeit, -en *f.*

personnel, *n.* Personal' *nt.*

perspective, *n.* Perspekti've, -n *f.*

perspiration, *n.* Schweiß *m.*

perspire, *vb.* schwitzen.

persuade, *vb.* überre'den.

persuasive, *adj.* überzeu'gend.

pertain, *vb.* betref'fen*.

pertinent, *adj.* zugehörig.

perturb, *vb.* beun'ruhigen.

perverse, *adj.* verkehrt', widernatürlich; pervers'.

perversion, *n.* Verdre'hung, -en *f.*

pervert, 1. *n.* perver'ser Mensch, -en, -en *m.* **2.** *vb.* verdre'hen; verfüh'ren.

pessimism, *n.* Pessimis'mus *m.*

pestilence, *n.* Pest *f.*

pet, 1. *n.* Liebling, -e *m.; (animal)* Haustier, -e *m.* **2.** *vb.* streicheln.

petal, *n.* Blütenblatt, ⸗er *nt.*

petition, *n.* Eingabe, -n *f.*, Antrag, ⸗e *m.*

petrify, *vb.* verstei'nern; **(be petrified)** wie gelähmt' sein*.

petrol, *n.* Benzin' *nt.*

petroleum, *n.* Petro'leum *nt.*

petticoat, *n.* steifer Unterrock, -e *m.*

petty, *adj.* gering'fügig; kleinlich.

petulant, *adj.* mürrisch.

pew, *n.* Kirchenstuhl, ⸗e *m.*

phantom, *n.* Phantom', -e *nt.*

pharmacist, *n.* Apothe'ker, - *m.*

pharmacy, *n.* Apothe'ke, -n *f.*

phase, *n.* Phase, -n *f.*

pheasant, *n.* Fasan', -e(n) *m.*

phenomenal, *adj.* erstaun'lich.

phenomenon, *n.* Erschei'nung, -en *f.*, Phänomen', -e *nt.*

philanthropy, *n.* Menschenliebe *f.*, Wohltätigkeit, -en *f.*

philately, *n.* Briefmarkenkunde *f.*

philosopher, *n.* Philosoph', -en, -en *m.*

philosophical, *adj.* philoso'phisch.

philosophy, *n.* Philosophie', -i'en *f.*

phlegm, *n.* Phlegma *nt.; (med.)* Schleim *m.*

phlegmatic, *adj.* phlegma'tisch.

phobia, *n.* krankhafte Angst *f.*, Phobie', -i'en *f.*

phonetic, *adj.* phone'tisch.

phonetics, *n.* Phone'tik *f.*

phonograph, *n.* Grammophon', -e *nt.*

phosphorus, *n.* Phosphor *m.*

photocopier, *n.* Photokopier'maschine, -n *f.*

photocopy, *n.* Photokopie', -en *f.; Ablichtung, -en *f.*

photocopy, *vb.* photokopie'ren.

photogenic, *adj.* photogen'.

photograph, *n.* Photographie', -i'en *f.*, Lichtbild, -er *nt.*

photographer, *n.* Photograph', -en, -en *m.*

photography, *n.* Photographie' *f.*

photostat, 1. *n.* Photokopie', -i'en *f.* **2.** *vb.* photokopie'ren.

phrase, 1. *n.* Satz, ⸗e *m.;* Redewendung, -en *f.* **2.** *vb.* ausdrücken.

physical, *adj.* körperlich, physisch.

physician, *n.* Arzt, ⸗e *m.*

physicist, *n.* Physiker, - *m.*

physics, *n.* Physik' *f.*

physiology, *n.* Physiologie' *f.*

physiotherapy, *n.* Physiotherapie' *f.*

physique, *n.* Körperbau *m.*

pianist, *n.* Klavier'spieler, - *m.*, Pianist', -en, -en *m.*

piano, *n.* Klavier', -e *nt.*

piccolo, *n.* Piccoloflöte, -n *f.*

pick, 1. *n.* Spitzhacke, -n *f.* **2.** *vb. (gather)* pflücken; *(select)* aus·wählen.

picket, 1. *n.* Holzpfahl, ⸗e *m.; (striker)* Streikposten, - *m.* **2.** *vb.* Streikposten stehen*.

pickle, *n.* saure Gurke *f.*

pickpocket, *n.* Taschendieb, -e *m.*

picnic, *n.* Picknick, -s *nt.*

picture, 1. *n.* Bild, -er *nt.; (fig.)* Vorstellung, -en *f.* **2.** *vb.* darstellen; sich vor·stellen.

picturesque, *adj.* malerisch.

pie, *n.* eine Art Backwerk.

piece, *n.* Stück, -e *nt.*

pier, *n.* Pier, -s *m.*

pierce, *vb.* durchboh'ren.

piety, *n.* Frömmigkeit *f.*

pig, *n.* Schwein, -e *nt.; (young)* Ferkel, -e *nt.*

pigeon, *n.* Taube, -n *f.*

pigment, *n.* Pigment', -e *nt.*

pile, 1. *n. (heap)* Haufen, *m.; (post)* Pfahl, ⸗e *m.* **2.** *vb.* auf·häufen.

pilfer, *vb.* stehlen*.

pilgrim, *n.* Pilger, - *m.*

pilgrimage, *n.* Wallfahrt, -en *f.*

pill, *n.* Pille, -n *f.*

pillage, 1. *n.* Plünderung, -en *f.* **2.** *vb.* plündern.

pillar, *n.* Säule, -n *f.*

pillow, *n.* Kissen, - *nt.*

pillowcase, *n.* Kissenbezug, ⸗e *m.*

pilot, *n.* Pilot', -en, -en *m.; (ship)* Lotse, -n, -n *m.*

pimple, *n.* Pickel, - *m.*

pin, 1. *n.* Stecknadel, -n *f.* **2.** *vb.* stecken.

pinch, 1. *n. (of salt, etc.)* Prise, - n *f.* **2.** *vb.* kneifen*, zwicken.

pine, 1. *n.* Fichte, -n *f.;* Keifer, -n *f.* **2.** *vb.* sich sehnen.

pineapple, *n.* Ananas, -se *f.*

ping-pong, *n.* Tischtennis *nt.*

pink, *adj.* rosa.

pinnacle, *n.* Gipfel, - *m.*

pint, *n.* etwa ein halber Liter.

pioneer, *n.* Pionier', -e *m.*

pious, *adj.* fromm(⸗, -).

pipe, *n.* Rohr, -e *nt.;* Röhre, -n *f.; (smoking)* Pfeife, -n *f.*

piquant, *adj.* pikant'.

pirate, *n.* Seeräuber, - *m.*

pistol, *n.* Pisto'le, -n *f.*

piston, *n.* Kolben, - *m.*

pit, *n. (stone)* Kern, -e *m; (hole)* Grube, -n *f.*

pitch, 1. *n. (tar)* Pech *nt.; (resin)* Harz, -e *nt.; (throw)* Wurf, ⸗e *m.; (music)* Tonhöhe, -n. **2.** *vb. (throw)* werfen*; *(a tent)* auf·schlagen*.

pitcher, *n. (jug)* Krug, ⸗e *m.; (thrower)* Ballwerfer beim Baseball *m.*

pitchfork, *n.* Heugabel, -n *f.*, Mistgabel, -n *f.; (music)* Stimmgabel, -n *f.*

pitfall, *n.* Falle, -n *f.*

pitiful, *adj.* erbärm'lich.

pitiless, *adj.* erbar'mungslos.

pity, *n.* Mitleid *nt.*, Erbar'men *nt.*

pivot, *n.* Drehpunkt, -e *m.*

pizza, *n.* Pizza, -s *f.*

placard, *n.* Plakat', -e *nt.*

placate, *vb.* beschwich'tigen.

place, 1. *n.* Platz, ⸗e *m.*, Ort, -e *m.* **2.** *vb.* setzen, stellen, legen; unter·bringen*.

placid, *adj.* gelas'sen.

plagiarism, *n.* Plagiat' *nt.*

plague, 1. *n.* Seuche, -n *f.* **2.** *vb.* plagen.

plain, 1. *n.* Ebene, -n *f.* **2.** *adj.* eben; *(fig.)* einfach, schlicht.

plaintiff, *n.* Kläger, - *m.*

plan, 1. *n.* Plan, ⸗e *m.* **2.** *vb.* planen.

plane, 1. *n. (geom.)* Fläche -n *f.; (tool)* Hobel, - *m.; (airplane)* Flugzeug, -e *nt.* **2.** *vb.* hobeln.

planet, *n.* Planet', -en, -en *m.*

planetarium, *n.* Planeta'rium, -ien *nt.*

plank, *n.* Brett, -er *nt.*, Planke, -n *f.*

plant, 1. *n.* Pflanze, -n *f.; (factory)* Fabrik', -en *f.; (installation)* Werk, -e *nt.* **2.** *vb.* pflanzen.

planter, *n.* Pflanzer, - *m.*

plasma, *n.* Plasma, -men *nt.*

plaster, *n.* Gips *m.; (med.)* Pflaster, - *nt.; (walls)* Verputz' *m.*

plastic, 1. *n.* Kunststoff, -e *m.* **2.** *adj.* plastisch.

plate, *n.* Platte, -n *f.; (dish)* Teller, - *m.*

plateau, *n.* Hochebene, -n *f.*, Plateau', -s *nt.*

platform, *n.* Plattform, -en *f.; (train)* Bahnsteig, -e *m.*

platinum, *n.* Platin *nt.*

platitude, *n.* Plattheit, -en *f.*

platoon, *n.* Zug, ⸗e *m.*

platter, *n.* Servier'platte, -n *f.*

plausible, *adj.* einleuchtend.

play, 1. *n.* Spiel, -e *nt.; (theater)* Thea'terstück, -e *nt.* **2.** *vb.* spielen.

player, *n. (game)* Mitspieler, -

m.; *(theater)* Schauspieler, -m.; *(music)* Spieler, - m.
playful, *adj.* spielerisch.
playground, n. Spielplatz, -e m.
playmate, n. Spielgefährte, -n, -n m.
playwright, n. Drama'tiker, - m.
plea, n. Bitte, -n f.; *(excuse)* Vorwand, -e m.; *(jur.)* Plä-doyer', -s nt.
plead, vb. bitten*, plädie'ren.
pleasant, adj. angenehm.
please, 1. vb. gefal'len*. **2.** *interj.* bitte.
pleasing, adj. angenehm.
pleasure, n. Vergnü'gen nt., Freude, -n f.
pleat, n. Falte, -n f.
plebiscite, n. Volksabstim-mung, -en f.
pledge, 1. n. Gelüb'de, - nt. **2.** vb. gelo'ben.
plentiful, adj. reichlich.
plenty, n. Fülle f.; **(p. of)** reich-lich, genug'.
pleurisy, n. Rippenfellentzün-dung, -en f.
pliable, pliant, adj. biegsam.
pliers, n. Zange, -n f., Kneif-zange, -n f.
plight, n. schwierige Lage, -n f.
plot, 1. n. Stück Erde nt.; *(story)* Handlung, -en f.; *(in-trigue)* Komplott', -e nt. **2.** vb. intrigie'ren; *(plan)* entwer'-fen*.
plow, 1. n. Pflug, -e m. **2.** vb. pflügen.
pluck, 1. n. Mut m. **2.** vb. rup-fen.
plug, 1. n. Stöpsel, - m., Pfrop-fen, - m.; **(spark p.)** Zünd-kerze, -n f.; **(fire p.)** Feuerhydrant, -en, -en m. **2.** vb. zu·stopfen.
plum, n. Pflaume, -n f.
plumage, n. Gefie'der nt.
plumber, n. Klempner, - m.
plume, n. Feder, -n f.
plump, adj. dicklich.
plunder, 1. n. Beute f., Raub m. **2.** vb. plündern.
plunge, vb. rauchen, stürzen.
plural, n. Mehrzahl, -en f., Plu-ral, -e m.
plus, prep. plus.
plutocrat, n. Plutokrat', -en, - en m.
pneumatic, adj. pneuma'tisch.
pneumonia, n. Lungenentzün-dung, -en f.
poach, vb. *(hunt illegally)* wil-dern; *(eggs)* pochie'ren.
pocket, n. Tasche, -n f.
pocketbook, n. Handtasche, -n f.
pod, n. Schote, -n f.
podiatry, n. Fußheilkunde f.
poem, n. Gedicht', -e nt.
poet, n. Dichter, - m.
poetic, adj. dichterisch, poe'-tisch.
poetry, n. Dichtung, -en f., Poesie' f.

poignant, adj. treffend.
point, 1. n. Punkt, -e m. **2.** vb. zeigen, hin·weisen*.
pointed, adj. spitz.
pointless, adj. sinnlos, witzlos.
poise, n. Schwebe f.; *(assured-ness)* sicheres Auftreten nt.
poison, 1. n. Gift, -e nt. **2.** vb. vergif'ten.
poisonous, adj. giftig.
poke, vb. stoßen*.
Poland, n. Polen nt.
polar, adj. polar'.
pole, n. *(post)* Pfahl, -e m.; *(rod)* Stange, -n f.; *(electrical, geographic)* Pol, -e m.
Pole, n. Pole, -n, -n m.
police, n. Polizei' f.
policeman, n. Polizist', -en, -en m.
policy, n. Politik' f.; *(insur-ance)* Poli'ce, -n f.
polish, 1. n. Politur', -en f.; **(shoe p.)** Schuhkrem, -s f. **2.** vb. polie'ren, putzen.
Polish, adj. polnisch.
polite, adj. höflich.
politeness, n. Höflichkeit, -en f.
politic, political, adj. poli'tisch.
politician, n. Poli'tiker, - m.
politics, n. Politik' f.
poll, 1. n. Wahl, -en f., Abstim-mung, -en f.; Meinungsum-frage, -n f. **2.** vb. befra'gen.
pollen, n. Blütenstaub m.
pollute, vb. verun'reinigen.
polonaise, n. Poloña'se, -n f.
polygamy, n. Polygamie' f.
pomp, n. Pomp m.
pompous, adj. prunkvoll; *(fig.)* hochtrabend.
poncho, n. Poncho, -s m.
pond, n. Teich, -e m.
ponder, vb. *(tr.)* erwä'gen; *(intr.)* nach·denken*.
ponderous, adj. schwerfällig.
pontiff, n. Papst, -e m.
pontoon, n. Schwimmer, - m.
pony, n. Pony, -s nt.
pool, n. *(pond)* Tümpel, - m.; *(swimming p.)* Schwimmbad, -er, nt.; *(group)* Interes'sengemein-schaft, -en f. **2.** vb. zusam'-men·legen.
poor, adj. arm (-).
pop, 1. n. Knall, -e m.; *(father)* Papi, -s m. **2.** vb. knallen.
pope, n. Pabst, -e m.
popular, adj. volkstümlich; be-liebt'.
popularity, n. Beliebt'heit f.
population, n. Bevöl'kerung, -en f.
porcelain, n. Porzellan', -e nt.
porch, n. Veran'da, -den f.
pore, n. Pore, -n f.
pork, n. Schweinefleisch nt.
pornography, n. Pornographie' f.
porous, adj. porös'.
port, n. Hafen, - m.; *(wine)* Port m.

portable, adj. tragbar.
portal, n. Portal', -e nt.
portend, vb. Unheil verkün'-den.
porter, n. Gepäck'träger, -m.
portfolio, n. Mappe, -n f.; Portefeuille' nt.
porthole, n. Luke, -n f.
portion, n. Teil, -e m.; *(serving)* Portion', -en f.
portrait, n. Porträt', -s nt.
portray, vb. schildern.
Portugal, n. Portugal nt.
Portuguese, 1. n. Portugie'se, - n, -n m. **2.** adj. portugie'sisch.
pose, 1. n. Haltung, -en f., Pose, -n f. **2.** vb. stellen; **(p. as)** sich aus·geben* für.
position, n. Stellung, -en f.
positive, adj. positiv.
possess, vb. besit'zen*.
possession, n. Besitz, -e m., Ei-gentum, -er nt.
possessive, adj. besitz'gierig.
possessor, n. Besit'zer, - m., Ei-gentümer, - m.
possibility, n. Möglichkeit, -en f.
possible, adj. möglich.
possibly, adv. möglicherweise.
post, 1. n. *(pole)* Pfahl, -e m.; *(place)* Posten, - m.; *(mail)* Post f. **2.** vb. auf·stellen; zur Post geben*.
postage, n. Porto nt.
postal, adj. Post- *(cpds.)*.
postcard, n. Postkarte, -n f.
poster, n. Plakat', -e nt.
posterior, adj. hinter-; Hinter- *(cpds.)*.
posterity, n. Nachwelt f.
postmark, n. Postempel, - m.
postman, n. Postbote, -n, -n m., Briefträger, - m.
post office, n. Post f., Postamt, -er nt.
postpone, vb. auf·schieben*, verschie'ben*.
postscript, n. Nachschrift, -en f.
posture, n. Haltung, -en f.
pot, n. Topf, -e m.; *(marijuana)* Hasch m.
potassium, n. Kalium nt.
potato, n. Kartof'fel, -n f.
potent, adj. stark (-).
potential, 1. n. Möglichkeit, - en f. **2.** adj. möglich.
potion, n. Trank, -e m.
pottery, n. Töpferware, -n f.
pouch, n. Tasche, -n f., Beutel, - m.
poultry, n. Geflü'gel nt.
pound, 1. n. Pfund, -e nt. **2.** vb. hämmern, schlagen*.
pour, vb. gießen*.
poverty, n. Armut f.
powder, 1. n. Pulver, - nt.; *(cos-metic)* Puder, - m. **2.** vb. pu-dern.
power, n. Macht, -e f.
powerful, adj. mächtig.
powerless, adj. machtlos.

practicable, *adj.* durchführbar.

practical, *adj.* praktisch.

practice, 1. *n.* Übung, -en *f.;* *(carrying out)* Ausübung *f.;* *(custom)* Gewohn'heit, -en *f.;* *(doctor)* Praxis, -xen *f.* **2.** *vb.* üben; *(carry out)* aus·üben.

practitioner, *n.* Vertre'ter, - *m.;* *(med.)* praktischer Arzt, -̈e *m.*

prairie, *n.* Prairie', -'i'en *f.*

praise, 1. *n.* Lob, -e *nt.* **2.** *vb.* loben.

prank, *n.* Streich, -e *m.*

pray, *vb.* beten.

prayer, *n.* Gebet', -e *nt.*

preach, *n.* predigen.

preacher, *n.* Prediger, - *m.*

precarious, *adj.* heikel.

precaution, *n.* Vorsichtsmaßre-gel, -n *f.*

precede, *vb.* voran'·gehen*.

precedence, *n.* Vorrang *m.*

precedent, *n.* Präzedenz'fall, -̈e *m.*

precept, *n.* Vorschrift, -en *f.*

precinct, *n.* Bezirk', -e *m.*

precious, *adj.* kostbar.

precipice, *n.* Abgrund, -̈e *m.*

precipitate, 1. *adj.* überstürzt'. **2.** *vb.* überstür'zen.

precise, *adj.* genau.

precision, *n.* Genau'igkeit *f.,* Präzision' *f.*

preclude, *vb.* aus·schließen*.

precocious, *adj.* frühreif, alt-klug (-').

predecessor, *n.* Vorgänger, - *m.*

predestination, *n.* Prädestina-tion' *f.*

predicament, *n.* Dilem'ma, -s *nt.*

predicate, 1. *n.* Prädikat', -e *nt.* **2.** *vb.* begrün'den.

predict, *vb.* voraus'·sagen.

predisposed, *adj.* geneigt'; *(med.)* anfällig.

predominant, *adj.* vorherr-schend.

prefabricated, *adj.* Fertig-*(cpds.).*

preface, *n.* Vorwort, -e *nt.*

prefer, *vb.* vor·ziehen*.

preferable, *adj.* vorzuziehen; **(is p.)** ist vorzuziehen.

preferably, *adv.* vorzugsweise.

preference, *n.* Vorzug *m.,* Vor-liebe *f.*

prefix, *n.* Vorsilbe, -n *f.,* Prä-fix, -e *nt.*

pregnancy, *n.* Schwanger-schaft, -en *f.*

pregnant, *adj.* schwanger.

prehistoric, *adj.* vorgeschicht-lich, prähisto'risch.

prejudice, *n.* Vorurteil, -e *nt.*

prejudiced, *adj.* voreingenom-men.

preliminary, *adj.* einleitend.

prelude, *n.* Einleitung, -en *f.,* Vorspiel, -e *nt.*

premature, *adj.* vorzeitig.

premeditate, *vb.* vorher über-le'gen.

premeditated, *adj.* vorbedacht; mit Vorbedacht.

premier, *n.* Minis'terpräsident, -en, -en *m.*

première, *n.* Uraufführung, -en *f.*

premise, *n.* Prämis'se, -n *f.*

premium, *n.* Prämie, -n *f.*

premonition, *n.* Vorahnung, -en *f.*

prenatal, *adj.* vorgeburtlich.

preparation, *n.* Vorbereitung, -en *f.;* *(of food)* Zubereitung *f.*

preparatory, *adj.* vorbereitend; Vorbereitungs- *(cpds.).*

prepare, *vb.* vor·bereiten; *(food)* zu·bereiten.

preponderant, *adj.* überwie'-gend.

preposition, *n.* Präposition', -en *f.*

preposterous, *adj.* widersinnig.

prerequisite, *n.* Vorbedingung, -en *f.*

prerogative, *n.* Vorrecht, -e *nt.*

prescribe, *vb.* vor·schreiben*; *(med.)* verschrei'ben*.

prescription, *n.* Rezept', -e *nt.*

presence, *n.* Anwesenheit *f.,* Gegenwart *f.*

present, 1. *n.* *(time)* Gegenwart *f.;* *(gram.)* Präsens *nt.;* *(gift)* Geschenk', -e *nt.* **2.** *adj.* an-wesend, gegenwärtig. **3.** *vb.* dar·bieten*; *(introduce)* vor-stellen; *(arms)* präsentie'ren.

presentable, *adj.* präsenta'bel.

presentation, *n.* Darstellung, -en *f.;* Vorstellung, -en *f.*

presently, *adv.* gleich.

preservation, *n.* Erhal'tung *f.*

preservative, *n.* Konservie'-rungsmittel, - *nt.*

preserve, *vb.* bewah'ren, erhal'-ten*; *(food)* konservie'ren, ein·machen.

preside, *vb.* den Vorsitz füh-ren.

presidency, *n.* Vorsitz, -e *m.;* Präsident'schaft *f.*

president, *n.* Präsident', -en, -en *m.*

press, 1. *n.* Presse *f.* **2.** *vb.* pres-sen, drücken; *(iron)* bügeln.

pressing, *adj.* dringend.

pressure, *n.* Druck *m.*

pressure cooker, *n.* Dampf-kochtopf, -̈e *m.*

prestige, *n.* Prestige' *nt.*

presume, *vb.* an·nehmen*; vor-aus'·setzen.

presumptuous, *adj.* anmaßend.

presuppose, *vb.* voraus'·setzen.

pretend, *vb.* vor·geben*.

pretense, *n.* Vorwand, -̈e *m.*

pretentious, *adj.* prätentiös'.

pretext, *n.* Vorwand, -̈e *m.*

pretty, 1. *adj.* hübsch, niedlich. **2.** *adv.* ziemlich.

prevail, *vb.* vor·herrschen; *(win)* siegen; **(p. upon)** über-re'den.

prevalent, *adj.* vorherrschend.

prevent, *vb.* verhin'dern, ver-hü'ten.

prevention, *n.* Verhin'derung *f.,* Verhü'tung, -en *f.*

preventive, *adj.* Verhü'tungs-, Präventiv'- *(cpds.).*

preview, *n.* Vorschau *f.,* Vor-anzeige, -n *f.*

previous, *adj.* vorher'gehend.

prey, *n.* Raub *m.,* Beute *f.*

price, *n.* Preis, -e *m.*

priceless, *adj.* unbezahl'bar.

prick, *vb.* stechen*.

pride, *n.* Stolz *m.,* Hochmut *m.*

priest, *n.* Priester, - *m.,* Pfarrer, - *m.*

prim, *adj.* spröde, prüde.

primary, *adj.* primär'.

prime, 1. *n.* Blüte *f.* **2.** *adj.* Haupt- *(cpds.);* erstklassig; **(p. number)** Primzahl, -en *f.*

prime minister, *n.* Premier'mi-nister, - *m.*

primitive, *adj.* primitiv'.

prince, *n.* *(king's son)* Prinz, -en, -en *m.;* *(other ruler)* Fürst, -en, -en *m.*

princess, *n.* Prinzes'sin, -nen *f.*

principal, 1. *n.* *(school)* Schul-direktor, -o'ren *m.* **2.** *adj.* hauptsächlich, Haupt-*(cpds.).*

principle, *n.* Prinzip', -ien *nt.,* Grundsatz, -̈e *m.*

print, 1. *n.* Druck, -e *m.* **2.** *vb.* drucken.

printing, *n.* Buchdruck *m.*

printing-press, *n.* Drucker-presse, -n *f.*

printout, *n.* Printout, -s *m.*

priority, *n.* Vorrang *m.,* Priori-tät', -en *f.*

prism, *n.* Prisma, -men *nt.*

prison, *n.* Gefäng'nis, -se *nt.*

prisoner, *n.* Gefan'gen- *m.&f.*

privacy, *n.* ungestörtes Allein-sein *nt.*

private, 1. *n.* *(mil.)* Soldat', -en, -en *m.* **2.** *adj.* privat'.

privation, *n.* Berau'bung, *f.;* Not, -̈e *f.*

privilege, *n.* Vorrecht, -e *nt.,* Privileg', -ien *nt.*

privy, 1. *n.* Abort, -e *m.* **2.** *adj.* geheim'.

prize, 1. *n.* Preis, -e *m.* **2.** *vb.* schätzen.

probability, *n.* Wahrschein'-lichkeit, -en *f.*

probable, *adj.* wahrschein'lich.

probation, *n.* Probezeit, -en *f.;* *(jur.)* Bewäh'rungsfrist *f.*

probe, *n.* sondie'ren.

problem, *n.* Problem', -e *nt.*

procedure, *n.* Verfah'ren *nt.*

proceed, *vb.* *(go on)* fort·fah-ren*; *(act)* verfah'ren*.

process, *n.* Verfah'ren, - *nt.*

procession, *n.* Prozession', -en *f.*

proclaim, *vb.* aus·rufen*, ver-kün'den.

proclamation, *n.* Bekannt'ma-chung, -en *f.,* Proklamation', -en *f.*

procrastinate, *vb.* zögern.

procure, *vb.* besor'gen, verschaf'fen.

prodigy, *n.* Wunder, - *nt.;* (**infant p.**) Wunderkind, -er *nt.*

produce, *vb. (show)* vor'legen, vor'führen; *(create)* erzeu'gen, her'stellen, produzie'ren.

product, *n.* Erzeug'nis, -se *nt.,* Produkt', -e *nt.*

production, *n.* Herstellung, -en *f.,* Produktion', -en *f.*

productive, *adj.* produktiv'.

profane, *adj.* profan'.

profanity, *n.* Fluchen *nt.*

profess, *vb.* beken'nen*; *(pretend)* vor'geben*.

profession, *n.* Bekennt'nis, -se *nt.; (calling)* Beruf', -e *m.*

professional, *adj.* berufs'mäßig.

professor, *n.* Profes'sor, -o'ren *m.*

proficient, *adj.* erfah'ren, beschla'gen.

profile, *n.* Profil', -e *nt.*

profit, **1.** *n.* Gewinn' *m.* **2.** *vb.* profitie'ren.

profitable, *adj.* einträglich; *(fig.)* vorteilhaft.

profiteer, *n.* Schieber, - *m.*

profound, *adj.* tief, tiefsinnig.

profundity, *n.* Tiefe *f.;* Tiefgründigkeit *f.*

profuse, *adj.* überreich.

program, *n.* Programm', -e *nt.*

progress, **1.** *n.* Fortschritt, -e *m.* **2.** *vb.* fort'schreiten*.

progressive, *adj.* fortschrittlich.

prohibit, *vb.* verbie'ten*; verhin'dern.

prohibition, *n.* Verbot', -e *nt.*

prohibitive, *adj.* verbie'terisch.

project, **1.** *n.* Projekt', -e *nt.* **2.** *vb.(plan)* projizie'ren; *(stick out)* vor'springen*.

projectile, *n.* Geschoß', -sse *nt.*

projection, *n.* Projektion', -en *f.*

projector, *n.* Projek'tor, -o'ren *m.*

proliferation, *n.* Verbreitung *f.*

prolific, *adj.* fruchtbar.

prologue, *n.* Prolog', -e *m.*

prolong, *vb.* verlän'gern, aus'dehnen.

prominent, *adj.* prominent'.

promiscuous, *adj.* unterschiedslos; sexuell' zügellos.

promise, **1.** *n.* Verspre'chen, - *nt.* **2.** *vb.* verspre'chen*.

promote, *vb.* fördern; *(in rank)* beför'dern.

promotion, *n.* Förderung *f.;* Beför'derung, -en *f.*

prompt, *adj.* prompt.

promulgate, *vb.* verkün'den.

pronoun, *n.* Fürwort, -er *nt.,* Prono'men, -mina *nt.*

pronounce, *vb.* aus'sprechen*.

pronunciation, *n.* Aussprache, -n *f.*

proof, *n.* Beweis, -e *m.; (printing)* Korrektur'bogen, -̈ *m.; (photo)* Abzug, -̈e *m.*

prop, **1.** *n.* Stütze, -n *f.* **2.** *vb.* stützen.

propaganda, *n.* Propagan'da *f.*

propagate, *vb.* fort'pflanzen; verbrei'ten.

propel, *vb.* an'treiben*.

propeller, *n.* Propel'ler, - *m.*

proper, *adj.* passend, angebracht.

property, *n.* Besitz' *m.,* Eigentum *nt.*

prophecy, *n.* Prophezei'ung, -en *f.*

prophesy, *vb.* prophezei'en.

prophet, *n.* Prophet', -en, -en *m.*

prophetic, *adj.* prophe'tisch.

propitious, *adj.* günstig.

proponent, *n.* Verfech'ter, - *m.*

proportion, *n.* Verhält'nis, -se *nt.,* Proportion', -en *f.,* Ausmaß, -e *nt.*

proportionate, *adj.* angemessen.

proposal, *n.* Vorschlag, -̈e *m.; (marriage)* Heiratsantrag, -̈e *m.*

propose, *vb.* vor'schlagen*; *(intend)* beab'sichtigen; einen Heiratsantrag machen.

proposition, *n.* Vorschlag, -̈e *m.; (logic)* Lehrsatz, -̈e *m.*

proprietor, *n.* Inhaber, - *m.,* Eigentümer, - *m.*

propriety, *n.* Anstand *m.*

prosaic, *adj.* prosa'isch.

prose, *n.* Prosa *f.*

prosecute, *vb.* verfol'gen; *(jur.)* an'klagen.

prospect, *n.* Aussicht, -en *f.*

prospective, *adj.* voraus'sichtlich.

prosper, *vb.* gedei'hen*.

prosperity, *n.* Wohlstand *m.*

prosperous, *adj.* blühend, wohlhabend.

prostitute, *n.* Prostituiert'- *f.*

prostrate, **1.** *adj.* hingestreckt. **2.** *vb.* zu Boden werfen*.

protect, *vb.* schützen, beschüt'zen.

protection, *n.* Schutz *m.*

protective, *adj.* Schutz- *(cpds.).*

protector, *n.* Beschüt'zer, - *m.*

protégé, *n.* Protegé', -s *m.*

protein, *n.* Protein' *nt.*

protest, **1.** *n.* Einspruch, -̈e *m.,* Protest', -e *m.* **2.** *vb.* Einspruch erhe'ben*, protestie'ren.

Protestant, **1.** *n.* Protestant', -en, -en *m.* **2.** *adj.* protestan'tisch.

Protestantism, *n.* Protestantis'mus *m.*

protocol, *n.* Protokoll', -e *nt.*

proton, *n.* Proton, -o'nen *nt.*

protrude, *vb.* hervor'stehen*.

protuberance, *n.* Auswuchs, -̈e *m.,* Buckel, - *m.*

proud, *adj.* stolz.

prove, *vb.* bewei'sen*.

proverb, *n.* Sprichwort, -̈er *nt.*

proverbial, *adj.* sprichwörtlich.

provide, *vb.* (**p. for**) sorgen für; (**p. with**) versor'gen mit, verse'hen-* mit.

provided, *adv.* voraus'gesetzt daß.

providence, *n.* Vorsehung *f.;* Vorsorge *f.*

province, *n.* Provinz', -en *f.*

provincial, *adj.* provinziell'.

provision, *n. (stipulation)* Bestim'mung, -en *f.; (food)* Proviant' *m.; (stock)* Vorrat, -̈e *m.*

provocation, *n.* Provokation', -en *f.*

provoke, *vb.* provozie'ren; *(call forth)* hervor'rufen*.

prowess, *n.* Tüchtigkeit *f.*

prowl, *vb.* umher'schleichen*.

proximity, *n.* Nähe *f.*

proxy, *n. (thing)* Vollmacht, -en *f.; (person)* Stellvertreter, - *m.*

prudence, *n.* Vorsicht *f.;* Klugheit *f.*

prudent, *adj.* klug (-̈); umsichtig.

prune, *n.* Backpflaume, -n *f.*

pry, *vb. (break open)* auf'brechen*; *(peer about)* herum'schnüffeln.

psalm, *n.* Psalm, -en *m.*

pseudonym, *n.* Pseudonym', -e *nt.*

psychedelic, *adj.* psychede'lisch, halluzinie'rend

psychiatrist, *n.* Psychia'ter, - *m.*

psychiatry, *n.* Psychiatrie' *f.*

psychoanalysis, *n.* Psychoanaly'se, -n *f.*

psychological, *adj.* psycholo'gisch.

psychology, *n.* Psychologie' *f.*

psychosis, *n.* Psycho'se, -n *f.*

ptomaine, *n.* Ptomain', -e *nt.*

public, **1.** *n.* Öffentlichkeit *f.* **2.** *adj.* öffentlich.

publication, *n.* Veröf'fentlichung, -en *f.,* Publikation', -en *f.*

publicity, *n.* Rekla'me *f.,* Propagan'da *f.*

publish, *vb.* veröf'fentlichen, publizie'ren; *(make known)* bekannt'machen.

publisher, *n.* Heraus'geber, - *m.,* Verle'ger, - *m.*

pudding, *n.* Pudding, -s *m.*

puddle, *n.* Pfütze, -n *f.*

puff, **1.** *n. (wind)* Windstoß, -̈e *m.; (smoke)* Rauchwolke, - *n f.; (powder)* Puderquaste, -n *f.* **2.** *vb.* blasen*; paffen.

pull, **1.** *n.* Zug *m.,* Anziehungskraft *f.; (influence)* Bezie'hung, -en *f.* **2.** *vb.* ziehen*.

pulley, *n.* Flaschenzug, -̈e *m.*

pulmonary, *adj.* Lungen- *(cpds.).*

pulp, *n.* Brei *m.; (fruit)* Fruchtfleisch *nt.*

pulpit, *n.* Kanzel, -n *f.*

pulsar, *n.* Pulsar *m.*

pulsate, vb. pulsie'ren.

pulse, n. Puls, -e m.

pump, 1. n. Pumpe, -n f.; (shoe) Pump -s m. **2.** vb. pumpen.

pumpkin, n. Kürbis, -se m.

pun, n. Wortspiel, -e nt.

punch, 1. n. Schlag, ̈e m., Stoß, ̈e m.; (drink) Punsch m. **2.** vb. schlagen*, stossen*; (make holes) lochen.

punctual, adj. pünktlich.

punctuate, vb. interpunktie'ren.

punctuation, n. Interpunktion' f.

puncture, 1. n. Loch, ̈er m.; (tire) Reifenpanne, -n f.; (med.) Punktion', -en f. **2.** vb. durchste'chen*.

pungent, adj. stechend, beißend.

punish, vb. strafen, bestra'fen.

punishment, n. Strafe, -n f.

puny, adj. mickrig.

pupil, n. Schüler, - m.; Schülerin, -nen f.

puppet, n. Marionet'te, -n f.

puppy, n. junger Hund, -e m.

purchase, 1. n. Kauf, ̈e m., Einkauf, ̈e m. **2.** vb. kaufen, erwer'ben*.

pure, adj. rein.

purée, n. Püree', -s nt.

purgative, n. Abführmittel, - nt.

purge, 1. n. Säuberungsaktion, -en f. **2.** vb. säubern.

purify, vb. reinigen, läutern.

puritanical, adj. purita'nisch.

purity, n. Reinheit f., Echtheit f.

purple, adj. purpurn, lila.

purport, 1. n. Sinn m. **2.** vb. den Anschein erwecken als ob.

purpose, n. Zweck, -e m.; Absicht, -en f.

purposely, adv. absichtlich.

purse, n. (handbag) Handtasche, -n f.; Geldbeutel, - m.

pursue, vb. verfol'gen.

pursuit, n. Verfol'gung, -en f.

push, 1. n. Stoß, ̈e m.; (fig.) Energie', -i'en f. **2.** vb. stossen*, schieben*.

put, vb. setzen; stellen; legen.

putrid, adj. faul, verfault'.

puzzle, 1. n. Rätsel, - nt.; (game) Puzzle, -s nt. **2.** vb. verwir'ren, zu denken geben*.

pyjamas, n.pl. Pyja'ma, -s m.

pyramid, n. Pyrami'de, -n f.

Q

quadrangle, n. Viereck, -e nt.

quadraphonic, adj. quadraphon'.

quadruped, n. Vierfüßler, - m.

quail, n. Wachtel, -n f.

quaint, adj. seltsam; altmodisch.

quake, 1. n. Beben nt. **2.** vb. beben, zittern.

qualification, n. Befä'higung, -en f., Qualifikation', -en f.; (reservation) Einschränkung, -en f.

qualified, adj. geeig'net; (limited) eingeschränkt.

qualify, vb. qualifizie'ren; (limit) einschränken.

quality, n. (characteristic) Eigenschaft, -en f.; (grade) Qualität, -en f.

qualm, n. Beden'ken nt.

quandary, n. Dilem'ma nt.

quantity, n. Menge, -n f., Quantität', -en f.

quarantine, n. Quarantä'ne f.

quarrel, 1. n. Streit m., Zank m. **2.** vb. streiten*, sich streiten*, sich zanken.

quarry, n. Steinbruch, ̈e m.

quarter, 1. n. Viertel, - nt. **2.** vb. einquartieren.

quarterly, 1. n. Vierteljah'resschrift, -en f. **2.** adj. vierteljähr'lich.

quartet, n. Quartett', -e nt.

quasar, n. Quasar m.

queen, n. Königin, -nen f.

queer, adj. merkwürdig, sonderbar.

quell, vb. unterdrü'cken.

quench, vb. löschen, stillen.

query, 1. n. Frage, -n f. **2.** vb. fragen.

quest, n. Suche, -n f.

question, 1. n. Frage, -n f. **2.** vb. fragen, befra'gen; anzweifeln.

questionable, adj. fraglich, fragwürdig.

question mark, n. Fragezeichen, - nt.

questionnaire, n. Fragebogen, ̈ m.

quick, adj. schnell, rasch.

quiet, 1. adj. leise, ruhig, still. **2.** vb. beru'higen.

quilt, n. Steppdecke, -n f.

quinine, n. Chinin' nt.

quintet, n. Quintett', -e nt.

quip, 1. n. witziger Seitenheib, -e m., spitze Bemer'kung, -en f. **2.** vb. witzeln.

quit, vb. (leave) verlas'sen*; (stop) aufhören; (resign) kündigen.

quite, adj. ziemlich; (completely) ganz, völlig.

quiver, 1. n. Köcher, - m. **2.** vb. beben, zittern.

quiz, 1. n. Quiz m.; (school) Klassenarbeit, -en f. **2.** vb. ausfragen.

quorum, n. beschluß'fähige Versamm'lung f.

quota, n. Quote, -n f.

quotation, n. Zitat', -e nt.; (price) Notie'rung, -en f.

quotation mark, n. Anführungsstrich, -e m., Anführungszeichen, - nt.

quote, vb. anführen, zitie'ren.

R

rabbi, n. Rabbi'ner, - m.

rabbit, n. Kanin'chen, - nt.

rabble, n. Volksmenge f., Pöbel m.

rabid, adj. fana'tisch.

rabies, n. Tollwut f.

race, 1. n. (contest) Rennen, - nt., Wettrennen, - nt.; (breed) Rasse, -n f. **2.** vb. rennen*, um die Wette rennen*.

race-track, n. Rennbahn, -en f.

rack, 1. n. (torture) Folterbank, ̈e f.; (feed) Futtergestell, -e nt.; (luggage) Ständer, - m.; (train) Gepäcknetz, -e nt. **2.** vb. foltern.

racket, n. (tennis) Schläger, -m.; (uproar) Krach m.; (crime) Schiebung, -en f.

radar, n. Radar nt.

radiance, n. Glanz m., Strahlen nt.

radiant, adj. strahlend.

radiate, vb. ausstrahlen.

radiation, n. Ausstrahlung, -en f.

radiator, n. Heizkörper, - m.; (auto) Kühler, - m.

radical, adj. radikal'.

radio, n. Rundfunk m.; Rundfunkgerät, -e nt.; Radio, -s nt.

radioactive, adj. radioaktiv'; (r. fall-out) radioakti'ver Niederschlag, ̈e m.

radish, n. Radies'chen, - nt.; (white) Rettich, -e m.; (horser.) Meerrettich, -e m.

radium, n. Radium nt.

radius, n. Radius, -ien m.

raffle, 1. n. Lotterie', -i'en f. **2.** vb. (r. off) auslosen.

raft, n. Floß, ̈e nt.

rag, n. Lumpen, - m., Lappen, - m.

rage, 1. n. Wut f.; (fashion) Schrei m. **2.** vb. wüten, rasen.

ragged, adj. zerlumpt'; (jagged) zackig.

raid, 1. n. Überfall, ̈e m., Razzia, -ien f. **2.** vb. überfal'len*, plündern.

rail, n. Schiene, -n f.

railing, n. Gelän'der, - nt.

railroad, n. Eisenbahn, -en f.

rain, 1. n. Regen m. **2.** vb. regnen.

rainbow, n. Regenbogen, ̈ m.

raincoat, n. Regenmantel, ̈ m.

rainy, adj. regnerisch.

raise, 1. n. (pay) Gehalts'erhöhung, -en f. **2.** vb. (increase) erhö'hen; (lift) heben*; (erect) aufstellen; (collect) auf·treiben*; (bring up) groß·ziehen*.

raisin, n. Rosi'ne, -n f.

rake, 1. n. (tool) Harke, -n f., Rechen, - m.; (person) Roué', -s m. 2. vb. harken.

rally, 1. n. (recovery) Erho'lung, -en f.; (meeting) Kundgebung, -en f.; Massenversammlung, -en f. 2. vb. sich erho'len; sich sammeln.

ram, 1. n. Widder, - m. 2. vb. rammen.

ramble, vb. umher'·schweifen.

ramp, n. Rampe, -n f.

rampart, n. Burgwall, =e m.

ranch, n. Ranch, -es f.

rancid, adj. ranzig.

rancor, n. Groll m.

random, n. (at r.) aufs Geratewohl'.

range, 1. n. (distance) Entfer'nung, -en f.; (scope) Spielraum, =e m.; (mountains) Bergkette, -n f.; (stove) Herd, -e m. 2. vb. (extend) sich erstre'cken.

rank, 1. n. Rang, =e m. 2. vb. ein·reihen.

ransack, vb. durchwüh'len.

ransom, n. Lösegeld, -er nt.

rap, vb. schlagen*, klopfen.

rape, 1. n. Vergewal'tigung, -en f. 2. vb. vergewal'tigen.

rapid, adj. schnell.

rare, adj. selten.

rascal, n. Schlingel, - m.

rash, adj. übereilt', waghalsig.

raspberry, n. Himbeere, -n f.

rat, n. Ratte, -n f.

rate, 1. n. (proportion) Maßstab, =e m.; (price) Preis, -e m.; (exchange r.) Kurs, -e m.; (speed) Geschwin'digkeit, -en f. 2. vb. ein·schätzen.

rather, adv. (preferably) lieber; (on the other hand) vielmehr.

ratify, vb. ratifizie'ren.

ratio, n. Verhält'nis, -se nt.

ration, 1. n. Ration', -en f. 2. vb. rationie'ren.

rational, adj. vernunft'gemäß.

rattle, vb. klappern.

ravage, 1. n. Verwüs'tung, -en f. 2. vb. verwüs'ten.

rave, vb. (fury) toben; (enthusiasm) schwärmen.

raven, 1. n. Rabe, -n, -n m. 2. adj. rabenschwarz.

raw, adj. rauh; (uncooked) roh.

ray, n. Strahl, -en m.

rayon, n. Kunstseide, -n f.

razor, n. (straight) Rasier'messer, - nt.; (safety) Rasier'apparat, -e m.

reach, 1. n. Reichweite f. 2. vb. (tr.) errei'chen; (intr.) reichen.

react, vb. reagie'ren.

reaction, n. Wirkung, -en f., Reaktion', -en f.

reactionary, 1. n. Reaktionär', -e m. 2. adj. reaktionär'.

reactor, n. Reak'tor, -o'ren m.

read, vb. lesen*.

reader, n. (person) Leser, - m.; (book) Lesebuch, =er nt.

readily, adv. gern; (easily) leicht.

reading, n. Lesen nt.

ready, adj. (prepared) bereit'; (finished) fertig.

real, adj. wirklich, tatsächlich; (genuine) echt.

realist, n. Realist', -en m.

reality, n. Wirklichkeit f.

realization, n. (understanding) Erkennt'nis, -se f.; (making real) Verwirk'lichung, -en f., Realisie'rung, -en f.

realize, vb. (understand) erken'nen, begrei'fen, (I r. it) ich bin mir darüber im klaren; (make real, attain) verwirk'lichen, realisie'ren.

realm, n. Reich, -e nt.; (fig.) Bereich', -e m.

reap, vb. ernten.

rear, 1. n. (back) Rückseite, -n f.; (r.·guard) Nachhut, -en f. 2. vb. (bring up) erzie'hen*; (erect) errich'ten; (of horses) sich bäumen.

rear·view mirror, n. Rückspiegel, - m.

reason, 1. n. Vernunft' f.; (cause) Grund, =e m. 2. vb. überle'gen, denken*; (r. with) vernünf'tig reden mit.

reasonable, adj. vernünf'tig.

reassure, vb. versi'chern; beru'higen.

rebate, n. Rabatt', -e m.

rebel, 1. n. Rebell', -en, -en m. 2. vb. rebellie'ren.

rebellion, n. Aufstand, =e m., Rebellion', -en f.

rebellious, adj. rebel'lisch.

rebound, vb. zurück'·prallen.

rebuild, vb. wieder auf·bauen.

rebuke, 1. n. Tadel, - m. 2. vb. tadeln.

rebuttal, n. Widerle'gung, -en f.

recalcitrant, adj. starrköpfig.

recall, vb. zurück'·rufen*; (remember) sich erin'nern an, (revoke) widerru'fen*.

recapitulate, vb. zusam'men·fassen.

recede, vb. zurück'·weichen*.

receipt, n. Quittung, -en f.; (recipe) Rezept', -e nt.

receiver, n. Empfän'ger, - m.; (telephone) Hörer, - m.

recent, adj. neu.

recently, adv. neulich, kürzlich.

receptacle, n. Behäl'ter, - m.

reception, n. Aufnahme, -n f.; (ceremony) Empfang', =e m.

receptive, adj. empfäng'lich.

recess, n. (in wall) Nische, -n f.; (intermission) Pause, -n f.

recipe, n. Rezept', -e nt.

recipient, n. Empfän'ger m.

reciprocate, vb. aus·tauschen; erwi'dern.

recitation, n. Rezitation', -en f.

recite, vb. auf·sagen, vor·tra·gen*.

reckless, adj. rücksichtslos; leichtsinnig.

reclaim, vb. ein·fordern; (land) urbar machen; (waste product) aus·werten.

reclamation, n. (land) Urbarmachung f.

recline, vb. sich zurück'·lehnen.

recognition, n. (acknowledgment) Anerkennung, -en f.; (know again) Wiedererkennung, -en f.

recognize, vb. (acknowledge) an·erkennen*; (know again) wieder·erkennen*.

recoil, vb. zurück'·prallen.

recollect, vb. sich erin'nern an.

recommend, vb. empfeh'len*.

recommendation, n. Empfeh'lung, -en f.

recompense, 1. n. Erstat'tung, -en f. 2. vb. wieder·erstatten.

reconcile, vb. versöh'nen.

reconsider, vb. wieder erwä'gen.

reconstruct, vb. rekonstru·ie'ren.

record, 1. n. (document) Urkunde, -n f.; (top achievement) Rekord', -e m.; (phonograph) Schallplatte, -n f.; (r. player) Plattenspieler, - m. 2. vb. ein·tragen*; auf·zeichnen; (phonograph, tape) auf·nehmen*.

recording, n. (phonograph, tape) Aufnahme, -n f.

recourse, n. Zuflucht f.

recover, vb. wieder·gewinnen*; (health) sich erho'len, gene'sen.

recovery, n. Wiedergewin'nung, -en f.; (health) Erho'lung, -en f.; Gene'sung, -en f.

recruit, 1. n. Rekrut', -en, -en m. 2. vb. an·werben*.

rectangle, n. Rechteck, -e nt.

rectifier, n. Gleichrichter, - m.

rectify, vb. berich'tigen.

recuperate, vb. sich erho'len.

recur, vb. wieder·kommen*, zurück'·kommen*.

recycle, vb. wieder auf·bereiten.

red, adj. rot (-).

Red Cross, n. Rotes Kreuz nt.

redeem, vb. ein·lösen; (eccles.) erlö'sen.

redeemer, n. (eccles.) Erlö'ser m., Heiland m.

redemption, n. Einlösung, -en f.; (eccles.) Erlö'sung f.

reduce, vb. verrin'gern, mindern, reduzie'ren; (prices) herab'·setzen; (weight) ab·nehmen*.

reduction, n. Vermin'derung, -en f.; Herab'setzung, -en f.

Ermäßigung, -en *f.;* Reduktion', -en *f.*

reed, *n.* Schilf *nt.; (music)* Rohrflöte, -n *f.*

reef, 1. *n.* Riff, -e *nt.; (sail)* Reff, -e *nt.* 2. *vb.* reffen.

reel, 1. *n.* Winde, -n *f.,* Spule, -n *f.,* Rolle, -n *f.* 2. *vb.* wickeln, spulen, drehen.

refer, *vb.* (r. to) sich bezie'hen* auf; sich beru'fen* auf; verwei'sen* auf.

referee, *n.* Schiedsrichter, - *m.*

reference, *n.* Bezug'nahme, -n *f.,* Hinweis, -e *m.; (recommendation)* Zeugnis, -se *nt.;* (cross-r.) Querverweis, -e *m.;* (r. library) Handbibliothek, -en *f.*

refill, *vb.* wiederfüllen, nachfüllen.

refine, *vb.* verfei'nern; (tech.) raffinie'ren.

refinement, *n.* Verfei'nerung, -en *f.;* (culture) Bildung *f.*

reflect, *vb.* zurück'strahlen; widerspiegeln; (think) nachdenken*.

reflection, *n.* Widerspiegelung, -en *f.,* Reflexion', -en *f.*

reflex, *n.* Reflex', -e *m.*

reform, 1. *n.* Reform', -en *f.* 2. *vb.* verbes'sern, reformie'ren.

reformation, *n.* Reformation' *f.*

refrain, 1. *n.* Refrain', -s *m.* 2. *vb.* sich enthal'ten*.

refresh, *vb.* auf·frischen; erfri'schen.

refreshment, *n.* Erfri'schung, -en *f.*

refrigerator, *n.* Kühlschrank, ˭ e *m.*

refuge, *n.* Zuflucht *f.*

refugee, *n.* Flüchtling, -e *m.*

refund, 1. *n.* Rückzahlung, -en *f.* 2. *vb.* zurück'zahlen.

refusal, *n.* Verwei'gerung, -en *f.*

refuse, 1. *n.* (waste matter) Abfall, ˭e *m.* 2. *vb.* verwei'gern; ab·schlagen*.

refute, *vb.* widerle'gen.

regain, *vb.* wieder·gewinnen*.

regal, *adj.* königlich.

regard, 1. *n.* Achtung, *f.;* (greetings) Grüße *pl.;* (in r. to) hinsichtlich. 2. *vb.* betrach'ten.

regarding, *prep.* hinsichtlich.

regardless, *adv.* (r. of) ohne Rücksicht auf.

regime, *n.* Regi'me, -s *nt.*

regiment, *n.* Regiment', ˭er *nt.*

region, *n.* Gebiet', -e *nt.,* Gegend, -en *f.*

register, 1. *n.* Verzeich'nis, -se *nt.;* (music) Regis'ter, - *nt.* 2. *vb.* verzeich'nen; eintragen*; (letter) ein·schreiben*.

registration, *n.* Registrie'rung, -en *f.*

regret, 1. *n.* Bedau'ern *nt.* 2. *vb.* bedau'ern, bereu'en.

regular, *adj.* regelmäßig; ordentlich; gewöhn'lich.

regularity, *n.* Regelmäßigkeit *f.*

regulate, *vb.* regeln, ordnen, regulie'ren.

regulation, *n.* Regelung, -en *f.,* Vorschrift, -en *f.*

rehabilitate, *vb.* rehabilitie'ren.

rehearsal, *n.* Probe, -n *f.*

rehearse, *vb.* proben.

reign, 1. *n.* Herrschaft *f.* 2. *vb.* herrschen.

reimburse, *vb.* zurück'erstatten.

rein, *n.* Zügel, - *m.*

reindeer, *n.* Renntier, -e *nt.*

reinforce, *vb.* verstär'ken.

reinforcement, *n.* Verstär'kung, -en *f.*

reinstate, *vb.* wiederein'setzen.

reiterate, *vb.* wiederho'len.

reject, *vb.* ab·lehnen, verwer'fen*.

rejoice, *vb.* frohlo'cken.

rejuvenate, *vb.* verjün'gen.

relapse, 1. *n.* Rückfall, ˭e *m.* 2. *vb.* zurück'fallen*.

relate, *vb.* (tell) berich'ten erzäh'len; (connect) verknüp'fen; (be connected with) sich bezie'hen*.

related, *adj.* verwandt'.

relate (to), *vb.* gemein haben (mit), zurechtkommen* (mit).

relation, *n.* (story) Erzäh'lung, -en *f.;* (connection) Beziehung, -en *f.;* (person) Verwandt' *m.&f.*

relationship, *n.* Bezie'hung, -en *f.;* (kinship) Verwandt'schaft, -en *f.*

relative, 1. *n.* Verwandt'- *m.&f.* 2. *adj.* relativ'.

relativity, *n.* Relativität' *f.*

relax, *vb.* sich entspan'nen; lockern.

relay, 1. *n.* Relais', - *nt.* 2. *vb.* übermit'teln.

release, 1. *n.* Entlas'sung, -en *f.,* Befrei'ung, -en *f.* 2. *vb.* entlas'sen*; frei'lassen*.

relent, *vb.* sich erwei'chen lassen*.

relevant, *adj.* einschlägig.

reliable, *adj.* zuverlässig.

relic, *n.* Reli'quie, -n *f.;* Überrest, -e *m.*

relief, *n.* Erleich'terung, -en *f.;* (social work) Unterstüt'zung, -en *f.;* (replacement) Ablösung, -en *f.;* (art) Relief', -s *nt.*

relieve, *vb.* erleich'tern; ab·lösen.

religion, *n.* Religion', -en *f.*

religious, *adj.* religiös', fromm.

relinquish, *vb.* auf·geben*.

relish, 1. *n.* Genuß', ˭sse *m.* 2. *vb.* genie'ßen*.

reluctance, *n.* Widerstre'ben *nt.*

reluctant, *adj.* widerstre'bend.

rely, *vb.* (r. on) sich verlas'sen* auf.

remain, *vb.* bleiben*; übrig bleiben*.

remainder, *n.* Rest, -e *m.*

remark, 1. *n.* Bemer'kung, -en *f.* 2. *vb.* bemer'ken.

remarkable, *adj.* bemer'kenswert, beacht'lich.

remedy, 1. *n.* Heilmittel, - *nt.* 2. *vb.* heilen; ab·helfen*.

remember, *vb.* sich erin'nern an.

remind, *vb.* erin'nern; ermah'nen.

reminiscence, *n.* Erin'nerung, -en *f.*

remiss, *adj.* nachlässig.

remit, *vb.* (send) übersen'den*; (send money) überwei'sen*; (forgive) verzei'hen*.

remittance, *n.* Überwei'sung, -en *f.*

remnant, *n.* Rest, -e *m.*

remorse, *n.* Gewis'senbiß, -sse *m.*

remote, *adj.* entle'gen.

removable, *adj.* abnehmbar, entfern'bar.

removal, *n.* Entfer'nung *f.,* Besei'tigung *f.*

remove, *vb.* entfer'nen, weg·räumen, besei'tigen.

renaissance, *n.* Renaissance' *f.*

rend, *vb.* zerrei'ßen*.

render, *vb.* geben*; erwei'sen*.

rendezvous, *n.* Stelldichein, - *nt.,* Rendezvous', - *nt.*

rendition, *n.* Wiedergabe, -n *f.*

renew, *vb.* erneu'ern; (subscription) verlän'gern.

renewal, *n.* Erneu'erung, -en *f.;* (subscription) Verlän'gerung, -en *f.*

renounce, *vb.* entsa'gen, verzich'ten auf.

renovate, *vb.* renovie'ren.

renowned, *adj.* berühmt', namhaft.

rent, 1. *n.* Miete, -n *f.* 2. *vb.* (from someone) mieten; (to someone) vermie'ten.

rental, *n.* Miete, -n *f.*

repair, 1. *n.* Ausbesserung, -en *f.,* Reparatur', -en *f.* 2. *vb.* aus·bessern, reparie'ren.

reparation, *n.* Reparation', -en *f.*

repatriate, 1. *n.* Repatriiert'- *m.&f.* 2. *vb.* repatriie'ren.

repay, *vb.* zurück'zahlen.

repeat, *vb.* wiederho'len.

repel, *vb.* zurück'treiben*; ab·schlagen*.

repent, *vb.* bereu'en.

repentance, *n.* Reue *f.*

repercussion, *n.* Auswirkung, -en *f.*

repertoire, *n.* Repertoire', -s *nt.*

repetition, *n.* Wiederho'lung, -en *f.*

replace, *vb.* erset'zen.

replenish, *vb.* wieder auf·füllen.

reply, 1. *n.* Antwort, -en *f.* **2.** *vb.* antworten, erwi'dern.

report, 1. *n.* Bericht', -e *m.;* (bang) Knall, -e *m.;* (rumor) Gerücht', -e *nt.* **2.** *vb.* berich'ten; (complain of) an-zeigen.

reporter, *n.* Bericht'erstatter, - *m.,* Repor'ter, - *m.*

repose, 1. *n.* Ruhe *f.* **2.** *vb.* ru-hen.

represent, *vb.* dar-stellen; ver-tre'ten*.

representation, *n.* Darstellung, -en *f.;* Vertre'tung, -en *f.*

representative, 1. *n.* Vertre'ter, - *m.;* (pol.) Abgeordnet- *m.&f.* **2.** *adj.* bezeich'nend, typisch.

repress, *vb.* unterdrü'cken.

repression, *n.* Unterdrü'ckung, -en *f.,* Repression', -en *f.*

reprimand, 1. *n.* Tadel, - *m.,* Verweis', -e *m.* **2.** *vb.* einen Verweis' ertei'len.

reprisal, *n.* Vergel'tungsmaßnahme, -n *f.*

reproach, 1. *n.* Vorwurf, -e *m.* **2.** *vb.* vor-werfen*.

reproduce, *vb.* reprodu'ren.

reproduction, *n.* Wiedergabe, - n *f.,* Reproduktion', -en *f.*

reptile, *n.* Reptil', -e *nt.*

republic, *n.* Republik', -en *f.*

republican, 1. *n.* Republika'ner, - *m.* **2.** *adj.* republika'nisch.

repudiate, *vb.* ab-leugnen.

repudiation, *n.* Zurück'weisung, -en *f.,* Nichtanerkennung, -en *f.*

repulse, *vb.* zurück'schlagen*.

repulsive, *adj.* widerwärtig.

reputation, *n.* Ruf *m.,* Ansehen *nt.*

repute, *n.* Ansehen *nt.*

request, 1. *n.* Bitte, -n *f.,* Gesuch', -e *nt.* **2.** *vb.* bitten*, ersu'chen.

require, *vb.* verlan'gen, erfor'dern.

requirement, *n.* Erfor'dernis, -se *nt.;* Bedin'gung, -en *f.*

requisite, 1. *n.* Erfor'dernis, -se *nt.* **2.** *adj.* erfor'derlich.

requisition, 1. *n.* Forderung, - en *f.,* Requisition', -en *f.* **2.** *vb.* an-fordern; beschlag'nahmen.

rescind, *vb.* rückgängig machen, auf-heben*.

rescue, 1. *n.* Rettung, -en *f.* **2.** *vb.* retten.

research, *n.* Forschung, -en *f.*

resemble, *vb.* gleichen*, ähneln.

resent, *vb.* übel-nehmen*.

reservation, *n.* vorbehalt *m.;* (tickets) Vorbestellung, -en *f.* **(Indian r.)** Reservation', -en *f.*

reserve, 1. *n.* Reser've, -n *f.* **2.** *vb.* vor-behalten*; (seats) reservie'ren.

reservoir, *n.* Reservoir', -s *nt.*

reside, *vb.* wohnen.

residence, *n.* Wohnsitz, -e *m.*

resident, 1. *n.* Einwohner, - *m.* **2.** *adj.* wohnhaft.

residue, *n.* Rest, -e *m.,* Restbestand, -e *m.*

resign, *vb.* zurück'treten*; (r. oneself) sich ab-finden* mit, resignie'ren.

resignation, *n.* Rücktritt, -e *m.;* Resignation', -en *f.*

resist, *vb.* widerste'hen*.

resistance, *n.* Widerstand, -e *m.*

resolute, *adj.* entschlos'sen.

resolution, *n.* Beschluß', -sse *m.;* Entschlos'senheit *f.*

resolve, *vb.* entschei'den*; beschlie'ßen*.

resonance, *n.* Resonanz', -en *f.*

resonant, *adj.* resonant'.

resort, *n.* Ferienort, -e *m.;* Kurort, -e *m.*

resound, *vb.* wider-hallen.

resources, *n.pl.* Hilfsquellen *pl.;* (natural r.) Bodenschätze *pl.*

respect, 1. *n.* (esteem) Achtung *f.;* (reference) Hinsicht, -en *f.* **2.** *vb.* achten.

respectable, *adj.* angesehen, ansehnlich.

respectful, *adj.* ehrerbietig, höflich.

respective, *adj.* entspre'chend.

respiration, *n.* Atmung *f.*

respite, *n.* Frist, -en *f.;* Atempause, -n *f.*

respond, *vb.* (answer) antworten; (react) reagie'ren.

response, *n.* Antwort, -en *f.;* Reaktion', -en *f.*

responsibility, *n.* Verant'wortung, -en *f.*

responsible, *adj.* verant'wortlich.

responsive, *adj.* zugänglich.

rest, 1. *n.* (remainder) Rest, -e *m.;* (repose) Ruhe *f.* **2.** *vb.* ruhen; (be based on) beru'hen auf.

restaurant, *n.* Restaurant', -s *nt.*

restful, *adj.* ausruhsam.

restitution, *n.* Wiedergut'machung, -en *f.*

restless, *adj.* unruhig.

restoration, *n.* Wiederher'stellung, -en *f.*

restore, *vb.* wiederher'stellen.

restrain, *vb.* zurück'halten*.

restraint, *n.* Zurück'haltung *f.*

restrict, *vb.* beschrän'ken, ein-schränken.

restriction, *n.* Einschränkung, -en *f.,* Beschrän'kung, -en *f.*

result, 1. *n.* Ergeb'nis, -se *nt.,* Resultat', -e *nt.* **2.** *vb.* erge'ben*; zur Folge haben*.

resume, *vb.* wieder auf-nehmen*.

résumé, *n.* Resümee', -s *nt.*

resurrect, *vb.* wieder-erwecken; wieder hervor'holen.

resurrection, *n.* (eccles.) Aufer'stehung *f.*

retail, 1. *n.* Einzelhandel *m.* **2.** *vb.* im Einzelhandel vertrei'ben*.

retain, *vb.* bei-behalten*; zurück'halten*; auf-halten*.

retaliate, *vb.* vergel'ten*.

retaliation, *n.* Vergel'tung, -en *f.*

retard, *vb.* verzö'gern. zurück'halten*.

retention, *n.* Beibehaltung, -en *f.*

reticence, *n.* Zurück'haltung *f.;* Verschwie'genheit *f.*

reticent, *adj.* zurück'haltend, schweigsam.

retina, *n.* Netzhaut, -e *f.*

retinue, *n.* Gefol'ge *nt.*

retire, *vb.* sich zurück'zie-hen*; (from office) sich pensionie'ren lassen*, in den Ruhestand treten*.

retort, 1. *n.* Retor'te, -n *f.;* (answer) Erwi'derung, -en *f.* **2.** *vb.* erwi'dern.

retract, *vb.* (pull back) zurück'ziehen*, (recant) wider'ru'fen*.

retreat, 1. *n.* (withdrawal) Rückzug, -e *m.;* (refuge) Zuflucht *f.;* (privacy) Zurück'gezogenheit *f.* **2.** *vb.* zurück'weichen*.

retribution, *n.* Strafe, -en *f.,* Vergel'tung *f.*

retrieve, *vb.* wieder-erlangen.

retroactive, *adj.* rückwirkend.

retrospect, *n.* Rückblick *m.*

return, 1. *n.* Rückkehr *f.,* Heimkehr *f.;* Rückgabe *f.* **2.** *vb.* zurück'kehren, zurück'kommen; zurück'geben*.

reunion, *n.* Wiederzusam'menkommen *nt.*

reunite, *vb.* wieder verei'nigen.

reveal, *vb.* offenba'ren; zeigen.

revel, *vb.* schwelgen.

revelation, *n.* Offenba'rung, -en *f.*

revelry, *n.* Schwegerei', -en *f.*

revenge, 1. *n.* Rache *f.* **2.** *vb.* rächen.

revenue, *n.* Einkommen, - *nt.*

reverberate, *vb.* wider-hallen.

revere, *vb.* vereh'ren.

reverence, *n.* Vereh'rung, -en *f.;* Ehrfurcht *f.*

reverend, *adj.* ehrwürdig.

reverent, *adj.* ehrerbietig.

reverie, *n.* Träumerei', -en *f.*

reverse, 1. *n.* (opposite) Gegenteil *m.;* (back) Rückseite, -n *f.;* (misfortune) Rückschlag, - e *m.;* (auto) Rückwärtsgang, - e *m.* **2.** *vb.* um-drehen; (auto) rückwärts-fahren*; (tech.) um-steuern.

revert, *vb.* zurück'kehren.

review, 1. *n.* nochmalige Durchsicht, -en *f.,* Überblick, -e *m.;* (book r.) Kritik', -en *f.,* Bespre'chung, -en *f.* **2.** *vb.* überbli'cken, revidie'ren; bespre'chen*.

revise, vb. ab-ändern, revidie'ren.

revision, n. Revision', -en f.

revival, n. Wiederbelebung, -en f., Neubelebung, -en f.

revive, vb. (person) wieder zu Bewußt'sein bringen*; (fashion) wieder auf-leben lassen*.

revocation, n. Aufhebung, -en f.

revoke, vb. widerru'fen*, aufheben*.

revolt, 1. n. Aufstand, -e m. **2.** vb. revoltie'ren.

revolution, n. Revolution', -en f.; (turn) Umdre'hung, -en f.

revolutionary, adj. revolutionär'.

revolve, vb. sich drehen.

revolver, n. Revol'ver, - m.

reward, 1. n. Beloh'nung, -en f. **2.** vb. beloh'nen.

rhetorical, adj. rheto'risch.

rheumatic, adj. rheuma'tisch.

rheumatism, n. Rheumatis'mus m.

rhinoceros, n. Nashorn, -er nt.

rhubarb, n. Rhabar'ber m.

rhyme, n. Reim, -e m.

rhythm, n. Rhythmus, -men m.

rhythmical, adj. rhythmisch.

rib, n. Rippe, -n f.

ribbon, n. Band, -er nt.

rice, n. Reis m.

rich, adj. reich.

rid, vb. los-werden*; sich los-machen.

riddle, n. Rätsel, - nt.

ride, 1. n. (horse) Ritt, -e m.; (vehicles) Fahrt, -en f. **1.** vb. reiten*; fahren*.

rider, n. Reiter, - m.

ridge, n. (mountain) Grat, -e m.; (mountain range) Bergrücken, - m.

ridicule, 1. n. Spott m. **2.** vb. lächerlich machen, bespöt'teln.

ridiculous, adj. lächerlich.

rifle, n. Gewehr', -e nt.

rig, 1. n. (gear) Ausrüstung, -en f.; (ship) Takela'ge, -n f.; (oil) Ölbohrer, -m. **2.** vb. auf-takeln.

right, 1. n. Recht, -e nt. **2.** adj. (side) recht-; (just) gerecht'; (be r.) recht haben*. **3.** adv. rechts. **4.** vb. (set upright) auf-richten; (correct) wiedergut'-machen.

righteous, adj. rechtschaffen; (smug) selbstgerecht.

righteousness, n. Rechtschaffenheit f.; Selbstgerechtheit f.

right of way, n. Vorfahrtsrecht, -e nt.

rigid, adj. steif; starr.

rigidity, n. Starrheit f.

rigor, n. Härte, -n f.

rigorous, adj. hart (-), streng.

rim, n. Rand, -er m.

ring, 1. n. Ring, -e m; (circle) Kreis, -e m.; (of bell) Klingeln nt. **2.** vb. klingeln.

rinse, vb. spülen.

riot, 1. n. Aufruhr, -e m. **2.** vb. in Aufruhr gera'ten*.

rip, vb. reißen*; auf-trennen.

ripe, adj. reif.

ripen, n., vb. reifen.

ripoff, n. Übervor'teilung f.

rip off, vb. jemand reinlegen

ripple, 1. n. leichte Welle, -n f. **2.** vb. leichte Wellen schlagen*.

rise, 1. n. (increase) Zuwachs m.; (emergence) Aufgang, -e m.; (advance) Aufstieg, -e m. **2.** vb. an-steigen*; auf-gehen*; (get up) auf-stehen*.

risk, 1. n. Risiko, -s nt. **2.** vb. wagen.

rite, n. Ritus, -ten m.

ritual, 1. n. Rituell', -e nt. **2.** adj. rituell'.

rival, 1. n. Riva'le, -n, -n m., Konkurrenz', -en f. **2.** adj. Konkurrenz- (cpds.). **3.** vb. wetteifern, rivalisie'ren.

rivalry, n. Konkurrenz', -en f., Wettstreit m.

river, n. Fluß, -sse m.

rivet, 1. n. Niete, -n f. **2.** vb. nieten.

road, n. Straße, -n f., Landstraße, -n f.

roam, vb. umher-schweifen.

roar, 1. n. Gebrüll' nt. **2.** vb. brüllen; brausen.

roast, 1. n. Braten, - m. **2.** vb. braten*; rösten.

rob, vb. rauben; berau'ben.

robber, n. Räuber, - m.; Dieb, -e m.

robbery, n. Raub m.

robe, n. Gewand', -er m.

robin, n. Rotkehlchen, - nt.

robot, n. Roboter, - m.

robust, adj. robust'.

rock, 1. n. Stein, -e m.; Felsen, - m.; (music) Rock m., Rockmusik f. **2.** vb. schaukeln.

rocker, n. Schaukelstuhl, -e m.

rocket, n. Rake'te, -n f.

rocky, adj. felsig; (shaky) wackelig.

rod, n. Stab, -e m., Stange, -n f.

rodent, n. Nagetier, -e nt.

roe, n. Rogen, - m.; (deer) Reh, -e nt.

role, n. Rolle, -n f.

roll, 1. n. Rolle, -n f.; Walze, -n f.; (bread) Brötchen, - nt. **2.** vb. rollen; (ship) schlingern.

roller, n. Rolle, -n f.; Walze, -n f.

Roman, 1. n. Römer, - m. **2.** adj. römisch.

romance, n. Roman'ze, -n f.; Liebesaffäre, -n f.

Romance, adj. roma'nisch.

romantic, adj. roman'tisch.

romanticism, n. Roman'tik f.

Rome, n. Rom nt.

roof, n. Dach, -er nt.

room, n. Zimmer, - nt., Raum, -e m.; (space) Raum m.

roommate, n. Zimmergenosse, -n, -n m.

rooster, n. Hahn, -e m.

root, 1. n. Wurzel, -n f. **2.** vb. (be rooted) wurzeln.

rope, n. Tau, -e nt., Seil, -e nt., Strick, -e m.

rosary, n. Rosenkranz, -e m.

rose, n. Rose, -n f.

rosy, adj. rosig.

rot, vb. verfau'len, verwe'sen.

rotate, vb. rotie'ren; sich ab-wechseln.

rotation, n. Umdre'hung, -en f., Rotation', -en f.; Wechsel. - m.

rotten, adj. faul; (base) niederträchtig.

rouge, n. Rouge nt.

rough, adj. rauh; (coarse) grob (-); (sea) stürmisch.

round, 1. n. Runde, -n f. **2.** adj. rund. **3.** prep. um, um . . . herum'.

rout, 1. n. wilde Flucht f. **2.** vb. in die Flucht schlagen*.

route, n. Weg, -e m. Route, -n f.

routine, 1. n. Routi'ne, -n f. **2.** adj. alltäglich.

rove, vb. umher-streifen.

row, 1. n. (line, series) Reihe, -n f.; (fight) Krach m. **2.** vb. rudern.

rowboat, n. Ruderboot, -e nt.

royal, adj. königlich.

royalty, n. Königstum nt.; Mitglied eines Königshauses; (share of profit) Gewinn'anteil, -e m.

rub, vb. reiben*.

rubber, n. Gummi nt.

rubbish, n. Abfall, -e m.; (nonsense) Quatsch m.

ruby, n. Rubin', -e m.

rudder, n. Steuerruder, - nt.

rude, adj. rauh, unhöflich.

rudiment, n. erster Anfang, -e m.; Anfangsgrund, -e m.

ruffle, 1. n. Rüsche, -n f. **2.** vb. kräuseln.

rug, n. Teppich, -e m.

rugged, adj. rauh, hart (-).

ruin, 1. n. Untergang m.; Rui'ne, -n f.; (r.s) Trümmer pl. **2.** vb. ruinie'ren.

ruinous, adj. verderb'lich, katastrophal'.

rule, 1. n. (reign) Herrschaft f.; (regulation) Regel, -n f. **2.** vb. herrschen; entschei'den*.

ruler, n. Herrscher, - m.; (measuring stick) Lineal', -e nt.

rum, n. Rum m.

rumor, 1. n. Gerücht', -e nt. **2.** vb. munkeln.

run, 1. n. Lauf m.; (stocking) Laufmasche, -n f. **2.** vb. laufen*; (flow) fließen*.

rung, n. Sprosse, -n f.

runner, n. Läufer, - m.

runway, n. Startbahn, -en f.

rupture, 1. n. Bruch, -e m. **2.** vb. brechen*; reißen*.

rural, adj. ländlich.

rush, 1. *n.* Andrange *m.;* *(hurry)* Eile *f.* 2. *vb.* draͤngen; eilen, sich stuͤrzen.

Russia, *n.* Rußland *nt.*

Russian, 1. *n.* Russe, -n, -n *m.* 2. *adj.* russisch.

rust, 1. *n.* Rost *m.* 2. *vb.* rosten.

rustic, *adj.* baͤurisch.

rustle, *vb.* rascheln.

rusty, *adj.* rostig.

rut, *n.* Rinne, *f.;* Radspur, -en *f.*

ruthless, *adj.* erbar'mungslos, ruͤcksichtslos.

rye, *n.* Roggen *m.*

S

Sabbath, *n.* Sabbat, -e *m.*

saber, *n.* Saͤbel, - *m.*

sable, *n.* Zobel *m.*

sabotage, 1. *n.* Sabota'ge *f.* 2. *vb.* sabotie'ren.

saboteur, *n.* Saboteur', -e *m.*

saccharine, *n.* Sacharin' *f.*

sack, 1. *n.* Sack, ͤe *m.* 2. *vb.* *(plunder)* pluͤndern; *(discharge)* auf der Stelle entlas'-sen*.

sacrament, *n.* Sakrament', -e *nt.*

sacred, *adj.* heilig.

sacrifice, 1. *n.* Opfer, - *nt.* 2. *vb.* opfern.

sacrilege, *n.* Sakrileg', -e *nt.*

sacrilegious, *adj.* gottesläster-lich.

sad, *adj.* traurig.

sadden, *vb.* betruͤ'ben.

saddle, 1. *n.* Sattel, - *m.* 2. *vb.* satteln.

sadism, *n.* Sadis'mus *m.*

safe, 1. *n.* Geldschrank, ͤe *m.* 2. *adj.* sicher.

safeguard, 1. *n.* Schutz *m.* 2. *vb.* schuͤtzen; sichern.

safety, *n.* Sicherheit *f.*

safety-pin, *n.* Sicherheitsnadel, -n *f.*

sage, *adj.* weise.

sail, 1. *n.* Segel, - *nt.* 2. *vb.* se-geln.

sailboat, *n.* Segelboot, -e *nt.*

sailor, *n.* Matro'se, -n, -n *m.*

saint, 1. *n.* Heilig- *m.&f.* 2. *adj.* heilig.

sake, *n.* **(for the s. of)** um . . . willen.

salad, *n.* Salat', -e *m.*

salary, *n.* Gehalt', ͤer *nt.*

sale, *n.* Verkauf' *m.;* **(bargain s.)** Ausverkauf *m.*

salesman, *n.* Verkaͤufer, - *m.;* **(traveling s.)** Handelsreisend-*m.*

sales tax, *n.* Umsatzsteuer, -n *f.*

saliva, *n.* Speichel *m.*

salmon, *n.* Lachs *m.*

salon, *n.* Salon', -s *m.*

salt, 1. *n.* Salz, -e *nt.* 2. *vb.* sal-zen.

salty, *adj.* salzig.

salutation, *n.* Gruß, ͤe *m.;* Be-gruͤ'ßung, -en *f.*

salute, 1. *n.* Gruß, ͤe *m.* 2. *vb.* salutie'ren.

salvage, 1. *n.* *(act)* Bergung *f.;* *(material)* Bergegut *nt.* 2. *vb.* bergen*, retten.

salvation, *n.* Rettung *f.,* Heil *nt.*

salve, *n.* Salbe, -n *f.*

same, *adj.* selb-; **(the s.)** der-selbe, dasselbe, dieselbe.

sample, 1. *n.* Probe, -n *f.,* Mus-ter, - *nt.* 2. *vb.* probie'ren.

sanatorium, *n.* Sanato'rium, -rien *nt.*

sanctify, *vb.* heiligen.

sanction, 1. *n.* Sanktion', -en *f.* 2. *vb.* sanktionie'ren.

sanctity, *n.* Heiligkeit *f.*

sanctuary, *n.* Heiligtum, ͤer *nt.;* *(refuge)* Zufluchtsort, -e *m.*

sand, *n.* Sand, -e *m.*

sandal, *n.* Sanda'le, -n *f.*

sandwich, *n.* belegtes Brot, -e *nt.*

sandy, *adj.* sandig.

sane, *adj.* vernuͤnf'tig; geistig gesund.

sanitary, *adj.* Gesund'heits-*(cpds.);* hygie'nisch.

sanitation, *n.* Gesund'heitswe-sen *nt.*

sanity, *n.* geistige Gesund'heit *f.*

Santa Claus, *n.* Weihnachts-mann, ͤer *m.*

sap, 1. *n.* Saft, ͤe *m.* 2. *vb.* schwaͤchen.

sapphire, *n.* Saphir', -e *m.*

sarcasm, *n.* Sarkas'mus *m.*

sarcastic, *adj.* sarkas'tisch.

sardine, *n.* Sardi'ne, -n *f.*

sash, *n.* Schaͤrpe, -n *f.;* *(window)* Fensterrahmen, - *m.*

satellite, *n.* Satellit', -en, -en *m.*

satin, *n.* Satin', -s *m.*

satire, *n.* Sati're, -n *f.*

satirize, *vb.* verspot'ten.

satisfaction, *n.* Genug'tuung, -en *f.;* Befrie'digung, -en *f.*

satisfactory, *adj.* befrie'digend, genuͤ'gend.

satisfy, *vb.* befrie'digen, genuͤ'-gen.

saturate, *vb.* saͤttigen.

saturation, *n.* Saͤttigung *f.*

Saturday, *n.* Sonnabend, -e *m.,* Samstag, -e *m.*

sauce, *n.* Soße, -n *f.*

saucer, *n.* Untertasse, -n *f.*

sausage, *n.* Wurst, ͤe *f.*

savage, 1. *n.* Wild- *m.&f.* 2. *adj.* wild.

save, 1. *vb.* *(preserve)* bewah'-ren; *(rescue)* retten; *(econo-mize)* sparen. 2. *prep.* außer.

savings, *n.pl.* Erspar'nisse *pl.*

savior, *n.* Retter, - *m.;* *(eccles.)* Heiland *m.*

savor, 1. *n.* Geschmack', ͤe *m.* 2. *vb.* aus·kosten.

saw, 1. *n.* Saͤge, -n *f.;* *(proverb)*

Sprichwort, ͤer *nt.* 2. *vb.* saͤ-gen.

say, *vb.* sagen.

saying, *n.* Redensart, -en *f.*

scab, *n.* Schorf *m.;* *(strike breaker)* Streikbrecher, - *m.*

scaffold, *n.* Geruͤst', -e *nt.;* *(ex-ecution)* Schafott', -e *nt.*

scald, *vb.* bruͤhen; verbruͤ'hen.

scale, 1. *n.* Maßstab, ͤe *m.,* Skala, -len *f.;* *(music)* Tonlei-ter, -n *f.;* *(weight measuring)* Waage, -n *f.;* *(fish)* Schuppe, -n *f.* 2. *vb.* *(climb)* erklet'tern.

scalp, *n.* Kopfhaut, ͤe *f.;* *(In-dian)* Skalp, -e *m.*

scan, *vb.* uͤberflie'gen*; *(verse)* skandie'ren.

scandal, *n.* Skandal', -e *m.*

scandalous, *adj.* schimpflich, unerhoͤrt'.

scant, *adj.* knapp.

scar, *n.* Narbe, -n *f.*

scarce, *adj.* selten; knapp.

scarcely, *adv.* kaum.

scarcity, *n.* Knappheit *f.,* Man-gel *m.*

scare, 1. *n.* Schreck *m.* 2. *vb.* erschre'cken; **(be s.d)** er-schre'cken*.

scarf, *n.* Schal, -s *m.,* Halstuch, ͤer *nt.*

scarlet, *adj.* scharlachrot.

scarlet fever, *n.* Scharlach *m.*

scatter, *vb.* zerstreu'en.

scenario, *n.* Inszenie'rung, -en *f.;* *(film)* Drehbuch, ͤer *nt.*

scene, *n.* Szene, -n *f.*

scenery, *n.* Landschaft, -en *f.;* *(stage)* Buͤhnenausstattung, -en *f.*

scent, *n.* Geruch', ͤe *m.;* *(track)* Spur, -en *f.*

schedule, 1. *n.* Liste, -n *f.;* Pro-gramm', -e *nt.;* *(timetable)* Fahrplan, ͤe *m.;* *(school)* Stundenplan, ͤe *m.* 2. *vb.* an·setzen.

scheme, 1. *n.* Plan, ͤe *m.,* Schema, -s *nt.* 2. *vb.* intrigie'-ren.

scholar, *n.* Gelehrt'- *m.&f.*

scholarship, *n.* *(knowledge)* Ge-lehr'samkeit *f.;* *(stipend)* Sti-pen'dium, -dien *nt.*

school, *n.* Schule, -n *f.*

science, *n.* Wissenschaft, -en *f.*

science fiction, *n.* Science fic-tion *f.*

scientific, *adj.* wissenschaft-lich.

scientist, *n.* Natur'wissen-schaftler, - *m.*

scissors, *n.pl.* Schere, -n *f.*

scold, *vb.* schelten*.

scolding, *n.* Schelte *f.*

scoop, *n.* *(ladle)* Schoͤpfkelle, -n *f.;* *(newspaper)* Erstmel-dung, -en *f.*

scope, *n.* Reichweite *f.,* Be-reich', -e *m.*

scorch, *vb.* sengen, brennen*.

score, 1. *n.* *(points)* Punktzahl, -en *f.;* **(what's the s.?)** wie steht das Spiel?; *(music)* Partitur', -en *f.* **2.** *vb.* an·schreiben*; *(mark)* markie'ren.

scorn, 1. *n.* Verach'tung *f.* **2.** *vb.* verach'ten.

scornful, *adj.* verächt'lich.

Scotland, *n.* Schottland *nt.*

Scotsman, *n.* Schotte, -n, -n *m.*

Scottish, *adj.* schottisch.

scour, *vb.* scheuern.

scout, 1. *n.* Kundschafter, - *m.; (boy s.)* Pfadfinder, - *m.* **2.** *vb.* erkun'den.

scowl, *vb.* finster blicken.

scramble, *vb. (tr.)* durcheinan'der·werfen*; *(intr.)* klettern; **(s. for)** sich reißen*um.

scrambled eggs, *n.* Rührei, -er *nt.*

scrap, 1. *n.* Fetzen, - *m.; (fight)* Streit *m.* **2.** *vb.* aus·rangieren; *(fight)* streiten*.

scrape, *vb.* kratzen.

scratch, 1. *n.* Schramme, -n *f.* **2.** *vb.* kratzen; streichen*; **(start from s.)** von Anfang an begin'nen*.

scream, 1. *n.* Schrei, -e *m.* **2.** *vb.* schreien*, brüllen.

screen, 1. *n. (furniture)* Wandschirm, -e *m.; (window)* Fliegengitter, - *nt.; (movie)* Leinwand, ¨-e *f.; (TV, radar)* Schirm, -e *m.; (camouflage)* Tarnung, -en *f.* **2.** *vb. (sift)* sieben; *(hide)* tarnen.

screw, 1. *n.* Schraube, -n *f.* **2.** *vb.* schrauben.

scribble, *vb.* kritzeln, schmieren.

scripture, *n. (eccles.)* Heilige Schrift, -en *f.*

scroll, *n.* Schriftrolle, -n *f.*

scrub, *vb.* schrubbern.

scruple, *n.* Skrupel - *m.,* Bedenʾken, - *nt.*

scrupulous, *adj.* gewisʾsenhaft.

scrutinize, *vb.* genau' betrach'ten.

sculptor, *n.* Bildhauer, - *m.*

sculpture, 1. *n.* Skulptur', -en *f.* **2.** *vb.* bildhauern.

scythe, *n.* Sense, -n *f.*

sea, *n.* See, Seʾen *f.,* Meer, -e *nt.; (waves)* Seegang *m.*

seabed, *n.* Meeresboden *m.*

seal, 1. *n.* Siegel, - *nt.; (animal)* Seehund, -e *m.,* Robbe, -n *f.* **2.** *vb.* siegeln, versieʾgeln.

seam, 1. *n.* Saum, ¨-e *m.* **2.** *vb.* säumen.

seaport, *n.* Hafen, ¨- *m.*

search, 1. *n.* Suche *f.;* Durch·suʾchung, -en *f.* **2.** *vb.* suchen; durch·suʾchen.

seasick, *adj.* seekrank (¨-).

seasickness, *n.* Seekrankheit *f.*

season, 1. *n.* Jahreszeit, -en *f.;* Saison', -s *f.* **2.** *vb.* würzen.

seasoning, *n.* Gewürz', -e *nt.*

seat, 1. *n.* Platz, ¨-e *m.,* Sitzplatz, ¨-e *m.; (headquarters)* Sitz, -e *m.* **2.** *vb.* Sitzplätze habenʾ* für.

second, 1. *n.* Sekunʾde, -n *f.* **2.**

---

adj. zweit-. **3.** *vb.* **(s. a motion)** einen Antrag unterstütʾzen.

secondary, *adj.* sekundär'.

secret, 1. *n.* Geheim'nis, -se *nt.* **2.** *adj.* geheim', heimlich.

secretary, *n.* Sekretär', -e *m.;* Sekretäʾrin, -nen *f.; (organization)* Schriftführer, - *m.*

sect, *n.* Sekte, -n *f.*

section, *n.* Schnitt, -e *m.;* Teil, -e *m.;* Abschnitt, -e *m.;* Abteiʾlung, -en *f.*

secular, *adj.* weltlich.

secure, 1. *adj.* sicher. **2.** *vb.* sichern.

security, *n.* Sicherheit, -en *f.*

sedative, *n.* Beruʾhigungsmittel, - *nt.*

seduce, *vb.* verfüh'ren.

seductive, *adj.* verfüh'rerisch.

see, *vb.* sehen*, schauen.

seed, *n. (individual)* Samen, - *m.; (collective & fig.)* Saat, -en *f.*

seek, *vb.* suchen.

seem, *vb.* scheinen*.

seep, *vb.* sickern.

seesaw, *n.* Wippe, -n *f.*

segment, *n.* Segment', -e *nt.*

segregate, *vb.* ab·sondern.

seize, *vb.* fassen, ergrei'fen*; *(confiscate)* beschlag'nahmen.

seldom, *adv.* selten.

select, 1. *adj.* ausgesucht. **2.** *vb.* aus·wählen, aus·suchen.

selection, *n.* Auswahl, -en *f.*

selective, *adj.* auswählend.

self, *adv.* selbst, selber.

selfish, *adj.* selbstsüchtig.

selfishness, *n.* Selbstsucht *f.*

sell, *vb.* verkau'fen.

semantic, *adj.* seman'tisch.

semantics, *n.* Seman'tik *f.*

semester, *n.* Semesʾter, - *nt.*

semicircle, *n.* Halbkreis, -e *m.*

semicolon, *n.* Strichpunkt, -e *m.,* Semikoʾlon *nt.*

seminary, *n.* Seminar', -e *nt.*

senate, *n.* Senat', -e *m.*

senator, *n.* Senaʾtor, -oʾren *m.*

send, *vb.* senden*, schicken.

senile, *adj.* senil'.

senior, *adj.* älter-.

senior citizen, *n.* Senior, -oʾren *m.;* Senioʾrin, -nen *f.*

sensation, *n.* Sensation', -en *f.; (feeling)* Gefühl', -e *nt.*

sensational, *adj.* sensationell'.

sense, 1. *n.* Sinn, -e *m.; (feeling)* Gefühl', -e *nt.; (meaning)* Bedeuʾtung, -en *f.* **2.** *vb.* fühlen, empfin'den*.

sensible, *adj.* vernünf'tig.

sensitive, *adj.* empfind'lich; sensitiv'.

sensual, *adj.* sinnlich.

sentence, 1. *n.* Satz, ¨-e *m.; (judgment)* Urteil, -e *nt.* **2.** *vb.* verur'teilen.

sentiment, *n.* Gefühl', -e *nt.,* Empfin'dung, -en *f.*

sentimental, *adj.* gefühl'voll, sentimental'.

---

separate, 1. *adj.* getrennt'. **2.** *vb.* trennen.

separation, *n.* Trennung, -en *f.*

September, *n.* Septem'ber, - *m.*

sequence, *n.* Reihenfolge, -n *f.*

serenade, *n.* Ständchen, - *nt.*

serene, *adj.* klar, ruhig.

sergeant, *n.* Unteroffizier, -e *m.; (police)* Wachtmeister, - *m.*

serial, 1. *n.* fortlaufende Erzäh'lung, -en *f.* **2.** *adj.* Reihen- *(cpds.).*

series, *n.* Reihe, -n *f.*

serious, *adj.* ernst.

seriousness, *n.* Ernst *m.*

sermon, *n.* Predigt, -en *f.*

serpent, *n.* Schlange, -n *f.*

serum, *n.* Serum, -ra *nt.*

servant, *n.* Diener, - *m.; (domestic)* Hausangestellt- *m.&f.*

serve, *vb.* dienen; *(offer food)* servie'ren.

service, *n.* Dienst, -e *m.; (hotel, etc.)* Bedie'nung *f.; (china, etc.)* Servi'ce *nt.; (church)* Gottesdienst, -e *m.*

session, *n.* Sitzung, -en *f.*

set, 1. *n. (dishes, tennis)* Satz, -¨ e *m.; (articles belonging together)* Garnitur', -en *f.* **2.** *adj.* bestimmt'. **3.** *vb.* setzen; stellen; legen; *(sun)* unter·gehen*.

settle, *vb. (dwell)* sich niederlassen*; *(conclude)* erle'digen; *(decide)* entschei'den*.

settlement, *n.* Niederlassung, -en *f.;* Siedlung, -en *f.; (decision)* Übereinʾkommen, - *nt.*

settler, *n.* Siedler, - *m.*

seven, *num.* sieben.

seventeen, *num.* siebzehn.

seventeenth, 1. *adj.* siebzehnt-. **2.** *n.* Siebzehntel, - *nt.*

seventh, 1. *adj.* sieb(en)t-. **2.** *n.* Sieb(en)tel, - *nt.*

seventieth, 1. *adj.* siebzigst-. **2.** *n.* Siebzigstel, - *nt.*

seventy, *num.* siebzig.

sever, *vb.* ab·trennen, ab·brechen*.

several, *adj.* mehrer-.

severe, *adj.* streng; hart (¨-); ernst.

severity, *n.* Strenge *f.;* Härte *f.;* Ernst *m.*

sew, *vb.* nähen.

sewer, *n.* Kanalisation' *f.*

sex, *n.* Geschlecht', -er *nt.;* Sexus *m.*

sexism, *n.* Vorurteil gegen das andere Geschlecht *nt.*

sexist, *n.* jemand, der ein Vorurteil gegen das andere Geschlecht hat.

sexton, *n.* Küster, - *m.*

sexual, *adj.* geschlecht'lich, sexuell'.

shabby, *adj.* schäbig.

shack, *n.* Bretterbude, -n *f.*

shade, 1. *n.* Schatten, - *m.;*

(color) Farbton, ⸚e *m.* **2.** *vb.* beschat'ten; schattie'ren.

shadow, *n.* Schatten, - *m.*

shady, *adj.* schattig; *(dubious)* zwielechtig.

shaft, *n.* Schaft, ⸚e *m.; (mine)* Schacht, ⸚e *m.; (transmission)* Welle, -n *f.; (wagon)* Deichsel, -n *f.*

shaggy, *adj.* zottig.

shake, *vb.* schütteln.

shall, *vb.* **(we s. do it)** wir werden* es tun; **(what s. we do?)** was sollen* wir tun?

shallow, *adj.* flach.

shame, 1. *n.* Schande *f.; (what a s.)* wie schade. **2.** *vb.* beschä'men.

shameful, *adj.* schandbar.

shameless, *adj.* schamlos.

shampoo, 1. *n.* Schampun', -s *nt.* **2.** *vb.* die Haare waschen*.

shape, 1. *n.* Form, -en *f.,* Gestalt', -en *f.* **2.** *vb.* formen, gestal'ten.

share, 1. *n.* Anteil, -e *m.; (stock)* Aktie, -n *f.* **2.** *vb.* teilen; teil·haben*.

shark, *n.* Haifisch, -e *m.*

sharp, 1. *n. (music)* Kreuz, -e *nt.* **2.** *adj.* scharf (⸚); *(clever)* schlau.

sharpen, *vb.* schärfen.

sharpness, *n.* Schärfe *f.*

shatter, *vb.* zerbre'chen*.

shave, 1. *vb.* rasie'ren. **2.** *n.* Rasie'ren *nt.; (get a s.)* sich rasie'ren lassen.

shawl, *n.* Schal, -s *m.*

she, *pron.* sie.

shear, *vb.* scheren*.

shears, *n.pl.* Schere, -n *f.*

sheath, *n.* Scheide, -n *f.; (dress)* körperenges Kleid, -er *nt.*

shed, 1. *n.* Schuppen, - *m.* **2.** *vb.* ab·werfen*; *(tears, blood)* vergie'ßen*.

sheep, *n.* Schaf, -e *nt.*

sheet, *n. (bed)* Laken, - *nt.; (paper)* Bogen, ⸚ *m.; (metal)* Platte, -n *f.*

shelf, *n.* Bord, -e *nt.*

shell, 1. *n.* Schale, -n *f.; (conch)* Muschel, -n *f.; (explosive)* Grana'te, -n *f.* **2.** *vb.* beschie'ßen*.

shellac, *n.* Schellack, -e *m.*

shelter, 1. *n.* Schutz *m.,* Obdach *nt.* **2.** *vb.* beschir'men; beher'bergen.

shepherd, *n.* Schäfer, - *m.,* Hirt, -en, -en *m.*

sherbet, *n.* Sorbett, -e *nt.*

sherry, *n.* Sherry, -s *m.*

shield, 1. *n.* Schild, -e *nt.* **2.** *vb.* schützen.

shift, 1. *n.* Wechsel, - *m.; (workers)* Schicht, -en *f.; (auto)* Schalthebel, - *m.* **2.** *vb.* wechseln; schalten; verschie'ben*.

shin, *n.* Schienbein, -e *nt.*

shine, *vb.* scheinen*, glänzen*; *(shoes)* putzen.

shingle, 1. *n.* Schindel, -n *f.,* Dachschindel, -n *f.*

shiny, *adj.* glänzend.

ship, 1. *n.* Schiff, -e *nt.* **2.** *vb.* senden*.

shipment, *n.* Ladung, -en *f.,* Sendung, -en *f.*

shipper, *n.* Verfrach'ter, - *m.,* Verla'der, - *m.*

shipping agent, *n.* Spediteur', -e *m.*

shipwreck, *n.* Schiffbruch, ⸚e *m.*

shirk, *vb.* sich drücken vor.

shirt, *n.* Hemd, -en *nt.*

shiver, *vb.* zittern.

shock, 1. *n.* Schock, -s *m.* **2.** *vb.* schockie'ren.

shoe, *n.* Schuh, -e *m.*

shoelace, *n.* Schnürsenkel, - *m.*

shoemaker, *n.* Schuhmacher, - *m.,* Schuster, -m.

shoot, 1. *n. (sprout)* Schößling, -e *m.* **2.** *vb. (gun)* schießen*; *(person)* erschie'ßen*.

shop, 1. *n.* Laden, ⸚ *m.,* Geschäft', -e *nt.; (factory)* Werkstatt, ⸚en *f.* **2.** *vb.* Einkäufe machen.

shopping, *n.* Einkaufen *nt.*

shore, *n.* Küste, -n *f.; (beach)* Strand, -e *m.*

short, *adj.* kurz (⸚); *(scarce)* knapp.

shortage, *n.* Knappheit, -en *f.*

shorten, *vb.* kürzen.

shorthand, *n.* Stenographie' *f.*

shortly, *adv.* bald (⸚).

shorts, *n.pl.* Shorts, *pl.*

shot, *n.* Schuß, ⸚sse *m.; (photo)* Aufnahme, -n *f.*

should, *vb.* sollte (-); **(s. have)** hätte . . . sollen.

shoulder, 1. *n.* Schulter, -n *f.* **2.** *vb.* schultern.

shout, *vb.* schreien*.

shovel, *n.* Schaufel, -n *f.*

show, 1. *n. (theater, film)* Vorstellung, -en *f.; (spectacle)* Thea'ter, - *nt.; (exhibit)* Ausstellung, -en *f.* **2.** *vb.* zeigen; vor·führen; aus·stellen.

shower, *n. (rain)* Schauer, - *m.; (bath)* Dusche, -n *f.*

shrapnel, *n.* Schrapnell', -s *nt.*

shrewd, *adj.* scharfsinnig; *(derogatory)* geris'sen.

shriek, *vb.* kreischen.

shrill, *adj.* schrill, gellend.

shrimp, *n.* Garne'le, -n *f.,* Krabbe, -n *f.; (small person)* Dreikä'sehoch, -s *m.*

shrine, *n.* Schrein, -e *m.*

shrink, *vb.* schrumpfen; *(cloth)* ein·laufen*.

shroud, *n.* Leichentuch, ⸚er *nt.*

shrub, *n.* Strauch, ⸚er *m.,* Busch, ⸚e *m.*

shudder, *vb.* schaudern.

shun, *vb.* vermei'den*.

shut, 1. *vb.* schließen*, zu·ma-

chen. **2.** *adj.* geschlos'sen. **3.** *adv.* zu.

shutter, *n.* Fensterladen, ⸚ *m.; (camera)* Verschluß', ⸚sse *m.*

shy, 1. *adj.* scheu, schüchtern. **2.** *vb.* scheuen.

Sicily, *n.* Sizi'lien *nt.*

sick, *adj.* krank (-); **(be s. of)** satt·haben*.

sickness, *n.* Krankheit, -en *f.*

side, *n.* Seite, -n *f.; (edge)* Rand, ⸚er *m.*

sidewalk, *n.* Bürgersteig, -e *m.*

siege, *n.* Bela'gerung, -en *f.*

sieve, *n.* Sieb, -e *nt.*

sift, *vb.* sieben; sichten.

sigh, 1. *n.* Seufzer, - *m.* **2.** *vb.* seufzen.

sight, 1. *n.* Sicht *f.; (vision)* Sehkraft *f.; (view)* Anblick, -e *m.; (sights)* Sehenswürdigkeit, -en *f.* **2.** *vb.* sichten.

sightseeing, *n.* Besich'tigung *(f.)* von Sehenswürdigkeiten.

sign, 1. *n.* Zeichen, -*nt.;* Schild, -er *nt.* **2.** *vb.* unterzeich'nen, unterschrei'ben*.

signal, 1. *n.* Signal', -e *nt.* **2.** *vb.* signalisie'ren.

signature, *n.* Unterschrift, -en *f.*

significance, *n.* Bedeu'tung, -en *f.,* Wichtigkeit *f.*

significant, *adj.* bezeich'nend, bedeu'tend.

signify, *vb.* bezeich'nen, bede'ten.

silence, 1. *n.* Schweigen *nt.,* Ruhe *f.* **2.** *vb.* zum Schweigen bringen*.

silent, *adj.* still, schweigsam.

silk, 1. *n.* Seide *f.* **2.** *adj.* seiden.

silken, silky, *adj.* seidig.

sill, *n. (door)* Schwelle, -n *f.; (window)* Fensterbrett, -er *nt.*

silly, *adj.* albern.

silo, *n.* Silo, -s *m.*

silver, 1. *n.* Silber *nt.* **2.** *adj.* silbern.

silverware, *n.* (silbernes) Besteck', -e *nt.*

similar, *adj.* ähnlich.

similarity, *n.* Ähnlichkeit, -en *f.*

simple, *adj.* einfach, schlicht; *(ignorant)* einfältig.

simplicity, *n.* Einfachheit *f.,* Schlichtheit *f.*

simplify, *vb.* verein'fachen.

simulate, *vb.* vor·geben*; nach·ahmen.

simultaneous, *adj.* gleichzeitig.

sin, 1. *n.* Sünde, -n *f.* **2.** *vb.* sündigen.

since, 1. *prep.* seit. **2.** *conj.* seit, seitdem'; *(because)* da. **3.** *adv.* seitdem'.

sincere, *adj.* aufrichtig, ehrlich.

sincerely, *adv.* **(s. yours)** Ihr erge'bener, Ihre erge'bene.

sincerity, *n.* Aufrichtigkeit *f.*

sinful, *adj.* sündhaft.

sing, *vb.* singen*.

singe, vb. sengen.

singer, n. Sänger, - m.

single, adj. einzeln; (unmarried) ledig.

singular, 1. n. (gram.) Einzahl f., Singular m. 2. adj. einzig; (unusual) eigentümlich.

sinister, adj. düster, unheimlich.

sink, 1. n. Ausguß, -sse m., Spülstein, -e m. 2. vb. (tr.) versen'ken; (intr.) sinken*.

sinner, n. Sünder, - m.

sinus, n. Stirnhöhle, -n f.

sinusitis, n. Stirnhöhlenentzündung, -en f.

sip, 1. n. Schluck, -e m. 2. vb. schlürfen.

siphon, n. Siphon, -s m.

sir, n. (yes, s.) jawohl'.

siren, n. Sire'ne, -n f.

sirloin, n. Lendenstück, -e nt.

sister, n. Schwester, -n f.

sister-in-law, n. Schwägerin, -nen f.

sit, vb. sitzen*; (s. down) sich (hin·)setzen.

site, n. Lage, -n f.

sitting, n. Sitzung, -en f.

situated, adj. gele'gen.

situation, n. Lage, -n f., Situation', -en f.

six, num. sechs.

sixteen, num. sechzehn.

sixteenth, 1. adj. sechzehnt-. 2. n. Sechzehntel, - nt.

sixth, 1. adj. sechst-. 2. n. Sechstel, - nt.

sixtieth, 1. adj. sechzigst-. 2. n. Sechzigstel, - nt.

sixty, num. sechzig.

size, n. Größe, -n f., Ausmaß, -e nt.

skate, 1. n. Schlittschuh, -e m. 2. vb. Schlittschuh laufen*.

skateboard, n. Skatebord m.; Rollbrett nt.

skeleton, n. Skelett', -e nt.

skeptic, n. Skeptiker, - m.

skeptical, adj. skeptisch.

sketch, 1. n. Skizze, -n f.; Sketch, -e m. 2. vb. skizzie'ren.

ski, 1. n. Ski, -er m. 2. vb. Ski'laufen*.

skid, 1. n. Hemmschuh, -e m. 2. vb. rutschen.

skill, n. Geschick', nt., Fertigkeit, -en f.

skillful, adj. geschickt'.

skim, vb. (remove cream) entrah'men; (go over lightly) flüchtig lesen*.

skim milk, n. Magermilch f.

skin, 1. n. Haut, -e f.; (fur) Fell, -e nt.; (of fruit) Schale, -n f. 2. vb. häuten.

skip, vb. springen*; (omit) überschla'gen*.

skirt, 1. n. Rock, -e m. 2. vb. umge'hen*.

skull, n. Schädel, - m.

skunk, n. Stinktier, -e nt.; (person) Schuft, -e m.

sky, n. Himmel, - m.

skyscraper, n. Wolkenkratzer, - m.

slab, n. Platte, -n f.

slack, adj. schlaff, flau.

slacken, vb. nach·lassen*.

slacks, n.pl. Slacks pl.

slam, vb. knallen, zu·knallen.

slander, 1. n. Verleum'dung, -en f. 2. vb. verleum'den.

slang, n. Slang m., Jargon', -s m.

slant, 1. n. Neigung, -en f.; schiefe Ebene, -n f.; Aspekt', -e m. 2. vb. neigen.

slap, 1. n. Klaps, -e m. 2. vb. schlagen*.

slash, 1. n. Schlitz, -e m.; Schnittwunde, -n f. 2. vb. schlitzen.

slat, n. Latte, -n f.

slate, n. Schiefer m.; (list) Liste, -n f.

slaughter, 1. n. Schlachten nt.; Gemet'zel, - nt. 2. vb. schlachten; nieder·metzeln.

Slav, n. Slawe, -n, -n m.

slave, n. Sklave, -n, -n m.

slavery, n. Sklaverei' f.

Slavic, adj. slawisch.

slay, vb. erschla'gen*.

sled, n. Schlitten, - m.; (go sledding) Schlitten fahren*, rodeln.

sleek, adj. glatt (-, -); geschniegelt.

sleep, 1. n. Schlaf m. 2. vb. schlafen*. (go to s.) ein·schlafen*.

sleeper, sleeping car, n. Schlafwagen, - m.

sleepy, adj. schläfrig, müde.

sleet, n. Eisregen m.

sleeve, n. Ärmel, - m.

sleigh, n. Schlitten, - m.

slender, adj. schlank; (slight) schwach (-).

slice, 1. n. Scheibe, -n f. 2. vb. in Scheiben schnei(d·en*.

slide, vb. gleiten*, rutschen.

slight, adj. leicht, gering'; (thin) schmächtig.

slim, adj. schlank; gering'.

slime, n. Schlamm m.; Schleim m.

slip, 1. n. (plant) Steckling, -e m.; (error) Verse'hen, - nt.; (underwear) Unterrock, -e m.; (paper) Zettel, - m.; (bedding) Bezug, -e m. 2. vb. gleiten*, aus·leiten*.

slipper, n. Hausschuh, -e m., Pantof'fel, -n m.

slippery, adj. glatt (-, -), schlüpfrig.

slit, 1. n. Schlitz, -e m. 2. vb. schlitzen.

slogan, n. Schlagwort, -e or -er nt.; (election s.) Wahlspruch, -e m.

slope, n. Abhang, -e m.; Neigung, -en f.

sloppy, adj. schlampig.

slot, n. Schlitz, -e m.

slovenly, adj. liederlich.

slow, adj. langsam; (be s., of a clock) nach·gehen*.

slowness, n. Langsamkeit f.

sluggish, adj. träge.

slum, n. Elendsviertel, - nt.

slur, 1. n. Anwurf, -e m. 2. vb. nuscheln.

slush, n. Matsch m.

sly, adj. schlau, verschla'gen.

small, adj. klein.

smallpox, n. Blattern, pl.

smart, adj.. intelligent'; elegant'.

smash, vb. zerschla'gen*, zerschmei'ßen*.

smear, vb. schmieren, beschmie'ren.

smell, 1. n. Geruch', -e m. 2. vb. riechen*.

smelt, n. Stint, -e m. 2. vb. schmelzen, ein·schmelzen.

smile, 1. n. Lächeln nt. 2. vb. lächeln.

smock, n. Kittel, - m.

smoke, 1. n. Rauch f. 2. vb. rauchen; (meat, fish) räuchern.

smooth, 1. adj. glatt (-, -). 2. vb. glätten.

smother, vb. ersti'cken.

smug, adj. selbstgefällig; blasiert'.

smuggle, vb. schmuggeln.

snack, n. Imbiß, -sse m.

snag, n. (stocking) Zugmasche, -n f.; (obstacle) Hindernis, -se nt.

snail, n. Schnecke, -n f.

snake, n. Schlange, -n f.

snap, 1. n. Druckknopf, -e m. 2. vb. schnappen; (break) zerrei'ßen*.

snapshot, n. Schnappschuß, -sse m.

snare, n. Falle, -n f.

snarl, 1. n. Verhed'derung, -en f. 2. vb. verhed'dern; (growl) drohend knurren.

snatch, vb. erha'schen, weg·schnappen.

sneak, vb. schleichen*.

sneer, vb. höhnisch grinsen.

sneeze, vb. niesen.

snob, n. Snob, -s m.

snore, vb. schnarchen.

snow, 1. n. Schnee m. 2. vb. schneien.

snub, 1. n. Affront', -s m. 2. vb. schneiden*.

snug, adj. eng; (fig.) mollig.

so, adv. so.

soak, vb. durchnäs'sen; ein·weichen.

soap, n. Seife, -n f.

soar, vb. sich empor'·schwingen*.

sob, vb. schluchzen.

sober, adj. nüchtern.

sociable, adj. gesel'lig.

social, adj. gesell'schaftlich, sozial'.

socialism, n. Sozialis'mus f.

socialist, n. Sozialist', -en, -en m.

society, n. Gesell'schaft, -en f.

sociology, n. Soziologie' f.

sock, 1. n. Socke, -n f. 2. vb. schlagen*.

socket, n. (eye) Augenhöhle, -n f.; (elec.) Steckdose, -n f.

sod, n. Sode, -n f.

soda, n. Soda nt.

sofa, n. Sofa, -s nt.

soft, adj. (not hard) weich; (not loud) leise; (not rough) sanft, sacht.

soft drink, n. alkoholfreies Getränk', -e nt.

soften, vb. weich machen*; (fig.) mildern.

soil, 1. n. Boden, ∺ m. 2. vb. beschmut'zen.

soiled, adj. schmutzig.

sojourn, 1. n. Aufenthalt, -e m. 2. vb. sich auf·halten*.

solace, n. Trost m.

solar, n. Sonnen- (cpds.).

soldier, n. Soldat', -en, -en m.

sole, 1. n. Sohle, -n f.; (fish) Seezunge, -n f. 2. adj. allei'nig, einzig.

solemn, adj. feierlich.

solicit, vb. an·halten* um.

solicitous, adj. besorgt'; eifrig.

solid, adj. fest; solid', kompakt'.

solidify, vb. festigen; verdich'ten.

solitary, adj. einzeln.

solitude, n. Einsamkeit, -en f.

solo, n. Solo, -s nt.

soloist, n. Solist', -en, -en m.

so long, interj. Wiedersehen.

solution, n. Lösung, -en f.

solve, vb. lösen.

solvent, 1. n. Lösungsmittel, -nt. 2. adj. (financially capable) zahlungsfähig.

somber, adj. düster.

some, pron.&adj. (with singulars) etwas; (with plurals) einig-, ein paar.

somebody, pron. jemand.

somehow, adv. irgendwie.

someone, pron. jemand.

somersault, n. Purzelbaum, ∺e m.

something, pron. etwas.

sometime, adv. irgendwann.

sometimes, adv. manchmal.

somewhat, adv. etwas.

somewhere, adv. irgendwo.

son, n. Sohn, ∺e m.

song, n. Lied, -er nt.

son-in-law, n. Schwiegersohn, ∺e m.

soon, adv. bald.

soot, n. Ruß m.

soothe, vb. beschwich'tigen.

soothing, adj. wohltuend.

sophisticated, adj. anspruchsvoll verfei'nert, lebenserfahren, weltgewandt.

soprano, n. Sopran', -e m.

sorcery, n. Zauberei' f.

sordid, adj. dreckig; gemein'.

sore, 1. n. wunde Stelle, -n f.; offene Wunde, -n f. 2. adj. wund; schmerzhaft; (angry)

eingeschnappt; (be s.) weh·tun*.

sorrow, n. Kummer, - m.

sorrowful, adj. kummervoll.

sorry, adj. traurig, betrübt'; (I am s.) es tut* mir leid.

sort, 1. n. Sorte, -n f., Art, -en f. 2. vb. sortie'ren.

soul, n. Seele, -n f.

sound, 1. n. Ton, ∺e m., Laut, -e m., Klang, ∺e m. 2. adj. gesund (:, -); (valid) einwandfrei. 3. vb. Klingen*; (take soundings) loten.

soup, n. Suppe, -n f.

source, n. Quelle, -n f.

south, 1. n. Süden m. 2. adj. südlich; Süd- (cpds.).

southeast, 1. n. Südos'ten m. 2. adj. südöst'lich; Südost'- (cpds.).

southeastern, adj. südlich.

southern, adj. südlich.

South Pole, n. Südpol m.

southwest, 1. n. Südwes'ten m. 2. adj. südwest'lich; Südwest'- (cpds.).

southwestern, adj. südwest'lich.

souvenir, n. Andenken, - nt.; Reiseandenken, - nt.

Soviet, 1. n. Sowjet, -s m. 2. adj. sowje'tisch.

sow, 1. n. Sau, ∺e f. 2. vb. säen.

space, n. Raum, ∺e m.

space shuttle, n. Raumtransporter, - m.

spacious, adj. geräu'mig.

spade, n. Spaten, - m.; (cards) Pik nt.

spaghetti, n. Spaghet'ti pl.

Spain, n. Spanien nt.

span, 1. n. Spanne, -n f. 2. vb. überspan'nen.

Spaniard, n. Spanier, - m.

Spanish, adj. spanisch.

spank, vb. hauen*.

spanking, n. Haue f.

spar, 1. n. Sparren, - m. 2. vb. boxen.

spare, 1. adj. Ersatz'-, Reser've- (cpds.). 2. vb. sparen, scheuen.

spark, n. Funke(n), - m.

sparkle, vb. funkeln.

spark-plug, n. Zündkerze, -n f.

sparrow, n. Sperling, -e m.

sparse, adj. spärlich.

spasm, n. Krampf, ∺e m.

spasmodic, adj. krampfhaft; sprunghaft.

spatter, vb. spritzen, besprit'zen.

speak, vb. sprechen*, reden.

speaker, n. Redner, - m.; (presiding officer) Präsident', -en, -en m.

spear, 1. n. Speer, -e m.; Spieß, -e m. 2. vb. auf·spießen.

special, adj. beson'der-.

specialist, n. Spezialist', -en, -en m.

specially, adv. beson'ders.

specialty, n. Spezialität', -en f.

species, n. Art, -en f.; Gattung, -en f.

specific, adj. spezi'fisch.

specify, vb. spezifizie'ren; (stipulate) bestim'men.

specimen, n. Muster, - nt., Exemplar', -e nt., Probe, -n f.

spectacle, n. Schauspiel, -e nt.; Anblick, -e m.; (s.s) Brille, -n f.

spectacular, adj. aufsehenerregend.

spectator, n. Zuschauer, - m.

spectrum, n. Spektrum, -tren nt.

speculate, vb. spekulie'ren.

speculation, n. Spekulation', -en f.

speech, n. Sprache, -n f.; (address) Rede, -n.

speechless, adj. sprachlos.

speed, 1. n. Geschwin'digkeit, -en f., Tempo nt. 2. vb. hasten; (s. up) beschleu'nigt erle'digen; (auto) die Geschwin'digkeitsgrenze überschrei'ten*.

speedometer, n. Geschwin'digkeitsmesser, - m.

speedy, adj. schnell; unverzüglich.

spell, 1. n. Zauber, - m. 2. vb. buchstabie'ren.

spelling, n. Rechtschreibung f.

spend, vb. (money) aus·geben*; (time) verwen'den*, verbrin'gen*.

sphere, n. Kugel, -n f., Sphäre, -n f.

spice, n. Gewürz', -e nt.

spider, n. Spinne, -n f.

spike, n. langer Nagel, ∺ m.; (thorn) Dorn, -en m., Stachel, -n m.

spill, vb. verschüt'ten; (make a spot) kleckern.

spin, vb. spinnen*.

spinach, n. Spinat' m.

spine, n. Rückgrat, -e nt.

spiral, 1. n. Spira'le, -n f. 2. adj. spiral'förmig.

spire, n. spitzer Turm, ∺e m.

spirit, n. Geist, m.; (ghost) Gespenst', -er nt.; (vivacity) Schwung m.; (s.s) Spirituo'sen pl.

spiritual, 1. n. geistliches Negerlied, -er nt. 2. adj. geistig, seelisch.

spiritualism, n. Spiritualis'mus m.; Spiritis'mus m.

spit, 1. n. (saliva) Speichel m.; (roasting) Spieß, -e m. 2. vb. spucken.

spite, 1. n. Trotz m.; (in s. of) trotz. 2. vb. ärgern.

splash, vb. spritzen; planschen.

splendid, adj. prächtig.

splendor, n. Pracht f.

splice, vb. spleißen.

splint, n. Schiene, -n f.

splinter, n. Splitter, - m.

split, 1. n. Spalt, -e m. 2. vb. spalten.

spoil, vb. verder'ben*; schlecht

werden*; *(child)* verwöh'nen, verzie'hen*.

spoke, *n.* Speiche, -n *f.*

spokesman, *n.* Sprecher, - *m.*

sponge, 1. *n.* Schwamm, ⁼e *m.* **2.** *vb. (live off)* nassauern.

sponsor, 1. *n.* Bürge, -n, -n *m.;* Förderer, - *m.; (radio, TV, etc.)* Rekla'meauftraggeber, - *m.* **2.** *vb.* fördern; *(advertising)* in Auftrag geben*.

spontaneity, *n.* Impulsivität' *f.*

spontaneous, *adj.* spontan'.

spool, *n.* Spule, -n *f.*

spoon, *n.* Löffel, - *m.*

sport, *n.* Sport *m.;* Vergnü'gen, - *nt.*

spot, *n. (place)* Stelle, -n *f.; (blot)* Fleck, -en *m.*

spouse, *n.* Gatte, -n, -n *m.;* Gattin, -nen *f.*

spout, 1. *n.* Tülle, -n *f.; (water)* Strahl, -en *m.* **2.** *vb.* hervor'-sprudeln; speien*.

sprain, 1. *n.* Verren'kung, -en *f.,* Verstau'chung, -en *f.* **2.** *vb.* verren'ken, verstau'chen.

sprawl, *vb.* sich aus·breiten; alle Viere aus·strecken.

spray, 1. *n.* spritzen; zerstäu'ben.

spread, 1. *n.* Spanne, -n *f.;* Umfang, ⁼e *m.* **2.** *vb.* aus·breiten.

spree, *n.* Bummel, - *m.* Ausflug, ⁼e *m.*

sprightly, *adj.* munter.

spring, 1. *n. (season)* Frühling, -e *m.;* Frühjahr, -e *nt.; (source)* Quelle, -n *f.; (leap)* Sprung, ⁼e *m.; (metal)* Feder, -n *f.* **2.** *vb.* springen*.

sprinkle, *vb.* sprengen; streuen

sprint, 1. *n.* Kurzstreckenlauf, ⁼e *m.* **2.** *vb.* sprinten.

sprout, 1. *n.* Sproß, sse *m.* **2.** *vb.* sprießen*.

spry, *adj.* flink.

spur, 1. *n.* Sporn, Sporen *m.* **2.** *vb.* an·spornen.

spurn, *vb.* verschmä'hen.

spurt, *vb.* hervor'·schießen*.

spy, 1. *n.* Spion', -e *m.* **2.** *vb.* spionie'ren.

squabble, 1. *n.* Zank *m.* **2.** *vb.* zanken.

squad, *n.* Trupp, -s *m.; (sport)* Mannschaft, -en *f.*

squadron, *n. (air)* Staffel, -n *f.; (navy)* Geschwa'der, - *nt.*

squall, *n.* Bö, -en *f.*

squalor, *n.* Schmutz *m.*

squander, *vb.* vergeu'den.

square, 1. *n.* Viereck, -e *nt.,* Quadrat', -e *nt.; (open place)* Platz, ⁼e *m.* **2.** *adj.* viereckig, quadra'tisch. **3.** *vb.* quadrieren.

squash, 1. *n.* Kürbis, -se *m.* **2.** *vb.* quetschen, zerquet'schen.

squat, 1. *adj.* kurz und dick. **2.** *vb.* hocken, kauern.

squeak, *vb.* quietschen.

squeamish, *adj.* zimperlich.

squeeze, *vb.* drücken; *(juice)* aus·pressen.

squirrel, *n.* Eichhörnchen, - *nt.*

squirt, *vb.* spritzen.

stab, 1. *n.* Stich, -e *m.* **2.** *vb.* stechen*; erste'chen*.

stability, *n.* Bestän'digkeit *f.,* Stabilität' *f.*

stabilize, *vb.* stabilisie'ren.

stable, 1. *n.* Stall, ⁼e *m.* **2.** *adj.* bestän'dig; stabil'.

stack, 1. *n.* Haufen, - *m.* **2.** *vb.* auf·stapeln.

stadium, *n.* Stadion, -dien *nt.*

staff, *n.* Stab, ⁼e *m.; (personnel)* Personal' *nt.; (music)* Notenlinien *pl.*

stag, *n.* Hirsch, -e *m.*

stage, 1. *n. (theater)* Bühne, -n *f.; (phase)* Stadium, -dien *nt.* **2.** *vb.* inszenie'ren.

stagflation, *n.* Stagflation' *f.*

stagger, *vb.* taumeln; *(amaze)* verblüf'fen; *(alternate)* staffeln.

stagnant, *adj.* stagnie'rend.

stagnate, *vb.* stagnie'ren.

stain, 1. *n.* Fleck, -e *m.; (color)* Färbstoff, -e *m.; (paint)* Beize *f.* **2.** *vb.* befle'cken, färben; beizen.

staircase, stairs, *n.* Treppe, -n *f.*

stake, 1. *n. (post)* Pfahl, ⁼e *m.; (sum, bet)* Einsatz, ⁼e *m.* **2.** *vb.* aufs Spiel setzen.

stale, *adj.* alt (⁻), schal.

stalk, *n.* Stiel, -e *m.,* Halm, -e *m.*

stall, 1. *n.* Stall, ⁼e *m.; (vendor's)* Bude, -n *f.* **2.** *vb. (hesitate)* Zeit schinden*; *(engine)* ab·würgen.

stamina, *n.* Energie' *f.,* Ausdauer *f.*

stammer, *vb.* stammeln.

stamp, 1. *n.* Stempel, - *m.; (mark)* Geprä'ge *nt.; (postal)* Freimarke, -n *f.,* Briefmarke, -n *f.* **2.** *vb.* stempeln; prägen.

stand, 1. *n.* Stellung, -en *f.; (vendor's)* Bude, -n *f.; (grandstand)* Tribü'ne, -n *f.* **2.** *vb.* stehen*; *(endure)* ertra'gen*.

standard, 1. *n.* Norm, -en *f.,* Standard, -s *m.* **2.** *adj.* Standard- *(cpds.).*

standardize, *vb.* standardisie'ren.

standing, *n.* Bestand' *m.; (reputation)* Ruf *m.*

standpoint, *n.* Standpunkt, -e *m.*

star, *n.* Stern, -e *m.; (movie)* Star, -s *m.*

starch, 1. *n.* Stärke *f.* **2.** *vb.* stärken.

stare, *vb.* starren, glotzen.

stark, *adj.* kraß; *(bare)* kahl.

start, 1. *n.* Anfang, ⁼e *m.,* Start, -s *m.* **2.** *vb.* an·fangen*, starten.

startle, *vb.* erschre'cken, auf·schrecken.

starvation, *n.* Verhun'gern *nt.;* Hungertod *m.*

starve, *vb.* hungern; **(s. to death)** verhun'gern.

state, 1. *n.* Staat, -en *m.; (condition)* Zustand, ⁼e *m.* **2.** *vb.* dar·legen, erklä'ren.

statement, *n.* Erklä'rung, -en *f.;* Behaup'tung, -en *f.*

stateroom, *n.* Kabi'ne, -n *f.*

statesman, *n.* Staatsmann, ⁼er *m.*

static, 1. *n.* atmosphä'rische Störung, -en *f.* **2.** *adj.* statisch.

station, *n.* Station', -en *f.; (position)* Stellung, -en *f.; (R.R.)* Bahnhof, ⁼e *m.*

stationary, *adj.* feststehend, stationär'.

stationer, *n.* Schreibwarenhändler, - *m.*

stationery, *n.* Schreibwaren *pl.;* Briefpapier *nt.*

station wagon, *n.* Kombiwagen, - *m.*

statistics, *n.pl.* Statis'tik *f.*

statue, *n.* Statue, -n *f.*

stature, *n.* Wuchs *m.,* Statur' *f.; (fig.)* Format', -e *nt.*

status, *n.* Stand, ⁼e *m.*

statute, *n.* Statut', -e *nt.,* Satzung, -en *f.*

staunch, *adj.* treu, wacker.

stay, 1. *n. (sojourn)* Aufenthalt *m.; (delay)* Einstellung, -en *f.* **2.** *vb.* bleiben*; *(hold back)* zurück'·halten*.

steady, *adj.* fest; sicher; bestän'dig.

steak, *n.* Beefsteak, -s *nt.*

steal, *vb.* stehlen*.

stealth, *n.* Verstoh'lenheit *f.*

stealthy, *adj.* verstoh'len.

steam, 1. *n.* Dampf, ⁼e *m.* **2.** *vb.* dampfen.

steamboat, *n.* Dampfboot, -e *nt.*

steamship, *n.* Dampfer, - *m.*

steel, 1. *n.* Stahl, -e *m.* **2.** *adj.* stählern; Stahl- *(cpds.).*

steep, *adj.* steil; *(price)* hoch (hoh-, höher, höchst-).

steeple, *n.* Kirchturm, ⁼e *m.*

steer, 1. *n.* Stier, -e *m.* **2.** *vb.* steuern.

stellar, *adj.* Sternen- *(cpds.).*

stem, 1. *n.* Stiel, -e *m.* **2.** *vb.* stammen.

stenographer, *n.* Stenotypis't'in, -nen *f.*

stenography, *n.* Kurzschrift, -en *f.;* Stenographie', -i'en *f.*

step, 1. *n.* Schritt, -e *m.; (stair)* Stufe, -n *f.* **2.** *vb.* treten*.

stepfather, *n.* Stiefvater, ⁼ *m.*

stepladder, *n.* Trittleiter, -n *f.*

stepmother, *n.* Stiefmutter, ⁼ *f.*

stereophonic, *adj.* stereophon'.

sterile, *adj.* unfruchtbar; steril'.

sterility, *n.* Sterilität' *f.*

sterilize, *vb.* sterilisie'ren.

sterling, *adj.* münzecht; *(silver)*

echt; **(pound s.)** Pfund Sterling *nt.*

stern, *adj.* streng.

stethoscope, *n.* Stethoskop', -e *nt.*

stew, 1. *n.* Stew, -s *nt.* **2.** *vb.* dämpfen.

steward, *n.* Steward, -s *m.*

stewardess, *n.* Stewardess', -en *f.*

stick, 1. *n.* Stock, ⸗e *m.* **2.** *vb. (adhere)* kleben; *(pin)* stecken.

sticker, *n.* Etiket'te, -n *f.*

sticky, *adj.* klebrig.

stiff, *adj.* steif.

stiffen, *vb.* steif werden*; *(fig.)* verhär'ten.

stiffness, *n.* Steifheit, -en *f.*

stifle, *vb.* ersti'cken.

stigma, *n.* Stigma, -men *nt.,* Schandfleck, -e *m.*

still, 1. *n.* Destillier'apparat, -e *m.* **2.** *adj.* still, **3.** *vb.* stillen. **4.** *adv.* noch; doch; dennoch.

stillness, *n.* Stille *f.*

stimulant, *n.* Reizmittel, - *nt.*

stimulate, *vb.* an·regen.

stimulus, *n.* Anreiz, -e *m.*

sting, 1. *n.* Stache-, - *m.; (bite)* Stich, -e *m.* **2.** *vb.* stechen*; *(burn)* brennen.

stingy, *adj.* geizig.

stink, *vb.* stinken*.

stipulate, *vb.* bestim'men.

stir, 1. *n.* Aufregung, -en *f.* **2.** *vb.* rühren; erre'gen.

stitch, 1. *n.* Stich, -e *m.; (knitting)* Masche, -n *f.* **2.** *vb.* step-pen.

stock, 1. *n. (supply)* Vorrat, ⸗e *m.,* Lager, - *nt.; (lineage)* Fami'lie, -n *f.; (livestock)* Viehbestand, ⸗e *m.; (gun)* Schaft, ⸗e *m.* **2.** *vb.* versor'gen; auf Lager haben*.

stockbroker, *n.* Börsenmakler, - *m.*

stock exchange, *n.* Börse, -n *f.*

stocking, *n.* Strumpf, ⸗e *m.*

stodgy, *adj.* schwerfällig; untersetzt'.

stole, *n.* Stola, -len *f.*

stomach, 1. *n.* Magen, ⸗ *m.* **2.** *vb. (fig.)* schlucken.

stone, 1. *n.* Stein, -e *m.; (fruit)* Kern, -e *m.* **2.** *vb.* steinigen.

stool, *n.* Schemel, - *m.*

stoop, *vb.* sich bücken; *(demean oneself)* sich ernied'rigen.

stop, 1. *n.* Haltestelle, -n *f.* **2.** *vb.* halten*; stoppen; *(cease)* auf·hören.

stop-over, *n.* Fahrtunterbrechung, -en *f.*

storage, *n.* Lagern *nt.;* Lagerhaus, ⸗er *nt.*

store, 1. *n.* Laden, ⸗ *m.,* Geschäft', -e *nt.; (supplies)* Vorräte *pl.* **2.** *vb.* lagern.

storehouse, *n.* Lagerhaus, ⸗er *nt.*

storm, 1. *n.* Sturm, ⸗e *m.* **2.** *vb.* stürmen.

stormy, *adj.* stürmisch.

story, *n.* Erzäh'lung, -en *f.,* Geschich'te, -n *f.*

stout, *adj.* dick; *(strong)* wacker.

stove, *n. (cooking)* Herd, -e *m.; (heating)* Ofen, ⸗ *m.*

straight, *adj.* gera'de; *(honest)* ehrlich.

straighten, *vb.* gera'de machen*; in Ordnung bringen*.

straightforward, *adj.* offen.

strain, 1. *n.* Anstrengung, -en *f.;* Belas'tung, -en *f.* **2.** *vb.* an·strengen; belas'ten; *(filter)* seihen.

strait, *n.* Meeresenge, -n *f.*

strand, 1. *n.* Strähne, -n *f.* **2.** *vb.* stranden.

strange, *adj.* merkwürdig; *(foreign)* fremd.

stranger, *n.* Fremd- *m.&f.*

strangle, *vb.* erwür'gen.

strap, *n.* Riemen, - *m.*

stratagem, *n.* Kriegslist, -en *f.*

strategic, *adj.* strate'gisch.

strategy, *n.* Strategie' *f.*

stratosphere, *n.* Stratosphä're *f.*

stratum, *n.* Schicht, -en *f.*

straw, *n.* Stroh, *nt.; (for drinking)* Strohalm, -e *m.*

strawberry, *n.* Erdbeere, -n *f.*

stray, 1. *adj.* verein'zelt. **2.** *vb.* ab·weichen; ab·schweifen.

streak, *n.* Strähne, -n *f.*

stream, *n.* Strom, ⸗e *m.; (small)* Bach, ⸗e *m.*

streamlined, *adj.* stromlinienförmig.

street, *n.* Straße, -n *f.*

streetcar, *n.* Straßenbahn, -en *f.*

strength, *n.* Kraft, ⸗e *f.,* Stärke, -n *f.*

strengthen, *vb.* stärken.

strenuous, *adj.* anstrengend.

stress, 1. *n.* Belas'tung, -en *f.; (accent)* Beto'nung, -en *f.* **2.** *vb.* belas'ten; beto'nen.

stretch, 1. *n.* Strecke, -n *f.;* Spanne, -n *f.* **2.** *vb.* strecken; spannen.

stretcher, *n.* Tragbahre, -n *f.*

strew, *vb.* streuen.

stricken, *adj.* getroffen.

strict, *adj.* streng.

stride, 1. *n.* Schritt, -e *m.* **2.** *vb.* schreiten*.

strife, *n.* Streit *m.*

strike, 1. *n. (workers')* Streik, -s *m.* **2.** *vb.* streiken; *(hit)* schlagen*.

string, 1. *n.* Bindfaden, ⸗ *m.,* Schnur, ⸗e *f.; (music)* Saite, -n *f.* **2.** *vb.* auf·reihen.

string bean, *n.* grüne Bohne, -n *f.*

strip, 1. *n.* Streifen, - *m.* **2.** *vb.* ab·streifen; entklei'den.

stripe, *n.* Streifen, - *m.*

strive, *vb.* streben.

stroke, 1. *n.* Schlag, ⸗e *m.; (pen, brush, etc.)* Strich, -e *m.;*

(med.) Schlaganfall, ⸗e *m.* **2.** *vb.* streicheln.

stroll, 1. *n.* kleiner Spazier'gang, ⸗e *m.* **2.** *vb.* spazie'ren·gehen*.

stroller, *n.* Spazier'gänger, *m.; (baby-carriage)* Kindersportwagen, - *m.*

strong, *adj.* stark (⸗), kräftig.

stronghold, *n.* Feste, -n *f.*

structure, *n.* Struktur', -en *f.*

struggle, 1. *n.* Ringen *nt.* **2.** *vb.* ringen*.

strut, *vb.* stolzie'ren.

stub, 1. *n.* Kontroll'abschnitt, -e *m.* **2.** *vb.* an·stoßen*.

stubborn, *adj.* hartnäckig; *(person)* dickköpfig.

student, *n.* Student', -en, -en *m.*

studio, *n.* Atelier', -s *nt.*

studious, *adj.* eifrig.

study, 1. *n.* Studium, -dien *nt.; (room)* Arbeitszimmer, - *nt.* **2.** *vb.* studie'ren; *(do homework)* arbeiten.

stuff, 1. *n.* Zeug *nt.* **2.** *vb.* stopfen.

stuffing, *n.* Füllung, -en *f.*

stumble, *vb.* stolpern.

stump, *n.* Stumpf, ⸗e *m.*

stun, *vb.* betäu'ben; verblüffen.

stunt, *n.* Kunststück, -e *nt.*

stupid, *adj.* dumm (⸗), blöde.

stupidity, *n.* Dummheit, -en *f.*

stupor, *n.* Betäu'bungszustand *m.*

sturdy, *adj.* stark (⸗), stämmig.

stutter, *vb.* stottern.

sty, *n.* Schweinestall, ⸗e *m.; (eye)* Gerstenkorn, ⸗er *nt.*

style, *n.* Stil, -e *m.*

stylish, *adj.* elegant'.

suave, *adj.* verbind'lich.

subconscious, *adj.* unterbewußt.

subdue, *vb.* unterdrü'cken.

subject, 1. *n. (gram.)* Subjekt, -e *nt.; (topic)* Thema, -men *nt.; (of king)* Untertan, -en, -en *m.* **2.** *adj.* unterwor'fen. **3.** *vb.* unterwer'fen*; aus·setzen.

subjugate, *vb.* unterjo'chen.

subjunctive, *n.* Konjunktiv, -e *m.*

sublime, *adj.* erha'ben.

submarine, *n.* Unterseeboot, -e *nt.,* U-Boot, -e *nt.*

submerge, *vb.* unter·tauchen.

submission, *n.* Unterwer'fung, -en *f.*

submit, *vb. (lay before)* unterbrei'ten; *(offer opinion)* anheim'·stellen; *(yield)* sich fügen; *(surrender)* sich unterwer'fen*.

subnormal, *adj.* unternormal.

subordinate, 1. *n.* Unterge'ben- *m.* **2.** *adj.* untergeordnet; **(s. clause)** Nebensatz, ⸗e *m.*

subscribe, *vb. (underwrite)* zeichnen; *(take regularly)* abonnie'ren; *(approve)* billigen.

subscription, *n.* Abonnement', -s *nt.;* Zeichnung, -en *f.*

subsequent, *adj.* folgend.

subside, *vb.* nach·lassen*.

subsidy, *n.* Zuschuß, ·sse *m.*

substance, *n.* Substanz', -en *f.*

substantial, *adj.* wesentlich; beträcht'lich.

substitute, 1. *n.* Ersatz' *m.;* Vertre'tung, -en *f.* **2.** *vb.* er·set'zen; als Ersatz' geben*; die Vertre'tung überneh'men*.

substitution, *n.* Erset'zung, -en *f.*

subtle, *adj.* subtil', fein.

subtract, *vb.* ab·ziehen*.

suburb, *n.* Vorort, -e *m.*

subversive, *adj.* zerset'zend, stattsfeindlich.

subway, *n.* Untergrundbahn, -en *f.,* U-Bahn, -en *f.*

succeed, *vb.* erfolg'reich sein*; *(come after)* folgen.

success, *n.* Erfolg', -e *m.*

successful, *adj.* erfolg'reich.

succession, *n.* *(to throne)* Erbfolge, -n *f.;* *(sequence)* Reihenfolge, -n *f.*

successive, *adj.* aufeinan'derfolgend.

successor, *n.* Nachfolger, - *m.*

succumb, *vb.* erlie'gen*.

such, *adj.* solch.

suck, *vb.* saugen, lutschen.

suction, *n.* Saugen *nt.;* Saug- *(cpds.).*

sudden, *adj.* plötzlich, jäh.

sue, *vb.* verkla'gen, gericht'lich belan'gen.

suffer, *vb.* leiden*.

suffice, *vb.* genü'gen, aus·reichen.

sufficient, *adj.* genü'gend.

suffocate, *vb.* ersti'cken.

sugar, *n.* Zucker *m.*

suggest, *vb.* vor·schlagen*.

suggestion, *n.* Vorschlag, ·-e *m.*

suicide, *n.* Selbstmord, -e *m.*

suit, 1. *n.* *(man's clothing)* Anzug, ·-e *m.;* *(woman's clothing)* Kostüm', -e *nt.;* *(cards)* Farbe, -n *f.;* *(law)* Prozeß', -sse *m.* **2.** *vb.* passen; *(be becoming)* stehen*.

suitable, *adj.* passend; angemessen.

suitcase, *n.* Koffer, - *m.*

suitor, *n.* Freier, - *m.*

sullen, *adj.* griesgrämig.

sum, *n.* Summe, -n *f.*

summarize, *vb.* zusam'men·fassen.

summary, 1. *n.* Übersicht, -en *f.* **2.** *adj.* summa'risch.

summer, *n.* Sommer, - *m.*

summit, *n.* Gipfel, - *m.*

summon, *vb.* zusam'men·rufen*, ein·berufen*; *(law)* vor·laden*.

sun, *n.* Sonne, -n *f.*

sunburn, *n.* Sonnenbrand, ·-e *m.*

sunburned, *adj.* sonnenverbrannt.

Sunday, *n.* Sonntag, -e *m.*

sunken, *adj.* versun'ken.

sunny, *adj.* sonnig.

sunshine, *n.* Sonnenschein *m.*

superb, *adj.* hervor'ragend.

superficial, *adj.* oberflächlich.

superfluous, *adj.* überflüssig.

super-highway, *n.* Autobahn -en *f.*

superior, 1. *n.* Vorgesetztm.&f. **2.** *adj.* höher; überle'gen.

superiority, *n.* Überle'genheit *f.*

superlative, 1. *n.* Superlativ, -e *m.* **2.** *adj.* überra'gend.

supernatural, *adj.* übernatür'lich.

supersede, *vb.* verdrän'gen; er·set'zen.

supersonic, *adj.* Überschall- *(cpds.).*

superstar, *n.* Superstar, -s *m.*

superstition, *n.* Aberglaube (n), -n *m.*

superstitious, *adj.* abergläubisch.

supervise, *vb.* beauf'sichtigen.

supper, *n.* Abendbrot, -e *nt.,* Abendessen, - *nt.;* **(Lord's S.)** Abendmahl, -e *nt.*

supplement, *n.* Ergän'zung, -en *f.,* Nachtrag, ·-e *m.*

supply, 1. *n.* Versor'gung *f.;* Vorrat, ·-e *m.;* **(s. and demand)** Angebot *(nt.)* und Nachfrage *(f.).* **2.** *vb.* versor'gen, liefern.

support, 1. *n.* Stütze, -n *f.;* Unterstüt'zung, -en *f.* **2.** *vb.* stüt'zen; unterstüt'zen.

suppose, *vb.* an·nehmen*, vermu'ten.

suppress, *vb.* unterdrü'cken.

suppression, *n.* Unterdrü'ckung, -en *f.*

supreme, *adj.* oberst-, höchst-; Ober- *(cpds.).*

sure, *adj.* sicher.

surely, *adv.* sicherlich, gewiß'.

surf, *n.* Brandung, -en *f.*

surface, *n.* Oberfläche, -n *f.*

surge, *vb.* wogen, branden.

surgeon, *n.* Chirurg', -en, -en *m.*

surgery, *n.* Chirurgie' *f.;* Operation', -en *f.*

surmise, 1. *n.* Vermu'tung, -en *f.* **2.** *vb.* vermu'ten.

surmount, *vb.* überwin'den*.

surname, *n.* Zuname(n), - *m.,* Fami'lienname(n), - *m.*

surpass, *vb.* überstei'gen*, übertref'fen*.

surplus, 1. *n.* Überschuß, ·-sse *m.* **2.** *adj.* überschüssig; Über- *(cpds.).*

surprise, 1. *n.* Überra'schung, -en *f.* **2.** *vb.* überra'schen.

surrender, 1. *n.* Übergabe *f.,* Erge'bung, -en *f.*

surround, *vb.* umge'ben*; umzin'geln.

surroundings, *n.pl.* Umge'bung, -en *f.*

survey, 1. *n.* Überblick, -e *m.;* *(measuring)* Vermes'sung, -en *f.* **2.** *vb.* überbli'cken; vermes'sen*.

survival, *n.* Überle'ben *nt.*

survive, *vb.* überle'ben.

susceptible, *adj.* empfäng'lich, zugänglich.

suspend, *vb.* *(debar)* suspendie'ren; *(stop temporarily)* zeitweilig auf·heben*; *(payment)* ein·stellen; *(sentence)* aus·setzen; *(hang)* auf·hängen.

suspense, *n.* Schwebe *f.;* Spannung, -en *f.*

suspension, *n.* Schwebe *f.;* Suspension', -en *f.*

suspicion, *n.* Verdacht' *m.,* Argwohn *m.*

suspicious, *adj.* *(doubting)* misstrauisch; *(doubtful looking)* verdäch'tig.

sustain, *vb.* aufrecht·erhalten*; *(suffer)* erlei'den*.

swallow, 1. *n.* *(bird)* Schwalbe, -n *f.;* *(gulp)* Schluck, -e *m.* **2.** *vb.* schlucken.

swamp, 1. *n.* Sumpf, ·-e *m.* **2.** *vb.* überschwem'men.

swan, *n.* Schwan, ·-e *m.*

swarm, 1. *n.* Schwarm, ·-e *m.* **2.** *vb.* schwärmen; *(fig.)* wimmeln.

sway, *vb.* schwingen*; schwanken.

swear, *vb.* schwören; *(curse)* fluchen.

sweat, 1. *n.* Schweiß *m.* **2.** *vb.* schwitzen.

sweater, *n.* Pullo'ver, - *m.,* Strickjacke, -n *f.*

Swede, *n.* Schwede, -n, -n *m.*

Sweden, *n.* Schweden *nt.*

Swedish, *adj.* schwedisch.

sweet, *adj.* süß.

sweetheart, *n.* Liebst- *m.&f.*

sweetness, *n.* Süße *f.;* *(fig.)* Anmut *f.*

swell, 1. *adj.* prima. **2.** *vb.* schwellen*.

swift, *adj.* rasch, geschwind'.

swim, *vb.* schwimmen*.

swindle, *vb.* schwindeln.

swindler, *n.* Schwindler, - *m.*

swine, *n.* Schwein, -e *nt.*

swing, 1. *n.* Schaukel, -n *f.* **2.** *vb.* schwingen*, schaukeln.

Swiss, 1. *n.* Schweizer, - *m.* **2.** *adj.* schweizerisch; Schweizer- *(cpds.).*

switch, 1. *n.* *(whip)* Gerte, -n *f.;* *(railway)* Weiche, -n *f.;* *(elec.)* Schalter, - *m.* **2.** *vb.* *(railway)* rangie'ren; um·schalten; *(exchange)* vertau'schen.

Switzerland, *n.* die Schweiz *f.*

sword, *n.* Schwert, -er *nt.*

syllabic, *adj.* silbisch.

syllable, *n.* Silbe, -n *f.*

symbol, *n.* Symbol', -e *nt.*

symbolic, *adj.* symbo'lisch.

sympathetic, *adj.* mitfühlend; *(med.)* sympa'thisch.

sympathize, *vb.* mit·fühlen.

sympathy, *n.* Sympathie', -i'en *f.*

symphonic, *adj.* sympho'nisch.

symphony, *n.* Symphonie', -i'en *f.*

symptom, *n.* Anzeichen, - *nt.,* Symptom', -e *nt.*

symptomatic, *adj.* symptoma'tisch; charakteris'tisch.

syndicate, *n.* Syndikat', -e *nt.*

syndrome, *n.* Syndrom', -e *nt.*

synonym, *n.* Synonym', -e *nt.*

synonymous, *adj.* sinnverwandt, synonym'.

synthetic, *adj.* synthe'tisch, künstlich; Kunst- *(cpds.).*

syphilis, *n.* Syphilis *f.*

syringe, *n.* Spritze, -n *f.*

syrup, *n.* Sirup *m.*

system, *n.* System', -e *nt.*

systematic, *adj.* systema'tisch.

T

table, *n.* Tisch, -e *m.; (list)* Verzeich'nis, -se *nt.*

tablecloth, *n.* Tischdecke, -n *f.,* Tischtuch, =er *nt.*

tablespoon, *n.* Eßlöffel, - *m.*

tablet, *n.* Tafel, -n *f.; (pill)* Tablet'te, -n *f.*

tack, 1. *n.* Stift, -e *m.; (thumb t.)* Heftzwecke, -n *f.* 2. *vb. (sew)* heften; *(sail)* kreuzen.

tact, *n.* Takt *m.*

tag, *n.* Etikett, -e *nt.; (play t.)* Fangen spielen.

tail, *n.* Schwanz, =e *m.*

tailor, *n.* Schneider, - *m.*

take, *vb.* nehmen*; *(carry)* bringen*; *(need)* erfor'dern.

tale, *n.* Geschich'te, -n *f.,* Erzäh'lung, -en *f.*

talent, *n.* Bega'bung, -en *f.,* Talent', -e *nt.*

talk, 1. *n.* Gespräch', -e *nt.; (lecture)* Vortrag, =e *m.* 2. *vb.* reden, sprechen*.

talkative, *adj.* gesprä'chig.

tall, *adj.* groß (=); hoch (hoh-, höher, höchst-); lang (=).

tame, 1. *adj.* zahm. 2. *vb.* zähmen.

tamper, *vb.* herum'pfuschen.

tan, 1. *n. (sun)* Sonnenbräune *f.* 2. *adj.* gelbbraun. 3. *vb.* bräunen; *(leather)* gerben.

tangle, 1. *n.* Gewirr' *nt.* 2. *vb.* sich zu schaffen machen mit.

tank, *n.* Tank, -s *m.; (mil.)* Panzer, - *m.*

tap, 1. *n. (blow)* Taps, -e *m.; (faucet)* Hahn, =e *m.* 2. *vb.* leicht schlagen*; an·zapfen.

tape, *n.* Band, =er *nt.*

tape recorder, *n.* Tonbandgerät, -e *nt.,* Magnetophon', -e *nt.*

tapestry, *n.* Wandteppich, -e *m.;* Tapisserie', -i'en *f.*

tar, 1. *n.* Teer *m.* 2. *vb.* teeren.

target, *n.* Ziel, -e *nt.;* Zielscheibe, -n *f.*

tariff, *n.* Zolltarif, -e *m.*

tarnish, *vb. (fig.)* befle'cken; *(silver)* sich beschla'gen*.

tart, 1. *n.* Törtchen, - *nt.* 2. *adj.* sauer, herb.

task, *n.* Aufgabe, -n *f.*

taste, 1. *n.* Geschmack', =e *m.* 2. *vb.* schmecken, kosten.

tasty, *adj.* schmackhaft.

taut, *adj.* straff.

tavern, *n.* Bierlokal, -e *nt.*

tax, 1. *n.* Steuer, -n *f.* 2. *vb.* besteu'ern, belas'ten.

taxi, *n.* Taxe, -n *f.,* Taxi, -s *nt.*

taxpayer, *n.* Steuerzahler, - *m.*

tea, *n.* Tee, -s *m.*

teach, *vb.* lehren, unterrich'ten.

teacher, *n.* Lehrer, - *m.*

tea-pot, *n.* Teekanne, -n *f.*

tear, 1. *n.* Träne, -n *f.; (rip)* Riß, -sse *m.* 2. *vb.* reißen*.

tease, *vb.* necken.

teaspoon, *n.* Teelöffel, - *m.*

technical, *adj.* technisch.

technique, *n.* Technik, -en *f.,* Kunstfertigkeit *f.*

tedious, *adj.* langweilig, mühsam.

telegram, *n.* Telegramm', -e *nt.*

telegraph, 1. *n.* Telegraph', -en, -en *m.* 2. *vb.* telegraphie'ren.

telephone, 1. *n.* Telephon', -e *nt.,* Fernsprecher, - *m.* 2. *vb.* telephonie'ren.

telescope, *n.* Fernrohr, -e *nt.*

televise, *vb.* im Fernsehen übertra'gen*.

television, *n.* Fernsehen *nt.*

television set, *n.* Fernsehapparat, -e *m.*

tell, *vb.* erzäh'len, berich'ten, sagen.

teller, *n.* Kassie'rer, - *m.*

temper, 1. *n.* Laune, -n *f.;* Temperament' *nt.; (anger)* Zorn *m.* 2. *vb.* mäßigen; *(steel)* härten.

temperament, *n.* Gemüts'art, -en *f.*

temperamental, *adj.* Gemüts'- *(cpds.);* temperament'voll.

temperate, *adj.* mäßig.

temperature, *n.* Temperatur', -en *f.*

tempest, *n.* Sturm, =e *m.*

temple, *n.* Tempel, -s *m.*

temporary, *adj.* zeitweilig, vorü'bergehend, proviso'risch.

tempt, *vb.* versu'chen; reizen.

temptation, *n.* Versu'chung, -en *f.*

ten, *num.* zehn.

tenant, *n.* Mieter, - *m.;* Pächter, - *m.*

tend, *vb.* pflegen, hüten; *(incline)* neigen zu.

tendency, *n.* Neigung, -en *f.,* Tendenz', -en *f.*

tender, 1. *n. (money)* Zahlungsmittel, - *nt.; (train, boat)* Tender, - *m.* 2. *adj.* zart; zärtlich. 3. *vb.* an·bieten*.

tenderness, *n.* Zartheit, -en *f.,* Zärtlichkeit, -en *f.*

tendon, *n.* Sehne, -n *f.*

tennis, *n.* Tennis *nt.*

tenor, *n.* Tenor', -e *m.*

tense, *adj.* gespannt'; kribbelig.

tension, *n.* Spannung, -en *f.*

tent, *n.* Zelt, -e *nt.*

tentative, *adj.* probeweise.

tenth, 1. *adj.* zehnt-. 2. *n.* Zehntel, - *nt.*

term, *n.* Perio'de, -n *f.; (of office)* Amtszeit, -en *f.; (college)* Semes'ter, - *nt.; (expression)* Ausdruck, =e *m.; (condition)* Bedin'gung, -en *f.*

terminate, *vb.* been'den; begren'zen.

terrace, *n.* Terras'se, -n *f.*

terrible, *adj.* schrecklich, furchtbar.

terrify, *vb.* erschre'cken.

territory, *n.* Gebiet', -e *nt.*

terror, *n.* Schrecken, - *m.*

test, 1. *n.* Prüfung, -en *f.;* Probe, -n *f.;* Test, -s *m.;* Versuch', -e *m.* 2. *vb.* prüfen.

testify, *vb.* bezeu'gen; *(court)* aus·sagen.

testimony, *n.* Zeugnis, -se *nt.;* Zeugenaussage, -n *f.*

text, *n.* Text, -e *m.*

textile, 1. *n.* Textil'ware, -n *f.* 2. *adj.* Textil'- *(cpds.).*

texture, *n.* Gewe'be, - *nt.;* Aufbau *m.;* Beschaf'fenheit, -en *f.*

than, *conj.* als.

thank, *vb.* danken.

thankful, *adj.* dankbar.

that, 1. *pron.&adj.* der, das, die; *jener,* -es, -e. 2. *conj.* daß.

the, *art.* der, das, die.

theater, *n.* Thea'ter, - *nt.; (fig.)* Schauplatz, =e *m.*

thee, *pron.* dich; dir.

theft, *n.* Diebstahl, =e *m.*

their, *adj.* ihr, -, -e.

theirs, *pron.* ihrer, -es, -e.

them, *pron.* sie; ihnen.

theme, *n.* Thema, -men *nt.*

then, *adv. (after that)* dann; *(at that time)* damals; *(therefore)* dann, also.

thence, *adv.* von da, von dort.

theology, *n.* Theologie' *f.*

theoretical, *adj.* theore'tisch.

theory, *n.* Theorie', -i'en *f.*

therapy, *n.* Therapie' *f.*

there, *adv. (in that place)* da, dort; *(to that place)* dahin', dorthin'; *(from t.)* daher', dorther'.

therefore, *adv.* daher, darum, deshalb, deswegen, also.

thermometer, *n.* Thermom'e'ter, - *nt.*

thermonuclear, *adj.* kernphysikalisch.

these, *adj.* diese.

they, *pron.* sie.

thick, *adj.* dick; *(dense)* dicht.

thicken, *vb.* dicken, verdi'cken; verdich'ten.

thickness, *n.* Dicke *f.;* Dichtheit *f.; (layer)* Schicht, -en *f.*

thief, *n.* Dieb, -e *m.*

thigh, *n.* Schenkel, - *m.*

thimble, *n.* Fingerhut, -e *m.*

thin, *adj.* dünn; mager.

thing, *n.* Ding, -e *nt.;* Sache, -n *f.*

think, *vb.* meinen, glauben; denken*, nach·denken*.

thinker, *n.* Denker, - *m.*

third, 1. *adj.* dritt-. **2.** *n.* Drittel, - *nt.*

Third World, *n.* Dritte Welt *f.*

thirst, 1. *n.* Durst *m.* **2.** *vb.* dürsten.

thirsty, *adj.* durstig.

thirteen, *num.* dreizehn.

thirteenth, 1. *adj.* dreizehnt-. **2.** *n.* Dreizehntel, - *nt.*

thirtieth, 1. *adj.* dreißigst-. **2.** *n.* Dreißigstel, - *nt.*

thirty, *num.* dreißig.

this, *pron.&adj.* dieser, -es, -e.

thorough, *adj.* gründlich.

thou, *pron.* du.

though, 1. *adv.* doch. **2.** *conj.* obwohl', obgleich'.

thought, *n.* Gedan'ke(n), - *m.*

thoughtful, *adj.* gedan'kenvoll; *(considerate)* rücksichtsvoll.

thousand, *num.* tausend.

thousandth, 1. *adj.* tausendst-. **2.** *n.* Tausendstel, - *nt.*

thread, *n.* Faden, - *m.;* Garn, -e *nt.*

threat, *n.* Drohung, -en *f.*

threaten, *vb.* drohen.

three, *num.* drei.

thrift, *n.* Sparsamkeit *f.*

thrill, 1. *n.* Aufregung, -en *f.;* Sensation', -en *f.;* Nervenkitzel, - *m.* **2.** *vb.* erre'gen, packen.

throat, *n.* Hals, -e *m.,* Kehle, -n *f.*

throb, *vb.* pochen, pulsie'ren.

throne, *n.* Thron, -e *m.*

through, 1. *prep.* durch. **2.** *adj.* fertig.

throughout, 1. *adv.* überall; völlig. **2.** *prep.* durch.

throw, 1. *n.* Wurf, -e *m.* **2.** *vb.* werfen*, schleudern.

thrust, 1. *n.* Stoß, -e *m.;* *(tech.)* Schub *m.* **2.** *vb.* stoßen*.

thumb, *n.* Daumen, - *m.*

thunder, 1. *n.* Donner, - *m.* **2.** *vb.* donnern.

thunderstorm, *n.* Gewit'ter, - *nt.*

Thursday, *n.* Donnerstag, -e *m.*

thus, *adv.* so.

ticket, *n.* Karte, -n *f.,* Billett', -s or -e *nt.; (admission)* Eintrittskarte, -n *f.; (travel)* Fahrkarte, -n *f.,* Fahrschein, -

e *m.; (traffic)* Strafmandat, -e *nt.*

tickle, *vb.* kitzeln.

ticklish, *adj.* kitzlig; *(delicate, risky)* heikel.

tide, *n.* Gezei'ten *pl.;* **(low t.)** Ebbe *f.;* **(high t.)** Flut *f.*

tidy, *adj.* sauber, ordentlich.

tie, 1. *n. (bond)* Band, -e *nt.; (necktie)* Krawat'te, -n *f.;* Schlips, -e *m.; (equal score)* Punktgleichheit *f.,* Stimmengleichheit *f.* **2.** *vb.* binden*, knüpfen.

tiger, *n.* Tiger, - *m.*

tight, *adj.* eng; *(taut)* straff; *(firm)* fest; *(drunk)* beschwipst'.

tighten, *vb.* straffen, enger machen.

tile, *n. (wall, stove)* Kachel, - *f.; (floor)* Fliese, -n *f.; (roof)* Ziegel, -e *m.*

till, 1. *n.* Ladenkasse, -n *f.* **2.** *vb.* bebau'en, bestel'len. **3.** *adv., conj.* bis.

tilt, 1. *n.* Neigung, -en *f.* **2.** *vb.* neigen, kippen.

timber, *n.* Holz *nt.*

time, 1. *n.* Zeit, -en *f.; (o'clock)* Uhr *f.* **2.** *vb.* die Zeit nehmen*.

timetable, *n.* Fahrplan, -e *m.,* Kursbuch, -er *nt.*

timid, *adj.* ängstlich, schüchtern.

timidity, *n.* Ängstlichkeit *f.,* Schüchternheit *f.*

tin, *n. (metal)* Zinn *nt.; (t. plate)* Blech *nt.; (t. can)* Konser'vendose, -n *f.*

tint, *n.* Farbtönung, -en *f.*

tiny, *adj.* winzig.

tip, 1. *n. (end)* Spitze, -n *f.; (gratuity)* Trinkgeld, -er *nt.* **2.** *vb. (tilt)* kippen; *(give gratuity)* ein Trinkgeld geben*.

tire, 1. *n.* Reifen, - *m.* **2.** *vb.* ermü'den.

tired, *adj.* müde.

tissue, *n.* Gewe'be, - *nt.; (facial t.)* Papier'taschentuch, -er *nt.*

title, *n.* Titel, - *m.; (heading)* Überschrift, -en *f.*

to, *prep.* zu.

toast, 1. *n.* Toast *m.; (drink to health)* Trinkspruch, -e *m.* **2.** *vb.* rösten; auf jemandes Wohl trinken*.

tobacco, *n.* Tabak *m.*

today, *adv.* heute.

toe, *n.* Zehe, -n *f.*

together, *adv.* zusam'men.

toil, 1. *n.* Arbeit, -en *f.,* Mühe, -n *f.* **2.** *vb.* arbeiten, sich ab·mühen.

toilet, *n.* Toilet'te, -n *f.*

token, *n.* Zeichen, - *nt.;* Symbol', -e *nt.*

tolerance, *n.* Duldsamkeit *f.,* Toleranz' *f.*

tolerant, *adj.* duldsam, tolerant'.

tolerate, *vb.* dulden.

toll, 1. *n.* Zoll *m.; (highway)*

Wegegeld, -er *nt., (bridge)* Brückengeld, -er *nt.* **2.** *vb.* läuten.

tomato, *n.* Toma'te, -n *f.*

tomb, *n.* Grab, -er *nt.,* Grabmal, -er *nt.*

tomorrow, *adv.* morgen.

ton, *n.* Tonne, -n *f.*

tone, *n.* Ton, -e *m.*

tongue, *n.* Zunge, -n *f.*

tonic, 1. *n.* Stärkungsmittel *nt.* **2.** *adj.* tonisch.

tonight, *adv.* heute abend.

tonsil, *n.* Mandel, -n *f.*

too, *adv.* zu; *(also)* auch.

tool, *n.* Werkzeug, -e *nt.*

tooth, *n.* Zahn, -e *m.*

toothache, *n.* Zahnschmerzen *pl.*

toothbrush, *n.* Zahnbürste, -n *f.*

toothpaste, *n.* Zahnpaste, -n *f.*

top, 1. *n.* Spitze, -n *f.,* oberstes Ende, -n *nt.; (surface)* Oberfläche, -n *f.;* **(on t. of all)** auf. **2.** *vb. (fig.)* krönen.

topcoat, *n.* Mantel, -e *m.*

topic, *n.* Thema, -men *nt.*

torch, *n.* Fackel, -n *f.*

torment, 1. *n.* Qual, -en *f.* **2.** *vb.* quälen.

torrent, *n.* reißender Strom, -e *m.*

torture, 1. *n.* Folter, -n *f.,* Qual, -en *f.* **2.** *vb.* foltern, quälen.

toss, *vb.* werfen*, schleudern.

total, 1. *n.* Summe, -n *f.* **2.** *adj.* gesamt'; total'.

totalitarian, *adj.* totalitär'.

touch, 1. *n.* Berüh'rung, -en *f.; (sense of t.)* Tastsinn *m.; (final t.)* letzter Schliff, -e *f.; (t. of fever, etc.)* Anflug *m.* **2.** *vb.* berüh'ren.

touching, *adj.* rührend.

tough, 1. *n.* Rabau'ke, -n, -n *m.* **2.** *adj.* zäh; *(hard)* hart (-).

tour, 1. *n.* Reise, -n *f.,* Tour, -en *f.* **2.** *vb.* berei'sen.

tourist, *n.* Tourist', -en, -en *m.*

tow, *vb.* schleppen.

toward, *prep.* nach; gegen; zu.

towel, *n.* Handtuch, -er *nt.*

tower, *n.* Turm, -e *m.*

town, *n.* Stadt, -e *f.,* Ort, -e *m.*

toy, 1. *n.* Spielzeug, -e *nt.* **2.** *vb.* spielen.

trace, 1. *n.* Spur, -en *f.* **2.** *vb. (delineate)* nach·zeichnen; *(track)* zurück'verfolgen.

track, 1. *n.* Spur, -en *f.,* Fährte, -n *f.; (sports)* Leichtathletik *f.; (R.R.)* Gelei'se, - *nt.,* Gleis, -e *nt.* **2.** *vb.* **(t. down)** nach·spüren.

tract, *n. (land)* Gebiet', -e *nt.; (pamphlet)* Traktat', -e *nt.*

tractor, *n.* Trecker, - *m.*

trade, 1. *n.* Handel *m.; (exchange)* Tausch *m.* **2.** *vb.* Handel treiben*; aus·tauschen.

trader, *n.* Händler, - *m.*

tradition, n. Tradition', -en f.

traditional, adj. traditionell'.

traffic, n. Verkehr' m.; (trade) Handel m.

traffic light, n. Verkehrs'licht, -er nt., Verkehrs'ampel, -n f.

tragedy, n. Tragö'die, -n f.

tragic, adj. tragisch.

trail, n. Fährte, -n f.

trailer, n. Anhänger, - m.; (for living) Wohnwagen, - m.

train, 1. n. Zug, ⁓e m.; (of dress) Schleppe, -n f. **2.** vb. aus'bilden.

traitor, n. Verrä'ter, - m.

tramp, n. Landstreicher, - m.

tranquil, adj. ruhig.

tranquillity, n. Ruhe f.

transaction, n. Transaktion', -en f.

transfer, 1. n. (ticket) Umsteigefahrschein, -e m. **2.** vb. (change cars) um'steigen*; (money) überwei'sen*; (ownership) übertra'gen*; (move to new location) verset'zen.

transfix, vb. durchboh'ren.

transform, vb. um'wandeln, um'formen.

transfusion, n. Transfusion', -en f.

transition, n. Übergang, ⁓e m.

translate, vb. überset'zen.

translation, n. Überset'zung, -en f.

transmit, vb. übertra'gen*; übersen'den.

transparent, adj. durchsichtig.

transport, 1. n. Beför'derung, -en f., Transport', -e m. **2.** vb. beför'dern, transportie'ren.

transportation, n. Beför'derung, -en f.

transsexual, adj. transsexual',

transvestite, n. Transvestit', -en, -en m.

trap, n. Falle, -n f.

trash, n. Abfall, ⁓e m.; (fig.) Kitsch m.

travel, 1. n. Reise, -n f. **2.** vb. reisen.

travel agency, n. Reisebüro, -s nt.

traveler, n. Reisend - m.&f.

traveler's check, n. Travelerscheck, -s m.; Reisecheck, -s m.

tray, n. Tablett', -e nt.

treacherous, adj. verrä'terisch; tückisch.

tread, 1. n. Schritt, -e m. **2.** vb. treten*.

treason, n. Verrat' m.

treasure, 1. n. Schatz, ⁓e m. **2.** vb. hoch'schätzen.

treasurer, n. Schatzmeister, - m.

treasury, n. Finanz'ministerium, -rien nt.

treat, 1. n. Extragenuß, ⁓sse m. **2.** vb. gehandeln; (pay for) frei'halten*.

treatment, n. Behand'lung, -en f.

treaty, n. Vertrag', ⁓e m.

tree, n. Baum, ⁓e m.

tremble, vb. zittern.

tremendous, adj. ungeheuer.

trench, n. Graben, ⁓ m.

trend, n. Trend, -s m.

trespass, vb. widerrechtlich betre'ten*; übertre'ten*.

triage, n. Einteilung je nach Priorität f.

trial, n. Versuch', -e m.; (law) Prozeß', -sse m.

triangle, n. Dreieck, -e nt.

tribute, n. Tribut', -e m.; (fig.) Ehrung, -en f.

trick, 1. n. Kniff, -e m., Trick, -s m. **2.** vb. rein'legen.

tricky, adj. knifflig; heikel.

trifle, n. Kleinigkeit, -en f., Lappa'lie, -n f.

trigger, n. (gun) Abzug, ⁓e m.

trim, 1. adj. adrett'. **2.** vb. (clip) stutzen; (adorn) beset'zen.

trip, 1. n. Reise, -n f. **2.** vb. stolpern; (tr.) einem ein Bein stellen.

triple, 1. adj. dreifach. **2.** vb. verdrei'fachen.

trite, adj. abgedroschen.

triumph, 1. n. Triumph', -e m. **2.** vb. triumphie'ren.

triumphant, adj. triumphie'rend.

trivial, adj. trivial'.

trolley-bus, n. Obus, -se m.

trolley-car, n. Strassenbahn, -en f.

troop, n. Trupp, -s m.

troops, n.pl. Truppen pl.

trophy, n. Trophä'e, -n f.

tropic, n. Wendekreis, -e m.

tropical, adj. tropisch.

tropics, n.pl. Tropen pl.

trot, 1. n. Trab m. **2.** vb. traben.

trouble, 1. n. Mühe, -n f.; (difficulty) Schwierigkeit, -en f.; (unpleasantness) Unannehmlichkeit, -en f.; (jam) Klemme, -n f. **2.** vb. bemü'hen; beun'ruhigen.

troublesome, adj. lästig.

trough, n. Trog, ⁓e m.

trousers, n.pl. Hose, -n f.

trousseau, n. Aussteuer, -n f.

trout, n. Forel'le, -n f.

truce, n. Waffenstillstand, -e m.

truck, n. Lastauto, -s nt., Lastwagen, - m., Lastkraftwagen, - m.

true, adj. wahr; wahrhaf'tig; (faithful) treu.

truly, adv. wahrhaf'tig; (yours t.) Ihr erge'bener, Ihre erge'bene.

trumpet, n. Trompe'te, -n f.

trunk, n. (tree) Stamm, ⁓e m.; (luggage) Koffer, - m.

trust, 1. n. Zuversicht f., Vertrau'en nt.; (comm.) Trust, -s m.; (in t.) zu treuen Händen. **2.** vb. vertrau'en.

trustworthy, adj. zuverlässig.

truth, n. Wahrheit, -en f.

truthful, adj. wahr; ehrlich.

try, 1. n. Versuch', -e m. **2.** vb. versu'chen, probie'ren.

T-shirt, n. T-shirt nt.

tub, n. Wanne, -n f.

tube, n. Röhre, -n f.; (container) Tube, -n f.

tuberculosis, n. Tuberkulo'se f.

tuck, 1. n. Falte, -n f. **2.** vb. falten.

Tuesday, n. Dienstag, -e m.

tuft, n. Büschel, - nt., Quaste, -n f.

tug, vb. ziehen*.

tuition, n. Schulgeld, -er nt.; (university) Studiengeld, -er nt.

tulip, n. Tulpe, -n f.

tumor, n. Tumor, -o'ren m.

tumult, n. Tumult', -e m.

tuna, n. Thunfisch, -e m.

tune, 1. n. Melodie', -i'en f. **2.** vb. stimmen.

tuneful, adj. melo'disch.

tunnel, n. Tunnel, - m.

turbine, n. Turbi'ne, -n f.

turbo-jet, n. (plane) Turbi'nenjäger, - m.

turbo-prop, n. Turbi'nenpropellertriebwerk, -e nt.

Turk, n. Türke, -n, -n m.

turkey, n. Truthahn, ⁓e m., Puter, - m.

Turkey, n. die Türkei' f.

Turkish, adj. türkisch.

turmoil, n. Durcheinan'der nt.

turn, 1. n. Umdre'hung, -en f.; Wendung, -en f., Kurve, -n f.; (to take t.s) sich ab'wechseln; (it's my t.) ich bin dran. **2.** vb. drehen, wenden*; (t. around) um'drehen.

turnip, n. Steckrübe, -n f.

turret, n. Turm, ⁓e m.

turtle, n. Schildkröte, -n f.

tutor, 1. n. Lehrer, - m.; Nachhilfelehrer, - m. **2.** vb. Nachhilfeunterricht geben*.

twelfth, 1. adj. zwölft-. **2.** n. Zwölftel, - nt.

twelve, num. zwölf.

twentieth, 1. adj. zwanzigst-. **2.** n. Zwanzigstel, - nt.

twenty, num. zwanzig.

twice, adv. zweimal.

twig, n. Zweig, -e m.

twilight, n. Dämmerung, -en f., Zwielicht nt.

twin, n. Zwilling, -e m.

twine, 1. n. (thread) Zwirn, -e m.; (rope) Tau, -e nt. **2.** vb. winden*.

twist, 1. n. Drehung, -en f.; (distortion) Verdre'hung, -en f. **2.** vb. drehen; verdre'hen.

two, num. zwei.

type, 1. n. Typ, -en m., Typus, -pen m.; (printing) Schriftsatz, ⁓e m.; (letter) Type, -n f. **2.** vb. kennzeichnen; (write on typewriter) tippen.

typewriter, n. Schreibmaschine, -n f.

typhoid fever, n. Typhus m.

typical, *adj.* typisch.
typist, *n.* Schreibdame, -n *f.*
tyranny, *n.* Tyrannei' *f.*
tyrant, *n.* Tyrann', -en, -en *m.*

U

ugliness, *n.* Häßlichkeit *f.*
ugly, *adj.* häßlich.
ulcer, *n.* Geschwür', -e *nt.*
ulterior, *adj.* höher; weiter; (**u. motives**) Hintergedanken *pl.*
ultimate, *adj.* äußerst-.
umbrella, *n.* Regenschirm, -e *m.*
umpire, *n.* Schiedsrichter, - *m.*
un- *prefix* un-.
unable, *adj.* unfähig.
unanimous, *adj.* einstimmig.
unbecoming, *adj.* unschicklich; (*of clothes*) unkleidsam.
uncertain, *adj.* ungewiß.
uncertainty, *n.* Ungewißheit, -en *f.*
uncle, *n.* Onkel, - *m.*
unconscious, *adj.* bewußt'los; (*unaware*) unbewußt.
uncover, *vb.* auf·decken; entblö'ßen.
under, *prep.* unter.
underground, **1.** *n.* Untergrundbahn, -en *f.* **2.** *adj.* unter der Erde gelegen; Untergrund- (*cpds.*).
underline, *vb.* unterstrei'chen*.
underneath, **1.** *adv.* unter, drunter. **2.** *prep.* unter.
undershirt, *n.* Unterhemd, -en *nt.*
undersign, *vb.* unterzeich'nen.
understand, *vb.* verste'hen*, begrei'fen*.
understanding, *n.* Verständ'nis *nt.;* (*agreement*) Einvernehmen, - *nt.*
undertake, *vb.* unterneh'men*.
undertaker, *n.* Leichenbestatter, - *m.*
underwear, *n.* Unterwäsche *f.*
underworld, *n.* Unterwelt *f.*
undo, *vb.* auf·machen, lösen; ungeschehen machen.
undress, *vb.* entklei'den, (sich) aus·ziehen*.
uneasy, *adj.* unruhig, unbehaglich.
unemployed, *adj.* arbeitslos.
unemployment, *n.* Arbeitslosigkeit *f.*
unequal, *adj.* ungleich.
uneven, *adj.* uneben; ungleich; (*numbers*) ungerade.
unexpected, *adj.* unerwartet.
unfair, *adj.* ungerecht.
unfamiliar, *adj.* unbekannt; ungeläufig.
unfavorable, *adj.* ungünstig.
unfit, *adj.* untauglich.
unfold, *vb.* entfal'ten.
unforgettable, *adj.* unvergeßlich.

unfortunate, *adj.* unglücklich; bedau'erlich.
unhappy, *adj.* unglücklich.
uniform, **1.** *n.* Uniform', -en *f.* **2.** *adj.* einheitlich.
unify, *vb.* verei'nen; verein'heitlichen.
union, *n.* Verei'nigung, -en *f.;* (**labor u.**) Gewerk'schaft, -en *f.*
unique, *adj.* einzigartig.
unisex, *adj.* unisex.
unit, *n.* Einheit, -en *f.*
unite, *vb.* verei'nigen.
United Nations, *n.* die Verein'ten Natio'nen *pl.*
United States, *n.* Die Verei'nigten Staaten *pl.*
unity, *n.* Einigkeit *f.*
universal, *adj.* universal'.
universe, *n.* Weltall *nt.*
university, *n.* Universität', -en *f.*
unjust, *adj.* ungerecht.
unknown, *adj.* unbekannt.
unleaded, *adj.* bleifrei.
unless, *conj.* wenn nicht; es sei denn, daß.
unlike, *adj.* ungleich.
unlikely, *adj.* unwahrscheinlich.
unload, *vb.* ab·laden*, aus·laden*.
unlock, *vb.* auf·schließen*.
unlucky, *adj.* (**be u.**) kein Glück haben*, Pech haben*.
unmarried, *adj.* unverheiratet.
unpack, *vb.* aus·packen.
unpleasant, *adj.* unangenehm.
unqualified, *adj.* (*unfit*) ungeeignet; (*unreserved*) uneingeschränkt.
unsettled, *adj.* unsicher, in der Schwebe.
unsteady, *adj.* unstet.
unsuccessful, *adj.* erfolg'los.
untie, *vb.* auf·knüpfen.
until, **1.** *prep.* bis; (**not u.**) erst. **2.** *conj.* bis; (**not u.**) erst wenn; erst als.
untruth, *n.* Unwahrheit, -en *f.*
untruthful, *adj.* unwahr.
unusual, *adj.* ungewöhnlich.
unwell, *adj.* unpäßlich, nicht wohl.
up, **1.** *prep.* auf. **2.** *adv.* auf, hinauf', herauf'.
upbraid, *vb.* schelten*.
uphill, **1.** *adj.* (*fig.*) mühsam. **2.** *adv.* bergan', bergauf'.
uphold, *vb.* aufrecht·erhalten*.
upholster, *vb.* bezie'hen*.
upholsterer, *n.* Tapezie'rer, - *m.*
upon, *prep.* auf.
upper, *adj.* ober-.
upright, *adj.* aufrecht.
uprising, *n.* Aufstand, -̈e *m.*
uproar, *n.* Getö'se *nt.*
uproot, *vb.* entwur'zeln.
upset, **1.** *n.* Rückschlag, -̈e *m.;* (**stomach u.**) Magenverstimmung, -en *f.* **2.** *vb.* (*overturn*) um·werfen*; (*disturb*) über den Haufen werfen, verstim'-

men; (*discompose*) aus der Fassung bringen*.
upside down, *adv.* umgekehrt, verkehrt' herum'.
upstairs, *adv.* oben; nach oben.
uptight, *adj.* unsicher, verklemmt.
urban, *adj.* städtisch.
urge, **1.** *n.* Drang, -̈e *m.;* (*sex*) Trieb, -e *m.* **2.** *vb.* drängen, nötigen.
urgency, *n.* Dringlichkeit *f.*
urgent, *adj.* dringend.
urinal, *n.* Harnglas, -̈er *nt.;* (*public*) öffentliche Bedürf'nisanstalt, -en *f.*
urinate, *vb.* urinie'ren.
urine, *n.* Urin', -e *nt.*
us, *pron.* uns.
usage, *n.* Gebrauch', -̈e *m.*
use, 1. *n.* Gebrauch', -̈e *m.,* Benut'zung, -en *f.* **2.** *vb.* gebrau'chen, verwen'den, benut'zen.
useful, *adj.* nützlich.
useless, *adj.* nutzlos.
user, *n.* Benut'zer, - *m.*
usher, *n.* (*theater, etc.*) Platzanweiser, - *m.;* (*wedding*) Brautführer, - *m.*
usual, *adj.* gewöhn'lich.
usury, *n.* Wucher *m.*
utensil, *n.* Gerät', -e *nt.*
uterus, *n.* Gebär'mutter, -̈ *f.*
utility, *n.* Nutzbarkeit *f.*
utilize, *vb.* aus·nutzen.
utmost, *adj.* äusserst.
utter, 1. *adj.* völlig. **2.** *vb.* äußern.
utterance, *n.* Äußerung, -en *f.*

V

vacancy, *n.* (*position*) freie Stellung, -en *f.;* (*hotel, etc.*) unvermietetes Zimmer, - *nt.*
vacant, *adj.* frei; (*empty*) leer.
vacate, *vb.* räumen.
vacation, *n.* Ferien *pl.*
vaccinate, *vb.* impfen.
vaccination, *n.* Impfung, -en *f.*
vaccine, *n.* Impfstoff, -e *m.*
vacuum, *n.* Vakuum, -kua *nt.*
vagrant, 1. *n.* Landstreicher, *m.;* (*worker*) Saison'arbeiter, - *m.* **2.** *adj.* vagabundie'rend.
vague, *adj.* unbestimmt, vage.
vain, 1. *adj.* (*conceited*) eitel; (*useless*) vergeb'lich. **2.** *n.* (**in v.**) umsonst', verge'bens.
valet, *n.* Diener, - *m.*
valiant, *adj.* tapfer.
valid, *adj.* gültig.
valise, *n.* Reisetasche, -n *f.*
valley, *n.* Tal, -̈er *nt.*
valor, *n.* Tapferkeit *f.*
valuable, *adj.* wertvoll.
value, *n.* Wert, -e *m.*
valve, *n.* Ventil', -e *nt.;* (*med.*) Klappe, -n *f.*
van, *n.* (*delivery truck*) Lieferwagen, - *m.;* (*moving v.*) Möbelwagen, - *m.*

vandal, *n.* Vanda'le, -n, -n *m.*

vanguard, *n.* Vorhut *f.; (person)* Vorkämpfer, - *m.*

vanilla, *n.* Vanil'le *f.*

vanish, *vb.* verschwin'den*.

vanity, *n.* Eitelkeit *f.*

vanquish, *vb.* besie'gen.

vapor, *n.* Dampf, -̈e *m.*

variance, *n.* Widerstreit *m.*

variation, *n.* Abwechslung, -en *f.;* Abänderung, -en *f.,* Variation', -en *f.*

varied, *adj.* verschie'den; mannigfaltig.

variety, *n.* Mannigfaltigkeit *f.; (choice)* Auswahl *f.; (theater)* Varieté *nt.*

various, *adj.* verschie'den.

varnish, **1.** *n.* Firnis, -se *m.* **2.** *vb.* firnissen.

vary, *vb.* variie'ren, verän'dern.

vase, *n.* Vase, -n *f.*

vasectomy, *n.* Vasektomie' *f.*

vast, *adj.* riesig.

vat, *n.* Faß, -̈sser *nt.*

vaudeville, *n.* Varieté' *nt.*

vault, **1.** *n.* Gewöl'be, - *nt.; (burial chamber)* Gruft, -̈e *f.; (bank)* Tresor', -e *m.; (jump)* Sprung, -̈e *m.* **2.** *vb.* springen*.

veal, *n.* Kalbfleisch *nt.*

vegetable, *n.* Gemü'se, - *nt.*

vehement, *adj.* heftig.

vehicle, *n.* Fahrzeug, -e *nt.*

veil, **1.** *n.* Schleier, - *m.* **2.** *vb.* verschlei'ern.

vein, *n.* Vene, -n *f.,* Ader, -n *f.*

velocity, *n.* Geschwin'digkeit, -en *f.*

velvet, *n.* Samt *m.*

veneer, *n.* Furnier', -e *nt.*

vengeance, *n.* Rache *f.*

venom, *n.* Gift, -e *nt.*

vent, **1.** *n.* Öffnung, -en *f.; (escape passage)* Abzugsröhre, -n *f.* **2.** *vb.* freien Lauf lassen*.

ventilate, *vb.* lüften, ventilie'ren.

ventilation, *n.* Lüftung *f.,* Ventilation' *f.*

venture, **1.** *n.* Wagnis, -se *nt.* **2.** *vb.* wagen.

verb, *n.* Verb, -en *nt.,* Zeitwort, -̈er *nt.*

verbal, *adj.* verbal'; *(oral)* mündlich.

verdict, *n.* Urteil, -e *nt.*

verge, **1.** *n. (fig.)* Rand, -̈er *m.* **2.** *vb.* (v. on) grenzen an.

verification, *n.* Bestä'tigung, - en *f.*

verify, *vb.* bestä'tigen.

vernacular, **1.** *n.* Umgangssprache, -n *f.* **2.** *adj.* umgangssprachlich.

versatile, *adj.* vielseitig.

verse, *n.* Vers, -e *m.*

versify, *vb.* in Verse bringen*.

version, *n.* Fassung, -en *f.,* Version', -en *f.*

versus, *prep.* gegen.

vertebrate, **1.** *n.* Wirbeltier, -e *nt.* **2.** *adj.* Wirbel- *(cpds.).*

vertical, *adj.* senkrecht.

very, *adv.* sehr.

vespers, *n.* Vesper, -n *f.*

vessel, *n.* Schiff, -e *nt.; (container)* Gefäß', -e *nt.*

vest, *n.* Weste, -n *f.*

vestige, *n.* Spur, -en *f.*

veteran, *n.* Veteran', -en, -en *m.*

veterinary, **1.** *n.* Tierarzt, -̈e *m.* **2.** *adj.* tierärztlich.

veto, **1.** *n.* Veto, -s *nt.* **2.** *vb.* das Veto ein·legen.

vex, *vb.* ärgern; verblüf'fen.

via, *prep.* über.

viaduct, *n.* Viadukt', -e *m.*

vibrate, *vb.* vibrie'ren, schwingen*.

vibration, *n.* Vibration', -en *f.,* Schwingung, -en *f.; (tremor)* Erschüt'terung, -en *f.*

vice, *n.* Laster, - *nt.*

vicinity, *n.* Nähe *f.,* Umgebung, -en *f.*

vicious, *adj.* gemein', heimtückisch.

victim, *n.* Opfer, - *nt.*

victor, *n.* Sieger, - *m.*

victorious, *adj.* siegreich.

victory, *n.* Sieg, -e *m.*

videodisc, *n.* Videoscheibe, -n *f.*

Vienna, *n.* Wien *nt.*

view, **1.** *n.* Aussicht, -en *f.* **2.** *vb.* bese'hen*, betrach'ten.

vigil, *n.* Nachtwache, -n *f.*

vigilant, *adj.* wachsam.

vigor, *n.* Kraft, -̈e *f.,* Energie', -i'en *f.*

vigorous, *adj.* kräftig, kraftstrozend.

vile, *adj.* gemein', niederträchtig.

village, *n.* Dorf, -̈er *nt.*

villain, *n.* Bösewicht, -e *m.,* Schurke, -n, -n *m.*

vindicate, *vb.* rechtfertigen.

vine, *n.* Rebstock, -̈e *m.; (creeper)* Ranke, -n *f.*

vinegar, *n.* Essig *m.*

vineyard, *n.* Weingarten, - *m.,* Weinberg, -e *m.*

vintage, *n. (gathering)* Weinlese *f.; (year)* Jahrgang, -̈e *m.*

viol, viola, *n.* Bratsche, -n *f.*

violate, *vb.* verlet'zen; *(oath)* brechen*; *(law, territory)* übertre'ten*.

violation, *n.* Verlet'zung, -en *f.;* Bruch, -̈e *m.;* Übertre'tung, -en *f.*

violator, *n.* Verlet'zer, - *m.;* Übertre'ter, - *m.*

violence, *n.* Gewalt'tätigkeit, -en *f.; (vehemence)* Gewalt'samkeit *f.,* Heftigkeit *f.*

violent, *adj.* gewalt'tätig; gewalt'sam, heftig.

violet, **1.** *n.* Veilchen, - *nt.* *adj.* violett', veilchenblau.

violin, *n.* Geige, -n *f.*

virgin, *n.* Jungfrau, -en *f.*

virile, *adj.* männlich.

virtue, *n.* Tugend, -en *f.*

virtuous, *adj.* tugendhaft, tugendsam.

virus, *n.* Virus, -ren *m.*

visa, *n.* Visum, -sa *nt.*

vise, *n.* Schraubstock, -̈e *m.*

visible, *adj.* sichtbar.

vision, *n.* Sehkraft, -̈e *f.; (visual image)* Vision', -en *f.*

visit, **1.** *n.* Besuch', -e *m.* **2.** *vb.* besu'chen.

visitor, *n.* Besu'cher, - *m.*

visual, *adj.* visuell'.

vital, *adj. (essential)* wesentlich; *(strong)* vital'.

vitality, *n.* Lebenskraft *f.,* Vitalität' *f.*

vitamin, *n.* Vitamin', -e *nt.*

vivacious, *adj.* lebhaft, temperament'voll.

vivid, *adj.* leben'dig, lebhaft.

vocabulary, *n.* Wortschatz, -̈e *m.; (list of words)* Wörterverzeichnis, -se *nt.*

vocal, *adj.* Stimm-, Gesang'- *(cpds.);* lautstark.

vogue, *n.* Mode, -n *f.*

voice, *n.* Stimme, -n *f.*

void, *adj.* ungültig.

volcano, *n.* Vulkan', -e *m.*

volt, *n.* Volt, - *m.*

voltage, *n.* Stromspannung, -en *f.*

volume, *n.* Volu'men, - *nt.; (book)* Band, -̈e *m.; (quantity)* Umfang, -̈e *m.*

voluntary, *adj.* freiwillig.

volunteer, **1.** *n.* Freiwillig-*m.&f.* **2.** *vb.* sich freiwillig melden.

vomit, *vb.* erbre'chen*.

vote, **1.** *n. (individual ballot)* Wahlstimme, -n *f.; (casting)* Stimmabgabe, -n *f.; (v. of confidence)* Vertrau'ensvotum *nt.* **2.** *vb.* wählen, stimmen, ab·stimmen.

voter, *n.* Wähler, - *m.*

vouch for, *vb.* verbür'gen für.

vow, **1.** *n.* Gelüb'de - *nt.* **2.** *vb.* gelo'ben.

vowel, *n.* Vokal', -e *m.*

voyage, *n.* Reise, -n *f.*

vulgar, *adj.* vulgär', ordinär', -en *f.*

vulgarity, *n.* Ordinär'heit, -en *f.*

vulnerable, *adj.* verletz'bar; angreifbar.

W

wad, *n.* Bündel, - *nt.; (of cotton)* Wattebausch, -̈e *m.; (roll)* Rolle, -n *f.*

wade, *vb.* waten.

wag, **1.** *n.* Spaßvogel, -̈ *m.* **2.** *vb.* wedeln.

wage, **1.** *n.* Lohn, -̈e *m.* **2.** *vb.* (w. war) Krieg führen.

wager, **1.** *n.* Wette, -n *f.* **2.** *vb.* wetten.

wagon, *n.* Wagen - *m.*

wail, *vb.* wehklagen.

waist, *n.* Taille, -n *f.*

waistcoat, n. Weste, -n f.
wait, 1. n. Wartezeit, -en f. 2. vb. warten; **(w. for)** warten auf.
waiter, n. Kellner, - m.
waitress, n. Kellnerin, -nen f.
waiver, n. Verzicht'leistung, -en f.
wake, 1. n. (vigil) Totenwache, -n f.; (of boat) Kielwasser nt. 2. vb. (tr.) wecken; (intr.) erwa'chen.
walk, 1. n. Spazier'gang, "e m. 2. vb. gehen*, laufen*.
wall, n. Wand, "e f.; (of stone or brick) Mauer, -n f.
wallcovering, n. Wandverkleidung f.
wallet, n. Brieftasche, -n f.
wallpaper, n. Tape'te, -n f.
walnut, n. Walnuß, "sse f.
walrus, n. Walross, -sse nt.
waltz, 1. n. Walzer, - m. 2. vb. Walzer tanzen.
wander, vb. wandern; **(w. around)** umher'wandern.
want, 1. n. Mangel, " m.; (needs) Bedarf' m.; (poverty) Armut f. 2. vb. wollen, wünschen.
war, n. Krieg, -e m.
ward, n. Mündel, - nt.; (city) Bezirk', -e m.; (hospital, prison) Abtei'lung, -en f.
ware, n. Ware, -n f.
warlike, adj. kriegerisch.
warm, 1. adj. warm (-). 2. vb. wärmen.
warmth, n. Wärme f.
warn, vb. warnen.
warning, n. Warnung, -en f.
warp, vb. krümmen; (fig.) Verdre'hen, entstel'len.
warrant, 1. n. (authorization) Vollmacht, -en f.; (writ of arrest) Haftbefehl, -e m. 2. vb. gewähr'leisten, garantie'ren.
warrior, n. Krieger, - m.
warship, n. Kriegsschiff, -e nt.
wash, 1. n. Wäsche, -n f. 2. vb. waschen*.
wash-basin, n. Waschbecken, - nt.
washroom, n. Waschraum, "e m.
wasp, n. Wespe, -n f.
waste, 1. n. Abfall, "e m. 2. adj. (superfluous) überflüssig; (bare) öde. 3. vb. verschwen'den, vergeu'den.
watch, 1. n. (guard) Wache, -n f.; (timepiece) Uhr, -en f.; (wrist w.) Armbanduhr, -en f.; (pocket w.) Taschenuhr, -en f. 2. vb. (guard) bewa'chen, passen auf; (observe) beob'achten, acht'geben; **(w. out)** auf'passen; **(w. out!)** Vorsicht!
watchful, adj. wachsam.
watchmaker, n. Uhrmacher, - m.
water, 1. n. Wasser, - nt. 2. vb. wässern, begie'ßen*.

waterbed, n. Matratze mit Wasser gefüllt f.
waterfall, n. Wasserfall, "e m.
waterproof, adj. wasserdicht.
wave, 1. n. Welle, -n f. 2. vb. wellen, wogen; (flag) wehen; (hand) winken.
waver, vb. schwanken.
wax, 1. n. Wachs, -e nt. 2. vb. wachsen; (moon) zunehmen*.
way, n. Weg, -e m.
we, pron. wir.
weak, adj. schwach (-).
weaken, vb. (tr.) schwächen; (intr.) schwach werden*.
weakness, n. Schwäche, -n f.
wealth, n. Reichtum, "er m.; (possessions) Vermö'gen, - nt.; (abundance) Fülle f.
wealthy, adj. reich, vermö'gend.
weapon, n. Waffe, -n f.
wear, vb. tragen*, an'haben*, (hat) auf'haben*; **(w. out)** ab'tragen*, (fig.) erschöp'fen; **(w. away)** aus'höhlen.
weary, adj. müde, erschöpft'.
weasel, n. Wiesel, - nt.
weather, 1. n. Wetter nt. 2. vb. (fig.) durch'stehen*.
weave, vb. weben(*).
weaver, n. Weber, - m.
web, n. Netz, -e nt., Gewe'be nt.; **(spider w.)** Spinnennetz, -e nt., Spinngewebe nt.
wedding, n. Hochzeit, -en f.
wedge, 1. n. Keil, -e m. 2. vb. ein'klemmen.
Wednesday, n. Mittwoch, -e m.
weed, 1. n. Unkraut nt. 2. vb. jäten.
week, n. Woche, -n f.
weekday, n. Wochentag, -e m.
week end, n. Wochenende, -n nt.
weekly, 1. n. Wochenschrift, -en f. 2. adj. wöchentlich.
weep, vb. weinen.
weigh, vb. wiegen*; (ponder) wägen.
weight, n. Gewicht', -e nt.; (burden) Last, -en f.
weird, adj. unheimlich.
welcome, 1. n. Willkom'men nt. 2. vb. bewill'kommnen, begrü'ßen. 3. adj. willkom'men; **(you're w.)** bitte.
welfare, n. Wohlergehen nt.; (social) Wohlfahrt f.
well, 1. n. Brunnen, - m. 2. quellen*. 3. adv. gut; (health) gesund' (-, -), wohl.
well-known, adj. bekannt'.
west, n. Westen m. 2. adj. westlich; West- (cpds.).
western, adj. westlich.
westward, adv. nach Westen.
wet, 1. adj. naß (-, -). 2. vb. nässen, naß machen.
whale, n. Walfisch, -e m.
what, 1. pron. was. 2. adj. welcher, -es, -e.
whatever, 1. pron. was . . .

wheat, n. Weizen m.
wheel, 1. n. Rad, "er nt. 2. vb. rollen.
when, 1. adv. (question) wann. 2. conj. (once in the past) als; (future; whenever) wenn; (indirect question) wann.
whence, adv. woher', von wo.
whenever, 1. conj. wenn. 2. adv. wann . . . auch.
where, adv. (in what place) wo; (to what place) wohin'; **(w. . . . from)** woher'.
wherever, adv. wo(hin) . . . auch.
whether, conj. ob.
which, pron.&adj. welcher, -es, -e.
whichever, pron.&adj. welcher, -es, -e . . . auch.
while, 1. n. Weile f. 2. conj. während.
whim, n. Laune, -n f.
whip, 1. n. Peitsche, -n f. 2. vb. peitschen, schlagen*.
whirl, vb. wirbeln.
whirlpool, n. Strudel, - m.
whirlwind, n. Wirbelwind, -e m.
whisker, n. Barthaar, -e nt.
whiskey, n. Whisky, -s m.
whisper, vb. flüstern.
whistle, 1. n. Flöte, -n f.; Pfeife, -n f. 2. vb. flöten, pfeifen*.
white, adj. weiß.
who, pron. (interrogative) wer; (relative) der, das, die.
whoever, pron. wer . . . auch.
whole, 1. n. Ganz- nt. 2. adj. ganz; (unbroken) heil.
wholesale, 1. n. Großhandel m. 2. adv. en gros.
wholesome, adj. gesund' (-, -)
why, adv. warum', wieso', weshalb.
wicked, adj. böse, verrucht'.
wickedness, n. Verrucht'heit f.
wide, adj. weit; breit.
widen, vb. erwei'tern.
widespread, adj. weit verbrei'tet.
widow, n. Witwe, -n f.
widower, n. Witwer, - m.
width, n. Weite, -n f.; Breite, -n f.
wield, vb. handhaben*; (fig.) aus'üben.
wife, n. Frau, -en f.
wig, n. Perü'cke, -n f.
wild, adj. wild.
wilderness, n. Wildnis, -se f.
wildlife, n. Tiere und Pflanzen in freier Natur.
wilful, adj. eigensinnig; (intentional) vorsätzlich.
will, 1. n. Wille(n) m.; (testament) Testament', -e nt. 2. vb. (future) werden*; (want to) wollen*; (bequeath) verma'chen.

willing, *adj.* willig; gewillt'; **(be w.)** wollen*.

willow, *n.* Weide, -n *f.*

wilt, *vb.* welken, verwel'ken.

wilted, *adj.* welk.

win, *vb.* gewin'nen*.

wind, 1. *n.* Wind, -e *m.* **2.** *vb.* winden*, wickeln; *(watch)* auf·ziehen*.

window, *n.* Fenster, - *nt.*

windy, *adj.* windig.

wine, *n.* Wein, -e *m.*

wing, *n.* Flügel, - *m.*

wink, *vb.* blinzeln.

winner, *n.* Gewin'ner, - *m.,* Sieger, - *m.*

winter, *n.* Winter, - *m.*

wintry, *adj.* winterlich.

wipe, *vb.* wischen.

wire, 1. *n.* Draht, ⁼e *m.; (telegram)* Telegramm', -e *nt.* **2.** *vb.* telegrafie'ren.

wire recorder, *n.* Drahtaufnahmegerät, -e *nt.*

wisdom, *n.* Weisheit, -en *f.*

wise, *adj.* weise, klug (⁼).

wish, 1. *n.* Wunsch, ⁼e *m.;* **(make a w.)** sich etwas wünschen. **2.** *vb.* wünschen.

wit, *n.* Verstand' *m.; (humor)* Humor' *m.*

witch, *n.* Hexe, -n *f.*

with, *prep.* mit.

withdraw, *vb.* zurück'·ziehen*.

wither, *vb.* verdor'ren.

withhold, *vb.* zurück'·halten*; ein·behalten*.

within, 1. *adv.* drinnen. **2.** *prep.* innerhalb.

without, 1. *adv.* draußen. **2.** *prep.* ohne.

witness, 1. *n.* Zeuge, -n, -n *m.* **2.** *vb.* Zeuge sein* von.

witty, *adj.* witzig; geistreich.

woe, *n.* Leid *nt.*

wolf, *n.* Wolf, ⁼e *m.*

woman, *n.* Frau, -en *f.*

womb, *n.* Mutterleib *m.*

wonder, 1. *n.* Wunder, - *nt.* **2.** *vb.* **(I w.)** ich möchte gern wissen.

wonderful, *adj.* wunderbar, herrlich.

woo, *vb.* umwer'ben*.

wood, *n.* Holz, ⁼er *nt.; (forest)* Wald, ⁼er *m.*

wooden, *adj.* hölzern.

wool, *n.* Wolle *f.*

woolen, *adj.* wollen.

word, *n. (single)* Wort, ⁼er *nt.; (connected)* Wort, -e *nt.*

wordy, *adj. (fig.)* langatmig.

work, 1. *n. (labor)* Arbeit,

-en *f.; (thing produced)* Werk, -e *nt.; (gas w.s)* Gaswerke *pl.* **2.** *vb.* arbeiten; *(function)* gehen*, funktionie'ren.

worker, *n.* Arbeiter, - *m.*

workman, *n.* Arbeiter, - *m.*

world, *n.* Welt, -en *f.*

worldly, *adj.* weltlich.

worm, *n.* Wurm, ⁼er *m.*

worn-out, *adj.* abgenutzt.

worry, 1. *n.* Sorge, -n *f.* **2.** *vb.* sich sorgen.

worse, *adj.* schlimmer, schlechter.

worship, 1. *n.* Vereh'rung, -en *f.; (church)* Gottesdienst, -e *m.* **2.** *vb.* vereh'ren, an·beten.

worst, *adj.* schlimmst-, schlechtest-.

worth, 1. *n.* Wert, -e *m.* **2.** *adj.* wert.

worthless, *adj.* wertlos.

worthy, *adj.* würdig, ehrenwert.

wound, 1. *n.* Wunde, -n *f.* **2.** *vb.* verwun'den.

wrap, 1. *n.* Umhang, ⁼e *m.* **2.** *vb.* wickeln.

wrapping, *n.* Verpa'ckung, -en *f.*

wrath, *n.* Zorn *m.*

wreath, *n.* Kranz, ⁼e *m.*

wreck, 1. *n.* Wrack, -s *nt.* **2.** *vb.* demolie'ren, kaputt'machen.

wrench, 1. *n.* Ruck *m.; (tool)* Schraubenschlüssel, - *m.* **2.** *vb.* verren'ken.

wrestle, *vb.* ringen*.

wretched, *adj.* erbärm'lich.

wring, *vb. (hands)* ringen*; *(laundry)* wringen*; *(neck)* ab·drehen.

wrinkle, 1. *n.* Falte, -n *f.,* Runzel, -n *f.* **2.** *vb.* runzeln; *(cloth)* knittern.

wrist, *n.* Handgelenk, -e *nt.*

wrist-watch, *n.* Armbanduhr, -en *f.*

write, *vb.* schreiben*.

writer, *n.* Schreiber, - *m.; (by profession)* Schriftsteller, - *m.; (author)* Verfas'ser, - *m.*

writing, *n.* Schrift, -en *f.; (in w.)* schriftlich.

wrong, 1. *n.* Unrecht *nt.* **2.** *adj.* falsch; unrecht; **(be w.)** unrecht haben*, sich irren. **3.** *vb.* Unrecht tun*.

X

x-ray, 1. *n.* Röntgenaufnahme, -n *f.* **2.** *vb.* röntgen.

x-rays, *n.pl.* Röntgenstrahlen *pl.*

xylophone, *n.* Xylophon', -e *nt.*

Y

yacht, *n.* Jacht, -en *f.*

yard, *n. (garden)* Garten, ⁼ *m.; (railroad)* Verschie'bebahnhof, ⁼e *m.; (measure)* Yard, -s *nt.*

yarn, *n.* Garn, -e *nt.; (story)* Geschich'te, -n *f.*

yawn, *vb.* gähnen.

year, *n.* Jahr, -e *nt.*

yearly, *adj.* jährlich.

yearn, *vb.* sich sehnen.

yell, 1. *n.* Schrei, -e *m.* **2.** *vb.* schreien*, brüllen.

yellow, *adj.* gelb.

yes, *interj.* ja.

yesterday, *adv.* gestern.

yet, 1. *adv. (still)* noch; *(already)* schon; *(not y.)* noch nicht. **2.** *conj.* doch.

yield, 1. *n.* Ertrag', ⁼e *m.* **2.** *vb.* ein·bringen*; *(cede)* nach·geben*.

yoke, *n.* Joch, -e *nt.*

yolk, *n.* Eigelb, - *nt.*

you, *pron.* du, Sie.

young, *adj.* jung (⁼).

youth, *n.* junger Mann, ⁼er *m.,* Jüngling, -e *m.; (young people; time of life)* Jugend, -en *f.*

youthful, *adj.* jugendlich.

Yugoslav, *n.* Jugosla'we, -n, -n *m.*

Yugoslavia, *n.* Jugosla'wien *nt.*

Yugoslavian, 1. *n.* Jugosla'we, -n, -n *m.* **2.** *adj.* jugosla'wisch.

Z

zap, *vb. (lit.)* töten; *(slang)* fertig machen, zerschmettern.

zeal, *n.* Eifer *m.*

zebra, *n.* Zebra, -s *nt.*

zero, *n.* Null, -en *f.*

zest, *n. (zeal)* Eifer *m.; (relish)* Genuß' *m.*

zinc, *n.* Zink *nt.*

zip code, *n.* Postleitzahl, -en *f.*

zipper, *n.* Reißverschluß, ⁼sse *m.*

zone, *n.* Zone, -n *f.*

zoo, *n.* Zoo, -s *m.*

zoological, *adj.* zoolo'gisch.

zoology, *n.* Zoologie' *f.*